RHCSA®
Red Hat® Enterprise Linux® 9

Training
and
Exam Preparation
Guide

Exam Code
EX200

Third Edition
February 2023

Asghar Ghori

1246 Heil Quaker Blvd., La Vergne, TN USA 37086
Chapter House, Pitfield, Kiln Farm, Milton Keynes, UK MK11 3LW
Unit A1/A3, 7 Janine Street, Scoresby, Victoria 3179, Australia
www.ingramspark.com

Technical Reviewers: Many of author's students and peers
Editors: FirstEditing.com and Zainab Ghori
Cover Design: Nid n Nad Graphics Printing Inc. (www.nidnnad.ca)
Printers and Distributors: IngramSpark Inc.

Printed in the USA, Canada, UK, France, Germany, Italy, Spain, and Australia.

ISBN-13: **978-1-7750621-6-5**
ISBN-10: **1-7750621-6-3**

To order in bulk at special quantity discounts for sales promotions or training programs, please contact the author directly at *asghar_ghori2002@yahoo.com*

The following are registered trademarks in the U.S. and other countries:

Red Hat® is a registered trademark of Red Hat, Inc.

RHCSA® is a registered trademark of Red Hat, Inc.

Linux® is a registered trademark of Linus Torvalds.

Oracle® and VirtualBox® are registered trademarks of Oracle Corporation, Inc.

UNIX® is a registered trademark of The Open Group.

Microsoft® and Windows® are US registered trademarks of Microsoft Corporation.

Docker and the Docker logo are trademarks or registered trademarks of Docker, Inc.

Intel® is the trademark or registered trademark of Intel Corporation or its subsidiaries.

All other trademarks, registered trademarks, or logos used in this book are the property of their respective owners.

The author has made his best efforts to prepare this book. The contents are based on Red Hat® Enterprise Linux® version 9.1. The author makes no representation or warranties of any kind with regard to the completeness or accuracy of the contents herein and accepts no liability whatsoever including but not limited to merchantability, fitness for any particular purpose, or any losses or damages of any kind caused or allegedly caused directly or indirectly from this material.

This book is not a replacement for the official Red Hat RH124 and RH134 training courses offered by Red Hat, Inc. for the preparation of the Red Hat Certified System Administrator (RHCSA) exam, EX200. However, it may be used to get ready for this exam based on the latest version of the exam objectives available on Red Hat's training and certification website. Neither author nor publisher warrants that use of this publication will ensure passing the relevant exam or that the information contained herein is endorsed by Red Hat, Inc.

Preface

Red Hat Enterprise Linux 9 was released on May 18, 2022. The official objectives for the Red Hat Certified System Administrator (RHCSA) certification exam were updated for the public shortly thereafter. There were no major enhancements or changes introduced; however, a few minor updates made to the exam objectives resulted in this publication: **RHCSA Red Hat Enterprise Linux 9: Training and Exam Preparation Guide**. This book presents a single, definitive resource to self-learners, instructor-led learners, and Linux instructors.

The RHCSA exam is performance-based and presents several tasks that are to be completed on virtual machines within a stipulated time. This book provides the necessary coverage from both theoretical and practical standpoints to assist learners in passing the exam. Moreover, this book may be used for in-class and live virtual trainings, and as an on-the-job deskside reference.

Keeping in mind the hands-on nature of the exam, I have included a multitude of step-by-step exercises and Do-It-Yourself (DIY) challenge labs throughout this publication. Chapter 01 describes how to obtain copies of VirtualBox Manager and RHEL 9 software, and the steps for building a lab environment to practice the procedures and perform labs.

I suggest that you study the material presented in each chapter thoroughly before proceeding to the relevant hands-on exercise(s). I have provided several review questions with answers at the end of each chapter. Take the quiz and then attempt the DIY challenge labs offered thereafter. I have not furnished solutions to these labs intentionally, as I am confident that the knowledge and skills you will have gained by that time will be sufficient to accomplish the labs on your own; and, in essence, this is what I want you to eventually get at. After you have read and understood the material, performed the exercises, completed review questions, and accomplished DIY challenge labs fully, take time to attempt the sample RHCSA exams provided in Appendices.

While performing exercises and labs, if a command does not produce the published result, I advise you to check the message the command has generated and browse through relevant log files. Minor issues such as a wrong path, typing error, or an incorrect option prevent commands from running. Sometimes, syntax errors in command constructs could result in execution failures. You will have to address the issue with the command to run it as expected. RHEL manual pages prove useful in comprehending commands and their syntaxes.

There are four areas I suggest you focus on to develop expertise with RHEL, as well as to prepare for the exam: 1) grasping concepts; 2) mastering implementation procedures, exercises, and labs; 3) learning commands, understanding configuration files, and knowing service processes; and 4) being able to analyze logs, and troubleshoot and resolve issues. An advanced knowledge of commands and key options, and the files they update should also be developed along with what processes handle which corresponding services, and so on. This will help you obtain a greater overall understanding of what exactly happens behind the scenes when a command runs. Debugging becomes easier when concepts are clear and working knowledge is solid.

I maintain *www.nixeducation.com* where I add errata, additional certification information, helpful videos on Linux concepts and administration topics, and links to other useful resources. I encourage you to visit this website.

To conclude, I would like to request your constructive feedback be sent to my personal email asghar_ghori2002@yahoo.com regarding any grammatical or technical errors or mistakes in the book, as well as any suggestions. Please be specific in your description. Improvement is a continuous process, and I believe your feedback will help me to continue delivering quality books.

Good luck in your endeavors.

Asghar Ghori | February 2023 | Toronto, Canada

Acknowledgments

As always, I am grateful to God who enabled me to write this book successfully.

I would like to acknowledge the valuable feedback my students, friends, and colleagues provided on my previous publications on RHCSA, RHCE, CompTIA Linux+, and HP-UX. I am thankful for their help in making this book better in all respects.

I recognize the constructive feedback I had received from the readers of my previous publications. I have used their comments toward the improvement of this edition.

I would like to express my special thanks to my wife, daughters, and sons, who endured my mental absence while writing this book. I could not have accomplished this project without their continuous support and encouragement.

Lastly, I would like to offer my very special tributes to my deceased parents and sisters.

Asghar Ghori

About the Author

Asghar Ghori is a seasoned Linux | Cloud | DevOps consultant, trainer, curriculum developer, and author. As a consultant with 30+ years of experience, he has architected, implemented, and administered complex technology solutions for both private and public sector organizations. As a trainer and curriculum developer with 20+ years of experience, he has designed, developed, and delivered numerous training programs on Linux/UNIX fundamentals, RHCSA, RHCE, Microsoft Azure (Fundamentals, Administrator, and Solution Architect), AWS (Practitioner and Solution Architect), Automation (Terraform and Ansible), UNIX administration and networking, high-availability clusters, and backup and recovery. As a published author with 20+ years of writing experience, he has 11 books on Linux (Red Hat Enterprise Linux and CompTIA Linux+) and UNIX to his credit.

Asghar is an engineer by education. He holds several technical certifications including RHCSA, RHCE, HPCSA, HPCSE, SCSA, IBM Certified Specialist for AIX, and CNE, as well as IT Infrastructure Library (ITIL) Foundation and Project Management Professional (PMP) certifications. He is 5x Azure Certified, 4x AWS Certified, MCP, and HashiCorp Certified Terraform Associate (HCTA). Asghar is Microsoft Certified Trainer (MCT) and a big advocate of cloud adoption.

Asghar lives in Toronto, Canada with his wife and children, and can be reached via email asghar_ghori2002@yahoo.com or LinkedIn https://www.linkedin.com/in/asghar-ghori-0315632/.

Publications of Asghar Ghori including this are:

1. RHCSA Red Hat Enterprise Linux 9: Training and Exam Preparation Guide (EX200) (ISBN: 978-1775062165) (RHEL version 9), published February 2023

2. RHCSA Red Hat Enterprise Linux 8 (UPDATED): Training and Exam Preparation Guide (EX200) (ISBN: 978-1775062141) (RHEL version 8), published November 2020

3. RHCSA Red Hat Enterprise Linux 8: Training and Exam Preparation Guide (EX200) (ISBN: 978-1775062127) (RHEL version 8), published January 2020

4. CompTIA Linux+/LPIC-1: Training and Exam Preparation Guide (Exam Codes: LX0-103/101-400 and LX0-104/102-400) (ISBN: 978-1775062103), published 2017

5. RHCSA & RHCE Red Hat Enterprise Linux 7: Training and Exam Preparation Guide (EX200 and EX300) (ISBN: 978-1495148200) (RHEL version 7), published 2015

6. Red Hat Certified System Administrator & Engineer: Training Guide and a Quick Deskside Reference (ISBN: 978-1467549400) (RHEL version 6), published 2012

7. Red Hat Certified Technician & Engineer (RHCT and RHCE) Training Guide and Administrator's Reference (ISBN: 978-1615844302) (RHEL version 5), published 2009

8. HP-UX: HP Certified Systems Administrator, Exam HP0-A01, Training Guide and Administrator's Reference (ISBN: 978-1606436547) (HP-UX 11iv3), published 2008

9. HP Certified Systems Administrator, Exam HP0-095, Training Guide and Administrator's Reference (ISBN: 978-1424342310) (HP-UX 11iv2 and 11iv3), published 2007

10. Certified System Administrator for HP-UX: Study Guide and Administrator's Reference (ISBN: 978-1419645938) (HP-UX 11iv1), published 2006

11. Fundamentals of UNIX: published 2002

Conventions Used in this Book

The following typographic and other conventions are used in this book:

Book Antiqua Italic 10 pt. is used in text paragraphs to introduce new terms. For example:

> "Red Hat renamed the Red Hat Linux operating system series *Red Hat Enterprise Linux (RHEL)* in 2003."

Times Roman Italic 10 pt. is used in text paragraphs to highlight names of files, directories, commands, daemons, users, groups, hosts, domains, and URLs. This font also highlights file and directory paths. For example:

> "To go directly from */etc* to a subdirectory *dir1* under *user1*'s home directory, create *dir1*, as . . . . ."

Times New Roman 9 pt. is used to segregate command output, script/file contents, and information expected to be entered in configuration files from the surrounding text. It is also used in tables, index, and side notes.

Times Roman Bold 10 pt. is used to highlight commands and command line arguments that the user is expected to type and execute at the command prompt. For example:

> [user1@server1 ~]$ **ls -lt**

Two white spaces (**cp -p file1 /tmp**) are employed between parts of a typed command for the sake of clarity in text.

Hundreds of screenshots taken directly from the Linux terminal screens showing commands and output are included. These screenshots will give the readers of this book an idea of what they should expect to see in their own lab environments.

All headings and sub-headings are in California FB font, and are bolded.

Ctrl+x key sequence implies that you hold down the Ctrl key and then press the other key. Courier New font is used to highlight such combinations. This font is also used to identify keystrokes, such as Enter and Esc.

. . . . Dotted lines represent truncated command output.

Pictures at chapter start are the property of their respective owners or taken from public domain.

Times Roman 8 pt. is used for notes.

Times Roman 8 pt. is used for warning messages.

 Exam Tip surrounded by a solid box is included where necessary.

The RHCSA 9 Exam and Exam Objectives

The Red Hat Certified System Administrator (RHCSA) certification exam is a performance-based hands-on exam designed for certification aspirants. This exam is presented on a live server running Red Hat Enterprise Linux 9. This server has two RHEL 9-based virtual machines to accomplish the exam tasks. During the exam, the candidates do not have access to any external resources such as the internet, printed material, electronic content, and mobile devices, except for the manuals and other documentation that is installed on the exam virtual machines.

The official exam objectives (68 in total as of February 21, 2023) are available for reference at *http://www.redhat.com/training/courses/ex200/examobjective*. Visit the URL for up-to-date information.

There are no pre-requisites to earn this certification.

The exam objectives are covered in detail in the chapters throughout this book. An enumerated list of the objectives are presented below along with the chapter number where each objective is discussed.

Understand and Use Essential Tools

1. Access a shell prompt and issue commands with correct syntax (chapter 2)
2. Use input-output redirection (>, >>, |, 2>, etc) (chapter 7)
3. Use grep and regular expressions to analyze text (chapter 7)
4. Access remote systems using ssh (chapters 01 and 18)
5. Log in and switch users in multi-user targets (chapter 6)
6. Archive, compress, unpack, and uncompress files using tar, star, gzip, and bzip2 (chapter 3)
7. Create and edit text files (chapter 3)
8. Create, delete, copy, and move files and directories (chapter 3)
9. Create hard and soft links (chapter 3)
10. List, set, and change standard ugo/rwx permissions (chapter 4)
11. Locate, read, and use system documentation including man, info, and files in /usr/share/doc (chapter 2)

Create Simple Shell Scripts

12. Conditionally execute code (use of: if, test, [], etc.) (chapter 21)
13. Use Looping constructs (for, etc.) to process file, command line input (chapter 21)
14. Process script inputs ($1, $2, etc.) (chapter 21)
15. Processing output of shell commands within a script (chapter 21)

Operate Running Systems

16. Boot, reboot, and shut down a system normally (chapter 12)
17. Boot systems into different targets manually (chapter 12)
18. Interrupt the boot process in order to gain access to a system (chapter 11)
19. Identify CPU/memory intensive processes and kill processes (chapter 8)
20. Adjust process scheduling (chapter 8)
21. Manage tuning profiles (chapter 12)
22. Locate and interpret system log files and journals (chapter 12)
23. Preserve system journals (chapter 12)
24. Start, stop, and check the status of network services (chapter 12)
25. Securely transfer files between systems (chapter 18)

Configure Local Storage

26. List, create, and delete partitions on MBR and GPT disks (chapter 13)
27. Create and remove physical volumes (chapter 13)
28. Assign physical volumes to volume groups (chapter 13)
29. Create and delete logical volumes (chapter 13)
30. Configure systems to mount file systems at boot by Universally Unique ID (UUID) or label (chapter 14)
31. Add new partitions and logical volumes, and swap to a system non-destructively (chapters 13 and 14)

Create and Configure File Systems

32. Create, mount, unmount, and use vfat, ext4, and xfs file systems (chapter 14)
33. Mount and unmount network file systems using NFS (chapter 16)
34. Configure autofs (chapter 16)
35. Extend existing logical volumes (chapters 13 and 14)
36. Create and configure set-GID directories for collaboration (chapter 4)
37. Diagnose and correct file permission problems (chapter 4)

Deploy, Configure, and Maintain Systems

38. Schedule tasks using at and cron (chapter 8)
39. Start and stop services and configure services to start automatically at boot (chapter 12)
40. Configure systems to boot into a specific target automatically (chapter 12)
41. Configure time service clients (chapter 17)
42. Install and update software packages from Red Hat Network, a remote repository, or from the local file system (chapter 9 and 10)
43. Modify the system bootloader (chapter 11)

Manage Basic Networking

44. Configure IPv4 and IPv6 addresses (chapter 15)
45. Configure hostname resolution (chapter 17)
46. Configure network services to start automatically at boot (chapter 12)
47. Restrict network access using firewall-cmd/firewall (chapter 19)

Manage Users and Groups

48. Create, delete, and modify local user accounts (chapter 5)
49. Change passwords and adjust password aging for local user accounts (chapter 5 and 6)
50. Create, delete, and modify local groups and group memberships (chapter 6)
51. Configure superuser access (chapter 6)

Manage Security

52. Configure firewall settings using firewall-cmd/firewalld (chapter 19)
53. Manage default file permissions (chapter 04)
54. Configure key-based authentication for SSH (chapter 18)
55. Set enforcing and permissive modes for SELinux (chapter 20)
56. List and identify SELinux file and process context (chapter 20)
57. Restore default file contexts (chapter 20)
58. Manage SELinux port labels (chapter 20)
59. Use Boolean settings to modify system SELinux settings (chapter 20)
60. Diagnose and address routine SELinux policy violations (chapter 20)

Manage Containers

Taking the Exam

1. Save time wherever possible, as time is of the essence during the exam
2. Make certain that any changes you make **must** survive system reboots
3. Use any available text editor you feel comfortable with to modify text configuration files
4. Exam tasks are split into two groups and each group must be performed in its own assigned virtual machine
5. Inform the proctor right away if you encounter any issues with your exam system or the virtual machines
6. The exam is administered with no access to the Internet, electronic devices, or written material
7. Read each exam task fully and understand it thoroughly before attempting it
8. Read all storage tasks carefully and use the lsblk command as explained in the book to identify the right disk to perform each task on.

Exam Fee and Registration Procedure

The fee for the RHCSA exam is US$400 (plus any applicable taxes), or equivalent in local currencies. To register, visit *http://www.redhat.com/training/courses/ex200/examobjective*, select your location, and click Get Started to log in with your Red Hat credentials to continue through the registration process. The RHCSA exam is based on version 9, and it lasts for 3 hours.

About this Book

RHCSA Red Hat Enterprise Linux 9: Training and Exam Preparation Guide, Third Edition provides an in-depth coverage of the latest RHCSA (version 9) EX200 exam objectives. The most definitive guide available on the subject, this book explains concepts, analyzes configuration files, describes command outputs, provides step-by-step procedures (includes screenshots of actual commands executed and outputs they produced), and challenges the readers' comprehension of the concepts and procedures by presenting plenty of supplementary labs and sample realistic exam tasks to perform on their own.

This book has **22 chapters** that are organized logically, from building a lab environment to the fundamentals of Linux to sophisticated Linux administration topics. The book covers the topics on local RHEL 9 installation; initial interaction with the system; essential Linux commands; file compression and archiving; file editing and manipulation; standard and special permissions; file searching and access controls; user monitoring and authentication files; users, groups, and password aging; bash shell features and startup files; processes and job scheduling; basic and advanced software administration techniques; system boot process and bootloader; kernel management and system initialization; logging and system tuning; basic and advanced storage management tools and solutions; local file systems and swap regions; network device and connection configuration; hostname resolution and time synchronization; remote file systems and automounting; the secure shell service; firewall and SELinux controls; bash shell scripting; and operating system virtualization using containers.

Each chapter highlights the major topics and relevant exam objectives at the beginning and ends with several review questions & answers and Do-It-Yourself challenge labs. Throughout the book, figures, tables, screenshots, examples, warnings, notes, and exam tips are furnished to support explanation and exam preparation. There are four sample RHCSA exams that are expected to be performed using the knowledge and skills attained from reading the material, following the in-chapter exercises, and completing the end-of-chapter challenge labs. The labs and the sample exams include hints to relevant topics and/or exercises.

This book may be used as a self-learning guide by RHCSA 9 exam aspirants, a resource by instructors and students to follow in physical and virtual training sessions, an on-the-job resource for reference, and an easy-to-understand guide by novice and non-RHEL administrators.

TABLE OF CONTENTS

15. Networking, Network Devices, and Network Connections 339

List of Figures

List of Tables

## Chapter 01

Local Installation

This chapter describes the following major topics:

➢ A quick look at Linux and Open Source
➢ Linux distribution from Red Hat
➢ Recommended lab setup for RHCSA exam preparation
➢ Overview of the installer program
➢ Where are installation messages stored?
➢ What are virtual console screens?
➢ Download and install VirtualBox
➢ Create virtual machine
➢ Download and install Red Hat Enterprise Linux in virtual machine
➢ Log in and out at the graphical console
➢ Log in and out over the network

RHCSA Objectives:

04. Access remote systems using ssh
This chapter sets up the foundation for learning and practicing the exam
objectives for RHCSA

L inux is a free operating system that has been in existence and use for just over three decades. Its source code is available to developers, amateurs, and the general public for enhancements and customization. Red Hat Inc. modifies a copy of a selected version of Linux source code and introduces features, adds improvements, and fixes bugs. The company packages the updated version as a Linux distribution of their own for commercial purposes. This distribution is thoroughly tested to run smoothly and perform well on a wide range of computer hardware platforms. It is stable, robust, feature-rich, and ready to host a workload of any size.

Red Hat Enterprise Linux may be downloaded for learning, practicing, and preparing for the RHCSA exam. It is available as a single installable image file. A lab environment is necessary to practice the procedures to solidify the understanding of the concepts and tools learned. The installation process requires careful planning to identify critical system configuration pieces prior to launching the installer program. Once the operating system is installed, users can log in at the console or over the network.

A Quick Look at Linux Development

Linux is a free computer operating system (OS) that is similar to the UNIX OS in terms of concepts, features, functionality, and stability. It is referred to as a UNIX-like operating system.

Linux powers an extensive range of computer hardware platforms, from laptop and desktop computers to massive mainframes and supercomputers. Linux also runs as the base OS on networking, storage, gaming, smart television, and mobile devices. Numerous vendors, including Red Hat, IBM, Canonical, Oracle, Microsoft, DXC Technology, Novell, and Dell, offer commercial support to Linux users worldwide.

Linux is the main alternative to proprietary UNIX and Windows operating systems because of its functionality, adaptability, portability, and cost-effectiveness. Currently, over one hundred different Linux distributions are circulating from various vendors, organizations, non-profit groups, and individuals, though only a few are popular and widely recognized.

Linux is largely used in government agencies, corporate businesses, academic institutions, scientific organizations, as well as in home computers. Linux development, adoption, and usage are constantly on the rise.

Linux History in a Nutshell

In 1984, Richard Stallman, an American software engineer, had a goal to create a completely free UNIX-compatible open-source (non-proprietary) operating system. The initiative was called the GNU Project (*GNU's Not Unix*) and by 1991, significant software had been developed. The only critical piece missing was a core software component called *kernel* to drive and control the GNU software and to regulate its communication with the hardware.

Around the same time, Finnish computer science student Linus Torvalds developed a kernel and proclaimed its availability. The new kernel was named *Linux*, and it was gradually integrated with the GNU software to form what is now referred to as *GNU/Linux*, *Linux operating system*, or simply *Linux*.

Linux was released under the GNU *General Public License* (GPL). Initially written to run on Intel x86-based computers, the first version (0.01) was released in September 1991 with little more than 10,000 lines of code. In 1994, the first major release (1.0.0) was introduced, followed by a series of successive major and minor versions until the release of version 5.0 in 2019. At the time of this writing, version 5.10 with millions of lines of code, is the latest long-term stable kernel.

The Linux kernel, and the operating system in general, has been enhanced with contributions from tens of thousands of software programmers, amateurs, and organizations around the world into a large and complex system under GNU GPL, which provides public access to its source code free of charge and with full consent to amend, package, and redistribute.

Linux from Red Hat

Red Hat, Inc. used the available Linux source code and created one of the first commercial Linux operating system distribution called *Red Hat Linux* (RHL). The company released the first version 1.0 in November 1994. Several versions followed until the last version in the series, Red Hat Linux 9 (later referred to as RHEL 3), based on kernel 2.4.20, was released in March 2003. Red Hat renamed their Red Hat Linux brand as *Red Hat Enterprise Linux* (RHEL) commencing 2003.

RHL was originally assembled and enhanced within the Red Hat company. In 2003, Red Hat sponsored and facilitated the *Fedora Project* and invited the user community to join hands in enhancing and updating the source code. This project served as the test bed for developing and testing new features and enabled Red Hat to include the improved code in successive versions of RHEL.

The Fedora distribution is completely free, while RHEL is commercial. RHEL 4 was based on kernel 2.6.9 and released in February 2005, RHEL 5 on kernel 2.6.18 with release date in March 2007, RHEL 6 on kernel 2.6.32 and released in November 2010, RHEL 7 on kernel 3.10 and released in June 2014, RHEL 8 on kernel 4.18 and released in May 2019, and RHEL 9 was based on kernel 5.14 with release date in May 2022). These RHEL releases were built using Fedora distributions 3, 6, 13, 20, 28, and 34 respectively.

RHEL 9 has been tested to run on bare-metal computer hardware, virtualized platforms, cloud-based virtual machines, high-end graphics workstations, IBM Power servers, IBM System Z, etc.

Lab Environment for Practice

RHEL 9 is available as a free download from Red Hat for Intel and AMD processor machines. You will need to create a free Red Hat user account in order to download it. The downloaded image file can then be attached to a *Virtual Machine* (VM) as an ISO image, burned to a DVD to support installation on a physical computer, or placed on a remote server for network-based installations via HTTP, FTP, or NFS protocol.

 An ISO image is a single file that represents the content of an entire DVD or CD.

Burning the image to a DVD and configuring a server for network-based installations are beyond the scope of this book. This chapter will focus on local installation of the operating system with an ISO image.

Lab Environment for In-Chapter Exercises

Throughout this book, there will be several discussions around system, network, and security, along with examples on how to implement and administer them. Each chapter will contain a number of exercises that will help you perform certain tasks and execute commands.

You'll need a laptop or a desktop computer with at least a dual-core processor, 8GB of physical memory (16GB preferred), and 50GB of free storage space to run two virtual machines with required storage. If you want to use the static IP addresses on your home router, make sure that you keep a mapping between them, and the ones provided below to avoid any confusion. The computer must have hardware virtualization support enabled in the BIOS/firmware to allow for 64-bit OS installation. Here is a summary of what is needed and how it will be configured:

Base/Host Operating System:	Windows 10/11 or MacOS 10.12 or higher
Hypervisor Software:	Oracle VM VirtualBox Manager (VirtualBox or VB in short) 7.0 or higher
Number of VMs:	2
vCPUs in each VM:	2
OS in each VM:	RHEL 9.1
VM1 (RHEL9-VM1):	*server1.example.com* with static IP 192.168.0.110/24, 2048MB memory, 1x20GB virtual disk for OS, and one virtual network device. This VM will be built using the RHEL 9.1 ISO image. Exercises 1-1 and 1-2 will walk through the process of installation. In Chapter 15, "Networking, Network Devices, and Network Connections", you will add another virtual network device and will rename this server to *server10.example.com*.

VM2 (RHEL9-VM2): *server2.example.com* with static IP 192.168.0.120/24, 2048MB memory, 1x20GB virtual disk for OS, and one virtual network device. In Chapter 13, "Storage Management", you will add 4x250MB and 1x5GB data disks for numerous upcoming exercises. You will build this VM using the RHEL 9.1 ISO image by referencing the steps outlined in Exercise 1-1 and Exercise 1-2. In Chapter 15, "Networking, Network Devices, and Network Connections", you will add another virtual network device and will rename this server to *server20.example.com*.

Check your Windows/MacOS IP assignments and make sure to use the same network subnet for your RHEL VMs. For instance, use 172.16.3.110/24 and 172.16.3.120/24 for your VMs if your Windows/MacOS is on the 172.16.3.0/24 subnet.

The setup for the lab is shown in Figure 1-1.

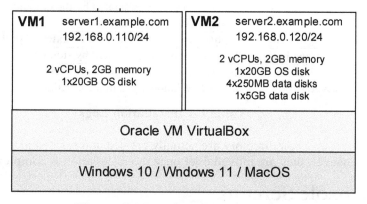

Figure 1-1 Lab Setup for Exercises

You will install VirtualBox 7.0 (or higher) on Windows 10/11 or MacOS 10.12 (or higher). You may use VMware or other virtualization software as an alternative; however, all exercises and examples in this book reference VirtualBox.

Lab Environment for End-of-Chapter Labs
For the end-of-chapter labs, I recommend you build a new environment with two virtual machines with the exact same specifications in terms of CPU, memory, network interface, and storage as RHEL-VM1 (*server1*) and RHEL-VM2 (*server2*). You may name the new systems RHEL-VM3 (*server3*) and RHEL-VM4 (*server4*). This new environment may be created after you have completed all in-chapter exercises and you are ready to perform the labs with minimal assistance (hints included but no solutions provided).

The RHEL Installer Program
The RHEL installer program is called *Anaconda*. There are several configuration options on the main screen that require modification before the installation process begins. Some of the questions are compulsory and must be answered appropriately while others are optional and may be skipped for post-installation setup.

The configuration can be done in any sequence. You should have the minimum mandatory configuration data handy and be ready to enter it. Some of the key configuration items are language, keyboard type, time zone, disk partitioning, hostname/IP, software selection, root password, and user information.

Installation Logs

There are plenty of log files created and updated as the installation progresses. These files record configuration and status information. You can view their contents after the installation has been completed to check how the installation proceeded. Most of these files are described in Table 1-1.

File	Description
/root/anaconda-ks.cfg	Records the configuration entered
/var/log/anaconda/anaconda.log	Contains informational, debug, and other general messages
/var/log/anaconda/journal.log	Stores messages generated by many services and components during system installation
/var/log/anaconda/packaging.log	Records messages generated by the dnf and rpm commands during software installation
/var/log/anaconda/program.log	Captures messages generated by external programs
/var/log/anaconda/storage.log	Records messages generated by storage modules
/var/log/anaconda/syslog	Records messages related to the kernel
/var/log/anaconda/X.log	Stores X Window System information

Table 1-1 Installation Logs

Files in the */var/log/anaconda* directory are actually created and resided in the */tmp* directory during the installation; however, they are moved over once the installation is complete.

Virtual Console Screens

During the installation, there are six text-based virtual console screens available to monitor the process, view diagnostic messages, and discover and fix any issues encountered. The information displayed on the console screens is captured in the installation log files (Table 1-1). You can switch between screens by pressing a combination of keys as described below.

Console 1 (Ctrl+Alt+F1): This is the main screen. Before Anaconda begins, you will select a language to use during installation, and then it will switch the default console to the sixth screen (Console 6).

Console 2 (Ctrl+Alt+F2): Presents the shell interface to run commands as the *root* user.

Console 3 (Ctrl+Alt+F3): Displays installation messages and stores them in */tmp/anaconda.log* file. This file also captures information on detected hardware, in addition to other data.

Console 4 (Ctrl+Alt+F4): Shows storage messages and records them in */tmp/storage.log* file.

Console 5 (Ctrl+Alt+F5): Exhibits program messages and logs them to */tmp/program.log* file.

Console 6 (Ctrl+Alt+F6): Default graphical configuration and installation console screen.

Exercise 1-1: Download and Install VirtualBox Software, and Create a Virtual Machine

In this exercise, you will download and install VirtualBox software. You will create a virtual machine to set up the foundation to install RHEL 9 for the next exercise.

> **EXAM TIP:** Downloading and installing VirtualBox software and creating a virtual machine are not part of the exam objectives. These tasks have been included here only to support readers with building their own lab environment for practice.

Downloading and Installing VirtualBox

VirtualBox is available for free download and use. At the time of this writing, the latest version is 7.0; however, you can use any previous 6.x or a future version. Here is a quick guide on how to download and install the current version of VirtualBox on a Windows 11 (works on Windows 10 as well) computer.

1. Go to *www.virtualbox.org* (Figure 1-2) and click "Download VirtualBox 7.0".

Figure 1-2 VirtualBox Website

2. On the next screen, click on "Windows hosts". This will start a download to your computer.

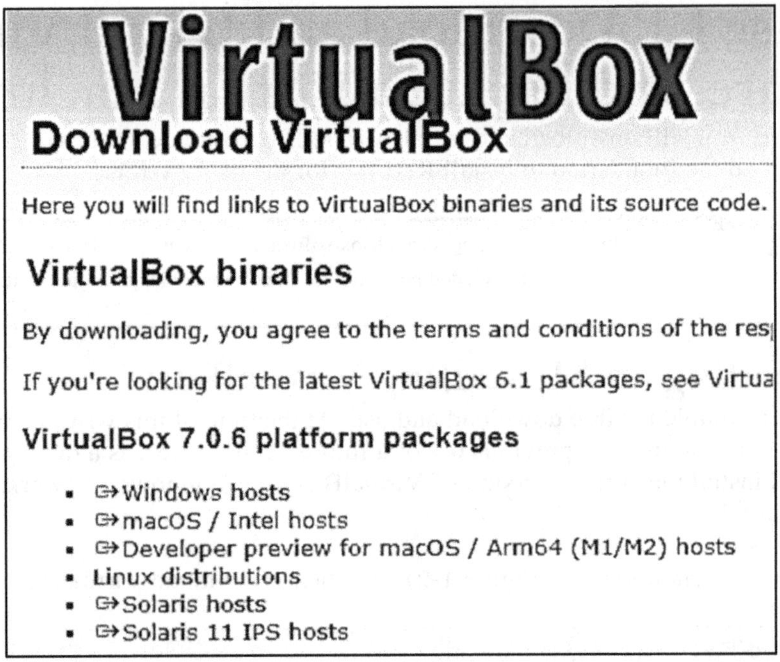

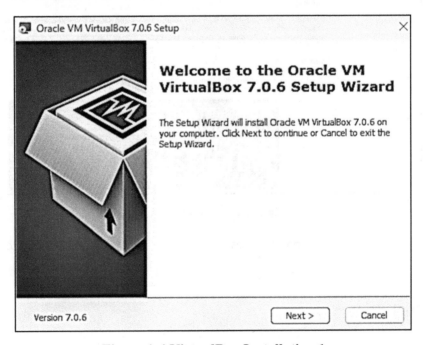

VirtualBox
Download VirtualBox

Here you will find links to VirtualBox binaries and its source code.

VirtualBox binaries

By downloading, you agree to the terms and conditions of the res|

If you're looking for the latest VirtualBox 6.1 packages, see Virtua

VirtualBox 7.0.6 platform packages

- ↪Windows hosts
- ↪macOS / Intel hosts
- ↪Developer preview for macOS / Arm64 (M1/M2) hosts
- Linux distributions
- ↪Solaris hosts
- ↪Solaris 11 IPS hosts

Figure 1-3 VirtualBox Download

The software is now available on your computer.

3. Double-click on the VirtualBox binary to start the installation. Click Next to proceed on the first screen that appears.

Figure 1-4 VirtualBox Installation 1

4. If needed, choose a different location on the disk for installation. Click Next to continue.

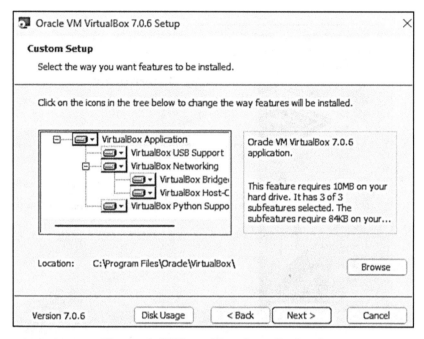

Figure 1-5 VirtualBox Installation 2

5. Accept the warning and continue by pressing Yes.

Figure 1-6 VirtualBox Installation 3

6. The installation process will report if any Python Core and/or win32api dependencies are missing. Click Yes to proceed.

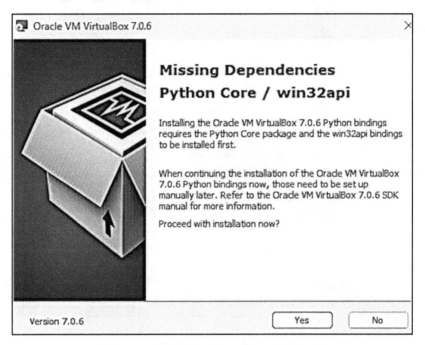

Figure 1-7 VirtualBox Installation 4

7. The setup wizard is now ready to begin the installation. Click Install to proceed.

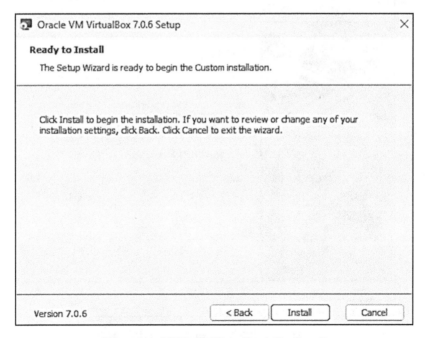

Figure 1-8 VirtualBox Installation 5

8. Click Finish to continue.

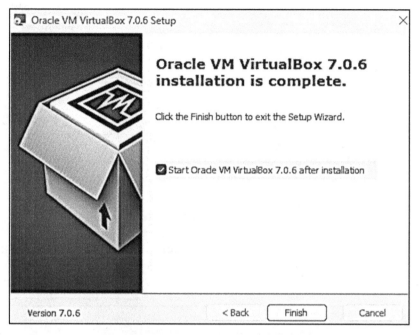

Figure 1-9 VirtualBox Installation 6

This brings the installation of VirtualBox to a successful completion. It will also launch the application when you click Finish.

Creating a Virtual Machine

Use VirtualBox to create the first virtual machine called *RHEL9-VM1* with specifications described earlier in this chapter. Here are the steps for the creation.

1. Launch VirtualBox if it is not already running. The interface looks similar to what is shown in Figure 1-10.

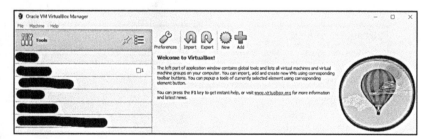

Figure 1-10 Virtual Machine Creation 1

2. Click on New on the top menu bar to start the virtual machine creation wizard as shown in Figure 1-11. Enter the name *RHEL9-VM1*, select Linux as the operating system type, and Red Hat (64-bit) as the version. For this demonstration, accept the default location to store the VM files on the C drive. Click Next to continue.

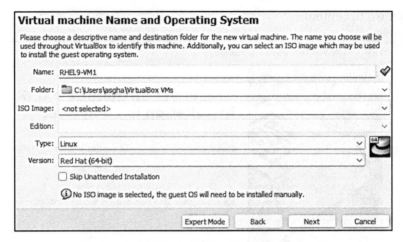

Figure 1-11 Virtual Machine Creation 2

3. In the next window, specify the memory size and number of processors you want allocated to the VM. Accept the recommended 2GB for memory and move the slider to the right to select 2 vCPUs and click Next.

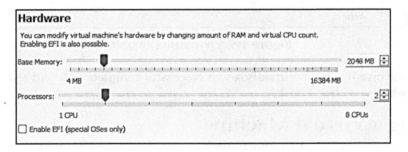

Figure 1-12 Virtual Machine Creation 3

4. The VM will need a virtual hard disk to store RHEL 9 operating system. For this demonstration, choose the creation of a virtual hard disk now with a size of 20GB. Both are also the defaults.

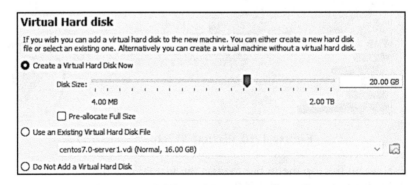

Figure 1-13 Virtual Machine Creation 4

5. Clicking Next on the previous window completes the VM creation process and displays a summary of the selections. Click Finish to end the wizard.

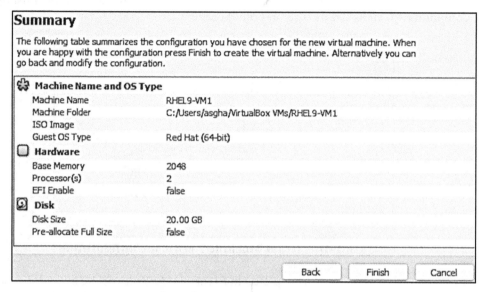

Figure 1-14 Virtual Machine Creation 5

6. VirtualBox will have the VM listed along with its configuration. See Figure 1-15.

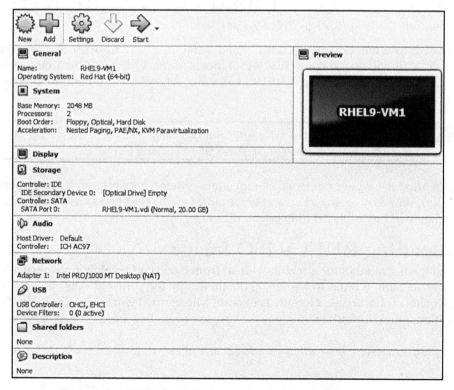

Figure 1-15 Virtual Machine Configuration Summary

7. On the VM configuration page above (Figure 1-15), click Network and choose Bridged Adapter from the dropdown and ensure that the right network connection name is selected. See Figure 1-16. This will allow the RHEL VM to communicate with the hosting Windows computer as well as the internet in both directions.

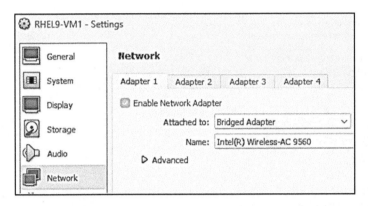

Figure 1-16 Virtual Machine Network Configuration

There are other configurable items as depicted in Figure 1-15. You will be attaching a bootable RHEL 9 OS image to the VM under Storage (Optical Drive Empty) shortly and may be making additional changes later.

Exercise 1-2: Download and Install RHEL

This exercise will build *server1* in *RHEL9-VM1*.

In this exercise, you will download RHEL 9 and install it in *RHEL9-VM1* that you created in Exercise 1-1. You will attach the RHEL 9 ISO image to the VM, name the Linux system *server1.example.com*, and configure IP 192.168.0.110/24. Additional configuration will be supplied as the installation advances.

> **EXAM TIP:** Downloading and installing RHEL 9 are beyond the scope of the exam. They have been included here only to support the readers with building their own lab environment for practice.

The user creation, base environments, storage management, network device and connection configuration, time synchronization, and other topics are not explained as part of this exercise; however, they will be discussed in later chapters.

Downloading RHEL 9 ISO Image

RHEL 9 image is available for a free download from Red Hat Developer's website. You need to create a user account in order to log in and obtain a copy for yourself. Alternatively, you can use your credentials on Facebook, Google, LinkedIn, Microsoft, Twitter, etc. for login. For this demonstration, you will find instructions on how to open a new account and download the software.

1. Visit *https://developers.redhat.com/login* and click "Register for a Red Hat Account".

Figure 1-17 Red Hat User Account Creation 1

2. Fill out the form by providing a unique username, email address, and password. Make sure to checkmark the boxes to accept terms and conditions. Click "Create My Account" at the bottom of the screen to continue.

Figure 1-18 Red Hat User Account Creation 2

3. After an account has been created, go back to the login page *https://developers.redhat.com/login* and submit the credentials to log in.
4. Click on "Explore Products" and then "Red Hat Enterprise Linux" under Featured Downloads.
5. Click "Download RHEL at no-cost". An ISO file of the latest version of RHEL will begin downloading for x86_64 computer. The latest version of RHEL available at the time of this writing is 9.1.

Figure 1-19 Red Hat Developer Login

The filename of the downloaded image for RHEL version 9.1 will be *rhel-baseos-9.1-x86_64-dvd.iso* and it will be around 8.4GB in size. You can move the file to a disk location on your computer where you want it stored.

Attaching RHEL 9 ISO Image to the Virtual Machine

We now attach the RHEL 9 ISO image to *RHEL9-VM1* to boot and install the OS in the VM. Click "[Optical Drive] Empty" under Storage in VirtualBox for this VM and select Choose Disk File. Navigate to where you have the ISO image stored. Highlight the image and click Open to attach it to the VM. After the image has been attached, the VirtualBox Storage configuration will look like as depicted in Figure 1-20.

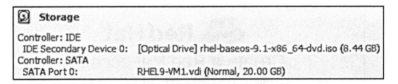

Figure 1-20 ISO Image Attached to VM

Leave the rest of the settings to their default values.

Launching the Installer

6. While the VM is highlighted in VirtualBox, click the Start button at the top to power up the VM.
7. A console screen pops up displaying the boot menu (Figure 1-21) with three options. Press the Spacebar key to halt the autoboot process.

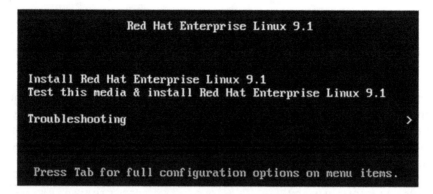

Figure 1-21 Boot Menu

The first option, "Install Red Hat Enterprise Linux 9.1", is used for installing the highlighted RHEL version unless you want the installation media tested for integrity before continuing, in which case you will select the second option. Anaconda awaits 60 seconds for you to alter the selection, or it proceeds and autoboots using the second option on the list, which is also the default. The third option, "Troubleshooting", allows you to address some boot-related issues that might occur during installation.

Use the Up or Down arrow key to select the "Install Red Hat Enterprise Linux 9.1" entry and press Enter. The installer is launched in graphical mode.

8. The installer program shows a welcome screen with a long list of supported languages that you could use during installation. The default is set to English. Click Continue to accept the default and move on.

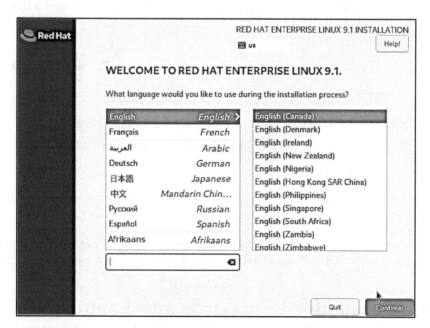

Figure 1-22 Language Selection

💡 If all the content does not fit on the console screen, try changing the Graphics Controller to VMSVGA under Settings | Display in the VirtualBox Manager for the VM. You will need to power off the VM to make this change.

9. The "Installation Summary" screen appears next, as shown in Figure 1-23. You have the opportunity to make all necessary configuration changes prior to starting the installation. This screen presents a unified interface to configure localization (keyboard, language, date, time, and time zone), software (installation source and software selection), system (disk partitioning, network assignments, hostname setting, etc.), and user settings (root password and user creation).

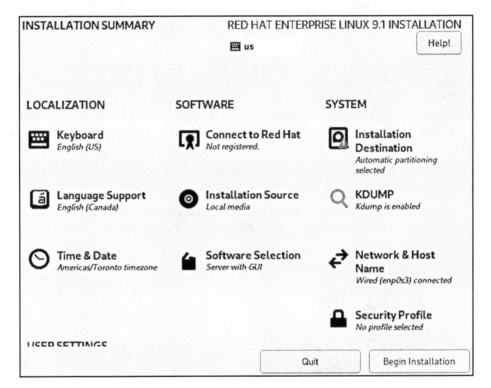

Figure 1-23 Installation Summary | Main

💡 Any items highlighted in red and with a warning sign must be configured before the Begin Installation button at the bottom right of the screen is enabled.

There is no particular sequence to configure these items. If you do not wish to change a non-highlighted item, simply leave it intact and the installation program will apply the default settings for it.

Adding Support for Keyboards and Languages

10. Anaconda presents additional choices for keyboard layouts and languages for use during and after the installation. The default is the US English for the keyboard and Canadian English as the language (for my location). Go ahead and change them as required.

Configuring Time & Date

11. Click Time & Date to set the time zone (region and city), date, and time for the system. See Figure 1-24. Click Done in the upper left corner to save the changes and return to the Installation Summary screen.

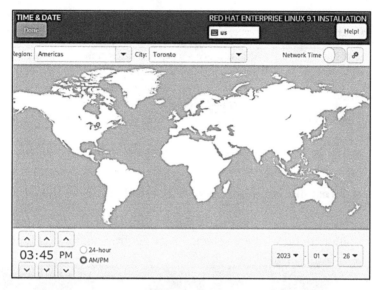

Figure 1-24 Installation Summary | Time & Date

Figure 1-24 reflects three adjustments from the default. The city is changed to Toronto, the clock format is switched to AM/PM, and the network time is turned off.

Choosing an Installation Source

12. You can set the installation source for RHEL 9. By default, Anaconda chooses the auto-detected installation media (DVD, USB flash drive, or ISO image) that was used to start this installation. For this demonstration, leave the installation source to the default. Click Done to return to the Installation Summary page.

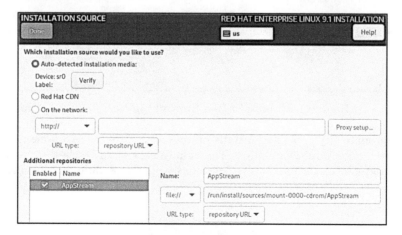

Figure 1-25 Installation Summary | Installation Source

Selecting Software to be Installed

13. You can choose the base operating environment that you want installed. Base environments are predefined groups of software packages designed for specific use cases. The six available base environments are described in Table 1-2.

Base Environment	Description
Server with GUI	Infrastructure server with graphics support
Server	Infrastructure server without graphics support
Minimal Install	Installs a minimum number of packages for basic system use
Workstation	Ideal for desktop and laptop users who require graphical support and with a minimal set of services
Custom Operating System	Gives you a set of basic building blocks for custom installations
Virtualization Host	Infrastructure plus virtualization support to host virtual machines

Table 1-2 Installation Summary | Software Selection | Base Environments

Choosing a base environment in the left pane reveals additional components on the right that may be ticked for installation along with the selected base environment. See Figure 1-26.

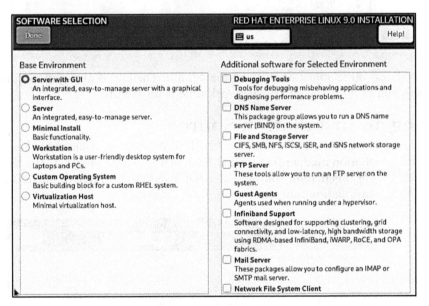

Figure 1-26 Installation Summary | Software Selection

The installer automatically picks and installs prerequisite software components to fulfill dependency requirements for a successful installation. The default base environment is "Server with GUI" for this demonstration. Leave add-ons to the default as well. Click Done to return to the Installation Summary page.

Configuring Installation Destination

14. The Installation Destination allows you to choose an available local or remote disk for partitioning and installing the OS on. Anaconda selects "Automatic partitioning selected" (highlighted in red) on the Installation Summary page (Figure 1-23), which you can change on Installation Destination (Figure 1-27). By default, the 20GB virtual disk you assigned to the VM is automatically picked up by the installer as the target and it is represented as *sda*. The "Encrypt my data" checkbox under Encryption (scroll down to see it) encrypts all partitions on the disk. If you choose this option, you will be prompted to enter a passphrase to access the partitions later. The "Full disk summary and bootloader" link at the bottom left allows you to choose a disk to place the bootloader program on. This does not need to be modified on a single disk system. The default and the only bootloader program available in RHEL 9 is called GRUB2, and it is explained at length in Chapter 11, "Boot Process, GRUB2, and the Linux Kernel".

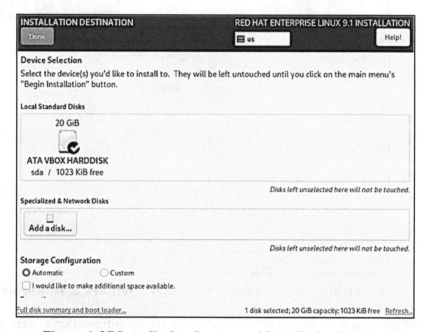

Figure 1-27 Installation Summary | Installation Destination

For this demonstration, stick to the default automatic partitioning scheme. Simply click Done to return to the previous screen. This scheme will create three partitions—*/boot*, */*, and swap—and together they will consume the entire selected disk space.

Configuring Network and Hostname

15. Assigning appropriate IP and hostname are essential for system functionality in a network environment. Click Network & Hostname on the Installation Summary page and a window similar to the one shown in Figure 1-28 will appear. Anaconda detects all attached network interfaces, but it does not automatically assign them IPs. Also, the default hostname field is empty. You need to modify these assignments so that your system can communicate with other systems on the network. Currently, there is one network device assigned to the system, which is represented as *enp0s3*.

The terms "network interface" and "network device" refer to the same network hardware component. These terms are used interchangeably throughout this book. These terms are different from the term "network connection", which is the software configuration applied to a network interface/device.

The default naming convention for network devices vary based on the underlying virtualization software being used.

Enter the hostname *server1.example.com* in the Hostname field and click Apply next to the field to activate it. For IP assignments, click Configure at the bottom right and enter IP information manually. You also need to ensure that the network connection is set to autostart.

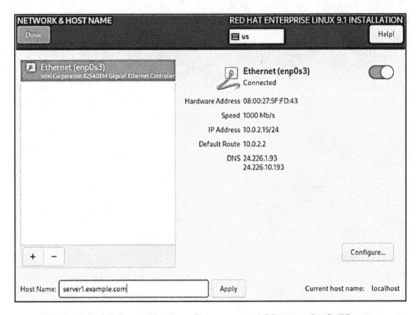

Figure 1-28 Installation Summary | Network & Hostname

There are multiple tabs available on the network connection configuration screen, as depicted in Figure 1-29. Go to IPv4 Settings and choose Manual from the drop-down list against Method. Click Add and enter address 192.168.0.110, netmask 24, and gateway 192.168.0.1. Click Save to save the configuration and return to the Network & Hostname window.

Check your Windows/MacOS host computer IP assignments and make sure to use the same subnet for your RHEL VMs. For instance, use 172.16.3.110/120 for your VMs if your host system is on the 172.16.3 subnet.

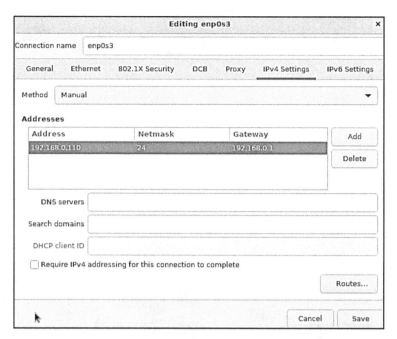

Figure 1-29 Installation Summary | Network & Hostname | Configure

On the Network & Hostname window, slide the ON/OFF switch to the ON position so that the new assignments take effect right away. This will also ensure that the assignments are applied automatically on subsequent system reboots.

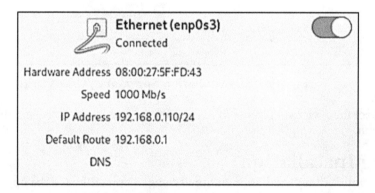

Figure 1-30 Installation Summary | Network & Hostname

Now click Done to return to the Installation Summary page. Chapter 16 "Networking, Network Devices, and Network Connections" discusses configuring hostnames, network interfaces, and network connections in detail.

Configuring User Settings

16. Setting the *root* user password is essential on a Linux system. Click Root Password on the Installation Summary page and a window similar to the one shown in Figure 1-31 will appear. Enter a password twice. Also tick the box "Allow root SSH login with password" to enable direct root login access to the VM. Click Done to return to the previous page.

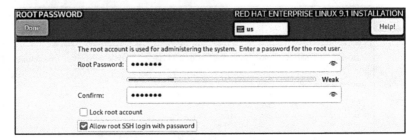

Figure 1-31 Installation Summary | Root Password

You will need to click Done twice if the password you entered is weak or too short.

17. Next, click User Creation (not shown earlier on the Installation Summary page image) under User Settings and create a user account called *user1* and assign it a password. Click Done (two clicks if the password entered is too short or simple) to return to the previous screen.

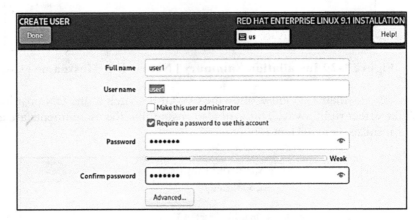

Figure 1-32 Installation Summary | User Creation

Anaconda will set the *root* user password and create the user account during the configuration part of the installation.

Beginning Installation

18. You're now on the Installation Summary page. You still have the opportunity to go back and configure or reconfigure any items you've missed. Once you are satisfied, click Begin Installation at the bottom right to initiate the installation based on the configuration entered in the previous steps. Anaconda will partition the selected disk, install the software, and perform all the configuration. Any data previously stored on the disk will be erased and unrecoverable.

The Begin Installation button remains inactive until all the items highlighted in red and with a warning sign are configured.

The configuration and software copy will take some time to complete. The progress will depend on the system performance and resources allocated to the VM.

Concluding Installation

19. When the required setup is complete and all software packages are installed, the Reboot System button at the bottom right on the Installation Progress screen (Figure 1-33) will become active. Click this button to reboot the new system.

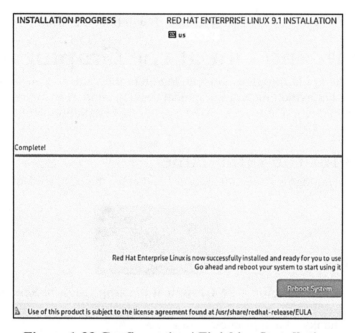

Figure 1-33 Configuration | Finishing Installation

By default, VirtualBox does not automatically change the default boot order for the VM. This may result in rebooting the VM from the ISO image again and restarting the installation. To avoid this situation, power off the virtual machine from VirtualBox Manager and alter the boot sequence.

Changing Default Boot Order

20. Power off the VM from VirtualBox Manager.
21. The current boot sequence, as shown in Figure 1-34, is set to boot with floppy first and then optical (DVD/CD) followed by hard disk.

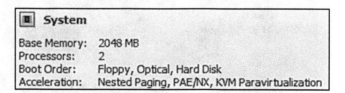

Figure 1-34 VirtualBox Manager | System | Boot Order

22. Change this sequence to hard disk first and optical next. See Figure 1-35. Untick Floppy, as it is not needed.

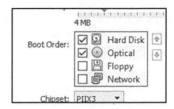

Figure 1-35 VirtualBox Manager | System | Boot Order | Alter

Power on the VM from the VirtualBox Manager. It will boot the installed OS.

Logging In and Out at the Graphical Console

Now that the installation is complete, you can log on to the system. You selected the Server with GUI base environment, which includes graphical desktop support to interact with the system. You also entered credentials for a user account, *user1*, during installation. You can now use this account to log in.

Logging In for the First Time

1. On the graphical logon screen, click *user1* and enter the password when prompted.

Figure 1-36 Graphical Desktop | Sign-in Screen

2. Select "No Thanks" when prompted for a tour.
3. The default graphical desktop included in RHEL 9 is the GNOME desktop environment (Figure 1-37). You should now be able to start using the system as *user1*.

Figure 1-37 GNOME Desktop Environment

Close the System Not Registered message as you skipped Connect to Red Hat under Installation Summary | Software during configuration.

GNOME stands for *GNU Network Object Model Environment*. It is the default graphical display manager and desktop environment for users in RHEL 9. Chapter 02 "Initial Interaction with the System" provides more details on this topic.

Logging Out

4. Logging out of the system is easy. Click on any icon in the top right corner, expand Power Off/Log Out, and click Log Out. See Figure 1-38. The user will be signed out and the main login screen will reappear.

Figure 1-38 GNOME Desktop Environment| Log Out

Now, let's look at how to connect and log in to the system remotely from over the network.

Exercise 1-3: Logging In from Windows

This exercise should be done on the Windows computer hosting the virtual machine for *server1*.

In this exercise, you will use a program called PuTTY to access *server1* using its IP address and as *user1*. You will run some basic commands on the server for validation. You will log off to terminate the session.

1. On Windows desktop, download PuTTY free of charge from the Internet. Launch this program and enter the target host's IP address. Leave the rest of the settings to their defaults.

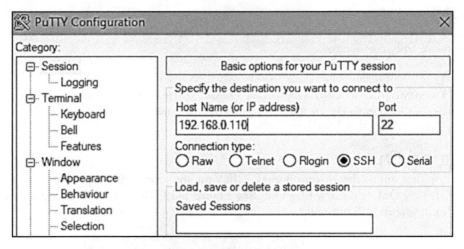

Figure 1-39 PuTTY Interface

You may assign a name to this session (typically the hostname is used as the session name) in the Saved Sessions field and click Save to store this information so as to avoid retyping in the future.

2. Click on the "Open" button at the bottom of the screen to try a connection.
3. Click Yes to accept a potential security breach warning. This alert only appears once.
4. Enter *user1* and password at the "login as" prompt to log in:

```
login as: user1
user1@192.168.0.110's password:
Register this system with Red Hat Insights: insights-client --register
Create an account or view all your systems at https://red.ht/insights-
Last login: Thu Jan 26 17:02:25 2023
[user1@server1 ~]$
```

5. Issue the basic Linux commands *whoami*, *hostname*, and *pwd* to confirm that you are logged in as *user1* on *server1* and placed in the correct home directory:

```
[user1@server1 ~]$
[user1@server1 ~]$ whoami
user1
[user1@server1 ~]$ hostname
server1.example.com
[user1@server1 ~]$ pwd
/home/user1
[user1@server1 ~]$
```

6. Run the *logout* or the *exit* command or press the key combination Ctrl+d to log off *server1* and terminate the login session:

```
[user1@server1 ~]$ logout
```

This concludes the exercise. Going forward, you should be doing all the exercises and labs presented in this book in PuTTY (ssh) terminal sessions.

Chapter 02 will explore how to navigate within the GNOME desktop environment, execute basic Linux commands at the command prompt, and obtain necessary help.

Chapter Summary

In this chapter, we started by looking at Linux history and exploring available versions of Linux from Red Hat. We examined various pre-installation items for our lab environment to prepare for a smooth installation in order to practice the exercises and labs presented in this book. We demonstrated downloading the images for VirtualBox Manager software and RHEL 9. We built a virtual machine and installed RHEL 9 in it. Finally, we logged in to the new system at the console and over the network via PuTTY to verify the installation.

Review Questions

1. RHEL 9 cannot be installed over the network. True or False?
2. Can you install RHEL 9 in text mode?
3. You can use the */boot* partition within LVM to boot RHEL. True or False?
4. Which kernel version is the initial release of RHEL 9 based on?
5. Several log files are created and updated in the */tmp* directory during the installation process. Where are these files moved to after the completion of installation?
6. The Minimal Install base environment includes the graphical support. True or False?
7. Name the RHEL installer program.
8. How many console screens do you have access to during the installation process?
9. RHEL 9 may be downloaded from Red Hat's developer site. True or False?
10. What is the name of the default graphical user desktop if Server with GUI is installed?

Answers to Review Questions

1. False. RHEL 9 can be installed with installation files located on a network server.
2. Yes, RHEL 9 can be installed using text mode.
3. False. */boot* cannot reside within LVM.
4. The initial release of RHEL 9 is based on kernel version 5.14.
5. These files are moved to the */var/log* directory.
6. False. Minimal Install base environment does not include graphics support.
7. The name of the RHEL installer program is Anaconda.
8. There are six console screens available to you during the installation process.
9. True. RHEL 9 may be downloaded from *developers.redhat.com*. You need to open a new account or use an existing before you can download it.
10. The default graphical desktop is called GNOME desktop environment.

Do-It-Yourself Challenge Labs

The following labs are useful to strengthen most of the concepts and topics learned in this chapter. It is expected that you perform the labs without external help. A step-by-step guide is not supplied, as the knowledge and skill required to implement the lab have already been disseminated in the chapter; however, hints to the relevant major topic(s) are included.

Lab 1-1: Build RHEL9-VM2 (server2)

Create another virtual machine called *RHEL9-VM2* in VirtualBox, attach the ISO image to it, and install RHEL 9.1. Use the configuration provided in "Lab Environment for Practice" and follow the procedures outlined in Exercise 1-1 and Exercise 1-2. Use PuTTY with the IP address of the new server to connect to it.

## Chapter 02

Initial Interaction with the System

This chapter describes the following major topics:

➤ Interact with display manager and understand graphical interface
➤ Overview of Linux directory structure
➤ Recognize top-level directories
➤ Understand command construct
➤ Describe and run basic Linux commands
➤ Obtain help using multiple native tools and RHEL documentation

RHCSA Objectives:

01. Access a shell prompt and issue commands with correct syntax
11. Locate, read, and use system documentation including man, info, and files in /usr/share/doc

Wayland

Wayland is an advanced display protocol that sets up the foundation for running graphical applications in RHEL, which includes system administration tools, user applications, as well as graphical display and desktop manager programs. Working in a graphical environment to interact with the system is convenient for users with limited command line knowledge or specific requirements.

Linux files are organized logically for ease of administration. This file organization is maintained in hundreds of directories located in larger containers called file systems. Red Hat Enterprise Linux follows the File system Hierarchy Standard for file organization, which describes names, locations, and permissions for many file types and directories.

Linux offers a variety of commands for users and system managers. User commands are general purpose that are intended for execution by any user on the system. However, system management commands require elevated privileges of the superuser. Knowledge of these tools is essential for productive usage and efficient administration of the system. This chapter provides an analysis of command components and how to construct a command. Following that, it introduces a few basic user-level commands.

The availability of native help on the system simplifies task execution for Linux users and system administrators alike. This assistance is available on commands and configuration files via locally installed searchable manual pages and documentation for installed packages. In addition, Red Hat documentation website provides a wealth of information on various topics, procedures, and command usage.

Linux Graphical Environment

RHEL allows users to work in both text and graphical environments. Text interface might be cumbersome, but it is the preferred choice for administrators and developers. Nevertheless, a graphical environment provides easier and convenient interaction with the OS by hiding the challenges that users may otherwise experience when working in text-mode.

Wayland is a client/server display protocol that sets up the foundation for running graphical programs and applications in RHEL 9. It is available alongside the legacy X Window System, which has been around in RHEL for decades. Wayland provides superior graphics capabilities, features, and performance than X. There are two components that are critical to the functionality of a graphical environment: a *display manager* (a.k.a. *login manager*) and a *desktop environment*. Both are launched following the completion of the groundwork established by Wayland.

Display/Login Manager

A display/login manager handles the presentation of graphical login screen. It allows users to enter credentials to log on to the system. A preconfigured graphical *desktop manager* appears after the credentials are verified. In RHEL 9, the default display manager is called *GNOME Display Manager* (GDM). Figure 2-1 provides an image of GDM.

Figure 2-1 GNOME Display Manager

The login screen presents a list of all normal user accounts that exist on the system. You can log in as any one of them by selecting the desired account. If you wish to sign in as an unlisted user or the *root* user, click "Not Listed?" and enter the username and password for the desired account. The current system date and time also appear at the top of the login screen.

There are two downward arrowheads at the top right of the login screen. The arrowhead on the left is to enable or disable an accessibility feature. The arrowhead on the right allows you to power off or reboot the system and change the system volume. More controls become available after you have logged in. There are three additional icons at the top right that show the network connectivity, sound level, and battery/power status.

Desktop Environment

Once the credentials are validated for a user, the display/login manager establishes a *Desktop Environment* (DE) to work in. RHEL 9 comes with several graphical desktop software with GNOME desktop environment set as the default. It provides an easy and point-and-click GUI for users to run programs and operating system tools. Figure 2-2 is an image of the default GNOME desktop environment for *root*.

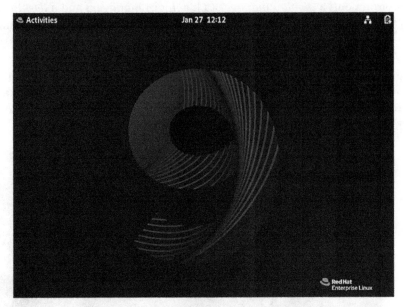

Figure 2-2 GNOME Desktop Environment

If you have worked with Microsoft Windows or MacOS, you should have no difficulty using this desktop environment. The default screen has an Activities icon at the top left, which allows you to search and access programs. Figure 2-3 depicts a list of application icons at the bottom when you click on Activities.

Figure 2-3 GNOME Desktop Environment | Activities

These application icons represent (from the left) the Firefox web browser, file manager, software updates, GNOME help, and shell terminal. The icon with nine dots displays all available programs, including Settings. The Settings application includes administrative and user-level controls to view or modify configuration for Wi-Fi, Bluetooth, desktop background, notifications, regional settings, privacy, sound, power, screensaver, network, and more.

Linux Directory Structure and File Systems

Linux files are organized logically in a hierarchy for ease of administration and recognition. This organization is maintained in hundreds of directories located in larger containers called *file systems*. Red Hat Enterprise Linux follows the *Filesystem Hierarchy Standard* (FHS) for file organization, which describes names, locations, and permissions for many file types and directories.

Linux file systems contain files and subdirectories. A subdirectory, also referred to as a *child* directory, is located under a *parent* directory. The parent directory is a subdirectory of a higher-level directory. The Linux directory structure is analogous to an inverted tree, where the top of the tree is the root of the directory, tree branches are subdirectories, and leaves are files. The root of the directory is represented by the forward slash character (/), and this is where the entire directory structure is ultimately connected. The forward slash is also used as a directory separator in a path, such as */etc/rc.d/init.d/README*.

In this example, the *etc* subdirectory is located under /, making *root* the parent of *etc* (which is a child), *rc.d* (child) is located under *etc* (parent), *init.d* (child) is located under *rc.d* (parent), and *README* (leaf) is located under *init.d* (parent) at the bottom.

 The term *subdirectory* is used for a directory that has a parent directory.

Each directory has a parent directory and a child directory, with the exception of the root and the lowest level subdirectories. The root directory has no parent, and the lowest level subdirectory has no child.

Top-Level Directories

The key top-level directories under the / are shown in Figure 2-4. Some of these hold *static* data while others contain *dynamic* or *variable* information. Static data refers to file content that remains unchanged unless modified explicitly. Dynamic or variable data, in contrast, refers to file content that is modified and updated as required by system processes. Static directories normally contain commands, configuration files, library routines, kernel files, device files, etc., and dynamic directories contain log files, status files, temporary files, etc.

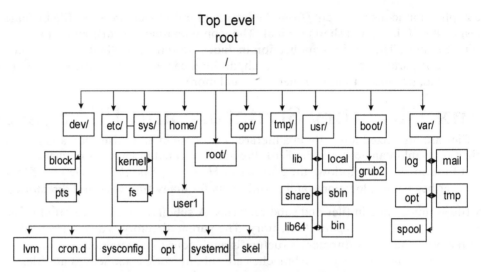

Figure 2-4 Linux Directory Structure

The hierarchical directory structure keeps related information together in a logical fashion. Compare this concept with a file cabinet containing several drawers, with each drawer storing multiple file folders.

File System Categories

There are a variety of file system types supported in RHEL that can be categorized in three basic groups: *disk-based*, *network-based*, and *memory-based*. Disk-based file systems are typically created on physical media such as a hard drive or a USB flash drive. Network-based file systems are essentially disk-based file systems that are shared over the network for remote access. Memory-based file systems are virtual; they are created automatically at system startup and destroyed when the system goes down. The first two types of file systems store information persistently, while any data saved in virtual file systems is lost at system reboots.

During RHEL installation, two disk-based file systems are created when you select the default partitioning. These file systems are referred to as the root and boot file systems. Furthermore, several memory-based file systems are vital to the operation of a RHEL system.

The Root File System (/), Disk-Based

The *root* directory is the top-level file system in the FHS and contains many higher-level directories that store specific information. Some of the key directories are:

/etc: The *etcetera* (or *extended text configuration*) directory holds system configuration files. Some common subdirectories are *systemd*, *sysconfig*, *lvm*, and *skel*, which comprise configuration files for systemd, most system services, the Logical Volume Manager, and per-user shell startup template files, respectively.

/root: This is the default home directory location for the *root* user.

/mnt: This directory is used to mount a file system temporarily.

The size of the root file system is automatically determined by the installer program based on the available disk space when you select the default partitioning; however, it may be altered at the time of installation if required.

The Boot File System (/boot), Disk-Based

The *boot* file system contains the Linux kernel, boot support files, and boot configuration files. Just like the *root* file system, the size of this file system is also automatically determined by the installer program based on the available disk space when you select the default partitioning; however, it may be set to a different size during or after the installation if required.

The Home Directory (/home)

The */home* directory is designed to store user *home* directories and other user contents. Each user is assigned a home directory to save personal files, and the user can block access to other users.

The Optional Directory (/opt)

This directory can be used to hold additional software that may need to be installed on the system. A subdirectory is created for each installed software.

The UNIX System Resources Directory (/usr)

This directory contains most of the system files. Some of the important subdirectories are:

/usr/bin: The *binary* directory contains crucial user executable commands.

/usr/sbin: Most commands are required at system boot, and those that require the *root* user privileges in order to run are located in this *system binary* directory. In other words, this directory contains crucial system administration commands that are not intended for execution by normal users (although they can still run a few of them). This directory is not included in the default search path for normal users because of the nature of data it holds.

/usr/lib and **/usr/lib64:** The *library* directories contain shared library routines required by many commands and programs located in the */usr/bin* and */usr/sbin* directories, as well as by the kernel and other applications and programs for their successful installation and operation. The */usr/lib* directory also stores system initialization and service management programs. The subdirectory */usr/lib64* contains 64-bit shared library routines.

/usr/include: This directory contains header files for *C* language.

/usr/local: This directory serves as a system administrator repository for storing commands and tools downloaded from the web, developed in-house, or obtained elsewhere. These commands and tools are not generally included with the original Linux distribution. In particular, */usr/local/bin* holds executables, */usr/local/etc* holds configuration files, and */usr/local/lib* and */usr/local/lib64* holds library routines.

/usr/share: This is the directory location for manual pages, documentation, sample templates, configuration files, etc., that may be shared with other Linux platforms.

/usr/src: This directory is used to store source code.

The Variable Directory (/var)

The */var* directory contains data that frequently changes while the system is operational. Files in this directory contain log, status, spool, lock, and other dynamic data. Some common subdirectories under */var* are:

/var/log: This is the storage for most system log files, such as system logs, boot logs, user logs, failed user logs, installation logs, cron logs, mail logs, etc.

/var/opt: This directory stores log, status, and other variable data files for additional software installed in */opt*.

/var/spool: Directories that hold print jobs, cron jobs, mail messages, and other queued items before being sent out to their intended destinations are located here.

/var/tmp: Large temporary files or temporary files that need to exist for longer periods of time than what is typically allowed in another temporary directory, */tmp*, are stored here. These files survive system reboots and are automatically deleted if they are not accessed or modified for a period of 30 days.

The Temporary Directory (/tmp)

This directory is a repository for temporary files. Many programs create temporary files here during runtime or installation. These files survive system reboots and are automatically removed if they are not accessed or modified for a period of 10 days.

The Devices File System (/dev), Virtual

The *Devices* (*dev file system*) file system is accessible via the */dev* directory, and it is used to store device nodes for physical hardware and virtual devices. The Linux kernel communicates with these devices through corresponding device nodes located here. These device nodes are automatically created and deleted by the *udevd* service (a Linux service for dynamic device management) as necessary.

There are two types of device files: *character* (or *raw*) device files, and *block* device files. The kernel accesses devices using one of these files or both.

Character devices are accessed serially with streams of bits transferred during kernel and device communication. Examples of such devices are console, serial printers, mice, keyboards, terminals, etc.

Block devices are accessed in a parallel fashion with data exchanged in blocks (parallel) during kernel and device communication. Data on block devices is accessed randomly. Examples of block devices are hard disk drives, optical drives, parallel printers, etc.

The Procfs File System (/proc), Virtual

The *Procfs* (*process file system*) file system is accessible via the */proc* directory, and it is used to maintain information about the current state of the running kernel. This includes the details for current hardware configuration and status information on CPU, memory, disks, partitioning, file systems, networking, running processes, and so on. This information is stored in a hierarchy of subdirectories that contain thousands of zero-length pseudo files. These files point to relevant data maintained by the kernel in the memory. This virtual directory structure simply provides an easy interface to interact with kernel-maintained information. The Procfs file system is dynamically managed by the system.

The contents in */proc* are created in memory at system boot time, updated during runtime, and destroyed at system shutdown.

The Runtime File System (/run), Virtual

This virtual file system is a repository of data for processes running on the system. One of its subdirectories, */run/media*, is also used to automatically mount external file systems such as those that are on optical (CD and DVD) and flash USB.

The contents of this file system are automatically deleted at system shutdown.

The System File System (/sys), Virtual

Information about hardware devices, drivers, and some kernel features is stored and maintained in the */sys* file system. This information is used by the kernel to load necessary support for the devices, create device nodes in */dev*, and configure the devices. This file system is auto-maintained as well.

Essential System Commands

There are hundreds of commands available in RHEL that range from simple to complex in terms of their construct and usage. Commands can be combined to build complex structures for innovative use cases. Some commands offer a few options, while others have as many as 70 or more. This section furnishes an understanding of how commands are formed and demonstrates the use of some of the basic, common Linux commands. You will learn more commands and their advanced usages throughout this book.

Starting a Remote Terminal Session

In order to issue commands and run programs at the command prompt, you need access to a terminal session. Follow the steps identified in Exercise 1-3 to log in to the system remotely as the *root* user. Figure 2-5 below shows a session with *root* user logged in.

```
  root@server1:~                                                    —
  login as: root
  root@192.168.0.110's password:
Activate the web console with: systemctl enable --now cockpit.socket

Register this system with Red Hat Insights: insights-client --register
Create an account or view all your systems at https://red.ht/insights-dash
Last login: Fri Jan 27 14:28:12 2023 from 192.168.0.4
[root@server1 ~]#
[root@server1 ~]# []
```

Figure 2-5 Remote Terminal Session

The header bar displays the logged-in username, hostname, and your current directory location.

The "[root@server1 ~]#" is the default representation of the command prompt. It reflects the logged-in username (*root*, *user1*, etc.), hostname of the system (*server1*, *server2*, etc.), and your current directory location, all enclosed within square brackets []. The command prompt ends with the hash sign (#) for the *root* user or the dollar sign ($) for normal users outside of the closing square bracket. Commands are typed at the cursor position and executed by pressing the Enter key.

Understanding the Command Mechanics

To practice the commands provided in this chapter, you can log in as *user1*, run the commands, and observe their outputs. However, as you are learning Linux system administration, it's important to feel comfortable working as *root* in the beginning. If something breaks, *server1* and *server2* are lab servers and they can be rebuilt.

The basic syntax of a Linux command is:

command option(s) argument(s)

Options (a.k.a. a *switch* of *flag*) are optional. You can specify zero or more options with a command. Arguments, in contrast, may be optional or mandatory depending on the command and its usage. Many commands have preconfigured default options and arguments. You are not required to specify them. Other commands do require at least one option or argument in order to work. An option modifies the behavior of the command. An argument supplies a target on which to perform the command action.

An option may start with a single hyphen character (-la, for instance), and it is referred to as the short-option format. Each individual letter in this depiction represents a separate option (l and a are two options in -la). This is a frequent format throughout this book.

An option may also begin with two hyphen characters (--all, for instance), and it is referred to as the long-option format. All letters in this representation are collectively identified as a single option (--all is one option).

The following examples express some command structures with a description on the right that states the number of options and arguments supplied:

# **ls**	No option, no explicit argument; the default argument is the current directory name
# **ls -l**	One option, no explicit argument; the default argument is the current directory name
# **ls -al**	Two options, no explicit argument; the default argument is the current directory name
# **ls --all**	One option, no explicit argument; the default argument is the current directory name
# **ls -l directory_name**	One option, one explicit argument

EXAM TIP: Use online help on the usage of a command if needed. Refer to "Getting Help" later in this chapter for details on how to access and use help.

Now let's take a look at some essential Linux commands and understand their usage.

Listing Files and Directories

One of the most rudimentary commands in Linux is the *ls* (*list*) command. It is used to show the list of files and directories. This command supports a multitude of options, some of which are listed in Table 2-1 along with a short explanation.

Option	Description
-a	Includes hidden files and directories in the output. A file or directory name that begins with the period character (.) is considered hidden.
-l	Displays long listing with detailed file information including the file type, permissions, link count, owner, group, size, date and time of last modification, and name of the file
-ld	Displays long listing of the specified directory but hides its contents
-lh	Displays long listing with file sizes shown in human-friendly format
-lt	Lists all files sorted by date and time with the newest file first
-ltr	Lists all files sorted by date and time with the oldest file first (reverse)
-R	Lists contents of the specified directory and all its subdirectories (recursive listing)

Table 2-1 ls Command Options

A grasp of the usage of this command and the output it produces is important. The following examples will illustrate the impact of options used with the *ls* command.

To list files in the current directory with the assumption that you are in the */root* directory:

```
[root@server1 ~]# ls
anaconda-ks.cfg  Documents  Music     Public     Videos
Desktop          Downloads  Pictures  Templates
```

To list files in the current directory with detailed information:

```
[root@server1 ~]# ls -l
total 4
-rw-------. 1 root root 1203 Jan 26 16:51 anaconda-ks.cfg
drwxr-xr-x. 2 root root    6 Jan 27 12:10 Desktop
drwxr-xr-x. 2 root root    6 Jan 27 12:10 Documents
drwxr-xr-x. 2 root root    6 Jan 27 12:10 Downloads
drwxr-xr-x. 2 root root    6 Jan 27 12:10 Music
drwxr-xr-x. 2 root root    6 Jan 27 12:10 Pictures
drwxr-xr-x. 2 root root    6 Jan 27 12:10 Public
drwxr-xr-x. 2 root root    6 Jan 27 12:10 Templates
drwxr-xr-x. 2 root root    6 Jan 27 12:10 Videos
```

The long listing in the output above furnishes a unique piece of information about the file or directory in nine discrete columns:

Column 1: The first character (hyphen or d) divulges the file type, and the next nine characters (rw-rw-r--) indicate permissions.
Column 2: Displays the number of links (links are explained later in this chapter)
Column 3: Shows the owner name
Column 4: Exhibits the owning group name
Column 5: Identifies the file size in bytes. For directories, this number reflects the number of blocks being used by the directory to hold information about its contents.
Columns 6, 7, and 8: Displays the month, day, and time of creation or last modification
Column 9: Indicates the name of the file or directory

As an alternative to **ls -l**, you may use its shortcut **ll** for brevity and convenience unless there is a specific need to use the former.

To show the long listing of only the specified directory without showing its contents:

```
[root@server1 ~]# ls -ld /usr
drwxr-xr-x. 12 root root 144 Jan 26 16:37 /usr
```

To display all files in the current directory with their sizes in human-friendly format:

```
[root@server1 ~]# ls -lh
total 4.0K
-rw-------. 1 root root 1.2K Jan 26 16:51 anaconda-ks.cfg
drwxr-xr-x. 2 root root    6 Jan 27 12:10 Desktop
drwxr-xr-x. 2 root root    6 Jan 27 12:10 Documents
drwxr-xr-x. 2 root root    6 Jan 27 12:10 Downloads
drwxr-xr-x. 2 root root    6 Jan 27 12:10 Music
drwxr-xr-x. 2 root root    6 Jan 27 12:10 Pictures
drwxr-xr-x. 2 root root    6 Jan 27 12:10 Public
drwxr-xr-x. 2 root root    6 Jan 27 12:10 Templates
drwxr-xr-x. 2 root root    6 Jan 27 12:10 Videos
```

To list all files, including the hidden files, in the current directory with detailed information:

```
[root@server1 ~]# ls -la
total 52
dr-xr-x---. 13 root root 4096 Jan 27 19:18 .
dr-xr-xr-x. 18 root root  235 Jan 26 16:37 ..
-rw-------.  1 root root 1203 Jan 26 16:51 anaconda-ks.cfg
-rw-------.  1 root root 1230 Jan 27 19:21 .bash_history
-rw-r--r--.  1 root root   18 Aug 10  2021 .bash_logout
-rw-r--r--.  1 root root  141 Aug 10  2021 .bash_profile
-rw-r--r--.  1 root root  429 Aug 10  2021 .bashrc
drwx------.  8 root root  120 Jan 27 12:11 .cache
drwx------.  7 root root 4096 Jan 27 12:11 .config
-rw-r--r--.  1 root root  100 Aug 10  2021 .cshrc
drwxr-xr-x.  2 root root    6 Jan 27 12:10 Desktop
drwxr-xr-x.  2 root root    6 Jan 27 12:10 Documents

. . . . . . . .
```

To repeat the previous example with the output sorted by date and time and with the newest file first:

```
[root@server1 ~]# ls -lt
total 4
drwxr-xr-x. 2 root root    6 Jan 27 12:10 Desktop
drwxr-xr-x. 2 root root    6 Jan 27 12:10 Documents
drwxr-xr-x. 2 root root    6 Jan 27 12:10 Downloads
drwxr-xr-x. 2 root root    6 Jan 27 12:10 Music
drwxr-xr-x. 2 root root    6 Jan 27 12:10 Pictures
drwxr-xr-x. 2 root root    6 Jan 27 12:10 Public
drwxr-xr-x. 2 root root    6 Jan 27 12:10 Templates
drwxr-xr-x. 2 root root    6 Jan 27 12:10 Videos
-rw-------. 1 root root 1203 Jan 26 16:51 anaconda-ks.cfg
```

To list contents of the */etc* directory recursively:

```
[root@server1 ~]# ls -R /etc
/etc:
accountsservice     gshadow-            profile
adjtime             gss                 profile.d
aliases             host.conf           protocols
alsa                hostname            pulse
alternatives        hosts               qemu-ga
anacrontab          hp                  ras
appstream.conf      inittab             rc.d
asound.conf         inputrc             rc.local
at.deny             insights-client     redhat-release
. . . . . . . .
```

Run **man ls** at the command prompt to view the manual pages of the *ls* command with all the options it supports and how to use them.

Printing Working Directory

The *pwd* (*print working directory* or *present working directory*) command displays a user's current location in the directory tree. The following example shows that *root* is currently in the */root* directory:

```
[root@server1 ~]# pwd
/root
```

/root is the home directory for the *root* user. The *pwd* command always returns the absolute path to a file or directory.

Navigating Directories

Files are placed in various directories in Linux, and there are tens of thousands of them. Each file and directory is recognized by a unique path in the directory tree. A *path* (or *pathname*) is like a road map that shows you how to get from one place in the directory hierarchy to another. It uniquely identifies a particular file or directory by its absolute or relative location in the directory structure.

An *absolute path* (a.k.a. a *full path* or a *fully qualified pathname*) points to a file or directory in relation to the top of the directory tree. It always starts with the forward slash (/). You can use the *pwd* command to view your current absolute path in the tree:

```
[root@server1 ~]# pwd
/root
```

The output indicates that */root* is the current location for the *root* user in the directory hierarchy, and the leading / identifies this location as a full path.

A *relative path*, on the other hand, points to a file or directory in relation to your current location. This file path never begins with the forward slash (/). It may begin with two period characters (..) or with a subdirectory name without a leading /, such as *etc/sysconfig*.

It's easy to navigate in the directory hierarchy if you have a good understanding of the absolute and relative paths and the key difference between them. Let's run a couple of examples using the *cd* (*change directory*) command, which is used to switch between directories, and verify the result with the *pwd* command.

To determine the current location and then go one level up into the parent directory using the relative path:

```
[root@server1 ~]# pwd
/root
[root@server1 ~]# cd ..
[root@server1 /]# pwd
/
```

The above sequence of commands display the current location (*/root* output of *pwd*), then move one level up (*cd* .. is relative to the current location), and finally verify the new location (/ output of *pwd*). You may want to use the absolute path (**cd** /) instead of (**cd** ..) to go to the top of the directory tree (parent directory of */root*).

Now, let's switch to the directory *sysconfig*, which is located under */etc*. There are two options: the absolute path (*/etc/sysconfig*), or the relative path (*etc/sysconfig*):

```
# cd /etc/sysconfig
```
or
```
# cd etc/sysconfig
```

To change into the */usr/bin* directory, for instance, you can run either of the following:

```
# cd /usr/bin
```
or
```
# cd ../../usr/bin
```

The above example indicates that the absolute path can be used to switch into a target directory regardless of your current location in the hierarchy. However, a relative path must be entered based on your current location in order to move to a target directory.

At this point, if you want to return to your home directory, you can simply run the *cd* command without inputting a path or by supplying the *tilde* character (~) with it. Either of the two will produce the desired result.

```
# cd
```
or
```
# cd ~
```

In the above example, you could also use the absolute path (**cd** /root) or a relative path (**cd** ../../root) instead.

To switch between the current and previous directories, issue the *cd* command with the hyphen character (-). See the following example and observe the output:

```
[root@server1 ~]# pwd
/root
[root@server1 ~]# cd -
/usr/bin
[root@server1 bin]# cd -
/root
[root@server1 ~]# pwd
/root
```

The example shows the use of the hyphen character (-) with the *cd* command to switch between the current and previous directories.

Viewing Directory Hierarchy

The *tree* command lists a hierarchy of directories and files. There are a number of options with this command that can be specified to include additional information. Table 2-2 describes some common options.

Option	Description
-a	Includes hidden files in the output
-d	Excludes files from the output
-h	Displays file sizes in human-friendly format
-f	Prints the full path for each file
-p	Includes file permissions in the output

Table 2-2 tree Command Options

To list only the directories in the *root* user home directory (*/root*):

```
[root@server1 ~]# tree -d
.
├── Desktop
├── Documents
├── Downloads
├── Music
├── Pictures
├── Public
├── Templates
└── Videos

8 directories
```

The output indicates that there are eight directories under */root*.

To list files in the */etc/sysconfig* directory along with their sizes in human-readable format, permissions, and full path:

```
[user1@server1 ~]$ tree -hpf /etc/sysconfig/
/etc/sysconfig
├── [-rw-r--r--    112]  /etc/sysconfig/anaconda
├── [-rw-r--r--    403]  /etc/sysconfig/atd
├── [-rw-r--r--    339]  /etc/sysconfig/autofs
├── [-rw-r--r--     50]  /etc/sysconfig/chronyd
├── [-rw-r--r--    150]  /etc/sysconfig/cpupower
├── [-rw-r--r--    110]  /etc/sysconfig/crond
├── [-rw-r--r--     73]  /etc/sysconfig/firewalld
├── [-rw-r--r--    903]  /etc/sysconfig/irqbalance
├── [-rw-r--r--   2.5K]  /etc/sysconfig/kdump
├── [-rw-r--r--    185]  /etc/sysconfig/kernel
├── [-rw-r--r--    310]  /etc/sysconfig/man-db
. . . . . . . . .
```

The output shows permissions in column 1, sizes in column 2, and full path of the files in column 3.

Run **man tree** at the command prompt to view the manual pages of this command for additional options and their usage.

Identifying Terminal Device File

Linux allocates unique *pseudo* (or *virtual*) numbered device files to represent terminal sessions opened by users on the system. It uses these files to communicate with individual sessions. By default, these files are stored in the */dev/pts* (*pseudo terminal session*) directory. These files are created by the system when a user opens a new terminal session and they are removed on its closure. The destroyed files are recreated and reused for new terminal sessions.

Linux provides a command called *tty* (*teletype*) to identify your current active terminal session. Here is an example:

```
[root@server1 ~]# tty
/dev/pts/0
```

The output discloses the filename "0" and its location (*/dev/pts* directory).

Inspecting System's Uptime and Processor Load

The *uptime* command is used to display the system's current time, length of time it has been up for, number of users currently logged in, and the average CPU (processing) load over the past 1, 5, and 15 minutes. See the following output:

```
[root@server1 ~]# uptime
 14:49:51 up 21:48,  2 users,  load average: 0.00, 0.00, 0.00
```

The output shows the current system time (14:49:51), up duration (21 hours and 48 minutes), number of logged-in users (2), and the CPU load averages over the past 1, 5, and 15 minutes (0.00, 0.00, and 0.00), respectively.

The load average numbers correspond to the percentage of CPU load with 0.00 and 1.00 represent no load and full load, and a number greater than 1.00 signifies excess load (over 100%).

Clearing the Screen

The *clear* command clears the terminal screen and places the cursor at the top left of the screen. This command is useful to clear the screen of any distractive content and run new commands on a clean slate.

```
# clear
```

You can also use Ctrl+l for this command.

Determining Command Path

RHEL provides a set of tools that can be used to identify the absolute path of the command that will be executed when you run it without specifying its full path. These tools are the *which*, *whereis*, and *type* commands. The following examples show the full location of the *uptime* command:

```
[root@server1 ~]# which uptime
/usr/bin/uptime
[root@server1 ~]# whereis uptime
uptime: /usr/bin/uptime /usr/share/man/man1/uptime.1.gz
[root@server1 ~]# type uptime
uptime is hashed (/usr/bin/uptime)
```

As shown above, all three commands responded with an identical path location for the *uptime* command, which is */usr/bin/uptime*. This implies that there is no need to type the entire path */usr/bin/uptime* to run *uptime*, as the system will automatically determine its location based on some predefined settings. Refer to Chapter 07 "The Bash Shell" for more guidance.

Viewing System Information

There are several elements in the RHEL system that identify various information regarding the operating system, hardware, kernel, storage, networking, and so on. The *uname* command identifies elementary information about the system including its hostname. Without any options, the output of this command is restricted to displaying the operating system name only; however, it reports other details by adding the -a option.

```
[root@server1 ~]# uname -a
Linux server1.example.com 5.14.0-162.6.1.el9_1.x86_64 #1 SMP PREEMPT_DYNAMIC Fri S
ep 30 07:36:03 EDT 2022 x86_64 x86_64 x86_64 GNU/Linux
```

The data returned by the second command above is elaborated below:

Linux	Kernel name
server1.example.com	Hostname of the system
5.14.0-162.6.1.el9_1.x86_64	Kernel release
#1 SMP PREEMPT_DYNAMIC Fri Sep 30 07:36:03 EDT 2022	Date and time of the kernel built
x86_64	Machine hardware name
x86_64	Processor type
x86_64	Hardware platform
GNU/Linux	Operating system name

Try running the *uname* command with the -s (kernel name), -n (node name), -r (kernel release), -v (kernel build date), -m (hardware name), -p (processor type), -i (hardware platform), and -o (OS name) options separately to view specific information.

Viewing CPU Specs

A CPU has many architectural pieces that can be looked at using the *lscpu* command. These pieces include the CPU architecture, its operating modes, vendor, family, model, speed, cache memory, and whether it supports virtualization. The following example shows the CPU information from *server1*:

```
[root@server1 ~]# lscpu
Architecture:              x86_64
  CPU op-mode(s):          32-bit, 64-bit
  Address sizes:           39 bits physical, 48 bits virtual
  Byte Order:              Little Endian
CPU(s):                    2
  On-line CPU(s) list:     0,1
Vendor ID:                 GenuineIntel
  Model name:              Intel(R) Core(TM) i7-10510U CPU @ 1.80GHz
    CPU family:            6
    Model:                 142
    Thread(s) per core:    1
    Core(s) per socket:    2
    Socket(s):             1
    Stepping:              12
    BogoMIPS:              4608.01
    Flags:                 fpu vme de pse tsc msr pae mce cx8 apic sep mtrr pge mca
                           cmov pat pse36 clflush mmx fxsr sse sse2 ht syscall nx rd
                           tscp lm constant_tsc rep_good nopl xtopology nonstop_tsc
                           cpuid tsc_known_freq pni pclmulqdq ssse3 cx16 pcid sse4_1
                            sse4_2 movbe popcnt aes rdrand hypervisor lahf_lm abm 3d
                           nowprefetch invpcid_single ibrs_enhanced fsgsbase bmi1 bm
                           i2 invpcid rdseed clflushopt md_clear flush_l1d arch_capa
                           bilities
Virtualization features:
  Hypervisor vendor:       KVM
  Virtualization type:     full
Caches (sum of all):
  L1d:                     64 KiB (2 instances)
  L1i:                     64 KiB (2 instances)
  L2:                      512 KiB (2 instances)
  L3:                      16 MiB (2 instances)
NUMA:
  NUMA node(s):            1
. . . . . . . .
```

The output indicates the architecture of the CPU (x86_64), supported modes of operation (32-bit and 64-bit), number of CPUs (2), vendor ID (GenuineIntel), model name (Intel …), threads per core (1), cores per socket (2), number of sockets (1), the amount and levels of cache memory (L1d, L1i, L2, and L3), and other information.

Getting Help

While working on the system, you may require help to obtain information about a command or a configuration file. RHEL offers online help via *manual* pages. Manual pages are online documentation that provides details on commands, configuration files, etc. They are installed under the */usr/share/man* directory when associated software packages are installed.

In addition to the manual pages, *apropos* and *whatis* commands as well as documentation located in the */usr/share/doc* directory are also available on the system.

> **EXAM TIP:** If you need help with a command or configuration file, do not hesitate to use the man pages, refer to the documentation available in the /usr/share/doc directory, or employ one of the other help tools.

Accessing Manual Pages

Use the *man* command to view manual pages. The following example shows how to check manual pages for the *passwd* command:

```
[root@server1 ~]# man passwd
PASSWD(1)                       User utilities                       PASSWD(1)

NAME
       passwd - update user's authentication tokens

SYNOPSIS
       passwd [-k] [-l] [-u [-f]] [-d] [-e] [-n mindays] [-x maxdays] [-w warn☐
       days] [-i inactivedays] [-S] [--stdin] [-?] [--usage] [username]

DESCRIPTION
       The passwd utility is used to update user's authentication token(s).

       This task is achieved through calls to the Linux-PAM  and  Libuser  API.
       Essentially,  it initializes itself as a "passwd" service with Linux-PAM
       and utilizes configured password modules to authenticate and then update
       a user's password.

       A  simple entry in the global Linux-PAM configuration file for this ser☐
       vice would be:

       #
       # passwd service entry that does strength checking of
       # a proposed password before updating it.
       #
       passwd password requisite pam_cracklib.so retry=3
       passwd password required pam_unix.so use_authtok
       #

       Note, other module types are not required for this application to  func☐
       tion correctly.

OPTIONS
       -k, --keep-tokens
Manual page passwd(1) line 1 (press h for help or q to quit)
```

The output returns the name of the command, the section of the manual pages it is documented in within the parentheses, and the type (User utilities) of the command on line 1. It then shows a short description (NAME), the command's usage (SYNOPSIS), and a long description (DESCRIPTION), followed by a detailed explanation of each option (OPTIONS) that the command supports and other relevant data. The highlighted line at the bottom indicates the line number of the manual page. Press h to get help on navigation, press q to quit and return to the command prompt, use the Up and Down arrow keys to scroll up and down, and the PgUp and PgDn keys to scroll one page at a time.

Table 2-3 summarizes the six keys described above and introduces more to assist in navigation.

Key	Action
Enter / Down arrow	Moves forward one line
Up arrow	Moves backward one line
f / Spacebar / Page down	Moves forward one page
b / Page up	Moves backward one page
d / u	Moves down / up half a page
g / G	Moves to the beginning / end of the man pages
:f	Displays the line number and bytes being viewed
q	Quits the man pages
/pattern	Searches forward for the specified pattern
?pattern	Searches backward for the specified pattern
n / N	Finds the next / previous occurrence of a pattern
h	Gives help on navigational keys

Table 2-3 Navigating within Manual Pages

Run *man* on any of the commands that you have reviewed so far and navigate using the keys provided in Table 2-3 for practice.

Headings in the Manual

Each page in the manual organizes information under several headings. Some common headings are NAME of the command or file with a short description, SYNOPSIS (syntax summary), long DESCRIPTION, available OPTIONS, EXAMPLES to explain the usage, a list of related FILES, SEE ALSO (reference) to other manual pages or topics, any reported BUGS or issues, and AUTHOR information. You may find a subset of these headings or additional headings depending on what information is documented for that command or file.

Manual Sections

Depending on the type of information, the manual information is split into nine sections for organization and clarity. For instance, section 1 refers to user commands (see "NAME" for an example of the *passwd* command), section 4 contains special files, section 5 describes file formats for many system configuration files, and section 8 documents system administration and privileged commands that are designed for execution by the *root* user.

The default behavior of the *man* command is to search through section 1 and each successive section until it finds a match. There are a few commands in Linux that also have a configuration file with an identical name. One instance is the *passwd* command and the *passwd* file. The former is located in the */usr/bin* directory and the latter in the */etc* directory.

When you run **man passwd**, the *man* command scans through the manual pages and the first occurrence it finds is of the *passwd* command that's stored in section 1. If you want to consult the manual pages of the *passwd* configuration file, you will need to specify the section number with the command (**man 5 passwd**) to instruct it to scan that particular section only.

```
PASSWD(5)                       Linux Programmer's Manual                       PASSWD(5)

NAME
        passwd - password file

DESCRIPTION
        The  /etc/passwd  file is a text file that describes user login accounts
        for the system.  It should have read permission allowed  for  all  users
        (many  utilities,  like  ls(1) use it to map user IDs to usernames), but
        write access only for the superuser.

        In the good old days there was no great problem with this  general  read
. . . . . . . .
```

The header at the top in the above output is an indication that this help is for the *passwd* file and it is documented in section 5.

Searching by Keyword

Sometimes you need to use a command, but you can't recall its name. Linux allows you to perform a keyword search on manual pages using the *man* command with the -*k* (lowercase) flag, or the *apropos* command. These commands search all sections of the manual pages and show a list of all entries matching the specified keyword in their names or descriptions.

Before you can perform keyword searches on a new Linux installation, you'll need to run the *mandb* command in order to build an indexed database of the manual pages. This activity depends on the speed and the number of RHEL packages installed on the system, and it should not take long to perform. Simply type the command at the prompt and press the Enter key as follows:

```
[root@server1 ~]# mandb
Processing manual pages under /usr/share/man/overrides...
Updating index cache for path `/usr/share/man/overrides/man3'. Wait...done.
Checking for stray cats under /usr/share/man/overrides...
Checking for stray cats under /var/cache/man/overrides...
Processing manual pages under /usr/share/man...
Updating index cache for path `/usr/share/man/man1'. Wait...mandb: warning: /usr/s
hare/man/man1/grub2-emu.1.gz: whatis parse for grub2-emu(1) failed
mandb: warning: /usr/share/man/man1/grub2-mount.1.gz: whatis parse for grub2-mount
(1) failed
Updating index cache for path `/usr/share/man/man8'. Wait...mandb: can't open /usr
/share/man/man8/nss-resolve.8: No such file or directory
mandb: warning: /usr/share/man/man8/libnss_resolve.so.2.8.gz: bad symlink or ROFF
`.so' request
Updating index cache for path `/usr/share/man/mann'. Wait...done.
. . . . . . . .
Updating index cache for path `/usr/local/share/man/mann'. Wait...done.
Checking for stray cats under /usr/local/share/man...
Checking for stray cats under /var/cache/man/local...
121 man subdirectories contained newer manual pages.
7815 manual pages were added.
0 stray cats were added.
0 old database entries were purged.
```

Now you are ready to run keyword lookups. As an example, to find a forgotten XFS administration command, search for a string "xfs" by running either **man -k xfs** or **apropos xfs**. Both will produce an identical result.

```
[root@server1 ~]# man -k xfs
attr (1)                 - extended attributes on XFS filesystem objects
filesystems (5)          - Linux filesystem types: ext, ext2, ext3, ext4, hpfs, i...
fs (5)                   - Linux filesystem types: ext, ext2, ext3, ext4, hpfs, i...
fsck.xfs (8)             - do nothing, successfully
fsfreeze (8)             - suspend access to a filesystem (Ext3/4, ReiserFS, JFS,...
mkfs.xfs (8)             - construct an XFS filesystem
xfs (5)                  - layout, mount options, and supported file attributes f...
xfs_admin (8)            - change parameters of an XFS filesystem
xfs_bmap (8)             - print block mapping for an XFS file
. . . . . . . .
```

Once you have identified the command you were looking for, you can check that command's manual pages for usage.

Some commands also support the use of the --help and -? parameters. These parameters provide a brief list of options and a description without going through the manual pages. For example, to get quick help on the *passwd* command, run either **passwd --help** or **passwd -?**:

```
[root@server1 ~]# passwd --help
Usage: passwd [OPTION...] <accountName>
  -k, --keep-tokens        keep non-expired authentication tokens
  -d, --delete             delete the password for the named account (root
                           only); also removes password lock if any
  -l, --lock               lock the password for the named account (root only)
  -u, --unlock             unlock the password for the named account (root only)
  -e, --expire             expire the password for the named account (root only)
  -f, --force              force operation

. . . . . . . .
```

 Not all commands support the --help and -? parameters.

Exposing Short Description

The *whatis* command searches for a short description of the specified command or file in the manual database. It quickly scans through the installed manual pages for the specified string and displays all matching entries. For instance, the following shows outputs of the command when run on *yum.conf* and *passwd* files:

```
[root@server1 ~]# whatis yum.conf
yum.conf (5)            - redirecting to DNF Configuration Reference
[root@server1 ~]# whatis passwd
passwd (5)              - password file
passwd (1ossl)          - OpenSSL application commands
passwd (1)              - update user's authentication tokens
```

The first output indicates that the specified file is a configuration file associated with the *yum* command, and the second output points to three entries for the *passwd* file (one configuration file and two commands).

You may alternatively run **man -f yum.conf** and **man -f passwd** for the exact same results. Both *man -f* and *whatis* produce identical output.

Documentation in the /usr/share/doc Directory

The */usr/share/doc* directory stores general documentation for installed packages under subdirectories that match their names. For example, the documentation for the gzip package includes the following files:

```
[root@server1 ~]# ls -l /usr/share/doc/gzip/
total 168
-rw-r--r--. 1 root root     98 Dec 31  2018 AUTHORS
-rw-r--r--. 1 root root 113573 Apr  7  2022 ChangeLog
-rw-r--r--. 1 root root  24523 Apr  7  2022 NEWS
-rw-r--r--. 1 root root   6134 Jan  3  2022 README
-rw-r--r--. 1 root root  13273 Mar 30  2022 THANKS
-rw-r--r--. 1 root root   3467 Jan  3  2022 TODO
```

These text files contain general information about the gzip package. However, the manual pages and the info documentation prove to be more resourceful to Linux users and administrators.

Red Hat Enterprise Linux 9 Documentation

The website at *docs.redhat.com* hosts documentation for Red Hat's various products including RHEL 9 in HTML, PDF, and EPUB formats. See Figure 2-6.

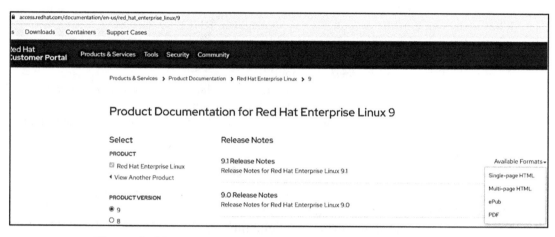

Figure 2-6 Red Hat's Webpage for RHEL 9 Documentation

This set of documentation includes release notes, as well as guides on planning, installation, administration, security, storage management, virtualization, and so on. For reference, you can download any of these guides for free in a format of your choice.

Chapter Summary

This chapter touched upon a few basic topics. We started by looking at a new display protocol that has replaced the legacy X Window System in RHEL 9. We interacted with the operating system at the graphical console screen and examined various settings.

Next, we reviewed the Linux file system structure standard and significant higher-level subdirectories that consisted of static and variable files, and were grouped logically into lower-level subdirectories.

We analyzed command construct, and learned and run selected user level commands for familiarity. These tools included listing, viewing, and identifying basic information, and navigating in the directory hierarchy.

Finally, we learned how to access online help for commands and configuration files. We saw how to search through manual pages for desired text. Explanations regarding what commands to use were offered for additional help.

Review Questions

1. What type of information does section 5 in manual pages contain?
2. Which protocol is used as the default display protocol in RHEL 9?
3. Which command can be used to determine the time the kernel was build?
4. RHEL follows the Filesystem Hierarchy Standard. True or False?
5. Consider a Linux system with six processor cores. How many times do you have to run the *lscpu* command to pull information for all the cores?

6. Which three categories can Linux file systems be divided into?
7. Which three commands may be used to identify the full path of a command?
8. Which Linux command displays the hierarchy of a directory?
9. Linux commands may be categorized into two groups: privileged and non-privileged. True or False?
10. What is the name of the default display manager in RHEL 9?
11. What is the use of the *apropos* command?
12. Which Linux service creates device nodes at system startup?
13. What is the function of the *pwd* command?
14. Which three formats RHEL 9 documentation is available in at *docs.redhat.com*?
15. What are the -R and -a options used for with the *ls* command?
16. What is the default number of days files in */tmp* are kept before they are automatically deleted if not accessed or modified.

Answers to Review Questions

1. Section 5 of the manual pages contain information on configuration files.
2. Wayland is the default display protocol in RHEL 9.
3. The *uname* command shows the kernel build time.
4. True.
5. Only one time.
6. Linux file systems may be divided into disk-based, network-based, and memory-based file systems.
7. The *which*, *whereis*, and *type* commands may be used to determine the full path for a specified command.
8. The *tree* command shows the hierarchy of a directory.
9. True.
10. GNOME Display Manager is the default display manager in RHEL 9.
11. The *apropos* command can be used to perform a keyword search in the manual pages.
12. The *udevd* service.
13. The *pwd* command shows the absolute path of the current working directory.
14. The RHEL 9 documentation is available in PDF, EPUB, and HTML formats.
15. The -R option is used for recursive directory listing and the -a option for listing hidden files.
16. Ten days.

Do-It-Yourself Challenge Labs

The following labs are useful to strengthen most of the concepts and topics learned in this chapter. It is expected that you perform the labs without external help. A step-by-step guide is not supplied, as the knowledge and skill required to implement the labs have already been disseminated in the chapter; however, hints to the relevant major topic(s) are included.

Use the lab environment built specifically for end-of-chapter labs. See sub-section "Lab Environment for End-of-Chapter Labs" in Chapter 01 "Local Installation" for details.

Lab 2-1: Navigate Linux Directory Tree

As *user1* on *server3*, execute the *pwd* command to check your location in the directory tree. Run the **ls** command with appropriate switches to show files in the current directory including the hidden files. Change directory into */etc* and run *pwd* again to confirm the directory change. Switch back to the directory where you were before and run *pwd* again to verify. (Hint: Essential System Commands).

Lab 2-2: Miscellaneous Tasks

As *user1* on *server3*, execute the *tty* command to identify the terminal device file. Observe the terminal number reported. Open a couple of more terminal sessions, and run the *tty* command and compare the terminal numbers. Execute the *uptime* command and analyze the system uptime and processor load information. Use the three commands—*which*, *whereis*, and *type*—and identify the location of the *vgs* command. (Hint: Essential System Commands).

Lab 2-3: Identify System and Kernel Information

As *user1* on *server3*, issue *uname -a*. Analyze the basic information about the system and kernel reported. Run the *lscpu* command and examine the key items relevant to the processor. (Hint: Essential System Commands).

Lab 2-4: Use Help

As *user1* on *server3*, run *man uname* and *man 5 shadow*, and browse various headings and understand what they contain. Try *apropos ext4* and *man -k ext4*, *whatis group*, and observe their outputs. (Hint: Getting Help).

Chapter 03

Basic File Management

This chapter describes the following major topics:

➤ Common types of file in Linux
➤ Compress and uncompress files
➤ Archive and compress files and directories
➤ Edit files with the vim editor
➤ Create, list, display, copy, move, rename, and remove files and directories
➤ Create file and directory links
➤ Identify differences between copying and linking

RHCSA Objectives:

06. Archive, compress, unpack, and uncompress files using tar, star, gzip, and bzip2
07. Create and edit text files
08. Create, delete, copy, and move files and directories
09. Create hard and soft links

L inux supports different file types that are identified based on the kind of data they store. There are files that save information in plain text or binary format. This file type is very common. There are other files that store device information or simply point to the same data on the disk. A good comprehension of Linux file types is important for both Linux users, developers, and administrators.

Compressing and archiving one or more large files or an entire directory hierarchy allows users to conserve disk space or remote copy them at a faster pace. The resulting compressed archive can be easily uncompressed and unarchived whenever and wherever needed. RHEL offers native tools to support both user needs.

Normal and application users and database and system administrators all need to edit text files on a regular basis as part of their job. Linux delivers several text editors for this purpose, including the vim editor, which is popular within the Linux community. A sound, working knowledge of this tool is essential for all these roles.

There are a number of common operations that can be performed on files and directories in addition to viewing their contents. These operations include creating, listing, copying, moving, renaming, and removing both files and directories. Normal users will require higher privilege in order to perform these operations outside of their realm.

There is a tool available in the operating system that helps in linking files and directories for various use cases. An understanding of when to link files or directories versus when to copy them is important.

Common File Types

RHEL supports seven types of files: regular, directory, block special device, character special device, symbolic link, named pipe, and socket. The first two are the most common. The two types of device files are used by the operating system to communicate with peripheral devices. There are many instances of symbolic links as well. The last two types—named pipes and sockets—are used in inter-process communication.

Linux does not require an extension to a file to identify its type. It provides two elementary commands called *file* and *stat*, in addition to the *ls* command, to ascertain the type of data that a file may contain. This chapter discusses the first five file types and skips the last two (named pipes and sockets), as they are beyond the scope of this book.

Regular Files

Regular files may contain text or binary data. These files may be shell scripts or commands in the binary form. When you list a directory, all line entries for files in the output that begin with the hyphen character (-) represent regular files. The following truncated output is of the */root* directory:

```
[root@server1 ~]# ls -l
total 4
-rw-------. 1 root root 1203 Jan 26 16:51 anaconda-ks.cfg
```

Notice the hyphen in field 1 of column 1 before rw. This character indicates that the listed file is a regular file. Now, let's run the *file* and *stat* commands on this file and see what they report:

```
[root@server1 ~]# file anaconda-ks.cfg
anaconda-ks.cfg: ASCII text
[root@server1 ~]#
[root@server1 ~]# stat anaconda-ks.cfg
  File: anaconda-ks.cfg
  Size: 1203          Blocks: 8          IO Block: 4096    regular file
Device: fd00h/64768d    Inode: 19521538    Links: 1
Access: (0600/-rw-------)  Uid: (    0/    root)   Gid: (    0/    root)
Context: system_u:object_r:admin_home_t:s0
Access: 2023-01-27 19:03:59.429000000 -0500
Modify: 2023-01-26 16:51:53.225000000 -0500
Change: 2023-01-26 16:51:53.225000000 -0500
 Birth: 2023-01-26 16:51:53.050000000 -0500
```

The two commands report the file type differently. The first command returns the specific type of data that the file contains (ASCII text), and the latter simply states that it is a regular file.

Directory Files

Directories are logical containers that hold files and subdirectories. The following *ls* command output shows a few directories from */usr/bin*:

```
[root@server1 ~]# ls -l /usr
total 236
dr-xr-xr-x.   2 root root 49152 Jan 26 16:43 bin
drwxr-xr-x.   2 root root     6 Aug  9  2021 games
drwxr-xr-x.   3 root root    23 Jan 26 16:39 include
dr-xr-xr-x.  38 root root  4096 Jan 26 16:43 lib
dr-xr-xr-x. 111 root root 69632 Jan 26 16:49 lib64
drwxr-xr-x.  47 root root  8192 Jan 26 16:43 libexec
drwxr-xr-x.  12 root root   131 Jan 26 16:37 local
dr-xr-xr-x.   2 root root 20480 Jan 26 16:43 sbin
drwxr-xr-x. 199 root root  8192 Jan 26 16:43 share
drwxr-xr-x.   4 root root    34 Jan 26 16:37 src
lrwxrwxrwx.   1 root root    10 Aug  9  2021 tmp -> ../var/tmp
```

The letter "d" at the beginning of each line entry identifies the file as a directory. Try running the **file** and **stat** commands on /usr and see what they report.

Block and Character Special Device Files

Each piece of hardware in the system has an associated file in the /dev directory that is used by the system to communicate with that device. This type of file is called a *device file*. There are two types of device files: *character* (or *raw*) and *block*. In the example below, the *ls* command in field 1 of column 1 distinguishes between the two with a "c" for character and a "b" for block:

```
[root@server1 ~]# ls -l /dev/console
crw--w----. 1 root tty 5, 1 Jan 26 17:01 /dev/console
[root@server1 ~]#
[root@server1 ~]# ls -l /dev/sd*
brw-rw----. 1 root disk 8, 0 Jan 26 17:01 /dev/sda
brw-rw----. 1 root disk 8, 1 Jan 26 17:01 /dev/sda1
brw-rw----. 1 root disk 8, 2 Jan 26 17:01 /dev/sda2
```

Use the **file** and **stat** commands on /dev/console and /dev/sda files for additional verification.

Every hardware device such as a disk, CD/DVD, printer, and terminal has an associated device driver loaded in the kernel. The kernel communicates with hardware devices through their respective device drivers. Each device driver is assigned a unique number called the *major* number, which the kernel uses to recognize its type.

Furthermore, there may be more than one instance of the same device type in the system. In that case, the same driver is used to control all those instances. For example, SATA device driver controls all SATA hard disks and CD/DVD drives. The kernel in this situation allots a *minor* number to each individual device within that device driver category to identify it as a unique device. This scheme applies to disk partitions as well. In short, a major number points to the device driver, and a minor number points to a unique device or partition that the device driver controls.

In the above long listing, columns 5 and 6 depict the major and minor number association for each device instance. Major number 8 represents the block device driver for SATA disks. Similarly (not shown in the above output), major number 253 denotes the driver for device mapper (VDO volumes, LVM logical volumes, etc.), and 11 signifies optical devices. VDO and LVM volumes are discussed in Chapter 13 "Storage Management".

Symbolic Links

A *symbolic link* (a.k.a. a *soft link* or a *symlink*) may be considered a shortcut to another file or directory. If you issue *ls -l* on a symbolically linked file or directory, the line entry will begin with the letter "l", and an arrow will be pointing to the target link. For example:

```
[root@server1 ~]# ls -l /usr/sbin/vigr
lrwxrwxrwx. 1 root root 4 Dec 18  2018 /usr/sbin/vigr -> vipw
```

Run the **file** and **stat** commands on /usr/sbin/vigr for additional confirmation.

Compression and Archiving

Compression tools are used to compress one or more files to conserve space. They may be used with archive commands, such as *tar* or *star*, to create a single compressed archive of hundreds of files and directories. A compressed archive can then be copied to a remote system faster than a non-compressed archive or stored at a backup location. RHEL offers a multitude of compression tools such as *gzip* (*gunzip*) and *bzip2* (*bunzip2*).

The *tar* and *star* commands have the ability to preserve general file attributes such as ownership, owning group, and timestamp as well as extended attributes such as SELinux contexts.

SELinux context is set on files and directories to provide an enhanced level of protection from unauthorized users and processes. Refer to Chapter 20 "Security Enhanced Linux" for details around SELinux.

The syntax and usage of *tar* and *star* commands are similar, and most of the common options are identical. We discuss only the *tar* command.

Using gzip and gunzip

The *gzip/gunzip* compression utility pair has been available in Linux for over two decades. The *gzip* command is used to create a compressed file of each of the specified files and it adds the *.gz* extension to each file for identification. This tool can be used with the -r option to compress an entire directory tree, and with the -l option to display compression information about a gzipped file. The -l option also instructs the command to display the filename that will be given to the file when it is uncompressed.

To compress the file *fstab* located in the */etc* directory, copy this file in the *root* user's home directory */root* using the *cp* command and confirm with *ls*:

```
[root@server1 ~]# pwd
/root
[root@server1 ~]# cp /etc/fstab .
[root@server1 ~]# ls -l fstab
-rw-r--r--. 1 root root 579 Jan 28 17:06 fstab
```

Now use the *gzip* command to compress this file and *ls* to confirm:

```
[root@server1 ~]# gzip fstab
[root@server1 ~]# ls -l fstab.gz
-rw-r--r--. 1 root root 351 Jan 28 17:06 fstab.gz
```

Notice that the original file is compressed, and it now has the *.gz* extension added to it. If you wish to view compression information for the file, run the *gzip* command again with the -l option:

```
[root@server1 ~]# gzip -l fstab.gz
         compressed        uncompressed  ratio uncompressed_name
               351                 579  43.5% fstab
```

To decompress this file, use the *gunzip* command:

```
[root@server1 ~]# gunzip fstab.gz
[root@server1 ~]# ls -l fstab
-rw-r--r--. 1 root root 579 Jan 28 17:06 fstab
```

Check the file after the decompression with the *ls* command. It will be the same file with the same size, timestamp, and other attributes.

Using bzip2 and bunzip2

The *bzip2/bunzip2* is another compression pair that has been available in Linux for a long time. The *bzip2* command creates a compressed file of each of the specified files and it adds the *.bz2* extension to each file for identification.

Let's compress the *fstab* file again, but this time with *bzip2* and confirm with *ls*:

```
[root@server1 ~]# bzip2 fstab
[root@server1 ~]# ls -l fstab.bz2
-rw-r--r--. 1 root root 389 Jan 28 17:06 fstab.bz2
```

Notice that the original file is compressed, and it now has the *.bz2* extension. To decompress this file, use the *bunzip2* command:

```
[root@server1 ~]# bunzip2 fstab.bz2
[root@server1 ~]# ls -l fstab
-rw-r--r--. 1 root root 579 Jan 28 17:06 fstab
```

Check the file after the decompression with the *ls* command. It will be the same file with the same size, timestamp, and other attributes.

Differences between gzip and bzip2

The function of both *gzip* and *bzip2* is the same: to compress and decompress files. However, in terms of the compression and decompression rate, *bzip2* has a better compression ratio (smaller target file size), but it is slower. These differences are evident on fairly large files. On small files, you can use either of the two. Both commands support several identical options.

Using tar

The *tar* (*tape archive*) command is used to create, append, update, list, and extract files or an entire directory tree to and from a single file, which is called a *tarball* or *tarfile*. This command can be instructed to also compress the tarball after it has been created.

tar supports a multitude of options such as those described in Table 3-1.

Option	Definition
-c	Creates a tarball.
-f	Specifies a tarball name.
-p	Preserve file permissions. Default for the root user. Specify this option if you create an archive as a normal user.
-r	Appends files to the end of an extant uncompressed tarball.
-t	Lists contents of a tarball.

Option	Definition
-u	Appends files to the end of an extant uncompressed tarball provided the specified files being added are newer.
-v	Verbose mode.
-x	Extracts or restores from a tarball.

Table 3-1 tar Command Options

The -r and -u options do not support adding files to an existing compressed tarball.

A few examples are provided below to elucidate the use of *tar*. Pay special attention to the syntax and options used in each command and observe the output.

To create a tarball called */tmp/home.tar* of the entire */home* directory, use the -v option for verbosity and the -f option to specify the name of the archive file with the command. The following is a truncated output of the command:

```
[root@server1 ~]# tar -cvf /tmp/home.tar /home
tar: Removing leading `/' from member names
/home/
/home/user1/
/home/user1/.mozilla/
/home/user1/.mozilla/extensions/
/home/user1/.mozilla/plugins/
/home/user1/.bash_logout
/home/user1/.bash_profile
```

The resulting tarball will not include the leading forward slash (/) in the file paths as indicated on line 1 of the output even though the full path of */home* is supplied. This is the default behavior of the *tar* command, which gives you the flexibility to restore the files at any location of your choice without having to worry about the full pathnames. Use the -P option at the creation time to override this behavior.

To create a tarball called */tmp/files.tar* containing only a select few files (two files in this example) from the */etc* directory:

```
[root@server1 ~]# tar -cvf /tmp/files.tar /etc/passwd /etc/yum.conf
tar: Removing leading `/' from member names
/etc/passwd
tar: Removing leading `/' from hard link targets
/etc/yum.conf
```

To append files located in the */etc/yum.repos.d* directory to the existing tarball */tmp/files.tar*:

```
[root@server1 ~]# tar -rvf /tmp/files.tar /etc/yum.repos.d
tar: Removing leading `/' from member names
/etc/yum.repos.d/
/etc/yum.repos.d/redhat.repo
tar: Removing leading `/' from hard link targets
```

To list what files are included in the *files.tar* tarball:

```
[root@server1 ~]# tar -tvf /tmp/files.tar
-rw-r--r-- root/root        2092 2023-01-26 16:50 etc/passwd
lrwxrwxrwx root/root           0 2022-09-15 08:05 etc/yum.conf -> dnf/dnf.conf
drwxr-xr-x root/root           0 2023-01-26 17:23 etc/yum.repos.d/
-rw-r--r-- root/root         358 2023-01-26 17:23 etc/yum.repos.d/redhat.repo
```

To restore a single file, *etc/yum.conf*, from */tmp/files.tar* under */root* and confirm the output with *ls*:

```
[root@server1 ~]# cd
[root@server1 ~]# tar -xf /tmp/files.tar etc/yum.conf
[root@server1 ~]# ls -l etc/yum.conf
lrwxrwxrwx. 1 root root 12 Sep 15 08:05 etc/yum.conf -> dnf/dnf.conf
```

To restore all files from */tmp/files.tar* under */root* and confirm the output with *ls*:

```
[root@server1 ~]# tar -xf /tmp/files.tar
[root@server1 ~]# ls -l etc
total 4
-rw-r--r--. 1 root root 2092 Jan 26 16:50 passwd
lrwxrwxrwx. 1 root root   12 Sep 15 08:05 yum.conf -> dnf/dnf.conf
drwxr-xr-x. 2 root root   25 Jan 26 17:23 yum.repos.d
```

tar also supports options to directly compress the target file while being archived using the *gzip* or *bzip2* command. These options are described in Table 3-2.

Option	Description
-j	Compresses a tarball with bzip2
-z	Compresses a tarball with gzip

Table 3-2 tar with Compression Options

You will use the options in Table 3-2 to create compressed archives in Exercise 3-1.

EXAM TIP: Archiving and compression are tasks usually done together to produce smaller archive files.

Exercise 3-1: Create Compressed Archives

This exercise should be done on *server1* as *root*.

In this exercise, you will create a tarball called *home.tar.gz* of the */home* directory under */tmp* and compress it with *gzip*. You will create another tarball called *home.tar.bz2* of the */home* directory under */tmp* and compress it with *bzip2*. You will list the content of *home.tar.gz* without uncompressing it and then extract all the files in the current directory. Finally, you will extract the *bzip2*-compressed archive in the */tmp* directory.

1. Create (-c) a *gzip*-compressed (-z) tarball under */tmp* (-f) for */home*:

   ```
   [root@server1 ~]# tar -czf /tmp/home.tar.gz /home
   ```

2. Create (-c) a *bzip2*-compressed (-j) tarball under */tmp* (-f) for */home*:

```
[root@server1 ~]# tar -cjf /tmp/home.tar.bz2 /home
```

3. List (-t) the content of the *gzip*-compressed archive (-f) without uncompressing it:

```
[root@server1 ~]# tar -tf /tmp/home.tar.gz
home/
home/user1/
home/user1/.mozilla/
home/user1/.mozilla/extensions/
. . . . . . . .
```

4. Extract (-x) files from the *gzip*-compressed tarball (-f) in the current directory:

```
[root@server1 ~]# tar -xf /tmp/home.tar.gz
```

5. Extract (-x) files from the *bzip2*-compressed (-f) tarball under */tmp* (a different directory location than the current directory) (-C):

```
[root@server1 ~]# tar -xf /tmp/home.tar.bz2 -C /tmp
```

Run **ls /tmp** to view the list of extracted files.

File Editing

The *vim editor* is an interactive, full-screen *visual* text-editing tool that allows you to create and modify text files. This tool is available as a standard editor in all vendor UNIX versions and Linux distributions. It does not require the graphical capability and it is not heavy on compute resources. All text editing within *vim* takes place in a *buffer* (a small chunk of memory used to hold file updates). Changes can either be written to the disk or discarded.

It is essential for you as a system administrator to master the *vim* editor skills. The best way to learn *vim* is to practice by opening or creating a file and run the *vim* commands. See the manual pages of *vim* for details. Alternatively, you can run the *vimtutor* command to view the tutorial.

Modes of Operation

The *vim* editor has three modes of operation: the command mode, the input mode, and the last line mode. The fourth mode is referred to as the visual mode, but it is not discussed in the book.

The *command* mode is the default mode of vim. The *vim* editor places you into this mode when you start it. While in the command mode, you can carry out tasks such as copy, cut, paste, move, remove, replace, change, and search on text, in addition to performing navigational operations. This mode is also known as the *escape* mode because the Esc key is used to enter the mode.

In the *input* mode, anything that is typed on the keyboard is entered into the file as text. Commands cannot be run in this mode. The input mode is also called the *edit* mode or the *insert* mode. You need to press the Esc key to return to the command mode.

While in the command mode, you may carry out advanced editing tasks on text by pressing the colon character (:), which places the cursor at the beginning of the last line of the screen, and hence it is referred to as the *last line* or *extended* mode. This mode is considered a special type of command mode.

Starting vim

The *vim* editor may be started by typing the command *vim* at the command prompt, and it may follow an existing or a new filename as an argument. Without a specified filename, it simply opens an empty screen where you can enter text. You can save the text in a file or discard using commands provided in subsequent subsections.

```
[root@server1 ~]# vim
```

Alternatively, you can supply a filename as an argument. This way, *vim* will open the specified file for editing if the file exists, or it will create a file by that name if it does not exist.

```
[root@server1 ~]# vim <filename>
```

There are options available that you may specify at the time of starting this editing tool. Refer to the manual pages for more information.

Inserting text

Once *vim* is started, there are six commands that can switch into the edit mode. These commands are simple lower and uppercase i, a, and o, and are described in Table 3-3.

Command	Action
i	Inserts text before the current cursor position
I	Inserts text at the beginning of the current line
a	Appends text after the current cursor position
A	Appends text to the end of the current line
o	Opens a new line below the current line
O	Opens a new line above the current line

Table 3-3 vim Editor | Inserting Text

Press the Esc key when you've finished entering text in the edit mode to return to the command mode.

Navigating within vim

Navigation keys are helpful in editing small and large files. They allow you to make rapid moves in the file. There are multiple key sequences available within *vim* to control the cursor movement. Some of the elementary keystrokes are elaborated in Table 3-4.

Command	Action
h	Moves backward one character
j	Moves downward one line
k	Moves upward one line
l	Moves forward one character
w	Moves to the start of the next word
b	Moves backward to the start of the preceding word
e	Moves to the ending character of the next word
$	Moves to the end of the current line
Enter	Moves to the beginning of the next line

Command	Action
Ctrl+f	Scrolls down to the next page
Ctrl+b	Scrolls up to the previous page

Table 3-4 vim Editor | Navigating

You can precede any of the commands listed in Table 3-4 by a numeral to repeat the command action that many times. For instance, 3h would move the cursor three places to the left, 5Enter would move the cursor five lines below, and 2Ctrl+f would move the cursor two screens down.

In addition, you can use 0 (zero) to move to the beginning of the current line, [[to move to the first line of the file, and]] to move to the last line of the file.

Revealing Line Numbering

While working with large files in the *vim* editor, you deal with hundreds or even thousands of lines. You may need to delete, copy, paste, or move one or more lines within the file. To perform these operations with accuracy, vim offers a way to enable line numbering within the editor. Table 3-5 describes the command.

Command	Action
:set nu	Shows line numbering
:set nonu	Hides line numbering

Table 3-5 vim Editor | Revealing Line Numbering

Line numbers are not recorded when you save the file. They are for a reference purpose only.

Deleting Text

vim provides several commands to carry out delete operations. Some of the commands are described in Table 3-6.

Command	Action
x	Deletes the character at the cursor position
X	Deletes the character before the cursor location
dw	Deletes the word or part of the word to the right of the cursor location
dd	Deletes the current line
D	Deletes at the cursor position to the end of the current line
:6,12d	Deletes lines 6 through 12

Table 3-6 vim Editor | Deleting Text

You can precede any of the commands listed in Table 3-6, except for the last line mode command, by a numeral to repeat the command action that many times. For instance, 2X would delete two characters before the cursor position, and 3dd would delete the current line and the two lines below it.

Undoing and Repeating

Table 3-7 explicates the commands that undo the last change made and repeat the last command run.

Command	Action
u	Undoes the previous command
U	Undoes all the changes done on the current line
:u	Undoes the previous last line mode command
. (dot)	Repeats the last command run

Table 3-7 vim Editor | Undoing and Repeating

You can precede any of the commands listed in Table 3-7, except for the U and :u commands, by a numeral to repeat the command action that many times. For instance, 2u would undo the previous two changes, and 2U would undo all the changes done on the current and the previous lines.

Searching for Text

You can perform forward and reverse searches while in the command mode by using the / and ? characters followed by the string to be searched. For instance, in a file with numerous occurrences of the string "profile," you can run /profile or ?profile for a forward or reverse search.

Table 3-8 summarizes these actions.

Command	Action
/string	Searches forward for a string
?string	Searches backward for a string
n	Finds the next occurrence of a string
N	Finds the previous occurrence of a string

Table 3-8 vim Editor | Searching for Text

For forward searches, repeating "n" takes the cursor to the previous occurrences of the searched string, and repeating "N" moves the cursor to the next occurrences.

The behavior is reversed for backward searches. Repeating "n" takes the cursor to the next occurrences of the searched string, and repeating "N" moves the cursor to the previous occurrences.

Replacing Text

Table 3-9 describes two last line mode commands that are used to perform a search and replace operation.

Command	Action
:%s/old/new	Replaces the first occurrence of *old* with *new* in a file. For example, to replace the first occurrence of profile with Profile, use *:%s/profile/Profile*.
:%s/old/new/g	Replaces all occurrences of *old* with *new* in a file. For example, to replace all the occurrences of profile with Profile in a file, use *:%s/profile/Profile/g*.

Table 3-9 vim Editor | Replacing Text

If you have used either of these and would like to undo it, use the last line mode command :u.

Copying, Moving, and Pasting Text

vim allows you to copy some text and paste it to the desired location within the file. You can copy (yank) a single character, a single word, or an entire line, and then paste it wherever you need it. The copy function can be performed on multiple characters, words, or lines simultaneously. Table 3-10 describes the copy, move, and paste commands.

Command	Action
yl	Yanks the current letter into buffer
yw	Yanks the current word into buffer
yy	Yanks the current line into buffer
p	Pastes yanked data below the current line
P	Pastes yanked data above the current line
:1,3co6	Copies lines 1 through 3 and pastes them after line 6
:4,6m9	Moves lines 4 through 6 after line 9

Table 3-10 vim Editor | Copying, Moving, and Pasting Text

You can precede any of the commands listed in Table 3-10, except for the last line mode commands, by a numeral to repeat the command action that many times. For instance, 2yw would yank two words, 2yy would yank two lines, and 2p would paste two times.

Changing Text

There are numerous commands available within *vim* to change and modify text as summarized in Table 3-11. Most of these commands switch into the edit mode, so you will have to press the Esc key to return to the command mode.

Command	Action
cl	Changes the letter at the cursor location
cw	Changes the word (or part of the word) at the cursor location to the end of the word
cc	Changes the entire line
C	Changes text at the cursor position to the end of the line
r	Replaces the character at the cursor location with the character entered following this command
R	Overwrites or replaces the text on the current line
J	Joins the next line with the current line
xp	Switches the position of the character at the cursor position with the character to the right of it
~	Changes the letter case (uppercase to lowercase, and vice versa) at the cursor location

Table 3-11 vim Editor | Changing Text

You can precede any of the commands listed in Table 3-11 by a numeral to repeat the command action that many times. For instance, 2cc would change the entire current and the next line, and 2r would replace the current character and the next character.

Saving and Quitting vim

When you are done with modifications, you can save or discard them. Use one of the commands listed in Table 3-12 as required.

Command	Action
:w	Writes changes into the file without quitting vim
:w file2	Writes changes into a new file called *file2* without quitting vim
:w!	Writes changes to the file even if the file owner does not have write permission on the file
:wq	Writes changes to the file and quits vim
:wq!	Writes changes to the file and quits vim even if the file owner does not have write permission on the file
:q	Quits vim if no modifications were made
:q!	Quits vim if modifications were made, but we do not wish to save them

Table 3-12 vim Editor | Saving and Quitting

The exclamation mark (!) can be used to override the write protection placed on the file for the owner.

> **EXAM TIP:** You may be required to edit configuration files or write scripts. Working knowledge of the vim editor is crucial.

File and Directory Operations

This section elaborates on various management operations that can be performed on files and directories. These operations include creating, displaying contents, copying, moving, renaming, and deleting files and directories. These common operations can be performed by normal users who own or have appropriate permissions. The *root* user can accomplish these tasks on any file or directory on the system, regardless of who owns it. In case there's a lack of user permissions, an error message is generated.

Creating Files and Directories

Files can be created in multiple ways using different commands; however, there is only one command to create directories.

Creating Empty Files Using touch

The *touch* command creates an empty file. If the file already exists, it simply updates the timestamp on it to match the current system date and time. Execute the following as *root* in the *root* user's home directory to create *file1* and then run *ls* to verify:

```
[root@server1 ~]# cd
[root@server1 ~]# touch file1
[root@server1 ~]# ls -l file1
-rw-r--r--. 1 root root 0 Jan 28 17:17 file1
```

As expected, column 5 (the size column) in the output is 0, meaning that *file1* is created with zero bytes in size. If you rerun the *touch* command on this file after a minute or so, a new timestamp is placed on it:

```
[root@server1 ~]# touch file1
[root@server1 ~]# ls -l file1
-rw-r--r--. 1 root root 0 Jan 28 17:18 file1
```

The *touch* command has a few interesting options. The -d and -t options set a specific date and time on a file; the -a and -m options enable you to change only the access or the modification time on a file to the current system time; and the -r option sets the modification time on a file to that of a reference file's. Let's use a couple of these options in the examples below:

To set the date on *file1* to January 31, 2023:

```
[root@server1 ~]# touch -d 2023-01-31 file1
[root@server1 ~]# ls -l file1
-rw-r--r--. 1 root root 0 Jan 31  2023 file1
```

To change the modification time on *file1* to the current system time:

```
[root@server1 ~]# touch -m file1
[root@server1 ~]# ls -l file1
-rw-r--r--. 1 root root 0 Jan 28 17:20 file1
```

Try the rest of the options for practice.

Creating Short Files Using cat

The *cat* command allows you to create short text files. The ending angle bracket ">" must be used to redirect the output to the specified file (*catfile1* in this example):

```
[root@server1 ~]# cat > catfile1
```

Nothing is displayed when you execute the above, as the system is waiting for you to input something. Type some text. Press the Enter key to open a new line and continue typing. When you are done, press Ctrl+d to save the text in *catfile1* and return to the command prompt. You can verify the file creation with the *ls* command.

Creating Files Using vim

You can use the *vim* editor to create and modify text files of any size. Refer to the previous section in this chapter on how to use vim.

Making Directories Using mkdir

The *mkdir* command is used to create directories. This command shows an output if you run it with the -v option. The following example demonstrates the creation of a directory called *dir1* in the *root* user's home directory:

```
[root@server1 ~]# mkdir dir1 -v
mkdir: created directory 'dir1'
[root@server1 ~]# ls -ld dir1
drwxr-xr-x. 2 root root 6 Jan 28 17:21 dir1
```

You can create a hierarchy of subdirectories by specifying the -p (parent) option with *mkdir*. In the following example, *mkdir* is used to create the hierarchy *dir2/perl/perl5*:

```
[root@server1 ~]# mkdir -vp dir2/perl/perl5
mkdir: created directory 'dir2'
mkdir: created directory 'dir2/perl'
mkdir: created directory 'dir2/perl/perl5'
```

Notice the placement of options in the two examples. Many commands in Linux accept either format.

Displaying File Contents

RHEL offers a variety of tools for showing file contents. Directory contents are simply the files and subdirectories that it contains. Use the *ls* command as explained earlier to view directory contents.

For viewing files, you can use the *cat*, *more*, *less*, *head*, and *tail* commands. These tools are explained below.

Using cat

cat displays the contents of a text file. It is typically used to view short files. It shows the entire file on the screen. The following example shows the *.bash_profile* file in the *root* user's home directory with the *cat* command:

```
[root@server1 ~]# cat .bash_profile
# .bash_profile

# Get the aliases and functions
if [ -f ~/.bashrc ]; then
        . ~/.bashrc
fi

# User specific environment and startup programs
```

You can add the -n option to the *cat* command to view the output in numbered format.

Using less and more

Both *less* and *more* are text filters that are used for viewing long text files one page at a time, starting at the beginning. The *less* command is more capable than the *more* command. *less* does not need to read the entire file before it starts to display its contents, thus making it faster. The *more* command is limited to forward text searching only, whereas *less* is able to perform both forward and backward searches. Run the *less* and *more* commands one at a time and observe the visual difference in the outputs:

```
[root@server1 ~]# less /usr/bin/znew
[root@server1 ~]# more /usr/bin/znew
```

You can navigate with the keys described in Table 3-13 while viewing the files with either tool.

Key	Purpose
Spacebar / f	Scrolls forward one screen
Enter	Scrolls forward one line
b	Scrolls backward one screen
d	Scrolls forward half a screen
h	Displays help
q	Quits and returns to the command prompt
/string	Searches forward for a string
?string	Searches backward for a string; only applies to the less command
n	Finds the next occurrence of a string
N	Finds the previous occurrence of a string; only applies to the less command

Table 3-13 Navigating with less and more

If the */usr/bin/znew* file is unavailable, use */etc/profile* instead.

Using head and tail

head displays the starting few lines of the specified text file. By default, it returns the first ten lines. See the example below:

```
[root@server1 ~]# head /etc/profile
# /etc/profile

# System wide environment and startup programs, for login setup
# Functions and aliases go in /etc/bashrc

# It's NOT a good idea to change this file unless you know what you
# are doing. It's much better to create a custom.sh shell script in
# /etc/profile.d/ to make custom changes to your environment, as this
# will prevent the need for merging in future updates.
```

The above output includes three empty lines as well. You can pass a numeral to the command as an argument to limit the number of lines in the output. For example, run the following to view only the top three lines from */etc/profile*:

```
[root@server1 ~]# head -3 /etc/profile
```

On the other hand, the *tail* command displays the ending ten lines from the specified file by default unless a numeral is passed as an argument to alter the behavior. Issue the following two commands on your terminal to witness the difference:

```
[root@server1 ~]# tail /etc/services
[root@server1 ~]# tail -3 /etc/services
```

The *tail* command is particularly useful when watching a log file while it is being updated. The -f (follow) option enables this function. The following example enables us to view the updates to the system log file */var/log/messages* in real time:

```
[root@server1 ~]# tail -f /var/log/messages
```

You may have to wait for some time before you see an update. Press `Ctrl+c` to quit when you are done.

Counting Words, Lines, and Characters in Text Files

The *wc* (*word count*) command displays the number of lines, words, and characters (or bytes) contained in a text file or input supplied. For example, when you run this command on the */etc/profile* file, you will see output similar to the following:

```
[root@server1 ~]# wc /etc/profile
   78   247 1899 /etc/profile
```

Column 1 in the output discloses the number of lines (78) in the file followed by the number of words (247), the number of characters (or bytes) (1899), and the filename (*/etc/profile*).

You can use the options listed in Table 3-14 to restrict the output as desired.

Option	Action
-l	Prints a count of lines
-w	Prints a count of words
-c	Prints a count of bytes
-m	Prints a count of characters

Table 3-14 wc Command Options

The following example displays only the count of characters in */etc/profile*:

```
[root@server1 ~]# wc -m /etc/profile
1899 /etc/profile
```

Try running *wc* with the other options and observe the outcomes.

Copying Files and Directories

The copy operation duplicates a file or directory. RHEL provides the *cp* command for this purpose, and it has a variety of options.

Copying Files

The *cp* command copies one or more files within a directory or to another directory. To duplicate a file in the same directory, you must give a different name to the target file. However, if the copy is being made to a different directory, you can use either the same filename or assign a different one. Consider the following examples:

To copy *file1* as *newfile1* within the same directory:

```
[root@server1 ~]# cp file1 newfile1
```

To copy *file1* by the same name to another existing directory *dir1*:

```
[root@server1 ~]# cp file1 dir1
```

By default, the copy operation overwrites the destination file if it exists without presenting a warning. To alter this behavior, use the -i (interactive) option to instruct *cp* to prompt for confirmation before overwriting:

```
[root@server1 ~]# cp file1 dir1 -i
cp: overwrite 'dir1/file1'? y
```

Press Enter after keying in a "y" for yes or an "n" for no to proceed.

By default, you do not need to specify the -i option for yes/no confirmation if you attempt to copy a file to overwrite the destination file as *root*. The predefined alias—"alias cp='cp -i'"—in the *.bashrc* file in the *root* user's home directory takes care of that.

Copying Directories

The *cp* command with the -r (recursive) option copies an entire directory tree to another location. In the following example, *dir1* is copied to *dir2* and then the directory contents of *dir2* are listed for validation:

```
[root@server1 ~]# cp -r dir1 dir2
[root@server1 ~]# ls -l dir2
total 0
drwxr-xr-x. 2 root root 19 Jan 28 17:26 dir1
drwxr-xr-x. 3 root root 19 Jan 28 17:22 perl
```

You may use the -i option for overwrite confirmation if the destination already has a matching file or directory.

Try running **ls -l dir2 -R** to view the entire *dir2* hierarchy.

The *cp* command can also use -p, which can provide the ability to preserve the attributes (timestamp, permissions, ownership, etc.) of a file or directory being copied. Try running **cp -p file1 /tmp** and then use *ls -l* to compare the attributes for both files.

Moving and Renaming Files and Directories

A file or directory can be moved within the same file system or to another. Within the file system move, an entry is added to the target directory and the source entry is removed, which leaves the actual data intact. On the other hand, a move to a different file system physically moves the file or directory content to the new location and deletes the source.

A rename simply changes the name of a file or directory; data is not touched.

Moving and Renaming Files

The *mv* command is used to move or rename files. The -i option can be specified for user confirmation if a file by that name already exists. The following example moves *file1* to *dir1* and prompts for confirmation:

```
[root@server1 ~]# mv -i file1 dir1
mv: overwrite 'dir1/file1'? y
```

By default, you do not need to specify the -i option for yes/no confirmation if you attempt to move a file to overwrite the destination file as *root*. The predefined alias—"alias mv='mv -i'"—in the *.bashrc* file in the *root* user's home directory takes care of that.

To rename *newfile1* as *newfile2*:

```
[root@server1 ~]# mv newfile1 newfile2
```

Verify the above operations with **ls -l**.

Moving and Renaming Directories

Use the *mv* command to move a directory and its contents to somewhere else or to change the name of the directory. For example, you can move *dir1* into *dir2* (*dir2* must exist, otherwise it will be a simple rename operation):

```
[root@server1 ~]# mv dir1 dir2
```

To rename *dir2* as *dir20*:

```
[root@server1 ~]# mv dir2 dir20
```

Verify the above operations with **ls -l**.

Removing Files and Directories

The remove operation deletes a file entry from the directory structure and marks its data space as free. For a directory, the remove operation weeds corresponding entries out from the file system structure.

Removing Files

You can remove a file using the *rm* command, which deletes one or more specified files. For example, issue the following command to erase *newfile2*:

```
[root@server1 ~]# rm -i newfile2
rm: remove regular empty file 'newfile2'? y
```

By default, you do not need to specify the -i option for yes/no confirmation if you attempt to remove a file as *root*. The predefined alias—"alias rm='rm -i'"—in the *.bashrc* file in the *root* user's home directory takes care of that.

The *rm* command can also be used to erase a file that has a wildcard character, such as an asterisk (*) or a question mark (?), embedded in its name. These characters have special meaning to the shell, and filenames containing them must be prepended with the backslash character (\) to instruct the shell to treat them as regular characters.

 A careful use of the *rm* command is particularly important when you have administrative rights on the system.

For example, if a file exists by the name * under the */tmp* directory (use **touch /tmp/*** to create it), you can remove it by executing **rm /tmp/***. If you mistakenly run **rm /tmp/*** instead, all files under */tmp* will be deleted.

Wildcard characters are used in filename globbing and in commands where an action needs to occur on multiple files matching certain criteria. They are discussed in Chapter 07 "The Bash Shell".

Removing Directories

The *rmdir* and *rm* commands erase directories. The *rmdir* command is used to delete empty directories, while *rm* requires the -d option to accomplish the same. In addition, the -r or -R (recursive) flag with *rm* will remove a directory and all of its contents. Both commands support the -v switch for reporting what they are doing. Let's look at a few examples.

To erase an empty directory called *emptydir* (assuming *emptydir* exists), use either of the following:

```
[root@server1 ~]# rmdir emptydir -v      or
[root@server1 ~]# rm -dv emptydir
```

To remove *dir20* and all its contents recursively, use either -r or -R with the command:

```
[root@server1 ~]# rm -r dir20
```

The *rm* command supports the -i flag for interactive deletions.

> **EXAM TIP:** Manipulating files and directories is one of the most common tasks performed in any operating system. Working knowledge of the tools learned in this section is crucial.

The same rules that apply on filenames with wildcard characters in their names, apply on directory names as well. See the previous topic for details.

File Linking

Each file within a file system has a multitude of attributes assigned to it at the time of its creation. These attributes are collectively referred to as the file's *metadata*, and they change when the file is accessed or modified. A file's metadata includes several pieces of information, such as the file type, size, permissions, owner's name, owning group name, last access/modification times, link count, number of allocated blocks, and pointers to the data storage location. This metadata takes 128 bytes of space for each file. This tiny storage space is referred to as the file's *inode* (*index node*).

An inode is assigned a unique numeric identifier that is used by the kernel for accessing, tracking, and managing the file. In order to access the inode and the data it points to, a filename is assigned to recognize it and access it. This mapping between an inode and a filename is referred to as a *link*. It is important to note that the inode does not store the filename in its metadata; the filename and corresponding inode number mapping is maintained in the directory's metadata where the file resides.

Linking files or directories creates additional instances of them, but all of them eventually point to the same physical data location in the directory tree. Linked files may or may not have identical inode numbers and metadata depending on how they are linked.

There are two ways to create file and directory links in RHEL, and they are referred to as hard links and soft links. Links are created between files or between directories, but not between a file and a directory.

Hard Link

A *hard* link is a mapping between one or more filenames and an inode number, making all hard-linked files indistinguishable from one another. This implies that all hard-linked files will have identical metadata. Changes to the file metadata and content can be made by accessing any of the filenames.

Figure 3-1 shows two filenames—*file10* and *file20*—both sharing the same inode number 10176147. Here, each filename is essentially a hard link pointing to the same inode.

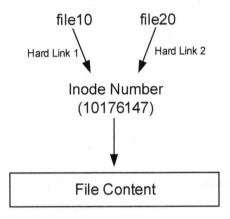

Figure 3-1 Hard Link

A hard link cannot cross a file system boundary, and it cannot be used to link directories because of the restrictions placed within Linux designed to avoid potential issues with some commands.

The following example creates an empty file called *file10* and then uses the *ln* command to create a hard link called *file20* in the same directory:

```
[root@server1 ~]# touch file10
[root@server1 ~]# ln file10 file20
```

After creating the link, run *ls* with the -li flags as follows:

```
[root@server1 ~]# ls -li file*
10176147 -rw-r--r--. 2 root root 0 Sep  6 14:29 file10
10176147 -rw-r--r--. 2 root root 0 Sep  6 14:29 file20
```

Look at columns 1 and 3. Column 1 shows the shared inode number (10176147), and column 3 provides a *link count* of the hard links that each file has (*file10* points to *file20*, and vice versa). If you remove the original file (*file10*), you will still have access to the data through *file20*. Each time you add a hard link to an extant file, the link count will increase by 1. Similarly, if you delete a hard link, the link count will go down by 1. When all the hard links (files) are erased, the link count will set to 0. The increase and decrease in the number of links is reflected on all hard-linked files.

Soft Link

A *soft* link (a.k.a. a *symbolic* link or a *symlink*) makes it possible to associate one file with another. The concept is analogous to that of a shortcut in Microsoft Windows where the actual file is resident somewhere in the directory structure, but there can be one or more shortcuts with different names pointing to it. With a soft link, you can access the file directly via the actual filename as well as any of the shortcuts. Each soft link has a unique inode number that stores the pathname to the file it is linked with. For a symlink, the link count does not increase or decrease, rather each symlinked file receives a new inode number. The pathname can be absolute or relative depending on what was specified at the time of its creation. The size of the soft link is the number of characters in the pathname to the target.

Figure 3-2 shows the file *file10* with a soft link called *soft10* pointing to it.

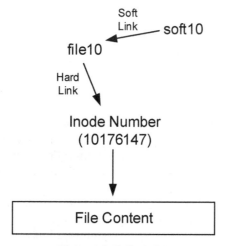

Figure 3-2 Soft Link

A soft link can cross a file system boundary and it can be used to link directories, as it simply uses the pathname of the destination object.

To create a soft link for *file10* as *soft10* in the same directory, use the *ln* command with the -s switch:

```
[root@server1 ~]# ln -s file10 soft10
```

After you have created the link, issue *ls -l* and notice the letter "l" as the first character in column 2 of the output. Also notice the arrow that is pointing from the linked file to the original file. Both of these indicate that *soft10* is merely a pointer to *file10*. The -i option displays the associated inode numbers in the first column. See the output of **ls -il** below:

```
[root@server1 ~]# ls -il file10 soft10
10176147 -rw-r--r--. 2 root root 0 Sep  6 14:29 file10
10185731 lrwxrwxrwx. 1 root root 6 Sep  6 18:22 soft10 -> file10
```

If you remove the original file (*file10* in this case), the link *soft10* will stay but points to something that does not exist.

RHEL 9 has four soft-linked directories under /. They are:

```
lrwxrwxrwx.  1 root root   7 Aug 9 2021 bin -> usr/bin
lrwxrwxrwx.  1 root root   7 Aug 9 2021 lib -> usr/lib
lrwxrwxrwx.  1 root root   9 Aug 9 2021 lib64 -> usr/lib64
lrwxrwxrwx.  1 root root   8 Aug 9 2021 sbin -> usr/sbin
```

The syntax for creating soft-linked directories is exactly the same as that for soft-linked files.

Differences between Copying and Linking

There are key differences between copying and linking operations. This subsection will discuss when to use copy and when to opt for a soft or hard link. Table 3-15 highlights the main differences between the two:

Copying	Linking
Creates a duplicate of the source file. If either file is modified, the other file will remain intact.	Creates a shortcut that points to the source file. The source can be accessed or modified using either the source file or the link.
Each copied file stores its own data at a unique location.	All linked files point to the same data.
Each copied file has a unique inode number with its unique metadata.	**Hard Link:** All hard-linked files share the same inode number, and hence the metadata. **Symlink:** Each symlinked file has a unique inode number, but the inode number stores only the pathname to the source.
If a copy is moved, erased, or renamed, the source file will have no impact, and vice versa.	**Hard Link:** If the hard link is weeded out, the other file and the data will remain untouched. **Symlink:** If the source is deleted, the soft link will be broken and become meaningless. If the soft link is removed, the source will have no impact.
Copy is used when the data needs to be edited independent of the other.	Links are used when access to the same source is required from multiple locations.
Permissions on the source and the copy are managed independent of each other.	Permissions are managed on the source file.

Table 3-15 Copying vs. Linking

Keep these differences in mind when you need to decide whether to use copy or a link.

Exercise 3-2: Create and Manage Hard Links

This exercise should be done on *server1* as *root*.

In this exercise, you will create an empty file *hard1* under */tmp* and display its attributes (the inode number, permissions, number of links, owning user, owning group, size, and timestamp). You will create two hard links *hard2* and *hard3* for it and list the attributes for all three files. You will edit *hard2* and add some text. You will list the attributes for all three files again and observe identicalness in all attributes except for the names of files. You will remove *hard1* and *hard3* and list the attributes again for the remaining file. You will notice a decrease in the link count by 2.

1. Create an empty file */tmp/hard1*, and display the long file listing including the inode number:

```
[root@server1 ~]# touch /tmp/hard1
[root@server1 ~]# ls -li /tmp/hard1
17389466 -rw-r--r--. 1 root root 0 Jan 28 21:42 /tmp/hard1
```

The file listing indicates the inode number in column 1, followed by permissions (column 2), number of links (column 3), owning user and group (columns 4 and 5), size (column 6), timestamp (columns 7, 8, and 9), and filename (column 10).

2. Create two hard links called *hard2* and *hard3* under */tmp*, and display the long listing:

```
[root@server1 ~]# ln /tmp/hard1 /tmp/hard2
[root@server1 ~]# ln /tmp/hard1 /tmp/hard3
[root@server1 ~]# ls -li /tmp/hard*
17389466 -rw-r--r--. 3 root root 0 Jan 28 21:42 /tmp/hard1
17389466 -rw-r--r--. 3 root root 0 Jan 28 21:42 /tmp/hard2
17389466 -rw-r--r--. 3 root root 0 Jan 28 21:42 /tmp/hard3
```

Observe the file listing. All attributes are identical.

3. Edit file *hard2* and add some random text. Display the long listing for all three files again:

```
[root@server1 ~]# vim /tmp/hard2
[root@server1 ~]# ls -li /tmp/hard*
17389466 -rw-r--r--. 3 root root 16 Jan 28 21:44 /tmp/hard1
17389466 -rw-r--r--. 3 root root 16 Jan 28 21:44 /tmp/hard2
17389466 -rw-r--r--. 3 root root 16 Jan 28 21:44 /tmp/hard3
```

Observe the size and timestamp columns for all three files. They are identical.

4. Erase file *hard1* and *hard3*, and display the long listing for the remaining file:

```
[root@server1 ~]# rm -f /tmp/hard1 /tmp/hard3
[root@server1 ~]# ls -li /tmp/hard*
17389466 -rw-r--r--. 1 root root 16 Jan 28 21:44 /tmp/hard2
```

The number of links reduced to 1, all other attributes are the same. You can still access the same data through this last file.

Exercise 3-3: Create and Manage Soft Links

This exercise should be done on *server1* as *root*.

In this exercise, you will create a soft link *soft1* under */root* pointing to */tmp/hard2*. You will display the attributes (the inode number, permissions, number of links, owning user, owning group, size, and timestamp) for both files. You will open *soft1* for edit and list the attributes after editing. You will remove *hard2* and then list *soft1*. You will notice that *soft1* becomes invalid, pointing to something that does not exist. Remove *soft1* to complete the exercise.

1. Create soft link */root/soft1* pointing to */tmp/hard2*, and display the long file listing for both:

```
[root@server1 ~]# ln -s /tmp/hard2 /root/soft1
[root@server1 ~]# ls -li /tmp/hard2 /root/soft1
17389472 lrwxrwxrwx. 1 root root 10 Jan 28 21:45 /root/soft1 -> /tmp/hard2
17389466 -rw-r--r--. 1 root root 16 Jan 28 21:44 /tmp/hard2
```

The file listing indicates the inode number in column 1, followed by permissions (column 2), number of links (column 3), owning user and group (columns 4 and 5), size (column 6), timestamp (columns 7, 8, and 9), and filename (column 10). The soft link file has an "l" prefixed to column 2 and an arrow pointing to the actual file after column 10. Both are indications of a soft link. Notice the file size (10 bytes for the full path *tmp/hard2*) for *soft1*. Observe similarities and other differences.

2. Edit *soft1* and display the long listing again:

```
[root@server1 ~]# vim /root/soft1
[root@server1 ~]# ls -li /tmp/hard2 /root/soft1
17389472 lrwxrwxrwx. 1 root root 10 Jan 28 21:45 /root/soft1 -> /tmp/hard2
17389466 -rw-r--r--. 1 root root 34 Jan 28 21:47 /tmp/hard2
```

The number of bytes for *hard1* and the timestamp reflects the editing. The rest of the attributes are the same.

3. Remove *hard2* and display the long listing:

```
[root@server1 ~]# rm -f /tmp/hard2
[root@server1 ~]# ls -li /tmp/hard2 /root/soft1
ls: cannot access '/tmp/hard2': No such file or directory
17389472 lrwxrwxrwx. 1 root root 10 Jan 28 21:45 /root/soft1 -> /tmp/hard2
```

The actual file, *hard2*, is gone and the soft link is now invalid. You can remove it with **rm -f /root/soft1**.

Chapter Summary

This chapter started with an introduction of common file types that are available in RHEL. A file's type is determined by the type of data it stores. Regular is the most common type of file that stores plain text or binary information. Directories are also very common and there are thousands of them on a typical RHEL system. Other file types include device files and linked files.

We looked at creating and manipulating compressed files and compressed archives. This is a common practice among Linux users for storing old files and transferring a large amount of data to remote systems.

We learned about the vim editor, which is a favorite text file creation and editing tool. We looked at its various modes of operations and switching between them. The basics of vim were discussed, including how to start and insert text, navigate and search for text, copy and paste text, modify and delete text, save edits, and quit with or without saving the changes.

Next, we described file and directory manipulation tools for operations such as creating, listing, displaying, copying, moving, renaming, and removing them. Normal and super users perform these tasks on Linux systems very often.

We examined soft and hard links, and their advantages and limitations. Based on the knowledge gained, we can identify and create the type of link we need for a particular use case.

Finally, we explored the differences between file copying and file linking.

Review Questions

1. A file compressed with *bzip2* can be uncompressed with the *gunzip* command. True or False?
2. The *tar* command can be used to archive files with their SELinux contexts. True or False?
3. Which numeric identifier does the kernel use to determine the uniqueness of a device within a device driver type?
4. What are the two indications in the output of *ls -l* that tells us if the file is a symlink?
5. The *rmdir* command without any switches can be used to erase an entire directory structure. True or False?
6. What would the command *tar pczf output.file /usr/local* do if it is executed by a normal user?
7. The *ls -l* command produces 9 columns in the output by default. True or False?
8. Which three Linux utilities can be used to determine a file's type?
9. There are two hard linked files in a directory. How would you identify them?
10. Which *vim* mode allows to execute advanced copy and move functions?
11. What would the command *wc -c file1* show?
12. What does the kernel use the major number for?
13. The *tail* command can be used to view a file while it is being updated. True or False?
14. Soft linked directories cannot cross file system boundaries, but hard linked directories can. True or False?
15. A file must have the *.exe* extension in order to run. True or False?
16. What would the command *touch file1* do on an existing *file1* file?

Answers to Review Questions

1. False. The file will have to be uncompressed with either *bzip2* or *bunzip2*.
2. True. The *tar* command has the --selinux switch that provides this support.
3. The kernel uses the minor number to identify the uniqueness of a device within a particular device category.
4. A symlink file line entry in the *ls -l* command output begins with the letter l and has an arrow pointing to the source file.
5. False. The *rmdir* command is used to erase empty directories.
6. This command will create a gzip'ed tar archive called *output.file* of the */usr/local* directory with file permissions preserved.
7. True.
8. The *stat, file*, and *ls* commands can be used to determine a file's type.
9. You can identify them by running *ls -li*.
10. The last line mode (extended mode) allows users to copy or move lines.
11. This command will show the number of bytes in *file1*.
12. The kernel employs the major number to identify the device type.
13. True. You need to include the -f switch in the command.
14. False. Soft linked directories can cross file system boundaries but hard linked directories cannot.
15. False.
16. This command will update the access time on *file1*.

Do-It-Yourself Challenge Labs

The following labs are useful to strengthen most of the concepts and topics learned in this chapter. It is expected that you perform the labs without external help. A step-by-step guide is not supplied, as the knowledge and skill required to implement the labs have already been disseminated in the chapter; however, hints to the relevant major topic(s) are included.

Use the lab environment built specifically for end-of-chapter labs. See sub-section "Lab Environment for End-of-Chapter Labs" in Chapter 01 "Local Installation" for details.

Lab 3-1: Archive, List, and Restore Files

As *root* on *server3*, execute the *tar* command to create a *gzip*-compressed archive of the */etc* directory. Run the *tar* command again to create a *bzip2*-compressed archive of the */etc* directory. Compare the file sizes of the two archives. Run the *tar* command and uncompress and restore both archives without specifying the compression tool used. (Hint: Compression and Archiving).

Lab 3-2: Practice the vim Editor

As *user1* on *server3*, create a file called *vipractice* in the home directory using *vim*. Type (do not copy and paste) each sentence from Lab 3-1 on a separate line (do not worry about line wrapping). Save the file and quit the editor. Open *vipractice* in *vim* again and copy lines 2 and 3 to the end of the file to make the total number of lines in the file to 6. Move line 3 to make it line 1. Go to the last line and append the contents of the *.bash_profile*. Substitute all occurrences of the string "Profile" with "Pro File", and all occurrences of the string "profile" with "pro file". Erase lines 5 to 8. Save the file and quit *vim*. Provide a count of lines, words, and characters in the *vipractice* file using the *wc* command. (Hint: File Editing).

Lab 3-3: File and Directory Operations

As *user1* on *server3*, create one file and one directory in the home directory. List the file and directory and observe the permissions, ownership, and owning group. Try to move the file and the directory to the */var/log* directory and notice what happens. Try again to move them to the */tmp* directory. Duplicate the file with the *cp* command, and then rename the duplicated file using any name. Erase the file and directory created for this lab. (Hint: File and Directory Operations).

Chapter 04

Advanced File Management

This chapter describes the following major topics:

➤ Understand ugo/rwx access permissions on files and directories
➤ Know symbolic and octal notations of permission allocation
➤ Modify permissions for file owner, owning group, and others
➤ Calculate and set default permissions on new files and directories
➤ Comprehend and configure special permission bits: setuid, setgid, and sticky
➤ Use setgid bit for group collaboration
➤ Apply sticky bit on public and shared writable directories
➤ Search for files in a variety of different ways

RHCSA Objectives:

10. List, set, and change standard ugo/rwx permissions
36. Create and configure set-GID directories for collaboration
37. Diagnose and correct file permission problems
53. Manage default file permissions

Permissions are set on files and directories to prevent access from unauthorized users. Users are grouped into three distinct categories. Each user category is then assigned required permissions. Permissions may be modified using one of two available methods. The user mask may be defined for individual users so new files and directories they create always get preset permissions. Every file in Linux has an owner and a group.

RHEL offers three additional permission bits to control user access to certain executable files and shared directories. A directory with one of these bits can be used for group collaboration. A public or group writable directory may also be configured with one of these bits to prevent file deletion by non-owners.

```
# ls -l file
-rw-r--r-- 1 root root 0 Nov 19 23:49 file
```

```
           Other (r--)          r = Readable
         Group (r--)            w = Writeable
       Owner (rw-)              x = Executable
                                - = Denied
File type
```

There is a tool available in RHEL that proves to be very helpful in searching for files at the specified location using a range of options to specify the search criteria. This tool may be set to execute an action on the output files as they are found.

File and Directory Access Permissions

Linux is a multi-user operating system that allows hundreds of users the ability to log in and work concurrently. In addition, the OS has hundreds of thousands of files and directories that it must maintain securely to warrant a successful system and application operation from a security standpoint. Given these factors, it is imperative to regulate user access to files and directories and grant them appropriate rights to carry out their designated functions without jeopardizing system security. This control of permissions on files and directories may also be referred to as user *access rights*.

Determining Access Permissions

Access permissions on files and directories allow administrative control over which users (permission classes) can access them and to what level (permission types). File and directory permissions discussed in this section are referred to as *standard ugo/rwx permissions*.

Permission Classes

Users are categorized into three unique classes for maintaining file security through access rights. These classes are *user* (u), *group* (g), and *other* (o, also referred to as *public*). These permission classes represent the owner, the set of users with identical access requirements, and everyone else on the system, respectively. There is another special user class called *all* (a) that represents the three user classes combined.

Permission Types

Permissions control what actions can be performed on a file or directory and by whom. There are three types of permissions bits—*read* (r), *write* (w), and *execute* (x)—and they behave differently for files and directories. For files, the permissions allow viewing and copying (read), modifying (write), and running (execute). And in the case of directories, they allow listing contents with *ls* (read); creating, erasing, and renaming files and subdirectories (write); and enter (with the *cd* command) into it (execute).

If a read, write, or execute permission bit is not desired, the hyphen character (-) is used to represent its absence.

Permission Modes

A permission mode is used to *add* (+), *revoke* (-), or *assign* (=) a permission type to a permission class. You can view the permission settings on files and directories in the long listing of the *ls* command. This information is encapsulated in column 1 of the output, a sample of which is shown below:

```
-  rwx  rw-  r--
```

The first character indicates the type of file: - for regular file, d for directory, l for symbolic link, c for character device file, b for block device file, p for named pipe, s for socket, and so on.

The next nine characters—three groups of three characters—show the read (r), write (w), and execute (x) permissions for the three user classes: user (owner), group, and other (public), respectively. The hyphen character (-) represents a permission denial for that level.

Modifying Access Permission Bits

The *chmod* command modifies access rights. It works identically on files and directories. *chmod* can be used by *root* or the file owner, and can modify permissions specified in one of two ways: *symbolic* or *octal*. Symbolic notation uses a combination of letters (ugo/rwx) and symbols (+, -, =) to add, revoke, or assign permission bits. The octal notation (a.k.a. the *absolute* representation) uses a three-digit numbering system ranging from 0 to 7 to express permissions for the three user classes. Octal values are given in Table 4-1.

Octal Value	Binary Notation	Symbolic Notation	Explanation
0	000	---	No permissions
1	001	--x	Execute permission only
2	010	-w-	Write permission only
3	011	-wx	Write and execute permissions
4	100	r--	Read permission only
5	101	r-x	Read and execute permissions
6	110	rw-	Read and write permissions
7	111	rwx	Read, write, and execute permissions

Table 4-1 Octal Permission Notation

In Table 4-1, each "1" corresponds to an r, w, or x, and each "0" corresponds to the hyphen character (-) for no permission at that level. Figure 4-1 shows weights associated with each digit position in the 3-digit octal numbering model.

Figure 4-1 Permission Weights

The position to the right is weight 1, the middle position is weight 2, and the left position is weight 4. If we assign a permission of 6, for example, it will correspond to the left and middle positions. Similarly, a permission of 2 would point to the middle position only.

Exercise 4-1: Modify Permission Bits Using Symbolic Form

This exercise should be done on *server1* as *user1*.

For this exercise, presume that a file called *permfile1* exists with read permission for the owner (*user1*), owning group (*user1*), and other, as shown below. If the permissions vary, bring them to the desired state by executing **chmod 444 permfile1** prior to starting the exercise.

```
-r--r--r--. 1 user1 user1 0 Sep  6 20:02 permfile1
```

In this exercise, you will add an execute bit for the owner and a write bit for group and public. You will then revoke the write bit from public and assign read, write, and execute bits to the three user categories at the same time. Finally, you will revoke write from the owning group and write and execute bits from public. The *chmod* command accepts the -v switch to display what it has changed. You may alternatively view the long listing after each command execution for verification.

1. Add an execute bit for the owner:

```
[user1@server1 ~]$ chmod u+x permfile1 -v
mode of 'permfile1' changed from 0444 (r--r--r--) to 0544 (r-xr--r--)
```

2. Add a write bit for group members and public:

```
[user1@server1 ~]$ chmod -v go+w permfile1
mode of 'permfile1' changed from 0544 (r-xr--r--) to 0566 (r-xrw-rw-)
```

3. Remove the write permission for public:

```
[user1@server1 ~]$ chmod -v o-w permfile1
mode of 'permfile1' changed from 0566 (r-xrw-rw-) to 0564 (r-xrw-r--)
```

4. Assign read, write, and execute permission bits to all three user categories:

```
[user1@server1 ~]$ chmod a=rwx -v permfile1
mode of 'permfile1' changed from 0564 (r-xrw-r--) to 0777 (rwxrwxrwx)
```

5. Revoke write bit from the group members and write and execute bits from public:

```
[user1@server1 ~]$ chmod g-w,o-wx permfile1 -v
mode of 'permfile1' changed from 0777 (rwxrwxrwx) to 0754 (rwxr-xr--)
```

Exercise 4-2: Modify Permission Bits Using Octal Form

This exercise should be done on *server1* as *user1*.

For this exercise, a file called *permfile2* exists with read permission for the owner (*user1*), owning group (*user1*), and other, as shown below. If the permissions vary, bring them to the desired state by executing **chmod 444 permfile2** prior to starting the exercise.

```
-r--r--r--. 1 user1 user1 0 Sep  6 21:12 permfile2
```

In this exercise, you will add an execute bit for the owner and a write permission bit for group and public. You will then revoke the write bit from public and assign read, write, and execute permissions to the three user categories at the same time. The *chmod* command accepts the -v flag to display what it has changed. You may alternatively view the long listing after each command execution for verification.

1. Add an execute bit for the owner:

```
[user1@server1 ~]$ chmod -v 544 permfile2
mode of 'permfile2' changed from 0444 (r--r--r--) to 0544 (r-xr--r--)
```

2. Add a write permission bit for group and public:

```
[user1@server1 ~]$ chmod -v 566 permfile2
mode of 'permfile2' changed from 0544 (r-xr--r--) to 0566 (r-xrw-rw-)
```

3. Revoke the write bit for public:

```
[user1@server1 ~]$ chmod -v 564 permfile2
mode of 'permfile2' changed from 0566 (r-xrw-rw-) to 0564 (r-xrw-r--)
```

4. Assign read, write, and execute permission bits to all three user categories:

```
[user1@server1 ~]$ chmod 777 -v permfile2
mode of 'permfile2' changed from 0564 (r-xrw-r--) to 0777 (rwxrwxrwx)
```

Default Permissions

Linux assigns *default permissions* to a file or directory at the time of its creation. Default permissions are calculated based on the *umask* (*user mask*) permission value subtracted from a preset *initial* permissions value.

The umask is a three-digit octal value (also represented in symbolic notation) that refers to read, write, and execute permissions for owner, group, and public. Its purpose is to set default permissions on new files and directories without touching the permissions on existing files and directories. The default umask value is set to 0022 for all users including the *root* user. Note that the

---

left-most 0 bit has no significance. Run the *umask* command without any options and it will display the current umask value in octal notation:

```
[user1@server1 ~]$ umask
0022
```

Run the command again but with the -S option to display the umask in symbolic form:

```
[user1@server1 ~]$ umask -S
u=rwx,g=rx,o=rx
```

The predefined initial permission values are 666 (rw-rw-rw-) for files and 777 (rwxrwxrwx) for directories. Even if the umask is set to 000, the new files will always get a maximum of 666 permissions; however, you can add the executable bits explicitly with the *chmod* command if desired.

Calculating Default Permissions

Consider the following example to calculate the default permission values on files:

Initial Permissions	666	
umask	− 022	(subtract)
========================		
Default Permissions	644	

This is an indication that every new file will have read and write permissions assigned to the owner, and a read-only permission to the owning group and others.

To calculate the default permission values on directories:

Initial Permissions	777	
umask	− 022	(subtract)
========================		
Default Permissions	755	

This indicates that every new directory created will have read, write, and execute permissions assigned to the owner, and read and execute permissions to the owning group and everyone else.

If you want different default permissions set on new files and directories, you will need to modify the umask. You first need to ascertain the desired default values. For instance, if you want all new files and directories to get 640 and 750 permissions, you can set umask to 027 by running either of the following:

```
[user1@server1 ~]$ umask 027                          or
[user1@server1 ~]$ umask u=rwx,g=rx,o=
```

The new value becomes effective right away, and it will only be applied to files and directories created thereafter. The existing files and directories will remain intact. Now create *tempfile1* and *tempdir1* as *user1* under */home/user1* to test the effect of the new umask:

```
[user1@server1 ~]$ touch tempfile1
[user1@server1 ~]$ ls -l tempfile1
-rw-r-----. 1 user1 user1 0 Sep  6 21:42 tempfile1
[user1@server1 ~]$ mkdir tempdir1
[user1@server1 ~]$ ls -ld tempdir1
drwxr-x---. 2 user1 user1 6 Sep  6 21:42 tempdir1
```

The above examples show that the new file and directory were created with different permissions. The file got (666 – 027 = 640) and the directory got (777 – 027 = 750) permissions.

The umask value set at the command line will be lost as soon as you log off. In order to retain the new setting, place it in an appropriate shell startup file discussed in Chapter 07 "The Bash Shell".

Special File Permissions

Linux offers three types of special permission bits that may be set on binary executable files or directories that respond differently to non-*root* users for certain operations. These permission bits are *set user identifier* bit (commonly referred to as *setuid* or *suid*), *set group identifier* bit (a.k.a. *setgid* or *sgid*), and *sticky* bit.

The setuid and setgid bits may be defined on binary executable files to provide non-owners and non-group members the ability to run them with the privileges of the owner or the owning group, respectively. The setgid bit may also be set on shared directories for group collaboration. The sticky bit may be set on public directories for inhibiting file erasures by non-owners.

 The setuid and sticky bits may be set on directories and files; however, they will have no effect.

The use of the special bits should be regulated and monitored to evade potential security issues to system operation and applications.

The setuid Bit on Binary Executable Files

The setuid flag is set on binary executable files at the file owner level. With this bit set, the file is executed by non-owners with the same privileges as that of the file owner. A common example is the *su* command that is owned by the *root* user. This command has the setuid bit enabled on it by default. See the underlined "s" in the owner's permission class below:

```
[root@server1 ~]# ls -l /usr/bin/su
-rwsr-xr-x. 1 root root 56936 Aug 24 11:22 /usr/bin/su
```

The su (*switch user*) command allows a user to switch to a different user account with the password for the target user. However, the *root* user can switch into any other user account without being prompted for a password. When a normal user executes this command, it will run as if *root* (the owner) is running it and, therefore, the user is able to run it successfully and gets the desired result.

Exercise 4-3: Test the Effect of setuid Bit on Executable Files

This exercise should be done on *server1* as *root* and *user1*.

In this exercise, you will need two terminal windows, one with a *root* session running and another with *user1* on it. As *user1*, you will switch into *root* and observe what happens. As *root*, you will then revoke the setuid bit from the */usr/bin/su* file and retry switching into *root* again. After the completion of the exercise, you will restore the setuid bit on */usr/bin/su*.

1. Log in as *root* and have a terminal window open (let's call it Terminal 1). Open another terminal (let's name it Terminal 2) and run the following to switch into *user1*:

```
[root@server1 ~]# su - user1
```

2. On Terminal 2, run the *su* command to switch into *root*:

```
[user1@server1 ~]$ su - root
Password:
[root@server1 ~]#
```

The output confirms the switch.

3. On Terminal 1, revoke the setuid bit from */usr/bin/su*:

```
[root@server1 ~]# chmod -v u-s /usr/bin/su
mode of '/usr/bin/su' changed from 4755 (rwsr-xr-x) to 0755 (rwxr-xr-x)
```

The file is still executable by everyone as indicated by the execute flag; however, it will prevent regular non-owning users from switching accounts, as they have lost that special elevated privilege.

4. On Terminal 2, press Ctrl+d to log off as *root*.
5. On Terminal 2, switch back into *root* and see what happens:

```
[user1@server1 ~]$ su -
Password:
su: Authentication failure
```

user1 gets an "authentication failure" message even though they entered the correct password.

6. On Terminal 1, restore the setuid bit on */usr/bin/su*:

```
[root@server1 ~]# chmod -v +4000 /usr/bin/su
mode of '/usr/bin/su' changed from 0755 (rwxr-xr-x) to 4755 (rwsr-xr-x)
```

With the argument +4000, the *chmod* command enables setuid on the specified file without altering any existing underlying permissions. Alternatively, you can use the symbolic notation as follows:

```
[root@server1 ~]# chmod u+s /usr/bin/su
```

If the file already has the "x" bit set for the user (owner), the long listing will show a lowercase "s", otherwise it will list it with an uppercase "S".

The setuid bit has no effect on directories.

The setgid Bit on Binary Executable Files

The setgid attribute is set on binary executable files at the group level. With this bit set, the file is executed by non-owners with the exact same privileges as that of the group members. A common example is the *write* command that is owned by the *root* user with *tty* as the owning group. This command has the setgid bit enabled on it by default. See the "s" in the group's permission class below:

```
[root@server1 ~]# ls -l /usr/bin/write
-rwxr-sr-x. 1 root tty 23792 Aug 24 11:22 /usr/bin/write
```

The *write* command allows users to write a message on another logged-in user's terminal. By default, normal users are allowed this special elevated privilege because of the presence of the setgid flag on the file. When a normal user executes this command to write to the terminal of another user, the command will run as if a member of the *tty* group is running it, and the user is able to execute it successfully.

Exercise 4-4: Test the Effect of setgid Bit on Executable Files

This exercise should be done on *server1* as *root* and *user1*.

In this exercise, you will need two terminal windows, one with a *root* session running and the other with *user1* on it. Both terminal sessions must be opened with ssh. As *user1*, you will produce a list of logged-in users; try to send the *root* user a message and observe what happens. As *root*, you will then revoke the setgid bit from the */usr/bin/write* file and retry sending another message to *root* as *user1*. After the completion of the exercise, you will restore the setgid bit on */usr/bin/write*.

1. Open a terminal window (let's call it Terminal 1) and log in as *root*. Open another terminal (let's name it Terminal 2) and log in as *user1*.
2. On Terminal 2, run the *who* command to list users who are currently logged on:

```
[user1@server1 ~]$ who
root      pts/0       2023-01-28 21:52 (192.168.0.4)
user1     pts/1       2023-01-28 22:10 (192.168.0.4)
```

The output discloses that there are two users—*root* and *user1*—currently signed in.

3. On Terminal 2, execute the *write* command as follows to send a message to *root*:

```
[user1@server1 ~]$ write root
```

4. On Terminal 1, you will see the following message from *user1*:

```
[root@server1 ~]#
Message from user1@server1.example.com on pts/1 at 13:56 ...
```

Any text you type on Terminal 2 will appear on Terminal 1. Press Ctrl+d on Terminal 2 to end the write session.

5. On Terminal 1, press Enter to get the command prompt back

---

6. Revoke the setgid bit from */usr/bin/write*:

```
[root@server1 ~]# chmod g-s /usr/bin/write -v
mode of '/usr/bin/write' changed from 2755 (rwxr-sr-x) to 0755 (rwxr-xr-x)
```

The file is still executable by everyone as indicated by the execute flag; however, it will prevent them from writing to the terminals of other users, as they have lost that special elevated privilege.

7. On Terminal 2, rewrite to *root* and see what happens:

```
[user1@server1 ~]$ write root
write: effective gid does not match group of /dev/pts/1
```

user1 gets an error as indicated in the above output.

8. On Terminal 1, restore the setgid bit on */usr/bin/write*:

```
[root@server1 ~]# chmod -v +2000 /usr/bin/write
mode of '/usr/bin/write' changed from 0755 (rwxr-xr-x) to 2755 (rwxr-sr-x)
```

With the argument +2000, the *chmod* command enables setgid on the specified file without altering any existing underlying permissions. Alternatively, you can use the symbolic form as follows:

```
[root@server1 ~]# chmod g+s /usr/bin/write
```

If the file already has the "x" bit set for the group, the long listing will show a lowercase "s", otherwise it will list it with an uppercase "S".

The setgid bit has an impact on shared (and public) directories (next subsection).

The setgid Bit on Shared Directories

The setgid bit can also be set on group-shared directories to allow files and subdirectories created underneath to automatically inherit the directory's owning group. This saves group members who are sharing the directory contents from changing the group ID for every new file and subdirectory that they add. The standard behavior for new files and subdirectories is to always receive the creator's group.

Exercise 4-5: Set up Shared Directory for Group Collaboration

This exercise should be done on *server1* as *root* and two test users *user100* and *user200*. Create the user accounts by running **useradd user100** and **useradd user200** (if they don't already exist) as *root*. Assign both user accounts passwords by running **passwd user100** and **passwd user200** and entering a password twice.

In this exercise, you will create a group called *sgrp* with GID 9999, and add *user100* and *user200* to this group as members with shared data needs. You will create a directory called */sdir* with ownership and owning group belonging to *root* and *sgrp*, then set the setgid bit on */sdir* and test. For details on managing users and groups, consult Chapter 05 "Basic User Management" and Chapter 06 "Advanced User Management".

1. Add group *sgrp* with GID 9999 with the *groupadd* command:

```
[root@server1 ~]# groupadd -g 9999 sgrp
```

2. Add *user100* and *user200* as members to *sgrp* using the *usermod* command:

```
[root@server1 ~]# usermod -aG sgrp user100
[root@server1 ~]# usermod -aG sgrp user200
```

3. Create */sdir* directory:

```
[root@server1 ~]# mkdir /sdir
```

4. Set ownership and owning group on */sdir* to *root* and *sgrp*, using the *chown* command:

```
[root@server1 ~]# chown root:sgrp /sdir
```

5. Set the setgid bit on */sdir* using the *chmod* command:

```
[root@server1 ~]# chmod g+s /sdir
```

6. Add write permission to the group members on */sdir* and revoke all permissions from public:

```
[root@server1 ~]# chmod g+w,o-rx /sdir
```

7. Verify the attributes set in the previous three steps using the *ls* command on */sdir*:

```
[root@server1 ~]# ls -ld /sdir
drwxrws---. 2 root sgrp 6 Sep  7 11:57 /sdir
```

8. Switch or log in as *user100* and change to the */sdir* directory:

```
[root@server1 ~]# su - user100
[user100@server1 ~]$ cd /sdir
[user100@server1 sdir]$
```

9. Create a file and check the owner and owning group on it:

```
[user100@server1 sdir]$ touch file100
[user100@server1 sdir]$ ls -l file100
-rw-rw-r--. 1 user100 sgrp 0 Sep  7 12:07 file100
```

10. Log out as *user100*, and switch or log in as *user200* and change to the */sdir* directory:

```
[user100@server1 sdir]$ exit
logout
[root@server1 ~]# su - user200
[user200@server1 ~]$ cd /sdir
[user200@server1 sdir]$
```

11. Create a file and check the owner and owning group on it:

```
[user200@server1 sdir]$ touch file200
[user200@server1 sdir]$ ls -l file200
-rw-rw-r--. 1 user200 sgrp 0 Sep  7 12:11 file200
```

As shown above, the owning group for each file is the same, *sgrp*, and the group members have identical rights (read and write). Both can modify or delete each other's file. The group members own the files, but the owning group will always be *sgrp* to which they both belong.

> **EXAM TIP:** Some of the steps provided above for setting up a directory for group collaboration may not have to be run in that order.

The Sticky Bit on Public and Shared Writable Directories

The sticky bit is set on public and shared writable directories to protect files and subdirectories owned by normal users from being deleted or moved by other normal users. This attribute is set on the */tmp* and */var/tmp* directories by default as depicted below; however, it can be applied to any writable directory:

```
[root@server1 ~]# ls -l /tmp /var/tmp -d
drwxrwxrwt. 14 root root 4096 Jan 28 22:10 /tmp
drwxrwxrwt. 10 root root 4096 Jan 28 22:10 /var/tmp
```

Notice the underlined letter "t" in other's permission fields. This indicates the presence of this attribute on the two directories.

Exercise 4-6: Test the Effect of Sticky Bit

This exercise should be done on *server1* as *root* and two test users *user100* and *user200* that were created in the previous exercise.

In this exercise, you will create a file under */tmp* as *user100* and then try to delete it as *user200*. You will unset the sticky bit on */tmp* and try to erase the file again. After the completion of the exercise, you will restore the sticky bit on */tmp*. For details on managing users and groups, consult Chapter 05 "Basic User Management" and Chapter 06 "Advanced User Management".

1. Switch or log in as *user100* and change to the */tmp* directory:

```
[root@server1 ~]# su - user100
[user100@server1 ~]$ cd /tmp
```

2. Create a file called *stickyfile*:

```
[user100@server1 tmp]$ touch stickyfile
```

3. Log out as *user100* and switch or log in as *user200* and change to the */tmp* directory:

```
[user100@server1 tmp]$ exit
logout
[root@server1 ~]# su - user200
[user200@server1 ~]$ cd /tmp
```

4. Try to erase the file and observe the system reaction:

```
[user200@server1 tmp]$ rm stickyfile
rm: remove write-protected regular empty file 'stickyfile'? y
rm: cannot remove 'stickyfile': Operation not permitted
```

It says, "Operation not permitted". The user cannot remove the file owned by another user.

5. Log out as *user200* and revoke the sticky bit from */tmp* as *root* and confirm:

```
[user200@server1 ~]$ exit
logout
[root@server1 ~]# chmod o-t /tmp
[root@server1 ~]# ls -ld /tmp
drwxrwxrwx. 15 root root 4096 Jan 28 22:20 /tmp
```

6. Switch or log back in as *user200* and retry the removal:

```
[root@server1 ~]# su - user200
[user200@server1 ~]$ cd /tmp
[user200@server1 tmp]$ rm stickyfile
rm: remove write-protected regular empty file 'stickyfile'? y
[user200@server1 tmp]$
```

The file is gone. A normal user, *user200*, was able to successfully delete a file, *stickyfile*, that was owned by a different normal user, *user100*, in a public writable directory, */tmp*.

7. Log out as *user200* and restore the sticky bit back on */tmp*:

```
[user200@server1 tmp]$ exit
logout
[root@server1 ~]# chmod -v +1000 /tmp
mode of '/tmp' changed from 0777 (rwxrwxrwx) to 1777 (rwxrwxrwt)
```

With the argument +1000, the *chmod* command sets the sticky bit on the specified directory without altering any existing underlying permissions. Alternatively, you can use the symbolic notation as follows:

```
[root@server1 ~]# chmod o+t /tmp
```

If the directory already has the "x" bit set for public, the long listing will show a lowercase "t", otherwise it will list it with an uppercase "T".

The sticky bit can also be set on group writable directories such as */sdir* that you created in the previous exercise.

File Searching

A typical running RHEL system has a few hundred thousand files distributed across several file systems. At times, it is imperative to look for one or more files based on certain criteria. One example would be to find all files owned by employees who left the company over a year ago. Another example would be to search for all the files that have been modified in the past 20 days by a specific user. For such situations, RHEL offers a command called *find*. You supply your search criteria and this command gets you the result. You can also instruct this utility to execute a command on the files as they are found.

Using the find Command

The *find* command recursively searches the directory tree, finds files that match the specified criteria, and optionally performs an action on the files as they are discovered. This powerful tool can be tailored to look for files in a number of ways. The search criteria may include tracking files by name or part of the name, ownership, owning group, permissions, inode number, last access or modification time in days or minutes, size, and file type. Figure 4-2 shows the command syntax.

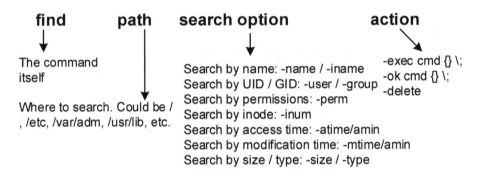

Figure 4-2 find Command Syntax

With *find*, files that match the criteria are located and their full paths are displayed.

To search for a file called *file10* (execute **touch file10** if it does not already exist) by its name (-name) in *root*'s home directory, run the *find* command as follows. The period character (.) represents the current directory, which is */root* in this example.

```
[root@server1 ~]# find . -name file10 -print
./file10
```

-print is optional. The *find* command, by default, displays the results on the screen. You do not need to specify this option.

To perform a case-insensitive (-iname) search for files and directories in */dev* that begin with the string "usb" followed by any characters:

```
[root@server1 ~]# find /dev -iname usb*
/dev/bus/usb
/dev/usbmon1
/dev/usbmon0
```

To find files smaller than 1MB (-1M) in size (-size) in the *root* user's home directory (~). You do not need to issue the command from this user's home directory. In fact, you can be anywhere in the directory tree.

```
[root@server1 ~]# find ~ -size -1M
```

 The tilde character (~) represents a user's home directory.

To search for files larger than 40MB (+40M) in size (-size) in the */usr* directory:

```
[root@server1 ~]# find /usr -size +40M
```

To find files in the entire root file system (/) with ownership (-user) set to user *daemon* and owning group (-group) set to any group other than (-not or ! for negation) *user1*:

```
[root@server1 ~]# find / -user daemon -not -group user1
```

To search for directories (-type) by the name "src" (-name) in */usr* at a maximum of two subdirectory levels below (-maxdepth):

```
[root@server1 ~]# find /usr -maxdepth 2 -type d -name src
```

To run the above search but at least three subdirectory levels beneath */usr*, substitute -maxdepth 2 with -mindepth 3.

To find files in the */etc* directory that were modified (-mtime) more than (the + sign) 2000 days ago:

```
[root@server1 ~]# find /etc -mtime +2000
```

To run the above search for files that were modified exactly 12 days ago, replace "+2000" with "12".

To find files in the */var/log* directory that have been modified (-mmin) in the past (the - sign) 100 minutes:

```
[root@server1 ~]# find /var/log -mmin -100
```

To run the above search for files that have been modified exactly 25 minutes ago, replace "-100" with "25".

To search for block device files (-type) in the */dev* directory with permissions (-perm) set to exactly 660:

```
[root@server1 ~]# find /dev -type b -perm 660
```

To search for character device files (-type) in the */dev* directory with at least (-222) world writable permissions (this example would ignore checking the write and execute permissions):

```
[root@server1 ~]# find /dev -type c -perm -222
```

To find files in the /etc/systemd directory that are executable by at least their owner or group members:

```
[root@server1 ~]# find /etc/systemd -perm /110
```

To search for symlinked files (-type) in /usr with permissions (-perm) set to read and write for the owner and owning group:

```
[root@server1 ~]# find /usr -type l -perm -ug=rw
```

find is a very useful and powerful file-searching tool with numerous other options available to use. Refer to its manual pages, as there are a ton of examples there. Try some of them out for additional practice.

Using find with -exec and -ok Flags

An advanced use of the *find* command is to perform an action on the files as they are found based on any criteria outlined in the previous subsection and in the command's manual pages. The action may include performing basic file management operations such as copying, erasing, renaming, changing ownership, or modifying permissions on each file found. This is done with the -exec switch. An equivalent option -ok may be used instead, which requires user confirmation before taking an action.

> **EXAM TIP:** The find command is very flexible and has a ton of options available to search for files. You should know the use of the exec option well.

To search for directories in the entire directory tree (/) by the name "core" (-name) and list them (ls -ld) as they are discovered without prompting for user confirmation (-exec):

```
[root@server1 ~]# find / -name core -type d -exec ls -ld {} \;
```

The *find* command replaces {} for each filename as it is found. The semicolon character (;) marks the termination of the command and it is escaped with the backslash character (\).

In the next example, the *find* command uses the -ok switch to prompt for confirmation (you need to enter a y) before it copies each matched file (-name) in /etc/sysconfig to /tmp:

```
[root@server1 ~]# find /etc/sysconfig -name *.conf -ok cp {} /tmp \;
< cp ... /etc/sysconfig/nftables.conf > ? y
```

The destination directory (/tmp) is specified between {} and \;. There are many advanced examples provided in the *find* command's manual pages. I suggest trying a few of them.

Chapter Summary

This chapter covered four topics: file and directory permissions, default permissions, special permissions, and file searching.

We learned classes, types, and modes of permissions, looked at octal and symbolic notations of changing permissions, and applied the knowledge to modify user access on files and directories. We examined the concept of default permissions and how they could be employed on parent directories to enable files and subdirectories created underneath to automatically get the desired permissions. We analyzed the role of the umask value in determining the new default permissions.

We looked at special permission bits that could be set on executable files to gain privileged access, applied on shared directories for content sharing, and enabled on shared and public writable directories to prevent file deletion by non-owning users.

Finally, we explored the criteria and the tool to search for files at the specified directory location. We also employed an extended flag for optional execution of an action on the outcome of the search command.

Review Questions

1. What would the *find / -name core -ok rm {} \;* command do?
2. Default permissions are calculated by subtracting the initial permissions from the umask value. True or False?
3. What would be the effect of the sticky bit on an executable file?
4. Name the permission classes, types, and modes.
5. The default umask for a normal user in bash shell is 0027. True or False?
6. What digit represents the setuid bit in the *chmod* command?
7. The output generated by the *umask* command shows the current user mask in four digits. What is the significance of the left-most digit?
8. What would the command *find /dev -type c -perm 660* do?
9. What would the command *chmod g-s file1* do?
10. The sticky bit is recommended for every system directory. True or False?
11. The setgid bit enables group members to run a command at a higher priority. True or False?
12. What is the equivalent symbolic value for permissions 751?
13. What permissions would the owner of the file get if the *chmod* command is executed with 555?
14. Which special permission bit is set on a directory for team sharing?

Answers to Review Questions

1. The *find* command provided will display all files by the name core in the entire directory hierarchy and ask for removal confirmation as it finds them.
2. permissions of 660.
3. False. Default permissions are calculated by subtracting the umask value from the initial permission values.
4. Nothing. The sticky bit is meant for directories only.
5. Permission classes are user, group, and public; permission types are read, write, and execute; and permission modes are add, revoke, and assign.
6. False. The default umask for bash shell users is 0022.
7. The left-most digit has no significance in the umask value.
8. The *find* command provided will find all character device files under */dev* with exact The digit 4 represents the setuid bit.
9. It would erase the setgid bit from *file1*.
10. False.

11. False.
12. The equivalent for octal 751 is rwxr-x--x.
13. The owner will get read and execute permissions.
14. The setgid bit is set for team sharing.

Do-It-Yourself Challenge Labs

The following labs are useful to strengthen most of the concepts and topics learned in this chapter. It is expected that you perform the labs without external help. A step-by-step guide is not supplied, as the knowledge and skill required to implement the labs have already been disseminated in the chapter; however, hints to the relevant major topic(s) are included.

Use the lab environment built specifically for end-of-chapter labs. See sub-section "Lab Environment for End-of-Chapter Labs" in Chapter 01 "Local Installation" for details.

Lab 4-1: Manipulate File Permissions

As *user1* on *server3*, create file *file11* and directory *dir11* in the home directory. Make a note of the permissions on them. Run the *umask* command to determine the current umask. Change the umask value to 0035 using symbolic notation. Create *file22* and directory *dir22* in the home directory. Observe the permissions on *file22* and *dir22,* and compare them with the permissions on *file11* and *dir11*. Use the *chmod* command and modify the permissions on *file11* to match those on *file22*. Use the *chmod* command and modify the permissions on *dir22* to match those on *dir11*. Do not remove *file11*, *file22*, *dir11*, and *dir22* yet. (Hint: File and Directory Access Permissions).

Lab 4-2: Configure Group Collaboration and Prevent File Deletion

As *root* on *server3*, create directory */sdir*. Create group *sgrp* and add *user1000* and *user2000* (create the users). Set up appropriate ownership (*root*), owning group (*sgrp*), and permissions (rwx for group, --- for public, s for group, and t for public) on the directory to support group collaboration and ensure non-owners cannot delete files. Log on as *user1000* and create a file under */sdir*. Log on as *user2000* and try to edit that file. You should be able to edit the file successfully. As *user2000* try to delete the file. You should not be able to. (Hint: Special File Permissions).

Lab 4-3: Find Files

As *root* on *server3*, execute the *find* command to search for all files in the entire directory structure that have been modified in the last 300 minutes and display their type. Use the *find* command again and search for named pipe and socket files. (Hint: File Searching).

Lab 4-4: Find Files Using Different Criteria

As *root* on *server3*, issue the *find* command to search for regular files under */usr* that were accessed more than 100 days ago, are not bigger than 5MB in size, and are owned by the user *root*. (Hint: File Searching).

## Chapter 05

Basic User Management

This chapter describes the following major topics:

➤ Show who is currently logged in
➤ Review history of successful user login attempts and system reboots
➤ Report history of failed user log in attempts
➤ View recent user login attempts
➤ Examine user and group information
➤ Understand the content and syntax of local user authentication files
➤ Analyze user configuration files
➤ Add, modify, and delete local user accounts with default and custom values
➤ Set and modify user passwords
➤ Add user account with nologin access

RHCSA Objectives:

48. Create, delete, and modify local user accounts
49. Change passwords and adjust password aging for local user accounts (only the first part of this objective "change passwords for local user accounts" is covered in this chapter; the second part is in Chapter 06)

U ser login activities are monitored and recorded in various files. RHEL offers a set of tools that read the activity data from these files and display the results. In addition to user activities, a history of system reboots is also maintained, and it may be viewed with one of the tools. This information may be useful in debugging, testing, or auditing purposes.

In order for an authorized person to gain access to the system, a unique username must be designated, and a user account must be created for them. This user is assigned a password and is allowed to change it themselves. User account information is recorded in several files. These files may be edited manually if necessary; however, this practice is discouraged. A good knowledge and grasp of the syntax and the type of information these files store is paramount for Linux administrators. User attributes may be modified later, or the account may be removed from the system altogether if not required anymore.

Though service user accounts are added to the system when a corresponding service is installed, there may be situations when they need to be added manually. These accounts do not require login access; their presence is needed to support an installed application.

User Login Activity and Information

On a busy RHEL system, many users sign in and run jobs as themselves, or they switch into the *root* or another user account to run tasks that only those users have the privilege to execute. As an administrator, it is one of your responsibilities to ensure that only authorized users are able to log in to the system. You can keep track of user logins, such as who is currently logged in and their previous and recent successful and unsuccessful login attempts. This information can be of immense help in determining any suspicious login activity. For instance, multiple failed attempts of logging in by an authorized user could be due to a forgotten or lost password, or it might be a result of an unauthorized individual trying to hack in.

There are many log files in RHEL that various services running on the system update automatically and instantly as activities occur. These logs capture user login activities among many others. This section will focus on the log files and tools that are relevant to user logins only. Others will be discussed in later chapters.

Listing Logged-In Users

A list of the users who have successfully signed on to the system with valid credentials can be printed using one of the two basic Linux tools: *who* and *w*. These commands show various pieces of information separated in multiple columns.

The *who* command references the */run/utmp* file and displays the information. Here is a sample from *server1*:

```
[root@server1 ~]# who
root      pts/0        2023-01-28 21:52 (192.168.0.4)
user1     pts/1        2023-01-28 22:10 (192.168.0.4)
```

Column 1 displays the login name of the user. Column 2 shows the terminal session device filename (pts stands for *pseudo terminal session*, and tty identifies a terminal window on the console). Columns 3 and 4 show the date and time of the user login, and column 5 indicates if the terminal session is graphical (:0), remote (IP address), or textual on the console.

The *w* (*what*) command displays information in a similar format as the *who* command, but it also tells the length of time the user has been idle for (IDLE), along with the CPU time used by all processes attached to this terminal (JCPU), the CPU time used by the current process (PCPU), and current activity (WHAT). In the following example, line 1 displays the current system time (22:29:41), the system up duration (2 days, 5 hours, and 28 minutes), number of users currently logged in (2), and the CPU load averages over the past 1, 5, and 15 minutes (0.00, 0.00, and 0.00), respectively. This is exactly what the *uptime* command shows, which was also discussed in Chapter 02 "Initial Interaction with the System".

```
[root@server1 ~]# w
 22:29:41 up 2 days,  5:28,  2 users,  load average: 0.00, 0.00, 0.00
USER      TTY        LOGIN@   IDLE   JCPU    PCPU WHAT
root      pts/0      21:52    1.00s  0.21s   0.02s w
user1     pts/1      22:10    16:16  0.04s   0.04s -bash
```

The load average numbers represent the percentage of CPU load with 0.00 and 1.00 correspond to no load and full load, and a number greater than 1.00 signifies excess load (over 100%).

Inspecting History of Successful Login Attempts and System Reboots

The *last* command reports the history of successful user login attempts and system reboots by consulting the *wtmp* file located in the */var/log* directory. This file keeps a record of all login and logout activities, including the login time, duration a user stayed logged in, and tty (where the user session took place). Consider the following two examples.

To list all user login, logout, and system reboot occurrences, issue the *last* command without any arguments:

```
[root@server1 ~]# last
user1      pts/1       192.168.0.4       Sat Jan 28 22:10   still logged in
root       pts/1       192.168.0.4       Sat Jan 28 22:03 - 22:10  (00:06)
user1      pts/1       192.168.0.4       Sat Jan 28 21:52 - 21:52  (00:00)
root       pts/0       192.168.0.4       Sat Jan 28 21:52   still logged in
root       pts/0       192.168.0.4       Fri Jan 27 19:21 - 21:51 (1+02:30)
root       pts/0       192.168.0.4       Fri Jan 27 19:17 - 19:17  (00:00)
root       pts/0       192.168.0.4       Fri Jan 27 19:16 - 19:16  (00:00)
root       pts/2       192.168.0.4       Fri Jan 27 14:28 - 19:21  (04:53)
root       pts/1       192.168.0.4       Fri Jan 27 14:28 - 14:28  (00:00)
root       tty2        tty2              Fri Jan 27 12:10 - 22:04 (1+09:53)
user1      pts/0       192.168.0.4       Fri Jan 27 11:30 - 14:49  (03:19)
user1      pts/0       192.168.0.3       Thu Jan 26 17:36 - 06:50  (13:14)
user1      tty2        tty2              Thu Jan 26 17:02 - 17:08  (00:05)
reboot     system boot 5.14.0-162.6.1.e  Thu Jan 26 17:01   still running
reboot     system boot 5.14.0-162.6.1.e  Thu Jan 26 16:56 - 16:59  (00:03)

wtmp begins Thu Jan 26 16:56:08 2023
```

The output has information that is distributed across eight to nine columns. Here is the description for each column for user history:

Column 1: Login name of the user
Column 2: Terminal name assigned upon logging in
Column 3: Terminal name or IP address from where the connection was established
Column 4 to 7: Day, month, date, and time when the connection was established
Column 8: Log out time. If the user is still logged on, it will say "still logged in"
Column 9: Duration of the login session

For system reboots, this is what it shows:

Column 1: Action name (reboot)
Column 2: Activity name (system boot)
Column 3: Linux kernel version
Column 4 to 7: Day, month, date, and time when the *reboot* command was issued
Column 8: System restart time
Column 9: Duration the system remained down. If the system is running, it will say "still running".

The last line in the output indicates the log filename (*wtmp*) being used to record this information and the time when it started to log events.

To list system reboot details only, you can issue the last command and specify reboot as an argument:

```
[root@server1 ~]# last reboot
reboot     system boot 5.14.0-162.6.1.e  Thu Jan 26 17:01   still running
reboot     system boot 5.14.0-162.6.1.e  Thu Jan 26 16:56 - 16:59  (00:03)

wtmp begins Thu Jan 26 16:56:08 2023
```

The output includes the same information that it depicts with the *last* command executed without any argument.

Viewing History of Failed User Login Attempts

The *lastb* command reports the history of unsuccessful user login attempts by reading the *btmp* file located in the */var/log* directory. This file keeps a record of all unsuccessful login attempts, including the login name, time, and tty (where the attempt was made). Consider the following example.

To list all unsuccessful login attempts, type the *lastb* command without any arguments. You must be *root* in order to run this command.

```
[root@server1 ~]# lastb
root      ssh:notty      192.168.0.4      Fri Jan 27 14:28 - 14:28  (00:00)
root      ssh:notty      192.168.0.4      Fri Jan 27 14:27 - 14:27  (00:00)
root      ssh:notty      192.168.0.4      Fri Jan 27 14:11 - 14:11  (00:00)
root      ssh:notty      192.168.0.4      Fri Jan 27 14:11 - 14:11  (00:00)
root      ssh:notty      192.168.0.4      Fri Jan 27 14:09 - 14:09  (00:00)
root      ssh:notty      192.168.0.4      Fri Jan 27 14:08 - 14:08  (00:00)

btmp begins Fri Jan 27 14:08:57 2023
```

The output has information that is presented in nine columns. Here is the description for each column:

Column 1: Name of the user who made the login attempt
Column 2: Name of the protocol used. No tty was assigned as the attempt failed
Column 3: Terminal name or IP address from where the connection attempt was launched
Column 4 to 7: Day, month, date, and time of the attempt
Column 8: Duration the login attempt was tried
Column 9: Duration the login attempt lasted for

The last line in the output discloses the log filename (*btmp*) being used to record this information and the time when it started to log events.

Reporting Recent User Login Attempts

The *lastlog* command reports the most recent login evidence information for every user account that exists on the system. This information is captured in the *lastlog* file located in the */var/log* directory. This file keeps a record of the most recent user login attempts, including the login name, time, and port (or tty). Consider the following example.

```
[root@server1 ~]# lastlog
Username        Port     From                             Latest
root            pts/0    192.168.0.3                      Sun Jan 29 12:29:22
500 2023
bin                                                       **Never logged in**
daemon                              .                     **Never logged in**
adm                                                       **Never logged in**
lp                                                        **Never logged in**
sync                                                      **Never logged in**
shutdown                                                  **Never logged in**
. . . . . . . .
```

```
 user1              pts/1      192.168.0.4                          Sat Jan 28 22:10:07
 500 2023
 user100            pts/0                                           Sat Jan 28 22:18:52
 500 2023
 user200            pts/0                                           Sat Jan 28 22:23:09
 500 2023
```

The output displays the information across four columns. Here is the description for each column:

Column 1: Login name of the user
Column 2: Terminal name assigned upon logging in
Column 3: Terminal name or IP address from where the session was initiated
Column 4: Timestamp for the latest login or "Never logged in" if the user never signed in

Note that service accounts are used by their respective services, and they are not meant for logging. More information on service accounts is discussed in the next section.

Examining User and Group Information

The *id* (*identifier*) command displays the calling user's UID (*User IDentifier*), username, GID (*Group IDentifier*), group name, all secondary groups the user is a member of, and SELinux security context. Here is a sample output for the *root* user when this command is executed without an option or argument:

```
[root@server1 ~]# id
uid=0(root) gid=0(root) groups=0(root) context=unconfined_u:unconfined_r:unconfined_t:s0-s0:c0.c1023
```

Each user and group has a corresponding number (called UID and GID) for identification purposes. These will be discussed in subsequent sections of this chapter. For SELinux, see Chapter 20 "Security Enhanced Linux".

The *id* command can be executed by a user to view other users' identification information. The following example shows an instance with the *root* user viewing another user's id:

```
[root@server1 ~]# id user1
uid=1000(user1) gid=1000(user1) groups=1000(user1)
```

The *groups* command, in contrast, lists all groups the calling user is a member of:

```
[root@server1 ~]# groups
root
```

The first group listed is the primary group for the user who executed this command; all other groups are secondary (or supplementary). The *groups* command can also be used to view group membership information for a different user. Try running it as **groups user1** and observe the outcome.

Local User Authentication Files

RHEL supports three fundamental user account types: *root*, *normal*, and *service*. The *root* user (a.k.a. the *superuser* or the *administrator*), has full access to all services and administrative functions on the system. This user is created by default during installation. Normal users have user-level privileges; they cannot perform any administrative functions but can run applications and programs that have been authorized. Service accounts take care of their respective services, which include apache, ftp, mail, and chrony.

User account information for local users is stored in four files that are located in the */etc* directory. These files—*passwd, shadow, group,* and *gshadow*—are updated when a user or group account is created, modified, or deleted. The same files are referenced to check and validate the credentials for a user at the time of their login attempt, and hence the files are referred to as user authentication files. These files are so critical to the operation of the system that the system creates their automatic backups by default as *passwd-, shadow-, group-,* and *gshadow-* in the */etc* directory.

Here is the list of the four files and their backups from the */etc* directory:

```
[root@server1 ~]# ls -l /etc/passwd* /etc/group* /etc/shadow* /etc/gshadow*
-rw-r--r--. 1 root root  872 Jan 28 22:16 /etc/group
-rw-r--r--. 1 root root  864 Jan 28 22:16 /etc/group-
----------. 1 root root  700 Jan 28 22:16 /etc/gshadow
----------. 1 root root  692 Jan 28 22:16 /etc/gshadow-
-rw-r--r--. 1 root root 2182 Jan 28 22:15 /etc/passwd
-rw-r--r--. 1 root root 2137 Jan 28 22:15 /etc/passwd-
----------. 1 root root 1192 Jan 28 22:15 /etc/shadow
----------. 1 root root 1162 Jan 28 22:15 /etc/shadow-
```

All files are short in size, but they grow bigger as new users are added. Two of the files—*gshadow* and *shadow*—along with their backups have no access permissions for any user, not even for *root*. Let's analyze these files and see what information they store and how.

The passwd File

The *passwd* file is a simple plaintext file but it contains vital user login data. Each row in the file holds information for one user account. There are seven colon-separated fields per line entry. A sample row from the file is displayed in Figure 5-1.

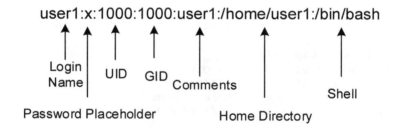

Figure 5-1 The passwd File

Here is a description for each field:

> **Field 1 (Login Name):** Contains the login name for signing in. Login names with up to 255 characters, including the underscore (_) and hyphen (-) characters, are supported. It is not recommended to include special characters and uppercase letters in login names.
> **Field 2 (Password):** Can contain an "x" (points to the */etc/shadow* file for the actual password), an asterisk * to identify a disabled account, or a hashed password.

A hashed password—a combination of random letters, numbers, and special characters—is an irreversible, unique, and scrambled string of characters to safeguard a clear text password. It is generated as a result of a conversion process of a password using one of the available hashing algorithms. By default, RHEL uses the SHA-512 algorithm for this purpose.

An algorithm is a set of well-defined but complex mathematical instructions used in data encryption and decryption techniques.

Field 3 (UID): Comprises a numeric UID between 0 and approximately 4.2 billion. UID 0 is reserved for the *root* account, UIDs between 1 and 200 are used by Red Hat to statically assign them to core service accounts, UIDs between 201 and 999 are reserved for non-core service accounts, and UIDs 1000 and beyond are employed for normal user accounts. By default, RHEL begins assigning UIDs to new users at 1000.

Field 4 (GID): Holds a GID that corresponds with a group entry in the */etc/group* file. By default, RHEL creates a group for every new user matching their login name and the same GID as their UID. The GID defined in this field represents the user's primary group.

Field 5 (Comments): Called GECOS (*General Electric Comprehensive Operating System* and later changed to GCOS), optionally stores general comments about the user that may include the user's name, phone number, location, or other useful information to help identify the person for whom the account is set up.

Field 6 (Home Directory): Defines the absolute path to the user home directory. A *home* directory is the location where a user is placed after signing in and it is used for personal storage. The default location for user home directories is */home*.

Field 7 (Shell): Consists of the absolute path of the shell file that the user will be using as their primary shell after logging in. The default shell used in RHEL is the Bash shell (*/bin/bash*). Consult Chapter 07 "The Bash Shell" for details on the Bash shell.

A *head* and *tail* from the *passwd* file for the first and last three lines is shown below:

```
[root@server1 ~]# head -3 /etc/passwd ; tail -3 /etc/passwd
root:x:0:0:root:/root:/bin/bash
bin:x:1:1:bin:/bin:/sbin/nologin
daemon:x:2:2:daemon:/sbin:/sbin/nologin
user1:x:1000:1000:user1:/home/user1:/bin/bash
user100:x:1002:1002::/home/user100:/bin/bash
user200:x:1003:1003::/home/user200:/bin/bash
```

The output indicates the *root* user with UID 0 followed by two service accounts (*bin* and *daemon*). The last three lines display the three user accounts that were created earlier as part of some of the exercises.

Let's verify the permissions and ownership on the *passwd* file:

```
[root@server1 ~]# ls -l /etc/passwd
-rw-r--r--. 1 root root 2182 Jan 28 22:15 /etc/passwd
```

The access permissions on the file are 644 (world-readable and owner-writable), and it is owned by the *root* user.

The shadow File

RHEL has a secure password control mechanism in place that provides an advanced level of password security for local users. This control is referred to as the *shadow password*. With this control mechanism in place, user passwords are hashed and stored in a more secure file */etc/shadow*, but there are certain limits on user passwords in terms of expiration, warning period, etc., that can also be applied on a per-user basis. These limits and other settings are defined in the */etc/login.defs* file, which the shadow password mechanism enforces on user accounts. This is called *password aging*. Unlike the *passwd* file, which is world-readable and owner-writable, the *shadow* file has no access permissions at all. This is done to safeguard the file's content.

With the shadow password mechanism active, a user is initially checked in the *passwd* file for existence and then in the *shadow* file for authenticity.

The *shadow* file contains user authentication and password aging information. Each row in the file corresponds to one entry in the *passwd* file. There are nine colon-separated fields per line entry. A sample row from this file is showcased in Figure 5-2.

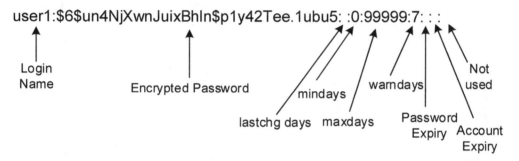

Figure 5-2 The shadow File

Here is a description for each field:

Field 1 (Login Name): Contains the login name as appears in the *passwd* file.

Field 2 (Encrypted Password): Consists of a hashed password. A single exclamation mark (!) at the beginning of this field implies that the user account is locked. If this field is empty, the user will have passwordless entry into the system.

Field 3 (Last Change): Sets the number of days (lastchg) since the UNIX epoch, a.k.a. UNIX time (January 01, 1970 00:00:00 UTC) when the password was last modified. An empty field represents the passiveness of password aging features, and a 0 forces the user to change their password upon next login.

Field 4 (Minimum): Expresses the minimum number of days (mindays) that must elapse before the user is allowed to change their password. This field can be altered using the *chage* command with the -m option or the *passwd* command with the -n option. A 0 or null in this field disables this feature.

Field 5 (Maximum): Defines the maximum number of days (maxdays) of password validity before the user password expires and it must be changed. This field may be altered using the *chage* command with the -M option or the *passwd* command with the -x option. A null value here disables this feature along with other features such as the maximum password age, warning alerts, and the user inactivity period.

Field 6 (Warning): Denotes the number of days (warndays) for which the user gets warnings for changing their password before it actually expires. This field may be altered using the *chage* command with the -W option or the *passwd* command with the -w option. A 0 or null in this field disables this feature.

Field 7 (Password Expiry): Contains the maximum allowable number of days for the user to be able to log in with the expired password. This period is referred to as the inactivity period. This field may be altered using the *chage* command with the -I option or the *passwd* command with the -i option. An empty field disables this feature.

Field 8 (Account Expiry): Determines the number of days since the UNIX time when the user account will expire and no longer be available. This field may be altered using the *chage* command with the -E option. An empty field disables this feature.

Field 9 (Reserved): Reserved for future use.

A *head* and *tail* from the *shadow* file for the first and last three lines is shown below:

```
[root@server1 ~]# head -3 /etc/shadow ; tail -3 /etc/shadow
root:$6$amGZvwoTHLhkMI8i$2fdXiLlaUSDATXRBxpDxYjvjauEL5v716bCgQ4kV
bg.uEsagY2am.ds4R7jt4K1::0:99999:7:::
bin:*:19121:0:99999:7:::
daemon:*:19121:0:99999:7:::
user1:$6$DmAkcx0gMaD0ssTL$Ta3im.nQMyNTX4BRY51Z/LWrQLAAaf/7dczKKt2
5iyQgx3yD5iKs9E8c1nOc.x/::0:99999:7:::
user100:!!:19386:0:99999:7:::
user200:!!:19386:0:99999:7:::
```

The output indicates the *root* user with UID 0 followed by two service accounts (*bin* and *daemon*). The last three lines display the three user accounts that were created earlier as part of some of the exercises. Notice that login names are used as a common key between the *shadow* and *passwd* files.

Let's verify the permissions and ownership on the *shadow* file:

```
[root@server1 ~]# ls -l /etc/shadow
----------. 1 root root 1192 Jan 28 22:15 /etc/shadow
```

The access permissions on the file are 000 (no permissions at all), and it is owned by the *root* user. There is a special mechanism in place that is employed in the background to update this file when a user account is added, modified, deleted, or the password changed. This will be discussed in Chapter 21 "Security Enhanced Linux".

The group File

The *group* file is a simple plaintext file and contains critical group information. Each row in the file stores information for one group entry. Every user on the system must be a member of at least one group, which is referred to as the *User Private Group* (UPG). By default, a group name matches the username it is associated with. Additional groups may be set up, and users with common file access requirements can be added to them. There are four colon-separated fields per line entry. A sample row from the file is exhibited in Figure 5-3.

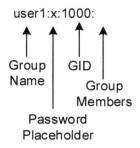

Figure 5-3 The group File

Here is a description for each field:

Field 1 (Group Name): Holds a group name that must begin with a letter. Group names with up to 255 characters, including the underscore (_) and hyphen (-) characters, are supported. It is not recommended to include special characters and uppercase letters in group names.

Field 2 (Encrypted Password): Can be empty or contain an "x" (points to the */etc/gshadow* file for the actual password), or a hashed group-level password. You can set a password on a group if you want non-members to be able to change their group identity temporarily using the *newgrp* command. The non-members must enter the correct password in order to do so.

Field 3 (GID): Holds a GID, which is also placed in the GID field of the *passwd* file. By default, groups are created with GIDs starting at 1000 and with the same name as the username. The system allows several users to belong to a single group; it also allows a single user to be a member of multiple groups at the same time.

Field 4 (Group Members): Lists the membership for the group. Note that a user's primary group is always defined in the GID field of the *passwd* file.

A *head* and *tail* from the *group* file for the first and last three lines is shown below:

```
[root@server1 ~]# head -3 /etc/group ; tail -3 /etc/group
root:x:0:
bin:x:1:
daemon:x:2:
sgrp:x:9999:user100,user200
user100:x:1002:
user200:x:1003:
```

The output discloses the *root* user with GID 0 followed by two group service accounts (*bin* and *daemon*). The last three lines showcase the three groups that were created earlier as part of some of the exercises.

Let's verify the permissions and ownership on the *group* file:

```
[root@server1 ~]# ls -l /etc/group
-rw-r--r--. 1 root root 872 Jan 28 22:16 /etc/group
```

The access permissions on the file are 644 (world-readable and owner-writable), and it is owned by the *root* user.

The gshadow File

The shadow password implementation also provides an added layer of protection at the group level. With this mechanism in place, the group passwords are hashed and stored in a more secure file */etc/gshadow*. Unlike the *group* file, which is world-readable and owner-writable, the *gshadow* file has no access permissions at all. This is done to safeguard the file's content.

The *gshadow* file stores hashed group-level passwords. Each row in the file corresponds to one entry in the *group* file. There are four colon-separated fields per line entry. A sample row from this file is exhibited in Figure 5-4.

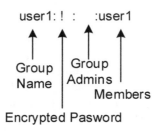

Figure 5-4 The gshadow File

Here is a description for each field:

> **Field 1 (Group Name):** Consists of a group name as appeared in the *group* file.
> **Field 2 (Encrypted Password):** Can contain a hashed password, which may be set with the *gpasswd* command for non-group members to access the group temporarily using the *newgrp* command. A single exclamation mark (!) or a null value in this field allows group members passwordless access and restricts non-members from switching into this group.
> **Field 3 (Group Administrators):** Lists usernames of group administrators that are authorized to add or remove members with the *gpasswd* command.
> **Field 4 (Members):** Holds a comma-separated list of members.

The gpasswd command is used to add group administrators, add or delete group members, assign or revoke a group-level password, and disable the ability of the newgrp command to access a group. This command picks up the default values from the /etc/login.defs file. Additional discussion on this command is beyond the scope; however, you can view the manual pages of this command for details on its usage.

A *head* and *tail* from the *gshadow* file for the first and last three lines is shown below:

```
[root@server1 ~]# head -3 /etc/gshadow ; tail -3 /etc/gshadow
root:::
bin:::
daemon:::
sgrp:!::user100,user200
user100:!::
user200:!::
```

The output indicates the *root* user with GID 0 followed by two group service accounts (*bin* and *daemon*). The last three lines exhibit the three groups that were created earlier as part of some of the exercises. Notice that group names are used as a common key between the *gshadow* and *group* files.

Let's verify the permissions and ownership on the *gshadow* file:

```
[root@server1 ~]# ls -l /etc/gshadow
----------. 1 root root 700 Jan 28 22:16 /etc/gshadow
```

The access permissions on the file are 000 (no permissions at all) and it is owned by the *root* user. There is a special mechanism in place that is employed in the background to update this file when a group account is added, modified, deleted, or the group password changed. This will be discussed further in Chapter 21 "Security Enhanced Linux".

The useradd and login.defs Configuration Files

The *useradd* command (discussed in the next section) picks up the default values from the */etc/default/useradd* and */etc/login.defs* files for any options that are not specified at the command line when executing it. Moreover, the *login.defs* file is also consulted by the *usermod*, *userdel*, *chage*, and *passwd* commands (also discussed in the next section) as needed. Both files store several defaults including those that affect the password length and password lifecycle. You can use the *cat* or *less* command to view the *useradd* file content or display the settings with the *useradd* command as follows:

```
[root@server1 ~]# useradd -D
GROUP=100
HOME=/home
INACTIVE=-1
EXPIRE=
SHELL=/bin/bash
SKEL=/etc/skel
CREATE_MAIL_SPOOL=yes
```

There are a multitude of defaults defined with the directives. These include the starting GID (GROUP) provided the USERGROUPS_ENAB directive in the *login.defs* file is set to no, home directory location (HOME), number of inactivity days between password expiry and permanent account disablement (INACTIVE), account expiry date (EXPIRE), login shell (SHELL), skeleton directory location to copy user initialization files from (SKEL), and whether to create mail spool directory (CREATE_MAIL_SPOOL). You will find a description for some of these in the next section.

The other file *login.defs* comprises of additional directives that set several defaults. User and group management commands consult this file to obtain information that is not supplied at the command line. A *grep* on the file with uncommented and non-empty lines is shown below:

```
[root@server1 ~]# grep -v ^# /etc/login.defs | grep -v ^$
MAIL_DIR          /var/spool/mail
UMASK             022
HOME_MODE         0700
PASS_MAX_DAYS     99999
PASS_MIN_DAYS     0
PASS_WARN_AGE     7
UID_MIN                     1000
UID_MAX                    60000
SYS_UID_MIN                  201
SYS_UID_MAX                 999
SUB_UID_MIN              100000
SUB_UID_MAX           600100000
SUB_UID_COUNT             65536
GID_MIN                     1000
GID_MAX                    60000
SYS_GID_MIN                  201
SYS_GID_MAX                 999
SUB_GID_MIN              100000
SUB_GID_MAX           600100000
SUB_GID_COUNT             65536
ENCRYPT_METHOD SHA512
USERGROUPS_ENAB yes
CREATE_HOME       yes
HMAC_CRYPTO_ALGO SHA512
```

 The grep command is discussed in detail in Chapter 07 "The Bash Shell".

Most of these directives are elaborated in Table 5-1.

Option	Description
MAIL_DIR	Specifies the mail directory location
UMASK	Defines the permissions to be set on the user home directory at creation based on this umask value
HOME_MODE	The mode for new user home directories. The umask value is used if not specified with the command.
PASS_MAX_DAYS, PASS_MIN_DAYS, and PASS_WARN_AGE	Define password aging attributes. See Chapter 06 "Advanced User Management" for details.
UID_MIN, UID_MAX, GID_MIN, and GID_MAX	Identify the ranges of UIDs and GIDs to be allocated to new users and groups
SYS_UID_MIN, SYS_UID_MAX, SYS_GID_MIN, and SYS_GID_MAX	Identify the ranges of UIDs and GIDs to be allocated to new service users and groups
ENCRYPT_METHOD	Specifies the encryption method for user passwords
USERGROUPS_ENAB	If set to yes, (1) the useradd command will create a group matching the name of the user and (2) the userdel command will delete a user's group if it contains no more members.
CREATE_HOME	Defines whether to create a home directory

Table 5-1 login.defs File Directives

There are many more directives available that can be added to this file for more control and flexibility. Check the manual pages of the file for details.

User Account Management

Managing user accounts involves creating, assigning passwords to, modifying, and deleting them. RHEL provides a set of tools for performing these operations. These tools are *useradd* to add a new user to the system, *usermod* to modify the attributes of an existing user, and *userdel* to remove a user from the system. In addition, the *passwd* command is available to set or modify a user's password.

The useradd, usermod, and userdel Commands

This set of commands is used to add, modify, and delete a user account from the system. The *useradd* command adds entries to the four user authentication files for each account added to the system. It creates a home directory for the user and copies the default user startup files from the *skeleton* directory */etc/skel* into the user's home directory. It can also be used to update the default settings that are used at the time of new user creation for unspecified settings. The *useradd* command supports a variety of flags; Table 5-2 lists some common options in both short and long versions.

Option	Description
-b (--base-dir)	Defines the absolute path to the base directory for placing user home directories. The default is /home.
-c (--comment)	Describes useful information about the user.
-d (--home-dir)	Defines the absolute path to the user home directory.
-D (--defaults)	Displays the default settings from the /etc/default/useradd file and modifies them.
-e (--expiredate)	Specifies a date on which a user account is automatically disabled. The format for the date specification is YYYY-MM-DD.
-f (--inactive)	Denotes maximum days of inactivity between password expiry and permanent account disablement.
-g (--gid)	Specifies the primary GID. Without this option, a group account matching the username is created with the GID matching the UID.
-G (--groups)	Specifies the membership to supplementary groups.
-k (--skel)	Specifies the location of the skeleton directory (default is /etc/skel), which stores default user startup files. These files are copied to the user's home directory at the time of account creation. Three hidden bash shell files—.bash_profile, .bashrc, and .bash_logout—are available in this directory by default. You can customize these files or add your own to be used for accounts created thereafter.
-m (--create-home)	Creates a home directory if it does not already exist.
-o (--non-unique)	Creates a user account sharing the UID of an existing user. When two users share a UID, both get identical rights on each other's files. This should only be done in specific situations.
-r (--system)	Creates a service account with a UID below 1000 and a never-expiring password.
-s (--shell)	Defines the absolute path to the shell file. The default is /bin/bash.

Option	Description
-u (--uid)	Indicates a unique UID. Without this option, the next available UID from the /etc/passwd file is used.
login	Specifies a login name to be assigned to the user account.

Table 5-2 useradd Command Options

You can modify the attributes of a user account with the *usermod* command. The syntax of this command is very similar to that of the *useradd*'s, with most switches identical. Table 5-3 describes the options that are specific to *usermod* only, and shows them in both short and long versions. There are two additional flags of interest that are discussed in Chapter 06 "Advanced User Management".

Option	Description
-a (--append)	Adds a user to one or more supplementary groups
-l (--login)	Specifies a new login name
-m (--move-home)	Creates a home directory and moves the content over from the old location

Table 5-3 usermod Command Options

The *userdel* command is straightforward. It removes entries for the specified user from the authentication files, and deletes the user's home directory if the -r flag is also specified. The -f option may be used to force the removal even if the user is still logged in.

Exercise 5-1: Create a User Account with Default Attributes

This exercise should be done on *server1* as *root*.

In this exercise, you will create a user account *user2* using the defaults defined in the *useradd* and *login.defs* files. You will assign this user a password and show the new line entries from all four authentication files.

1. Create *user2* with all the default values:

   ```
   [root@server1 ~]# useradd user2
   ```

2. Assign this user a password and enter it twice when prompted:

   ```
   [root@server1 ~]# passwd user2
   Changing password for user user2.
   New password:
   BAD PASSWORD: The password is shorter than 8 characters
   Retype new password:
   passwd: all authentication tokens updated successfully.
   ```

3. *grep* for *user2:* on the authentication files to examine what the *useradd* command has added:

```
[root@server1 ~]# cd /etc ; grep user2: passwd shadow group gshadow
passwd:user2:x:1003:1003::/home/user2:/bin/bash
shadow:user2:$y$j9T$qh2XZ/2/FFKybTfrbVez90$6zVCVP3ymy89cJriKNEBvx2wktWS
9386:0:99999:7:::
group:user2:x:1003:
gshadow:user2:!::
```

The command used the next available UID (1003) and GID (1003), and the default settings for the home directory (*/home/user2*) and shell file (*/bin/bash*).

4. Test this new account by logging in as *user2* and then run the *id* and *groups* commands to verify the UID, GID, and group membership information:

```
[root@server1 etc]# su - user2
[user2@server1 ~]$ id
uid=1003(user2) gid=1003(user2) groups=1003(user2) context=unconfined
onfined_t:s0-s0:c0.c1023
[user2@server1 ~]$ groups
user2
```

The above outputs confirmed the UID and username, GID and group name, and primary group name.

Exercise 5-2: Create a User Account with Custom Values

This exercise should be done on *server1* as *root*.

In this exercise, you will create an account *user3* with UID 1010, home directory */usr/user3a*, and shell */bin/sh*. You will assign this user a password and exhibit the new line entries from all four authentication files.

1. Create *user3* with UID 1010 (-u), home directory */usr/user3a* (-d), and shell */bin/sh* (-s):

```
[root@server1 ~]# useradd -u 1010 -d /usr/user3a -s /bin/sh user3
```

2. Assign user1234 as password (passwords assigned in the following way is not recommended; however, it is okay in a lab environment):

```
[root@server1 ~]# echo user1234 | passwd --stdin user3
Changing password for user user3.
passwd: all authentication tokens updated successfully.
```

3. *grep* for *user3:* on the four authentication files to see what was added for this user:

```
[root@server1 ~]# cd /etc ; grep user3: passwd shadow group gshadow
passwd:user3:x:1010:1010::/usr/user3a:/bin/sh
shadow:user3:$y$j9T$M/g7a2Bwi/PayyNJaSCWk1$cSCsE8IArr0.nS1Dv9Y2dRS5:.
9386:0:99999:7:::
group:user3:x:1010:
gshadow:user3:!::
```

4. Test this account by switching to or logging in as *user3* and entering user1234 as the password. Run the *id* and *groups* commands for further verification.

Exercise 5-3: Modify and Delete a User Account

This exercise should be done on *server1* as *root*.

In this exercise, you will modify certain attributes for *user2* and then delete it. You will change the login name to *user2new*, UID to 2000, home directory to */home/user2new*, and login shell to */sbin/nologin*. You will display the line entry for *user2new* from the *passwd* file for validation. Finally, you will remove this user and confirm the deletion.

1. Modify the login name for *user2* to *user2new* (-l), UID to 2000 (-u), home directory to */home/user2new* (-m and -d), and login shell to */sbin/nologin* (-s). Notice that the options are specified in a different sequence.

   ```
   [root@server1 ~]# usermod -l user2new -m -d /home/user2new -s /sbin/nologin -u 2
   000 user2
   ```

2. Obtain the information for *user2new* from the *passwd* file for confirmation:

   ```
   [root@server1 ~]# grep user2new /etc/passwd
   user2new:x:2000:1003::/home/user2new:/sbin/nologin
   ```

3. Remove *user2new* along with their home and mail spool directories (-r):

   ```
   [root@server1 ~]# userdel -r user2new
   ```

4. Confirm the user deletion:

   ```
   [root@server1 ~]# grep user2new /etc/passwd
   ```

Nothing is returned in the output, which means this user does not exist in the *passwd* file any longer. This confirms the removal.

No-Login (Non-Interactive) User Account

The *nologin* shell is a special purpose program that can be employed for user accounts that do not require login access to the system. It is located in the */usr/sbin* (or */sbin*) directory. With this shell assigned, the user is refused with the message, "This account is currently not available." displayed on the screen. If a custom message is required, you can create a file called *nologin.txt* in the */etc* directory and add the desired text to it. The content of this file is printed on the screen upon user access denial instead of the default message.

> **EXAM TIP:** If a no-login user is able to log in with their credentials, there is a problem. Use the grep command against the /etc/passwd file to ensure '/sbin/nologin' is there in the shell field for that user.

Typical examples of user accounts that do not require login access are the service accounts such as *ftp*, *mail*, and *sshd*. Let's take a look at the *passwd* file and list such users:

```
[root@server1 ~]# grep nologin /etc/passwd
bin:x:1:1:bin:/bin:/sbin/nologin
daemon:x:2:2:daemon:/sbin:/sbin/nologin
adm:x:3:4:adm:/var/adm:/sbin/nologin
lp:x:4:7:lp:/var/spool/lpd:/sbin/nologin
mail:x:8:12:mail:/var/spool/mail:/sbin/nologin
operator:x:11:0:operator:/root:/sbin/nologin
games:x:12:100:games:/usr/games:/sbin/nologin
ftp:x:14:50:FTP User:/var/ftp:/sbin/nologin
nobody:x:65534:65534:Kernel Overflow User:/:/sbin/nologin
```

This output returns a truncated list of non-interactive user accounts. There are tens of them, and they grow as you install more services on the system.

Exercise 5-4: Create a User Account with No-Login Access

This exercise should be done on *server1* as *root*.

In this exercise, you will create an account *user4* with all the default attributes but with a non-interactive shell. You will assign this user the nologin shell to prevent them from signing in. You will display the new line entry from the *passwd* file and test the account.

1. Create *user4* with non-interactive shell file */sbin/nologin*:

    ```
    [root@server1 ~]# useradd -s /sbin/nologin user4
    ```

2. Assign user1234 as password:

    ```
    [root@server1 ~]# echo user1234 | passwd --stdin user4
    ```

3. *grep* for *user4* on the *passwd* file and verify the shell field containing the nologin shell:

    ```
    [root@server1 ~]# grep user4 /etc/passwd
    user4:x:1011:1011::/home/user4:/sbin/nologin
    ```

4. Test this account by attempting to log in or switch:

    ```
    [root@server1 ~]# su - user4
    This account is currently not available.
    ```

As mentioned earlier, you may create the */etc/nologin.txt* file and add a custom message to it. The new message will appear on your next login attempt.

Chapter Summary

We started this chapter by discovering various tools that are employed to monitor user login and system reboot activities. This information is stored in several system files and may be used for testing, auditing, or troubleshooting reasons. Most of these tools can be executed by normal users to obtain desired results; however, others may require privileged access of the root user in order to be viewed.

Next, we looked closely at the four local user authentication files: *passwd, shadow, group*, and *gshadow*. We examined their contents and syntax to comprehend what they store and how. These files are critical to the user login process as well as the functioning of applications and services.

Finally, we explored user management tools and put them into action in exercises to create, modify, and delete user accounts. These tools offer a number of switches to add accounts with default and custom attributes, as well as user accounts that do not require login access.

Review Questions

1. UID 999 is reserved for normal users. True or False?
2. Which file is assigned to users to deny them login access?
3. You execute the *lastb* command as a normal user. The output reports an error. What do you need to do to run this command successfully?
4. What would the command *useradd -D* do?
5. What does the *lastlog* command do?
6. What would the command *useradd user500* do?
7. The *id* and *groups* commands are useful for listing a user identification. True or False.
8. Name the three fundamental user account classes in RHEL.
9. Every user in RHEL gets a private group by default. True or False?
10. What does the "x" in the password field in the *passwd* file imply?
11. Name the file that the *who* command consults to display logged-in users.
12. What information does the *lastb* command provide?
13. The *who* command may be used to view logged out users. True or False?
14. What would the *userdel* command do if it is run with the -r option?
15. Name the four local user authentication files.
16. The *passwd* file contains secondary user group information. True or False?
17. What is the first UID assigned to a normal user?
18. What is the first GID assigned to a group?
19. What is the name of the default backup file for *shadow*?
20. Which file does the *last* command consult to display reports?

Answers to Review Questions

1. False. UID 999 is reserved for system accounts.
2. The */sbin/nologin* file is assigned to users to deny them login.
3. You need to run the *lastb* command as *root* or with the *root* privilege.
4. This command displays the defaults settings used at the time of user creation or modification.
5. The *lastlog* command provides information about recent user logins.
6. The command provided will add *user500* with all predefined default values.
7. False. Only the *id* command is used for this purpose.
8. The three fundamental user account categories are root, normal, and system.
9. True.
10. The "x" in the password field implies that the hashed password is stored in the *shadow* file.
11. The *who* command consults the */run/utmp* file to list logged-in users.
12. The *lastb* command reports the history of unsuccessful user login attempts.
13. False. The *who* command shows currently logged-in users only.
14. The *userdel* command with -r will delete the specified user along with their home directory.
15. The *passwd, shadow, group*, and *gshadow* files.
16. False. The *passwd* file contains primary user group information.

17. The first UID assigned to a normal user is 1000.
18. The first GID assigned to a normal user is 1000.
19. The name of the default backup file for *shadow* is *shadow-*.
20. The *last* command consults the */var/log/wtmp* file to display reports.

Do-It-Yourself Challenge Labs

The following labs are useful to strengthen most of the concepts and topics learned in this chapter. It is expected that you perform the labs without external help. A step-by-step guide is not supplied, as the knowledge and skill required to implement the labs have already been disseminated in the chapter; however, hints to the relevant major topic(s) are included.

Use the lab environment built specifically for end-of-chapter labs. See sub-section "Lab Environment for End-of-Chapter Labs" in Chapter 01 "Local Installation" for details.

Lab 5-1: Check User Login Attempts

As *root* on *server3*, execute the *last*, *lastb*, and *lastlog* commands, and observe the outputs. Check which users recently logged in and out successfully (*last*) and unsuccessfully (*lastb*). List the timestamps when the system was last rebooted (*last*). Check the last login status for each user (*lastlog*). Use the *vim* editor to record your results. (Hint: User Login Activity and Information).

Lab 5-2: Verify User and Group Identity

As *user1* on *server3*, run the *who* and *w* commands one at a time, and compare the outputs. Execute the *id* and *groups* commands, and compare the outcomes. Examine the extra information that the *id* command shows, but not the *groups* command. (Hint: User Login Activity and Information).

Lab 5-3: Create Users

As *root* on *server3*, create user account *user4100* with UID 4100 and home directory under */usr*. Create another user account *user4200* with default attributes. Assign both users a password. View the contents of the *passwd*, *shadow*, *group*, and *gshadow* files, and observe what has been added for the two new users. (Hint: Local User Authentication Files, and User Account Management).

Lab 5-4: Create User with Non-Interactive Shell

As *root* on *server3*, create user account *user4300* with the disability of logging in. Assign this user a password. Try to log on with this user and see is displayed on the screen. View the content of the *passwd* file, and see what prevents this user from logging in. (Hint: Local User Authentication Files, and User Account Management).

Chapter 06

Advanced User Management

This chapter describes the following major topics:

➤ Configure password aging attributes on local user accounts
➤ Lock and unlock user account
➤ Understand, create, modify, and delete local groups and group memberships
➤ Switch into another user account
➤ Configure who can execute which privileged commands
➤ Identify and manage file owners and owning groups

RHCSA Objectives:

05. Log in and switch users in multi-user targets
49. Change passwords and adjust password aging for local user accounts (only the second part of this objective "adjust password aging for local user accounts" is covered in this chapter; the first part is in Chapter 05)
50. Create, delete, and modify local groups and group memberships
51. Configure superuser access

Password

Password aging attributes may be set on user accounts for increased control on their logins and passwords. This can be done for an individual user or applied to all users. Password aging information for users is stored in one of the authentication files that was discussed at length in the previous chapter. Individual user accounts may be prevented from logging in to the system by locking their access for a period of time or permanently. This lock may be lifted when required. Setting password aging and locking/unlocking accounts are administrative functions and must be performed by a user with elevated privileges of the root user.

Users are apportioned membership to a single group at the time of their addition to the system. Later, they may be assigned membership to additional groups. Members of the same group possess the same access rights on files and directories. Other users and members of other groups may optionally be given access to those files. Group membership information is stored in user and group authentication files that were examined in the previous chapter as well.

Users may switch into other user accounts, including the root user, provided they know the target user's password. Normal users may be allowed access to privileged commands by defining them appropriately in a configuration file. Each file that exists on the system regardless of its type has an owning user and an owning group. Similarly, every file that a user creates is in the ownership of that user. The ownership may be changed and given to another user by a super user.

Password Aging and its Management

As mentioned, password aging is a secure mechanism to control user passwords in Linux. The key advantages include setting restrictions on password expiry, account disablement, locking and unlocking users, and password change frequency. These controls are applied to all user accounts at the time of their creation and can be set explicitly on a per-user basis later. You can even choose to inactivate it completely for an individual user.

Password aging information is stored in the */etc/shadow* file (fields 4 to 8) and its default policies in the */etc/login.defs* configuration file. These files were thoroughly examined in Chapter 05 "Basic User Management". In this section, we explore the aging management tools—*chage* and *passwd*—and look at how to employ them to apply password controls on user accounts, *user100* and *user200*. Alongside *chage* and *passwd*, the *usermod* command can also be used to implement two aging attributes (user expiry and password expiry); however, this section focuses on this command's ability to lock and unlock user accounts.

The chage Command

The *chage* command is used to set or alter password aging parameters on a user account. This command changes various fields in the *shadow* file depending on which option(s) you pass to it. There are plenty of switches available with the command in both short and long formats. Table 6-1 describes most of them.

Option	Description
-d (--lastday)	Specifies an explicit date in the YYYY-MM-DD format, or the number of days since the UNIX time when the password was last modified. With -d 0, the user is forced to change the password at next login. It corresponds to field 3 in the shadow file.
-E (--expiredate)	Sets an explicit date in the YYYY-MM-DD format, or the number of days since the UNIX time on which the user account is deactivated. This feature can be disabled with -E -1. It corresponds to field 8 in the shadow file.
-I (--inactive)	Defines the number of days of inactivity after the password expiry and before the account is locked. The user may be able to log in during this period with their expired password. This feature can be disabled with -I -1. It corresponds to field 7 in the shadow file.
-l	Lists password aging attributes set on a user account.
-m (--mindays)	Indicates the minimum number of days that must elapse before the password can be changed. A value of 0 allows the user to change their password at any time. It corresponds to field 4 in the shadow file.
-M (--maxdays)	Denotes the maximum number of days of password validity before the user password expires and it must be changed. This feature can be disabled with -M -1. It corresponds to field 5 in the shadow file.
-W (--warndays)	Designates the number of days for which the user gets alerts to change their password before it expires. It corresponds to field 6 in the shadow file.

Table 6-1 chage Command Options

You will use most of these flags used in Exercise 6-1 and later in this chapter.

Exercise 6-1: Set and Confirm Password Aging with chage

This exercise should be done on *server1* as *root*.

In this exercise, you will configure password aging for *user100* using the *chage* command. You will set mindays to 7, maxdays to 28, and warndays to 5, and verify the new settings. You will then rerun the command and set account expiry to December 31, 2023. You will complete the exercise with another confirmation.

1. Set password aging parameters for *user100* to mindays (-m) 7, maxdays (-M) 28, and warndays (-W) 5:

```
[root@server1 ~]# chage -m 7 -M 28 -W 5 user100
```

2. Confirm the new settings:

```
[root@server1 ~]# chage -l user100
Last password change                              : Jan 29, 2023
Password expires                                  : Feb 26, 2023
Password inactive                                 : never
Account expires                                   : never
Minimum number of days between password change    : 7
Maximum number of days between password change    : 28
Number of days of warning before password expires : 5
```

The bottom three rows in the output confirm the new settings. The current password expiry (February 26, 2023) reflects the 28-day duration from January 29, 2023 when this command was executed.

3. Set the account expiry to December 31, 2023:

```
[root@server1 ~]# chage -E 2023-12-31 user100
```

4. Verify the new account expiry setting:

```
[root@server1 ~]# chage -l user100
Last password change                              : Jan 29, 2023
Password expires                                  : Feb 26, 2023
Password inactive                                 : never
Account expires                                   : Dec 31, 2023
Minimum number of days between password change    : 7
Maximum number of days between password change    : 28
Number of days of warning before password expires : 5
```

The middle row reflects the new account expiry for *user100*. Similarly, you can use the -d and -I options with the *chage* command as required.

The passwd Command

The common use of the *passwd* command is to set or modify a user's password; however, you can also use this command to modify the password aging attributes and lock or unlock their account. Table 6-2 lists some key options in both short and long formats.

Option	Description
-d (--delete)	Deletes a user password without expiring the user account.
-e (--expire)	Forces a user to change their password upon next logon.
-i (--inactive)	Defines the number of days of inactivity after the password expiry and before the account is locked. It corresponds to field 7 in the shadow file.
-l (--lock)	Locks a user account.
-n (--minimum)	Specifies the number of days that must elapse before the password can be changed. It corresponds to field 4 in the shadow file.

Option	Description
-S (--status)	Displays the status information for a user.
-u (--unlock)	Unlocks a locked user account.
-w (--warning)	Designates the number of days for which the user gets alerts to change their password before it actually expires. It corresponds to field 6 in the shadow file.
-x (--maximum)	Denotes the maximum number of days of password validity before the user password expires and it must be changed. It corresponds to field 5 in the shadow file.

Table 6-2 passwd Command Options

Most of these flags will be used in the next few exercises.

Exercise 6-2: Set and Confirm Password Aging with passwd

This exercise should be done on *server1* as *root*.

In this exercise, you will configure password aging for *user200* using the *passwd* command. You will set mindays to 10, maxdays to 90, and warndays to 14, and verify the new settings.

Next, you will set the number of inactivity days to 5 and ensure that the user is forced to change their password upon next login. You will complete the exercise with another verification.

1. Set password aging attributes for *user200* to mindays (-n) 10, maxdays (-x) 90, and warndays (-w) 14:

   ```
   [root@server1 ~]# passwd -n 10 -x 90 -w 14 user200
   ```

2. Confirm the new settings:

   ```
   [root@server1 ~]# passwd -S user200
   user200 PS 2023-01-28 10 90 14 5 (Password set, unknown crypt variant.)
   ```

The output confirms the three new settings (10, 90, and 14).

3. Set the number of inactivity days to 7:

   ```
   [root@server1 ~]# passwd -i7 user200
   ```

4. Confirm the new setting:

   ```
   [root@server1 ~]# passwd -S user200
   user200 PS 2023-01-28 10 90 14 7 (Password set, unknown crypt variant.)
   ```

The output verifies the new setting (7).

5. Ensure that the user is forced to change their password at next login:

   ```
   [root@server1 ~]# passwd -e user200
   ```

---

6. Display the new setting for confirmation:

```
[root@server1 ~]# passwd -S user200
user200 PS 1969-12-31 10 90 14 7 (Password set, unknown crypt variant.)
```

The output shows a date prior to the UNIX time. This user will be prompted to change their password when they attempt to log in the next time.

The usermod Command

The common use of the *usermod* command is to modify a user's attribute, but it can also lock or unlock their account. Table 6-3 explains the two options in both short and long formats.

Option	Description
-L (--lock)	Locks a user account by placing a single exclamation mark (!) at the beginning of the password field and before the hashed password string.
-U (--unlock)	Unlocks a user's account by removing the exclamation mark (!) from the beginning of the password field.

Table 6-3 usermod Command Options for User Lock/Unlock

Let's apply these options in the next exercise.

Exercise 6-3: Lock and Unlock a User Account with usermod and passwd

This exercise should be done on *server1* as *root*.

In this exercise, you will disable the ability for *user200* to log in using the *usermod* and *passwd* commands. You will verify the change and then reverse it.

1. Obtain the current password information for *user200* from the *shadow* file:

```
[root@server1 ~]# grep user200 /etc/shadow
user200:$y$j9T$.n6/qk6Pr6zJpwT.el.vl.$z0CJx4qo0FW86bsTsL62/tr/
0:14:7::
```

An unlocked user account never has its password field begin with an exclamation mark (!). The above output is indicative of the fact that the account is currently not locked.

2. Lock the account for *user200*:

```
[root@server1 ~]# usermod -L user200          or
[root@server1 ~]# passwd -l user200
```

3. Confirm the change:

```
[root@server1 ~]# grep user200 /etc/shadow
user200:!$y$j9T$.n6/qk6Pr6zJpwT.el.vl.$z0CJx4qo0FW86bsTsL62/tr/
90:14:7::
```

Notice that an exclamation mark (!) is prepended to the encrypted password, which indicates a locked account.

4. Unlock the account with either of the following:

```
[root@server1 ~]# usermod –U user200          or
[root@server1 ~]# passwd –u user200
```

Verify the reversal with the *grep* command as demonstrated in step 3. You can also try to log in as *user200* for an additional validation. The *grep* command is discussed in detail in Chapter 07 "The Bash Shell".

Linux Groups and their Management

Linux groups are collections of one or more users with identical permission requirements on files and directories. They allow group members to collaborate on files of common interest.

Group information is stored in the */etc/group* file and the default policies in the */etc/login.defs* configuration file. Furthermore, the */etc/gshadow* file stores group administrator information and group-level passwords. These files were thoroughly examined in Chapter 05 "Basic User Management".

This section explores group management tools—*groupadd*, *groupmod*, and *groupdel*—and looks at how to utilize them to create, alter, and erase groups. Additional group administration operations, such as adding and deleting group administrators, and setting and revoking group-level passwords, are beyond the scope.

The groupadd, groupmod, and groupdel Commands

This set of management commands is used to add, modify, and delete a group from the system. The *groupadd* command adds entries to the *group* and *gshadow* files for each group added to the system. Table 6-4 lists and explains some of the *groupadd* command options in both short and long formats.

Option	Description
-g (--gid)	Specifies the GID to be assigned to the group
-o (--non-unique)	Creates a group with a matching GID of an existing group. When two groups have an identical GID, members of both groups get identical rights on each other's files. This should only be done in specific situations.
-r	Creates a system group with a GID below 1000
groupname	Specifies a group name

Table 6-4 groupadd Command Options

The *groupadd* command picks up the default values from the *login.defs* file.

You can modify the attributes of a group with the *groupmod* command. The syntax of this command is very similar to the *groupadd* with most options identical. The only flag that is additional with this command is -n, which can change the name of an existing group.

The *groupdel* command is straightforward. It removes entries for the specified group from both *group* and *gshadow* files.

Exercise 6-4: Create a Group and Add Members

This exercise should be done on *server1* as *root*.

In this exercise, you will create a group called *linuxadm* with GID 5000 and another group called *dba* sharing the GID 5000. You will add *user1* as a secondary member to group *dba*.

1. Create the group *linuxadm* with GID 5000:

   ```
   [root@server1 ~]# groupadd -g 5000 linuxadm
   ```

2. Create a group called *dba* with the same GID as that of group *linuxadm*:

   ```
   [root@server1 ~]# groupadd -o -g 5000 dba
   ```

3. Confirm the creation of both groups:

   ```
   [root@server1 ~]# grep linuxadm /etc/group
   linuxadm:x:5000:
   [root@server1 ~]# grep dba /etc/group
   dba:x:5000:
   ```

The GID for both groups is identical.

4. Add *user1* as a secondary member of group *dba* using the *usermod* command. The existing membership for the user must remain intact.

   ```
   [root@server1 ~]# usermod -aG dba user1
   ```

5. Verify the updated group membership information for *user1* by extracting the relevant entry from the *group* file, and running the *id* and *groups* command for *user1*:

   ```
   [root@server1 ~]# grep dba /etc/group
   dba:x:5000:user1
   [root@server1 ~]#
   [root@server1 ~]# id user1
   uid=1000(user1) gid=1000(user1) groups=1000(user1),5000(dba)
   [root@server1 ~]# groups user1
   user1 : user1 dba
   ```

The output confirms the primary (*user1*) and secondary (*dba*) group memberships for *user1*.

Exercise 6-5: Modify and Delete a Group Account

This exercise should be done on *server1* as *root*.

In this exercise, you will change the *linuxadm* group name to *sysadm* and the GID to 6000. You will add *user200* to *sysadm* group as a secondary member. You will remove the *sysadm* group and verify.

1. Alter the name of *linuxadm* to *sysadm*:

```
[root@server1 ~]# groupmod -n sysadm linuxadm
```

2. Change the GID of *sysadm* to 6000:

```
[root@server1 ~]# groupmod -g 6000 sysadm
```

3. Add *user200* to *sysadm* as a secondary member:

```
[root@server1 ~]# usermod -aG sysadm user200
```

4. Confirm the above actions:

```
[root@server1 ~]# grep sysadm /etc/group
sysadm:x:6000:user1,user200
[root@server1 ~]# grep linuxadm /etc/group
[root@server1 ~]#
```

The outputs confirm both actions. The new group name is *sysadm* and the new GID is 6000. *user200* is a member of the *sysadm* group. Also notice that the *linuxadm* group does not exist anymore. The second command returned nothing for it.

5. Delete the *sysadm* group and confirm:

```
[root@server1 ~]# groupdel sysadm
[root@server1 ~]# grep sysadm /etc/group
[root@server1 ~]#
```

The second command returns nothing, which confirms the group deletion.

Substituting Users and Doing as Superuser

In real world Linux environments, you'll always sign in as a normal user. Normal users have limited rights on the system. Their profiles are set to allow them to accomplish routine jobs efficiently and securely. This is done to secure the overall system functionality and to prevent unexpected issues. There are times though when a normal user needs to assume the identity of a different user to carry out a task as that user or execute a command successfully that requires elevated privileges. Linux offers two fundamental tools to support users in both situations.

Substituting (or Switching) Users

Even though you can log in to the system directly as *root*, it is not a recommended practice. Instead, log in with a normal user account and then switch to the *root* account if necessary. This is safer and ensures system security and protection. In addition to becoming *root*, you can switch into another user account. In either case, you'll need to know the password for the target user in order for a successful switch. The *su* command has the ability to switch into other user accounts.

To switch from *user1* (assuming you are logged in as *user1*) into *root* without executing the startup scripts (startup scripts are explained later in this chapter) for the target user, run the *su* command and enter the *root* user password when prompted:

```
[user1@server1 ~]$ su
```

Press `Ctrl+d` key combination to return to the *user1* command prompt. Then rerun the *su* command with the hyphen character (-) specified to ensure that startup scripts for the target user are also executed to provide an environment similar to that of a real login:

```
[user1@server1 ~]$ su -
```

To switch into a different user account, such as *user100*, specify the name of the target user with the command. You must enter the password of the target user when prompted.

```
[user1@server1 ~]$ su - user100
```

RHEL offers two tools—*whoami* (*who am i*) and *logname* (*login name*)—that show a user's current identity (after *su*'ing into the target user) and the identity of the user who originally logged in. Let's see what they report after switching into *user100*:

```
[user100@server1 ~]$ whoami
user100
[user100@server1 ~]$ logname
user1
```

The *whoami* command returns the effective (current) username (*user100*), and the *logname* command reports the user's real (original) username (*user1*).

To issue a command as a different user without switching into that user, use the -c option with *su*. For example, the *firewall-cmd* command with the --list-services option requires superuser privileges. *user1* can use *su* as follows and execute this privileged command to obtain desired results:

```
[user1@server1 ~]$ su -c 'firewall-cmd --list-services'
```

The *root* user can switch into any user account that exists on the system without being prompted for that user's password.

The firewall-cmd command is used to manage the Linux firewall at the command line. It is discussed in detail in Chapter 19 "The Linux Firewall".

Although the *su* command does provide the flexibility and convenience, switching into the *root* account to execute privileged actions is not recommended. There is a preferred method available in Linux that should be used instead. The following section sheds light on it.

Doing as Superuser (or Doing as Substitute User)

On production Linux servers, there are necessary steps to ensure that users have the ability to carry out their assigned job without hassle. In most cases, this requires privileged access to certain tools and functions, which the *root* user is normally allowed to run.

RHEL provides normal users the ability to run a set of privileged commands or to access non-owning files without the knowledge of the *root* password. This allows the flexibility of assigning a specific command or a set of commands to an individual user or a group of users based on their needs. These users can then precede one of those commands with a utility called *sudo* (*superuser do*, a.k.a. *substitute user do*) at the time of executing that command. The users are prompted to enter their own password, and if correct, the command is executed successfully for them. The *sudo* utility is designed to provide protected access to administrative functions as defined in the */etc/sudoers* file or files in the drop-in directory */etc/sudoers.d*. It can also be used to allow a user or a group of users to run scripts and applications owned by a different user.

Any normal user that requires privileged access to administrative commands or non-owning files is defined in the *sudoers* file. This file may be edited with a command called *visudo*, which creates a copy of the file as *sudoers.tmp* and applies the changes there. After the *visudo* session is over, the updated file overwrites the original *sudoers* file and *sudoers.tmp* is deleted. This is done to prevent multiple users editing this file simultaneously.

The syntax for user and group entries in the file is similar to the following example entries for user *user1* and group *dba*:

```
user1       ALL=(ALL)       ALL
%dba        ALL=(ALL)       ALL
```

These entries may be added to the beginning of the file, and they are intended to provide full access to every administrative function to *user1* and members of the *dba* group (group is prefixed by the percentage sign (%)). In other words, *user1* and *dba* group members will have full *root* user authority on the system.

When *user1* or a *dba* group member attempts to access a privileged function, they will be required to enter their own password. For instance:

```
[user1@server1 ~]$ sudo head /etc/sudoers
[sudo] password for user1:
user1 ALL=(ALL) ALL
%dba ALL=(ALL) ALL
## Sudoers allows particular users to run various commands as
## the root user, without needing the root password.
##
## Examples are provided at the bottom of the file for collections
## of related commands, which can then be delegated out to particular
## users or groups.
##
## This file must be edited with the 'visudo' command.
```

If you want *user1* and *dba* group members not to be prompted for their passwords, modify the entries in the *sudoers* file to look like:

```
user1       ALL=(ALL)       NOPASSWD:ALL
%dba        ALL=(ALL)       NOPASSWD:ALL
```

Rather than allowing them full access to the system, you can restrict their access to the functions that they need access to. For example, to limit their access to a single command */usr/bin/cat*, modify the directives as follows:

```
user1       ALL=/usr/bin/cat
%dba        ALL=/usr/bin/cat
```

These users should now be able to use the *cat* command to view the content of the */etc/sudoers* or any other file that requires the *root* privilege. Try **cat /etc/sudoers** as *user1* and then again as **sudo cat /etc/sudoers**. You will see the difference.

Configuring sudo to work the way it has just been explained may result in a cluttered *sudoers* file with too many entries to fulfill diversified needs of users and groups. A preferred method is to use predefined aliases—User_Alias and Cmnd_Alias—to configure groups of users and commands, and assign access as required. For instance, you can define a Cmnd_Alias called PKGCMD containing *yum* and *rpm* package management commands, and a User_Alias called PKGADM for *user1*, *user100*, and *user200*. These users may or may not belong to the same Linux group.

Next, assign PKGCMD to PKGADM. This way one rule is set that allows a group of users access to a group of commands. You can add or remove commands and users anytime as needed, and the change will take effect right away. Here is what this configuration will look like:

```
Cmnd_Alias        PKGCMD = /usr/bin/yum, /usr/bin/rpm
User_Alias        PKGADM = user1, user100, user200
PKGADM            ALL = PKGCMD
```

Append the above to the bottom of the *sudoers* file and then run the *yum* or *rpm* command preceded by *sudo* as one of the users listed. You will be able to perform software management tasks just like the *root* user.

The *sudo* command logs successful authentication and command data to the */var/log/secure* file under the name of the actual user executing the command (and not *root*).

The *sudoers* file contains several examples with a brief explanation. It is a good idea to look at those examples for additional understanding.

Now that the normal user *user1* is added to the *sudoers* configuration file, you will be using this user account with *sudo* where appropriate in the examples and exercises in the remainder of the book.

Owning User and Owning Group

In Linux, every file and directory has an owner. By default, the creator assumes the ownership, but this may be altered and allocated to a different user if required.

Similarly, every user is a member of one or more groups. A group is a collection of users with common permission requirements. By default, the owner's group is assigned to a file or directory.

Let's create a file *file1* as *user1* in their home directory and exhibit the file's long listing:

```
[user1@server1 ~]$ touch file1
[user1@server1 ~]$ ls -l file1
-rw-r--r--. 1 user1 user1 0 Jan 29 18:53 file1
```

The output indicates that the owner of *file1* is *user1* who belongs to group *user1*. If you wish to view the corresponding UID and GID instead, you can specify the -n option with the command:

```
[user1@server1 ~]$ ls -ln file1
-rw-r--r--. 1 1000 1000 0 Jan 29 18:53 file1
```

Linux provides the *chown* and *chgrp* commands that can alter the ownership and owning group for files and directories; however, you must have the *root* user privilege to make these modifications.

Exercise 6-6: Modify File Owner and Owning Group

This exercise should be done on *server1* as *user1* with *sudo* where required.

In this exercise, you will first create a file *file10* and a directory *dir10* as *user1* under */tmp*, and then change the ownership for *file10* to *user100* and the owning group to *dba* in two separate transactions. Then you'll apply ownership on *file10* to *user200* and owning group to *user100* at the same time. Finally, you will change the two attributes on the directory to *user200:dba* recursively. Make sure to use *sudo* where necessary.

1. Change into the */tmp* directory and create *file10* and *dir10*:

   ```
   [user1@server1 ~]$ cd /tmp
   [user1@server1 tmp]$ touch file10
   [user1@server1 tmp]$ mkdir dir10
   ```

2. Check and validate that both attributes are set to *user1*:

   ```
   [user1@server1 tmp]$ ls -l file10
   -rw-r--r--. 1 user1 user1 0 Jan 29 18:54 file10
   [user1@server1 tmp]$ ls -ld dir10/
   drwxr-xr-x. 2 user1 user1 6 Jan 29 18:54 dir10/
   ```

3. Set the ownership to *user100* and confirm:

   ```
   [user1@server1 tmp]$ sudo chown user100 file10
   [user1@server1 tmp]$ ls -l file10
   -rw-r--r--. 1 user100 user1 0 Jan 29 18:54 file10
   ```

4. Alter the owning group to *dba* and verify:

   ```
   [user1@server1 tmp]$ sudo chgrp dba file10
   [user1@server1 tmp]$ ls -l file10
   -rw-r--r--. 1 user100 dba 0 Jan 29 18:54 file10
   ```

5. Change the ownership to *user200* and owning group to *user100* and confirm:

   ```
   [user1@server1 tmp]$ sudo chown user200:user100 file10
   [user1@server1 tmp]$ ls -l file10
   -rw-r--r--. 1 user200 user100 0 Jan 29 18:54 file10
   ```

6. Modify the ownership to *user200* and owning group to *dba* recursively on *dir10* and validate:

   ```
   [user1@server1 tmp]$ sudo chown -R user200:dba dir10/
   [user1@server1 tmp]$ ls -ld dir10/
   drwxr-xr-x. 2 user200 dba 6 Jan 29 18:54 dir10/
   ```

You can also use **ls -lR dir10** to view file and directory information under *dir10*; however, it will show nothing as the directory is currently empty.

Chapter Summary

At the outset, we described various aging attributes for user login and password controls that are available to us. We also looked at files that store default attributes that are applied to user accounts at the time of their creation. These defaults may be modified if necessary.

Next, we modified aging attributes for certain user accounts with the help of the tools we learned. We also employed a tool with a pair of flags to deny and restore user access to the system.

We examined group management commands and used them in exercises to create, modify, and delete group accounts, and add users to supplementary groups. The set of the management commands is straightforward and easy to use, but they require execution by a privileged user.

We looked at a couple of tools towards the end of the chapter to switch into other user accounts, including the root user, and to run privileged commands as a normal user. The use of the latter tool is recommended.

Finally, we discussed ownership and owning groups on files and directories, and how they are assigned. We performed exercises to understand who can modify them and how.

Review Questions

1. The *chown* command may be used to modify both ownership and group membership on a file. True or False?
2. What would the command *passwd -n 7 -x 15 -w 3 user5* do?
3. Write the two command names for managing all of the password aging attributes.
4. What would the command *chage -d 0 user60* do?
5. Which file has the default password aging settings defined?
6. What would the command *chage -E 2024-10-22 user10* do?
7. What would the command *chage -l user5* do?
8. Which two commands can be used to lock and unlock a user account?
9. When using *sudo*, log files record activities under the *root* user account. True or False?
10. What is the difference between running the *su* command with and without the hyphen sign?
11. What is the significance of the -o option with the *groupadd* and *groupmod* commands?
12. What would the entry user10 ALL=(ALL) NOPASSWD:ALL in the sudoers file imply?
13. Which command can be used to display the effective (current) username?
14. What is the recommended location to store custom *sudo* rules?
15. What would the command *passwd -l user10* do?
16. The *chgrp* command may be used to modify both ownership and group membership on a file. True or False?

Answers to Review Questions

1. True.
2. The command will set mindays to 7, maxdays to 15, and warndays to 3 for *user5*.
3. The *passwd* and *chage* commands.
4. The command provided will force *user60* to change their password at next login.
5. The */etc/login.defs* file has the defaults for password aging defined.
6. The command provided will set October 22, 2024, as the expiry date for *user10*.

7. The command provided will display password aging attributes for *user5*.
8. The *usermod* and *passwd* commands can be used to lock and unlock a user account.
9. False. The activities are registered under the username who invokes the *sudo* command.
10. With the dash sign the *su* command processes the specified user's startup files, and it won't without this sign.
11. The -o option lets the commands share a GID between two or more groups.
12. It will give *user10* passwordless access to all privileged commands.
13. The *whoami* command reports the effective username of the user running this command.
14. The custom sudo rules should be stored in files under the */etc/sudoers.d* directory.
15. This command will lock *user10*.
16. False.

Do-It-Yourself Challenge Labs

The following labs are useful to strengthen most of the concepts and topics learned in this chapter. It is expected that you perform the labs without external help. A step-by-step guide is not supplied, as the knowledge and skill required to implement the labs have already been disseminated in the chapter; however, hints to the relevant major topic(s) are included.

Use the lab environment built specifically for end-of-chapter labs. See sub-section "Lab Environment for End-of-Chapter Labs" in Chapter 01 "Local Installation" for details.

Lab 6-1: Create User and Configure Password Aging

As *root* on *server3*, create group *lnxgrp* with GID 6000. Create user *user5000* with UID 5000 and GID 6000. Assign this user a password, and establish password aging attributes so that this user cannot change their password within 4 days after setting it and with a password validity of 30 days. This user should start getting warning messages for changing password 10 days prior to account lock down. This user account needs to expire on the 20th of December 2023. (Hint1: Chapter 05: Local User Authentication Files, and User Account Management). (Hint2: Password Aging and its Management, and Linux Groups and their Management).

Lab 6-2: Lock and Unlock User

As *root* on *server3*, lock the user account for *user5000* using the *passwd* command, and confirm by examining the change in the */etc/shadow* file. Try to log in with *user5000* and observe what happens. Use the *usermod* command and unlock this account. Verify the unlocking by checking the entry for the user in the */etc/shadow* file. (Hint: Password Aging and its Management).

Lab 6-3: Modify Group

As *root* on *server3*, modify the GID from 6000 to 7000 for the *lnxgrp* group. Add users *user1000* and *user2000* as supplementary members (create users if needed). Change the group's name to *dbagrp*, and verify. (Hint: Linux Groups and their Management).

Lab 6-4: Configure sudo Access

As *root* on *server3*, add a rule for user5000 to the */etc/sudoers* file to allow this user full *root* access on the system. Make sure that this user is not prompted for a password when they use *sudo* to execute a command. Now switch into this user account and try running *sudo vgs*, and see if that works. (Hint: Substituting Users and Doing as Superuser).

Lab 6-5: Modify Owning User and Group

As *user1* on *server3*, create file *f6* and directory *d6* under */tmp*. Change owning user for *f6* to *user90* (create user) using *sudo chown*, and owning group to *dbagrp* with *sudo chgrp*. Change owning user and group on *d6* to *user90:g1* (create group) recursively using *sudo chown*. (Hint: Owing User and Owning Group).

Chapter 07

The Bash Shell

This chapter describes the following major topics:

➤ Introduction to the bash shell

➤ Understand, set, and unset shell and environment variables

➤ Comprehend and use command and variable expansions

➤ Grasp and utilize input, output, and error redirections

➤ Know and use history substitution, command line editing, tab completion, tilde substitution, and command aliasing

➤ Identify and use metacharacters, wildcard characters, pipes, and pipelines

➤ Discover the use of quoting mechanisms and regular expressions

➤ Identify and examine shell startup files

RHCSA Objectives:

02. Use input-output redirection (>, >>, |, 2>, etc.)

03. Use grep and regular expressions to analyze text

S hells allow users to interact with the operating system for execution of their instructions through programs, commands, and applications. RHEL supports a variety of shells of which the bash shell is the most common. It is also the default shell for users in RHEL 9. This shell offers a variety of features that help users and administrators perform their job with ease and flexibility. Some of these features include recalling a command from history and editing it at the command line before running it, sending output and error messages to non-default target locations, creating command shortcuts, sending output of one command as input to the next, assigning the output of a command to a variable, using special characters to match a string of characters, treating a special character as a literal character, and so on.

Regular expressions are text patterns for matching against an input provided in a search operation. Text patterns may include any sequenced or arbitrary characters or character range. RHEL offers a powerful command to work with pattern matching.

At login, plenty of system and user startup scripts are executed to set up the user environment. The system startup scripts may be customized for all users by the Linux administrator and the user startup scripts may be modified by individual users as per their need.

The Bourne-Again Shell

A *shell* is referred to as the command interpreter, and it is the interface between a user and the Linux kernel. The shell accepts instructions (commands) from users (or programs), interprets them, and passes them on to the kernel for processing. The kernel utilizes all hardware and software components required for a successful processing of the instructions. When concluded, it returns the results to the shell, which then exhibits them on the screen. The shell also shows appropriate error messages, if generated. In addition, the shell delivers a customizable environment to users.

A widely used shell by Linux users and administrators is the *bash* (*bourne-again shell*) shell. Bash is a replacement for the older *Bourne* shell with numerous enhancements and plenty of new features incorporated from other shells. It is the default shell in most popular Linux distributions including RHEL 9 and offers several features such as variable manipulation, variable substitution, command substitution, input and output redirections, history substitution, tab completion, tilde substitution, alias substitution, metacharacters, pattern matching, filename globbing, quoting mechanisms, conditional execution, flow control, and shell scripting. This section discusses all of these features except for the last three.

The bash shell is identified by the $ sign for normal users and the # sign for the *root* user. The bash shell is resident in the */usr/bin/bash* file.

Shell and Environment Variables

A *variable* is a transient storage for data in memory. It retains information that is used for customizing the shell environment and referenced by many programs to function properly. The shell stores a value in a variable, and one or more white space characters must be enclosed within quotation marks.

There are two types of variables: *local* (or *shell*) and *environment*. A local variable is private to the shell in which it is created, and its value cannot be used by programs that are not started in that shell. This introduces the concept of *current* shell and *sub*-shell (or *child* shell). The current shell is where a program is executed, whereas a sub-shell (or child shell) is created within a shell to run a program. The value of a local variable is only available in the current shell.

The value of an environment variable is inherited from the current shell to the sub-shell during the execution of a program. In other words, the value stored in an environment variable is accessible to the program, as well as any sub-programs that it spawns during its lifecycle. Any environment variable set in a sub-shell is lost when the sub-shell terminates.

There are a multitude of predefined environment variables that are set for each user upon logging in. Use the **env** or the **printenv** command to view their values. Run these commands on *server1* as *user1* and observe the output. There should be around 25 of them. Some of the common predefined environment variables are described in Table 7-1.

Variable	Description
DISPLAY	Stores the hostname or IP address for graphical terminal sessions
HISTFILE	Defines the file for storing the history of executed commands
HISTSIZE	Defines the maximum size for the HISTFILE
HOME	Sets the home directory path
LOGNAME	Retains the login name
MAIL	Contains the path to the user mail directory
PATH	Defines a colon-separated list of directories to be searched when executing a command. A correct setting of this variable eliminates the need to specify the absolute path of a command to run it.
PPID	Holds the identifier number for the parent program
PS1	Defines the primary command prompt
PS2	Defines the secondary command prompt
PWD	Stores the current directory location
SHELL	Holds the absolute path to the primary shell file
TERM	Holds the terminal type value
UID	Holds the logged-in user's UID
USER	Retains the name of the logged-in user

Table 7-1 Common Predefined Environment Variables

RHEL provides the *echo* command to view the values stored in variables. For instance, to view the value for the PATH variable, run the *echo* command and ensure to prepend the variable name (PATH) with the $ sign:

```
[user1@server1 ~]$ echo $PATH
/home/user1/.local/bin:/home/user1/bin:/usr/local/bin:/usr/bin:/usr/local/sbin:/
usr/sbin
```

Try running **echo $HOME, echo $SHELL, echo $TERM, echo $PPID, echo $PS1**, and **echo $USER** and see what values they store.

Setting and Unsetting Variables

Shell and environment variables may be set or unset at the command prompt or via programs, and their values may be viewed and used as necessary. We define and undefine variables and view their values using built-in shell commands such as *export, unset*, and *echo*. It is recommended to use uppercase letters to name variables so as to circumvent any possible conflicts with a command, program, file, or directory name that exist somewhere on the system. To understand how variables are defined, viewed, made environment, and undefined, a few examples are presented below. We run the commands as *user1*.

To define a local variable called VR1:

```
[user1@server1 ~]$ VR1=RHEL9
```

To view the value stored in VR1:

```
[user1@server1 ~]$ echo $VR1
```

Now type **bash** at the command prompt to enter a sub-shell and then run **echo $VR1** to check whether the variable is visible in the sub-shell. You will not find it there, as it was not an environment variable. Exit out of the sub-shell by typing **exit**.

To make this variable an environment variable, use the *export* command:

```
[user1@server1 ~]$ export VR1
```

Repeat the previous test by running the **bash** command and then the **echo $VR1**. You should be able to see the variable in the sub-shell, as it is now an environment variable. Exit out of the sub-shell with the **exit** command.

To undefine this variable and erase it from the shell environment:

```
[user1@server1 ~]$ unset VR1
```

To define a local variable that contains a value with one or more white spaces:

```
[user1@server1 ~]$ VR2="I love RHEL 9."
```

To define and make the variable an environment variable at the same time:

```
[user1@server1 ~]$ export VR3="I love RHEL 9."
```

The *echo* command is restricted to showing the value of a specific variable and the *env* and *printenv* commands display the environment variables only. If you want to view both local and environment variables, use the *set* command. Try running **set** and observe the output.

Command and Variable Substitutions

The primary command prompt ends in the # sign for the *root* user and in the $ sign for normal users. Customizing this prompt to exhibit useful information such as who you are, the system you are logged on to, and your current location in the directory tree is a good practice. By default, this setting is already in place through the PS1 environment variable, which defines the primary command prompt. You can validate this information by looking at the command prompt **[user1@server1 ~]$**.

You can also view the value stored in PS1 by issuing **echo $PS1**. The value is \u@\h \W\$. The \u translates into the logged-in username, \h represents the hostname of the system, \W shows your current working directory, and \$ indicates the end of the command prompt.

Exercise 7-1 demonstrates how to employ the command and variable substitution features to customize the primary command prompt for *user1*. You will use the *hostname* command and assign its output to the PS1 variable. This is an example of *command substitution*. Note that the command whose output you want assigned to a variable must be encapsulated within either backticks `hostname` or parentheses $(hostname).

There are two instances of the *variable substitution* feature employed in Exercise 7-1. The LOGNAME and the PWD environment variables to display the username and to reflect the current directory location.

Exercise 7-1: Modify Primary Command Prompt

This exercise should be done on *server1* as *user1*.

In this exercise, you will customize the primary shell prompt to display the information enclosed within the quotes "< username on hostname in pwd >: " using the variable and command substitution features. You will do this at the command prompt. You will then edit the *~/.bash_profile* file for *user1* and define the new value in there for permanence (see Shell Startup Files later in this chapter to understand the purpose of *.bash_profile*), otherwise, the value will be lost when *user1* closes the terminal window or logs off.

1. Change the value of the variable PS1 to reflect the desired information:

   ```
   [user1@server1 ~]$ export PS1="< $LOGNAME on $(hostname) in \$PWD > "
   < user1 on server1.example.com in /home/user1 >
   ```

The prompt has changed to display the desired information.

2. Edit the *.bash_profile* file for *user1* and define the value exactly as it was run in Step 1.
3. Test by logging off and logging back in as *user1*. The new command prompt will be displayed.

This concludes the exercise.

Input, Output, and Error Redirections

Programs read input from the keyboard and write output to the terminal window where they are initiated. Any errors, if encountered, are printed on the terminal window too. This is the default behavior. The bash handles input, output, and errors as character streams. If you do not want input to come from the keyboard or output and error to go to the terminal screen, the shell gives you the flexibility to redirect input, output, and error messages to allow programs and commands to read input from a non-default source, and forward output and errors to one or more non-default destinations.

> **EXAM TIP:** You may be asked to run a command and redirect its output and/or error messages to a file.

The default (or the standard) locations for the three streams are referred to as *standard input* (or *stdin*), *standard output* (or *stdout*), and *standard error* (or *stderr*). These locations may also be epitomized using the opening angle bracket symbol (<) for stdin, and the closing angle bracket symbol (>) for stdout and stderr. Alternatively, you may use the *file descriptors* (the digits 0, 1, and 2) to represent the three locations.

Redirecting Standard Input

Input redirection instructs a command to read input from an alternative source, such as a file, instead of the keyboard. The opening angle bracket (<) is used for input redirection. For example, run the following to have the *cat* command read the */etc/redhat-release* file and display its content on the standard output (terminal screen):

```
[user1@server1 ~]$ cat < /etc/redhat-release
Red Hat Enterprise Linux release 9.1 (Plow)
```

Redirecting Standard Output

Output redirection sends the output generated by a command to an alternative destination, such as a file, instead of to the terminal window. The closing angle bracket (>) is used for this purpose. For instance, the following directs the *ls* command output to a file called *ls.out*. This will overwrite any existing *ls.out* file if there is one; otherwise, a new file will be created.

```
[user1@server1 ~]$ ls > ls.out
```

The above can also be run as **ls 1> ls.out** where the digit "1" represents the standard output location.

If you want to prevent an inadvertent overwriting of the output file, you can enable the shell's noclobber feature with the *set* command and confirm its activation by re-issuing the above redirection example:

```
[user1@server1 ~]$ set -o noclobber
[user1@server1 ~]$ ls > ls.out
-bash: ls.out: cannot overwrite existing file
```

You are denied the action.

You can disable the noclobber option by running **set +o noclobber** at the command prompt.

To direct the *ls* command to append the output to the *ls.out* file instead of overwriting it, use the two closing angle brackets (>>):

```
[user1@server1 ~]$ ls >> ls.out
```

Again, the equivalent for the above is **ls 1>> ls.out**.

Redirecting Standard Error

Error redirection forwards any error messages generated to an alternative destination rather than to the terminal window. An alternative destination could be a file. For example, the following directs the *find* command issued as a normal user to search for all occurrences of files by the name *core* in the entire directory tree and sends any error messages produced to */dev/null* (*/dev/null* is a special file that is used to discard data). This way only the useful output is exhibited on the screen and errors are thrown away.

```
[user1@server1 ~]$ find / -name core -print 2> /dev/null
```

Redirecting both Standard Output and Error

You may redirect both output and error to alternative locations as well. For instance, issue the following to forward them both to a file called *outerr.out*:

```
[user1@server1 ~]$ ls /usr /cdr &> outerr.out
```

This example will produce a listing of the */usr* directory and save the result in *outerr.out*. At the same time, it will generate an error message complaining about the non-existence of */cdr*, and it will send it to the same file as well.

Another method to run the above command is by typing **ls /usr /cdr 1> outerr.out 2>&1**, which essentially means to redirect file descriptor 1 to file *outerr.out* as well as to file descriptor 2.

You can exchange &> with &>> in the above example to append the information in the file rather than overwriting it.

History Substitution

History substitution (a.k.a. *command history* or *history expansion*) is a time-saver bash shell feature that keeps a log of all commands or commandsets that you run at the command prompt in chronological order with one command or commandset per line. The history feature is enabled by default; however, you can disable and re-enable it if required. The bash shell stores command history in a file located in the user's home directory and in system memory. You may retrieve the commands from history, modify them at the command prompt, and rerun them.

There are three variables—HISTFILE, HISTSIZE, and HISTFILESIZE—that control the location and history storage. HISTFILE defines the name and location of the history file to be used to store command history, and the default is *.bash_history* in the user's home directory. HISTSIZE dictates the maximum number of commands to be held in memory for the current session. HISTFILESIZE sets the maximum number of commands allowed for storage in the history file at the beginning of the current session and are written to the HISTFILE from memory at the end of the current terminal session. Usually, HISTSIZE and HISTFILESIZE are set to a common value. These variables and their values can be viewed with the *echo* command. The following shows the settings for *user1*:

```
[user1@server1 ~]$ echo $HISTFILE
/home/user1/.bash_history
[user1@server1 ~]$ echo $HISTSIZE
1000
[user1@server1 ~]$ echo $HISTFILESIZE
1000
```

The values of any of these variables may be altered for individual users by editing the *.bashrc* or *.bash_profile* file in the user's home directory. A discussion on these files is provided later in this chapter.

In RHEL, the *history* command displays or reruns previously executed commands. This command gets the history data from the system memory as well as from the *.bash_history* file. By default, it shows all entries. Run this command at the prompt without any options and it will dump everything on the screen:

```
[user1@server1 ~]$ history
```

The *history* command has some useful options. Let's use them and observe the impact on the output.

To display this command and the ten preceding entries:

```
[user1@server1 ~]$ history 10
```

To re-execute a command by its line number (line 15 for example):

```
[user1@server1 ~]$ !15
```

To re-execute the most recent occurrence of a command that started with a particular letter or series of letters (ch for example):

```
[user1@server1 ~]$ !ch
```

To issue the most recent command that contained "grep":

```
[user1@server1 ~]$ !?grep?
```

To remove entry 24 from history:

```
[user1@server1 ~]$ history -d 24
```

To repeat the last command executed:

```
[user1@server1 ~]$ !!
```

The second exclamation mark (!) in the above example is used to retrieve the last executed command.

You may disable the shell's history expansion feature by issuing **set +o history** at the command prompt and re-enable it with **set -o history**. The *set* command is used in this way to enable or disable a bash shell feature.

Editing at the Command Line

While typing a command with a multitude of options and arguments at the command prompt, you often need to move the cursor backward to add or modify something. For instance, if you are typing a long command as a normal user and then realize the command needs to have *sudo* added at the beginning, move the cursor quickly to the start of the command. This is a shortcut to save time. There are plenty of key combinations for rapid movement on the command line. Table 7-2 lists and explains several of these.

Key Combinations	Action
Ctrl+a / Home	Moves the cursor to the beginning of the command line
Ctrl+e / End	Moves the cursor to the end of the command line
Ctrl+u	Erase the entire line
Ctrl+k	Erase from the cursor to the end of the command line
Alt+f	Moves the cursor to the right one word at a time
Alt+b	Moves the cursor to the left one word at a time
Ctrl+f / Right arrow	Moves the cursor to the right one character at a time
Ctrl+b / Left arrow	Moves the cursor to the left one character at a time

Table 7-2 Helpful Command Line Editing Shortcuts

For normal users and administrators who often work at the command line, these key combinations will be very helpful in saving time.

Tab Completion

Tab completion (a.k.a. *command line completion*) is a bash shell feature whereby typing one or more initial characters of a file, directory, or command name at the command line and then hitting the Tab key twice automatically completes the entire name. In case of multiple possibilities matching the entered characters, it completes up to the point they have in common and prints the rest of the possibilities on the screen. You can then type one or more following characters and press Tab again to further narrow down the possibilities. When the desired name appears, press Enter to accept it and perform the action. One of the major benefits of using this feature is the time saved on typing long file, directory, or command names.

Try this feature out on your Linux terminal window and get yourself familiarized with it.

Tilde Substitution

Tilde substitution (or *tilde expansion*) is performed on words that begin with the tilde character (~). The rules to keep in mind when using the ~ are:

1. If ~ is used as a standalone character, the shell refers to the $HOME directory of the user running the command. The following example displays the $HOME directory of *user1*:

```
[user1@server1 ~]$ echo ~
/home/user1
```

2. If the plus sign (+) follows the ~, the shell refers to the current directory. For example, if *user1* is in the */usr/bin* directory and does ~+, the output exhibits the user's current directory location:

```
[user1@server1 bin]$ echo ~+
/usr/bin
```

3. If the hyphen character (-) follows the ~, the shell refers to the previous working directory. For example, if *user1* switches into the */usr/share/man* directory from */usr/bin* and does ~-, the output displays the user's last working directory:

```
[user1@server1 bin]$ cd /usr/share/man
[user1@server1 man]$ echo ~-
/usr/bin
```

4. If a username has the ~ prepended, the shell refers to the $HOME directory of that user:

```
[user1@server1 man]$ echo ~user200
/home/user200
```

Tilde substitution can also be used with commands such as *cd* and *ls*. For instance, to *cd* into the home directory of *user1* (or any other user for that matter) from anywhere in the directory structure, specify the login name with the ~:

```
[user1@server1 man]$ cd ~user1
[user1@server1 ~]$ pwd
/home/user1
```

This command is only successful if *user1* has the right permissions to navigate into the target user's home directory. Let's try this example as the *root* user:

```
[root@server1 ~]# cd ~user100
[root@server1 user100]# pwd
/home/user100
```

The above example demonstrates the navigation into the home directory of *user100* as the *root* user. By default, *root* has full rights to *cd* into any users' home directory.

Another example below exhibits how a user can *cd* into one of their subdirectories (such as */home/user1/dir1*) directly from anywhere (*/etc/systemd/system*) in the directory structure (create *dir1* for this test):

```
[user1@server1 ~]$ cd
[user1@server1 ~]$ mkdir dir1
[user1@server1 ~]$ cd /etc/systemd/system/
[user1@server1 system]$ pwd
/etc/systemd/system
[user1@server1 system]$ cd ~/dir1
[user1@server1 dir1]$ pwd
/home/user1/dir1
```

Try using the ~ with the *ls* command. For example, run **sudo ls -ld ~root/Desktop** as *user1*.

Alias Substitution

Alias substitution (a.k.a. *command aliasing* or *alias*) allows you to define a shortcut for a lengthy and complex command or a set of commands. Defining and using aliases saves time and saves you from typing. The shell executes the corresponding command or commandset when an alias is run.

The bash shell includes several predefined aliases that are set during user login. These aliases may be viewed with the *alias* command. The following shows all the aliases that are currently set for *user1*:

```
[user1@server1 ~]$ alias
alias egrep='egrep --color=auto'
alias fgrep='fgrep --color=auto'
alias grep='grep --color=auto'
alias l.='ls -d .* --color=auto'
alias ll='ls -l --color=auto'
alias ls='ls --color=auto'
alias xzegrep='xzegrep --color=auto'
alias xzfgrep='xzfgrep --color=auto'
alias xzgrep='xzgrep --color=auto'
alias zegrep='zegrep --color=auto'
alias zfgrep='zfgrep --color=auto'
alias zgrep='zgrep --color=auto'
```

There are a few additional default aliases set for the *root* user. Run *alias* as *root*:

```
[root@server1 ~]# alias
alias cp='cp -i'
alias egrep='egrep --color=auto'
alias fgrep='fgrep --color=auto'
alias grep='grep --color=auto'
alias l.='ls -d .* --color=auto'
alias ll='ls -l --color=auto'
alias ls='ls --color=auto'
alias mv='mv -i'
alias rm='rm -i'
alias xzegrep='xzegrep --color=auto'
alias xzfgrep='xzfgrep --color=auto'
alias xzgrep='xzgrep --color=auto'
alias zegrep='zegrep --color=auto'
alias zfgrep='zfgrep --color=auto'
alias zgrep='zgrep --color=auto'
```

Many aliases have the option "color" set to auto, which implies that the output will highlight the file names and pattern matches in a color. Table 7-3 describes the common aliases from the previous two outputs.

Alias	Value	Definition
cp	cp -i	Issues the cp command in interactive mode
ll	ls -l	Shows the ls command output in long format
mv	mv -i	Executes the mv command in interactive mode
rm	rm -i	Runs the rm command in interactive mode

Table 7-3 Predefined Aliases

In addition to listing the set aliases, the *alias* command can also be used to define new aliases. The opposite function of unsetting an alias is performed with the *unalias* command. Both *alias* and *unalias* are internal shell commands. Let's look at a few examples.

Create an alias "search" to abbreviate the *find* command with several switches and arguments. Enclose the entire command within single quotation marks ('') to ensure white spaces are taken care of. Do not leave any spaces before and after the equal sign (=).

```
[user1@server1 ~]$ alias search='find / -name core -exec ls -l {} \;'
```

Now, when you type the string "search" at the command prompt and press the Enter key, the shell will trade the alias "search" with what is stored in it and will run it. Essentially, you have created a shortcut to that lengthy command.

Sometimes you define an alias by a name that matches the name of some system command or program. In this situation, the shell gives the execution precedence to the alias. This means the shell will run the alias and not the command or the program. For example, the *rm* command deletes a file without giving any warning if run as a normal user. To prevent accidental deletion of files with *rm*, you may create an alias by the same name as the command but with the interactive option added, as shown below:

```
[user1@server1 ~]$ alias rm='rm -i'
```

When you execute *rm* now to remove a file, the shell will run what is stored in the *rm* alias and not the command *rm*. If you wish to run the *rm* command instead, run it by preceding a backslash (\) with it:

```
[user1@server1 ~]$ \rm file1
```

You can use the *unalias* command to unset one or more specified aliases if they are no longer in need. The following will undefine the two aliases that were defined for our examples:

```
[user1@server1 ~]$ unalias search rm
```

Metacharacters and Wildcard Characters

Metacharacters are special characters that possess special meaning to the shell. Some of them are the dollar sign ($), caret (^), period (.), asterisk (*), question mark (?), pipe (|), angle brackets (<>), curly brackets ({}), square brackets ([]), parentheses (()), plus (+), exclamation mark (!), semicolon

(;), and backslash (\) characters. They are used in pattern matching (a.k.a. *filename expansion* or *file globbing*) and regular expressions. This sub-section discusses the metacharacters (* ? [] !) that are used in pattern matching. The *, ?, and [] characters are also referred to as *wildcard characters*.

The * Character

The asterisk (*) matches zero to an unlimited number of characters except for the leading period (.) in a hidden filename. See the following examples on usage.

To list all files in the */etc* directory that begin with letters "ma" and followed by any characters:

```
[user1@server1 ~]$ ls /etc/ma*
/etc/machine-id  /etc/mailcap                    /etc/man_db.conf
/etc/magic       /etc/makedumpfile.conf.sample
```

To list all hidden files and directories in */home/user1*:

```
[user1@server1 ~]$ ls -d .*
.    .bash_history  .bash_profile  .cache    .local
..   .bash_logout   .bashrc        .config   .mozilla
```

To list all files in the */var/log* directory that end in ".log":

```
[user1@server1 ~]$ ls /var/log/*.log
/var/log/boot.log          /var/log/dnf.log          /var/log/kdump.log
/var/log/dnf.librepo.log   /var/log/dnf.rpm.log
```

The * is probably the most common metacharacter that is used in pattern matching.

The ? Character

The question mark (?) matches exactly one character except for the leading period in a hidden filename. See the following example to understand its usage.

To list all files and directories under */var/log* with exactly four characters in their names:

```
[user1@server1 ~]$ ls -d /var/log/????
/var/log/btmp  /var/log/cups  /var/log/sssd
/var/log/cron  /var/log/rhsm  /var/log/wtmp
```

The ? is another metacharacter that is used widely in pattern matching.

The Square Brackets [] and the Exclamation Mark !

The square brackets ([]) can be used to match either a set of characters or a range of characters for a single character position.

For a set of characters specified in this enclosure, the order in which they are listed has no importance. This means the shell will interpret [xyz], [yxz], [xzy], and [zyx] alike during pattern matching. In the following example, two characters are enclosed within the square brackets. The output will include all files and directories that begin with either of the two characters and followed by any number of characters.

```
[user1@server1 ~]$ ls /usr/bin/[yw]*
/usr/bin/w               /usr/bin/whereis              /usr/bin/wvtag
/usr/bin/wait            /usr/bin/which                /usr/bin/wvunpack
/usr/bin/wall            /usr/bin/whiptail             /usr/bin/yelp
/usr/bin/watch           /usr/bin/who                  /usr/bin/yelp-build
/usr/bin/watchgnupg      /usr/bin/whoami               /usr/bin/yelp-check
/usr/bin/wavpack         /usr/bin/wireplumber          /usr/bin/yelp-new
/usr/bin/wc              /usr/bin/wnck-urgency-monitor /usr/bin/yes
/usr/bin/wdctl           /usr/bin/wpctl                /usr/bin/ypdomainname
/usr/bin/wget            /usr/bin/wpexec               /usr/bin/yum
/usr/bin/whatis          /usr/bin/write
/usr/bin/whatis.man-db   /usr/bin/wvgain
```

A range of characters must be specified in a proper sequence such as [a-z] or [0-9]. The following example matches all directory names that begin with any letter between "m" and "o" in the /etc/systemd/system directory:

```
[user1@server1 ~]$ ls -d /etc/systemd/system/[m-o]*
/etc/systemd/system/multi-user.target.wants
/etc/systemd/system/network-online.target.wants
```

The shell enables the exclamation mark (!) to inverse the matches. For instance, [!a-d]* would exclude all filenames that begin with any of the first four alphabets. The following example will produce the reverse of what the previous example did:

```
[user1@server1 ~]$ ls -d /etc/systemd/system/[!m-o]*
/etc/systemd/system/basic.target.wants
/etc/systemd/system/bluetooth.target.wants
/etc/systemd/system/ctrl-alt-del.target
/etc/systemd/system/dbus-org.bluez.service
/etc/systemd/system/dbus-org.fedoraproject.FirewallD1.service
/etc/systemd/system/dbus-org.freedesktop.Avahi.service
/etc/systemd/system/dbus-org.freedesktop.ModemManager1.service
/etc/systemd/system/dbus-org.freedesktop.nm-dispatcher.service
/etc/systemd/system/dbus.service
/etc/systemd/system/default.target
```

The output will have a multitude of filenames printed.

Piping Output of One Command as Input to Another

The *pipe*, represented by the vertical bar (|) and normally resides with the backslash (\) on most keyboards, is used to send the output of one command as input to the next. This character is also used to define alternations in regular expressions. You can use the pipe operator as many times in a command as you require.

The /etc directory contains plenty of files, but they all do not fit on one terminal screen when you want to see its long listing. You can use the pipe operator to pipe the output to the *less* command in order to view the directory listing one screenful at a time:

```
[user1@server1 ~]$ ls -l /etc | less
total 1320
drwxr-xr-x.  3 root root          28 Jan 26 16:38 accountsservice
-rw-r--r--.  1 root root          16 Jan 26 16:50 adjtime
-rw-r--r--.  1 root root        1529 Jun 23  2020 aliases
drwxr-xr-x.  3 root root          65 Jan 26 16:43 alsa
drwxr-xr-x.  2 root root        4096 Jan 26 16:43 alternatives
-rw-r--r--.  1 root root         541 Jul 11  2022 anacrontab
. . . . . . . .
```

In another example, the *last* command is run and its output is piped to the *nl* command to number
each output line:

```
[user1@server1 ~]$ last | nl
     1  user1    pts/1        192.168.0.3      Sun Jan 29 18:28 - 18:50  (00:21)
     2  root     pts/0        192.168.0.3      Sun Jan 29 12:29   still logged in
     3  reboot   system boot  5.14.0-162.6.1.e Sun Jan 29 12:29   still running
     4  user1    pts/1        192.168.0.4      Sat Jan 28 22:10 - 22:34  (00:23)
     5  root     pts/1        192.168.0.4      Sat Jan 28 22:03 - 22:10  (00:06)
     6  user1    pts/1        192.168.0.4      Sat Jan 28 21:52 - 21:52  (00:00)
     7  root     pts/0        192.168.0.4      Sat Jan 28 21:52 - 22:34  (00:42)
     8  root     pts/0        192.168.0.4      Fri Jan 27 19:21 - 21:51  (1+02:30)
     9  root     pts/0        192.168.0.4      Fri Jan 27 19:17 - 19:17  (00:00)
    10  root     pts/0        192.168.0.4      Fri Jan 27 19:16 - 19:16  (00:00)
    11  root     pts/2        192.168.0.4      Fri Jan 27 14:28 - 19:21  (04:53)
. . . . . . . .
```

 The nl command reveals numbering for each line in the output.

The following example sends the output of *ls* to *grep* for the lines that do not contain the pattern
"root". The new output is further piped for a case-insensitive selection of all lines that exclude the
pattern "dec". The filtered output is numbered, and the final result shows the last four lines on the
display.

```
[user1@server1 ~]$ ls -l /proc | grep -v root | grep -iv dec | nl | tail -4
    51  dr-xr-xr-x.  9 libstoragemgmt libstoragemgmt            0 Jan 29 12:29 740
    52  dr-xr-xr-x.  9 polkitd        polkitd                   0 Jan 29 12:29 742
    53  dr-xr-xr-x.  9 rtkit          rtkit                     0 Jan 29 12:29 745
    54  dr-xr-xr-x.  9 avahi          avahi                     0 Jan 29 17:37 756
```

A construct like the above with multiple pipes is referred to as a *pipeline*.

Quoting Mechanisms

As you know, metacharacters have special meaning to the shell. In order to use them as regular
characters, the bash shell offers three *quoting mechanisms* to disable their special meaning and
allow the shell to treat them as literal characters. These mechanisms are available through the use of
the backslash (\), single quotation ('), and double quotation ("") characters, and work by
prepending a special character to the backslash, or enclosing it within single or double quotation
marks.

Prefixing with a Backslash \

The backslash character (\), also referred to as the *escape* character in shell terminology, instructs the shell to mask the meaning of any special character that follows it. For example, if a file exists by the name * and you want to remove it with the *rm* command, you will have to escape the * so that it is treated as a regular character, not as a wildcard character.

```
[user1@server1 ~]$ rm \*
```

In the above example, if you forget to escape the *, the *rm* command will remove all files from the directory.

Enclosing within Single Quotes ''

The single quotation marks ('') instructs the shell to mask the meaning of all encapsulated special characters. For example, LOGNAME is a variable, and its value can be viewed with the *echo* command:

```
[user1@server1 ~]$ echo $LOGNAME
user1
```

If you encapsulate $LOGNAME within single quotes, the *echo* command will exhibit the entire string as is:

```
[user1@server1 ~]$ echo '$LOGNAME'
$LOGNAME
```

In the above example, the shell interprets the $ sign as a literal character, and that's why the *echo* command displays what is inside the enclosure, including the $ rather than the value of the variable.

Enclosing within Double Quotes ""

The double quotation marks ("") commands the shell to mask the meaning of all but the backslash (\), dollar sign ($), and single quotes (''). These three special characters retain their special meaning when they are enclosed within double quotes. Look at the following examples to understand its usage.

```
[user1@server1 ~]$ echo "$SHELL"
/bin/bash
[user1@server1 ~]$ echo "\$PWD"
$PWD
[user1@server1 ~]$ echo "'\'"
'\'
```

The above three instances confirm the use of the double quotes as a special character pair, as depicted in the outputs.

Regular Expressions

A *regular expression*, also referred to as a *regexp* or simply *regex*, is a text pattern or an expression that is matched against a string of characters in a file or supplied input in a search operation. The pattern may include a single character, multiple random characters, a range of characters, word, phrase, or an entire sentence. Any pattern containing one or more white spaces must be surrounded by quotation marks.

RHEL provides a powerful tool called *grep* (*global regular expression print* or *get regular expression and print*) to work with pattern matching in regular expressions. This tool searches the contents of one or more text files or input supplied for a match. If the expression is matched, *grep* prints every line containing that expression on the screen without changing the source content. *grep* has plenty of options and it accepts expressions in various forms.

> **EXAM TIP:** The grep command is a handy tool to extract needed information from a file or command output. The extracted information can then be redirected to a file. The sequence of the grep'ed data remains unchanged.

Let's consider the following examples to comprehend the usage of the *grep* command.

To search for the pattern "operator" in the */etc/passwd* file:

```
[user1@server1 ~]$ grep operator /etc/passwd
operator:x:11:0:operator:/root:/sbin/nologin
```

To search for the space-separated pattern "aliases and functions" in the $HOME/.bashrc file:

```
[user1@server1 ~]$ grep 'aliases and functions' .bashrc
# User specific aliases and functions
```

To search for the pattern "nologin" in the *passwd* file and exclude (-v) the lines in the output that contain this pattern. Add the -n switch to show the line numbers associated with the matched lines.

```
[user1@server1 ~]$ grep -nv nologin /etc/passwd
1:root:x:0:0:root:/root:/bin/bash
6:sync:x:5:0:sync:/sbin:/bin/sync
7:shutdown:x:6:0:shutdown:/sbin:/sbin/shutdown
8:halt:x:7:0:halt:/sbin:/sbin/halt
37:user1:x:1000:1000:user1:/home/user1:/bin/bash
38:user100:x:1001:1001::/home/user100:/bin/bash
39:user200:x:1002:1002::/home/user200:/bin/bash
40:user3:x:1010:1010::/usr/user3a:/bin/sh
```

To find any duplicate entries for the *root* user in the *passwd* file. Prepend the caret sign (^) to the pattern "root" to mark the beginning of a line.

```
[user1@server1 ~]$ grep ^root /etc/passwd
root:x:0:0:root:/root:/bin/bash
```

To identify all users in the *passwd* file with bash as their primary shell. Append the $ sign to the pattern "bash" to mark the end of a line.

```
[user1@server1 ~]$ grep bash$ /etc/passwd
root:x:0:0:root:/root:/bin/bash
user1:x:1000:1000:user1:/home/user1:/bin/bash
user100:x:1001:1001::/home/user100:/bin/bash
user200:x:1002:1002::/home/user200:/bin/bash
```

To show the entire *login.defs* file but exclude all the empty lines:

```
[user1@server1 ~]$ grep -v ^$ /etc/login.defs
```

To perform a case-insensitive search (-i) for all the lines in the */etc/bashrc* file that match the pattern "path."

```
[user1@server1 ~]$ grep -i path /etc/bashrc
    # Need to redefine pathmunge, it gets undefined at the end of /etc/profile
    pathmunge () {
        case ":${PATH}:" in
                PATH=$PATH:$1
                PATH=$1:$PATH
    unset -f pathmunge
```

To print all the lines from the */etc/lvm/lvm.conf* file that contain an exact match for a word (-w). You can use the period character (.) in the search string to match a single position. The following example searches for words in the *lvm.conf* file that begin with letters "acce" followed by exactly two characters:

```
[user1@server1 ~]$ grep -w acce.. /etc/lvm/lvm.conf
        # Commands also accept this as a prefix on volume group names.
        # This is a list of regular expressions used to accept or reject block
        # (or any character) and is preceded by 'a' to accept the path, or
        # device is rejected. Unmatching path names do not affect the accept
```

In addition to the caret (^), dollar ($), and period (.), the asterisk (*), question mark (?), square brackets ([]), and curly brackets ({}) are also used in regular expressions.

To print all the lines from the *ls* command output that include either (-E) the pattern "cron" or "ly". The pipe | character is used as an OR operator in this example. This is referred to as *alternation*. Regex allows you to add more patterns to this set if desired. For instance, if you search for three patterns, use 'pattern1|pattern2|pattern3'. The patterns must be enclosed within single or double quotes. Here is what you will issue when you want to look for the patterns "cron" and "ly" in the */etc* directory listing:

```
[user1@server1 ~]$ ls -l /etc | grep -E 'cron|ly'
-rw-r--r--.  1 root root     541 Jul 11  2022 anacrontab
drwxr-xr-x.  2 root root      21 Jan 26 16:38 cron.d
drwxr-xr-x.  2 root root       6 Mar 23  2022 cron.daily
-rw-r--r--.  1 root root       0 Jul 11  2022 cron.deny
drwxr-xr-x.  2 root root      22 Mar 23  2022 cron.hourly
drwxr-xr-x.  2 root root       6 Mar 23  2022 cron.monthly
-rw-r--r--.  1 root root     451 Mar 23  2022 crontab
drwxr-xr-x.  2 root root       6 Mar 23  2022 cron.weekly
drwxr-xr-x.  2 root root      28 Jan 26 16:39 plymouth
```

To show all the lines from the */etc/ssh/sshd_config* file but exclude (-v) the empty lines and the rows that begin with the hash (#) character (commented lines). Using the -e flag multiple times as shown below is equivalent to how "-E 'pattern1|pattern2'" was used in the above example.

```
[user1@server1 ~]$ sudo grep -ve ^$ -ve ^# /etc/ssh/sshd_config
Include /etc/ssh/sshd_config.d/*.conf
PermitRootLogin yes
AuthorizedKeysFile          .ssh/authorized_keys
Subsystem          sftp     /usr/libexec/openssh/sftp-server
```

You can combine options and employ diverse regular expression criteria to perform complex matches on input. Issue **man 7 regex** in a terminal window to learn more about regex. Also consult the manual pages of the *grep* command to view available options and other details.

Shell Startup Files

Earlier in this chapter, you used local and environment variables and learned how to modify the primary command prompt to add useful information to it. In other words, you modified the default shell environment to suit your needs. You stored the PS1 value in a shell startup file to ensure the changes are always available after you log off and log back in.

Modifications to the default shell environment can be stored in *startup* (or *initialization*) files. These files are sourced by the shell following user authentication at the time of logging in and before the command prompt appears. In addition, aliases, functions, and scripts can be added to these files as well. There are two types of startup files: *system-wide* and *per-user*.

System-wide Shell Startup Files

System-wide startup files set the general environment for all users at the time of their login to the system. These files are located in the */etc* directory and are maintained by the Linux administrator. System-wide files can be modified to include general environment settings and customizations.

Table 7-4 lists and describes system-wide startup files for bash shell users.

File	Comments
/etc/bashrc	Defines functions and aliases, sets umask for user accounts with a non-login shell, establishes the command prompt, etc. It may include settings from the shell scripts located in the /etc/profile.d directory.
/etc/profile	Sets common environment variables such as PATH, USER, LOGNAME, MAIL, HOSTNAME, HISTSIZE, and HISTCONTROL for all users, establishes umask for user accounts with a login shell, processes the shell scripts located in the /etc/profile.d directory, and so on.
/etc/profile.d	Contains scripts for bash shell users that are executed by the /etc/profile file.

Table 7-4 System-wide Startup Files

Excerpts from the *bashrc* and *profile* files and a list of files in the *profile.d* directory are displayed below:

```
[user1@server1 ~]$ head /etc/bashrc
# /etc/bashrc

# System wide functions and aliases
# Environment stuff goes in /etc/profile

# It's NOT a good idea to change this file unless you know what you
# are doing. It's much better to create a custom.sh shell script in
# /etc/profile.d/ to make custom changes to your environment, as this
# will prevent the need for merging in future updates.


[user1@server1 ~]$ head /etc/profile
# /etc/profile

# System wide environment and startup programs, for login setup
# Functions and aliases go in /etc/bashrc

# It's NOT a good idea to change this file unless you know what you
# are doing. It's much better to create a custom.sh shell script in
# /etc/profile.d/ to make custom changes to your environment, as this
# will prevent the need for merging in future updates.

[user1@server1 ~]$ ls -l /etc/profile.d/
total 100
-rw-r--r--. 1 root root  726 Aug  9 2021 bash_completion.sh
-rw-r--r--. 1 root root  196 Aug  9 2021 colorgrep.csh
-rw-r--r--. 1 root root  201 Aug  9 2021 colorgrep.sh
-rw-r--r--. 1 root root 1586 May 31 2022 colorls.csh
-rw-r--r--. 1 root root 1431 May 31 2022 colorls.sh
```

Any file in the *profile.d* directory can be edited and updated. Alternatively, you can create your own file and define any customization that you want.

Per-user Shell Startup Files

Per-user shell startup files override or modify system default definitions set by the system-wide startup files. These files may be customized by individual users to suit their needs. By default, two such files, in addition to the *.bash_logout* file, are located in the skeleton directory */etc/skel* and are copied into user home directories at the time of user creation.

You may create additional files in your home directories to set more environment variables or shell properties if required.

Table 7-5 lists and describes per-user startup files for bash shell users.

File	Comments
.bashrc	Defines functions and aliases. This file sources global definitions from the /etc/bashrc file.
.bash_profile	Sets environment variables and sources the .bashrc file to set functions and aliases.
.gnome2/	Directory that holds environment settings when GNOME desktop is started. Only available if GNOME is installed.

Table 7-5 Per-user Startup Files

Excerpts from the *.bashrc* and *.bash_profile* files are exhibited below:

```
[user1@server1 ~]$ cat .bashrc
# .bashrc

# Source global definitions
if [ -f /etc/bashrc ]; then
        . /etc/bashrc
fi

# User specific environment
if ! [[ "$PATH" =~ "$HOME/.local/bin:$HOME/bin:" ]]
then
    PATH="$HOME/.local/bin:$HOME/bin:$PATH"
fi
export PATH

........

[user1@server1 ~]$ cat .bash_profile
# .bash_profile

# Get the aliases and functions
if [ -f ~/.bashrc ]; then
        . ~/.bashrc
fi

# User specific environment and startup programs
```

The order in which the system-wide and per-user startup files are executed is important to grasp. The system runs the */etc/profile* file first, followed by *.bash_profile*, *.bashrc*, and finally the */etc/bashrc* file.

> **EXAM TIP:** For persistence, per-user settings must be added to an appropriate file.

There is also a per-user file *.bash_logout* in the user's home directory. This file is executed when the user leaves the shell or logs off. This file may be customized as well.

Chapter Summary

In this chapter, we explored the bash shell, which has numerous features that are essential for users and administrators alike. We touched upon a few that are more prevalent. These features included variable settings, command prompt customization using substitution techniques, input/output/error redirections, history expansion, command line editing, filename completion, tilde substitution, and command aliasing.

We continued to examine additional bash shell features and expanded on metacharacters, wildcard characters, pipe symbol, and quoting mechanisms. We demonstrated an example of building a pipeline by incorporating multiple pipe characters between commands.

Finally, we analyzed various system-wide and per-user shell initialization scripts that are executed upon logging in to set a user environment. These scripts may be customized for all users or individual users to suit specific needs.

Review Questions

1. What would the command *ls /cdr /usr > output* do? Assume */cdr* does not exist.
2. What is the name of the command that allows a user to define shortcuts to lengthy commands?
3. Which file typically defines the history variables for all users?
4. You have a command running that is tied to your terminal window. You want to get the command prompt back without terminating the running command. Which key combination would you press to return to the command prompt?
5. Name the three quoting mechanisms?
6. What would the command export *VAR1="I passed RHCSA"* do?
7. Name the default filename and location where user command history is stored?
8. What is the primary function of the shell in Linux?
9. What would the command *cd ~user20* do if executed as *user10*?
10. You want to change the command prompt for yourself. Where (the bash shell file) would you define it so that you get the custom command prompt whenever you log in?
11. What is the other name for the command line completion feature?
12. What is a common use of the pipe symbol?
13. Which directory location stores most, if not all, privileged commands?
14. You have a file called "?" in your home directory along with other one-letter files. What would you run to delete the "?" file only?
15. Which command would you use to display all matching lines from a text file?
16. What would the command *ls > ls.out* do?

Answers to Review Questions

1. The command provided will redirect *ls /usr* output to the specified file and *ls /cdr* (error) to the terminal.
2. The *alias* command.
3. */etc/profile* is the file where the history variables are defined for all users.
4. The Ctrl+z key combination will suspend the running program and give you access to the command prompt.
5. The three quoting mechanisms are backslash, single quotation mark, and double quotation mark.
6. The command provided will set an environment variable with the quoted string as its value.
7. The user command history is stored in *~/.bash_history* file.
8. The shell acts as an interface between a user and the system.
9. The command provided will allow *user10* to *cd* into *user20*'s home directory provided *user10* has proper access permissions.
10. You can define it in the *~/.bash_profile* file.
11. The other name for the command line completion feature is tab completion.
12. A common use of the pipe character is to receive the output of one command and pass it along to the next command as an input.
13. Privileged commands are stored in */usr/sbin* directory.
14. You can issue *rm \?* to remove the file.
15. The *grep* command.
16. The command provided will redirect the *ls* command output to the specified file.

Do-It-Yourself Challenge Labs

The following labs are useful to strengthen most of the concepts and topics learned in this chapter. It is expected that you perform the labs without external help. A step-by-step guide is not supplied, as the knowledge and skill required to implement the labs have already been disseminated in the chapter; however, hints to the relevant major topic(s) are included.

Use the lab environment built specifically for end-of-chapter labs. See sub-section "Lab Environment for End-of-Chapter Labs" in Chapter 01 "Local Installation" for details.

Lab 7-1: Customize the Command Prompt

As *user1* on *server3*, customize the primary shell prompt to display the information enclosed within the quotes "<user1@server1 in /etc >: " when this user switches into the */etc* directory. The prompt should always reflect the current directory path. Add this to the appropriate per-user startup file for permanence. (Hint: Command and Variable Substitutions).

Lab 7-2: Redirect the Standard Input, Output, and Error

As *user1* on *server3*, run the *ls* command on */etc*, */dvd*, and */var*. Have the output printed on the screen and the errors forwarded to file */tmp/ioerror*. Check both files after the command execution and analyze the results. (Hint: Input, Output, and Error Redirections).

## Chapter 08

Linux Processes and Job Scheduling

This chapter describes the following major topics:

➢ Identify and display system and user executed processes

➢ View process states and priorities

➢ Examine and change process niceness and priority

➢ Understand signals and their use in controlling processes

➢ Review job scheduling

➢ Control who can schedule jobs

➢ Schedule and manage jobs (tasks) using at

➢ Comprehend crontab and understand the syntax of crontables

➢ Schedule and manage jobs using cron

RHCSA Objectives:

19. Identify CPU/memory intensive processes, adjust process priority with renice, and kill processes
20. Adjust process scheduling
38. Schedule tasks using at and cron

A process is any program, command, or application running on the system. Every process has a unique numeric identifier, and it is managed by the kernel through its entire lifespan. It may be viewed, listed, and monitored, and can be launched at a non-default priority based on the requirement and available computing resources. A process may also be re-prioritized while it is running. A process is in one of several states at any given time during its lifecycle. A process may be tied to the terminal window where it is initiated, or it may run on the system as a service.

There are plenty of signals that may be passed to a process to accomplish various actions. These actions include hard killing a process, soft terminating it, and forcing it to restart with the same identifier.

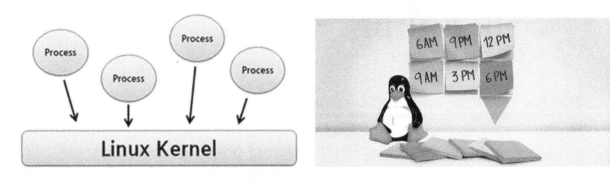

Job scheduling allows a user to schedule a command for a one-time or recurring execution in the future. A job is submitted and managed by authorized users only. All executed jobs are logged.

Processes and Priorities

A *process* is a unit for provisioning system resources. It is any program, application, or command that runs on the system. A process is created in memory when a program, application, or command is initiated. Processes are organized in a hierarchical fashion. Each process has a *parent process* (a.k.a. a *calling process*) that spawns it. A single parent process may have one or many *child processes* and passes many of its attributes to them at the time of their creation. Each process is assigned an exclusive identification number known as the *Process IDentifier* (PID), which is used by the kernel to manage and control the process through its lifecycle. When a process completes its lifespan or is terminated, this event is reported back to its parent process, and all the resources provisioned to it (cpu cycles, memory, etc.) are then freed and the PID is removed from the system.

Plenty of processes are spawned at system boot, many of which sit in the memory and wait for an event to trigger a request to use their services. These background system processes are called *daemons* and are critical to system operation.

Process States

A process changes its operating state multiple times during its lifecycle. Many factors, such as load on the processor, availability of free memory, priority of the process, and response from other applications, affect how often a process jumps from one operating state to another. It may be in a non-running condition for a while or waiting for other process to feed it information so that it can continue to run.

There are five basic process states: *running*, *sleeping*, *waiting*, *stopped*, and *zombie*. Each process is in one state at any given time. See Figure 8-1.

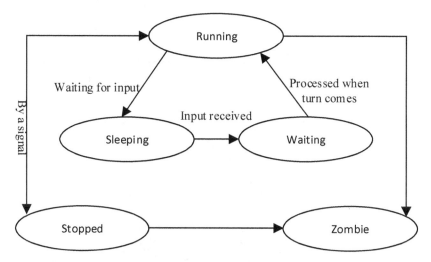

Figure 8-1 Process State Transition

Running: The process is being executed by the system CPU.

Sleeping: The process is waiting for input from a user or another process.

Waiting: The process has received the input it was waiting for and is now ready to run as soon as its turn comes.

Stopped: The process is currently halted and will not run even when its turn comes unless a signal is sent to change its behavior. (Signals are explained later in this chapter.)

Zombie: The process is dead. A zombie process exists in the process table alongside other process entries, but it takes up no resources. Its entry is retained until its parent process permits it to die. A zombie process is also called a *defunct* process.

Viewing and Monitoring Processes with ps

A system may have hundreds or thousands of processes running concurrently depending on the purpose of the system. These processes may be viewed and monitored using various native tools such as *ps* (*process status*) and *top* (*table of processes*). The *ps* command offers plentiful switches that influence its output, whereas *top* is used for real-time viewing and monitoring of processes and system resources.

Without any options or arguments, *ps* lists processes specific to the terminal where this command is issued:

```
[user1@server1 ~]$ ps
   PID TTY          TIME CMD
  2762 pts/0    00:00:00 bash
  2908 pts/0    00:00:00 ps
```

The above output returns the elementary information about processes in four columns. These processes are tied to the current terminal window. It exhibits the PID, the terminal (TTY) the

---

process spawned in, the cumulative time (TIME) the system CPU has given to the process, and the name of the actual command or program (CMD) being executed.

Some common options that can be used with the *ps* command to generate detailed reports include -e (every), -f (full-format), -F (extra full-format), and -l (long format). A combination of -e, -F, and -l (**ps -eFl**) produces a very thorough process report, however, that much detail may not be needed in most situations. Other common options such as --forest and -x will report the output in tree-like hierarchy and include the daemon processes as well. Check the manual pages of the command for additional options and their usage.

Here are a few sample lines from the beginning and end of the output when *ps* is executed with -e and -f flags on the system.

```
[user1@server1 ~]$ ps -ef
UID          PID     PPID  C STIME TTY          TIME CMD
root           1        0  0 12:28 ?        00:00:02 /usr/lib/systemd/systemd
root           2        0  0 12:28 ?        00:00:00 [kthreadd]
root           3        2  0 12:28 ?        00:00:00 [rcu_gp]
root           4        2  0 12:28 ?        00:00:00 [rcu_par_gp]
root           5        2  0 12:28 ?        00:00:00 [netns]
root           7        2  0 12:28 ?        00:00:00 [kworker/0:0H-events_high
root           9        2  0 12:28 ?        00:00:11 [kworker/0:1H-events_high
root          10        2  0 12:28 ?        00:00:00 [mm_percpu_wq]
root          12        2  0 12:28 ?        00:00:00 [rcu_tasks_kthre]
```

This output is disseminated across eight columns showing details about every process running on the system. Table 8-1 describes the content type of each column.

Column	Description
UID	User ID or name of the process owner
PID	Process ID of the process
PPID	Process ID of the parent process
C	CPU utilization for the process
STIME	Process start date or time
TTY	The controlling terminal the process was started on. "Console" represents the system console and "?" represents a daemon process.
TIME	Aggregated execution time for a process
CMD	The command or program name

Table 8-1 ps Command Output Description

The *ps* output above pinpoints several daemon processes running in the background. These processes are not associated with any terminal, which is why there is a ? in the TTY column. Notice the PID and PPID numbers. The smaller the number, the earlier it is started. The process with PID 0 is started first at system boot, followed by the process with PID 1, and so on. Each PID has an associated PPID in column 3. The owner of each process is exposed in the UID column along with the name of the command or program under CMD.

Information for each running process is recorded and maintained in the */proc* file system, which *ps* and many other commands reference to acquire desired data for viewing.

The *ps* command output may be customized to view only the desired columns. For instance, if you want to produce an output with the command name in column 1, PID in column 2, PPID in column 3, and owner name in column 4, run it as follows:

```
[user1@server1 ~]$ ps -o comm,pid,ppid,user
COMMAND              PID    PPID USER
bash                2762    2761 user1
ps                  2913    2762 user1
```

Make sure the -o option is specified for a user-defined format and there is no white space before or after the column names. You can add or remove columns and switch their positions as needed.

Another switch to look at with the *ps* command is -C (command list). This option is used to list only those processes that match the specified command name. For example, run it to check how many *sshd* processes are currently running on the system:

```
[user1@server1 ~]$ ps -C sshd
   PID TTY          TIME CMD
   873 ?        00:00:00 sshd
  1254 ?        00:00:00 sshd
  1668 ?        00:00:05 sshd
```

The output exhibits multiple background *sshd* processes.

Viewing and Monitoring Processes with top

The other popular tool for viewing process information is the *top* command. This command displays statistics in real time and continuously, and may be helpful in identifying possible performance issues on the system. A sample of a running *top* session is shown below:

```
[user1@server1 ~]$ top
top - 19:44:20 up  7:15,  1 user,  load average: 0.00, 0.01, 0.00
Tasks: 170 total,   1 running, 169 sleeping,   0 stopped,   0 zombie
%Cpu(s):  0.0 us,  0.0 sy,  0.0 ni, 99.8 id,  0.0 wa,  0.0 hi,  0.2 si,  0.0 st
MiB Mem :   1770.9 total,    755.9 free,    662.0 used,    516.4 buff/cache
MiB Swap:   2048.0 total,   2048.0 free,      0.0 used.   1108.9 avail Mem

   PID USER      PR  NI    VIRT    RES    SHR S  %CPU  %MEM     TIME+ COMMAND
   864 root      20   0  474112  20520  17796 S   0.3   1.1   0:07.78 NetworkMan
  1668 root      20   0   19352   7420   5144 S   0.3   0.4   0:05.39 sshd
  2911 root      20   0       0      0      0 I   0.3   0.0   0:00.05 kworker/0:
  2916 user1     20   0  225916   4176   3552 R   0.3   0.2   0:00.02 top
     1 root      20   0  106320  16052  10468 S   0.0   0.9   0:02.76 systemd
     2 root      20   0       0      0      0 S   0.0   0.0   0:00.14 kthreadd
     3 root       0 -20       0      0      0 I   0.0   0.0   0:00.00 rcu_gp
     4 root       0 -20       0      0      0 I   0.0   0.0   0:00.00 rcu_par_gp
     5 root       0 -20       0      0      0 I   0.0   0.0   0:00.00 netns
```

Press q or Ctrl+c to quit.

The *top* output may be divided into two major portions: the summary portion and the tasks portion. The summary area spreads over the first five lines of the output, and it shows the information as follows:

Line 1: Indicates the system uptime, number of users logged in, and system load averages over the period of 1, 5, and 15 minutes. See the description for the *uptime* command output in Chapter 02 "Initial Interaction with the System".

Line 2: Displays the task (or process) information, which includes the total number of tasks running on the system and how many of them are in running, sleeping, stopped, and zombie states.

Line 3: Shows the processor usage that includes the CPU time in percentage spent in running user and system processes, in idling and waiting, and so on.

Line 4: Depicts memory utilization that includes the total amount of memory allocated to the system, and how much of it is free, in use, and allocated for use in buffering and caching.

Line 5: Exhibits swap (virtual memory) usage that includes the total amount of swap allocated to the system, and how much of it is free and in use. The "avail Mem" shows an estimate of the amount of memory available for starting new processes without using the swap.

The second major portion in the *top* command output showcases the details for each process in 12 columns as described below:

Columns 1 and 2: Pinpoint the process identifier (PID) and owner (USER)

Columns 3 and 4: Display the process priority (PR) and nice value (NI)

Columns 5 and 6: Depict amounts of virtual memory (VIRT) and non-swapped resident memory (RES) in use

Column 7: Shows the amount of shareable memory available to the process (SHR)

Column 8: Represents the process status (S)

Columns 9 and 10: Express the CPU (%CPU) and memory (%MEM) utilization

Column 11: Exhibits the CPU time in hundredths of a second (TIME+)

Column 12: Identifies the process name (COMMAND)

While in *top*, you can press "o" to re-sequence the process list, "f" to add or remove fields, "F" to select the field to sort on, and "h" to obtain help. *top* is highly customizable. See the command's manual pages for details.

Listing a Specific Process

Though the tools discussed so far provide a lot of information about processes including their PIDs, Linux also offers the *pidof* and *pgrep* commands to list only the PID of a specific process. These commands have a few switches available to modify their behavior; however, their most elementary use is to pass a process name as an argument to view its PID. For instance, to list the PID of the *rsyslogd* daemon, use either of the following:

```
[user1@server1 ~]$ pidof rsyslogd
744
[user1@server1 ~]$ pgrep rsyslogd
744
```

Both commands produce an identical result if used without an option.

Listing Processes by User and Group Ownership

A process can be listed by its ownership or owning group. You can use the *ps* command for this purpose. For example, to list all processes owned by *user1*, specify the -U (or -u) option with the command and then the username:

```
[user1@server1 ~]$ ps -U user1
   PID TTY          TIME CMD
  2762 pts/0    00:00:00 bash
  2922 pts/0    00:00:00 ps
```

The command lists the PID, TTY, TIME, and CMD name for all the processes owned by *user1*. You can specify the -G (or -g) option instead and the name of an owning group to print processes associated with that group only:

```
[user1@server1 ~]$ ps -G root
   PID TTY          TIME CMD
     1 ?        00:00:02 systemd
     2 ?        00:00:00 kthreadd
     3 ?        00:00:00 rcu_gp
     4 ?        00:00:00 rcu_par_gp
     5 ?        00:00:00 netns
```

The above output reveals all the running processes with *root* as their owning group.

Understanding Process Niceness and Priority

Linux is a multitasking operating system. It runs numerous processes on a single processor core by giving each process a slice of time. The process scheduler on the system performs rapid switching of processes, giving the notion of concurrent execution of multiple processes.

A process is spawned at a certain priority, which is established at initiation based on a numeric value called *niceness* (a.k.a. a *nice* value). There are 40 niceness values, with -20 being the highest or the most favorable to the process, and +19 being the lowest or the least favorable to the process. Most system-started processes run at the default niceness of 0. A higher niceness lowers the execution priority of a process, and a lower niceness increases it. In other words, a process running at a higher priority gets more CPU attention. A child process inherits the niceness of its calling process in its priority calculation. Though programs are normally run at the default niceness, you can choose to initiate them at a different niceness to adjust their priority based on urgency, importance, or system load. As a normal user, you can only make your processes nicer, but the *root* user can raise or lower the niceness of any process.

RHEL provides the *nice* command to launch a program at a non-default priority and the *renice* command to alter the priority of a running program.

The default niceness can be viewed with the *nice* command as follows:

```
[user1@server1 ~]$ nice
0
```

The *ps* command with the -l option along with the -ef options can be used to list priority (PRI, column 7) and niceness (NI, column 8) for all processes:

```
[user1@server1 ~]$ ps -efl
F S UID          PID    PPID  C PRI   NI ADDR SZ WCHAN   STIME TTY           TIME CMD
4 S root           1       0  0  80    0 -  26580 -      12:28 ?       00:00:02 /usr/lib
1 S root           2       0  0  80    0 -      0 -      12:28 ?       00:00:00 [kthread
1 I root           3       2  0  60  -20 -      0 -      12:28 ?       00:00:00 [rcu_gp]
1 I root           4       2  0  60  -20 -      0 -      12:28 ?       00:00:00 [rcu_par
1 I root           5       2  0  60  -20 -      0 -      12:28 ?       00:00:00 [netns]
```

The output indicates that the first two processes are running at the default niceness of 0 and the next three at the highest niceness of -20. These values are used by the process scheduler to adjust the execution time of the processes on the CPU. The *ps* command maintains an internal mapping between niceness levels and priorities. A niceness of 0 (NI column) corresponds to priority 80 (PR column), and a niceness of -20 (NI column) maps to priority 60 (PR column).

In contrast to the niceness-priority mapping that the ps command uses, the top command displays it differently. For a 0-80 ps mapping, the top session will report it 0-20. Likewise, ps' (-20)-60 will be the same as the top's (-20)-0.

Exercise 8-1: Start Processes at Non-Default Priorities

This exercise should be done on *server1* as *user1* with *sudo* where required.

You will need two terminal sessions to perform this exercise. Let's call them Terminal 1 and Terminal 2.

In this exercise, you will launch the *top* program three times and observe how the *ps* command reports the priority and niceness values. You will execute the program the first time at the default priority, the second time at a lower priority, and the third time at a higher priority. You will control which priority to run the program at by specifying a niceness value with the *nice* command. You will verify the new niceness and priority after each execution of the *top* session.

1. Run the *top* command at the default priority/niceness in Terminal 1:

    ```
    [user1@server1 ~]$ top
    ```

2. Check the priority and niceness for the *top* command in Terminal 2 using the *ps* command:

    ```
    [user1@server1 ~]$ ps -efl | grep top
    0 S user1        3051    2762  0  80    0 -  56479 do_sel 20:32 pts/0    00:00:00 top
    ```

The command reports the values as 80 and 0, which are the defaults.

3. Terminate the *top* session in Terminal 1 by pressing the letter *q* and relaunch it at a lower priority with a nice value of +2:

    ```
    [user1@server1 ~]$ nice -n 2 top
    ```

4. Check the priority and niceness for the *top* command in Terminal 2 using the *ps* command:

    ```
    [user1@server1 ~]$ ps -efl | grep top
    0 S user1        3056    2762  0  82    2 -  56479 do_sel 20:33 pts/0    00:00:00 top
    ```

The command reports the new values as 82 and 2.

---

5. Terminate the *top* session in Terminal 1 by pressing the letter *q* and relaunch it at a higher priority with a nice value of -10. Use *sudo* for *root* privileges.

```
[user1@server1 ~]$ sudo nice -n -10 top
```

6. Check the priority and niceness for the *top* command in Terminal 2 using the *ps* command:

```
[user1@server1 ~]$ ps -efl | grep top
4 S root         3064    3062  0  70 -10 - 56479 -        20:34 pts/0     00:00:00 top
```

As you can see, the process is running at a higher priority (70) with a nice value of -10. Terminate the *top* session by pressing the letter *q*.

This concludes the exercise.

Exercise 8-2: Alter Process Priorities

This exercise should be done on *server1* as *user1* with *sudo* where required.

You will need two terminal sessions to perform this exercise. Let's call them Terminal 1 and Terminal 2.

In this exercise, you will launch the *top* program at the default priority and alter its priority without restarting it. You will set a new priority by specifying a niceness value with the *renice* command. You will verify the new niceness and priority after each execution of the *top* session.

1. Run the *top* command at the default priority/niceness in Terminal 1:

```
[user1@server1 ~]$ top
```

2. Check the priority and niceness for the *top* command in Terminal 2 using the *ps* command:

```
[user1@server1 ~]$ ps -efl | grep top
0 S user1        3079    2762  0  80   0 - 56479 do_sel 20:35 pts/0     00:00:00 top
```

The command reports the values as 80 and 0, which are the defaults.

3. While the *top* session is running in Terminal 1, increase its priority by renicing it to -5 in Terminal 2. Use the command substitution to get the PID of *top*. Prepend the *renice* command by *sudo*.

```
[user1@server1 ~]$ sudo renice -n -5 $(pidof top)
3079 (process ID) old priority 0, new priority -5
```

The output indicates the old (0) and new (-5) priorities for the process.

4. Validate the above change with *ps*. Focus on columns 7 and 8.

```
[user1@server1 ~]$ ps -efl | grep top
0 S user1        3079    2762  0  75  -5 - 56479 do_sel 20:35 pts/0     00:00:00 top
```

As you can see, the process is now running at a higher priority (75) with a nice value of -5.

---

5. Repeat the above but set the process to run at a lower priority by renicing it to 8:

```
[user1@server1 ~]$ sudo renice -n 8 $(pidof top)
3079 (process ID) old priority -5, new priority 8
```

The output indicates the old (-5) and new (8) priorities for the process.

6. Validate the above change with *ps*. Focus on columns 7 and 8.

```
[user1@server1 ~]$ ps -efl | grep top
0 S user1       3079    2762  0  88   8 - 56479 do_sel 20:35 pts/0    00:00:00 top
```

The process is reported to now running at a lower priority (88) with niceness 8.

This concludes the exercise.

Controlling Processes with Signals

A system may have hundreds or thousands of processes running on it. Sometimes it becomes necessary to alert a process of an event. This is done by sending a control signal to the process. Processes may use signals to alert each other as well. The receiving process halts its execution as soon as it gets the signal and takes an appropriate action as per the instructions enclosed in the signal. The instructions may include terminating the process gracefully, killing it abruptly, or forcing it to re-read its configuration.

There are plentiful signals available for use, but only a few are common. Each signal is associated with a unique numeric identifier, a name, and an action. A list of available signals can be viewed with the *kill* command using the -l option:

```
[user1@server1 ~]$ kill -l
 1) SIGHUP        2) SIGINT        3) SIGQUIT       4) SIGILL        5) SIGTRAP
 6) SIGABRT       7) SIGBUS        8) SIGFPE        9) SIGKILL      10) SIGUSR1
11) SIGSEGV      12) SIGUSR2      13) SIGPIPE      14) SIGALRM      15) SIGTERM
16) SIGSTKFLT    17) SIGCHLD      18) SIGCONT      19) SIGSTOP      20) SIGTSTP
21) SIGTTIN      22) SIGTTOU      23) SIGURG       24) SIGXCPU      25) SIGXFSZ
26) SIGVTALRM    27) SIGPROF      28) SIGWINCH     29) SIGIO        30) SIGPWR
31) SIGSYS       34) SIGRTMIN     35) SIGRTMIN+1   36) SIGRTMIN+2   37) SIGRTMIN+3
38) SIGRTMIN+4   39) SIGRTMIN+5   40) SIGRTMIN+6   41) SIGRTMIN+7   42) SIGRTMIN+8
43) SIGRTMIN+9   44) SIGRTMIN+10  45) SIGRTMIN+11  46) SIGRTMIN+12  47) SIGRTMIN+13
48) SIGRTMIN+14  49) SIGRTMIN+15  50) SIGRTMAX-14  51) SIGRTMAX-13  52) SIGRTMAX-12
53) SIGRTMAX-11  54) SIGRTMAX-10  55) SIGRTMAX-9   56) SIGRTMAX-8   57) SIGRTMAX-7
58) SIGRTMAX-6   59) SIGRTMAX-5   60) SIGRTMAX-4   61) SIGRTMAX-3   62) SIGRTMAX-2
63) SIGRTMAX-1   64) SIGRTMAX
```

The output returns 64 signals available for process-to-process and user-to-process communication. Table 8-2 describes the control signals that are most often used.

Signal Number	Signal Name	Action
1	SIGHUP	Hang up signal causes a process to disconnect itself from a closed terminal that it was tied to. Also used to instruct a running daemon to re-read its configuration without a restart.

Signal Number	Signal Name	Action
2	SIGINT	The ^c (Ctrl+c) signal issued on the controlling terminal to interrupt the execution of a process.
9	SIGKILL	Terminates a process abruptly
15	SIGTERM	Sends a soft termination signal to stop a process in an orderly fashion. This is the default signal if none is specified with the command.
18	SIGCONT	Same as using the bg command to resume
19	SIGSTOP	Same as using Ctrl+z to suspend a job
20	SIGTSTP	Same as using the fg command

Table 8-2 Control Signals

The commands used to pass a signal to a process are *kill* and *pkill*. These commands are usually used to terminate a process. Ordinary users can kill processes that they own, while the *root* user privilege is needed to kill any process on the system.

The *kill* command requires one or more PIDs, and the *pkill* command requires one or more process names to send a signal to. You can specify a non-default signal name or number with either utility.

Let's look at a few examples to understand the usage of these tools.

To pass the soft termination signal to the *crond* daemon, use either of the following:

```
[user1@server1 ~]$ sudo pkill crond
[user1@server1 ~]$ sudo kill $(pidof crond)
```

The *pidof* command in the above example is used to discover the PID of the *crond* process using command substitution and it is then passed to the *kill* command for termination. You may also use the *pgrep* command to determine the PID of a process, as demonstrated in the next example. Use **ps -ef | grep crond** to confirm the termination.

Using the *pkill* or *kill* command without specifying a signal name or number sends the default signal of 15 to the process. This signal may or not terminate the process. Some processes ignore the soft termination signal as they might be in a waiting state. These processes may be ended forcefully using signal 9 in any of the following ways:

```
[user1@server1 ~]$ sudo pkill -9 crond
[user1@server1 ~]$ sudo pkill -s SIGKILL crond
[user1@server1 ~]$ sudo kill -9 $(pgrep crond)
```

You may run the *killall* command to terminate all processes that match a criterion. Here is how you can use this command to kill all *crond* processes (assuming there are many of them running):

```
[user1@server1 ~]$ sudo killall crond
```

There are plenty of options available with the *kill*, *killall*, *pkill*, *pgrep*, and *pidof* commands. Consult respective manual pages for more details.

Job Scheduling

Job scheduling allows a user to submit a command for execution at a specified time in the future. The execution of the command could be one time or periodic based on a pre-determined time schedule. A one-time execution may be scheduled for an activity that needs to be performed at a time of low system usage. One example of such an activity would be the execution of a lengthy shell program. In contrast, a recurring activity could include creating a compressed archive, trimming log files, monitoring the system, running a custom script, or removing unwanted files from the system.

Job scheduling and execution is taken care of by two service daemons: *atd* and *crond*. While *atd* manages the jobs scheduled to run one time in the future, *crond* is responsible for running jobs repetitively at pre-specified times. At startup, this daemon reads the schedules in files located in the */var/spool/cron* and */etc/cron.d* directories, and loads them in the memory for on-time execution. It scans these files at short intervals and updates the in-memory schedules to reflect any modifications. This daemon runs a job at its scheduled time only and does not entertain any missed jobs. In contrast, the *atd* daemon retries a missed job at the same time next day. For any additions or changes, neither daemon needs a restart.

Controlling User Access

By default, all users are allowed to schedule jobs using the at and cron services. However, this access may be controlled and restricted to specific users only. This can be done by listing users in the allow or deny file located in the */etc* directory for either service. These files are named *at.allow* and *at.deny* for the at service and *cron.allow* and *cron.deny* for the cron service.

The syntax for the four files is identical. You only need to list usernames that are to be allowed or denied access to these scheduling tools. Each file takes one username per line. The *root* user is always permitted; it is affected neither by the existence or non-existence of these files nor by the inclusion or exclusion of its entry in these files.

Table 8-3 shows various combinations and their impact on user access.

at.allow / cron.allow	at.deny / cron.deny	Impact
Exists, and contains user entries	Existence does not matter	All users listed in allow files are permitted
Exists, but is empty	Existence does not matter	No users are permitted
Does not exist	Exists, and contains user entries	All users, other than those listed in deny files, are permitted
Does not exist	Exists, but is empty	All users are permitted
Does not exist	Does not exist	No users are permitted

Table 8-3 User Access Restrictions to Scheduling Tools

By default, the *deny* files exist and are empty, and the *allow* files are non-existent. This opens up full access to using both tools for all users.

EXAM TIP: One username is entered per line entry in an appropriate allow or deny file.

The following message appears if an unauthorized user attempts to execute *at*:

```
You do not have permission to use at.
```

And the following warning is displayed for unauthorized access attempt to the cron service:

```
You (user1) are not allowed to use this program (crontab)
See crontab(1) for more information
```

To generate the denial messages, you need to place entries for *user1* in the *deny* files.

Scheduler Log File

All activities for *atd* and *crond* services are logged to the */var/log/cron* file. Information such as the time of activity, hostname, process name and PID, owner, and a message for each invocation is captured. The file also keeps track of other events for the *crond* service such as the service start time and any delays. A few sample entries from the log file are shown below:

```
[user1@server1 ~]$ sudo cat /var/log/cron
Jan 29 12:29:12 server1 crond[950]: (CRON) STARTUP (1.5.7)
Jan 29 12:29:12 server1 crond[950]: (CRON) INFO (Syslog will be used inste
.)
Jan 29 12:29:12 server1 crond[950]: (CRON) INFO (RANDOM_DELAY will be scal
 10% if used.)
Jan 29 12:29:12 server1 crond[950]: (CRON) INFO (running with inotify supp
Jan 29 13:01:01 server1 CROND[1859]: (root) CMD (run-parts /etc/cron.hourl
Jan 29 13:01:01 server1 run-parts[1859]: (/etc/cron.hourly) starting 0anac
Jan 29 13:01:01 server1 anacron[1872]: Anacron started on 2023-01-29
```

The truncated output shows some past entries from the file. You need the *root* user privilege to be able to read the file content.

Using at

The *at* command is used to schedule a one-time execution of a program in the future. All submitted jobs are spooled in the */var/spool/at* directory and executed by the *atd* daemon at the specified time. Each submitted job will have a file created containing the settings for establishing the user's shell environment to ensure a successful execution. This file also includes the name of the command or program to be run. There is no need to restart the daemon after a job submission.

There are multiple ways and formats for expressing the time with *at*. Some examples are:

at 1:15am	(executes the task at the next 1:15 a.m.)
at noon	(executes the task at 12:00 p.m.)
at 23:45	(executes the task at 11:45 p.m.)
at midnight	(executes the task at 12:00 a.m.)
at 17:05 tomorrow	(executes the task at 5:05 p.m. on the next day)
at now + 5 hours	(executes the task 5 hours from now. We can specify minutes, days, or weeks in place of hours)
at 3:00 10/15/23	(executes the task at 3:00 a.m. on October 15, 2023)

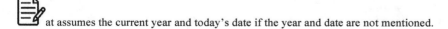 at assumes the current year and today's date if the year and date are not mentioned.

You may supply a filename with the *at* command using the -f option. The command will execute that file at the specified time. For instance, the following will run */home/user1/.bash_profile* file for *user1* 2 hours from now:

```
[user1@server1 ~]$ at -f ~/.bash_profile now + 2 hours
warning: commands will be executed using /bin/sh
job 1 at Sun Jan 29 22:47:00 2023
```

The above will be executed as scheduled and will have an entry placed for it in the log file.

Exercise 8-3: Submit, View, List, and Erase an at Job

This exercise should be done on *server1* as *user1*.

In this exercise, you will submit an at job as *user1* to run the *date* command at 11:30 p.m. on March 31, 2023, and have the output and any error messages generated redirected to the */tmp/date.out* file. You will list the submitted job, exhibit its contents for verification, and then remove the job.

1. Run the *at* command and specify the correct execution time and date for the job. Type the entire command at the first at> prompt and press Enter. Press Ctrl+d at the second at> prompt to complete the job submission and return to the shell prompt.

    ```
    [user1@server1 ~]$ at 11:30pm 3/31/23
    warning: commands will be executed using /bin/sh
    at> data &> /tmp/date.out
    at> <EOT>
    job 2 at Fri Mar 31 23:30:00 2023
    ```

The system assigned job ID 2 to it, and the output also pinpoints the job's execution time.

2. List the job file created in the */var/spool/at* directory:

    ```
    [user1@server1 ~]$ sudo ls -l /var/spool/at/
    total 4
    -rwx------. 1 user1 user1 2757 Jan 29 20:48 a0000201ab53d2
    ```

3. List the spooled job with the *at* command. You may alternatively use **atq** to list it.

    ```
    [user1@server1 ~]$ at -l
    2       Fri Mar 31 23:30:00 2023 a user1
    ```

4. Display the content of this file with the *at* command and specify the job ID:

    ```
    [user1@server1 ~]$ at -c 2
    #!/bin/sh
    # atrun uid=1000 gid=1000
    # mail root 0
    umask 22
    SHELL=/bin/bash; export SHELL
    HISTCONTROL=ignoredups; export HISTCONTROL
    HISTSIZE=1000; export HISTSIZE
    HOSTNAME=server1.example.com; export HOSTNAME
    PWD=/home/user1; export PWD
    LOGNAME=user1; export LOGNAME
    ```

5. Remove the spooled job with the *at* command by specifying its job ID. You may alternatively run **atrm 2** to delete it.

```
[user1@server1 ~]$ at -d 2
```

This should erase the job file from the */var/spool/at* directory. You can confirm the deletion by running **atq** or **at -l**.

Using crontab

Using the *crontab* command is the other method for scheduling tasks for running in the future. Unlike *atd*, *crond* executes cron jobs on a regular basis if they comply with the format defined in the */etc/crontab* file. Crontables (another name for crontab files) are located in the */var/spool/cron* directory. Each authorized user with a scheduled job has a file matching their login name in this directory.

For example, the crontable for *user1* would be */var/spool/cron/user1*. The other two locations where system crontables can be stored are the */etc/crontab* file and the */etc/cron.d* directory; however, only the *root* user is allowed to create, modify, and delete them. The *crond* daemon scans entries in the files at the three locations to determine job execution schedules. The daemon runs the commands or programs at the specified time and adds a log entry to the */var/log/cron* file for each invocation. There is no need to restart the daemon after submitting a new or modifying an existing cron job.

The *crontab* command is used to edit (-e), list (-l), and remove (-r) crontables. The -u option is also available for users who wish to modify a different user's crontable, provided they are allowed to do so and the other user is listed in the *cron.allow* file. The *root* user can also use the -u flag to alter other users' crontables even if the affected users are not listed in the *allow* file. By default, crontab files are opened in the *vim* editor when the *crontab* command is issued to edit them.

Syntax of User Crontables

The */etc/crontab* file specifies the syntax that each user cron job must comply with in order for *crond* to interpret and execute it successfully. Based on this structure, each line in a user crontable with an entry for a scheduled job is comprised of six fields. Fields 1 to 5 are for the schedule, field 6 may contain the login name of the executing user, and the rest for the command or program to be executed. See Figure 8-2 for the syntax.

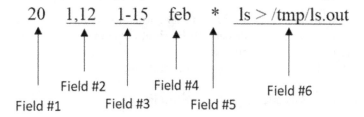

Figure 8-2 Syntax of Crontables

A description of each field is provided in Table 8-4.

Field	Field Content	Description
1	Minute of the hour	Valid values are 0 (the exact hour) to 59. This field can have one specific value as in field 1, multiple comma-separated values as in field 2, a range of values as in field 3, a mix of fields 2 and 3 (1-5,6-19), or an * representing every minute of the hour as in field 5.
2	Hour of the day	Valid values are 0 (midnight) to 23. Same usage applies as described for field 1.
3	Day of the month	Valid values are 1 to 31. Same usage applies as described for field 1.
4	Month of the year	Valid values are 1 to 12 or jan to dec. Same usage applies as described for field 1.
5	Day of the week	Valid values are 0 to 7 or sun to sat, with 0 and 7 representing Sunday, 1 representing Monday, and so on. Same usage applies as described for field 1.
6	Command or program to execute	Specifies the full path name of the command or program to be executed, along with any options or arguments that it requires.

Table 8-4 Crontable Syntax Explained

Furthermore, step values may be used with * and ranges in the crontables using the forward slash character (/). Step values allow the number of skips for a given value. For example, */2 in the minute field would mean every second minute, */3 would mean every third minute, 0-59/4 would mean every fourth minute, and so on. Step values are also supported in the same format in fields 2 to 5.

EXAM TIP: Make sure you understand and memorize the order of the fields defined in crontables.

Consult the manual pages of the *crontab* configuration file (**man 5 crontab**) for more details on the syntax.

Exercise 8-4: Add, List, and Erase a Cron Job

This exercise should be done on *server1* as *user1* with *sudo* where required.

For this exercise, assume that all users are currently denied access to cron.

In this exercise, you will submit a cron job as *user1* to echo "Hello, this is a cron test.". You will schedule this command to execute at every fifth minute past the hour between 10:00 a.m. and 11:00 a.m. on the fifth and twentieth of every month. You will have the output redirected to the */tmp/hello.out* file, list the cron entry, and then remove it.

1. Edit the */etc/cron.allow* file and add *user1* to it:

   ```
   [user1@server1 ~]$ sudo vim /etc/cron.allow
   user1
   ```

2. Open the crontable and append the following schedule to it. Save the file when done and exit out of the editor.

```
[user1@server1 ~]$ crontab -e
*/5 10-11 5,20 * * echo "Hello, this is a cron test." > /tmp/hello.out
```

3. Check for the presence of a new file by the name *user1* under the */var/spool/cron* directory:

```
[user1@server1 ~]$ sudo ls -l /var/spool/cron/
```

4. List the contents of the crontable:

```
[user1@server1 ~]$ crontab -l
*/5 10-11 5,20 * * echo "Hello, this is a cron test." > /tmp/hello.out
```

5. Remove the crontable and confirm the deletion:

```
[user1@server1 ~]$ crontab -r
[user1@server1 ~]$ crontab -l
no crontab for user1
```

Do not run **crontab -r** if you do not wish to remove the crontab file. Instead, edit the file with **crontab -e** and just erase the entry.

Chapter Summary

This chapter discussed two major topics: process management and job scheduling.

It is vital for users, developers, and administrators alike to have a strong grasp on running processes, resources they are consuming, process owners, process execution priorities, etc. They should learn how to list processes in a variety of ways. We looked at the five states a process is in at any given time during its lifecycle. We examined the concepts of niceness and reniceness for increasing or decreasing a process's priority. We analyzed some of the many available signals and looked at how they could be passed to running processes to perform an action on them.

The second and the last topic talked about submitting and managing tasks to run in the future one time or on a recurring basis. We learned about the service daemons that handle the task execution and the control files where we list users who can or cannot submit jobs. We looked at the log file that stores information for all executed jobs. We reviewed the syntax of the crontable and examined a variety of date/time formats for use with both at and cron job submission. We performed two exercises to gain a grasp on their usage.

Review Questions

1. The default location to send application error messages is the system log file. True or False?
2. What are the five process states?
3. Signal 9 is used for a hard termination of a process. True or False?
4. You must restart the *crond* service after modifying the */etc/crontab* file. True or False?
5. What are the background service processes normally referred to in Linux?
6. What is the default nice value?
7. The parent process gets the nice value of its child process. True or False?
8. When would the *cron* daemon execute a job that is submitted as */10 * 2-6 6 * /home/user1/script1.sh*?
9. What is the other command besides *ps* to view running processes?

10. Every process that runs on the system has a unique identifier called UID. True or False?
11. Why would you use the *renice* command?
12. What are the two commands to list the PID of a specific process?
13. By default the *.allow* files exist. True or False?
14. Where do the scheduling daemons store log information of executed jobs?
15. Which user does not have to be explicitly defined in either *.allow* or *.deny* file to run the at and cron jobs?
16. When would the *at* command execute a job that is submitted as at 01:00 12/12/2020?
17. What are the two commands that you can use to terminate a process?
18. What is the directory location where user crontab files are stored?
19. What would the *nice* command display without any options or arguments?
20. Which command can be used to edit crontables?

Answers to Review Questions

1. False. The default location is the user screen where the program is initiated.
2. The five process states are running, sleeping, waiting, stopped, and zombie.
3. True.
4. False. The *crond* daemon does not need a restart after a crontable is modified.
5. The background service processes are referred to as daemons.
6. The default nice value is zero.
7. False. The child process inherits its parent's niceness.
8. The *cron* daemon will run the script every tenth minute past the hour on the 2nd, 3rd, 4th, 5th, and 6th day of every sixth month.
9. The *top* command.
10. False. It is called the PID.
11. The *renice* command is used to change the niceness of a running process.
12. The *pidof* and *pgrep* commands.
13. False. By default, the *.deny* files exist.
14. The scheduling daemons store log information of executed jobs in the */var/log/cron* file.
15. The *root* user.
16. The *at* command will run it at 1am on December 12, 2020.
17. The *kill* and *pkill* commands.
18. The user crontab files are stored in the */var/spool/cron* directory.
19. The *nice* command displays the default nice value when executed without any options.
20. You can use the *crontab* command with the -e option to edit crontables.

Do-It-Yourself Challenge Labs

The following labs are useful to strengthen most of the concepts and topics learned in this chapter. It is expected that you perform the labs without external help. A step-by-step guide is not supplied, as the knowledge and skill required to implement the labs have already been disseminated in the chapter; however, hints to the relevant major topic(s) are included.

Use the lab environment built specifically for end-of-chapter labs. See sub-section "Lab Environment for End-of-Chapter Labs" in Chapter 01 "Local Installation" for details.

Lab 8-1: Nice and Renice a Process

As *user1* with *sudo* on *server3*, open two terminal sessions. Run the *top* command in terminal 1. Run the *pgrep* or *ps* command in terminal 2 to determine the PID and the nice value of *top*. Stop *top* on terminal 1 and relaunch at a lower priority (+8). Confirm the new nice value of the process in terminal 2. Issue the *renice* command in terminal 2 and increase the priority of *top* to -10, and validate. (Hint: Processes and Priorities).

Lab 8-2: Configure a User Crontab File

As *user1* on *server3*, run the *tty* and *date* commands to determine the terminal file (assume */dev/pts/1*) and current system time. Create a cron entry to display "Hello World" on the terminal. Schedule *echo "Hello World" > /dev/tty/1* to run 3 minutes from the current system time. As *root*, ensure *user1* can schedule cron jobs. (Hint: Job Scheduling).

## Chapter 09

Basic Package Management

This chapter describes the following major topics:

➢ Overview of Red Hat packages, naming, and management tools
➢ Package dependency and database
➢ Query, install, upgrade, freshen, overwrite, and remove packages
➢ Extract package files from installable package
➢ Validate package integrity and authenticity
➢ View GPG keys and verify package attributes
➢ Manage packages using the rpm command

RHCSA Objectives:

42. Install and update software packages from Red Hat Network, a remote
repository, or from the local file system (part of this objective is also
covered in Chapter 10)

The Red Hat software management system is known as RPM Package Manager (RPM). RPM also refers to one or more files that are packaged together in a special format and stored in files with the .rpm extension. These rpm files (also called rpms, rpm packages, or packages) are manipulated by the RPM package management system. Each package included in and available for RHEL is in this file format. Packages have meaningful names and contain necessary files, as well as metadata structures such as ownership, permissions, and directory location for each included file. Packages may be downloaded and saved locally or on a network share for quick access, and they may have dependencies over files or other packages. In other words, a package may require the presence of additional files, another package, or a group of packages in order to be installed successfully and operate properly. Once a package has been installed and its metadata information stored in a package database, future attempts to update the package are reflected in the metadata as well.

RHEL provides a powerful tool for the installation and administration of RPM packages. The rpm command is flexible and offers multitude of options and subcommands to perform functions such as querying, installing, upgrading, freshening, removing, and decompressing packages, and validating package integrity and authenticity.

Package Overview

RHEL is essentially a set of packages grouped together to create an operating system. They are prepackaged for installation and assembled for various intended use cases. They are built around the Linux kernel and include thousands of packages that are digitally signed, tested, and certified. There are several basic and advanced concepts associated with packages, packaging, and their management that are touched upon in this and the next chapter.

Packages and Packaging

A software *package* is a group of files organized in a directory structure along with metadata and intelligence that make up a software application. They are available in two types: *binary* (or *installable*) and *source*. Binary packages are installation-ready and are bundled for distribution. They have .rpm extension and contain install scripts, pre- and post-installation scripts, executables, configuration files, library files, dependency information, where to install files, and documentation. The documentation includes detailed instructions on how to install and uninstall the package, manual pages for the configuration files and commands, and other necessary information pertaining to the installation and usage of the package.

All metadata related to packages is stored at a central location and includes information such as package version, installation location, checksum values, and a list of included files with their attributes. This allows the package management toolset to handle package administration tasks efficiently by referencing this metadata.

The package intelligence is used by the package administration toolset for a successful completion of the package installation process. It may include information on prerequisites, user account setup (if required), and any directories and soft links that need to be created. The intelligence also includes the reverse of this process for uninstallation.

Source packages come with the original unmodified version of the software that may be unpacked, modified as desired, and repackaged in the binary format for installation or redistribution. They are identified with the .src extension.

Package Naming

Red Hat software packages follow a standard naming convention. Typically, there are five parts to a package name: (1) the package name, (2) the package version, (3) the package release (revision or build), (4) the Enterprise Linux the package is created for, and (5) the processor architecture the package is built for. An installable package name always has the .rpm extension; however, this extension is removed from the installed package name.

For example, if the name of an installable package is openssl-3.0.1-43.el9_0.x86_64.rpm, its installed name would be openssl-3.0.1-43.el9_0.x86_64. Here is a description of each part of the package name:

openssl: package name
3.0.1: version
43: release
el9_0: stands for *Enterprise Linux* 9.0 (not all packages have it)
x86_64: processor architecture the package is created for. You may see "noarch" for platform-independent packages that can be installed on any hardware architecture, or "src" for source code packages.
.rpm: the extension

Package Dependency

An installable package may require the presence of one or more additional packages in order to be installed successfully. Likewise, a software package component may require the functionality provided by one or more packages to exist in order to operate as expected. This is referred to as *package dependency*, where one package depends on one or more other packages for installation or execution. Package dependency information is recorded in each package's metadata from where it is read by package handling utilities.

Package Database

Metadata for installed packages and package files is stored and maintained in the */var/lib/rpm* directory. This directory location is referred to as the *package database,* and it is referenced by package manipulation utilities to obtain package name and version data and information about ownerships, permissions, timestamps, and sizes for each and every file that is part of the package. The package database also contains information on dependencies. All this data aids management commands in listing and querying packages, verifying dependencies and file attributes, installing new packages, upgrading and uninstalling existing packages, and carrying out other package handling tasks.

The package database does not update existing package information by simply adding available enhancements. It removes the metadata of the package being replaced and then adds the information of the replacement package. In RHEL 9, it can maintain multiple versions of a single package alongside their metadata.

Package Management Tools

The primary tool for package management on Red Hat Enterprise Linux is called *rpm* (*redhat package manager*). This tool offers abundant options for flexible package handling; however, a major caveat is that it does not automatically resolve package dependencies. To overcome this gap, a more innovative tool called *yum* (*yellowdog update, modified*) was introduced, which offered an easier method for package management that can find, get, and install all required dependent packages automatically.

Starting in RHEL 8, a major enhancement to *yum* was introduced known as *dnf. dnf* does not have an official acronym, but some documentation refers to it as *dandified* yum. You may still use the *yum* command; however, it is simply a soft link to *dnf.*

This chapter focuses on the use of the *rpm* command. Chapter 10 "Advanced Package Management" details the *dnf* command.

Package Management with rpm

The *rpm* command handles package management tasks including querying, installing, upgrading, freshening, overwriting, removing, extracting, validating, and verifying packages. As mentioned, this command has a major drawback as it does not have the ability to automatically satisfy package dependencies, which can be frustrating during software installation and upgrade. The *rpm* command works with both installed and installable packages.

The rpm Command

Before getting into the details, let's look at some common *rpm* command options. Table 9-1 describes query options in both short and long option formats. You may use either format.

Query Options	Description
-q (--query)	Queries and displays packages
-qa (--query --all)	Lists all installed packages
-qc (--query --configfiles)	Lists configuration files in a package
-qd (--query --docfiles)	Lists documentation files in a package
-qf (--query --file)	Exhibits what package a file comes from

Query Options	Description
-qi (--query --info)	Shows installed package information including version, size, installation status and date, signature, and description
-qip (--query --info --package)	Shows installable package information including version, size, installation status and date, signature, and description
-ql (--query --list)	Lists all files in a package
-qR (--query --requires)	Lists files and packages a package depends on (requires)
-q --whatprovides	Lists packages that provide the specified package or file
-q --whatrequires	Lists packages that require the specified package or file

Table 9-1 rpm Command Query Options

Table 9-2 describes options related to package installation, removal, and verification. These options are also available in both short and long formats. You may use either format.

Install/Remove Options	Description
-e (--erase)	Removes a package
--force	Installs and replaces a package or files of the same version
-F (--freshen)	Upgrades an installed package
-h (--hash)	Shows installation progress with hash marks
-i (--install)	Installs a package
--import	Imports a public key
-K	Validates the signature and package integrity
-U (--upgrade)	Upgrades an installed package or loads it if it is not already installed
-v (--verbose) or -vv	Displays detailed information
-V (--verify)	Verifies the integrity of a package or package files

Table 9-2 rpm Command Install/Remove/Verify Options

The examples in this chapter employ most of these options in short format to understand how they are used to achieve desired results.

Exercise 9-1: Mount RHEL 9 ISO Persistently

This exercise should be done on *server1* as *user1* with *sudo* where required.

In this exercise, you will attach the RHEL 9 ISO image to the *RHEL9-VM1* in VirtualBox and mount the image on */mnt* directory on *server1* to access and manipulate the software packages in it with the *rpm* command. You will ensure that the image is automatically mounted on each system reboot. You will confirm access to the packages by listing the subdirectories that store them.

1. Go to the VirtualBox VM Manager and make sure that the RHEL 9 image is attached to *RHEL9-VM1* as depicted below:

Storage

Controller: IDE
  IDE Secondary Device 0: [Optical Drive] rhel-baseos-9.1-x86_64-dvd.iso (8.44 GB)
Controller: SATA
  SATA Port 0: RHEL9-VM1.vdi (Normal, 20.00 GB)

2. Open the */etc/fstab* file in the *vim* editor (or another editor of your choice) and add the following line entry at the end of the file to mount the DVD image (*/dev/sr0*) in read-only (ro) mode on the */mnt* directory.

```
/dev/sr0  /mnt  iso9660  ro  0 0
```

 sr0 represents the first instance of the optical device and iso9660 is the standard format for optical file systems.

3. Mount the file system as per the configuration defined in the */etc/fstab* file using the *mount* command with the -a (all) option:

```
[user1@server1 ~]$ sudo mount -a
[user1@server1 ~]$
```

The command should return without displaying anything in the output. This will confirm that the new entry was placed correctly in the file. See Chapter 14 "Local File Systems and Swap" for details on mount and mount point concepts.

4. Verify the mount using the *df* command:

```
[user1@server1 ~]$ df -h | grep mnt
/dev/sr0                    8.5G  8.5G       0 100% /mnt
```

The image and the packages therein can now be accessed via the */mnt* directory just like any other local directory on the system.

5. List the two directories—*/mnt/BaseOS/Packages* and */mnt/AppStream/Packages*—that contain all the software packages (directory names are case sensitive):

```
[user1@server1 ~]$ ls -l /mnt/BaseOS/Packages/ | more
total 1027279
-r--r--r--. 1 root root     96227 Apr 12  2022 accel-config-3.4.6.3-1.el9.i686.r
-r--r--r--. 1 root root     92744 Apr 12  2022 accel-config-3.4.6.3-1.el9.x86_64
-r--r--r--. 1 root root     61211 Apr 12  2022 accel-config-libs-3.4.6.3-1.el9.i
-r--r--r--. 1 root root     60264 Apr 12  2022 accel-config-libs-3.4.6.3-1.el9.x
m
-r--r--r--. 1 root root     79170 Nov 20  2021 acl-2.3.1-3.el9.x86_64.rpm
-r--r--r--. 1 root root    991535 Nov 20  2021 acpica-tools-20210604-3.el9.x86_6
-r--r--r--. 1 root root    126699 Nov 20  2021 adcli-0.9.1-7.el9.x86_64.rpm

........
[user1@server1 ~]$ ls -l /mnt/AppStream/Packages/ | more
total 6980092
-r--r--r--. 1 root root   3047214 Oct  7 10:06 389-ds-base-2.1.3-4.el9_1.x86_64.rp
-r--r--r--. 1 root root   1551682 Oct  7 10:06 389-ds-base-libs-2.1.3-4.el9_1.x86_
-r--r--r--. 1 root root     36268 Nov 20  2021 a52dec-0.7.4-42.el9.x86_64.rpm
-r--r--r--. 1 root root    149889 Nov 20  2021 aajohan-comfortaa-fonts-3.001-10.el
ch.rpm
-r--r--r--. 1 root root   1022450 Aug 26 14:54 aardvark-dns-1.1.0-4.el9.x86_64.rpm

........
```

There are thousands of files in the two locations, each representing a single rpm package.

This concludes the exercise.

Querying Packages

You can query for packages in the package database or at the specified location. The following are some examples.

To query all installed packages:

```
[user1@server1 ~]$ rpm -qa
libgcc-11.3.1-2.1.el9.x86_64
fonts-filesystem-2.0.5-7.el9.1.noarch
linux-firmware-whence-20220708-127.el9.noarch
crypto-policies-20220815-1.git0fbe86f.el9.noarch

........
```

To query whether the specified package is installed:

```
[user1@server1 ~]$ rpm -q perl
package perl is not installed
```

To list all files in a package:

```
[user1@server1 ~]$ rpm -ql iproute
/etc/iproute2
/etc/iproute2/bpf_pinning
/etc/iproute2/ematch_map
/etc/iproute2/group

........
```

To list only the documentation files in a package:

```
[user1@server1 ~]$ rpm -qd audit
/usr/share/doc/audit/ChangeLog
/usr/share/doc/audit/README
/usr/share/doc/audit/auditd.cron

........
```

To list only the configuration files in a package:

```
[user1@server1 ~]$ rpm -qc cups
/etc/cups/classes.conf
/etc/cups/client.conf
/etc/cups/cups-files.conf
/etc/cups/cupsd.conf
/etc/cups/lpoptions

........
```

To identify which package owns the specified file:

```
[user1@server1 ~]$ rpm -qf /etc/passwd
setup-2.13.7-7.el9.noarch
```

To display information about an installed package including version, release, installation status, installation date, size, signatures, description, and so on:

```
[user1@server1 ~]$ rpm -qi setup
Name        : setup
Version     : 2.13.7
Release     : 7.el9
Architecture: noarch
Install Date: Thu 26 Jan 2023 04:37:45 PM
Group       : System Environment/Base
Size        : 726385
License     : Public Domain
Signature   : RSA/SHA256, Tue 26 Jul 2022 07:02:29 AM, Key ID 199e2f
Source RPM  : setup-2.13.7-7.el9.src.rpm
Build Date  : Mon 09 May 2022 07:19:12 AM
Build Host  : x86-vm-56.build.eng.bos.redhat.com
Packager    : Red Hat, Inc. <http://bugzilla.redhat.com/bugzilla>
Vendor      : Red Hat, Inc.
URL         : https://pagure.io/setup/
Summary     : A set of system configuration and setup files
Description :
The setup package contains a set of important system configuration a
setup files, such as passwd, group, and profile.
```

To list all file and package dependencies for a given package:

```
[user1@server1 ~]$ rpm -qR chrony
/bin/sh
/bin/sh
/bin/sh
/bin/sh
/usr/bin/bash
/usr/bin/sh
config(chrony) = 4.2-1.el9
libc.so.6()(64bit)
libc.so.6(GLIBC_2.12)(64bit)
libc.so.6(GLIBC_2.14)(64bit)

. . . . . . . .
```

To query an installable package for metadata information (version, release, architecture, description, size, signatures, etc.):

```
[user1@server1 ~]$ rpm -qip /mnt/BaseOS/Packages/zsh-5.8-9.el9.x86_64.rpm
Name        : zsh
Version     : 5.8
Release     : 9.el9
Architecture: x86_64
Install Date: (not installed)
Group       : Unspecified
Size        : 8018363
License     : MIT
Signature   : RSA/SHA256, Thu 24 Feb 2022 10:59:15 AM, Key ID 199e2f91fd4
Source RPM  : zsh-5.8-9.el9.src.rpm
Build Date  : Wed 23 Feb 2022 09:10:14 AM

. . . . . . . .
```

To determine what packages require the specified package in order to operate properly:

```
[user1@server1 ~]$ rpm -q --whatrequires lvm2
libblockdev-lvm-2.25-14.el9.x86_64
udisks2-lvm2-2.9.4-3.el9.x86_64
```

The above output lists all the packages that will require the specified package "lvm2" in order to work fully and properly.

Installing a Package

Installing a package creates the necessary directory structure for the package, installs the required files, and runs any post-installation steps. The following command installs a package called *zsh-5.8-9.el9.x86_64.rpm* on the system:

```
[user1@server1 ~]$ sudo rpm -ivh /mnt/BaseOS/Packages/zsh-5.8-9.el9.x86_64.rpm
warning: /mnt/BaseOS/Packages/zsh-5.8-9.el9.x86_64.rpm: Header V3 RSA/SHA256 S:
key ID fd431d51: NOKEY
Verifying...                          ################################## [100%]
Preparing...                          ################################## [100%]
Updating / installing...
   1:zsh-5.8-9.el9                     ################################## [100%]
```

If this package required the presence of any missing packages, you would see an error message related to failed dependencies. In that case, you would have to first install the missing packages for this package to be loaded successfully.

Upgrading a Package

Upgrading a package upgrades an installed version of the package. In the absence of an existing version, the upgrade simply installs the package.

To upgrade a package called *sushi*, use the -U option with the *rpm* command. Notice that the *sushi* package is located in a different directory than the *zsh* package in the previous example.

```
[user1@server1 ~]$ sudo rpm -Uvh /mnt/AppStream/Packages/sushi-3.38.1-2.el9.x86_64.rpm
warning: /mnt/AppStream/Packages/sushi-3.38.1-2.el9.x86_64.rpm: Header V3 RSA/SHA256 S
nature, key ID fd431d51: NOKEY
Verifying...                          ################################## [100%]
Preparing...                          ################################## [100%]
        package sushi-3.38.1-2.el9.x86 64 is already installed
```

The command makes a backup of all the affected configuration files during the upgrade process and adds the extension *.rpmsave* to them. In the above example, the *sushi* package was installed, as it was not already on the system.

Freshening a Package

Freshening a package requires that an older version of the package must already exist on the system.

To freshen the *sushi* package, use the -F option:

```
[user1@server1 ~]$ sudo rpm -Fvh /mnt/AppStream/Packages/sushi-3.38.1-2.el9.x86_64.rpm
warning: /mnt/AppStream/Packages/sushi-3.38.1-2.el9.x86_64.rpm: Header V3 RSA/SHA256 S
nature, key ID fd431d51: NOKEY
```

The above command did nothing because the same package version specified with the command is already installed on the system. It will only work if a new version of the installed package is available.

Overwriting a Package

Overwriting a package replaces the existing files associated with the package of the same version.

To overwrite the package *zsh-5.8-9.el9.x86_64* that was installed earlier, use the --replacepkgs option:

```
[user1@server1 ~]$ sudo rpm -ivh --replacepkgs /mnt/BaseOS/Packages/zsh-5.8-9.el9.x86_64
.rpm
warning: /mnt/BaseOS/Packages/zsh-5.8-9.el9.x86_64.rpm: Header V3 RSA/SHA256 Signature,
key ID fd431d51: NOKEY
Verifying...                          ################################# [100%]
Preparing...                          ################################# [100%]
Updating / installing...
   1:zsh-5.8-9.el9                     ################################# [100%]
```

The installation progress indicates that the *zsh* package was replaced successfully. This action is particularly useful when you suspect corruption in one or more installed package files and you want to start afresh.

Removing a Package

Removing a package uninstalls the package and all its associated files and the directory structure.

To remove the package *sushi*, use the -e option and specify -v for verbosity:

```
[user1@server1 ~]$ sudo rpm sushi -ve
Preparing packages...
sushi-3.38.1-2.el9.x86_64
```

This command performs a dependency inspection to check whether there are any packages that require the existence of the package being weeded out and fails the removal if it detects a dependency.

Extracting Files from an Installable Package

Files in an installable package can be extracted using the *rpm2cpio* command for reasons such as examining the contents of the package, replacing a corrupted or lost command, or replacing a critical configuration file of an installed package to its original state.

Assuming you have lost the */etc/chrony.conf* configuration file, which is part of a package called *chrony*, and want to retrieve it from its installable package and put it back, you'll first need to determine what package this file comes from:

```
[user1@server1 ~]$ rpm -qf /etc/chrony.conf
chrony-4.2-1.el9.x86_64
```

Now use the *rpm2cpio* command to extract (-i) all files from the *chrony* package (located under */mnt/BaseOS/Packages*) and create (-d) the necessary directory structure during the retrieval. Extract the files in a temporary location such as the */tmp* directory before you proceed with overwriting the destination under */etc*.

```
[user1@server1 tmp]$ sudo rpm2cpio /mnt/BaseOS/Packages/chrony-4.2-1.el9.x86_64.rpm | cp
io -imd
1230 blocks
```

Run *find* to locate the *chrony.conf* file:

```
[user1@server1 tmp]$ sudo find . -name chrony.conf
./etc/chrony.conf
```

The above output shows that the file is under */tmp/etc*. You can copy it to the */etc* directory now, and you're back in business.

Validating Package Integrity and Credibility

Before it is installed, a package may be checked for integrity (completeness and error-free state) and credibility (authenticity) after it has been copied to another location, downloaded from the web, or obtained elsewhere. Use the MD5 checksum for verifying its integrity and the *GNU Privacy Guard* (GnuPG or GPG) public key signature for ensuring the credibility of its developer or publisher. This will ensure an uncorrupted and genuine piece of software.

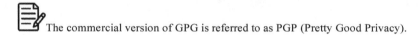 The commercial version of GPG is referred to as PGP (Pretty Good Privacy).

To check the integrity of a package such as *chrony-4.2-1.el9.x86_64.rpm* located in */mnt/BaseOS/Packages*:

```
[user1@server1 ~]$ rpm -K /mnt/BaseOS/Packages/chrony-4.2-1.el9.x86_64.rpm --nosignature
/mnt/BaseOS/Packages/chrony-4.2-1.el9.x86_64.rpm: digests OK
```

The OK in the output confirms that the package is free of corruption.

Red Hat signs their products and updates with a GPG key and includes necessary public keys in the products for verification. For RHEL, the keys are in files on the installation media and are copied to the */etc/pki/rpm-gpg/* directory during the OS installation. Refer to Table 9-3 for a list of files in that directory and a short explanation.

GPG File	Description
RPM-GPG-KEY-redhat-release	Used for packages shipped after November 2009 and their updates
RPM-GPG-KEY-redhat-beta	Used for beta test products shipped after November 2009

Table 9-3 Red Hat GPG Key Files

To check the credibility of a package, import the relevant GPG key and then verify the package. The table above shows that the GPG file for the recent packages is *RPM-GPG-KEY-redhat-release*. In the following example, run the *rpm* command to import the GPG key from this file and verify the signature for the *chrony-4.2-1.el9.x86_64.rpm* package using the -K option with the command:

```
[user1@server1 ~]$ sudo rpmkeys --import /etc/pki/rpm-gpg/RPM-GPG-KEY-redhat-release
[user1@server1 ~]$ sudo rpmkeys -K /mnt/BaseOS/Packages/chrony-4.2-1.el9.x86_64.rpm
/mnt/BaseOS/Packages/chrony-4.2-1.el9.x86_64.rpm: digests signatures OK
```

The OK validates the package signature and certifies the authenticity and integrity of the package.

Viewing GPG Keys

The GPG key imported in the previous subsection can be viewed with the *rpm* command. You can list the key and display its details as well. Run the command as follows to list the imported key:

```
[user1@server1 ~]$ rpm -q gpg-pubkey
gpg-pubkey-fd431d51-4ae0493b
gpg-pubkey-5a6340b3-6229229e
```

The output suggests that there are two GPG public keys currently imported on the system. Let's view the details for the second one:

```
[user1@server1 ~]$ rpm -qi gpg-pubkey-5a6340b3-6229229e
Name          : gpg-pubkey
Version       : 5a6340b3
Release       : 6229229e
Architecture: (none)
Install Date: Sun 29 Jan 2023 09:29:15 PM
Group         : Public Keys
Size          : 0
License       : pubkey
Signature     : (none)
Source RPM    : (none)
Build Date    : Wed 09 Mar 2022 04:56:46 PM
Build Host    : localhost
Packager      : Red Hat, Inc. (auxiliary key 3) <security@redhat.co
Summary       : Red Hat, Inc. (auxiliary key 3) <security@redhat.co
Description :
-----BEGIN PGP PUBLIC KEY BLOCK-----
Version: rpm-4.16.1.3 (NSS-3)

mQINBGIpIp4BEAC/o5e1WzLIsS6/JOQCs4XYATYTcf6B6ALzcP05G0W3uRpUQSrL
........
```

The output returns both the metadata and the key data for the specified GPG public key.

Verifying Package Attributes

Verifying the integrity of an installed package compares the attributes of files in the package with the original file attributes saved and stored in the package database at the time of package installation. The verification process uses the *rpm* command with the -V option to compare the owner, group, permission mode, size, modification time, digest, and type among other attributes. The command returns to the prompt without exhibiting anything if it detects no changes in the attributes. You can use the -v or -vv option with the command for increased verbosity.

Run this check on the *at* package:

```
[user1@server1 ~]$ sudo rpm -V at
```

The command returned nothing, which implies that the file attributes are intact. Now change the permissions on one of the files, */etc/sysconfig/atd*, in this package to 770 from the current value of 644, and then re-execute the verification test:

```
[user1@server1 ~]$ ls -l /etc/sysconfig/atd
-rw-r--r--. 1 root root 403 Apr  4  2022 /etc/sysconfig/atd
[user1@server1 ~]$ sudo chmod -v 770 /etc/sysconfig/atd
mode of '/etc/sysconfig/atd' changed from 0644 (rw-r--r--) to 0770 (rwxrwx---)
[user1@server1 ~]$ sudo rpm -V at
.M.......  c /etc/sysconfig/atd
```

The output is indicative of a change in the permission mode on the *atd* file in the *at* package. You may alternatively run the verification check directly on the file by adding the -f option to the command and passing the filename as an argument:

```
[user1@server1 ~]$ sudo rpm -Vf /etc/sysconfig/atd
.M.......  c /etc/sysconfig/atd
```

The output returns three columns: column 1 contains nine fields, column 2 shows the file type, and column 3 expresses the full path of the file. The command performs a total of nine checks, as illustrated by the codes in column 1 of the output, and displays any changes that have occurred since the package that contains the file was installed. Each of these codes has a meaning. Table 9-4 lists the codes with description as they appear from left to right. The period character (.) appears for an attribute that is not in an altered state.

Code	Description
S	Appears if the file size is different
M	Appears if the (mode) permission or file type is altered
5	Appears if MD5 checksum does not match
D	Appears if the file is a device file and its major or minor number has changed
L	Appears if the file is a symlink and its path has altered
U	Appears if the ownership has modified
G	Appears if the group membership has modified
T	Appears if timestamp has changed
P	Appears if capabilities have altered
.	Appears if no modification is detected

Table 9-4 Package Verification Codes

Column 2 in the output above exposes a code that represents the type of file. Table 9-5 lists them.

File Type	Description
c	Configuration file
d	Documentation file
g	Ghost file
l	License file
r	Readme file

Table 9-5 File Type Codes

Based on the information in the tables, the */etc/sysconfig/atd* is a configuration file with a modified permission mode. Reset the attribute to its previous value and rerun the check to ensure the file is back to its original state.

```
[user1@server1 ~]$ sudo chmod -v 644 /etc/sysconfig/atd
mode of '/etc/sysconfig/atd' changed from 0770 (rwxrwx---) to 0644 (rw-r--r--)
[user1@server1 ~]$ sudo rpm -V at
```

The command produced no output, which confirms the integrity of the file as well as the package.

Exercise 9-2: Perform Package Management Using rpm

This exercise should be done on *server1* as *user1* with *sudo* where required.

In this exercise, you will verify the integrity and authenticity of a package called *rmt* located in the */mnt/BaseOS/Packages* directory on the installation image and then install it. You will display basic information about the package, show files it contains, list documentation files, verify the package attributes, and erase the package.

1. Run the *ls* command on the */mnt/BaseOS/Packages* directory to confirm that the *rmt* package is available:

    ```
    [user1@server1 ~]$ ls -l /mnt/BaseOS/Packages/rmt-1.6-6.el9.x86_64.rpm
    -r--r--r--. 1 root root 49582 Nov 20  2021 /mnt/BaseOS/Packages/rmt-1.6-6.el9.x86_64.rpm
    ```

2. Run the *rpm* command and verify the integrity and credibility of the package:

    ```
    [user1@server1 ~]$ rpmkeys -K /mnt/BaseOS/Packages/rmt-1.6-6.el9.x86_64.rpm
    /mnt/BaseOS/Packages/rmt-1.6-6.el9.x86_64.rpm: digests signatures OK
    ```

3. Install the package:

    ```
    [user1@server1 Packages]$ sudo rpm -ivh /mnt/BaseOS/Packages/rmt-1.6-6.el9.x86_64.rpm
    Verifying...                      ################################# [100%]
    Preparing...                      ################################# [100%]
    Updating / installing...
       1:rmt-2:1.6-6.el9              ################################# [100%]
    ```

4. Show basic information about the package:

    ```
    [user1@server1 ~]$ rpm -qi rmt
    Name         : rmt
    Epoch        : 2
    Version      : 1.6
    Release      : 6.el9
    Architecture : x86_64
    Install Date : Tue 21 Feb 2023 06:15:32 PM
    Group        : Unspecified
    Size         : 88810
    License      : CDDL
    Signature    : RSA/SHA256, Sat 20 Nov 2021 10:46:44 AM, Key
    Source RPM   : star-1.6-6.el9.src.rpm
    Build Date   : Tue 10 Aug 2021 06:13:47 PM
    Build Host   : x86-vm-55.build.eng.bos.redhat.com

    . . . . . . . .
    ```

5. Show all the files the package contains:

```
[user1@server1 ~]$ rpm -ql rmt
/etc/default/rmt
/etc/rmt
/usr/lib/.build-id
/usr/lib/.build-id/c2
/usr/lib/.build-id/c2/6a51ea96fc4b4367afe
/usr/sbin/rmt
/usr/share/doc/star
/usr/share/doc/star/CDDL.Schily.txt
. . . . . . . .
```

6. List the documentation files the package has:

```
[user1@server1 ~]$ rpm -qd rmt
/usr/share/doc/star/CDDL.Schily.txt
/usr/share/doc/star/COPYING
/usr/share/man/man1/rmt.1.gz
```

7. Verify the attributes of each file in the package. Use verbose mode.

```
[user1@server1 ~]$ rpm -Vv rmt
. . . . . . . . .   c /etc/default/rmt
. . . . . . . . .     /etc/rmt
. . . . . . . . .   a /usr/lib/.build-id
. . . . . . . . .   a /usr/lib/.build-id/c2
. . . . . . . . .   a /usr/lib/.build-id/c2/6a51ea96fc4b4367
. . . . . . . . .     /usr/sbin/rmt
. . . . . . . . .     /usr/share/doc/star
. . . . . . . . .   d /usr/share/doc/star/CDDL.Schily.txt
. . . . . . . . .   d /usr/share/doc/star/COPYING
. . . . . . . . .   d /usr/share/man/man1/rmt.1.gz
```

8. Remove the package:

```
[user1@server1 ~]$ sudo rpm -ve rmt
Preparing packages...
rmt-2:1.6-6.el9.x86_64
```

This concludes the exercise.

Chapter Summary

This chapter is the first of the two chapters (second one being the next chapter) with coverage on software management. It covered the foundational topics and set the groundwork for more advanced features and functions.

We learned the concepts around packages, packaging, naming convention, dependency, and patch database. We looked at the variety of options available with the rpm utility to perform package administration tasks and put many of them into action to demonstrate their usage. Moreover, we employed appropriate options to view and validate package metadata information, GPG keys, and package attributes.

Review Questions

1. What would the *rpm -ql zsh* command do?
2. What is the difference between installing and upgrading a package?
3. Package database is located in the */var/lib/rpm* directory. True or False?
4. What would the *rpm -qf /bin/bash* command do?
5. Name the directory where RHEL 9 stores GPG signatures.
6. What would the options ivh cause the *rpm* command to do?
7. State the purpose of the *rpm2cpio* command.
8. What is the difference between freshening and upgrading a package?
9. The *rpm* command automatically takes care of package dependencies. True or False?
10. What would the *rpm -qa* command do?

Answers to Review Questions

1. The command provided will list all the files that are included in the installed *zsh* package.
2. Installing will install a new package whereas upgrading will upgrade an existing package or install it if it does not already exist.
3. True.
4. The command provided will display information about the */bin/bash* file.
5. RHEL 9 stores GPG signatures in the */etc/pki/rpm-gpg* directory.
6. The *rpm* command will install the specified package and show installation details and hash signs for progress.
7. The *rpm2cpio* command is used to extract files from the specified package.
8. Both are used to upgrade an existing package, but freshening requires an older version of the package to exist.
9. False.
10. The command provided will list all installed packages.

Do-It-Yourself Challenge Labs

The following labs are useful to strengthen most of the concepts and topics learned in this chapter. It is expected that you perform the labs without external help. A step-by-step guide is not supplied, as the knowledge and skill required to implement the labs have already been disseminated in the chapter; however, hints to the relevant major topic(s) are included.

Use the lab environment built specifically for end-of-chapter labs. See sub-section "Lab Environment for End-of-Chapter Labs" in Chapter 01 "Local Installation" for details.

Lab 9-1: Install and Verify Packages

As *user1* with *sudo* on *server3*, make sure the RHEL 9 ISO image is attached to the VM and mounted. Use the *rpm* command and install the *zsh* package by specifying its full path. Run the *rpm* command again and perform the following on the *zsh* package: (1) show information, (2) validate integrity, and (3) display attributes. (Hint: Package Management with rpm).

Lab 9-2: Query and Erase Packages

As *user1* with *sudo* on *server3*, make sure the RHEL 9 ISO image is attached to the VM and mounted. Use the *rpm* command to perform the following: (1) check whether the *setup* package is installed, (2) display the list of configuration files in the *setup* package, (3) show information for the *zlib-devel* package on the ISO image, (4) reinstall the *zsh* package (--reinstall -vh), and (5) remove the *zsh* package. (Hint: Package Management with rpm).

Chapter 10

Advanced Package Management

This chapter describes the following major topics:

➤ Describe package groups
➤ Understand application streams
➤ Software repositories and how to access them
➤ Perform software management operations using dnf
➤ List, install, update, and delete individual packages and package groups
➤ Show package information, determine provider, and search metadata
➤ Exhibit package group information

RHCSA Objectives:

42. Install and update software packages from Red Hat Network, a remote repository, or from the local file system (part of this objective is covered in Chapter 09)

This is the second of the two chapters that discusses software administration in RHEL. While the first chapter (Chapter 09) expounds upon the basic concepts of rpm package management and demonstrates a basic command to manipulate individual packages, this chapter elaborates on the concepts and handling of package groups. It also presents a coverage on the concept of software repositories and how to configure them.

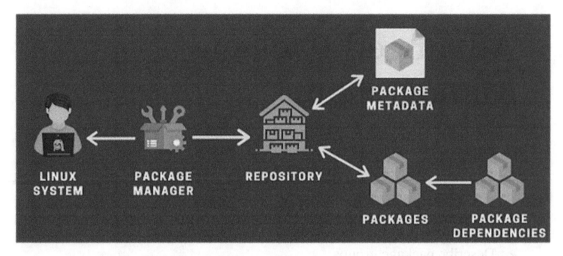

The dnf command is superior to the rpm tool in the sense that it performs automatic dependency checks and marks any identified extra packages for installation. There are numerous options and subcommands available with this advanced tool and it is capable of interacting with software repositories as well.

Advanced Package Management Concepts

We discussed and grasped the basic package management concepts and employed the *rpm* utility in a variety of ways to manipulate individual packages. The focus of this chapter will be on understanding advanced software packaging and distribution techniques, and using a tool that is capable of handling a single package, discrete packages, and collection of packages, efficiently.

RHEL 9 is shipped with two core repositories called *BaseOS* and *Application Stream* (AppStream).

Package Groups

A *package group* is a collection of correlated packages designed to serve a common purpose. It provides the convenience of querying, installing, and deleting as a single unit rather than dealing with packages individually. There are two types of package groups: *environment groups* and *package groups*. The environment groups available in RHEL 9 are server, server with GUI, minimal install, workstation, virtualization host, and custom operating system. These are listed on the software selection window during RHEL 9 installation. The package groups include container management, smart card support, security tools, system tools, network servers, etc.

BaseOS Repository

The BaseOS repository includes the core set of RHEL 9 components including the kernel, modules, bootloader, and other foundational software packages. These components lay the foundation to install and run software applications and programs. BaseOS repository components are available in the traditional rpm format.

AppStream Repository

The AppStream repository comes standard with core applications, as well as several add-on applications many of them in the traditional rpm format and some in the new modular format. These add-ons include web server software, development languages, database software, etc. and are shipped to support a variety of use cases and deployments.

Benefits of Segregation

There are two fundamental benefits to a segregation of the BaseOS components from other applications: (1) it separates the application components from the core operating system elements, and (2) it allows publishers to deliver and administrators to apply application updates more frequently. In RHEL version 7 and older, an OS update would update all installed components including the kernel, service, and application components to the latest versions by default. This could result in an unstable system or a misbehaving application due to an unwanted upgrade of one or more packages. By detaching the base OS components from the applications, either of the two can be updated independent of the other. This provides enhanced flexibility in tailoring the system components and application workloads without impacting the underlying stability of the system.

dnf Repository

A *dnf repository* (*yum repository* or simply a *repo*) is a digital library for storing software packages. A repository is accessed for package retrieval, query, update, and installation, and it may be free or for a fee. The two repositories—BaseOS and AppStream—come preconfigured with the RHEL 9 ISO image. There are a number of other repositories available on the Internet that are maintained by software publishers such as Red Hat and CentOS. Furthermore, you can build private custom repositories for internal IT use for stocking and delivering software. This may prove to be a good practice for an organization with a large Linux server base, as it manages dependencies automatically and aids in maintaining software consistency across the board. These repositories can also be used to store in-house developed packages.

It is important to obtain software packages from authentic and reliable sources such as Red Hat to prevent potential damage to your system and to circumvent possible software corruption.

There is a process to create repositories and to access preconfigured repositories. Creating repositories is beyond the scope of this book, but you will configure access to the BaseOS and AppStream repositories via a definition file to support the exercises and lab environment.

A sample repo definition file is shown below with some key directives:

```
[BaseOS_RHEL_9]
name= RHEL 9 base operating system components
baseurl=file:///mnt/BaseOS
enabled=1
gpgcheck=0
```

> **EXAM TIP:** Knowing how to configure a dnf repository using a URL plays an important role in completing some of the RHCSA exam tasks successfully. Use two forward slash characters (//) with the baseurl directive for an FTP, HTTP, or HTTPS source.

The above example shows five lines from a sample repo file. Line 1 defines an exclusive ID within the square brackets. Line 2 is a brief description of the repo with the "name" directive. Line 3 is the location of the repodata directory with the "baseurl" directive. Line 4 shows whether this repository is active. Line 5 shows if packages are to be GPG-checked for authenticity.

Each repository definition file must have a unique ID, a description, and a baseurl directive defined at a minimum; other directives are set as required. The baseurl directive for a local directory path is defined as file:///local_path (the first two forward slash characters represent the URL convention, and the third forward slash is for the absolute path to the destination directory), and for FTP and HTTP(S) sources as ftp://hostname/network_path and http(s)://hostname/network_path, respectively. The network path must include a resolvable hostname or an IP address.

Software Management with dnf

Software for enterprise Linux distributions such as Red Hat and CentOS is available in the rpm format. These distributions offer tools to work with individual packages as well as package groups. The *rpm* command was used in the previous chapter to query, list, install, and erase packages, in addition to a few other tasks that it can perform. This command is limited to managing one package at a time.

A more capable tool for managing a single package or a group of packages is referred to as *dnf* (or *yum*). This tool has an associated configuration file that can define settings to control its behavior.

dnf Configuration File

The key configuration file for *dnf* is *dnf.conf* that resides in the */etc/dnf* directory. The "main" section in the file sets directives that have a global effect on dnf operations. You can define separate sections for each custom repository that you plan to set up on the system. However, the preferred location to store configuration for each custom repository in their own definition files is in the */etc/yum.repos.d* directory, which is the default location created for this purpose. The default content of this configuration file is listed below:

```
[user1@server1 ~]$ cat /etc/dnf/dnf.conf
[main]
gpgcheck=1
installonly_limit=3
clean_requirements_on_remove=True
best=True
```

Table 10-1 explains the above and a few other directives that you may define in the file. The directives in Table 10-1 are listed in an alphabetical order.

Directive	Description
best	Specifies whether to install (or upgrade to) the latest available version
clean_requirements_on_remove	Defines whether to remove dependencies during a package removal process that are no longer in use
debuglevel	Sets the level between 1 (minimum) and 10 (maximum) at which the debug is to be recorded in the logfile. Default is 2. A value of 0 disables this feature.
gpgcheck	Indicates whether to check the GPG signature for package authenticity. Default is 1 (enabled).

Directive	Description
installonly_limit	Specifies a count of packages that can be installed concurrently. Default is 3.
keepcache	Defines whether to store the package and header cache following a successful installation. Default is 0 (disabled).
logdir	Sets the directory location to store the log files. Default is */var/log*.
obsoletes	Checks and removes any obsolete dependent packages during installs and updates. Default is 1 (enabled).

Table 10-1 Directive Settings in dnf.conf File

There are a multitude of additional directives available that you may want to set in the main section of this file or in custom repository definition files. Run **man 5 dnf.conf** for details.

The dnf Command

The *dnf* command is the advanced package management tool in RHEL. This utility requires the system to have access to a local or remote software repository or to a local installable package file. The *Red Hat Subscription Management* (RHSM) service available in the Red Hat Customer Portal offers access to official Red Hat software repositories. There are other web-based repositories that host packages that you may want to install and use. Alternatively, you can set up a local, custom repository on your RHEL system and add packages of your choice to it.

The primary benefit of using *dnf* over *rpm* is the former's ability to resolve dependencies automatically by identifying and installing any packages required for a successful installation of the specified software. With multiple repositories in place, *dnf* extracts the software from wherever it finds it.

dnf invokes the *rpm* utility in the background and can perform numerous operations on individual packages or package groups such as listing, querying, installing, and removing them.

Table 10-2 summarizes the software handling tasks that *dnf* can perform on packages. It also lists two subcommands (clean and repolist) that are for repository operations. The subcommands are sequenced alphabetically. Refer to the *dnf* command manual pages for additional subcommands, operators, options, and examples.

Subcommand	Description
check-update	Checks if updates are available for installed packages
clean	Removes cached data
history	Displays previous dnf activities as recorded in the /var/lib/dnf/history directory
info	Shows details for a package
install	Installs or updates a package
list	Lists installed and available packages
provides	Searches for packages that contain the specified file or feature
reinstall	Reinstalls the exact version of an installed package
remove	Removes a package and its dependencies
repolist	Lists enabled repositories
repoquery	Runs queries on available packages
search	Searches package metadata for the specified string

Subcommand	Description
upgrade	Updates each installed package to the latest version

Table 10-2 dnf Subcommands for Package and Repository Manipulation

Table 10-3 lists and describes *dnf* subcommands that are intended for operations on package groups.

Subcommand	Description
group install	Installs or updates a package group
group info	Returns details for a package group
group list	Lists available package groups
group remove	Removes a package group

Table 10-3 dnf Subcommands for Package Group Manipulation

You will use most of the subcommands from the two Tables in the examples and exercises that follow, but first you'll need to create a definition file and configure access to the two repositories available on the RHEL 9 ISO image.

Exercise 10-1: Configure Access to Pre-Built Repositories

This exercise should be done on *server1* as *user1* with *sudo* where required.

In this exercise, you will set up access to the two dnf repositories that are available on RHEL 9 image. You've already configured an automatic mounting of RHEL 9 image on */mnt* in Chapter 09 "Basic Package Management". You will create a definition file for the repositories and confirm.

1. Verify that the image is currently mounted:

    ```
    [root@server1 ~]# df -h | grep mnt
    /dev/sr0                8.5G  8.5G      0 100% /mnt
    ```

2. Create a definition file called *local.repo* in the */etc/yum.repos.d* directory using the *vim* editor and define the following data for both repositories in it:

    ```
    [BaseOS]
    name=Base OS software
    baseurl=file:///mnt/BaseOS
    enabled=1
    gpgcheck=0

    [AppStream]
    name=Application software
    baseurl=file:///mnt/AppStream
    enabled=1
    gpgcheck=0
    ```

3. Confirm access to the repositories:

    ```
    [user1@server1 ~]$ sudo dnf repolist -v
    ```

```
DNF version: 4.12.0
cachedir: /var/cache/dnf
Base OS software                                   14 MB/s | 1.7 MB    00:00
Application software                              8.7 MB/s | 6.1 MB    00:00
Repo-id                 : AppStream
Repo-name               : Application software
Repo-revision           : 1666858692
Repo-updated            : Thu 27 Oct 2022 04:18:12 AM
Repo-pkgs               : 5,472
Repo-available-pkgs: 5,367'
Repo-size               : 6.7 G
Repo-baseurl            : file:///mnt/AppStream
Repo-expire             : 172,800 second(s) (last: Mon 30 Jan 2023 01:50:47 PM)
Repo-filename           : /etc/yum.repos.d/local.repo

Repo-id                 : BaseOS
Repo-name               : Base OS software
Repo-revision           : 1666858715
Repo-updated            : Thu 27 Oct 2022 04:18:35 AM
Repo-pkgs               : 1,137
Repo-available-pkgs: 1,137
Repo-size               : 1.0 G
Repo-baseurl            : file:///mnt/BaseOS
Repo-expire             ': 172,800 second(s) (last: Mon 30 Jan 2023 01:50:46 PM)
Repo-filename           : /etc/yum.repos.d/local.repo
Total packages: 6,609
```

Ignore any lines that are related to subscription and system registration (not shown in the above output). The output provides details for the two repositories. It shows the rate at which the command read the repo data (lines 3 and 4) followed by separate metadata sections for each repository. Each section contains repository ID, name, count of packages, total size of all the packages, mount location, and the file holding the repo information. As depicted, the AppStream repo consists of 5,472 packages and the BaseOS repo contains 1,137 packages. Both repos are enabled and are ready for use.

We have divided software administration operations into two sections below to focus on individual packages and package groups.

Individual Package Management

The *dnf* command can be used to perform a variety of operations on individual packages, just like the *rpm* command. The following subsections elaborate with examples on using this tool to list, install, query, and remove packages.

Listing Available and Installed Packages

Listing the packages that are available for installation from one or more enabled repositories helps you understand what is in the current software inventory and what is needed. Likewise, listing the packages that are already installed on the system enables you to make important decisions as to whether they should be retained, upgraded, downgraded, or erased. The *dnf* command lists available packages as well as installed packages.

To list all packages available for installation from all enabled repos, run a query against the two repositories that we configured earlier, as those are the only ones you currently have access to. The following command will result in a long output.

```
[user1@server1 ~]$ sudo dnf repoquery
```

```
Last metadata expiration check: 0:49:15 ago on Mon 30 Jan 2023 10:38:44 PM.
389-ds-base-0:2.1.3-4.el9_1.x86_64
389-ds-base-libs-0:2.1.3-4.el9_1.x86_64
Box2D-0:2.4.1-7.el9.i686
Box2D-0:2.4.1-7.el9.x86_64
CUnit-0:2.1.3-25.el9.i686
CUnit-0:2.1.3-25.el9.x86_64

. . . . . . . .
```

To limit the above to the list of packages that are available only from a specific repo:

```
[user1@server1 ~]$ sudo dnf repoquery --repo "BaseOS"
Last metadata expiration check: 0:50:48 ago on Mon 30 Jan 2023 10:38:44 PM.
ModemManager-0:1.18.2-3.el9.x86_64
ModemManager-glib-0:1.18.2-3.el9.i686
ModemManager-glib-0:1.18.2-3.el9.x86_64
NetworkManager-1:1.40.0-1.el9.x86_64
NetworkManager-adsl-1:1.40.0-1.el9.x86_64

. . . . . . . .
```

You can *grep* for an expression to narrow down your search. For example, to find whether the BaseOS repo includes the *zsh* package, run the following:

```
[user1@server1 ~]$ sudo dnf repoquery --repo BaseOS | grep zsh
Last metadata expiration check: 0:51:38 ago on Mon 30 Jan 2023 10:38:44 PM.
zsh-0:5.8-9.el9.x86_64
```

To list all installed packages on the system:

```
[user1@server1 ~]$ sudo dnf list installed
Installed Packages
ModemManager.x86_64                      1.18.2-3.el9              @anaconda
ModemManager-glib.x86_64                 1.18.2-3.el9              @anaconda
NetworkManager.x86_64                    1:1.40.0-1.el9            @anaconda
NetworkManager-adsl.x86_64               1:1.40.0-1.el9            @anaconda
NetworkManager-bluetooth.x86_64          1:1.40.0-1.el9            @anaconda
NetworkManager-config-server.noarch      1:1.40.0-1.el9            @anaconda
NetworkManager-libnm.x86_64              1:1.40.0-1.el9            @anaconda
NetworkManager-team.x86_64               1:1.40.0-1.el9            @anaconda

. . . . . . . .
```

The graphic above shows the output in three columns: package name, package version, and the repo it was installed from. @anaconda means the package was installed at the time of RHEL installation.

To list all installed packages and all packages available for installation from all enabled repositories:

```
[user1@server1 ~]$ sudo dnf list
Installed Packages
ModemManager.x86_64                      1.18.2-3.el9              @anaconda
ModemManager-glib.x86_64                 1.18.2-3.el9              @anaconda
NetworkManager.x86_64                    1:1.40.0-1.el9            @anaconda
NetworkManager-adsl.x86_64               1:1.40.0-1.el9            @anaconda
NetworkManager-bluetooth.x86_64          1:1.40.0-1.el9            @anaconda
NetworkManager-config-server.noarch      1:1.40.0-1.el9            @anaconda
NetworkManager-libnm.x86_64              1:1.40.0-1.el9            @anaconda
NetworkManager-team.x86_64               1:1.40.0-1.el9            @anaconda
```

```
. . . . . . . .
Available Packages
389-ds-base.x86_64                              2.1.3-4.el9_1               AppStream
389-ds-base-libs.x86_64                         2.1.3-4.el9_1               AppStream
Box2D.i686                                      2.4.1-7.el9                AppStream
Box2D.x86_64                                    2.4.1-7.el9                AppStream
CUnit.i686                                      2.1.3-25.el9               AppStream
CUnit.x86_64                                    2.1.3-25.el9               AppStream
HdrHistogram_c.i686                             0.11.0-6.el9               AppStream
HdrHistogram_c.x86_64                           0.11.0-6.el9               AppStream
Judy.i686                                       1.0.5-28.el9               AppStream

. . . . . . . .
```

The @ sign that precedes a repository name in column 3 identifies the package as installed.

To list all packages available from all enabled repositories that should be able to update:

```
[user1@server1 ~]$ sudo dnf list updates
```

To list whether a package (*bc*, for instance) is installed or available for installation from any enabled repository:

```
[user1@server1 ~]$ sudo dnf list bc
```

To list all installed packages whose names begin with the string "gnome" followed by any number of characters:

```
[user1@server1 ~]$ sudo dnf list installed gnome*
Installed Packages
gnome-autoar.x86_64                             0.4.1-2.el9                @AppStream
gnome-bluetooth.x86_64                          1:3.34.5-3.el9             @AppStream
gnome-bluetooth-libs.x86_64                     1:3.34.5-3.el9             @AppStream
gnome-calculator.x86_64                         40.1-2.el9                 @AppStream

. . . . . . . .
```

To list recently added packages:

```
[user1@server1 ~]$ sudo dnf list recent
```

Refer to the *repoquery* and *list* subsections of the *dnf* command manual pages for more options and examples.

Installing and Updating Packages

Installing a package creates the necessary directory tree for the specified and dependent packages, installs the required files, and runs any post-installation steps. If the package being loaded is already present, the *dnf* command updates it to the latest available version. By default, *dnf* prompts for a yes or no confirmation unless the -y flag is entered with the command.

The following attempts to install a package called *keybinder3*, but proceeds with an update if it detects the presence of an older version:

```
[user1@server1 ~]$ sudo dnf install keybinder3
```

```
Dependencies resolved.
================================================================================
 Package        Architecture     Version          Repository          Size
================================================================================
Installing:
 keybinder3     x86_64           0.3.2-13.el9     AppStream           23 k

Transaction Summary
================================================================================
Install  1 Package

Total size: 23 k
Installed size: 32 k
Is this ok [y/N]: y
Downloading Packages:
Running transaction check
Transaction check succeeded.
Running transaction test
Transaction test succeeded.
Running transaction
  Preparing        :                                                     1/1
  Installing       : keybinder3-0.3.2-13.el9.x86_64                      1/1
  Running scriptlet: keybinder3-0.3.2-13.el9.x86_64                      1/1
  Verifying        : keybinder3-0.3.2-13.el9.x86_64                      1/1
Installed products updated.

Installed:
  keybinder3-0.3.2-13.el9.x86_64

Complete!                _
```

The above *dnf* command example resolved dependencies and showed a list of the packages that it would install. It exhibited the size of the packages and the amount of disk space that the installation would consume. It downloaded the packages after confirmation to proceed and installed them. It completed the installation after every package was verified. A list of the installed packages was displayed at the bottom of the output.

To install or update a package called *dcraw* located locally at */mnt/AppStream/Packages*:

```
[user1@server1 ~]$ sudo dnf localinstall /mnt/AppStream/Packages/dcraw-9.28.0-13.el9.x86_64
.rpm
```

To update an installed package (*autofs*, for example) to the latest available version. Note that *dnf* will fail if the specified package is not already installed.

```
[user1@server1 ~]$ sudo dnf update autofs
Package autofs available, but not installed.
No match for argument: autofs
Error: No packages marked for upgrade.
```

To update all installed packages to the latest available versions:

```
[user1@server1 ~]$ sudo dnf -y update
```

Refer to the *install* and *update* subsections of the *dnf* command manual pages for more options and examples.

Exhibiting Package Information

Displaying information for a package shows its name, architecture it is built for, version, release, size, whether it is installed or available for installation, repo name it was installed or is available from, short and long descriptions, license, and so on. This information can be viewed by supplying the *info* subcommand to *dnf*.

To view information about a package called *autofs*:

```
[user1@server1 ~]$ dnf info autofs
Available Packages
Name         : autofs
Epoch        : 1
Version      : 5.1.7
Release      : 31.el9
Architecture : x86_64
Size         : 389 k
Source       : autofs-5.1.7-31.el9.src.rpm
Repository   : BaseOS
Summary      : A tool for automatically mounting and unmounting filesystems
```

The output shows that *autofs* is not currently installed, but it is available for installation from the BaseOS repo. The *info* subcommand automatically determines whether the specified package is installed.

Refer to the *info* subsection of the *dnf* command's manual pages for more options available for viewing package information.

Removing Packages

Removing a package uninstalls it and removes all associated files and directory structure. It also erases any dependencies as part of the deletion process. By default, *dnf* prompts for a yes or no confirmation unless the -y flag is specified at the command line.

To remove a package called *keybinder3*:

```
[user1@server1 ~]$ sudo dnf remove keybinder3
. . . . . . . .
Removing:
 keybinder3           x86_64           0.3.2-13.el9

Transaction Summary
================================================================
Remove  1 Package

Freed space: 32 k
Is this ok [y/N]: y
Running transaction check
Transaction check succeeded.
Running transaction test
Transaction test succeeded.
Running transaction
  Preparing        :
  Erasing          : keybinder3-0.3.2-13.el9.x86_64
  Verifying        : keybinder3-0.3.2-13.el9.x86_64
Installed products updated.

Removed:
  keybinder3-0.3.2-13.el9.x86_64
```

The above output resolved dependencies and showed a list of the packages that it would remove. It displayed the amount of disk space that their removal would free up. After confirmation to proceed, it erased the identified packages and verified their removal. A list of the removed packages was exhibited at the bottom of the output.

Refer to the *remove* subsection of the *dnf* command's manual pages for more options and examples available for removing packages.

Exercise 10-2: Manipulate Individual Packages

This exercise should be done on *server1* as *user1* with *sudo* where required.

In this exercise, you will perform management operations on a package called *cifs-utils*. You will determine if this package is already installed and if it is available for installation. You will display its information before installing it. You will install the package and exhibit its information. Finally, you will erase the package along with its dependencies and confirm the removal.

1. Check whether the *cifs-utils* package is already installed:

    ```
    [user1@server1 ~]$ dnf list installed |grep cifs-utils
    [user1@server1 ~]$
    ```

The command returned to the prompt without any output, which implies that the specified package is not installed.

2. Determine if the *cifs-utils* package is available for installation:

    ```
    [user1@server1 ~]$ dnf repoquery cifs-utils
    cifs-utils-0:6.14-1.el9.x86_64
    ```

The package is available for installation. The output shows its version as well.

3. Display detailed information about the package:

    ```
    [user1@server1 ~]$ dnf info cifs-utils
    Available Packages
    Name         : cifs-utils
    Version      : 6.14
    Release      : 1.el9
    Architecture : x86_64
    Size         : 102 k
    Source       : cifs-utils-6.14-1.el9.src.rpm
    Repository   : BaseOS
    Summary      : Utilities for mounting and managing CIF
    URL          : http://linux-cifs.samba.org/cifs-utils/
    License      : GPLv3
    Description  : The SMB/CIFS protocol is a standard fil
                 : on Microsoft Windows machines. This pac
                 : shares on Linux using the SMB/CIFS prot
                 : work in conjunction with support in the
                 : SMB/CIFS share onto a client and use it
                 : file system.
    ```

The output is indicative of the fact that the package is available for installation from the BaseOS repo.

4. Install the package:

```
[user1@server1 ~]$ sudo dnf install -y cifs-utils
Dependencies resolved.
================================================================================
 Package              Architecture       Version               Repo
================================================================================
Installing:
 cifs-utils           x86_64             6.14-1.el9            Base
Installing dependencies:
 keyutils             x86_64             1.6.1-4.el9           Base

Transaction Summary
================================================================================
Install  2 Packages

Total size: 171 k
Installed size: 362 k
Is this ok [y/N]: y

. . . . . . . .
```

5. Display the package information again:

```
[user1@server1 ~]$ dnf info cifs-utils
Installed Packages
Name         : cifs-utils
Version      : 6.14
Release      : 1.el9
Architecture : x86_64
Size         : 220 k
Source       : cifs-utils-6.14-
Repository   : @System
From repo    : BaseOS
```

The output reveals that the package is now installed.

6. Remove the package:

```
[user1@server1 ~]$ sudo dnf remove -y cifs-utils
```

7. Confirm the removal:

```
[user1@server1 ~]$ dnf list installed | grep cifs-utils
[user1@server1 ~]$
```

The no output above confirms that the package is not loaded on the system.

Determining Provider and Searching Package Metadata

Determining package contents includes search operations on installed and available packages. For instance, you can determine what package a specific file belongs to or which package comprises a certain string. The following examples show how to carry out these tasks.

To search for packages that contain a specific file such as *etc/passwd*, use the *provides* or the *whatprovides* subcommand with *dnf*:

```
[user1@server1 ~]$ dnf provides /etc/passwd
setup-2.13.7-7.el9.noarch : A set of system co:
Repo         : @System
Matched from:
Filename     : /etc/passwd

setup-2.13.7-7.el9.noarch : A set of system co:
Repo         : BaseOS
Matched from:
Filename     : /etc/passwd
```

The output returns two instances of the file. The first one indicates that the *passwd* file is part of a package called *setup*, which was installed during RHEL installation, and the second instance shows it as part of the *setup* package from the BaseOS repository.

With the *provides* (*whatprovides*) subcommand, you can also use a wildcard character for filename expansion. For example, the following command will list all packages that contain filenames beginning with "system-config" followed by any number of characters:

```
[user1@server1 ~]$ dnf whatprovides /usr/bin/system-config*
policycoreutils-gui-3.4-4.el9.noarch : SELinux conf.
Repo         : AppStream
Matched from:
Filename     : /usr/bin/system-config-selinux
```

To search for all the packages that match the specified string in their name or summary:

```
[user1@server1 ~]$ dnf search system-config
=============================== Name Matched: system-config ==========:
system-config-printer-libs.noarch : Libraries and shared code for prir
                                  : tool
system-config-printer-udev.x86_64 : Rules for udev for automatic confi
                                  : printers
============================== Summary Matched: system-config =========:
cups-pk-helper.x86_64 : A helper that makes system-config-printer use
```

The above outcome depicts three matches, two in package names and one in summary.

Package Group Management

The *dnf* command can be used to perform ample operations on package groups by specifying the *group* subcommand with it. The following subsections elaborate with examples on using this tool to list, install, query, and remove groups of packages.

Listing Available and Installed Package Groups

The *group list* subcommand can be used with *dnf* to list the package groups available for installation from either or both repos, as well as to list the package groups that are already installed.

To list all available and installed package groups from all repositories:

```
[user1@server1 ~]$ dnf group list
Available Environment Groups:
    Server
    Minimal Install
    Workstation
    Custom Operating System
    Virtualization Host
Installed Environment Groups:
    Server with GUI
Installed Groups:
    Container Management
    Headless Management
Available Groups:
    Legacy UNIX Compatibility
    Console Internet Tools
    Development Tools
    .NET Development
    Graphical Administration Tools
    Network Servers
    RPM Development Tools
    Scientific Support
    Security Tools
    Smart Card Support
    System Tools
```

The output reveals two categories of package groups: an *environment group* and a *group*. An environment group is a larger collection of RHEL packages that provides all necessary software to build the operating system foundation for a desired purpose. The Server with GUI environment group was selected at the time of installing *server1*, which installed a multitude of packages as well as the GNOME desktop. See Table 1-2 in Chapter 01 "Local Installation" for a description of other environment groups.

A group, on the other hand, is a small bunch of RHEL packages that serve a common purpose. It also saves time on the deployment of individual and dependent packages. The above output shows two installed and several available package groups.

To display the number of installed and available package groups:

```
[user1@server1 ~]$ dnf group summary
Installed Groups: 2
Available Groups: 11
```

To list all installed and available package groups including those that are hidden:

```
[user1@server1 ~]$ dnf group list hidden
Available Environment Groups:
    Server
    Minimal Install
    Workstation
    Custom Operating System
    Virtualization Host
Installed Environment Groups:
    Server with GUI
Installed Groups:
    Hardware Support
    Server product core
    base-x
    Container Management
    Core
. . . . . . . .
```

Try *group list* with --installed and --available options to narrow down the output list.

To list all packages that a specific package group such as *Base* (not shown in the above output) contains:

```
[user1@server1 ~]$ dnf group info Base
Group: Base
 Description: The standard install.
 Mandatory Packages:
   acl
   at
   attr
   bc
   cpio
   crontabs
   cyrus-sasl-plain
   dbus
   ed
   file
 . . . . . . . .
```

You may use the -v option with *group info* for more information. Refer to the *group list* and *group info* subsections of the *dnf* command's manual pages for more details.

Installing and Updating Package Groups

Installing a package group creates the necessary directory structure for all the packages included in the group and all dependent packages, installs the required files, and runs any post-installation steps. If the package group is being loaded or part of it is already present, the command attempts to update all the packages included in the group to the latest available versions. By default, *dnf* prompts for a yes or no confirmation unless the -y flag is entered with the command.

The following example attempts to install a package group called *smart card support*, but proceeds with an update if it detects the presence of an older version. You may enclose the group name within either single or double quotation marks.

```
[user1@server1 ~]$ sudo dnf -y groupinstall "smart card support"
Dependencies resolved.
=================================================================================
 Package                 Architecture    Version            Repo:
=================================================================================
Installing group/module packages:
 esc                     x86_64          1.1.2-16.el9       AppSt
 pcsc-lite-ccid          x86_64          1.4.36-1.el9       Base(
Installing dependencies:
 opensc                  x86_64          0.22.0-2.el9       Base(
 pcsc-lite               x86_64          1.9.4-1.el9        Base(
 pcsc-lite-libs          x86_64          1.9.4-1.el9        Base(
Installing Groups:
 Smart Card Support

Transaction Summary
=================================================================================
Install  5 Packages

Total size: 1.9 M
Installed size: 6.1 M
```

```
. . . . . . . .
Installed:
  esc-1.1.2-16.el9.x86_64                          opensc-0.22.0
  pcsc-lite-1.9.4-1.el9.x86_64                      pcsc-lite-cci
  pcsc-lite-libs-1.9.4-1.el9.x86_64

Complete!
```

The output discloses that the command installed five packages located across the two repositories to complete the installation of the package group.

To update the *smart card support* group to the latest version:

```
[user1@server1 ~]$ sudo dnf groupupdate "smart card support" -y
```

The above command will update all the packages within the package group to their latest versions if it has access to them. Refer to the *group install* and *group update* subsections of the *dnf* command's manual pages for more details.

Removing Package Groups

Removing a package group uninstalls all the included packages and deletes all associated files and directory structure. It also erases any dependencies as part of the deletion process. By default, *dnf* prompts for a yes or no confirmation unless the -y flag is specified at the command line.

To erase the *smart card support* package group that was installed earlier:

```
[user1@server1 ~]$ sudo dnf -y groupremove 'smart card support'
Dependencies resolved.
===========================================================================
 Package              Architecture    Version              Reposit
===========================================================================
Removing:
 esc                  x86_64          1.1.2-16.el9         @AppSt
 pcsc-lite-ccid       x86_64          1.4.36-1.el9         @BaseO
Removing unused dependencies:
 opensc               x86_64          0.22.0-2.el9         @BaseO
 pcsc-lite            x86_64          1.9.4-1.el9          @BaseO
 pcsc-lite-libs       x86_64          1.9.4-1.el9          @BaseO
Removing Groups:
 Smart Card Support

Transaction Summary
===========================================================================
Remove   5 Packages

Freed space:  6.1 M

. . . . . . . .
Removed:
  esc-1.1.2-16.el9.x86_64                          opensc-0.22.0-2.el
  pcsc-lite-1.9.4-1.el9.x86_64                      pcsc-lite-ccid-1.4
  pcsc-lite-libs-1.9.4-1.el9.x86_64

Complete!
```

The above output resolved dependencies and showed a list of the packages that it would remove. It displayed the amount of disk space that their removal would free up. After confirmation to proceed, it erased the identified packages and verified their removal. A list of the removed packages was exposed at the bottom of the output.

Refer to the *remove* subsection of the *dnf* command's manual pages for more details.

Exercise 10-3: Manipulate Package Groups

This exercise should be done on *server1* as *user1* with *sudo* where required.

In this exercise, you will perform management operations on a package group called *system tools*. You will determine if this group is already installed and if it is available for installation. You will list the packages it contains and install it. Finally, you will remove the group along with its dependencies and confirm the removal.

1. Check whether the *system tools* package group is already installed:

```
[user1@server1 ~]$ dnf group list installed 'system tools'
```

The output does not show it installed.

2. Determine if this package group is available for installation:

```
[user1@server1 ~]$ dnf group list available 'system tools'
Available Groups:
    System Tools
```

The group is available for installation.

3. Display the list of packages this group contains:

```
[user1@server1 ~]$ dnf group info 'system tools'
Group: System Tools
 Description: This group is a collecti
t for connecting to SMB shares and too
 Default Packages:
    NetworkManager-libreswan
    chrony
    cifs-utils
    libreswan
    nmap
    openldap-clients
    samba-client
    setserial
    tigervnc
    tmux
    zsh
 Optional Packages:
    PackageKit-command-not-found
    aide
    autofs
 . . . . . . . .
```

The output returns a long list of packages that are included in this group. All the packages will be installed as part of the group installation.

4. Install the group:

```
[user1@server1 ~]$ sudo dnf group install 'system tools'
Dependencies resolved.
==============================================================
Package                 Architecture Version              Re
==============================================================
Installing group/module packages:
 NetworkManager-libreswan   x86_64     1.2.14-1.el9.3         Ap
 libreswan                  x86_64     4.6-3.el9             Ap
 nmap                       x86_64     3:7.91-10.el9          Ap
 openldap-clients           x86_64     2.6.2-3.el9           Ba
 samba-client               x86_64     4.16.4-101.el9         Ap
 setserial                  x86_64     2.17-54.el9           Ba
 tigervnc                   x86_64     1.12.0-4.el9           Ap
 tmux                       x86_64     3.2a-4.el9             Ba
Installing dependencies:
 fltk                       x86_64     1.3.8-1.el9           Ap
 ldns                       x86_64     1.7.1-11.el9           Ap
 nss-tools                  x86_64     3.79.0-14.el9_0        Ap
 tigervnc-icons             noarch     1.12.0-4.el9           Ap
 tigervnc-license           noarch     1.12.0-4.el9           Ap
 unbound-libs               x86_64     1.16.2-2.el9           Ap
Installing Groups:
 System Tools

Transaction Summary
==============================================================
Install  14 Packages

Total size: 10 M
Installed size: 39 M
..........
Installed:
  NetworkManager-libreswan-1.2.14-1.el9.3.x86_64    fltk-1.
  ldns-1.7.1-11.el9.x86_64                          libresw
  nmap-3:7.91-10.el9.x86_64                         nss-too
  openldap-clients-2.6.2-3.el9.x86_64               samba-c
  setserial-2.17-54.el9.x86_64                      tigervr
  tigervnc-icons-1.12.0-4.el9.noarch                tigervr
  tmux-3.2a-4.el9.x86_64                            unbounc

Complete!
```

5. Remove the group:

```
[user1@server1 ~]$ sudo dnf group remove 'system tools' -y
```

6. Confirm the removal:

```
[user1@server1 ~]$ dnf group list installed
```

```
Installed Environment Groups:
    Server with GUI
Installed Groups:
    Container Management
    Headless Management
```

The package group is not listed in the above output, which confirms its removal.

Chapter Summary

This chapter is the second of the two chapters (the first one being Chapter 09) with coverage on software management. This chapter covers advanced topics: yum repositories and package groups.

We looked at the concept of package repositories and demonstrated setting up access to a local repo. Employing repositories for package installation and automatic dependency selection make software installation much easier than to use the rpm command.

We learned about package groups and the benefits of using them in contrast to handling individual software packages.

Finally, we examined the dnf command and discovered its benefits over the standard rpm command. dnf offers a variety of options and subcommands that we employed in this chapter to demonstrate installing, listing, querying, updating, and deleting individual packages and package groups. Other management operations such as exhibiting package data, ascertaining provider, and searching metadata for information were also covered.

Review Questions

1. What *dnf* subcommand would we use to check available updates for installed packages?
2. What is the concept of module in RHEL 9?
3. What must be the extension of a yum repository file?
4. What would the *dnf list zsh* command do?
5. What would the *dnf list installed *gnome** command do?
6. How many package names can be specified at a time with the *dnf install* command?
7. Name the two default yum repositories that contain all the packages for RHEL 9?
8. What would the *dnf group info Base* command do?
9. Which *dnf* subcommand can be used to list all available repositories?
10. What is the use of the -y option with the *dnf group install* command?
11. What is the main advantage of using *dnf* over *rpm*?
12. We can update all the packages within a package group using the *groupupdate* subcommand with *dnf*. True or False?
13. What would the *dnf info zsh* command do?

Answers to Review Questions

1. The *check-update* subcommand.
2. A module is a collection of packages, including the dependent packages, that are required to install an application.
3. The extension of a yum repository configuration file must be *.repo* in order to be recognized as a valid repo file.
4. The command provided will display installed and available *zsh* package.

5. The command provided will display all installed packages that contain gnome in their names.
6. There is no limit.
7. The two yum repositories the BaseOS and AppStream.
8. The command provided will list all packages in the specified package group.
9. The *repolist* subcommand.
10. *dnf* will not prompt for user confirmation if the -y option is used with it.
11. *dnf* resolves and installs dependent packages automatically.
12. True.
13. The command provided will display the header information for the *zsh* package.

Do-It-Yourself Challenge Labs

The following labs are useful to strengthen most of the concepts and topics learned in this chapter. It is expected that you perform the labs without external help. A step-by-step guide is not supplied, as the knowledge and skill required to implement the labs have already been disseminated in the chapter; however, hints to the relevant major topic(s) are included.

Use the lab environment built specifically for end-of-chapter labs. See sub-section "Lab Environment for End-of-Chapter Labs" in Chapter 01 "Local Installation" for details.

Lab 10-1: Configure Access to RHEL 9 Repositories

As *user1* with *sudo* on *server3*, make sure the RHEL 9 ISO image is attached to the VM and mounted. Create a definition file under */etc/yum.repos.d*, and define two blocks (one for BaseOS and another for AppStream). Verify the configuration with *dnf repolist*. You should see numbers in thousands under the Status column for both repositories. (Hint1: Chapter 09: Package Management with rpm). (Hint2: Chapter 10: Software Management with dnf).

Lab 10-2: Install and Manage Individual Packages

As *user1* with *sudo* on *server3* and using the *dnf* command, list all installed and available packages separately. Show which package contains the */etc/group* file. Install the package *httpd*. Review */var/log/dnf.log* for confirmation. Perform the following on the *httpd* package: (1) show information, (2) list dependencies, and (3) remove it. (Hint: Individual Package Management).

Lab 10-3: Install and Manage Package Groups

As *user1* with *sudo* on *server3* and using the *dnf* command, list all installed and available package groups separately. Install package groups *Security Tools* and *Scientific Support*. Review */var/log/dnf.log* for confirmation. Show the packages included in the *Scientific Support* package group and delete this group. (Hint: Package Group Management).

Chapter 11

Boot Process, GRUB2, and the Linux Kernel

This chapter describes the following major topics:

➢ Linux boot process: firmware, bootloader, kernel, and initialization

➢ Understand and interact with GRUB2 to boot into different targets

➢ Modify GRUB2 configuration

➢ Boot system into specific targets

➢ Reset lost or forgotten root user password

➢ Linux kernel, packages, version anatomy, and key directories

➢ Download and install a new kernel version

RHCSA Objectives:

18. Interrupt the boot process in order to gain access to a system
43. Modify the system bootloader

RHEL goes through multiple phases during the boot process. It starts selective services during its transition from one phase into another. It presents the administrator an opportunity to interact with a preboot program to boot the system into a non-default target, pass an option to the kernel, or reset the lost or forgotten root user password. It launches a number of services during its transition to the default or specified target.

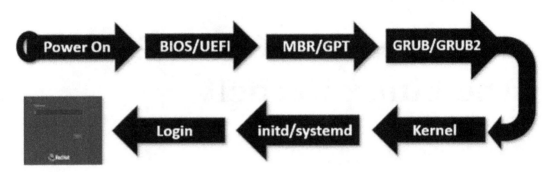

The kernel controls everything on the system. It controls the system hardware, enforces security and access controls, and runs, schedules, and manages processes and service daemons. The kernel is comprised of several modules. A new kernel must be installed or an existing kernel must be upgraded when the need arises from an application or functionality standpoint.

Linux Boot Process

RHEL goes through a *boot* process after the system has been powered up or restarted. The boot process lasts until all enabled services are started. A login prompt will appear on the screen, which allows users to log in to the system. The boot process is automatic, but you may need to interact with it to take a non-default action, such as booting an alternative kernel, booting into a non-default operational state, repairing the system, recovering from an unbootable state, and so on. The boot process on an x86 computer may be split into four major phases: (1) the firmware phase, (2) the bootloader phase, (3) the kernel phase, and (4) the initialization phase. The system accomplishes these phases one after the other while performing and attempting to complete the tasks identified in each phase.

The Firmware Phase (BIOS and UEFI)

The *firmware* is the BIOS (*Basic Input/Output System*) or the UEFI (*Unified Extensible Firmware Interface*) code that is stored in flash memory on the x86-based system board. It runs the *Power-On-Self-Test* (POST) to detect, test, and initialize the system hardware components. While doing so, it installs appropriate drivers for the video hardware and exhibit system messages on the screen. The firmware scans the available storage devices to locate a boot device, starting with a 512-byte image that contains 446 bytes of the bootloader program, 64 bytes for the partition table, and the last two bytes with the boot signature. This 512-byte tiny area is referred to as the *Master Boot Record* (MBR) and it is located on the first sector of the boot disk. As soon as it discovers a usable boot device, it loads the bootloader into memory and passes control over to it.

The BIOS is a small memory chip in the computer that stores system date and time, list and sequence of boot devices, I/O configuration, etc. This configuration is customizable. Depending on the computer hardware, you need to press a key to enter the BIOS setup or display a menu to choose a source to boot the system. The computer goes through the hardware initialization phase that involves detecting and diagnosing peripheral devices. It runs the POST on the devices as it finds them, installs drivers for the graphics card and the attached monitor, and begins exhibiting system messages on the video hardware. It discovers a usable boot device, loads the bootloader program into memory, and passes control over to it. Boot devices on most computers support booting from optical and USB flash devices, hard drives, network, and other media.

The UEFI is a new 32/64-bit architecture-independent specification that computer manufacturers have widely adopted in their latest hardware offerings replacing BIOS. This mechanism delivers enhanced boot and runtime services, and superior features such as speed over the legacy 16-bit BIOS. It has its own device drivers, is able to mount and read extended file systems, includes UEFI-compliant application tools, and supports one or more bootloader programs. It comes with a boot manager that allows you to choose an alternative boot source. Most computer manufacturers have customized the features for their hardware platform. You may find varying menu interfaces among other differences.

The Bootloader Phase

Once the firmware phase is over and a boot device is detected, the system loads a piece of software called *bootloader* that is located in the boot sector of the boot device. RHEL uses GRUB2 (*GRand Unified Bootloader*) version 2 as the bootloader program. GRUB2 supports both BIOS and UEFI firmware.

The primary job of the bootloader program is to spot the Linux kernel code in the */boot* file system, decompress it, load it into memory based on the configuration defined in the */boot/grub2/grub.cfg* file, and transfer control over to it to further the boot process. For UEFI-based systems, GRUB2 looks for the EFI system partition */boot/efi* instead, and runs the kernel based on the configuration defined in the */boot/efi/EFI/redhat/grub.efi* file. The next section details the interaction with the bootloader.

The Kernel Phase

The *kernel* is the central program of the operating system, providing access to hardware and system services. After getting control from the bootloader, the kernel extracts the *initial RAM disk* (initrd) file system image found in the */boot* file system into memory, decompresses it, and mounts it as read-only on */sysroot* to serve as the temporary root file system. The kernel loads necessary modules from the initrd image to allow access to the physical disks and the partitions and file systems therein. It also loads any required drivers to support the boot process. Later, it unmounts the initrd image and mounts the actual physical root file system on / in read/write mode.

At this point, the necessary foundation has been built for the boot process to carry on and to start loading the enabled services. The kernel executes the *systemd* process with PID 1 and passes the control over to it.

The Initialization Phase

This is the fourth and the last phase in the boot process. *systemd* takes control from the kernel and continues the boot process. It is the default system initialization scheme used in RHEL 9. It starts all enabled userspace system and network services and brings the system up to the preset boot target.

A boot target is an operational level that is achieved after a series of services have been started to get to that state. More on targets later in this chapter.

The system boot process is considered complete when all enabled services are operational for the boot target and users are able to log in to the system. A detailed discussion on *systemd* is furnished in Chapter 12 "System Initialization, Message Logging, and System Tuning".

The GRUB2 Bootloader

After the firmware phase has concluded, the bootloader presents a menu with a list of bootable kernels available on the system and waits for a predefined amount of time before it times out and boots the default kernel. You may want to interact with GRUB2 before the autoboot times out to boot with a non-default kernel, boot to a different target, or customize the kernel boot string.

Pressing a key before the timeout expires allows you to interrupt the autoboot process and interact with GRUB2. If you wish to boot the system using the default boot device with all the configured default settings, do not press any key, as shown in Figure 11-1, and let the system go through the autoboot process.

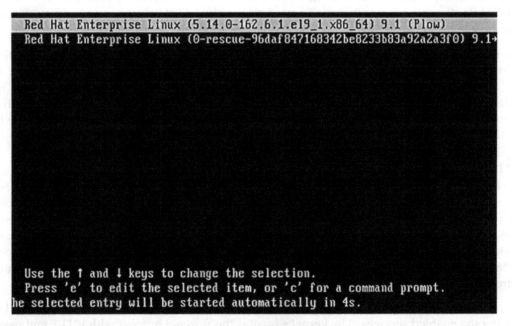

Figure 11-1 GRUB2 Menu

The line at the bottom in Figure 11-1 shows the autoboot countdown in seconds. The default value is 5 seconds. If you press no keys within the 5 seconds, the highlighted kernel will boot automatically.

Interacting with GRUB2

The GRUB2 main menu shows a list of bootable kernels at the top. You can change the selection using the Up or Down arrow key. It lets you edit a selected kernel menu entry by pressing an *e* or go to the grub> command prompt by pressing a *c*.

In the edit mode, GRUB2 loads the configuration for the selected kernel entry from the */boot/grub2/grub.cfg* file in an editor, enabling you to make a desired modification before booting the system. For instance, you can boot the system into a less capable operating target by adding "rescue", "emergency", or "3" to the end of the line that begins with the keyword "linux", as depicted in Figure 11-2. Press Ctrl+x when done to boot. Remember that this is a one-time temporary change and it won't touch the *grub.cfg* file.

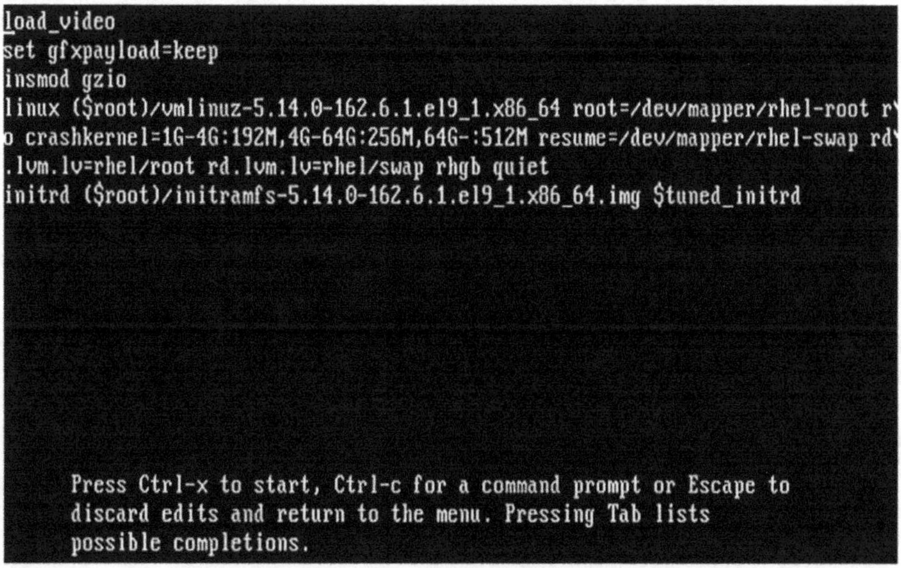

```
load_video
set gfxpayload=keep
insmod gzio
linux ($root)/vmlinuz-5.14.0-162.6.1.el9_1.x86_64 root=/dev/mapper/rhel-root r\
o crashkernel=1G-4G:192M,4G-64G:256M,64G-:512M resume=/dev/mapper/rhel-swap rd\
.lvm.lv=rhel/root rd.lvm.lv=rhel/swap rhgb quiet
initrd ($root)/initramfs-5.14.0-162.6.1.el9_1.x86_64.img $tuned_initrd




      Press Ctrl-x to start, Ctrl-c for a command prompt or Escape to
      discard edits and return to the menu. Pressing Tab lists
      possible completions.
```

Figure 11-2 GRUB2 Kernel Entry Edit

If you do not wish to boot the system at this time, you can press ESC to discard the changes and return to the main menu.

The grub> command prompt appears when you press Ctrl+c while in the edit window or a *c* from the main menu. The command mode provides you with the opportunity to execute debugging, recovery, and many other tasks. You can view available commands by pressing the TAB key. See Figure 11-3.

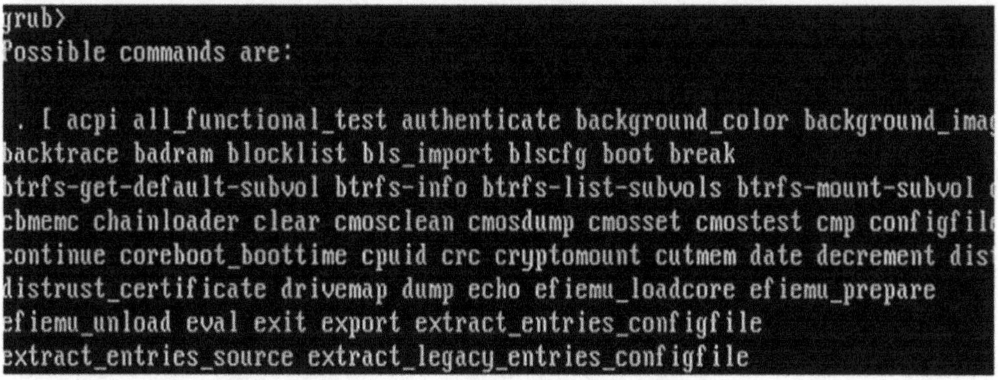

```
grub>
Possible commands are:

. [ acpi all_functional_test authenticate background_color background_ima\
backtrace badram blocklist bls_import blscfg boot break
btrfs-get-default-subvol btrfs-info btrfs-list-subvols btrfs-mount-subvol \
cbmemc chainloader clear cmosclean cmosdump cmosset cmostest cmp configfil\
continue coreboot_boottime cpuid crc cryptomount cutmem date decrement dis\
distrust_certificate drivemap dump echo efiemu_loadcore efiemu_prepare
efiemu_unload eval exit export extract_entries_configfile
extract_entries_source extract_legacy_entries_configfile
```

Figure 11-3 GRUB2 Commands

There are over one hundred commands available to perform a variety of tasks at the GRUB2 level.

Understanding GRUB2 Configuration Files

The GRUB2 configuration file, *grub.cfg*, is located in the */boot/grub2* directory. This file is referenced at boot time. This file is generated automatically when a new kernel is installed or upgraded, so it is not advisable to modify it directly, as your changes will be overwritten. The primary source file that is used to regenerate *grub.cfg* is called *grub*, and it is located in the */etc/default* directory. This file defines the directives that govern how GRUB2 should behave at boot time. Any changes made to the *grub* file will only take effect after the *grub2-mkconfig* utility has been executed.

Let's analyze the two files to understand their syntax and contents.

The /etc/default/grub File

The *grub* file defines the directives that control the behavior of GRUB2 at boot time. Any changes in this file must be followed by the execution of the *grub2-mkconfig* command in order to be reflected in *grub.cfg*.

Here is an enumerated list of the default settings from the *grub* file, followed by an explanation in Table 11-1:

```
[user1@server1 ~]$ nl /etc/default/grub
     1   GRUB_TIMEOUT=5
     2   GRUB_DISTRIBUTOR="$(sed 's, release .*$,,g' /etc/system-release)"
     3   GRUB_DEFAULT=saved
     4   GRUB_DISABLE_SUBMENU=true
     5   GRUB_TERMINAL_OUTPUT="console"
     6   GRUB_CMDLINE_LINUX="crashkernel=1G-4G:192M,4G-64G:256M,64G-:512M resume=
/dev/mapper/rhel-swap rd.lvm.lv=rhel/root rd.lvm.lv=rhel/swap rhgb quiet"
     7   GRUB_DISABLE_RECOVERY="true"
     8   GRUB_ENABLE_BLSCFG=true
```

Directive	Description
GRUB_TIMEOUT	Defines the wait time, in seconds, before booting off the default kernel. Default value is 5.
GRUB_DISTRIBUTOR	Sets the name of the Linux distribution
GRUB_DEFAULT	Boots the selected option from the previous system boot
GRUB_DISABLE_SUBMENU	Enables/disables the appearance of GRUB2 submenu
GRUB_TERMINAL_OUTPUT	Sets the default terminal
GRUB_CMDLINE_LINUX	Specifies the command line options to pass to the kernel at boot time
GRUB_DISABLE_RECOVERY	Lists/hides system recovery entries in the GRUB2 menu
GRUB_ENABLE_BLSCFG	Defines whether to use the new bootloader specification to manage bootloader configuration

Table 11-1 GRUB2 Default Settings

Generally, you do not need to make any changes to this file, as the default settings are good enough for normal system operation.

The grub.cfg File

The *grub.cfg* is the main GRUB2 configuration file that supplies boot-time configuration information. This file is located in the */boot/grub2* directory on BIOS-based systems and in the */boot/efi/EFI/redhat* directory on UEFI-based systems. This file can be recreated manually with the *grub2-mkconfig* utility, or it is automatically regenerated when a new kernel is installed or upgraded. In either case, this file will lose any previous manual changes made to it.

During the recreation process, the *grub2-mkconfig* command also uses the settings defined in helper scripts located in the */etc/grub.d* directory. There are plenty of files located here, as shown below:

```
[user1@server1 ~]$ sudo ls -l /etc/grub.d
total 108
-rwxr-xr-x. 1 root root  9346 Aug 25 14:04 00_header
-rwxr-xr-x. 1 root root  1046 Aug 19 14:28 00_tuned
-rwxr-xr-x. 1 root root   236 Aug 25 14:04 01_users
-rwxr-xr-x. 1 root root   835 Aug 25 14:04 08_fallback_counting
-rwxr-xr-x. 1 root root 19075 Aug 25 14:04 10_linux
-rwxr-xr-x. 1 root root   833 Aug 25 14:04 10_reset_boot_success
-rwxr-xr-x. 1 root root   892 Aug 25 14:04 12_menu_auto_hide
-rwxr-xr-x. 1 root root   410 Aug 25 14:04 14_menu_show_once
-rwxr-xr-x. 1 root root 13613 Aug 25 14:04 20_linux_xen
-rwxr-xr-x. 1 root root  2562 Aug 25 14:04 20_ppc_terminfo
-rwxr-xr-x. 1 root root 10869 Aug 25 14:04 30_os-prober
-rwxr-xr-x. 1 root root  1122 Aug 25 14:04 30_uefi-firmware
-rwxr-xr-x. 1 root root   703 Aug 10 08:27 35_fwupd
-rwxr-xr-x. 1 root root   218 Aug 25 14:04 40_custom
-rwxr-xr-x. 1 root root   219 Aug 25 14:04 41_custom
-rw-r--r--. 1 root root   483 Aug 25 14:04 README
```

The first script, *00_header*, sets the GRUB2 environment; the *10_linux* script searches for all installed kernels on the same disk partition; the *30_os-prober* searches for the presence of other operating systems; and *40_custom* and *41_custom* store user customizations. An example would be to add custom entries to the boot menu.

The *grub.cfg* file also sources the *grubenv* file located in the */boot/grub2* directory for kernel options and other settings. Here is what this file contains on *server1*:

```
[user1@server1 ~]$ sudo cat /boot/grub2/grubenv
# GRUB Environment Block
# WARNING: Do not edit this file by tools other than grub-editenv!!!
saved_entry=96daf847168342be8233b83a92a2a3f0-5.14.0-162.6.1.el9_1.x86_64
menu_auto_hide=1
boot_success=0
boot_indeterminate=0
################################################################################
################################################################################
################################################################################
```

If a new kernel is installed, the existing kernel entries remain intact. All bootable kernels are listed in the GRUB2 menu, and any of the kernel entries can be selected to boot.

Exercise 11-1: Change Default System Boot Timeout

This exercise should be done on *server1* as *user1* with *sudo* where required.

In this exercise, you will change the default system boot timeout value to 8 seconds persistently, and validate.

1. Edit the */etc/default/grub* file and change the setting as follows:

    ```
    GRUB_TIMEOUT=8
    ```

2. Execute the *grub2-mkconfig* command to reproduce *grub.cfg*:

    ```
    [user1@server1 ~]$ sudo grub2-mkconfig -o /boot/grub2/grub.cfg
    Generating grub configuration file ...
    done
    ```

3. Restart the system with *sudo reboot* and confirm the new timeout value when GRUB2 menu appears.

This concludes the exercise.

Booting into Specific Targets

RHEL boots into graphical target state by default if the Server with GUI software selection is made during installation. It can also be directed to boot into non-default but less capable operating targets from the GRUB2 menu. Additionally, in situations when it becomes mandatory to boot the system into an administrative state for implementing a function that cannot be otherwise performed in other target states or for system recovery, RHEL offers emergency and rescue boot targets. These special target levels can be launched from the GRUB2 interface by selecting a kernel, pressing *e* to enter the edit mode, and appending the desired target name to the line that begins with the keyword "linux".

> **EXAM TIP:** You must know how to boot a RHEL 9 system into a specific target from the GRUB2 menu to modify the fstab file or reset an unknown root user password.

Here is how you would append "emergency" to the kernel line entry:

```
load_video
set gfxpayload=keep
insmod gzio
linux ($root)/vmlinuz-5.14.0-162.6.1.el9_1.x86_64 root=/dev/mapper/rhel-root r\
o crashkernel=1G-4G:192M,4G-64G:256M,64G-:512M resume=/dev/mapper/rhel-swap rd\
.lvm.lv=rhel/root rd.lvm.lv=rhel/swap rhgb quiet emergency_
initrd ($root)/initramfs-5.14.0-162.6.1.el9_1.x86_64.img $tuned_initrd
```

Press Ctrl+x after making the modification to boot the system into the supplied target. You will be required to enter the *root* user password to log on. Run *reboot* after you are done to reboot the system.

```
You are in emergency mode. After logging in, type "journalctl -xb" to view
system logs, "systemctl reboot" to reboot, "systemctl default" or "exit"
to boot into default mode.
Give root password for maintenance
(or press Control-D to continue): _
```

Similarly, you can append "rescue" (or simply "1", "s", or "single") to the "linux" line and press Ctrl+x to boot into the rescue target.

Exercise 11-2: Reset the root User Password

This exercise should be done on *server1*.

For this exercise, assume that the *root* user password is lost, stolen, or forgotten, and it needs to be reset.

In this exercise, you will terminate the boot process at an early stage to be placed in a special debug shell to reset the *root* password.

1. Reboot or reset *server1*, and interact with GRUB2 by pressing a key before the autoboot times out. Highlight the rescue kernel entry in the GRUB2 menu and press *e* to enter the edit mode. Scroll down to the line entry that begins with the keyword "linux" and press the End key to go to the end of that line:

```
load_video
set gfxpayload=keep
insmod gzio
linux ($root)/vmlinuz-5.14.0-162.6.1.el9_1.x86_64 root=/dev/mapper/rhel-root r\
o crashkernel=1G-4G:192M,4G-64G:256M,64G-:512M resume=/dev/mapper/rhel-swap rd\
.lvm.lv=rhel/root rd.lvm.lv=rhel/swap rhgb quiet
initrd ($root)/initramfs-5.14.0-162.6.1.el9_1.x86_64.img $tuned_initrd
```

2. Modify this kernel string and append "rd.break" to the end of the line to make the boot process stop after the initial ram disk (rd) has been loaded into memory. It should look like:

```
load_video
set gfxpayload=keep
insmod gzio
linux ($root)/vmlinuz-5.14.0-162.6.1.el9_1.x86_64 root=/dev/mapper/rhel-root r\
o crashkernel=1G-4G:192M,4G-64G:256M,64G-:512M resume=/dev/mapper/rhel-swap rd\
.lvm.lv=rhel/root rd.lvm.lv=rhel/swap rhgb quiet rd.break
initrd ($root)/initramfs-5.14.0-162.6.1.el9_1.x86_64.img $tuned_initrd
```

3. Press Ctrl+x when done to boot to the special shell. The system mounts the root file system read-only on the */sysroot* directory. Press the Enter key when prompted to enter the maintenance mode:

```
Entering emergency mode. Exit the shell to continue.
Type "journalctl" to view system logs.
You might want to save "/run/initramfs/rdsosreport.txt" to a USB stick or /boot
after mounting them and attach it to a bug report.

switch_root:/#
```

4. Make */sysroot* appear as mounted on */* using the *chroot* command, and confirm:

```
sh-5.1# chroot /sysroot
sh-5.1# pwd
/
sh-5.1#
```

5. Remount the root file system in read/write mode to allow the *passwd* command to modify the *shadow* file and replace the password:

```
sh-5.1# mount -o remount,rw /
```

6. Enter a new password for *root* by invoking the *passwd* command:

```
sh-5.1# passwd
Changing password for user root.
New password:
BAD PASSWORD: The password is shorter than 8 characters
Retype new password:
passwd: all authentication tokens updated successfully.
```

7. Create a hidden file called *.autorelabel* to instruct the operating system to run SELinux relabeling on all files, including the *shadow* file that was updated with the new *root* password, on the next reboot:

```
sh-5.1# touch .autorelabel
```

 SELinux is discussed in detail in Chapter 20 "Security Enhanced Linux".

8. Issue the *exit* command to return to the chroot shell and then again to relabel SELinux and restart the system to boot to the default target.

```
sh-5.1# exit
exit
sh-5.1# exit
exit
[  608.973430] selinux-autorelabel[888]: *** Warning -- SELinux targeted policy relabel is required.
[  608.973903] selinux-autorelabel[888]: *** Relabeling could take a very long time, depending on fi
le
[  608.974653] selinux-autorelabel[888]: *** system size and speed of hard drives.
[  618.457965] selinux-autorelabel[894]: Relabeling / /boot /dev /dev/hugepages /dev/mqueue /dev/pts
 /dev/shm /run /sys /sys/fs/cgroup /sys/fs/pstore /sys/kernel/debug /sys/kernel/tracing
```

Depending on the system size and disk speed, it might take a few minutes for the system to complete the relabeling process and return to a fully functional state.

The Linux Kernel

The *kernel* is the core of the Linux system. It manages hardware, enforces security, regulates access to the system, as well as handles processes, services, and application workloads. It is a collection of software components called *modules* that work in tandem to provide a stable and controlled platform. Modules are *device drivers* that control hardware devices—the processor, memory, storage, controller cards, and peripheral equipment, and interact with software subsystems, such as storage management, file systems, networking, and virtualization.

Some of these modules are static to the kernel and are integral to system functionality, while others are loaded dynamically as needed, making the kernel speedier and more efficient in terms of overall performance and less vulnerable to crashes. RHEL 9 is shipped with kernel version 5.14.0 for the 64-bit Intel/AMD processor architecture computers with single, multi-core, and multi-processor configurations. On a Linux system, **uname -m** reveals the architecture of the system.

The default kernel installed during the installation is usually adequate for most system needs; however, it requires a rebuild when a new functionality is added or removed. The new functionality may be introduced by installing a new kernel, upgrading an existing one, installing a new hardware device, or changing a critical system component. Likewise, an existing functionality that is no longer needed may be removed to make the overall footprint of the kernel smaller, resulting in improved performance and reduced memory utilization.

To control the behavior of the modules, and the kernel in general, a variety of tunable parameters are set that define a baseline for kernel functionality. Some of these parameters must be tuned to allow certain applications and database software to be installed smoothly and operate properly.

RHEL allows you to generate and store several custom kernels with varied configuration and required modules, but only one of them can be active at a time. A different kernel may be loaded by interacting with GRUB2.

Kernel Packages

Just like any other software that comes in the rpm format for RHEL, the software comprising the kernel is no different. There is a set of core kernel packages that must be installed on the system at a minimum to make it work. Additional packages providing supplementary kernel support are also available. Table 11-2 lists and describes the core and some add-on kernel packages.

Kernel Package	Description
kernel	Contains no files, but ensures other kernel packages are accurately installed
kernel-core	Includes a minimal number of modules to provide core functionality
kernel-devel	Includes support for building kernel modules
kernel-headers	Includes files to support the interface between the kernel and userspace libraries and programs
kernel-modules	Contains modules for common hardware devices
kernel-modules-extra	Contains modules for not-so-common hardware devices
kernel-tools	Includes tools to manipulate the kernel
kernel-tools-libs	Includes the libraries to support the kernel tools

Table 11-2 Kernel Packages

Moreover, packages containing the source code for RHEL 9 are also available for those who wish to customize and recompile the code for their precise needs.

Currently, the following kernel packages are installed on *server1*:

```
[user1@server1 ~]$ rpm -qa |grep ^kernel
kernel-tools-libs-5.14.0-162.6.1.el9_1.x86_64
kernel-tools-5.14.0-162.6.1.el9_1.x86_64
kernel-core-5.14.0-162.6.1.el9_1.x86_64
kernel-modules-5.14.0-162.6.1.el9_1.x86_64
kernel-5.14.0-162.6.1.el9_1.x86_64
```

The output returns six kernel packages that were loaded during the OS installation.

Analyzing Kernel Version

Sometimes you need to ascertain the version of the kernel running on the system to check for compatibility with an application or database that you need to deploy. RHEL has a basic tool available to extract the version. The *uname* command with the -r switch depicts this information, as follows:

```
[user1@server1 ~]$ uname -r
5.14.0-162.6.1.el9_1.x86_64
```

The output shows the current kernel version in use is 5.14.0-162.6.1.el9_1.x86_64. An anatomy of the version is illustrated in Figure 11-4 and explained subsequently.

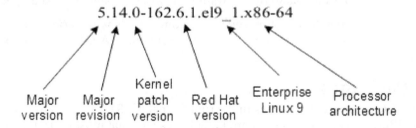

Figure 11-4 Anatomy of a Kernel Version

From left to right:

- ✓ (5) major version of the Linux kernel. It changes when significant alterations, enhancements, and updates to the previous major version are made.
- ✓ (14) major revision of the 5th major version
- ✓ (0) represents patched version of 5.14 with minor bug and security hole fixes, minor enhancements, and so on.
- ✓ (162.6.1) Red Hat customized version of 5.14.0
- ✓ (el9_1) Enterprise Linux this kernel is built for
- ✓ (x86_64) architecture this kernel is built for

A further analysis designates that 5.14.0 holds the general Linux kernel version information, the numbers and letters (162.6.1.el9_1) represent the Red Hat specific information, and x86_64 identifies the hardware architecture type.

Understanding Kernel Directory Structure

Kernel and its support files are stored at different locations in the directory hierarchy, of which three locations—*/boot*, */proc*, and */usr/lib/modules*—are noteworthy.

The /boot Location

/boot is essentially a file system that is created at system installation. It houses the Linux kernel, GRUB2 configuration, and other kernel and boot support files. A long listing produces the following output for this file system:

```
[user1@server1 ~]$ ls -l /boot
total 239936
-rw-r--r--. 1 root root    212826 Sep 30 07:49 config-5.14.0-162.6.1.el9_1.x86_64
drwxr-xr-x. 3 root root        17 Jan 26 16:38 efi
drwx------. 5 root root        97 Jan 31 14:03 grub2
-rw-------. 1 root root 124157674 Jan 26 16:46 initramfs-0-rescue-96daf847168342be8233b8
2a2a3f0.img
-rw-------. 1 root root  57917447 Jan 26 16:51 initramfs-5.14.0-162.6.1.el9_1.x86_64.img
-rw-------. 1 root root  34777600 Jan 31 08:37 initramfs-5.14.0-162.6.1.el9_1.x86_64kdump
.img
drwxr-xr-x. 3 root root        21 Jan 26 16:43 loader
lrwxrwxrwx. 1 root root        51 Jan 26 16:44 symvers-5.14.0-162.6.1.el9_1.x86_64.gz ->
ib/modules/5.14.0-162.6.1.el9_1.x86_64/symvers.gz
-rw-------. 1 root root   5316561 Sep 30 07:49 System.map-5.14.0-162.6.1.el9_1.x86_64
-rwxr-xr-x. 1 root root  11649784 Jan 26 16:45 vmlinuz-0-rescue-96daf847168342be8233b83a
2a3f0
-rwxr-xr-x. 1 root root  11649784 Sep 30 07:49 vmlinuz-5.14.0-162.6.1.el9_1.x86_64
```

The output displays several files, five of which are for the kernel and two for its rescue version. The *vmlinuz* is the main kernel file with *config*, *initramfs*, *symvers*, and *System.map* storing the kernel's configuration, boot image, CRC values of all the variables used in the kernel and modules, and mapping, respectively.

The files for the rescue version have the string "rescue" embedded within their names, as indicated in the above output.

The *efi* and *grub2* subdirectories under */boot* hold bootloader information specific to firmware type used on the system: UEFI or BIOS. For *server1*, *grub2* contains GRUB2 information as shown below:

```
[user1@server1 ~]$ sudo ls -l /boot/grub2
total 32
-rw-r--r--. 1 root root   64 Jan 26 16:50 device.map
drwxr-xr-x. 2 root root   25 Jan 26 16:50 fonts
-rw-------. 1 root root 7118 Jan 26 16:50 grub.cfg
-rw-------. 1 root root 1024 Jan 31 14:03 grubenv
drwxr-xr-x. 2 root root 8192 Jan 26 16:50 i386-pc
drwxr-xr-x. 2 root root 4096 Jan 26 16:50 locale
```

The files *grub.cfg* and *grubenv* contain critical data with the former holding bootable kernel information and the latter stores the environment information that the kernel uses.

The subdirectory *loader* under */boot* is the storage location for configuration of the running and rescue kernels. The configuration is stored in files under the *entries* subdirectory, as shown below:

```
[user1@server1 ~]$ sudo ls -l /boot/loader/entries/
total 8
-rw-r--r--. 1 root root 484 Jan 31 13:21 96daf847168342be8233b83a92a2a3f0-0-rescue.conf
-rw-r--r--. 1 root root 442 Jan 31 13:21 96daf847168342be8233b83a92a2a3f0-5.14.0-162.6.
9 1.x86 64.conf
```

The files are named using the machine id of the system as stored in the */etc/machine-id* file and the kernel version they are for. The content of the kernel file is presented below:

```
[user1@server1 ~]$ sudo cat /boot/loader/entries/96daf847168342be8233b83a92a2a3f0-5.14
2.6.1.el9_1.x86_64.conf
title Red Hat Enterprise Linux (5.14.0-162.6.1.el9_1.x86_64) 9.1 (Plow)
version 5.14.0-162.6.1.el9_1.x86_64
linux /vmlinuz-5.14.0-162.6.1.el9_1.x86_64
initrd /initramfs-5.14.0-162.6.1.el9_1.x86_64.img $tuned_initrd
options root=/dev/mapper/rhel-root ro crashkernel=1G-4G:192M,4G-64G:256M,64G-:512M res
dev/mapper/rhel-swap rd.lvm.lv=rhel/root rd.lvm.lv=rhel/swap rhgb quiet
grub_users $grub_users
grub_arg --unrestricted
grub_class rhel
```

The "title" is displayed on the bootloader screen where the countdown to autoboot a selected kernel entry runs. Other than the kernel version, and the default kernel and boot image filenames, the environment variables "kernelopts" and "tuned_params" supply various values to the booting kernel to control its behavior.

The /proc Location

/proc is a virtual, memory-based file system. Its contents are created and updated in memory at system boot and during runtime, and they are destroyed at system shutdown. It maintains information about the current state of the kernel, which includes hardware configuration and status information about processor, memory, storage, file systems, swap, processes, network interfaces and connections, routing, etc. This data is kept in tens of thousands of zero-byte files organized in a hierarchy of hundreds of subdirectories. A long directory listing of */proc* is provided below:

```
[user1@server1 ~]$ ls -l /proc
total 0
dr-xr-xr-x.  9 root         root             0 Jan 31 13:53 1
dr-xr-xr-x.  9 root         root             0 Jan 31 13:53 10
dr-xr-xr-x.  9 root         root             0 Jan 31 13:54 1102
dr-xr-xr-x.  9 root         root             0 Jan 31 13:54 1103
dr-xr-xr-x.  9 root         root             0 Jan 31 13:54 1104
. . . . . . . .
```

Some subdirectory names are numerical and contain information about a specific process, and the process ID matches the subdirectory name. Within each subdirectory are other files and subdirectories containing a plethora of information, such as memory segments for processes and configuration data for system components. You can view the configuration of a particular item using any text file viewing tool. The following show selections from the *cpuinfo* and *meminfo* files that hold processor and memory information:

RHCSA Red Hat Enterprise Linux 9: Training and Exam Preparation Guide

```
[user1@server1 ~]$ cat /proc/cpuinfo
processor        : 0
vendor_id        : GenuineIntel
cpu family       : 6
model            : 142
model name       : Intel(R) Core(TM) i7-10510U CPU @ 1.80GHz
stepping         : 12
microcode        : 0xffffffff
cpu MHz          : 2304.006
cache size       : 8192 KB
physical id      : 0
siblings         : 2
core id          : 0
cpu cores        : 2

. . . . . . . .
[user1@server1 ~]$ cat /proc/meminfo
MemTotal:         1813400 kB
MemFree:           763820 kB
MemAvailable:     1190180 kB
Buffers:             2792 kB
Cached:            547768 kB
SwapCached:             0 kB
Active:            213536 kB
Inactive:          664004 kB

. . . . . . . .
```

The data stored under *proc* is referenced by many system utilities, including *top*, *ps*, *uname*, *free*, *uptime*, and *w* to produce their output.

The /usr/lib/modules Location

This directory holds information about kernel modules. Underneath it are subdirectories specific to the kernels installed on the system. For example, the long listing of *usr/lib/modules* below shows that there is only one kernel installed. The name of the subdirectory corresponds with the installed kernel version.

```
[user1@server1 ~]$ ls -l /usr/lib/modules
total 4
drwxr-xr-x. 3 root root   19 Jan 26 16:39 5.14.0-162.5.1.el9_1.x86_64
drwxr-xr-x. 7 root root 4096 Jan 26 16:50 5.14.0-162.6.1.el9_1.x86_64
```

And this subdirectory contains:

```
[user1@server1 ~]$ ls -l /usr/lib/modules/5.14.0-162.6.1.el9_1.x86_64/
total 20584
lrwxrwxrwx. 1 root root       44 Sep 30 07:49 build -> /usr/src/kerne
_1.x86_64
-rw-r--r--. 1 root root   212826 Sep 30 07:49 config
drwxr-xr-x. 14 root root     156 Jan 26 16:39 kernel
-rw-r--r--. 1 root root   846660 Jan 26 16:50 modules.alias
-rw-r--r--. 1 root root   806978 Jan 26 16:50 modules.alias.bin
-rw-r--r--. 1 root root      461 Sep 30 07:49 modules.block
-rw-r--r--. 1 root root     9387 Sep 30 07:49 modules.builtin

. . . . . . . .
```

There are several files and a few subdirectories here; they hold module-specific information for the kernel version.

One of the key subdirectories is *usr/lib/modules/5.14.0-162.6.1.el9_1.x86_64/kernel/drivers*, which stores modules for a variety of hardware and software components in various subdirectories, as shown in the listing below:

```
[user1@server1 ~]$ ls -l /usr/lib/modules/5.14.0-162.6.1.el9_1.x86_64/kernel/drivers/
total 60
drwxr-xr-x. 5 root root 4096 Jan 26 16:39 acpi
drwxr-xr-x. 2 root root  169 Jan 26 16:39 ata
drwxr-xr-x. 3 root root   20 Jan 26 16:39 base
drwxr-xr-x. 2 root root   24 Jan 26 16:39 bcma
drwxr-xr-x. 4 root root  174 Jan 26 16:39 block
drwxr-xr-x. 2 root root 4096 Jan 26 16:39 bluetooth
drwxr-xr-x. 3 root root   17 Jan 26 16:39 bus

. . . . . . . .
```

Additional modules may be installed on the system to support more components.

Installing the Kernel

Installing kernel packages requires extra care because it could leave your system in an unbootable or undesirable state. It is advisable to have the bootable medium handy prior to starting the kernel install process. By default, the *dnf* command adds a new kernel to the system, leaving the existing kernel(s) intact. It does not replace or overwrite any existing kernel files.

> **EXAM TIP:** Always install a new version of the kernel instead of upgrading it. The upgrade process removes any existing kernel and replaces it with a new one. In case of a post-installation issue, you will not be able to revert to the old working kernel.

A new version of the kernel is typically required if an application needs to be deployed on the system that requires a different kernel to operate. When deficiencies or bugs are identified in the existing kernel, it can hamper the kernel's smooth operation. In either case, the new kernel addresses existing issues as well as adds bug fixes, security updates, new features, and improved support for hardware devices.

The *dnf* command is the preferred tool to install a kernel, as it resolves and installs any required dependencies automatically. The *rpm* command may alternatively be used; however, you must install any reported dependencies manually.

The kernel packages for RHEL 9 are available to subscribers for download on Red Hat's Customer Portal. You need a user account in order to log in and download.

Exercise 11-3: Download and Install a New Kernel

This exercise should be done on *server1* as *user1* with *sudo* where required.

In this exercise, you will download the latest available kernel packages from the Red Hat Customer Portal and install them using the *dnf* command. You will ensure that the existing kernel and its configuration remain intact.

1. Check the version of the running kernel:

```
[user1@server1 ~]$ uname -r
5.14.0-162.6.1.el9_1.x86_64
```

The output discloses the current active kernel version as 5.14.0-162.6.1.el9_1.x86_64.

2. List the kernel packages currently installed:

```
[user1@server1 ~]$ rpm -qa | grep ^kernel
kernel-tools-libs-5.14.0-162.6.1.el9_1.x86_64
kernel-tools-5.14.0-162.6.1.el9_1.x86_64
kernel-core-5.14.0-162.6.1.el9_1.x86_64
kernel-modules-5.14.0-162.6.1.el9_1.x86_64
kernel-5.14.0-162.6.1.el9_1.x86_64
```

There are five kernel packages on the system as reported.

3. Access the Red Hat Customer Portal webpage at *access.redhat.com* and click Log In to sign in to the portal using the credentials you used/created in Chapter 01 "Local Installation" for the developer account:

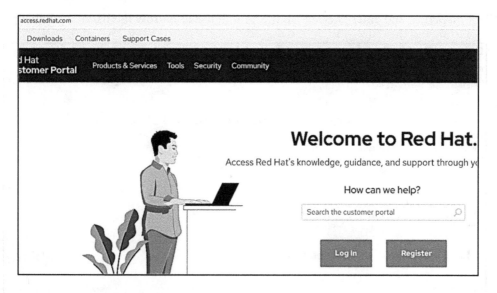

4. Click Downloads at the top:

5. Click "Red Hat Enterprise Linux" under "By Category" on the next screen:

6. Click Packages and enter "kernel" in the Search bar to narrow the list of available packages:

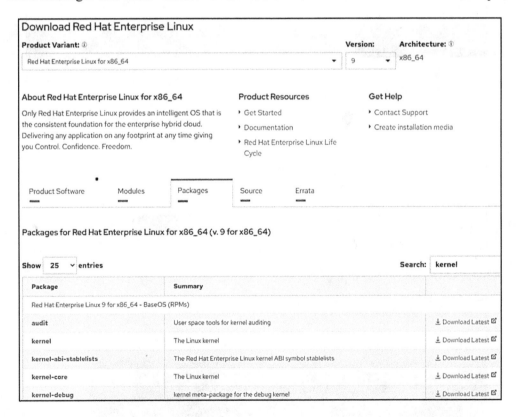

7. Click "Download Latest" beside the packages *kernel*, *kernel-core*, *kernel-modules*, *kernel-tools*, and *kernel-tools-libs* to download them. These are the new packages for the version you currently have on the system.
8. Once downloaded, move the packages to the */tmp* directory using the *mv* command.
9. List the packages after moving them:

```
[user1@server1 ~]$ ls /tmp/kernel*
/tmp/kernel-5.14.0-162.12.1.el9_1.x86_64.rpm
/tmp/kernel-core-5.14.0-162.12.1.el9_1.x86_64.rpm
/tmp/kernel-modules-5.14.0-162.12.1.el9_1.x86_64.rpm
/tmp/kernel-tools-5.14.0-162.12.1.el9_1.x86_64.rpm
/tmp/kernel-tools-libs-5.14.0-162.12.1.el9_1.x86_64.rpm
```

10. Install all five packages at once using the *dnf* command:

```
[user1@server1 ~]$ sudo dnf install /tmp/kernel* -y
Dependencies resolved.
===================================================================================
 Package              Architecture Version              Repository        Size
===================================================================================
Installing:
 kernel               x86_64       5.14.0-162.12.1.el9_1 @commandline     1.9 M
Upgrading:
 kernel-tools         x86_64       5.14.0-162.12.1.el9_1 @commandline     2.1 M
 kernel-tools-libs    x86_64       5.14.0-162.12.1.el9_1 @commandline     1.9 M
Installing dependencies:
 kernel-core          x86_64       5.14.0-162.12.1.el9_1 @commandline      46 M
 kernel-modules       x86_64       5.14.0-162.12.1.el9_1 @commandline      34 M

Transaction Summary
===================================================================================
Install  3 Packages
Upgrade  2 Packages

Total size: 85 M
Is this ok [y/N]: y

.........
Installed products updated.

Upgraded:
  kernel-tools-5.14.0-162.12.1.el9_1.x86_64 kernel-tools-libs-5.14.0-162.12.1
Installed:
  kernel-5.14.0-162.12.1.el9_1.x86_64          kernel-core-5.14.0-162.12.1.e
  kernel-modules-5.14.0-162.12.1.el9_1.x86_64

Complete!
```

11. Confirm the installation:

```
[user1@server1 ~]$ sudo dnf list installed kernel*
```

```
Installed Packages
kernel.x86_64                           5.14.0-162.6.1.el9_1            @anaconda
kernel.x86_64                           5.14.0-162.12.1.el9_1           @@commandline
kernel-core.x86_64                      5.14.0-162.6.1.el9_1            @anaconda
kernel-core.x86_64                      5.14.0-162.12.1.el9_1           @@commandline
kernel-modules.x86_64                   5.14.0-162.6.1.el9_1            @anaconda
kernel-modules.x86_64                   5.14.0-162.12.1.el9_1           @@commandline
kernel-tools.x86_64                     5.14.0-162.12.1.el9_1           @@commandline
kernel-tools-libs.x86_64                5.14.0-162.12.1.el9_1           @@commandline
```

The output indicates that packages for a higher kernel version 5.14.0-162.12.1.el9_1 have been installed. It also shows the presence of the previous kernel packages.

12. The */boot/grub2/grubenv* file now has the directive "saved_entry" set to the new kernel, which implies that this new kernel will boot on the next system restart:

```
[user1@server1 ~]$ sudo cat /boot/grub2/grubenv
# GRUB Environment Block
# WARNING: Do not edit this file by tools other than grub-editenv!!!
saved_entry=96daf847168342be8233b83a92a2a3f0-5.14.0-162.12.1.el9_1.x86_64
menu_auto_hide=1
boot_success=1
boot_indeterminate=2
####################################################################################
####################################################################################
```

13. Reboot the system. You will see the new kernel entry in the GRUB2 boot list at the top. The system will autoboot this new default kernel.

```
Red Hat Enterprise Linux (5.14.0-162.12.1.el9_1.x86_64) 9.1 (Plow)
Red Hat Enterprise Linux (5.14.0-162.6.1.el9_1.x86_64) 9.1 (Plow)
Red Hat Enterprise Linux (0-rescue-96daf847168342be8233b83a92a2a3f0) 9.1
```

14. Run the *uname* command after the system has been booted up to confirm the loading of the new kernel:

```
[user1@server1 ~]$ uname -r
5.14.0-162.12.1.el9_1.x86_64
```

The new kernel is active.

15. You can also view the contents of the *version* and *cmdline* files under */proc* to verify the active kernel:

```
[user1@server1 ~]$ cat /proc/version
Linux version 5.14.0-162.12.1.el9_1.x86_64 (mockbuild@x86-vm-07.build.eng.bos.redhat.co
gcc (GCC) 11.3.1 20220421 (Red Hat 11.3.1-2), GNU ld version 2.35.2-24.el9) #1 SMP PREI
DYNAMIC Tue Dec 20 06:06:30 EST 2022
[user1@server1 ~]$
[user1@server1 ~]$ cat /proc/cmdline
BOOT_IMAGE=(hd0,msdos1)/vmlinuz-5.14.0-162.12.1.el9_1.x86_64 root=/dev/mapper/rhel-root
crashkernel=1G-4G:192M,4G-64G:256M,64G-:512M resume=/dev/mapper/rhel-swap rd.lvm.lv=rhe
ot rd.lvm.lv=rhel/swap rhgb quiet
```

This concludes the process of downloading and installing a new kernel on RHEL 9.

Chapter Summary

This chapter presented a high-level look at the Linux boot process, highlighting the four phases the system passes through and the complexities involved. We reviewed firmware and looked at preboot administration tasks, which included interacting with the bootloader program, booting into specific targets, and an analysis of the bootloader configuration files. We performed a critical exercise that focused on resetting a forgotten or lost root user password.

The next major topic discussed the Linux kernel, its key components and management. We explored various packages that made up the core kernel software, performed an anatomy of its versioning, and examined key directories and file systems that are employed to hold kernel-specific information. Before the chapter was concluded, we downloaded and installed a new kernel without impacting the old one.

Review Questions

1. You want to view the parameters passed to the kernel at boot time. Which virtual file would you look at?
2. UEFI is replacing BIOS on new computers. True or False?
3. You have changed the timeout value in the *grub* configuration file located in the */etc/default* directory. Which command would you run now to ensure the change takes effect on next system reboots?
4. Name the location of the *grub.efi* file in the UEFI-based systems.
5. What is the name of the default bootloader program in RHEL 9?
6. Which file stores the location of the boot partition on the BIOS systems?
7. You have lost the *root* user password and you need to reset it. What would you add to the default kernel boot string to break the boot process at an early stage?
8. The *systemd* command may be used to rebuild a new kernel. True or False?
9. What does the *chroot* command do?
10. At what stage should you interrupt the boot sequence to boot the system into a non-default target?
11. Which two files would you view to obtain processor and memory information?
12. By default, GRUB2 is stored in the MBR on a BIOS-based system. True or False?
13. You have installed a new version of the kernel. What would you now have to do to make it the default boot kernel?
14. What is the system initialization and service management scheme called?

Answers to Review Questions

1. The *cmdline* file in the */proc* file system.
2. True.
3. You will need to run the *grub2-mkconfig* command.
4. The *grub.efi* file is located in the */boot/efi/EFI/redhat* directory.
5. GRUB2.
6. The *grub.cfg* file stores the location information of the boot partition.
7. You would add rd.break to the kernel boot string.
8. False.
9. The *chroot* command changes the specified directory path to /.
10. At the GRUB2 stage.
11. The *cpuinfo* and *meminfo* files in the */proc* file system.

12. True.
13. Nothing. The install process takes care of that.
14. It is called *systemd*.

Do-It-Yourself Challenge Labs

The following labs are useful to strengthen most of the concepts and topics learned in this chapter. It is expected that you perform the labs without external help. A step-by-step guide is not supplied, as the knowledge and skill required to implement the labs have already been disseminated in the chapter; however, hints to the relevant major topic(s) are included.

Use the lab environment built specifically for end-of-chapter labs. See sub-section "Lab Environment for End-of-Chapter Labs" in Chapter 01 "Local Installation" for details.

Lab 11-1: Enable Verbose System Boot

As *user1* with *sudo* on *server3*, remove "quiet" from the end of the value of the variable GRUB_CMDLINE_LINUX in the */etc/default/grub* file and run *grub2-mkconfig* to apply the update. Reboot the system and observe that the system now displays verbose information during the boot process. (Hint: The GRUB2 Bootloader and Exercise 11-1).

Lab 11-2: Reset root User Password

As *root* on *server4*, reset the *root* user password by booting the system into emergency mode with SELinux disabled. Log in with *root* and enter the new password after the reboot for validation. (Hint: The GRUB2 Bootloader and Exercise 11-2).

Lab 11-3: Install New Kernel

As *user1* with *sudo* on *server3*, check the current version of the kernel using the *uname* or *rpm* command. Download a higher version from the Red Hat Customer Portal and install it. Reboot the system and ensure the new kernel is listed on the bootloader menu. (Hint: The Linux Kernel and Exercise 11-3).

## Chapter 12

System Initialization, Message Logging, and System Tuning

This chapter describes the following major topics:

➢ Understand systemd, units, and targets
➢ Analyze service and target unit configuration files
➢ List and view status of running units
➢ Manage service units and target units
➢ Display and configure default system boot target
➢ Switch into non-default targets
➢ Analyze system log configuration file
➢ Examine log file rotation settings
➢ Review boot and system log files
➢ Record custom messages in system log file
➢ Describe systemd journal service
➢ Retrieve and scrutinize messages from journal
➢ Store journal information persistently
➢ Know system tuning and apply tuning profile

RHCSA Objectives:

16. Boot, reboot, and shut down a system normally
17. Boot systems into different targets manually
24. Start, stop, and check the status of network services
39. Start and stop services and configure services to start automatically at boot
40. Configure systems to boot into a specific target automatically
46. Configure network services to start automatically at boot
22. Locate and interpret system log files and journals
23. Preserve system journals
21. Manage tuning profiles

Systemd is the default system initialization and service management scheme in RHEL. It can boot the system into one of several predefined targets and it is used to handle operational states of services. It employs the concepts of units and targets for initialization, service administration, and state changes. A good grasp of what unit and target configuration files store is key to understanding how systemd operates.

Alerts and messages generated by system services and user activities are forwarded to predefined locations for storage. These alerts and messages include those that are produced during system boot time. The log data may be analyzed for debugging or auditing purposes. Log files grow over time and need to be rotated periodically to prevent the file system space from filling up. There are configuration files that define the default and custom locations to direct the log messages to and to configure rotation settings. The system log file records custom messages sent to it. systemd includes a service for viewing and managing system logs in addition to the traditional logging service. This service maintains a log of runtime activities for faster retrieval and can be configured to store the information permanently.

System tuning service is employed to monitor connected devices and to tweak their parameters to improve performance or conserve power. A recommended tuning profile may be identified and activated for optimal performance and power saving.

System Initialization and Service Management

systemd (short for *system daemon*) is the system initialization and service management mechanism. It has fast-tracked system initialization and state transitioning by introducing features such as parallel processing of startup scripts, improved handling of service dependencies, and on-demand activation of services. Moreover, it supports snapshotting of system states, tracks processes using control groups, and automatically maintains mount points. *systemd* is the first process with PID 1 that spawns at boot and it is the last process that is terminated at shut down.

systemd spawns several processes during a service startup. It places the processes in a private hierarchy composed of *control groups* (or *cgroups* for short) to organize processes for the purposes of monitoring and controlling system resources such as processor, memory, network bandwidth, and disk I/O. This includes limiting, isolating, and prioritizing their usage of resources. This way resources can be distributed among users, databases, and applications based on need and priority, resulting in overall improved system performance.

In order to benefit from parallelism, systemd initiates distinct services concurrently, taking advantage of multiple CPU cores and other compute resources. To that end, systemd creates sockets for all enabled services that support socket-based activation instantaneously at the very beginning of the initialization process. It passes them on to service daemon processes as they attempt to start in parallel. This approach lets systemd handle inter-service order dependencies and allows services to start without any delays. With systemd, dependent daemons need not be running; they only need the correct socket to be available. systemd creates sockets first, starts daemons next, and caches any client requests to daemons that have not yet started in the socket buffer. It fills the pending client requests when the daemons they were awaiting come online.

 Socket is a communication method that allows two processes on the same or different systems to talk.

During the operational state, systemd maintains the sockets and uses them to reconnect other daemons and services that were interacting with an old instance of a daemon before that daemon was terminated or restarted. Likewise, services that use activation based on D-Bus (*Desktop Bus*) are started when a client application attempts to communicate with them for the first time. Additional methods used by systemd for activation are device-based and path-based, with the former starting the service when a specific hardware type such as USB is plugged in, and the latter starting the service when a particular file or directory alters its state.

D-Bus is another communication method that allows multiple services running in parallel on a system to talk to one another on the same or remote system.

With on-demand activation, systemd defers the startup of services—Bluetooth and printing—until they are actually needed during the boot process or during runtime. Together, parallelization and on-demand activation save time and compute resources, and contribute to expediting the boot process considerably.

Another major benefit of parallelism witnessed at system boot is when systemd uses the autofs service to temporarily mount the configured file systems. During the boot process, the file systems are checked that may result in unnecessary delays. With autofs, the file systems are temporarily mounted on their normal mount points, and as soon as the checks on the file systems are finished, systemd remounts them using their standard devices. Parallelism in file system mounts does not affect the root and virtual file systems.

Units

Units are systemd objects used for organizing boot and maintenance tasks, such as hardware initialization, socket creation, file system mounts, and service startups. Unit configuration is stored in their respective configuration files, which are auto-generated from other configurations, created dynamically from the system state, produced at runtime, or user-developed. Units are in one of several operational states, including active, inactive, in the process of being activated or deactivated, and failed. Units can be enabled or disabled. An enabled unit can be started to an active state; a disabled unit cannot be started.

Units have a name and a type, and they are encoded in files with names in the form unitname.type. Some examples are tmp.mount, sshd.service, syslog.socket, and umount.target. There are two types of unit configuration files: (1) system unit files that are distributed with installed packages and located in the *usr/lib/systemd/system* directory, and (2) user unit files that are user-defined and stored in the */etc/systemd/user* directory (run **ls -l** on both directories to list their contents).

There are additional system units that are created at runtime and destroyed when they are no longer needed. They are located in the */run/systemd/system* directory. These runtime unit files take precedence over the system unit files, and the user unit files take priority over the runtime files.

Unit configuration files are a direct replacement of the initialization scripts found in the */etc/rc.d/init.d* directory in older RHEL releases.

systemd includes eleven unit types, which are described in Table 12-1.

Unit Type	Description
Automount	Offers automount capabilities for on-demand mounting of file systems
Device	Exposes kernel devices in systemd and may be used to implement device-based activation
Mount	Controls when and how to mount or unmount file systems
Path	Activates a service when monitored files or directories are accessed
Scope	Manages foreign processes instead of starting them
Service	Starts, stops, restarts, or reloads service daemons and the processes they are made up of
Slice	May be used to group units, which manage system processes in a tree-like structure for resource management
Socket	Encapsulates local inter-process communication or network sockets for use by matching service units
Swap	Encapsulates swap partitions
Target	Defines logical grouping of units
Timer	Useful for triggering activation of other units based on timers

Table 12-1 systemd Unit Types

Unit files contain common and specific configuration elements. Common elements fall under the [Unit] and [Install] sections, and comprise the description, documentation location, dependency information, conflict information, and other options that are independent of the type of unit. The unit-specific configuration data is located under the unit type section: [Service] for the service unit type, [Socket] for the socket unit type, and so forth. A sample unit file for *sshd.service* is shown below from the */usr/lib/systemd/system* directory:

```
[user1@server1 ~]$ cat /usr/lib/systemd/system/sshd.service
[Unit]
Description=OpenSSH server daemon
Documentation=man:sshd(8) man:sshd_config(5)
After=network.target sshd-keygen.target
Wants=sshd-keygen.target

[Service]
Type=notify
EnvironmentFile=-/etc/sysconfig/sshd
ExecStart=/usr/sbin/sshd -D $OPTIONS
ExecReload=/bin/kill -HUP $MAINPID
KillMode=process
Restart=on-failure
RestartSec=42s

[Install]
WantedBy=multi-user.target
```

Units can have dependency relationships among themselves based on a sequence (ordering) or a requirement. A sequence outlines one or more actions that need to be taken before or after the activation of a unit (the Before and After directives). A requirement specifies what must already be running (the Requires directive) or not running (the Conflicts directive) in order for the successful launch of a unit. For instance, the *graphical.target* unit file tells us that the system must already be operating in the multi-user mode and not in rescue mode in order for it to boot successfully into the graphical mode. Another option, Wants, may be used instead of Requires in the [Unit] or [Install] section so that the unit is not forced to fail activation if a required unit fails to start. Run **man systemd.unit** for details on systemd unit files.

There are a few other types of dependencies that you may see in other unit configuration files. systemd generally sets and maintains inter-service dependencies automatically; however, this can be done manually if needed.

Targets

Targets are simply logical collections of units. They are a special systemd unit type with the .target file extension. They share the directory locations with other unit configuration files. Targets are used to execute a series of units. This is typically true for booting the system to a desired operational run level with all the required services up and running. Some targets inherit services from other targets and add their own to them. systemd includes several predefined targets that are described in Table 12-2.

Target	Description
halt	Shuts down and halts the system
poweroff	Shuts down and powers off the system
shutdown	Shuts down the system
rescue	Single-user target for running administrative and recovery functions. All local file systems are mounted. Some essential services are started, but networking remains disabled.

Target	Description
emergency	Runs an emergency shell. The root file system is mounted in read-only mode; other file systems are not mounted. Networking and other services remain disabled.
multi-user	Multi-user target with full network support, but without GUI
graphical	Multi-user target with full network support and GUI
reboot	Shuts down and reboots the system
default	A special soft link that points to the default system boot target (multi-user.target or graphical.target)
hibernate	Puts the system into hibernation by saving the running state of the system on the hard disk and powering it off. When powered up, the system restores from its saved state rather than booting up.

Table 12-2 systemd Targets

Target unit files contain all information under the [Unit] section, and it comprises the description, documentation location, and dependency and conflict information. A sample file for the *graphical.target* target is shown below from the */usr/lib/systemd/system* directory:

```
[user1@server1 ~]$ cat /usr/lib/systemd/system/graphical.target
[Unit]
Description=Graphical Interface
Documentation=man:systemd.special(7)
Requires=multi-user.target
Wants=display-manager.service
Conflicts=rescue.service rescue.target
After=multi-user.target rescue.service rescue.target display-manager.service
AllowIsolate=yes
```

The file shows four dependencies: Requires, Wants, Conflicts, and After. It suggests that the system must have already accomplished the rescue.service, rescue.target, multi-user.target, and display-manager.service levels in order to be declared running in the graphical target. Run **man systemd.target** for details on systemd targets.

The systemctl Command

systemd comes with a set of management tools for querying and controlling operations. The primary tool for interaction in this command suite is *systemctl*. The *systemctl* command performs administrative functions and supports plentiful subcommands and flags. Table 12-3 lists and describes some common operations.

Subcommand	Description
daemon-reload	Re-reads and reloads all unit configuration files and recreates the entire user dependency tree.
enable (disable)	Activates (deactivates) a unit for autostart at system boot
get-default (set-default)	Shows (sets) the default boot target
get-property (set-property)	Returns (sets) the value of a property
is-active	Checks whether a unit is running
is-enabled	Displays whether a unit is set to autostart at system boot

Subcommand	Description
is-failed	Checks whether a unit is in the failed state
isolate	Changes the running state of a system
kill	Terminates all processes for a unit
list-dependencies	Lists dependency tree for a unit
list-sockets	Lists units of type socket
list-unit-files	Lists installed unit files
list-units	Lists known units. This is the default behavior when systemctl is executed without any arguments.
mask (unmask)	Prohibits (permits) auto and manual activation of a unit to avoid potential conflict
reload	Forces a running unit to re-read its configuration file. This action does not change the PID of the running unit.
restart	Stops a running unit and restarts it
show	Shows unit properties
start (stop)	Starts (stops) a unit
status	Presents the unit status information

Table 12-3 systemctl Subcommands

You will use a majority of these subcommands with *systemctl* going forward. Refer to the manual pages of the command for more details.

Listing and Viewing Units

The *systemctl* command is used to view and manage all types of units. The following examples demonstrate common operations pertaining to viewing and querying units.

To list all units that are currently loaded in memory along with their status and description, run the *systemctl* command without any options or subcommands. A long output is generated. The graphic below shows a few starting and concluding lines followed by a brief explanation.

```
[user1@server1 ~]$ systemctl
 UNIT
 proc-sys-fs-binfmt_misc.automount
 sys-devices-pci0000:00-0000:00:01.1-ata2-host1-target1:0:0-1:
 sys-devices-pci0000:00-0000:00:03.0-net-enp0s3.device
 sys-devices-pci0000:00-0000:00:05.0-sound-card0-controlC0.dev.
 sys-devices-pci0000:00-0000:00:0d.0-ata3-host2-target2:0:0-2:
 sys-devices-pci0000:00-0000:00:0d.0-ata3-host2-target2:0:0-2:
 sys-devices-pci0000:00-0000:00:0d.0-ata3-host2-target2:0:0-2:
 sys-devices-platform-serial8250-tty-ttyS0.device
 sys-devices-platform-serial8250-tty-ttyS1.device
 sys-devices-platform-serial8250-tty-ttyS2.device
 sys-devices-platform-serial8250-tty-ttyS3.device
 sys-devices-virtual-block-dm\x2d0.device
 sys-devices-virtual-block-dm\x2d1.device
 sys-devices-virtual-misc-rfkill.device
 sys-module-configfs.device
 sys-module-fuse.device
 sys-subsystem-net-devices-enp0s3.device
 -.mount
 boot.mount
 . . . . . . . .
```

```
LOAD   = Reflects whether the unit definition was properly loaded.
ACTIVE = The high-level unit activation state, i.e. generalization o
SUB    = The low-level unit activation state, values depend on unit
142 loaded units listed. Pass --all to see loaded but inactive unit:
To show all installed unit files use 'systemctl list-unit-files'.
lines 112-149/149 (END)
```

Here is a breakdown of the above graphic: the UNIT column shows the name of the unit and its location in the tree, the LOAD column reflects whether the unit configuration file was properly loaded (other possibilities are not found, bad setting, error, and masked), the ACTIVE column returns the high-level activation state (other possible states are active, reloading, inactive, failed, activating, and deactivating), the SUB column depicts the low-level unit activation state (reports unit-specific information), and the DESCRIPTION column illustrates the unit's content and functionality.

By default, the *systemctl* command lists only the active units. You can use the --all option to include the inactive units too.

To list all (--all) active and inactive units of type (-t) socket:

```
[user1@server1 ~]$ systemctl -t socket --all
  UNIT                    LOAD   ACTIVE   SUB       DESCRIPTION
  avahi-daemon.socket     loaded active   running   Avahi mDNS/DNS-SD S1
  cups.socket             loaded active   running   CUPS Scheduler
  dbus.socket             loaded active   running   D-Bus System Message
  dm-event.socket         loaded active   listening Device-mapper event
  iscsid.socket           loaded active   listening Open-iSCSI iscsid Sc
  iscsiuio.socket         loaded active   listening Open-iSCSI iscsiuio
  lvm2-lvmpolld.socket    loaded active   listening LVM2 poll daemon soc
  multipathd.socket       loaded inactive dead      multipathd control :
  sssd-kcm.socket         loaded active   listening SSSD Kerberos Cache
  syslog.socket           loaded inactive dead      Syslog Socket    .
. . . . . . . .
```

To list all units of type socket (column 2) currently loaded in memory and the service they activate (column 3), sorted by the listening address (column 1):

```
[user1@server1 ~]$ systemctl list-sockets
LISTEN                        UNIT                     ACTIVATES
/dev/rfkill                   systemd-rfkill.socket    systemd-rfkill.se
/run/.heim_org.h51.kcm-socket sssd-kcm.socket          sssd-kcm.service
/run/avahi-daemon/socket      avahi-daemon.socket      avahi-daemon.serv
/run/cups/cups.sock           cups.socket              cups.service
/run/dbus/system_bus_socket   dbus.socket              dbus-broker.servi
/run/dmeventd-client          dm-event.socket          dm-event.service
/run/dmeventd-server          dm-event.socket          dm-event.service
/run/initctl                  systemd-initctl.socket   systemd-initctl.s
/run/lvm/lvmpolld.socket      lvm2-lvmpolld.socket     lvm2-lvmpolld.ser
. . . . . . . .
```

To list all unit files (column 1) installed on the system and their current state (column 2). This will generate a long list of units in the output. The following only shows a selection.

```
[user1@server1 ~]$ systemctl list-unit-files
UNIT FILE                                STATE        VENDOR PR
proc-sys-fs-binfmt_misc.automount        static       -
-.mount                                  generated    -
boot.mount                               generated    -
dev-hugepages.mount                      static       -
dev-mqueue.mount                         static       -
mnt.mount                                generated    -
proc-sys-fs-binfmt_misc.mount            disabled     disabled
run-vmblock\x2dfuse.mount                disabled     disabled
sys-fs-fuse-connections.mount            static       -
sys-kernel-config.mount                  static       -
sys-kernel-debug.mount                   static       -
sys-kernel-tracing.mount                 static       -
tmp.mount                                disabled     disabled
........
```

To list all units that failed (--failed) to start at the last system boot:

```
[user1@server1 ~]$ systemctl --failed
  UNIT LOAD ACTIVE SUB DESCRIPTION
0 loaded units listed.
```

To list the hierarchy of all dependencies (required and wanted units) for the current default target:

```
[user1@server1 ~]$ systemctl list-dependencies
default.target
●   ├─accounts-daemon.service
●   ├─gdm.service
○   ├─nvmefc-boot-connections.service
●   ├─power-profiles-daemon.service
●   ├─rtkit-daemon.service
●   ├─switcheroo-control.service
○   ├─systemd-update-utmp-runlevel.service
●   ├─udisks2.service
●   ├─upower.service
●   └─multi-user.target
●      ├─atd.service
........
```

To list the hierarchy of all dependencies (required and wanted units) for a specific unit such as *atd.service*:

```
[user1@server1 ~]$ systemctl list-dependencies atd.service
atd.service
●   ├─system.slice
●   └─sysinit.target
●      ├─dev-hugepages.mount
●      ├─dev-mqueue.mount
●      ├─dracut-shutdown.service
........
```

There are other listing subcommands and additional flags available that can be used to produce a variety of reports.

Managing Service Units

The *systemctl* command offers several subcommands to manage service units, including starting, stopping, restarting, and checking their status. These and other management operations are summarized in Table 12-3 earlier. The following examples demonstrate their use on a service unit called *atd*.

To check the current operational status and other details for the *atd* service:

```
[user1@server1 ~]$ systemctl status atd
● atd.service - Deferred execution scheduler
     Loaded: loaded (/usr/lib/systemd/system/atd.service; enabled; vendor preset: enabled
     Active: active (running) since Tue 2023-01-31 16:56:13 EST; 44min ago
       Docs: man:atd(8)
   Main PID: 944 (atd)
      Tasks: 1 (limit: 10944)
     Memory: 304.0K
        CPU: 21ms
     CGroup: /system.slice/atd.service
             └─944 /usr/sbin/atd -f
```

The above output reveals a lot of information about the *atd* service. On line 1, it shows the service description (read from the */usr/lib/systemd/system/atd.service* file). Line 2 illustrates the load status, which reveals the current load status of the unit configuration file in memory. Other possibilities for "Loaded" include "error" (if there was a problem loading the file), "not-found" (if no file associated with this unit was found), "bad-setting" (if a key setting was missing), and "masked" (if the unit configuration file is masked). Line 2 also tells us whether the service is set (enabled or disabled) for autostart at system boot.

Line 3 exhibits the current activation status and the time the service was started. An activation status designates the current state of the service. Possible states include:

Active (running): The service is running with one or more processes
Active (exited): Completed a one-time configuration
Active (waiting): Running but waiting for an event
Inactive: Not running
Activating: In the process of being activated
Deactivating: In the process of being deactivated
Failed: If the service crashed or could not be started

The output also depicts the PID of the service process and other information.

To disable the *atd* service from autostarting at the next system reboot:

```
[user1@server1 ~]$ sudo systemctl disable atd
Removed /etc/systemd/system/multi-user.target.wants/atd.service.
```

To re-enable *atd* to autostart at the next system reboot:

```
[user1@server1 ~]$ sudo systemctl enable atd
Created symlink /etc/systemd/system/multi-user.target.wants/atd.service → /usr/lib/systemd/system/
atd.service.
```

To check whether *atd* is set to autostart at the next system reboot:

```
[user1@server1 ~]$ systemctl is-enabled atd
enabled
```

To check whether the *atd* service is running:

```
[user1@server1 ~]$ systemctl is-active atd
active
```

To stop and restart *atd*, run either of the following:

```
[user1@server1 ~]$ sudo systemctl stop atd ; sudo systemctl start atd
[user1@server1 ~]$ sudo systemctl restart atd
```

To show the details of the *atd* service:

```
[user1@server1 ~]$ systemctl show atd
Type=simple
ExitType=main
Restart=no
NotifyAccess=none
. . . . . . . .
```

To prohibit *atd* from being enabled or disabled:

```
[user1@server1 ~]$ sudo systemctl mask atd
Created symlink /etc/systemd/system/atd.service → /dev/null.
```

Try disabling or enabling *atd* and observe the effect of the previous command:

```
[user1@server1 ~]$ sudo systemctl disable atd
Unit /etc/systemd/system/atd.service is masked, ignoring.
[user1@server1 ~]$ sudo systemctl enable atd
Failed to enable unit: Unit file /etc/systemd/system/atd.service is masked.
```

Reverse the effect of the *mask* subcommand and try disable and enable operations:

```
[user1@server1 ~]$ sudo systemctl unmask atd
Removed /etc/systemd/system/atd.service.
[user1@server1 ~]$
[user1@server1 ~]$ sudo systemctl disable atd
Removed /etc/systemd/system/multi-user.target.wants/atd.service.
[user1@server1 ~]$ sudo systemctl enable atd
Created symlink /etc/systemd/system/multi-user.target.wants/atd.service → /usr/lib/systemd/system/
atd.service.
```

Notice that the *unmask* subcommand has removed the restriction that was placed on the *atd* service.

Managing Target Units

The *systemctl* command is also used to manage the target units. It can be used to view or change the default boot target, switch from one running target into another, and so on. These operations are briefed in Table 12-3 earlier. Let's look at some examples.

To view what units of type (-t) target are currently loaded and active:

```
[user1@server1 ~]$ systemctl -t target
  UNIT                        LOAD   ACTIVE SUB    DESCRIPTION
  basic.target                loaded active active Basic System
  cryptsetup.target           loaded active active Local Encrypted Volume
  getty.target                loaded active active Login Prompts
  graphical.target            loaded active active Graphical Interface
  integritysetup.target       loaded active active Local Integrity Protec
  local-fs-pre.target         loaded active active Preparation for Local
  local-fs.target             loaded active active Local File Systems
  multi-user.target           loaded active active Multi-User System
  network-online.target       loaded active active Network is Online
  network-pre.target          loaded active active Preparation for Networ
  network.target              loaded active active Network
  nss-user-lookup.target      loaded active active User and Group Name Lo
  paths.target                loaded active active Path Units
  remote-fs-pre.target        loaded active active Preparation for Remote
  remote-fs.target            loaded active active Remote File Systems
  slices.target               loaded active active Slice Units
  sockets.target              loaded active active Socket Units
. . . . . . . .
```

For each target unit, the above output returns the target unit's name, load state, high-level and low-level activation states, and a short description. Add the --all option to the above to see all loaded targets in either active or inactive state.

Viewing and Setting Default Boot Target

The *systemctl* command is used to view the current default boot target and to set it. Let's use the *get-default* and *set-default* subcommands with *systemctl* to perform these operations.

To check the current default boot target:

```
[user1@server1 ~]$ systemctl get-default
graphical.target
```

> **EXAM TIP:** You may have to modify the default boot target persistently.

To change the current default boot target from graphical.target to multi-user.target:

```
[user1@server1 ~]$ sudo systemctl set-default multi-user
Removed /etc/systemd/system/default.target.
Created symlink /etc/systemd/system/default.target → /usr/lib/systemd/system/multi-user.target.
```

The command simply removes the existing symlink (*default.target*) pointing to the old boot target and replaces it with the new target file path.

Execute **sudo systemctl set-default graphical** to revert the default boot target to graphical.

Switching into Specific Targets

The *systemctl* command can be used to transition the running system from one target state into another. There are a variety of potential targets available to switch into as listed in Table 12-2 earlier; however, only a few of them—graphical, multi-user, reboot, shutdown—are typically used. The rescue and emergency targets are for troubleshooting and system recovery purposes, poweroff and halt are similar to shutdown, and hibernate is suitable for mobile devices. Consider the following examples that demonstrate switching targets.

The current default target on *server1* is graphical. To switch into multi-user, use the *isolate* subcommand with *systemctl*:

```
[user1@server1 ~]$ sudo systemctl isolate multi-user
```

This should stop the graphical service on the system and display the text-based console login screen, as shown below:

```
Red Hat Enterprise Linux 9.1 (Plow)
Kernel 5.14.0-162.12.1.el9_1.x86_64 on an x86_64

Activate the web console with: systemctl enable --now cockpit.socket

server1 login: _
```

Type in a username such as *user1* and enter the password to log in:

```
server1 login: user1
Password:
Last login: Tue Jan 31 16:56:28 from 192.168.0.3
[user1@server1 ~]$
```

To return to the graphical target:

```
[user1@server1 ~]$ sudo systemctl isolate graphical
```

The graphical login screen should appear shortly and you should be able to log back in.

To shut down the system and power it off, use the following or simply run the *poweroff* command:

```
[user1@server1 ~]$ sudo systemctl poweroff
```

To shut down and reboot the system, use the following or simply run the *reboot* command:

```
[user1@server1 ~]$ sudo systemctl reboot
```

The *halt, poweroff,* and *reboot* commands are mere symbolic links to the *systemctl* command, as the following long listing suggests:

```
[user1@server1 ~]$ ls -l /usr/sbin/halt /usr/sbin/poweroff /usr/sbin/reboot
lrwxrwxrwx. 1 root root 16 Sep 23 10:35 /usr/sbin/halt -> ../bin/systemctl
lrwxrwxrwx. 1 root root 16 Sep 23 10:35 /usr/sbin/poweroff -> ../bin/systemctl
lrwxrwxrwx. 1 root root 16 Sep 23 10:35 /usr/sbin/reboot -> ../bin/systemctl
```

The *halt*, *poweroff*, and *reboot* commands are available in RHEL 9 for compatibility reasons. It is recommended to use the *systemctl* command instead when switching system states.

The three commands, without any arguments, perform the same action that the *shutdown* command would with the "-H now", "-P now", and "-r now" arguments, respectively. In addition, it also broadcasts a warning message to all logged-in users, blocks new user login attempts, waits for the specified amount of time for users to save their work and log off, stops the services, and eventually shut the system down to the specified target state.

System Logging

System logging (*syslog* for short) is one of the most rudimentary elements of an operating system. Its purpose is to capture messages generated by the kernel, daemons, commands, user activities, applications, and other events, and forwarded them to various log files, which store them for security auditing, service malfunctioning, system troubleshooting, or informational purposes.

The daemon that is responsible for system logging is called *rsyslogd* (*rocket-fast system for log processing*). This service daemon is multi-threaded, with support for enhanced filtering, encryption-protected message relaying, and a variety of configuration options. The *rsyslogd* daemon reads its configuration file */etc/rsyslog.conf* and the configuration files located in the */etc/rsyslog.d* directory at startup. The default depository for most system log files is the */var/log* directory. Other services such as audit, Apache, and GNOME desktop manager have subdirectories under */var/log* for storing their respective log files.

The *rsyslog* service is modular, allowing the modules listed in its configuration file to be dynamically loaded in the kernel as and when needed. Each module brings a new functionality to the system upon loading.

The *rsyslogd* daemon can be stopped manually using **systemctl stop rsyslog**. Replace stop with start, restart, reload, and status as appropriate.

A PID is assigned to the daemon at startup and a file by the name *rsyslogd.pid* is created in the */run* directory to save the PID. The reason this file is created and stores the PID is to prevent the initiation of multiple instances of this daemon.

The Syslog Configuration File

The *rsyslog.conf* is the primary syslog configuration file located in the */etc* directory . The default uncommented line entries from the file are shown below and explained thereafter. Section headings have been added to separate the directives in each section.

```
[user1@server1 ~]$ sudo grep -Ev '^#|^$' /etc/rsyslog.conf

#### GLOBAL DIRECTIVES ####
global(workDirectory="/var/lib/rsyslog")
module(load="builtin:omfile" Template="RSYSLOG_TraditionalFileFormat")
include(file="/etc/rsyslog.d/*.conf" mode="optional")
```

```
#### MODULES ####
module(load="imuxsock"      # provides support for local system logging (e.g. via l(
         SysSock.Use="off") # Turn off message reception via local log socket;
                            # local messages are retrieved through imjournal now.
module(load="imjournal"              # provides access to the systemd journal
         StateFile="imjournal.state") # File to store the position in the journal
global(workDirectory="/var/lib/rsyslog")


#### RULES ####
*.info;mail.none;authpriv.none;cron.none               /var/log/messages
authpriv.*                                             /var/log/secure
mail.*                                                 -/var/log/maillog
cron.*                                                 /var/log/cron
*.emerg                                                :omusrmsg:*
uucp,news.crit                                         /var/log/spooler
local7.*                                               /var/log/boot.log
```

As depicted, the syslog configuration file contains three sections: Global Directives, Modules, and Rules. The Global Directives section contains three active directives. The definitions in this section influence the overall functionality of the *rsyslog* service. The first directive sets the location for the storage of auxiliary files (*/var/lib/rsyslog*). The second directive instructs the *rsyslog* service to save captured messages using traditional file formatting. The third directive directs the service to load additional configuration from files located in the */etc/rsyslog.d/* directory.

The Modules section defines two modules—*imuxsock* and *imjournal*—and they are loaded on demand. The *imuxsock* module furnishes support for local system logging via the *logger* command, and the *imjournal* module allows access to the systemd journal.

The Rules section has many two-field line entries. The left field is called *selector*, and the right field is referred to as *action*. The selector field is further divided into two period-separated sub-fields called *facility* (left) and *priority* (right), with the former representing one or more system process categories that generate messages, and the latter identifying the severity associated with the messages. The semicolon (;) character is used as a distinction mark if multiple facility.priority groups are present. The action field determines the destination to send the messages to.

There are numerous supported facilities such as auth, authpriv, cron, daemon, kern, lpr, mail, news, syslog, user, uucp, and local0 through local7. The asterisk (*) character represents all of them.

Similarly, there are several supported priorities, and they include emerg, alert, crit, error, warning, notice, info, debug, and none. This sequence is in the descending criticality order. The asterisk (*) represents all of them. If a lower priority is selected, the daemon logs all messages of the service at that and higher levels.

Line 1 under the Rules section instructs the syslog daemon to catch and store informational messages from all services to the */var/log/messages* file and ignore all messages generated by mail, authentication, and cron services. Lines 2, 3, and 4 command the daemon to collect and log all messages produced by authentication, mail, and cron to the *secure, maillog,* and *cron* files, respectively. Line 5 orders the daemon to display emergency messages (omusrmsg stands for *user message output module*) on the terminals of all logged-in users. Line 6 shows two comma-separated facilities that are set at a common priority. These facilities tell the daemon to gather critical messages from uucp and news facilities and log them to the */var/log/spooler* file. Line 7 (the last line) is for recording the boot-time service startup status to the */var/log/boot.log* file.

If you have made any modifications to the syslog configuration file, you need to run the *rsyslogd* command with the -N switch and specify a numeric verbosity level to inspect the file for any syntax or typing issues:

```
[user1@server1 ~]$ sudo rsyslogd -N 1
rsyslogd: version 8.2102.0-105.el9, config validation run (level 1),
master config /etc/rsyslog.conf
rsyslogd: End of config validation run. Bye.
```

The validation returns the version of the command, verbosity level used, and the configuration file path. With no issues reported, the *rsyslog* service can be restarted (or reloaded) in order for the changes to take effect.

Rotating Log Files

RHEL records all system activities in log files that are stored in a central location under the */var/log* directory, as defined in the rsyslog configuration file. A long listing of this directory reveals the files along with subdirectories that may have multiple service-specific logs. Here is a listing from *server1*:

```
[user1@server1 ~]$ ls -l /var/log
total 2040
drwxr-xr-x. 2 root    root       4096 Jan 26 16:51 anaconda
drwx------. 2 root    root         23 Jan 26 16:56 audit
-rw-------. 1 root    root     142206 Jan 31 18:02 boot.log
-rw-------. 1 root    root      34870 Jan 28 00:00 boot.log-20230128
-rw-------. 1 root    root      14351 Jan 29 12:29 boot.log-20230129
-rw-------. 1 root    root       2720 Jan 30 00:00 boot.log-20230130
-rw-rw----. 1 root    utmp       4224 Jan 31 16:54 btmp
drwxr-x---. 2 chrony  chrony        6 Mar 24  2022 chrony
-rw-------. 1 root    root      22613 Jan 31 18:02 cron
-rw-------. 1 root    root      19853 Jan 28 22:01 cron-20230129
drwxr-xr-x. 2 lp      sys          57 Jan 26 16:40 cups
-rw-r--r--. 1 root    root      26800 Jan 31 17:43 dnf.librepo.log
-rw-r--r--. 1 root    root     182135 Jan 31 17:43 dnf.log
-rw-r--r--. 1 root    root       9953 Jan 31 17:43 dnf.rpm.log
-rw-r-----. 1 root    root          0 Jan 26 16:56 firewalld
```

The output shows log files for various services. Depending on the usage and the number of events generated and captured, log files may quickly fill up the */var* file system, resulting in unpredictable system behavior. Also, they may grow to an extent that would make it difficult to load, read, send, or analyze them. To avoid getting into any unwanted situation, it's important to ensure that they're rotated on a regular basis and their archives are removed automatically.

To that end, a systemd unit file called *logrotate.timer* under the */usr/lib/systemd/system* directory invokes the *logrotate* service (*/usr/lib/systemd/system/logrotate.service*) on a daily basis. Here is what this file contains:

```
[user1@server1 ~]$ systemctl cat logrotate.timer
# /usr/lib/systemd/system/logrotate.timer
[Unit]
Description=Daily rotation of log files
Documentation=man:logrotate(8) man:logrotate.conf(5)

[Timer]
OnCalendar=daily
AccuracySec=1h
Persistent=true

[Install]
WantedBy=timers.target
```

The *logrotate* service runs rotations as per the schedule and other parameters defined in the
/etc/logrotate.conf and additional log configuration files located in the */etc/logrotate.d* directory.
The following shows the content of */etc/logrotate.conf*:

```
[user1@server1 ~]$ grep -v ^$ /etc/logrotate.conf
# see "man logrotate" for details
# global options do not affect preceding include directives
# rotate log files weekly
weekly
# keep 4 weeks worth of backlogs
rotate 4
# create new (empty) log files after rotating old ones
create
# use date as a suffix of the rotated file
dateext
# uncomment this if you want your log files compressed
#compress
# packages drop log rotation information into this directory
include /etc/logrotate.d
```

The file content includes the default log rotation frequency (weekly). It indicates the period of time
(4 weeks) to retain the rotated logs before deleting them. Each time a log file is rotated, an empty
replacement file is created with the date as a suffix to its name, and the *rsyslog* service is restarted.
The script presents the option of compressing the rotated files using the *gzip* utility. During the
script execution, the *logrotate* command checks for the presence of files in the */etc/logrotate.d*
directory and includes them as necessary. The directives defined in the *logrotate.conf* file have a
global effect on all log files. You can define custom settings for a specific log file in *logrotate.conf*
or create a separate file under */etc/logrotate.d*. Any settings defined in user-defined files overrides
the global settings.

Here is the default list of additional log configuration files that reside in the */etc/logrotate.d*
directory:

```
[user1@server1 ~]$ ls -l /etc/logrotate.d/
total 56
-rw-r--r--. 1 root root  91 Mar 31  2021 bootlog
-rw-r--r--. 1 root root 130 Oct 14  2019 btmp
-rw-r--r--. 1 root root 160 Dec 16  2021 chrony
-rw-r--r--. 1 root root  88 Apr 27  2022 dnf
-rw-r--r--. 1 root root  93 Aug  5 07:20 firewalld
-rw-r--r--. 1 root root 172 Jul 29  2021 iscsiuiolog
-rw-r--r--. 1 root root 162 Dec 20 06:22 kvm_stat
-rw-r--r--. 1 root root 312 Nov  1  2021 psacct
-rw-r--r--. 1 root root 226 May 16  2022 rsyslog
-rw-r--r--. 1 root root 155 Aug 26 03:24 samba
-rw-r--r--. 1 root root 237 Aug 26 13:29 sssd
-rw-r--r--. 1 root root  88 Aug 11 11:17 subscription-manager
-rw-r--r--. 1 root root 100 May 13  2022 wpa_supplicant
-rw-r--r--. 1 root root 145 Oct 14  2019 wtmp
```

The above file listing shows files for a number of services—*chrony, dnf, rsyslog, samba, etc.*—all with their own rules defined. The following shows the file content for *btmp* (records of failed user login attempts) that is used to control the rotation behavior for the */var/log/btmp* file:

```
[user1@server1 ~]$ cat /etc/logrotate.d/btmp
# no packages own btmp -- we'll rotate it here
/var/log/btmp {
    missingok
    monthly
    create 0660 root utmp
    rotate 1
}
```

The rotation is once a month. The replacement file will get read/write permission bits for the owner (*root*) and the owning group (*utmp*), and the *rsyslog* service will maintain only one rotated copy of the *btmp* file.

The Boot Log File

Logs generated during the system startup display the service startup sequence with a status showing whether the service was started successfully. This information may help in any post-boot troubleshooting if required. Boot logs are stored in the *boot.log* file under */var/log*. Here are a few lines from the beginning of the file:

```
[user1@server1 ~]$ sudo head /var/log/boot.log
         Starting Load Kernel Module drm...
[  OK  ] Started User Login Management.
[  OK  ] Finished Load Kernel Module drm.
[  OK  ] Finished Rotate log files.
[  OK  ] Started Daemon for power management.
[  OK  ] Started Authorization Manager.
         Starting Modem Manager...
         Starting firewalld - dynamic firewall daemon...
[  OK  ] Started Power Profiles daemon.
[  OK  ] Started Accounts Service.
```

OK or FAILED within the square brackets indicates whether or not a service was started.

The System Log File

The default location for storing most system activities, as defined in the *rsyslog.conf* file, is the */var/log/messages* file. This file saves log information in plain text format and may be viewed with any file display utility, such as *cat*, *more*, *pg*, *less*, *head*, or *tail*. This file may be observed in real time using the *tail* command with the -f switch. The *messages* file captures the date and time of the activity, hostname of the system, name and PID of the service, and a short description of the event being logged.

> **EXAM TIP:** It is helpful to "tail" the messages file when starting or restarting a system service or during testing to identify any issues encountered.

The following illustrates some recent entries from this file:

```
[user1@server1 ~]$ sudo tail /var/log/messages
Feb  1 08:55:33 server1 systemd[2046]: Listening on D-Bus User Mess
Feb  1 08:55:33 server1 systemd[2046]: Reached target Sockets.
Feb  1 08:55:33 server1 systemd[2046]: Finished Create User's Volat
irectories.
Feb  1 08:55:33 server1 systemd[2046]: Reached target Basic System.
Feb  1 08:55:33 server1 systemd[1]: Started User Manager for UID 1(
Feb  1 08:55:33 server1 systemd[1]: Started Session 2 of User user:
Feb  1 08:55:33 server1 systemd[2046]: Reached target Main User Ta:
Feb  1 08:55:33 server1 systemd[2046]: Startup finished in 126ms.
Feb  1 08:55:33 server1 systemd[1]: Starting Hostname Service...
Feb  1 08:55:33 server1 systemd[1]: Started Hostname Service.
```

Each line entry represents the detail for a single event.

Logging Custom Messages

Many times, it is worthwhile to add a manual note to the system log file to mark the start or end of an activity for future reference. This is especially important when you run a script to carry out certain tasks and you want to record the status or add comments at various stages throughout its execution. This is also beneficial in debugging the startup of an application to know where exactly it is failing.

The Modules section in the *rsyslog.conf* file provides the support via the imuxsock module to record custom messages to the *messages* file using the *logger* command. This command may be run by normal users or the *root* user. The following example shows how to add a note indicating the calling user has rebooted the system:

```
[user1@server1 ~]$ logger -i "System rebooted by $USER"
```

tail the last line from the *messages* file and you'll observe the message recorded along with the timestamp, hostname, and PID:

```
[user1@server1 ~]$ sudo tail -1 /var/log/messages
Feb  1 08:57:42 server1 user1[2117]: System rebooted by user1
```

You may add the -p option and specify a priority level either as a numerical value or in the facility.priority format. The default priority at which the events are recorded is user.notice. See the manual pages for the *logger* command for more details.

The systemd Journal

In addition to the *rsyslog* service, RHEL offers a systemd-based logging service for the collection and storage of logging data. This service is implemented via the *systemd-journald* daemon. The function of this service is to gather, store, and display logging events from a variety of sources such as the kernel, *rsyslog* and other services, initial RAM disk, and alerts generated during the early boot stage. It stores these messages in the binary format in files called *journals* that are located in the */run/log/journal* directory. These files are structured and indexed for faster and easier searches, and may be viewed and managed using the *journalctl* command. As you know, */run* is a virtual file system that is created in memory at system boot, maintained during system runtime, and destroyed at shutdown. Therefore, the data stored therein is non-persistent, but you can enable persistent storage for the logs if desired.

RHEL runs both *rsyslogd* and *systemd-journald* concurrently. In fact, the data gathered by *systemd-journald* may be forwarded to *rsyslogd* for further processing and persistent storage in text format.

The main configuration file for this service is */etc/systemd/journald.conf*, which contains numerous default settings that affect the overall functionality of the service. These settings may be modified as required.

Retrieving and Viewing Messages

RHEL provides the *journalctl* command to retrieve messages from the journal for viewing in a variety of ways using different options. One common usage is to run the command without any options to see all the messages generated since the last system reboot. The following shows a few initial entries from the journal:

```
[user1@server1 ~]$ sudo journalctl
Feb 01 06:16:05 server1.example.com kernel: Linux version 5.14.0-162.:
Feb 01 06:16:05 server1.example.com kernel: The list of certified harc
Feb 01 06:16:05 server1.example.com kernel: Command line: BOOT_IMAGE=
Feb 01 06:16:05 server1.example.com kernel: x86/fpu: x87 FPU will use
Feb 01 06:16:05 server1.example.com kernel: signal: max sigframe size:
Feb 01 06:16:05 server1.example.com kernel: BIOS-provided physical RAM
Feb 01 06:16:05 server1.example.com kernel: BIOS-e820: [mem 0x0000000(
Feb 01 06:16:05 server1.example.com kernel: BIOS-e820: [mem 0x0000000(
```

Notice that the format of the messages is similar to that of the events logged to the */var/log/messages* file that you saw earlier. Each line begins with a timestamp followed by the system hostname, process name with or without a PID, and the actual message.

Let's run the *journalctl* command with different options to produce various reports.

To display detailed output for each entry, use the -o verbose option:

```
[user1@server1 ~]$ sudo journalctl -o verbose
Wed 2023-02-01 06:16:05.566418 EST [s=591ce68c6a194b8bbce6dek
    _SOURCE_MONOTONIC_TIMESTAMP=0
    _TRANSPORT=kernel
    PRIORITY=5
    SYSLOG_FACILITY=0
    SYSLOG_IDENTIFIER=kernel
    MESSAGE=Linux version 5.14.0-162.12.1.el9_1.x86_64 (mockk
    _BOOT_ID=6b01ff5357784939b0e2ac76bab16132
    _MACHINE_ID=96daf847168342be8233b83a92a2a3f0
    _HOSTNAME=server1.example.com
Wed 2023-02-01 06:16:05.566486 EST [s=591ce68c6a194b8bbce6dek
    _SOURCE_MONOTONIC_TIMESTAMP=0
    _TRANSPORT=kernel
    PRIORITY=5

 . . . . . . . .
```

To view all events since the last system reboot, use the -b options:

```
[user1@server1 ~]$ sudo journalctl -b
```

You may specify -0 (default, since the last system reboot), -1 (the previous system reboot), -2 (two reboots before), and so on to view messages from previous system reboots.

To view only kernel-generated alerts since the last system reboot:

```
[user1@server1 ~]$ sudo journalctl -kb0
```

To limit the output to view a specific number of entries only (3 in the example below), use the -n option:

```
[user1@server1 ~]$ sudo journalctl -n3
Feb 01 09:01:37 server1.example.com sudo[2171]: pam_unix(sudo:se:
Feb 01 09:02:01 server1.example.com sudo[2176]:     user1 : TTY=p
Feb 01 09:02:01 server1.example.com sudo[2176]: pam_unix(sudo:se:
```

To show all alerts generated by a particular service, such as *crond*:

```
[user1@server1 ~]$ sudo journalctl /usr/sbin/crond
Feb 01 06:16:36 server1.example.com crond[1124]: (CRON) STARTUP (1.5.7)
Feb 01 06:16:36 server1.example.com crond[1124]: (CRON) INFO (Syslog wil
Feb 01 06:16:36 server1.example.com crond[1124]: (CRON) INFO (RANDOM_DEL
Feb 01 06:16:36 server1.example.com crond[1124]: (CRON) INFO (running wi
```

To retrieve all messages logged for a certain process, such as the PID associated with the *chronyd* service:

```
[user1@server1 ~]$ sudo journalctl  PID=$(pgrep chronyd)
```

To reveal all messages for a particular system unit, such as sshd.service:

```
[user1@server1 ~]$ sudo journalctl _SYSTEMD_UNIT=sshd.service
```

To view all error messages logged between a date range, such as January 25, 2023, and January 31, 2023:

```
[user1@server1 ~]$ sudo journalctl --since 2023-01-25 --until 2023-01-31 -p err
```

To get all warning messages that have appeared today and display them in reverse chronological order:

```
[user1@server1 ~]$ sudo journalctl --since today -p warning -r
```

You can specify the time range in hh:mm:ss format, or yesterday, today, or tomorrow instead.

Similar to the -f (follow) option that is used with the *tail* command for real-time viewing of a log file, you can use the same switch with *journalctl* as well. Press Ctrl+c to terminate.

```
[user1@server1 ~]$ sudo journalctl -f
```

Check the manual pages of the *journalctl* command and the *systemd-journald* service for more details.

Preserving Journal Information

By default, journals are stored in the */run/log/journal* directory for the duration of system runtime. This data is transient and it does not survive across reboots. The *journalctl* command examples demonstrated earlier retrieve journal information from this temporary location. The *rsyslogd* daemon, by default, reads the temporary journals and stores messages in the */var/log/messages* file. You can enable a separate storage location for the journal to save all its messages there persistently. The default is under the */var/log/journal* directory. This will make the journal information available for future reference.

The *systemd-journald* service supports four options with the Storage directive in its configuration file *journald.conf* to control how the logging data is handled. These options are described in Table 12-4.

Option	Description
volatile	Stores data in memory only
persistent	Stores data permanently under /var/log/journal and falls back to memory-only option if this directory does not exist or has a permission or other issue. The service creates /var/log/journal in case of its non-existence.
auto	Similar to "persistent" but does not create /var/log/journal if it does not exist. This is the default option.
none	Disables both volatile and persistent storage options. Not recommended.

Table 12-4 Journal Data Storage Options

The default (auto) option appears more suitable as it stores data in both volatile and on-disk storage; however, you need to create the */var/log/journal* directory manually. This option provides two fundamental benefits: faster query responses from in-memory storage and access to historical log data from on-disk storage.

Exercise 12-1: Configure Persistent Storage for Journal Information

This exercise should be done on *server1* as *user1* with *sudo* where required.

In this exercise, you will run the necessary steps to enable and confirm persistent storage for the journals.

1. Create a subdirectory called *journal* under the */var/log* directory and confirm:

```
[user1@server1 ~]$ sudo mkdir /var/log/journal
[user1@server1 ~]$ ls -ld /var/log/journal/
drwxr-xr-x. 2 root root 6 Feb  1 10:59 /var/log/journal/
```

2. Restart the *systemd-journald* service and confirm:

```
[user1@server1 ~]$ sudo systemctl restart systemd-journald
[user1@server1 ~]$ sudo systemctl status systemd-journald
● systemd-journald.service - Journal Service
     Loaded: loaded (/usr/lib/systemd/system/systemd-journald.service; st
     Active: active (running) since Wed 2023-02-01 11:01:06 EST; 6s ago
TriggeredBy: ● systemd-journald.socket
             ● systemd-journald-dev-log.socket
       Docs: man:systemd-journald.service(8)
             man:journald.conf(5)
   Main PID: 2336 (systemd-journal)
. . . . . . . .
```

3. List the new directory and observe a subdirectory matching the machine ID of the system as defined in the */etc/machine-id* file is created:

```
[user1@server1 ~]$ ll /var/log/journal/
total 0
drwxr-sr-x+ 2 root systemd-journal 53 Feb  1 11:03 96daf847168342be8233b83a92a2a3f
0
[user1@server1 ~]$ cat /etc/machine-id
96daf847168342be8233b83a92a2a3f0
```

Compare the name of the subdirectory with the ID stored in the */etc/machine-id* file. They are identical.

This log file is rotated automatically once a month based on the settings in the *journald.conf* file. Check the manual pages of the configuration file for details and relevant directives.

This concludes the exercise.

System Tuning

RHEL uses a system tuning service called *tuned* to monitor storage, networking, processor, audio, video, and a variety of other connected devices, and adjusts their parameters for better performance

---

or power saving based on a chosen profile. There are several predefined tuning profiles for common use cases shipped with RHEL that may be activated either statically or dynamically.

The *tuned* service activates a selected profile at service startup and continues to use it until it is switched to a different profile. This is the static behavior and it is enabled by default.

The dynamic alternative adjusts the system settings based on the live activity data received from monitored system components to ensure optimal performance. In most cases, the utilization of system components varies throughout the day. For example, the disk and processor utilization increases during a program startup and the network connection use goes up during a large file transfer. A surge in a system component activity results in heightened power consumption.

Tuning Profiles

tuned includes nine predefined profiles to support a variety of use cases. In addition, you can create custom profiles from nothing or by using one of the existing profiles as a template. In either case, you need to store the custom profile under the */etc/tuned* directory in order to be recognized by the *tuned* service.

Tuning profiles may be separated into three groups: (1) optimized for better performance, (2) geared towards power consumption, and (3) those that offers a balance between the first two and the maximum performance/power combination. Table 12-5 lists and describes common profiles.

Profile	Description
Profiles Optimized for Better Performance	
Desktop	Based on the balanced profile for desktop systems. Offers improved throughput for interactive applications.
Latency-performance	For low-latency requirements
Network-latency	Based on the latency-performance for faster network throughput
Network-throughput	Based on the throughput-performance profile for maximum network throughput
Virtual-guest	Optimized for virtual machines
Virtual-host	Optimized for virtualized hosts
Profiles Optimized for Power Saving	
Powersave	Saves maximum power at the cost of performance
Balanced/Max Profiles	
Balanced	Preferred choice for systems that require a balance between performance and power saving
Throughput-performance	Provides maximum performance and consumes maximum power

Table 12-5 Tuning Profiles

Predefined profiles are located in the */usr/lib/tuned* directory in subdirectories matching their names. The following shows a long listing of the directory:

```
[user1@server1 ~]$ ll /usr/lib/tuned/
total 16
drwxr-xr-x. 2 root root    24 Jan 26 16:43 accelerator-performance
drwxr-xr-x. 2 root root    24 Jan 26 16:43 balanced
drwxr-xr-x. 2 root root    24 Jan 26 16:43 desktop
-rw-r--r--. 1 root root 15373 Aug 19 14:28 functions
drwxr-xr-x. 2 root root    24 Jan 26 16:43 hpc-compute
drwxr-xr-x. 2 root root    24 Jan 26 16:43 intel-sst
drwxr-xr-x. 2 root root    24 Jan 26 16:43 latency-performance
drwxr-xr-x. 2 root root    24 Jan 26 16:43 network-latency
drwxr-xr-x. 2 root root    24 Jan 26 16:43 network-throughput
drwxr-xr-x. 2 root root    24 Jan 26 16:43 optimize-serial-console
drwxr-xr-x. 2 root root    41 Jan 26 16:43 powersave
```

The default active profile set on *server1* and *server2* is the *virtual-guest* profile, as the two systems are hosted in a VirtualBox virtualized environment.

The tuned-adm Command

tuned comes with a single profile management command called *tuned-adm*. This tool can list active and available profiles, query current settings, switch between profiles, and turn the tuning off. This command can also recommend the best profile for the system based on many system attributes. Refer to the manual pages of the command for more details.

The following exercise demonstrates the use of most of the management operations listed above.

Exercise 12-2: Manage Tuning Profiles

This exercise should be done on *server1* as *user1* with *sudo* where required.

In this exercise, you will install and start the *tuned* service and enable it for auto-restart upon future system reboots. You will display all available profiles and the current active profile. You will switch to one of the available profiles and confirm. You will determine the recommended profile for the system and switch to it. Finally, you will deactivate tuning and reactivate it. You will confirm the activation to conclude the exercise.

1. Install the *tuned* package if it is not already installed:

    ```
    [user1@server1 ~]$ sudo dnf install -y tuned
    Package tuned-2.19.0-1.el9.noarch is already installed.
    Dependencies resolved.
    Nothing to do.
    Complete!
    ```

The output indicates that the software is already installed.

2. Start the *tuned* service and set it to autostart at reboots:

    ```
    [user1@server1 ~]$ sudo systemctl --now enable tuned
    ```

3. Confirm the startup:

```
[user1@server1 ~]$ sudo systemctl status tuned
● tuned.service - Dynamic System Tuning Daemon
     Loaded: loaded (/usr/lib/systemd/system/tuned.service; enabled;
     Active: active (running) since Wed 2023-02-01 11:17:18 EST; 8s
       Docs: man:tuned(8)
             man:tuned.conf(5)
             man:tuned-adm(8)
   Main PID: 2139 (tuned)
      Tasks: 4 (limit: 10944)
     Memory: 13.9M
        CPU: 685ms
     CGroup: /system.slice/tuned.service
             └─2139 /usr/bin/python3 -Es /usr/sbin/tuned -l -P
```

4. Display the list of available tuning profiles:

```
[user1@server1 ~]$ sudo tuned-adm list
Available profiles:
- accelerator-performance    - Throughput performance based tuning w
higher latency STOP states
- balanced                   - General non-specialized tuned profile
- desktop                    - Optimize for the desktop use-case
- hpc-compute                - Optimize for HPC compute workloads
- intel-sst                  - Configure for Intel Speed Select Base
- latency-performance        - Optimize for deterministic performanc
 of increased power consumption
- network-latency            - Optimize for deterministic performanc
 of increased power consumption, focused on low latency network perfc
- network-throughput         - Optimize for streaming network throug
ly only necessary on older CPUs or 40G+ networks
- optimize-serial-console    - Optimize for serial console use.
- powersave                  - Optimize for low power consumption
- throughput-performance     - Broadly applicable tuning that provid
performance across a variety of common server workloads
- virtual-guest              - Optimize for running inside a virtual
- virtual-host               - Optimize for running KVM guests
Current active profile: virtual-guest
```

The output shows several predefined profiles as well as the current active profile.

5. List only the current active profile:

```
[user1@server1 ~]$ sudo tuned-adm active
Current active profile: virtual-guest
```

6. Switch to the *powersave* profile and confirm:

```
[user1@server1 ~]$ sudo tuned-adm profile powersave
[user1@server1 ~]$ sudo tuned-adm active
Current active profile: powersave
```

The active profile is now *powersave*.

7. Determine the recommended profile for *server1* and switch to it:

```
[user1@server1 ~]$ sudo tuned-adm recommend
virtual-guest
[user1@server1 ~]$ sudo tuned-adm profile virtual-guest
[user1@server1 ~]$ sudo tuned-adm active
Current active profile: virtual-guest
```

The first instance of the command shows the best recommended profile for *server1* based on its characteristics, the second command instance switched to the recommended profile, and the third instance confirmed the switching.

8. Turn off tuning:

```
[user1@server1 ~]$ sudo tuned-adm off
[user1@server1 ~]$ sudo tuned-adm active
No current active profile.
```

The service will not perform any tuning until it is reactivated.

9. Reactivate tuning and confirm:

```
[user1@server1 ~]$ sudo tuned-adm profile virtual-guest
[user1@server1 ~]$ sudo tuned-adm active
Current active profile: virtual-guest
```

The tuning is re-enabled and the *virtual-guest* profile is in effect. This concludes the exercise.

Chapter Summary

This chapter started with a discussion of systemd, the default service management and system initialization scheme used in RHEL. We explored key components of systemd, its key directories, and examined unit and target configuration files. We utilized the lone systemd administration command to switch system operational states, identify and set default boot targets, and manage service start, stop, and status checking.

Next, we looked at the traditional system logging and systemd journaling services. Both mechanisms have similarities and differences in how they capture log data and where they direct it for storage and retrieval. We examined the system log configuration file and the configuration file that controls the log file rotation settings. The log subsystem proves valuable when records are needed for monitoring, troubleshooting, auditing, or reporting purpose.

Finally, we explored preconfigured tuning profiles and analyzed pros and cons associated with each one of them. We demonstrated how to determine a recommended profile for the system and how to set and activate it.

Review Questions

1. What is the PID of the *systemd* process?
2. What is a target in *systemd*?
3. You need to append a text string "Hello world" to the system log file. What would be the command to achieve this?
4. The *systemd* command may be used to rebuild a new kernel. True or False?

5. Which command is used to manage system services?
6. Which configuration file must be modified to ensure journal log entries are stored persistently?
7. What is the recommended location to store custom log configuration files?
8. What would the command *systemctl list-dependencies crond* do?
9. What would the command *systemctl restart rsyslog* do?
10. What are the two common *systemd* targets production RHEL servers are typically configured to run at?
11. By default, log files are rotated automatically every week. True or False?
12. Name the two directory paths where *systemd* unit files are stored.
13. What would you run to identify the recommended tuning profile for the system?
14. What would the command *systemctl get-default* do?
15. *systemd* starts multiple services concurrently during system boot. True or False?
16. What is the name of the boot log file?
17. Which *systemctl* subcommand is executed after a unit configuration file has been modified to apply the changes?
18. Which other logging service complements the *rsyslog* service?
19. A RHEL system is booted up. You want to view all messages that were generated during the boot process. Which log file would you look at?

Answers to Review Questions

1. The PID of the *systemd* process is 1.
2. A target is a collection of units.
3. The command to accomplish the desired result would be *logger -i "Hello world"*.
4. False.
5. The *systemctl* command.
6. The *journald.conf* file under the */etc/systemd* directory.
7. The recommended location to store custom log configuration files is */etc/rsyslog.d* directory.
8. The command provided will display all dependent units associated with the specified service.
9. The command provided will restart the *rsyslog* service.
10. The two common *systemd* boot targets are multi-user and graphical.
11. True.
12. The directory locations are */etc/systemd/system* and */usr/lib/systemd/system*.
13. The *tuned-adm recommend* command.
14. The command provided will reveal the current default boot target.
15. True.
16. The *boot.log* file in the */var/log* directory.
17. The *daemon-reload* subcommand.
18. The *systemd-journald* service.
19. The */var/log/boot.log* file.

Do-It-Yourself Challenge Labs

The following labs are useful to strengthen most of the concepts and topics learned in this chapter. It is expected that you perform the labs without external help. A step-by-step guide is not supplied, as the knowledge and skill required to implement the labs have already been disseminated in the chapter; however, hints to the relevant major topic(s) are included.

Use the lab environment built specifically for end-of-chapter labs. See sub-section "Lab Environment for End-of-Chapter Labs" in Chapter 01 "Local Installation" for details.

Lab 12-1: Modify Default Boot Target

As *user1* with *sudo* on *server3*, modify the default boot target from graphical to multi-user, and reboot the system to test it. Run the *systemctl* and *who* commands after the reboot for validation. Restore the default boot target back to graphical and reboot to verify. (Hint: System Initialization and Service Management).

Lab 12-2: Record Custom Alerts

As *user1* with *sudo* on *server3*, write the message "This is $LOGNAME adding this marker on $(date)" to the */var/log/messages* file. Ensure that variable and command expansions work. Verify the entry in the file. (Hint: System Logging).

Lab 12-3: Apply Tuning Profile

As *user1* with *sudo* on *server3*, identify the current system tuning profile with the *tuned-adm* command. List all available profiles. List the recommended profile for *server3*. Apply the "balanced" profile and verify with *tuned-adm*. (Hint: System Tuning).

Chapter 13

Storage Management

This chapter describes the following major topics:

➢ Master Boot Record vs. GUID Partition Table

➢ Identify and understand disk partitions

➢ The concept of thin provisioning, and its benefits

➢ Create and delete partition on MBR disk

➢ Create and delete partition on GPT disk

➢ Describe Logical Volume Manager and its components

➢ Understand various Logical Volume Manager management operations

➢ Know Logical Volume Manager administration commands

➢ Overview of Virtual Data Optimizer and how it conserves storage

➢ Create and confirm physical volumes, volume groups, LVM logical volumes, and VDO logical volumes

➢ Rename, reduce, extend, and remove logical volumes

➢ Extend, reduce, and remove volume groups

➢ Remove physical volumes

RHCSA Objectives:

26. List, create, and delete partitions on MBR and GPT disks
27. Create and remove physical volumes
28. Assign physical volumes to volume groups
29. Create and delete logical volumes
31. Add new partitions and logical volumes, and swap to a system non-destructively (the swap portion of this objective is covered in Chapter 14)
35. Extend existing logical volumes (additional coverage on this objective is available in Chapter 14)

Data is stored on disks that are logically divided into partitions. A partition can exist on a portion of a disk, on an entire disk, or it may span multiple disks. Each partition is accessed and managed independent of other partitions and may contain a file system or swap space. Partitioning information is stored at special disk locations that the system references at boot time. RHEL offers a number of tools for partition management. Partitions created with a combination of most of these tools can coexist on a single disk.

Thin provisioning is a powerful feature that guarantees an efficient use of storage space by allocating only what is needed and by storing data at adjacent locations. Many storage management solutions such as those we discuss later in this chapter and in the next incorporate thin provisioning technology in their core configuration.

Virtual Data Optimizer capitalizes on thin provisioning, de-duplication, and compression technologies to conserve storage space, improve data throughput, and save money.

The Logical Volume Manager solution sets up an abstraction layer between the operating system and the storage hardware. It utilizes virtual objects for storage pooling and allocation, and offers a slew of commands to carry out management operations.

Storage Management Overview

A disk in RHEL can be carved up into several partitions. This partition information is stored on the disk in a small region, which is read by the operating system at boot time. This region is referred to as the *Master Boot Record* (MBR) on the BIOS-based systems, and *GUID Partition Table* (GPT) on the UEFI-based systems. At system boot, the BIOS/UEFI scans all storage devices, detects the presence of MBR/GPT areas, identifies the boot disks, loads the bootloader program in memory from the default boot disk, executes the boot code to read the partition table and identify the */boot* partition, loads the kernel in memory, and passes control over to it. Though MBR and GPT are designed for different PC firmware types, their job is essentially the same: to store disk partition information and the boot code.

Master Boot Record (MBR)

The MBR resides on the first sector of the boot disk. MBR was the preferred choice for saving partition table information on x86-based computers. However, with the arrival of bigger and larger hard drives, a new firmware specification (UEFI) was introduced. MBR is still widely used, but its use is diminishing in favor of UEFI.

MBR allows the creation of three types of partition—*primary*, *extended*, and *logical*—on a single disk. Of these, only primary and logical can be used for data storage; the extended is a mere enclosure for holding the logical partitions and it is not meant for data storage. MBR supports the creation of up to four primary partitions numbered 1 through 4 at a time. In case additional partitions are required, one of the primary partitions must be deleted and replaced with an extended partition to be able to add logical partitions (up to 11) within that extended partition. Numbering for logical partitions begins at 5. MBR supports a maximum of 14 usable partitions (3 primary and 11 logical) on a single disk.

MBR cannot address storage space beyond 2TB. This is due to its 32-bit nature and its 512-byte disk sector size. The MBR is non-redundant; the record it contains is not replicated, resulting in an unbootable system in the event of corruption. If your disk is smaller than 2TB and you don't intend to build more than 14 usable partitions, you can use MBR without issues. For more information on MBR, refer to Chapter 11 "Boot Process, GRUB2, and the Linux Kernel".

GUID Partition Table (GPT)

With the increasing use of disks larger than 2TB on x86 computers, a new 64-bit partitioning standard called *Globally Unique Identifiers* (GUID) *Partition Table* (GPT) was developed and integrated into the UEFI firmware. This new standard introduced plenty of enhancements, including the ability to construct up to 128 partitions (no concept of extended or logical partitions), utilize disks larger than 2TB, use 4KB sector size, and store a copy of the partition information before the end of the disk for redundancy.

Moreover, this standard allows a BIOS-based system to boot from a GPT disk using the bootloader program stored in a protective MBR at the first disk sector. In addition, the UEFI firmware also supports the secure boot feature, which only allows signed binaries to boot. For more information on UEFI and GPT, refer to Chapter 11 "Boot Process, GRUB2, and the Linux Kernel".

Disk Partitions

The space on a storage device can be sliced into partitions. Care must be taken when adding a new partition to elude data corruption with overlapping an extant partition or wasting storage by leaving unused space between adjacent partitions. On *server1*, the disk that was allocated at the time of installation is recognized as *sda* (**s** for **S**ATA, **S**AS, or **S**CSI device) **d**isk **a**, with the first partition identified as *sda1* and the second partition as *sda2*. Any subsequent disks added to the system will be known as *sdb*, *sdc*, *sdd*, and so on, and will use 1, 2, 3, etc. for partition numbering.

RHEL offers a command called *lsblk* to list disk and partition information. The following graphic illustrates the current storage status on *server1*:

```
[user1@server1 ~]$ lsblk
NAME            MAJ:MIN RM   SIZE RO TYPE MOUNTPOINTS
sda               8:0    0    20G  0 disk
├─sda1            8:1    0     1G  0 part /boot
└─sda2            8:2    0    19G  0 part
  ├─rhel-root 253:0      0    17G  0 lvm  /
  └─rhel-swap 253:1      0     2G  0 lvm  [SWAP]
sr0              11:0    1   8.4G  0 rom  /mnt
```

It reveals the presence of one 20GB disk, *sda*, with two partitions: *sda1* and *sda2*. The first partition holds */boot*, and the second one is an LVM object encapsulating *root* (17GB) and *swap* (2GB) logical volumes within it. Both *sda1* and *sda2* partitions occupy the entire disk capacity. The *sr0* represents the ISO image mounted as an optical medium.

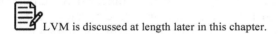 LVM is discussed at length later in this chapter.

There are additional tools such as *fdisk* and *parted* available that can be used to expose disk and partitioning information. Let's run *fdisk* with -l and see what it reveals:

```
[user1@server1 ~]$ sudo fdisk -l
Disk /dev/sda: 20 GiB, 21474836480 bytes, 41943040 sectors
Disk model: VBOX HARDDISK
Units: sectors of 1 * 512 = 512 bytes
Sector size (logical/physical): 512 bytes / 512 bytes
I/O size (minimum/optimal): 512 bytes / 512 bytes
Disklabel type: dos
Disk identifier: 0x9bfed139

Device     Boot    Start       End   Sectors  Size Id Type
/dev/sda1   *       2048   2099199   2097152   1G 83 Linux
/dev/sda2        2099200  41943039  39843840  19G 8e Linux LVM


Disk /dev/mapper/rhel-root: 17 GiB, 18249416704 bytes, 35643392 sectors
Units: sectors of 1 * 512 = 512 bytes
Sector size (logical/physical): 512 bytes / 512 bytes
I/O size (minimum/optimal): 512 bytes / 512 bytes


Disk /dev/mapper/rhel-swap: 2 GiB, 2147483648 bytes, 4194304 sectors
Units: sectors of 1 * 512 = 512 bytes
Sector size (logical/physical): 512 bytes / 512 bytes
I/O size (minimum/optimal): 512 bytes / 512 bytes
```

The output depicts the size of *sda* in GBs, bytes, and sectors, the type of disk label (dos) the disk has, and the disk's geometry in the top block. The second block shows the two disk partitions: *sda1* as the bootable partition marked with an asterisk (*) and *sda2* as an LVM partition. It also exposes the starting and ending sector numbers, size in 1KB blocks, and type of each partition. The identifiers 83 and 8e are hexadecimal values for the partition types. The last two blocks are specific to the LVM logical volumes that exist within the *sda2* partition.

Storage Management Tools

RHEL offers numerous tools and toolsets for storage management, and they include *parted*, *gdisk*, and LVM. There are other native tools available in the OS, but their discussion is beyond the scope of this book. Partitions created with a combination of most of these tools and toolsets can coexist on the same disk.

parted is a simple tool that understands both MBR and GPT formats. *gdisk* is designed to support the GPT format only, and it may be used as a replacement of *parted*. LVM is a feature-rich logical volume management solution that gives flexibility in storage management.

Thin Provisioning

Thin provisioning technology allows for an economical allocation and utilization of storage space by moving arbitrary data blocks to contiguous locations, which results in empty block elimination. With thin provisioning support in LVM, you can create a *thin pool* of storage space and assign volumes much larger storage space than the physical capacity of the pool. Workloads begin consuming the actual allocated space for data writing. When a preset custom threshold (80%, for instance) on the actual consumption of the physical storage in the pool is reached, expand the pool dynamically by adding more physical storage to it. The volumes will automatically start exploiting the new space right away. The thin provisioning technique helps prevent spending more money upfront.

Adding Storage for Practice

This and the next chapter have a considerable number of exercises that require block storage devices for practice. In Chapter 01 "Local Installation" under "Lab Environment for Practice", we mentioned that *server2* will have 4x250MB and 1x5GB virtual disks for storage exercises. We presume that *server2* was built as part of Lab 1-1 and it is now available for use.

Exercise 13-1: Add Required Storage to server2

This exercise will add the required storage disks to *server2* (*RHEL9-VM2*) using VirtualBox.

In this exercise, you will start VirtualBox and add 4x250MB and 1x5GB disks to *server2* in preparation for exercises in this and the next chapter.

1. Start VirtualBox on your Windows/Mac computer and highlight the *RHEL9-VM2* virtual machine that you created in Lab 1-1. See Figure 13-1.

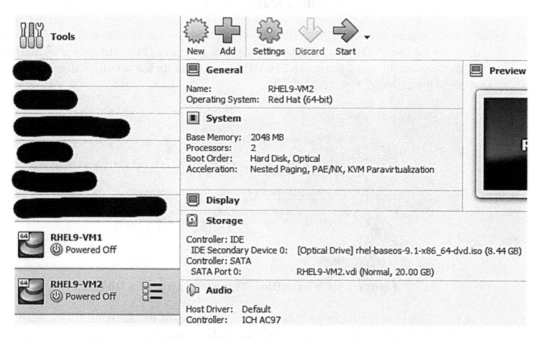

Figure 13-1 VirtualBox Manager | RHEL9-VM2 Selected

2. Click Settings at the top and then Storage on the window that pops up. Click on "Controller: SATA" to select it. Figure 13-2.

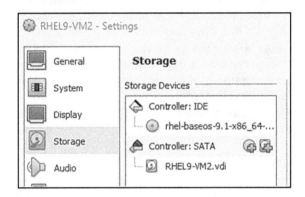

Figure 13-2 VirtualBox Manager | Add Storage

3. Click on the right-side icon next to "Controller: SATA" to add a hard disk and then click Create (on the Medium Selector screen). Figure 13-3.

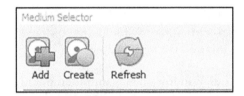

Figure 13-3 VirtualBox Manager | Medium Selector Screen

4. Follow this sequence to add a 250MB disk: Click Next on the next two screens to select the two defaults for the "VDI (Virtualization Disk Image)" and "Dynamically allocated" options. Adjust the size on the third screen to 250MB. Assign the disk a unique name and click Finish to complete the process. Figure 13-4.

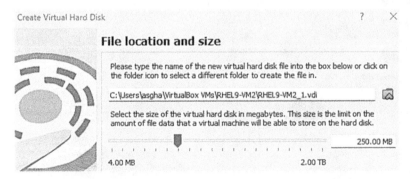

Figure 13-4 VirtualBox Manager | Create a Disk

5. Repeat step 4 three more times to create additional disks of the same size.
6. Repeat step 4 one time to create a disk of size 5GB.
7. On the Medium Selector screen, the five new disks will appear under the Not Attached list of disks. Double-click on each one of them to add to RHEL9-VM2.

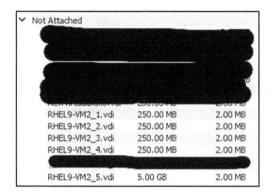

Figure 13-5 VirtualBox Manager | 5 New Disks Created

8. The final list of disks should look similar to what is shown in Figure 13-6 after the addition of all five disks (RHEL9-VM2_1 to RHEL9-VM2_5). Disk names may vary.

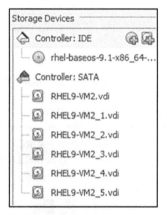

Figure 13-6 VirtualBox Manager | 5 New Disks Added

9. Click OK to return to the main VirtualBox interface.
10. Power on *RHEL9-VM2*.
11. When the server is booted up, log on as *user1* and run the *lsblk* command to verify the new storage:

```
[user1@server2 ~]$ lsblk
NAME            MAJ:MIN RM   SIZE RO TYPE MOUNTPOINTS
sda               8:0    0    20G  0 disk
├─sda1            8:1    0     1G  0 part /boot
└─sda2            8:2    0    19G  0 part
  ├─rhel-root 253:0    0    17G  0 lvm  /
  └─rhel-swap 253:1    0     2G  0 lvm  [SWAP]
sdb              8:16    0   250M  0 disk
sdc              8:32    0   250M  0 disk
sdd              8:48    0   250M  0 disk
sde              8:64    0   250M  0 disk
sdf              8:80    0     5G  0 disk
sr0             11:0     1   8.4G  0 rom
```

12. The five new disks added to *server2* are 250MB (*sdb*, *sdc*, *sdd*, and *sde*) and 5GB (*sdf*).

This concludes the exercise for storage addition to *server2*.

MBR Storage Management with parted

parted (*partition editor*) is a popular tool in RHEL that can be used to partition disks. This program may be run interactively or directly from the command prompt. It understands and supports both MBR and GPT schemes, and can be used to create up to 128 partitions on a single GPT disk. *parted* provides an abundance of subcommands to perform disk management operations such as viewing, labeling, adding, naming, and deleting partitions. Table 13-1 describes these subcommands in that sequence.

Subcommand	Description
print	Displays the partition table that includes disk geometry and partition number, start and end, size, type, file system type, and relevant flags.
mklabel	Applies a label to the disk. Common labels are gpt and msdos.
mkpart	Makes a new partition
name	Assigns a name to a partition
rm	Removes the specified partition

Table 13-1 Common parted Subcommands

For the basic partition creation and deletion operations, Exercises 13-2 and 13-3 will show the use of this tool by directly invoking it from the command prompt. You will use the */dev/sdb* disk for these exercises. After making a partition, use the *print* subcommand to ensure you created what you wanted. The */proc/partitions* file is also updated to reflect the results of partition management operations.

Exercise 13-2: Create an MBR Partition

This exercise should be done on *server2* as *user1* with *sudo* where required.

In this exercise, you will assign partition type "msdos" to */dev/sdb* for using it as an MBR disk. You will create and confirm a 100MB primary partition on the disk.

1. Execute *parted* on */dev/sdb* to view the current partition information:

```
[user1@server2 ~]$ sudo parted /dev/sdb print
Error: /dev/sdb: unrecognised disk label
Model: ATA VBOX HARDDISK (scsi)
Disk /dev/sdb: 262MB
Sector size (logical/physical): 512B/512B
Partition Table: unknown
Disk Flags:
```

There is an error on line 1 of the output, indicating an unrecognized label. This disk must be labeled before it can be partitioned.

2. Assign disk label "msdos" to the disk with *mklabel*. This operation is performed only once on a disk.

```
[user1@server2 ~]$ sudo parted /dev/sdb mklabel msdos
Information: You may need to update /etc/fstab.

[user1@server2 ~]$ sudo parted /dev/sdb print
Model: ATA VBOX HARDDISK (scsi)
Disk /dev/sdb: 262MB
Sector size (logical/physical): 512B/512B
Partition Table: msdos
Disk Flags:

Number  Start  End  Size  Type  File system  Flags
```

The *print* subcommand confirms the successful application of the label.

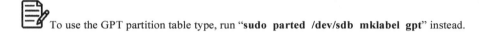 To use the GPT partition table type, run "**sudo parted /dev/sdb mklabel gpt**" instead.

3. Create a 100MB primary partition starting at 1MB (beginning of the disk) using *mkpart*:

```
[user1@server2 ~]$ sudo parted /dev/sdb mkpart primary 1 101m
```

4. Verify the new partition with *print*:

```
[user1@server2 ~]$ sudo parted /dev/sdb print
Number  Start   End    Size    Type      File system  Flags
   1    1049kB  101MB  99.6MB  primary
```

Partition numbering begins at 1 by default.

5. Confirm the new partition with the *lsblk* command:

```
[user1@server2 ~]$ lsblk /dev/sdb
NAME    MAJ:MIN RM  SIZE RO TYPE MOUNTPOINT
sdb       8:16   0  250M  0 disk
└─sdb1    8:17   0   95M  0 part
```

The device file for the first partition on the *sdb* disk is *sdb1* as identified on the bottom line. The partition size is 95MB.

Different tools will have variance in reporting partition sizes. You should ignore minor differences.

6. Check the */proc/partitions* file also:

```
[user1@server2 ~]$ cat /proc/partitions | grep sdb
   8       16     256000 sdb
   8       17      97280 sdb1
```

The virtual file is also updated with the new partition information. This completes the steps for creating and verifying an MBR partition using the *parted* command.

Exercise 13-3: Delete an MBR Partition

This exercise should be done on *server2* as *user1* with *sudo* where required.

In this exercise, you will delete the *sdb1* partition that was created in Exercise 13-2 and confirm the deletion.

1. Execute *parted* on */dev/sdb* with the *rm* subcommand to remove partition number 1:

   ```
   [user1@server2 ~]$ sudo parted /dev/sdb rm 1
   ```

2. Confirm the partition deletion with *print*:

   ```
   . . . . . . . .
   Number  Start  End  Size  Type  File system  Flags
   ```

The partition no longer exists.

3. Check the */proc/partitions* file:

   ```
   [user1@server2 ~]$ cat /proc/partitions | grep sdb
       8      16     256000 sdb
   ```

The virtual file has the partition entry deleted as well. You can also run the *lsblk* command for further verification. The partition has been removed successfully.

> **EXAM TIP:** Knowing either parted or gdisk for the exam is enough.

We will recreate partitions for use in LVM later in this chapter and then again in the next chapter to construct file system and swap structures.

GPT Storage Management with gdisk

The *gdisk* (*GPT disk*) utility partitions disks using the GPT format. This text-based, menu-driven program can show, add, verify, modify, and delete partitions among other operations. *gdisk* can create up to 128 partitions on a single disk on systems with UEFI firmware.

The main interface of *gdisk* can be invoked by specifying a disk device name such as */dev/sdc* with the command. Type *help* or *?* (question mark) at the prompt to view available subcommands.

```
[user1@server2 ~]$ sudo gdisk /dev/sdc
GPT fdisk (gdisk) version 1.0.7

Partition table scan:
  MBR: protective
  BSD: not present
  APM: not present
  GPT: present

Found valid GPT with protective MBR; using GPT.

Command (? for help): ?
b         back up GPT data to a file
c         change a partition's name
d         delete a partition
i         show detailed information on a partition
l         list known partition types
n         add a new partition
o         create a new empty GUID partition table (GPT)
p         print the partition table
q         quit without saving changes
r         recovery and transformation options (experts only)
s         sort partitions
t         change a partition's type code
v         verify disk
w         write table to disk and exit
x         extra functionality (experts only)
?         print this menu

Command (? for help): q
```

The output illustrates that there is no partition table defined on the disk at the moment. There are several subcommands in the main menu followed by a short description. Refer to the screenshot above for a list of subcommands. Enter *q* to quit and return to the command prompt.

Exercise 13-4: Create a GPT Partition

This exercise should be done on *server2* as *user1* with *sudo* where required.

In this exercise, you will assign partition type "gpt" to */dev/sdc* for using it as a GPT disk. You will create and confirm a 200MB partition on the disk.

1. Execute *gdisk* on */dev/sdc* to view the current partition information:

```
[user1@server2 ~]$ sudo gdisk /dev/sdc
GPT fdisk (gdisk) version 1.0.7

Partition table scan:
  MBR: protective
  BSD: not present
  APM: not present
  GPT: present

Found valid GPT with protective MBR; using GPT.

Command (? for help):
```

The disk currently does not have any partition table on it.

2. Assign "gpt" as the partition table type to the disk using the *o* subcommand. Enter "y" for confirmation to proceed. This operation is performed only once on a disk.

```
Command (? for help): o
This option deletes all partitions and creates a new protective MBR.
Proceed? (Y/N): Y
```

3. Run the *p* subcommand to view disk information and confirm the GUID partition table creation:

```
Command (? for help): p
Disk /dev/sdc: 512000 sectors, 250.0 MiB
Model: VBOX HARDDISK
Sector size (logical/physical): 512/512 bytes
Disk identifier (GUID): CFBCD800-847E-4D49-96E1-BA6EC693A4D1
Partition table holds up to 128 entries
Main partition table begins at sector 2 and ends at sector 33
First usable sector is 34, last usable sector is 511966
Partitions will be aligned on 2048-sector boundaries
Total free space is 511933 sectors (250.0 MiB)

Number  Start (sector)    End (sector)  Size        Code  Name
```

The output returns the assigned GUID and states that the partition table can hold up to 128 partition entries.

4. Create the first partition of size 200MB starting at the default sector with default type "Linux filesystem" using the *n* subcommand:

```
Command (? for help): n
Partition number (1-128, default 1):
First sector (34-511966, default = 2048) or {+-}size{KMGTP}:
Last sector (2048-511966, default = 511966) or {+-}size{KMGTP}: +200M
Current type is 8300 (Linux filesystem)
Hex code or GUID (L to show codes, Enter = 8300):
Changed type of partition to 'Linux filesystem'
```

5. Verify the new partition with *p*:

```
Command (? For help): p
. . . . . . . .
Number  Start (sector)    End (sector)  Size        Code  Name
    1             2048          411647  200.0 MiB   8300  Linux filesystem
```

6. Run *w* to write the partition information to the partition table and exit out of the interface. Enter "y" to confirm when prompted.

```
Command (? for help): w

Final checks complete. About to write GPT data. THIS WILL OVERWRITE EXISTING
PARTITIONS!!

Do you want to proceed? (Y/N): Y
OK; writing new GUID partition table (GPT) to /dev/sdc.
The operation has completed successfully.
```

You may need to run the partprobe command after exiting the gdisk utility to inform the kernel of partition table changes.

7. Verify the new partition by issuing either of the following at the command prompt:

```
[user1@server2 ~]$ grep sdc /proc/partitions
   8        32      256000 sdc
   8        33      204800 sdc1
[user1@server2 ~]$
[user1@server2 ~]$ lsblk /dev/sdc
NAME    MAJ:MIN RM  SIZE RO TYPE MOUNTPOINT
sdc        8:32   0  250M  0 disk
└─sdc1     8:33   0  200M  0 part
```

The device file for the first partition on the *sdc* disk is *sdc1* and it is 200MB in size as reported in the above outputs. This completes the steps for creating and verifying a GPT partition using the *gdisk* command.

Exercise 13-5: Delete a GPT Partition

This exercise should be done on *server2* as *user1* with *sudo* where required.

In this exercise, you will delete the *sdc1* partition that was created in Exercise 13-4 and confirm the removal.

1. Execute *gdisk* on */dev/sdc* and run *d1* at the utility's prompt to delete partition number 1:

```
Command (? for help): d1
Using 1
```

2. Confirm the partition deletion with *p*:

```
........
 Number  Start (sector)    End (sector)  Size        Code  Name
```

The partition no longer exists.

3. Write the updated partition information to the disk with *w* and quit *gdisk*:

```
Command (? for help): w

Final checks complete. About to write GPT data. THIS WILL OVERWRITE EXISTING
PARTITIONS!!

Do you want to proceed? (Y/N): Y
OK; writing new GUID partition table (GPT) to /dev/sdc.
The operation has completed successfully.
```

4. Verify the partition deletion by issuing either of the following at the command prompt:

```
[user1@server2 ~]$ grep sdc /proc/partitions
    8       32      256000 sdc
[user1@server2 ~]$
[user1@server2 ~]$ lsblk /dev/sdc
NAME MAJ:MIN RM  SIZE RO TYPE MOUNTPOINT
sdc   8:32   0  250M  0 disk
```

Both commands confirm the successful partition removal.

Logical Volume Manager (LVM)

The *Logical Volume Manager* (LVM) solution is widely used for managing block storage in Linux.
LVM provides an abstraction layer between the physical storage and the file system, enabling the
file system to be resized, span across multiple disks, use arbitrary disk space, etc. LVM accumulates
spaces taken from partitions or entire disks (called *Physical Volumes*) to form a logical container
(called *Volume Group*), which is then divided into logical partitions (called *Logical Volumes*). The
other key benefits of LVM include online resizing of volume groups and logical volumes, online
data migration between logical volumes and between physical volumes, user-defined naming for
volume groups and logical volumes, mirroring and striping across multiple disks, and snapshotting
of logical volumes. Figure 13-7 depicts the LVM components.

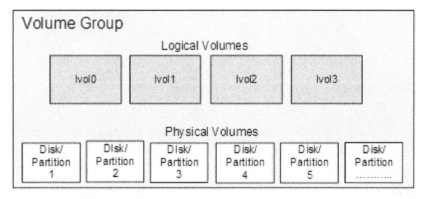

Figure 13-7 LVM Structure

As noted above, the LVM structure is made up of three key objects called physical volume, volume
group, and logical volume. These objects are further virtually broken down into *Physical Extents*
(PEs) and *Logical Extents* (LEs). The LVM components are explained in the following subsections.

Physical Volume

A *Physical Volume* (PV) is created when a block storage device such as a partition or an entire disk is initialized and brought under LVM control. This process constructs LVM data structures on the device, including a label on the second sector and metadata shortly thereafter. The label includes the UUID, size, and pointers to the locations of data and metadata areas. Given the criticality of metadata, LVM stores a copy of it at the end of the physical volume as well. The rest of the device space is available for use.

You can use an LVM command called *pvs* (*physical volume scan* or *summary*) to scan and list available physical volumes on *server2*:

```
[user1@server2 ~]$ sudo pvs
  PV         VG    Fmt  Attr PSize   PFree
  /dev/sda2  rhel  lvm2 a--  <19.00g    0
```

The output shows one physical volume (PV) */dev/sda2* of size 19GB in *rhel* volume group (VG). Additional information displays the metadata format (Fmt) used, status of the physical volume under the Attr column (a for allocatable), and the amount of free space available on the physical volume (PFree).

Try running this command again with the -v flag to view more information about the physical volume.

Volume Group

A *Volume Group* (VG) is created when at least one physical volume is added to it. The space from all physical volumes in a volume group is aggregated to form one large pool of storage, which is then used to build logical volumes. The physical volumes added to a volume group may be of varying sizes. LVM writes volume group metadata on each physical volume that is added to it. The volume group metadata contains its name, date and time of creation, how it was created, the extent size used, a list of physical and logical volumes, a mapping of physical and logical extents, etc. A volume group can have a custom name assigned to it at the time of its creation. For example, it may be called *vg01*, *vgora*, or *vgweb* that identifies the type of information it is constructed to store. A copy of the volume group metadata is stored and maintained at two distinct locations on each physical volume within the volume group.

You can use an LVM command called *vgs* (*volume group scan* or *summary*) to scan and list available volume groups on *server2*:

```
[user1@server2 ~]$ sudo vgs
  VG    #PV #LV #SN Attr   VSize   VFree
  rhel    1   2   0 wz--n- <19.00g    0
```

The output shows one volume group (VG) *rhel* on *server2* containing one physical volume (#PV). Additional information displays the number of logical volumes (#LV) and snapshots (#SN) in the volume group, status of the volume group under the Attr column (w for writeable, z for resizable, and n for normal), size of the volume group (VSize), and the amount of free space available in the volume group (VFree).

Try running this command again with the -v flag to view more information about the volume group.

Physical Extent

A physical volume is divided into several smaller logical pieces when it is added to a volume group. These logical pieces are known as *Physical Extents* (PE). An extent is the smallest allocatable unit of space in LVM. At the time of volume group creation, you can either define the size of the PE or leave it to the default value of 4MB. This implies that a 20GB physical volume would have approximately 5,000 PEs. Any physical volumes added to this volume group thereafter will use the same PE size.

You can use an LVM command called *vgdisplay* (*volume group display*) on *server2* and *grep* for 'PE Size' to view the PE size used in the *rhel* volume group:

```
[user1@server2 ~]$ sudo vgdisplay rhel | grep 'PE Size'
  PE Size               4.00 MiB
```

The output reveals the PE size used for the *rhel* VG.

Logical Volume

A volume group consists of a pool of storage taken from one or more physical volumes. This volume group space is used to create one or more *Logical Volumes* (LVs). A logical volume can be created or weeded out online, expanded or shrunk online, and can use space taken from one or multiple physical volumes inside the volume group.

The default naming convention used for logical volumes is *lvol0, lvol1, lvol2*, and so on; however, you may assign custom names to them. For example, a logical volume may be called *system, undo*, or *webdata1* so as to establish the type of information it is constructed to store.

You can use an LVM command called *lvs* (*logical volume scan* or *summary*) to scan and list available logical volumes on *server2*:

```
[user1@server2 ~]$ sudo lvs
  LV   VG   Attr       LSize   Pool Origin
  root rhel -wi-ao---- <17.00g
  swap rhel -wi-ao----   2.00g
```

The output shows two logical volumes *root* and *swap* in *rhel* volume group. Additional information displays the status of the logical volumes under the Attr column (w for writeable, i for inherited allocation policy, a for active, and o for open) and their sizes.

Try running this command again with the -v flag to view more information about the logical volumes.

Logical Extent

A logical volume is made up of *Logical Extents* (LE). Logical extents point to physical extents, and they may be random or contiguous. The larger a logical volume is, the more logical extents it will have. Logical extents are a set of physical extents allocated to a logical volume.

The LE size is always the same as the PE size in a volume group. The default LE size is 4MB, which corresponds to the default PE size of 4MB.

You can use an LVM command called *lvdisplay* (*logical volume display*) on *server2* to view information about the *root* logical volume in the *rhel* volume group.

```
[user1@server2 ~]$ sudo lvdisplay /dev/rhel/root
  --- Logical volume ---
  LV Path                /dev/rhel/root
  LV Name                root
  VG Name                rhel
  LV UUID                J04CAD-K4xZ-M0BQ-zr76-JygN-0TyW
  LV Write Access        read/write
  LV Creation host, time server2.example.com, 2023-02-01
  LV Status              available
  # open                 1
  LV Size                <17.00 GiB
  Current LE             4351
  Segments               1
  Allocation             inherit
  Read ahead sectors     auto
  - currently set to     256
  Block device           253:0
```

The output does not disclose the LE size; however, you can convert the LV size in MBs (17,000) and then divide the result by the Current LE count (4,351) to get the LE size (which comes close to 4MB).

LVM Operations and Commands

The LVM toolset offers a multitude of administrative commands to carry out various disk and volume management operations. These operations include creating and removing a physical volume, volume group, and logical volume; extending and reducing a volume group and logical volume; renaming a volume group and logical volume; and listing and displaying physical volume, volume group, and logical volume information.

Table 13-2 summarizes the common LVM tasks and the commands that are employed to accomplish them.

Command	Description
Create and Remove Operations	
pvcreate/pvremove	Initializes/uninitializes a disk or partition for LVM use
vgcreate/vgremove	Creates/removes a volume group
lvcreate/lvremove	Creates/removes a logical volume
Extend and Reduce Operations	
vgextend/vgreduce	Adds/removes a physical volume to/from a volume group
lvextend/lvreduce	Extends/reduces the size of a logical volume
lvresize	Resizes a logical volume. With the -r option, this command calls the fsadm command to resize the underlying file system as well.
Rename Operations	
vgrename	Renames a volume group
lvrename	Renames a logical volume
List and Display Operations	
pvs/pvdisplay	Lists/displays physical volume information
vgs/vgdisplay	Lists/displays volume group information
lvs/lvdisplay	Lists/displays logical volume information

Table 13-2 Common LVM Operations and Commands

All the tools accept the -v switch to support verbosity. Refer to the manual pages of the commands for usage and additional details.

As noted earlier, there are five disks available on *server2* for practice. Issue the *lsblk* command to confirm:

```
sdb          8:16    0    250M    0 disk
sdc          8:32    0    250M    0 disk
sdd          8:48    0    250M    0 disk
sde          8:64    0    250M    0 disk
sdf          8:80    0      5G    0 disk
```

You will use the *sdd* and *sde* disks for LVM activities in the following exercises.

Exercise 13-6: Create Physical Volume and Volume Group

This exercise should be done on *server2* as *user1* with *sudo* where required.

In this exercise, you will initialize one partition *sdd1* (90MB) and one disk *sde* (250MB) for use in LVM. You will create a volume group called *vgbook* and add both physical volumes to it. You will use the PE size of 16MB and list and display the volume group and the physical volumes.

1. Create a partition of size 90MB on *sdd* using the *parted* command and confirm. You need to label the disk first, as it is a new disk.

```
[user1@server2 ~]$ sudo parted /dev/sdd mklabel msdos
[user1@server2 ~]$ sudo parted /dev/sdd mkpart primary 1 91m
[user1@server2 ~]$ sudo parted /dev/sdd print
Model: ATA VBOX HARDDISK (scsi)
Disk /dev/sdd: 262MB
Sector size (logical/physical): 512B/512B
Partition Table: msdos
Disk Flags:

Number  Start    End      Size     Type     File system  Flags
 1      1049kB   91.2MB   90.2MB   primary
```

The *print* subcommand confirms the creation of the partition. It is the first partition on the disk.

2. Initialize the *sdd1* partition and the *sde* disk using the *pvcreate* command. Note that there is no need to apply a disk label on *sde* with *parted* as LVM does not require it.

```
[user1@server2 ~]$ sudo pvcreate /dev/sdd1 /dev/sde -v
    Wiping signatures on new PV /dev/sdd1.
    Wiping signatures on new PV /dev/sde.
    Set up physical volume for "/dev/sdd1" with 176128 available sectors.
    Zeroing start of device /dev/sdd1.
    Writing physical volume data to disk "/dev/sdd1".
  Physical volume "/dev/sdd1" successfully created.
    Set up physical volume for "/dev/sde" with 512000 available sectors.
    Zeroing start of device /dev/sde.
    Writing physical volume data to disk "/dev/sde".
  Physical volume "/dev/sde" successfully created.
```

The command generated a verbose output. You now have two physical volumes available for use.

3.   Create *vgbook* volume group using the *vgcreate* command and add the two physical volumes to it. Use the -s option to specify the PE size in MBs.

```
[user1@server2 ~]$ sudo vgcreate -vs 16 vgbook /dev/sdd1 /dev/sde
    Wiping signatures on new PV /dev/sdd1.
    Wiping signatures on new PV /dev/sde.
    Adding physical volume '/dev/sdd1' to volume group 'vgbook'
    Adding physical volume '/dev/sde' to volume group 'vgbook'
    Archiving volume group "vgbook" metadata (seqno 0).
    Creating volume group backup "/etc/lvm/backup/vgbook" (seqno 1).
  Volume group "vgbook" successfully created
```

The above command combines the two options with a single hyphen.

4.   List the volume group information:

```
[user1@server2 ~]$ sudo vgs vgbook
  VG       #PV #LV #SN Attr   VSize   VFree
  vgbook    2   0   0 wz--n- 320.00m 320.00m
```

The total capacity available in the *vgbook* volume group is 320MB.

5.   Display detailed information about the volume group and the physical volumes it contains:

```
[user1@server2 ~]$ sudo vgdisplay -v vgbook
  --- Volume group ---
  VG Name               vgbook
  System ID
  Format                lvm2
  Metadata Areas        2
  Metadata Sequence No  1
  VG Access             read/write
  VG Status             resizable
  MAX LV                0
  Cur LV                0
  Open LV               0
  Max PV                0
  Cur PV                2
  Act PV                2
  VG Size               320.00 MiB
  PE Size               16.00 MiB
  Total PE              20
  Alloc PE / Size       0 / 0
  Free  PE / Size       20 / 320.00 MiB
  VG UUID               hcgP0t-507k-ju1k-DjGO-x1O3-Rs

  --- Physical volumes ---
  PV Name               /dev/sdd1
  PV UUID               LAw1xd-CgN2-5nrH-X1ZG-paec-DZ
  PV Status             allocatable
  Total PE / Free PE    5 / 5

  PV Name               /dev/sde
  PV UUID               oaum6u-67xo-1Ud7-mO3O-6PkF-07
  PV Status             allocatable
  Total PE / Free PE    15 / 15
```

The verbose output includes the physical volume attributes as well. There are a total of 20 PEs in the volume group (5 in *sdd1* and 15 in *sde*), and each PE is 16MB in size. The collective size of all the physical volumes represents the total size of the volume group, which is 20x16 = 320MB.

6. List the physical volume information:

```
[user1@server2 ~]$ sudo pvs
  PV           VG      Fmt   Attr PSize    PFree
  /dev/sda2    rhel    lvm2  a--  <19.00g       0
  /dev/sdd1    vgbook  lvm2  a--   80.00m  80.00m
  /dev/sde     vgbook  lvm2  a--  240.00m 240.00m
```

The output shows the physical volumes in *vgbook*, along with their utilization status.

7. Display detailed information about the physical volumes:

```
[user1@server2 ~]$ sudo pvdisplay /dev/sdd1
  --- Physical volume ---
  PV Name               /dev/sdd1
  VG Name               vgbook
  PV Size               86.00 MiB / not usable 6.00 MiB
  Allocatable           yes
  PE Size               16.00 MiB
  Total PE              5
  Free PE               5
  Allocated PE          0
  PV UUID               LAw1xd-CgN2-5nrH-X1ZG-paec-DZjP-J

[user1@server2 ~]$ sudo pvdisplay /dev/sde
  --- Physical volume ---
  PV Name               /dev/sde
  VG Name               vgbook
  PV Size               250.00 MiB / not usable 10.00 MiB
  Allocatable           yes
  PE Size               16.00 MiB
  Total PE              15
  Free PE               15
  Allocated PE          0
  PV UUID               oaum6u-67xo-1Ud7-mO3O-6PkF-07M3-P₁
```

Once a partition or disk is initialized and added to a volume group, they are treated identically within the volume group. LVM does not prefer one over the other.

Exercise 13-7: Create Logical Volumes

This exercise should be done on *server2* as *user1* with *sudo* where required.

In this exercise, you will create two logical volumes, *lvol0* and *lvbook1*, in the *vgbook* volume group. You will use 120MB for *lvol0* and 192MB for *lvbook1* from the available pool of space. You will display the details of the volume group and the logical volumes.

1. Create a logical volume with the default name *lvol0* using the *lvcreate* command. Use the -L option to specify the logical volume size, 120MB. You may use the -v, -vv, or -vvv option with the command for verbosity.

```
[user1@server2 ~]$ sudo lvcreate -vL 120 vgbook
  Rounding up size to full physical extent 128.00 MiB
  Creating logical volume lvol0
  Archiving volume group "vgbook" metadata (seqno 1).
  Activating logical volume vgbook/lvol0.
  activation/volume_list configuration setting not defined: Checking
s for vgbook/lvol0.
  Creating vgbook-lvol0
  Loading table for vgbook-lvol0 (253:2).
  Resuming vgbook-lvol0 (253:2).
  Wiping known signatures on logical volume vgbook/lvol0.
  Initializing 4.00 KiB of logical volume vgbook/lvol0 with value 0.
  Logical volume "lvol0" created.
  Creating volume group backup "/etc/lvm/backup/vgbook" (seqno 2).
```

The size for the logical volume may be specified in units such as MBs, GBs, TBs, or as a count of LEs; however, MB is the default if no unit is specified (see the previous command). The size of a logical volume is always in multiples of the PE size. For instance, logical volumes created in *vgbook* with the PE size set at 16MB can be 16MB, 32MB, 48MB, 64MB, and so on. The output above indicates that the logical volume is 128MB (16x8), and not 120MB as specified.

2. Create *lvbook1* of size 192MB (16x12) using the *lvcreate* command. Use the -l switch to specify the size in logical extents and -n for the custom name. You may use -v for verbose information.

```
[user1@server2 ~]$ sudo lvcreate -l 12 -n lvbook1 vgbook
  Logical volume "lvbook1" created.
```

3. List the logical volume information:

```
[user1@server2 ~]$ sudo lvs
  LV       VG      Attr       LSize    Poc
  root     rhel    -wi-ao---- <17.00g
  swap     rhel    -wi-ao----   2.00g
  lvbook1  vgbook  -wi-a-----  192.00m
  lvol0    vgbook  -wi-a-----  128.00m
```

Both logical volumes are listed in the output with their attributes and sizes.

4. Display detailed information about the volume group including the logical volumes and the physical volumes:

```
[user1@server2 ~]$ sudo vgdisplay -v vgbook
........
```

```
--- Logical volume ---
LV Path                    /dev/vgbook/lvol0
LV Name                    lvol0
VG Name                    vgbook
LV UUID                    Zy7Gpw-Lv0T-NmlP-GA9y-kMn1-o0Ub
LV Write Access            read/write
LV Creation host, time     server2.example.com, 2023-02-02
LV Status                  available
# open                     0
LV Size                    128.00 MiB
Current LE                 8
Segments                   1
Allocation                 inherit
Read ahead sectors         auto
- currently set to         256
Block device               253:2

--- Logical volume ---
LV Path                    /dev/vgbook/lvbook1
LV Name                    lvbook1
VG Name                    vgbook
LV UUID                    kdkW0M-9BFX-rChN-TYxG-k6fO-VAbg
LV Write Access            read/write
LV Creation host, time     server2.example.com, 2023-02-02
LV Status                  available
# open                     0
LV Size                    192.00 MiB
Current LE                 12
Segments                   2
Allocation                 inherit
Read ahead sectors         auto
- currently set to         256
Block device               253:3
........
```

Alternatively, you can run the following to view only the logical volume details:

```
[user1@server2 ~]$ sudo lvdisplay /dev/vgbook/lvol0
[user1@server2 ~]$ sudo lvdisplay /dev/vgbook/lvbook1
```

Review the attributes of the logical volumes as detailed above.

Exercise 13-8: Extend a Volume Group and a Logical Volume

This exercise should be done on *server2* as *user1* with *sudo* where required.

In this exercise, you will add another partition *sdd2* of size 158MB to *vgbook* to increase the pool of allocatable space. You will initialize the new partition prior to adding it to the volume group. You will increase the size of *lvbook1* to 336MB. You will display basic information for the physical volumes, volume group, and logical volume.

1. Create a partition of size 158MB on *sdd* using the *parted* command. Display the new partition to confirm the partition number and size.

```
[user1@server2 ~]$ sudo parted /dev/sdd mkpart pri 92 250
[user1@server2 ~]$ sudo parted /dev/sdd set 2 lvm on
[user1@server2 ~]$ sudo parted /dev/sdd print
........
2        92.3MB   250MB    157MB   primary
```

2. Initialize *sdd2* using the *pvcreate* command:

```
[user1@server2 ~]$ sudo pvcreate /dev/sdd2
  Physical volume "/dev/sdd2" successfully created.
```

3. Extend *vgbook* by adding the new physical volume to it:

```
[user1@server2 ~]$ sudo vgextend vgbook /dev/sdd2
  Volume group "vgbook" successfully extended
```

4. List the volume group:

```
[user1@server2 ~]$ sudo vgs
  VG       #PV #LV #SN Attr   VSize    VFree
  rhel      1   2   0 wz--n- <19.00g    0
  vgbook    3   2   0 wz--n- 464.00m    0
```

The output reflects the addition of a third physical volume to *vgbook*. The total capacity of the volume group has now increased to 464MB with 144MB free.

5. Extend the size of *lvbook1* to 340MB by adding 144MB using the *lvextend* command:

```
[user1@server2 ~]$ sudo lvextend -L +144 /dev/vgbook/lvbook1
  Size of logical volume vgbook/lvbook1 changed from 192.00 MiB (12 extents) to 336.00 MiB (2
1 extents).
  Logical volume vgbook/lvbook1 successfully resized.
```

EXAM TIP: Make sure the expansion of a logical volume does not affect the file system and the data it contains. More details in Chapter 14.

6. Issue *vgdisplay* on *vgbook* with the -v switch for the updated details:

```
[user1@server2 ~]$ sudo vgdisplay -v vgbook
```

The output will show a lot of information about the volume group and the logical and physical volumes it contains. It will reflect the updates made in this exercise. In fact, each time a volume group or a logical volume is resized, *vgdisplay* will reflect those changes. The above output will display three physical volumes with the combined allocatable space grown to 464MB. The number of PEs will have increased to 29, with all of them allocated to logical volumes and 0 unused. The

Logical Volume sections will display the updated information for the logical volumes. And at the very bottom, the three physical volumes will show with their device names, and total and available PEs in each.

7. View a summary of the physical volumes:

```
[user1@server2 ~]$ sudo pvs
  PV          VG      Fmt   Attr  PSize     PFree
  /dev/sda2   rhel    lvm2  a--   <19.00g      0
  /dev/sdd1   vgbook  lvm2  a--    80.00m      0
  /dev/sdd2   vgbook  lvm2  a--   144.00m      0
  /dev/sde    vgbook  lvm2  a--   240.00m      0
```

8. View a summary of the logical volumes:

```
[user1@server2 ~]$ sudo lvs
  LV        VG      Attr        LSize     Pool
  root      rhel    -wi-ao----  <17.00g
  swap      rhel    -wi-ao----    2.00g
  lvbook1   vgbook  -wi-a-----  336.00m
  lvol0     vgbook  -wi-a-----  128.00m
```

This brings the exercise to an end.

Exercise 13-9: Rename, Reduce, Extend, and Remove Logical Volumes

This exercise should be done on *server2* as *user1* with *sudo* where required.

In this exercise, you will rename *lvol0* to *lvbook2*. You will decrease the size of *lvbook2* to 50MB using the *lvreduce* command and then add 32MB with the *lvresize* command. You will then remove both logical volumes. You will display the summary for the volume groups, logical volumes, and physical volumes.

1. Rename *lvol0* to *lvbook2* using the *lvrename* command and confirm with *lvs*:

```
[user1@server2 ~]$ sudo lvrename vgbook lvol0 lvbook2
  Renamed "lvol0" to "lvbook2" in volume group "vgbook"
[user1@server2 ~]$ sudo lvs
  LV        VG      Attr        LSize     Pool Origin Data%  ]
  root      rhel    -wi-ao----  <17.00g
  swap      rhel    -wi-ao----    2.00g
  lvbook1   vgbook  -wi-a-----  336.00m
  lvbook2   vgbook  -wi-a-----  128.00m
```

2. Reduce the size of *lvbook2* to 50MB with the *lvreduce* command. Specify the absolute desired size for the logical volume. Answer "Do you really want to reduce vgbook/lvbook2?" in the affirmative.

```
[user1@server2 ~]$ sudo lvreduce -L 50 /dev/vgbook/lvbook2
  Rounding size to boundary between physical extents: 64.00 MiB.
  WARNING: Reducing active logical volume to 64.00 MiB.
  THIS MAY DESTROY YOUR DATA (filesystem etc.)
Do you really want to reduce vgbook/lvbook2? [y/n]: y
  Size of logical volume vgbook/lvbook2 changed from 128.00 MiB (8 extents) t
o 64.00 MiB (4 extents).
  Logical volume vgbook/lvbook2 successfully resized.
```

3. Add 32MB to *lvbook2* with the *lvresize* command:

```
[user1@server2 ~]$ sudo lvresize -L +32 /dev/vgbook/lvbook2
  Size of logical volume vgbook/lvbook2 changed from 64.00 MiB (4 extents) to
  96.00 MiB (6 extents).
  Logical volume vgbook/lvbook2 successfully resized.
```

4. Use the *pvs*, *lvs*, *vgs*, and *vgdisplay* commands to view the updated allocation.
5. Remove both *lvbook1* and *lvbook2* logical volumes using the *lvremove* command. Use the -f option to suppress the "Do you really want to remove active logical volume" message.

```
[user1@server2 ~]$ sudo lvremove /dev/vgbook/lvbook1 -f
  Logical volume "lvbook1" successfully removed
[user1@server2 ~]$ sudo lvremove /dev/vgbook/lvbook2 -f
  Logical volume "lvbook2" successfully removed
```

Removing a logical volume is a destructive task. You need to ensure that you perform a backup of any data in the target logical volume prior to deleting it. You will need to unmount the file system or disable swap in the logical volume. See Chapter 15 on how to unmount a file system and disable swap.

6. Execute the *vgdisplay* command and *grep* for "Cur LV" to see the number of logical volumes currently available in *vgbook*. It should show 0, as you have removed both logical volumes.

```
[user1@server2 ~]$ sudo vgdisplay vgbook | grep 'Cur LV'
  Cur LV                 0
```

This concludes the exercise.

Exercise 13-10: Reduce and Remove a Volume Group

This exercise should be done on *server2* as *user1* with *sudo* where required.

In this exercise, you will reduce *vgbook* by removing the *sdd1* and *sde* physical volumes from it, and then remove the volume group. Confirm the deletion of the volume group and the logical volumes at the end.

1. Remove *sdd1* and *sde* physical volumes from *vgbook* by issuing the *vgreduce* command:

```
[user1@server2 ~]$ sudo vgreduce vgbook /dev/sdd1 /dev/sde
  Removed "/dev/sdd1" from volume group "vgbook"
  Removed "/dev/sde" from volume group "vgbook"
```

2. Remove the volume group using the *vgremove* command. This will also remove the last physical volume, *sdd2*, from it.

```
[user1@server2 ~]$ sudo vgremove vgbook
  Volume group "vgbook" successfully removed
```

📝 You can also use the -f option with the *vgremove* command to force the volume group removal even if it contains any number of logical and physical volumes in it.

📝 Remember to proceed with caution whenever you perform reduce and erase operations.

3. Execute the *vgs* and *lvs* commands for confirmation:

```
[user1@server2 ~]$ sudo vgs
  VG    #PV #LV #SN Attr   VSize    VFree
  rhel   1   2   0 wz--n- <19.00g     0
[user1@server2 ~]$
[user1@server2 ~]$ sudo lvs
  LV   VG   Attr       LSize    Pool Origin
  root rhel -wi-ao---- <17.00g
  swap rhel -wi-ao----   2.00g
```

This concludes the exercise.

Exercise 13-11: Uninitialize Physical Volumes

This exercise should be done on *server2* as *user1* with *sudo* where required.

In this exercise, you will uninitialize all three physical volumes—*sdd1*, *sdd2*, and *sde*—by deleting the LVM structural information from them. Use the *pvs* command for confirmation. Remove the partitions from the *sdd* disk and verify that all disks used in Exercises 13-6 to 13-10 are now in their original raw state.

1. Remove the LVM structures from *sdd1*, *sdd2*, and *sde* using the *pvremove* command:

```
[user1@server2 ~]$ sudo pvremove /dev/sdd1 /dev/sdd2 /dev/sde
  Labels on physical volume "/dev/sdd1" successfully wiped.
  Labels on physical volume "/dev/sdd2" successfully wiped.
  Labels on physical volume "/dev/sde" successfully wiped.
```

2. Confirm the removal using the *pvs* command:

```
[user1@server2 ~]$ sudo pvs
  PV         VG   Fmt  Attr PSize   PFree
  /dev/sda2  rhel lvm2 a--  <19.00g    0
```

The partitions and the disk are now back to their raw state and can be repurposed.

3. Remove the partitions from *sdd* using the *parted* command:

```
[user1@server2 ~]$ sudo parted /dev/sdd rm 1 ; sudo parted /dev/sdd rm 2
```

4. Verify that all disks used in previous exercises have returned to their original raw state using the *lsblk* command:

```
[user1@server2 ~]$ lsblk
NAME           MAJ:MIN RM   SIZE RO TYPE MOUNTPOINTS
sda               8:0    0    20G  0 disk
├─sda1            8:1    0     1G  0 part /boot
└─sda2            8:2    0    19G  0 part
  ├─rhel-root 253:0    0    17G  0 lvm  /
  └─rhel-swap 253:1    0     2G  0 lvm  [SWAP]
sdb               8:16   0   250M  0 disk
sdc               8:32   0   250M  0 disk
sdd               8:48   0   250M  0 disk
sde               8:64   0   250M  0 disk
sdf               8:80   0     5G  0 disk
sr0              11:0    1   8.4G  0 rom
```

This brings the exercise to an end.

We will recreate logical volumes and construct file system and swap structures in them in the next chapter.

Storage Optimization with Virtual Data Optimizer (VDO)

Virtual Data Optimizer (VDO) is a device driver layer that sits between the Linux kernel and the physical storage devices. The goals are to conserve disk space, improve data throughput, and save on storage cost. VDO employs thin provisioning, de-duplication, and compression technologies to help realize the goals.

How VDO Conserves Storage

VDO makes use of the thin provisioning technology to identify and eliminate empty (zero-byte) data blocks. This is referred to as *zero-block elimination*. VDO removes randomization of data blocks by moving in-use data blocks to contiguous locations on the storage device. This is the initial stage in the process.

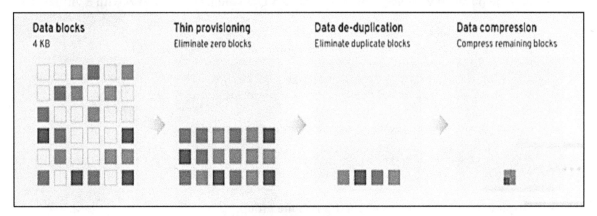

Figure 13-8 Storage Optimization with VDO

Next, VDO keeps an eye on data being written to the disk. If it detects that the new data is an identical copy of some existing data, it makes an internal note of it but does not actually write the redundant data to the disk. VDO uses the technique called *de-duplication* to this end. This technique is implemented with the inclusion of a kernel module called *UDS* (*Universal De-duplication Service*). This is the second stage in the process.

In the third and final stage, VDO calls upon another kernel module called *kvdo*, which compresses the residual data blocks and consolidates them on a lower number of blocks. This results in a further drop in storage space utilization.

VDO runs in the background and processes inbound data through the three stages on VDO-enabled volumes. VDO is not a CPU- or memory-intensive process; it consumes a low amount of system resources.

VDO Integration with LVM

RHEL 9 uses an LVM VDO implementation for managing VDO logical volumes. Unlike previous versions of RHEL, a separate set of VDO management tools are no longer necessary. The LVM utilities have been enhanced to include options to support VDO volumes.

VDO Components

VDO utilizes the concepts of *pool* and *volume*. A pool is a logical volume that is created inside an LVM volume group using a deduplicated storage space. A VDO volume is just like a regular LVM logical volume, but it is provisioned in a pool. A VDO volume needs to be formatted with file system structures before it can be used.

To create, mount, and manage LVM VDO volumes, two software packages are installed on the system by default. These packages are *vdo* and *kmod-kvdo*. The former installs the tools necessary to support the creation and management of VDO volumes and the latter implements fine-grained storage virtualization, thin provisioning, and compression.

Exercise 13-12: Create an LVM VDO Volume

This exercise should be done on *server2* as *user1* with *sudo* where required.

In this exercise, you will initialize the 5GB disk (*sdf*) for use in LVM VDO. You will create a volume group called *vgvdo* and add the physical volume to it. You will list and display the volume group and the physical volume. You will create a VDO volume called *lvvdo* with a virtual size of 20GB.

1. Initialize the *sdf* disk using the *pvcreate* command:

    ```
    [user1@server2 ~]$ sudo pvcreate /dev/sdf
      Physical volume "/dev/sdf" successfully created.
    ```

2. Create *vgvdo* volume group using the *vgcreate* command:

    ```
    [user1@server2 ~]$ sudo vgcreate vgvdo /dev/sdf
      Volume group "vgvdo" successfully created
    ```

3. Display basic information about the volume group:

```
[user1@server2 ~]$ sudo vgdisplay vgvdo
--- Volume group ---
VG Name                vgvdo
System ID
Format                 lvm2
Metadata Areas         1
Metadata Sequence No   3
VG Access              read/write
VG Status              resizable
MAX LV                 0
Cur LV                 2
Open LV                0
Max PV                 0
Cur PV                 1
Act PV                 1
VG Size                <5.00 GiB
PE Size                4.00 MiB
Total PE               1279
Alloc PE / Size        1279 / <5.00 GiB
Free   PE / Size       0 / 0
VG UUID                zNljB6-QZG7-gVe4-hfL9-oMfL-IjyV-tdJ
```

The volume group contains a total of 1279 PEs.

4. Create a VDO volume called lvvdo using the lvcreate command. Use the -l option to specify the number of logical extents (1279) to be allocated and the -V option for the amount of virtual space.

```
[user1@server2 ~]$ sudo lvcreate --type vdo -l 1279 -n lvvdo -V 20G vgvdo
    The VDO volume can address 2 GB in 1 data slab.
    It can grow to address at most 16 TB of physical storage in 8192 slabs.
    If a larger maximum size might be needed, use bigger slabs.
    Logical volume "lvvdo" created.
```

5. Display detailed information about the volume group including the logical volume and the physical volume:

```
[user1@server2 ~]$ sudo vgdisplay -v vgvdo
........
--- Logical volume ---
LV Path                /dev/vgvdo/vpool0
LV Name                vpool0
VG Name                vgvdo
LV UUID                DOSQN6-f0of-rrIw-h7od-KNbl-AHhg
LV Write Access        read/write
LV Creation host, time server2.example.com, 2023-02-02
LV VDO Pool data       vpool0_vdata
LV VDO Pool usage      60.00%
LV VDO Pool saving     100.00%
LV VDO Operating mode  normal
LV VDO Index state     online
LV VDO Compression st  online
LV VDO Used size       <3.00 GiB
LV Status              NOT available
LV Size                <5.00 GiB
Current LE             1279
Segments               1
Allocation             inherit
Read ahead sectors     auto
```

```
--- Logical volume ---
LV Path                 /dev/vgvdo/lvvdo
LV Name                 lvvdo
VG Name                 vgvdo
LV UUID                 TqqrCm-bFFT-zqNE-DahU-BW07-IIle
LV Write Access         read/write
LV Creation host, time  server2.example.com, 2023-02-02
LV VDO Pool name        vpool0
LV Status               available
# open                  0
LV Size                 20.00 GiB
Current LE              5120
Segments                1
Allocation              inherit
Read ahead sectors      auto
- currently set to      256
Block device            253:4
```

The output reflects the creation of two logical volumes: a pool called */dev/vgvdo/vpool0* and a volume called */dev/vgvdo/lvvdo*.

Exercise 13-13: Remove a Volume Group and Uninitialize Physical Volume

This exercise should be done on *server2* as *user1* with *sudo* where required.

In this exercise, you will remove the *vgvdo* volume group along with the VDO volumes and uninitialize the physical volume */dev/sdf*. You will confirm the deletion.

1. Remove the volume group along with the VDO volumes using the *vgremove* command:

   ```
   [user1@server2 ~]$ sudo vgremove vgvdo -f
     Logical volume "lvvdo" successfully removed.
     Volume group "vgvdo" successfully removed
   ```

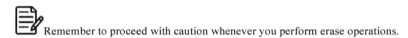 Remember to proceed with caution whenever you perform erase operations.

2. Execute *sudo vgs* and *sudo lvs* commands for confirmation.
3. Remove the LVM structures from *sdf* using the *pvremove* command:

   ```
   [user1@server2 ~]$ sudo pvremove /dev/sdf
     Labels on physical volume "/dev/sdf" successfully wiped.
   ```

4. Confirm the removal by running *sudo pvs*.

The disk is now back to its raw state and can be repurposed.

5. Verify that the *sdf* disk used in the previous exercises has returned to its original raw state using the *lsblk* command:

```
[user1@server2 ~]$ lsblk
NAME            MAJ:MIN RM   SIZE RO TYPE MOUNTPOINTS
sda                 8:0   0   20G  0 disk
├─sda1              8:1   0    1G  0 part /boot
└─sda2              8:2   0   19G  0 part
  ├─rhel-root   253:0   0   17G  0 lvm  /
  └─rhel-swap   253:1   0    2G  0 lvm  [SWAP]
sdb                8:16   0  250M  0 disk
sdc                8:32   0  250M  0 disk
sdd                8:48   0  250M  0 disk
sde                8:64   0  250M  0 disk
sdf                8:80   0    5G  0 disk
sr0               11:0    1  8.4G  0 rom
```

This brings the exercise to an end.

We will recreate logical volumes in Chapter 14 and construct file system and swap structures in them.

Chapter Summary

This chapter started with an overview of how and where disk partitioning information is stored. It presented a comparison between the two common schemes and explained which one to use and in which situation. A little later, we touched briefly on the common storage management solutions available in RHEL.

We examined the concept of thin provisioning and realized the benefits associated with this technology.

Next, we carved up available disk devices using both MBR and GPT partitioning schemes. We demonstrated the partition creation, display, and delete operations by running one command directly at the command prompt and launching the other in interactive mode.

Next, we explicated the Logical Volume Manager solution. We discovered how LVM works. We looked at various LVM objects and their relationship with one another. We explored LVM management commands and common options available with them. We performed a series of exercises to demonstrate the creation, expansion, renaming, reduction, and deletion of physical volumes, logical volumes, and volume groups.

Finally, we explored the VDO solution and how it exploits the underlying thin provisioning, de-duplication, and compression technologies to save cost, ensure efficient use of storage space, and improve data throughput. We performed a couple of exercises in the end to demonstrate the creation and deletion of VDO logical volumes under LVM.

Review Questions

1. Where is the partition table information stored on BIOS-based systems?
2. What is the name of the technology that VDO employs to remove randomization of data blocks?
3. What would *sdd3* represent?
4. Provide the command to add physical volumes */dev/sdd1* and */dev/sdc* to *vg20* volume group.
5. What are the two commands that you can use to add logical extents to a logical volume?

6. Provide the command to create a volume group called *vg20* on */dev/sdd* disk with physical extent size 64MB.
7. Thin provisioning technology allows us to create logical volumes of sizes larger than the actual physical storage size. True or False?
8. What is the maximum supported number of usable partitions on a GPT disk?
9. Which kernel module is responsible for data block compression in VDO volumes?
10. What are the three techniques VDO volumes employ for storage conservation?
11. What would the command *parted /dev/sdc mkpart pri 1 200m* do?
12. What is the maximum number of usable partitions that can be created on an MBR disk?
13. The *gdisk* utility can be used to store partition information in MBR format. True or False?
14. What would the command *parted /dev/sdd mklabel msdos* do?
15. Which file in the */proc* file system stores the in-memory partitioning information?
16. De-duplication is the process of zero-block elimination. True or False?
17. The *parted* utility may be used to create LVM logical volumes. True or False?
18. What are the two commands that you can use to reduce the number of logical extents from a logical volume?
19. A single disk can be used by both parted and LVM solutions at the same time. True or False?
20. Provide the command to erase */dev/sdd1* physical volume from *vg20* volume group.
21. Provide the command to remove *vg20* along with logical and physical volumes it contains.
22. What is the default size of a physical extent in LVM?
23. What is the default name for the first logical volume in a volume group?
24. What is one difference between the *pvs* and *pvdisplay* commands?
25. When can a disk or partition be referred to as a physical volume?
26. Provide the command to remove *webvol* logical volume from *vg20* volume group.
27. It is necessary to create file system structures in a logical volume before it can be used to store files in it. True or False?
28. Physical and logical extents are typically of the same size. True or False?
29. What is the purpose of the *pvremove* command?
30. What would the command *pvcreate /dev/sdd* do?
31. A disk or partition can be added to a volume group without being initialized. True or False?
32. Provide the command to create a logical volume called *webvol* of size equal to 100 logical extents in *vg20* volume group.
33. A volume group can be created without any physical volume in it. True or False?
34. A partition can be used as an LVM object. True or False?
35. Which command would you use to view the details of a volume group and its objects?

Answers to Review Questions

1. The partition table information is stored on the Master Boot Record.
2. VDO employs thin provisioning technology to remove data block randomization.
3. *sdd3* represents the third partition on the fourth disk.
4. *vgextend vg20 /dev/sdd1 /dev/sdc*
5. The *lvextend* and *lvresize* commands.
6. *vgcreate -s 64 vg20 /dev/sdd*
7. True.
8. 128.
9. The *kvdo* module is responsible for compressing data blocks in VDO volumes.
10. VDO volumes use thin provisioning, de-duplication, and compression techniques for storage conservation.

11. The command provided will create a primary partition of size 200MB on the *sdc* disk starting at the beginning of the disk.
12. 14.
13. False. The *gdisk* tool is only for GPT type tables.
14. The command provided will apply msdos label to the *sdd* disk.
15. The *partitions* file.
16. False. De-duplication is the process of removing blocks of identical data.
17. False.
18. The *lvreduce* and *lvresize* commands.
19. True. A single disk can be shared between parted-created partitions and LVM.
20. *vgreduce vg20 /dev/sdd1*
21. *vgremove -f vg20*
22. The default PE size is 4MB.
23. *lvol0* is the default name for the first logical volume created in a volume group.
24. The *pvs* command lists basic information about physical volumes whereas the *pvdisplay* command shows the details.
25. After the *pvcreate* command has been executed on it successfully.
26. *lvremove /dev/vg20/webvol*
27. True.
28. True.
29. The *pvremove* command is used to remove LVM information from a physical volume.
30. The command provided will prepare the */dev/sdd* disk for use in a volume group.
31. False. A disk or partition must be initialized before it can be added to a volume group.
32. *lvcreate -l 100 -n webvol vg20*
33. False.
34. True.
35. The *vgdisplay* command with the -v option.

Do-It-Yourself Challenge Labs

The following labs are useful to strengthen most of the concepts and topics learned in this chapter. It is expected that you perform the labs without external help. A step-by-step guide is not supplied, as the knowledge and skill required to implement the labs have already been disseminated in the chapter; however, hints to the relevant major topic(s) are included.

Use the lab environment built specifically for end-of-chapter labs. See sub-section "Lab Environment for End-of-Chapter Labs" in Chapter 01 "Local Installation" for details.

Add more storage to *server4* if required.

Lab 13-1: Create and Remove Partitions with parted

As *user1* with *sudo* on *server4*, create a 100MB primary partition on one of the available 250MB disks (*lsblk*) by invoking the *parted* utility directly at the command prompt. Apply label "msdos" if the disk is new. Create another 100MB partition by running *parted* interactively while ensuring that the second partition won't overlap the first. Verify the label and the partitions. Remove both partitions at the command prompt. (Hint: MBR Storage Management with parted).

Lab 13-2: Create and Remove Partitions with gdisk

As *user1* with *sudo* on *server4*, create two 80MB partitions on one of the 250MB disks (*lsblk*) using the *gdisk* utility. Make sure the partitions won't overlap. Verify the partitions. You may delete the partitions if you want. (Hint: GPT Storage Management with gdisk).

Lab 13-3: Create Volume Group and Logical Volumes

As *user1* with *sudo* on *server4*, initialize 1x250MB disk for use in LVM (use *lsblk* to identify available disks). Create volume group *vg100* with PE size 16MB and add the physical volume. Create two logical volumes *lvol0* and *swapvol* of sizes 90MB and 120MB. Use the *vgs*, *pvs*, *lvs*, and *vgdisplay* commands for verification. (Hint: Logical Volume Manager).

Lab 13-4: Expand Volume Group and Logical Volume

As *user1* with *sudo* on *server4*, create a partition on an available 250MB disk and initialize it for use in LVM (use *lsblk* to identify available disks). Add the new physical volume to *vg100*. Expand the *lvol0* logical volume to size 300MB. Use the *vgs*, *pvs*, *lvs*, and *vgdisplay* commands for verification. (Hint: Logical Volume Manager).

Lab 13-5: Add a VDO Logical Volume

As *user1* with *sudo* on *server4*, initialize the *sdf* disk for use in LVM and add it to *vg100*. Create a VDO logical volume named *vdovol* using the entire disk capacity. Use the *vgs*, *pvs*, *lvs*, and *vgdisplay* commands for verification. (Hint: Logical Volume Manager).

Lab 13-6: Reduce and Remove Logical Volumes

As *user1* with *sudo* on *server4*, reduce the size of *lvol0* logical volume to 80MB. Then erase all three logical volumes *swapvol*, *lvol0*, and *vdovol*. Confirm the deletion with *vgs*, *pvs*, *lvs*, and *vgdisplay* commands. (Hint: Logical Volume Manager).

Lab 13-7: Remove Volume Group and Physical Volumes

As *user1* with *sudo* on *server4*, remove the volume group and uninitialized the physical volumes. Confirm the deletion with *vgs*, *pvs*, *lvs*, and *vgdisplay* commands. Use the *lsblk* command and verify that the disks used for the LVM labs no longer show LVM information. (Hint: Logical Volume Manager).

## Chapter 14

Local File Systems and Swap

This chapter describes the following major topics:

➤ Understand file systems and their benefits, categories, and types
➤ Review file system types: Ext3/Ext4, XFS, VFAT, and ISO9660
➤ Know file system administration commandset
➤ Mount and unmount file systems manually and persistently
➤ Determine and use UUID
➤ Apply and use file system label
➤ Monitor file system and directory usage
➤ Create and mount different types of local file systems in partitions
➤ Create, mount, and resize Ext4 and XFS file systems in LVM
➤ Understand, create, and activate swap in partitions and LVM

RHCSA Objectives:

30. Configure systems to mount file systems at boot by Universally Unique ID (UUID) or label
31. Add new partitions and logical volumes, and swap to a system non-destructively (the first part of this objective is covered in more detail in Chapter 13)
32. Create, mount, unmount, and use vfat, ext4, and xfs file systems
35. Extend existing logical volumes (more details in Chapter 13 also)

File systems are the most common structures created in partitions and volumes regardless of the underlying storage management solution employed. They are logical containers employed for file storage and can be optimized, resized, mounted, and unmounted independently. They must be connected to the directory hierarchy in order to be accessed by users and applications. This may be accomplished automatically at system boot or manually as required. File systems can be mounted or unmounted using their unique identifiers, labels, or device files. There is a whole slew of commands available for file system creation and administration; some of them are file system type specific while others are general.

The other common structure created in partitions and logical volumes is the swap space. Swapping provides a mechanism to move out and in pages of idle data between physical memory and swap. Swap areas act as extensions to the physical memory, and they may be activated or deactivated independent of swap spaces located in other partitions and volumes.

This chapter elaborates on file systems and swap, and demonstrates their creation and management in several exercises. It also highlights the tools to monitor their usage.

File Systems and File System Types

A *file system* is a logical container that stores files and directories. Each file system is created in a discrete partition, VDO volume, or logical volume. A typical production RHEL system usually has numerous file systems. During OS installation, only two file systems—/ and */boot*—are created in the default disk layout, but you can design a custom disk layout and construct separate containers to store dissimilar information. Typical additional file systems that may be created during an installation are */home*, */opt*, */tmp*, */usr*, and */var*. The two mandatory file systems—/ and */boot*—are required for installation and booting.

Storing disparate data in distinct file systems versus storing all data in a single file system offers the following advantages:

✓ Make any file system accessible (mount) or inaccessible (unmount) to users independent of other file systems. This hides or reveals information contained in that file system.
✓ Perform file system repair activities on individual file systems
✓ Keep dissimilar data in separate file systems
✓ Optimize or tune each file system independently
✓ Grow or shrink a file system independent of other file systems

RHEL supports several types of file system that may be categorized in three basic groups: *disk-based*, *network-based*, and *memory-based*. Disk-based file systems are typically created on physical drives using SATA, USB, Fibre Channel, and other technologies. Network-based file systems are essentially disk-based file systems shared over the network for remote access. Memory-based file systems are virtual; they are created at system startup and destroyed when the system goes down. Disk-based and network-based file systems store information persistently, while any data saved in virtual file systems does not survive across system reboots.

Table 14-1 lists and explains various common disk- and network-based supported file system types.

File System Type	Category	Description
Ext3	Disk	The third generation of the extended file system. It supports metadata journaling for faster recovery, offers superior reliability, allows the creation of up to 32,000 subdirectories, and supports larger file systems and bigger files than its predecessor.
Ext4	Disk	The fourth generation of the extended file system developed as the successor to Ext3. It supports all features of Ext3 in addition to a larger file system size, bigger file size, an unlimited number of subdirectories, metadata and quota journaling, and extended user attributes.
XFS	Disk	XFS is a highly scalable and high-performing 64-bit file system. It supports metadata journaling for faster crash recovery, and online defragmentation, expansion, quota journaling, and extended user attributes. XFS is the default file system type in RHEL 9.
VFAT	Disk	This file system is used for post-Windows 95 file system formats on hard disks, USB drives, and floppy disks.
ISO9660	Disk	This is used for optical file systems such as CD and DVD.
NFS	Network	Network File System. A shared directory or file system for remote access by other Linux systems.
AutoFS	Network	Auto File System. An NFS file system set to mount and unmount automatically on remote client systems.

Table 14-1 File System Types

This chapter covers Ext3, Ext4, XFS, and VFAT file systems at length. It also touches upon mounting and unmounting ISO9660. For a brief discussion on memory-based file systems, see Chapter 02 "Initial Interaction with the System". NFS and AutoFS are discussed in Chapter 16 "Network File System".

Extended File Systems

Extended file systems have been part of RHEL for many years. The first generation is obsolete and is no longer supported. The second, third, and fourth generations are currently available and supported. The fourth generation is the latest in the series and is superior in features and enhancements to its predecessors.

The structure of an extended file system is built on a partition or logical volume at the time of file system creation. This structure is divided into two sets. The first set holds the file system's metadata and it is very tiny. The second set stores the actual data, and it occupies almost the entire partition or the logical volume (VDO and LVM) space.

The metadata includes the *superblock*, which keeps vital file system structural information, such as the type, size, and status of the file system, and the number of data blocks it contains. Since the superblock holds such critical information, it is automatically replicated and maintained at various known locations throughout the file system. The superblock at the beginning of the file system is referred to as the *primary superblock*, and all of its copies as *backup superblocks*. If the primary superblock is corrupted or lost, it renders the file system inaccessible. One of the backup superblocks is then used to supplant the corrupted or lost primary superblock to bring the file system back to its normal state.

The metadata also contains the *inode table*, which maintains a list of *index node* (*inode*) numbers. Each file is assigned an inode number at the time of its creation, and the inode number holds the file's attributes such as its type, permissions, ownership, owning group, size, and last access/modification time. The inode also holds and keeps track of the pointers to the actual data blocks where the file contents are located.

The Ext3 and Ext4 file systems support a journaling mechanism that provides them with the ability to recover swiftly after a system crash. Both Ext3 and Ext4 file systems keep track of recent changes in their metadata in a *journal* (or log). Each metadata update is written in its entirety to the journal after completion. The system peruses the journal of each extended file system following the reboot after a crash to determine if there are any errors, and it recovers the file system rapidly using the latest metadata information stored in its journal.

In contrast to Ext3 that supports file systems up to 16TiB and files up to 2TiB, Ext4 supports very large file systems up to 1EiB (ExbiByte) and files up to 16TiB (TebiByte). Additionally, Ext4 uses a series of contiguous physical blocks on the hard disk called *extents*, resulting in improved read and write performance with reduced fragmentation. Ext4 supports extended user attributes, metadata and quota journaling, and so on.

XFS File System

The *X File System* (XFS) is a high-performing 64-bit extent-based journaling file system type. XFS allows the creation of file systems and files up to 8EiB (ExbiByte). It does not run file system checks at system boot; rather, it relies on you to use the *xfs_repair* utility to manually fix any issues. XFS sets the extended user attributes and certain mount options by default on new file systems. It enables defragmentation on mounted and active file systems to keep as much data in contiguous blocks as possible for faster access. The only major caveat with using XFS is its inability to shrink.

Like Ext3 and Ext4, XFS also uses journaling for metadata operations, guaranteeing the consistency of the file system against abnormal or forced unmounting. The journal information is read and any pending metadata transactions are replayed when the XFS file system is remounted.

XFS uses sophisticated techniques in its architecture for speedy input/output performance. It can be snapshot in a mounted, active state. The snapshot can then be used for backup or other purposes.

VFAT File System

VFAT (*Virtual File Allocation Table*) is an extension to the legacy *FAT* file system type, also called *FAT16*, that was introduced in early versions of MS-DOS. The support for FAT16 was later added to Microsoft Windows, MacOS, and some UNIX versions, enabling them to read and write files

---

written in that format. FAT16 had limitations; it was designed to use no more than 8.3 characters in filenames, limiting filenames to a maximum of eight characters plus three characters as an extension. Moreover, it only allowed filenames to begin with a letter or number and to not contain spaces. FAT16 treated lowercase and uppercase letters alike.

VFAT was introduced with Microsoft Windows 95 and it has since been available. It supports 255 characters in filenames including spaces and periods; however, it still does not differentiate between lowercase and uppercase letters. VFAT support was added to Linux several years ago. A VFAT file system may be created on hard drives, but it is primarily used on removable media, such as floppy and USB flash drives, for exchanging data between Linux and Windows.

ISO9660 File System

This file system type conforms to the ISO 9660 standard, hence the name. It is used for removable optical disc media such as CD/DVD drives for transporting software and patches, and operating system images in ISO format between computers. The ISO9660 format originated from the *High-Sierra File System* (HSFS) format, and it has now been enhanced to include innovative features.

File System Management

Managing file systems involves such operations as creating, mounting, labeling, viewing, growing, shrinking, unmounting, and removing them. These management tasks are common to both Extended and XFS types. Most of these functions are also applicable to VFAT and a few to optical file systems.

In Chapter 13, you created several partitions and logical volumes. However, you did not initialize them with a file system type, and therefore you could not mount or use them. Later, you destroyed all the partitions and the volumes that were created. You also deleted the LVM volume group. All the disks were returned to their unused state after the completion of the exercises.

Here is a listing of the block devices to confirm the current state of the disks:

```
[user1@server2 ~]$ lsblk
NAME              MAJ:MIN RM   SIZE RO TYPE MOUNTPOINTS
sda               8:0     0    20G  0 disk
├─sda1            8:1     0     1G  0 part /boot
└─sda2            8:2     0    19G  0 part
  ├─rhel-root 253:0     0    17G  0 lvm  /
  └─rhel-swap 253:1     0     2G  0 lvm  [SWAP]
sdb               8:16    0   250M  0 disk
sdc               8:32    0   250M  0 disk
sdd               8:48    0   250M  0 disk
sde               8:64    0   250M  0 disk
sdf               8:80    0     5G  0 disk
sr0               11:0    1   8.4G  0 rom
```

The output verifies the unused state and availability status for all the disks—*sdb* through *sdf*. You should be able to reuse them in the exercises in this chapter.

File System Administration Commands

In order to create and manage file systems, RHEL offers a number of commands of which some are limited to their operations on the Extended, XFS, or VFAT file system type, while others are

---

general and applicable to all file system types. Table 14-2 describes common file system administration commands.

Command	Description
Extended File System	
e2label	Modifies the label of a file system
tune2fs	Tunes or displays file system attributes
XFS	
xfs_admin	Tunes file system attributes
xfs_growfs	Extends the size of a file system
xfs_info	Exhibits information about a file system
VFAT	
General File System Commands	
blkid	Displays block device attributes including their UUIDs and labels
df	Reports file system utilization
du	Calculates disk usage of directories and file systems
fsadm	Resizes a file system. This command is automatically invoked when the lvresize command is run with the -r switch.
lsblk	Lists block devices and file systems and their attributes including their UUIDs and labels
mkfs	Creates a file system. Use the -t option and specify ext3, ext4, vfat, or xfs file system type.
mount	Mounts a file system for user access. Displays currently mounted file systems.
umount	Unmounts a file system

Table 14-2 File System Management Commands

Most of these commands are used in this chapter.

Mounting and Unmounting File Systems

In order to enable users to access files and application programs in a file system, the file system must be connected to the directory structure at a desired attachment point, which is referred to as the *mount point*. A mount point in essence is any empty directory that is created and used for this purpose.

There are many file systems already mounted on your system, such as the root file system mounted on / and the boot file system mounted on /boot. Both of them are empty directories and are reserved to connect the two file systems to the directory hierarchy. You can use the *mount* command to view information about mounted file systems. The following shows the XFS file systems only:

```
[user1@server2 ~]$ mount -t xfs
/dev/mapper/rhel-root on / type xfs (rw,relatime,seclabel,attr2,inode64,logb
ufs=8,logbsize=32k,noquota)
/dev/sda1 on /boot type xfs (rw,relatime,seclabel,attr2,inode64,logbufs=8,lo
gbsize=32k,noquota)
```

The "-t xfs" option makes the command to only show the file systems initialized with the XFS type.

The *mount* command is also used for mounting a file system to a mount point, and this action is performed with the *root* user privileges. The command requires the absolute pathnames of the file system block device and the mount point name. It also accepts the UUID or label of the file system in lieu of the block device name. Options are available with this command to mount all or a specific type of file system. The *mount* command is also used to mount other types of file systems such as those located in removable media. Upon successful mount, the kernel places an entry for the file system in the */proc/self/mounts* file.

A mount point should be empty when an attempt is made to mount a file system on it, otherwise the content of the mount point will hide. As well, the mount point must not be in use or the mount attempt will fail.

The *mount* command supports numerous options that may be used as required to override its default behavior. We can also specify multiple comma-separated options. Table 14-3 describes some common options.

Option	Description
auto (noauto)	Mounts (does not mount) the file system when the -a option is specified
defaults	Mounts a file system with all the default values (async, auto, rw, etc.)
_netdev	Used for a file system that requires network connectivity in place before it can be mounted. NFS is an example.
remount	Remounts an already mounted file system to enable or disable an option
ro (rw)	Mounts a file system read-only (read/write)

Table 14-3 Common mount Command Options

The opposite of the *mount* command is *umount*, which is used to detach a file system from the directory hierarchy and make it inaccessible to users and applications. This command expects the absolute pathname to the block device containing the file system or its mount point name in order to detach it. Options are available with *umount* to unmount all or a specific type of file system. The kernel removes the corresponding file system entry from the */proc/self/mounts* file after it has been successfully disconnected.

Determining the UUID of a File System

Every Extended and XFS file system has a 128-bit (32 hexadecimal characters) UUID (*Universally Unique IDentifier*) assigned to it at the time of its creation. In contrast, UUIDs assigned to vfat file systems are 32-bit (8 hexadecimal characters) in length. Assigning a UUID makes the file system unique among many other file systems that potentially exist on the system. The primary benefit of using a UUID is the fact that it always stays persistent across system reboots. UUIDs are used by default in RHEL 9 in the */etc/fstab* file for any file system that is created by the system in a standard partition.

RHEL attempts to mount all file systems listed in the */etc/fstab* file at reboots. Each file system has an associated device file and UUID, but may or may not have a corresponding label. The system checks for the presence of each file system's device file, UUID, or label, and then attempts to mount it.

The *boot* file system, for instance, is located in a partition and the device file associated with it is on *server2* is */dev/sda1*. You can use the *xfs_admin* command, the *blkid* command, or the *lsblk* command as follows to determine its UUID:

```
[user1@server2 ~]$ sudo xfs_admin -u /dev/sda1
UUID = 22d05484-6ae1-4ef8-a37d-abab674a5e35
[user1@server2 ~]$
[user1@server2 ~]$ sudo blkid /dev/sda1
/dev/sda1: UUID="22d05484-6ae1-4ef8-a37d-abab674a5e35" TYPE="xfs"
[user1@server2 ~]$
[user1@server2 ~]$ sudo lsblk -f /dev/sda1
NAME FSTYPE FSVER LABEL UUID                                    FSAV:
sda1 xfs                 22d05484-6ae1-4ef8-a37d-abab674a5e35    7:
```

The UUID reported by the above commands for the */boot* file system is "22d05484-6ae1-4ef8-a37d-abab674a5e35". If you *grep* for the string "boot" on the */etc/fstab* file, you will see that the system uses this UUID to mount */boot*. A discussion on the */etc/fstab* file is provided later in this chapter.

📝 For extended file systems, you can use the *tune2fs* command in addition to the *blkid* and *lsblk* commands to determine the UUID.

A UUID is also assigned to a file system that is created in a VDO or LVM volume; however, it need not be used in the *fstab* file, as the device files associated with the logical volumes are always unique and persistent.

Labeling a File System

A unique label may be used instead of a UUID to keep the file system association with its device file exclusive and persistent across system reboots. A label is limited to a maximum of 12 characters on the XFS file system and 16 characters on the Extended file system. By default, no labels are assigned to a file system at the time of its creation.

The */boot* file system is located in the */dev/sda1* partition and its type is XFS. You can use the *xfs_admin* or the *lsblk* command as follows to determine its label:

```
[user1@server2 ~]$ sudo xfs_admin -l /dev/sda1
label = ""
[user1@server2 ~]$ sudo lsblk -f /dev/sda1
NAME FSTYPE FSVER LABEL UUID                                    FSAVAIL FSUSE% MOUNT:
sda1 xfs                 22d05484-6ae1-4ef8-a37d-abab674a5e35    730M    28%   /boot
```

The output discloses that there is currently no label assigned to the */boot* file system.

A label is not needed on a file system if you intend to use its UUID or if it is created in a logical volume; however, you can still apply one using the *xfs_admin* command with the -L option. Labeling an XFS file system requires that the target file system be unmounted.

The following example demonstrates the steps to unmount */boot*, set the label "bootfs" on its device file, and remount it:

```
[user1@server2 ~]$ sudo umount /boot
[user1@server2 ~]$ sudo xfs_admin -L bootfs /dev/sda1
writing all SBs
new label = "bootfs"
[user1@server2 ~]$ sudo mount /boot
```

You can confirm the new label by executing **sudo xfs_admin -l /dev/sda1** or **sudo lsblk -f /dev/sda1**.

For extended file systems, you can use the *e2label* command to apply a label and the *tune2fs*, *blkid*, and *lsblk* commands to view and verify.

Now you can replace the UUID="22d05484-6ae1-4ef8-a37d-abab674a5e35" for */boot* in the *fstab* file with LABEL=bootfs, and unmount and remount */boot* as demonstrated above for confirmation.

A label may also be applied to a file system created in a logical volume; however, it is not recommended for use in the *fstab* file, as the device files for logical volumes are always unique and remain persistent across system reboots.

Automatically Mounting a File System at Reboots

File systems defined in the */etc/fstab* file are mounted automatically at reboots. This file must contain proper and complete information for each listed file system. An incomplete or inaccurate entry might leave the system in an undesirable or unbootable state. Another benefit of adding entries to this file is that you only need to specify one of the four attributes—block device name, UUID, label, or mount point—of the file system that you wish to mount manually with the *mount* command. The *mount* command obtains the rest of the information from this file. Similarly, you only need to specify one of these attributes with the *umount* command to detach it from the directory hierarchy.

The default *fstab* file contains entries for file systems that are created at the time of installation. On *server2*, for instance, this file currently has the following three entries:

```
/dev/mapper/rhel-root    /                                    xfs   defaults  0 0
UUID=22d05484-6ae1-4ef8-a37d-abab674a5e35 /boot xfs   defaults  0 0
/dev/mapper/rhel-swap    none                      swap defaults  0 0
```

EXAM TIP: Any missing or invalid entry in this file may render the system unbootable. You will have to boot the system in emergency mode to fix this file. Ensure that you understand each field in the file for both file system and swap entries.

The format of this file is such that each row is broken out into six columns to identify the required attributes for each file system to be successfully mounted. Here is what the columns contain:

Column 1: Defines the physical or virtual device path where the file system is resident, or its associated UUID or label. There can be entries for network file systems here as well.
Column 2: Identifies the mount point for the file system. For swap partitions, use either "none" or "swap".

Column 3: Specifies the type of file system such as Ext3, Ext4, XFS, VFAT, or ISO9660. For swap, the type "swap" is used. You may use "auto" instead to leave it up to the *mount* command to determine the type of the file system.

Column 4: Identifies one or more comma-separated options to be used when mounting the file system. See Table 15-3 for a description of some of the options, consult the manual pages of the *mount* command or the *fstab* file for additional options and details.

Column 5: Is used by the *dump* utility to ascertain the file systems that need to be dumped. A value of 0 (or the absence of this column) disables this check. This field is applicable only on Extended file systems; XFS does not use it.

Column 6: Expresses the sequence number in which to run the *e2fsck* (file system check and repair utility for Extended file system types) utility on the file system at system boot. By default, 0 is used for memory-based, remote, and removable file systems, 1 for /, and 2 for */boot* and other physical file systems. 0 can also be used for /, */boot*, and other physical file systems you don't want to be checked or repaired. This field is applicable only on Extended file systems; XFS does not use it.

A 0 in columns 5 and 6 for XFS, virtual, remote, and removable file system types has no meaning. You do not need to add them for these file system types.

This file is edited manually, so care must be observed to circumvent syntax and typing errors.

Monitoring File System Usage

On a live system, you'll often need to check file system usage to know if a mounted file system requires an expansion for growth or a clean up to generate free space. This involves examining the used and available spaces for a file system. The *df* (*disk free*) command has been used for this purpose. It reports usage details for mounted file systems. By default, this command reports the numbers in KBs unless the -m or -h option is specified to view the sizes in MBs or human-readable format.

Let's run this command with the -h option on *server2*:

```
[user1@server2 ~]$ df -h
Filesystem              Size  Used Avail Use% Mounted on
devtmpfs                4.0M     0  4.0M   0% /dev
tmpfs                   886M     0  886M   0% /dev/shm
tmpfs                   355M  6.2M  348M   2% /run
/dev/mapper/rhel-root    17G  4.0G   14G  24% /
tmpfs                   178M   96K  177M   1% /run/user/987
tmpfs                   178M   36K  178M   1% /run/user/1000
/dev/sda1              1014M  285M  730M  29% /boot
```

The output shows the file system device file or type in column 1, followed by the total, used, and available spaces in columns 2, 3, and 4, and the usage percentage and mount point in the last two columns.

There are a few other useful flags available with the *df* command that can produce modified output. These flags include:

-T to add the file system type to the output (example: **df -hT**)

-x to exclude the specified file system type from the output (example: **df -hx tmpfs**)

-t to limit the output to a specific file system type (example: **df -t xfs**)

-i to show inode information (example: **df -hi**)

You may use -h with any of these examples to print information in human-readable format.

Calculating Disk Usage

In contrast to the *df* command that returns usage information for an entire file system, the *du* command reports the amount of space a file or directory occupies. By default, it shows the output in KBs; however, you can use the -m or -h option to view the output in MBs or human-readable format. In addition, you can view a usage summary with the -s switch and a grand total with -c.

Let's run this command on the */usr/bin* directory to view the usage summary:

```
[user1@server2 ~]$ du -sh /usr/bin
197M    /usr/bin
```

To add a "total" row to the output and with numbers displayed in KBs:

```
[user1@server2 ~]$ du -sc /usr/bin
201240  /usr/bin
201240  total
```

Try this command with different options on the */usr/sbin/lvm* file and observe the results.

Exercise 14-1: Create and Mount Ext4, VFAT, and XFS File Systems in Partitions

This exercise should be done on *server2* as *user1* with *sudo* where required.

In this exercise, you will create 2 x 100MB partitions on the */dev/sdb* disk, initialize them separately with the Ext4 and VFAT file system types, define them for persistence using their UUIDs, create mount points called */ext4fs1* and */vfatfs1*, attach them to the directory structure, and verify their availability and usage. Moreover, you will use the disk */dev/sdc* and repeat the above procedure to establish an XFS file system in it and mount it on */xfsfs1*.

1. Apply the label "msdos" to the *sdb* disk using the *parted* command:

    ```
    [user1@server2 ~]$ sudo parted /dev/sdb mklabel msdos
    Warning: The existing disk label on /dev/sdb will be destroyed and
    all data on this disk will be lost. Do you want to continue?

    Yes/No? Yes
    ```

2. Create 2 x 100MB primary partitions on *sdb* with the *parted* command:

    ```
    [user1@server2 ~]$ sudo parted /dev/sdb mkpart primary 1 101m
    [user1@server2 ~]$ sudo parted /dev/sdb mkpart primary 102 201m
    ```

3. Initialize the first partition (*sdb1*) with Ext4 file system type using the *mkfs* command:

```
[user1@server2 ~]$ sudo mkfs -t ext4 /dev/sdb1
mke2fs 1.46.5 (30-Dec-2021)
Creating filesystem with 97280 1k blocks and 24288 inodes
Filesystem UUID: e169c0c6-d1ef-4704-8b2f-c7431eea6f68
Superblock backups stored on blocks:
        8193, 24577, 40961, 57345, 73729

Allocating group tables: done
Writing inode tables: done
Creating journal (4096 blocks): done
Writing superblocks and filesystem accounting information: done
```

4. Initialize the second partition (*sdb2*) with VFAT file system type using the *mkfs* command:

```
[user1@server2 ~]$ sudo mkfs -t vfat /dev/sdb2
mkfs.fat 4.2 (2021-01-31)
```

5. Initialize the whole disk (*sdc*) with the XFS file system type using the *mkfs.xfs* command. Add the -f flag to force the removal of any old partitioning or labeling information from the disk.

```
[user1@server2 ~]$ sudo mkfs.xfs /dev/sdc -f
meta-data=/dev/sdc              isize=512    agcount=4, agsize=16000 blks
         =                      sectsz=512   attr=2, projid32bit=1
         =                      crc=1        finobt=1, sparse=1, rmapbt=0
         =                      reflink=1    bigtime=1 inobtcount=1
data     =                      bsize=4096   blocks=64000, imaxpct=25
         =                      sunit=0      swidth=0 blks
naming   =version 2             bsize=4096   ascii-ci=0, ftype=1
log      =internal log          bsize=4096   blocks=1368, version=2
         =                      sectsz=512   sunit=0 blks, lazy-count=1
realtime =none                  extsz=4096   blocks=0, rtextents=0
```

6. Determine the UUIDs for all three file systems using the *lsblk* command:

```
[user1@server2 ~]$ sudo lsblk -f /dev/sdb /dev/sdc
NAME    FSTYPE FSVER LABEL UUID
sdb
├─sdb1 ext4   1.0          e169c0c6-d1ef-4704-8b2f-c7431eea6f68
└─sdb2 vfat         FAT16   7EAA-4B6E
sdc    xfs                  26ba7989-32f0-494c-a2db-fe0dff8d4ea8
```

7. Open the */etc/fstab* file, go to the end of the file, and append entries for the file systems for persistence using their UUIDs:

```
UUID=e169c0c6-d1ef-4704-8b2f-c7431eea6f68 /ext4fs1 ext4 defaults 0 0
UUID=7EAA-4B6E                            /vfatfs1 vfat defaults 0 0
UUID=26ba7989-32f0-494c-a2db-fe0dff8d4ea8 /xfsfs1  xfs  defaults 0 0
```

8. Create mount points */ext4fs1*, */vfatfs1*, and */xfsfs1* for the three file systems using the *mkdir* command:

```
[user1@server2 ~]$ sudo mkdir /ext4fs1 /vfatfs1 /xfsfs1
```

9. Mount the new file systems using the *mount* command. This command will fail if there are any invalid or missing information in the file.

```
[user1@server2 ~]$ sudo mount -a
```

10. View the mount and availability status as well as the types of all three file systems using the *df* command:

```
[user1@server2 ~]$ df -hT
........
/dev/sdb1            ext4      84M   14K   77M   1% /ext4fs1
/dev/sdb2            vfat      95M    0    95M   0% /vfatfs1
/dev/sdc             xfs      245M   15M  231M   6% /xfsfs1
```

The output verifies the creation and availability status of the three file systems. They are added to the *fstab* file for persistence. A system reboot at this point will remount them automatically. These file systems may now be used to store files.

Exercise 14-2: Create and Mount Ext4 and XFS File Systems in LVM Logical Volumes

This exercise should be done on *server2* as *user1* with *sudo* where required.

In this exercise, you will create a volume group called *vgfs* comprised of a 172MB physical volume created in a partition on the */dev/sdd* disk. The PE size for the volume group should be set at 16MB. You will create two logical volumes called *ext4vol* and *xfsvol* of sizes 80MB each and initialize them with the Ext4 and XFS file system types. You will ensure that both file systems are persistently defined using their logical volume device filenames. You will create mount points called */ext4fs2* and */xfsfs2*, mount the file systems, and verify their availability and usage.

1. Create a 172MB partition on the *sdd* disk using the *parted* command:

```
[user1@server2 ~]$ sudo parted /dev/sdd mkpart pri 1 172
```

2. Initialize the *sdd1* partition for use in LVM using the *pvcreate* command:

```
[user1@server2 ~]$ sudo pvcreate /dev/sdd1
  Physical volume "/dev/sdd1" successfully created.
```

3. Create the volume group *vgfs* with a PE size of 16MB using the physical volume *sdd1*:

```
[user1@server2 ~]$ sudo vgcreate -s 16 vgfs /dev/sdd1
  Volume group "vgfs" successfully created
```

The PE size is not easy to alter after a volume group creation, so ensure it is defined as required at creation.

4. Create two logical volumes *ext4vol* and *xfsvol* of size 80MB each in *vgfs* using the *lvcreate* command:

```
[user1@server2 ~]$ sudo lvcreate -n ext4vol -L 80 vgfs
  Logical volume "ext4vol" created.
[user1@server2 ~]$ sudo lvcreate -n xfsvol -L 80 vgfs
  Logical volume "xfsvol" created.
```

5. Format the *ext4vol* logical volume with the Ext4 file system type using the *mkfs.ext4* command:

```
[user1@server2 ~]$ sudo mkfs.ext4 /dev/vgfs/ext4vol
mke2fs 1.46.5 (30-Dec-2021)
Creating filesystem with 81920 1k blocks and 20480 inodes
Filesystem UUID: d5b13978-909a-43dc-9284-d488764df754
Superblock backups stored on blocks:
        8193, 24577, 40961, 57345, 73729

Allocating group tables: done
Writing inode tables: done
Creating journal (4096 blocks): done
Writing superblocks and filesystem accounting information: done
```

You may alternatively use **sudo mkfs -t ext4 /dev/vgfs/ext4vol**.

6. Format the *xfsvol* logical volume with the XFS file system type using the *mkfs.xfs* command:

```
[user1@server2 ~]$ sudo mkfs.xfs /dev/vgfs/xfsvol
meta-data=/dev/vgfs/xfsvol        isize=512    agcount=4, agsize=5120 blks
         =                        sectsz=512   attr=2, projid32bit=1
         =                        crc=1        finobt=1, sparse=1, rmapbt=0
         =                        reflink=1
data     =                        bsize=4096   blocks=20480, imaxpct=25
         =                        sunit=0      swidth=0 blks
naming   =version 2               bsize=4096   ascii-ci=0, ftype=1
log      =internal log            bsize=4096   blocks=1368, version=2
         =                        sectsz=512   sunit=0 blks, lazy-count=1
realtime =none                    extsz=4096   blocks=0, rtextents=0
```

You may use **sudo mkfs -t xfs /dev/vgfs/xfsvol** instead.

7. Open the */etc/fstab* file, go to the end of the file, and append entries for the file systems for persistence using their device files:

```
/dev/vgfs/ext4vol /ext4fs2 ext4 defaults 0 0
/dev/vgfs/xfsvol  /xfsfs2  xfs  defaults 0 0
```

8. Create mount points */ext4fs2* and */xfsfs2* using the *mkdir* command:

```
[user1@server2 ~]$ sudo mkdir /ext4fs2 /xfsfs2
```

9. Mount the new file systems using the *mount* command. This command will fail if there is any invalid or missing information in the file.

```
[user1@server2 ~]$ sudo mount -a
```

Fix any issues in the file if reported.

10. View the mount and availability status as well as the types of the new LVM file systems using the *lsblk* and *df* commands:

```
[user1@server2 ~]$ lsblk /dev/sdd
NAME                 MAJ:MIN RM  SIZE RO TYPE MOUNTPOINTS
sdd                     8:48  0  250M  0 disk
└─sdd1                  8:49  0  163M  0 part
  ├─vgfs-ext4vol 253:5   0   80M  0 lvm  /ext4fs2
  └─vgfs-xfsvol  253:6   0   80M  0 lvm  /xfsfs2
[user1@server2 ~]$
[user1@server2 ~]$ df -hT | grep fs2
/dev/mapper/vgfs-ext4vol ext4      70M   14K   64M   1% /ext4fs2
/dev/mapper/vgfs-xfsvol  xfs       75M  4.8M   70M   7% /xfsfs2
```

The *lsblk* command output illustrates the LVM logical volumes (*ext4vol* and *xfsvol*), the disk they are located on (*sdd*), the sizes (80MB), and the mount points (*/ext4fs2* and */xfsfs2*) where the file system are connected to the directory structure.

The *df* command shows the size and usage information. Both file systems are added to the *fstab* file for persistence, meaning future system reboots will remount them automatically. They may now be used to store files.

Exercise 14-3: Resize Ext4 and XFS File Systems in LVM Logical Volumes

This exercise should be done on *server2* as *user1* with *sudo* where required.

In this exercise, you will grow the size of the *vgfs* volume group that was created in Exercise 14-2 by adding the whole *sde* disk to it. You will extend the *ext4vol* logical volume along with the file system it contains by 40MB using two separate commands. You will extend the *xfsvol* logical volume along with the file system it contains by 40MB using a single command. You will verify the new extensions.

1. Initialize the *sde* disk and add it to the *vgfs* volume group:

```
[user1@server2 ~]$ sudo pvcreate /dev/sde
  Physical volume "/dev/sde" successfully created.
[user1@server2 ~]$ sudo vgextend vgfs /dev/sde
  Volume group "vgfs" successfully extended
```

2. Confirm the new size of *vgfs* using the *vgs* and *vgdisplay* commands:

```
[user1@server2 ~]$ sudo vgs
  VG     #PV #LV #SN Attr   VSize    VFree
  rhel     1   2   0 wz--n- <19.00g      0
  vgfs     2   2   0 wz--n- 400.00m 240.00m
  vgvdo    1   2   0 wz--n-  <5.00g      0
[user1@server2 ~]$
[user1@server2 ~]$ sudo vgdisplay vgfs
```

```
--- Volume group ---
VG Name                 vgfs
System ID
Format                  lvm2
Metadata Areas          2
Metadata Sequence No    4
VG Access               read/write
VG Status               resizable
MAX LV                  0
Cur LV                  2
Open LV                 2
Max PV                  0
Cur PV                  2
Act PV                  2
VG Size                 400.00 MiB
PE Size                 16.00 MiB
Total PE                25
Alloc PE / Size         10 / 160.00 MiB
Free  PE / Size         15 / 240.00 MiB
VG UUID                 pvpkuY-mfh2-s2rB-cgUA-za3d-S0l
```

There are now two physical volumes in the volume group and the total size increased to 400MiB.

3. Grow the logical volume *ext4vol* and the file system it holds by 40MB using the *lvextend* and *fsadm* command pair. Make sure to use an uppercase L to specify the size. The default unit is MiB. The plus sign (+) signifies an addition to the current size.

```
[user1@server2 ~]$ sudo lvextend -L +40 /dev/vgfs/ext4vol
  Rounding size to boundary between physical extents: 48.00 MiB.
  Size of logical volume vgfs/ext4vol changed from 80.00 MiB (5 extents) to 128.
00 MiB (8 extents).
  Logical volume vgfs/ext4vol successfully resized.

[user1@server2 ~]$ sudo fsadm resize /dev/vgfs/ext4vol
resize2fs 1.44.3 (10-July-2018)
Filesystem at /dev/mapper/vgfs-ext4vol is mounted on /ext4fs2; on-line resizing
required
old_desc_blocks = 1, new_desc_blocks = 1
The filesystem on /dev/mapper/vgfs-ext4vol is now 131072 (1k) blocks long.
```

The *resize* subcommand instructs the *fsadm* command to grow the file system to the full length of the specified logical volume.

4. Grow the logical volume *xfsvol* and the file system (-r) it holds by (+) 40MB using the *lvresize* command:

```
[user1@server2 ~]$ sudo lvresize -r -L +40 /dev/vgfs/xfsvol
  Rounding size to boundary between physical extents: 48.00 MiB.
  Size of logical volume vgfs/xfsvol changed from 80.00 MiB (5 extents) to 128.0
0 MiB (8 extents).
  Logical volume vgfs/xfsvol successfully resized.
meta-data=/dev/mapper/vgfs-xfsvol isize=512    agcount=4, agsize=5120 blks
         =                        sectsz=512   attr=2, projid32bit=1
         =                        crc=1        finobt=1, sparse=1, rmapbt=0
         =                        reflink=1
data     =                        bsize=4096   blocks=20480, imaxpct=25
         =                        sunit=0      swidth=0 blks
```

5. Verify the new extensions to both logical volumes using the *lvs* command. You may also issue the *lvdisplay* or *vgdisplay* command instead.

```
[user1@server2 ~]$ sudo lvs | grep vol
   ext4vol vgfs -wi-ao---- 128.00m

   xfsvol  vgfs -wi-ao---- 128.00m
```

6. Check the new sizes and the current mount status for both file systems using the *df* and *lsblk* commands:

```
[user1@server2 ~]$ df -hT | grep -E 'ext4vol|xfsvol'
/dev/mapper/vgfs-ext4vol ext4       115M   14K  107M   1% /ext4fs2
/dev/mapper/vgfs-xfsvol  xfs        123M  5.4M  118M   5% /xfsfs2
[user1@server2 ~]$
[user1@server2 ~]$ lsblk /dev/sdd /dev/sde
NAME                MAJ:MIN RM  SIZE RO TYPE MOUNTPOINTS
sdd                    8:48  0  250M  0 disk
└─sdd1                 8:49  0  163M  0 part
  ├─vgfs-ext4vol 253:5  0  128M  0 lvm  /ext4fs2
  └─vgfs-xfsvol  253:6  0  128M  0 lvm  /xfsfs2
sde                    8:64  0  250M  0 disk
├─vgfs-ext4vol 253:5  0  128M  0 lvm  /ext4fs2
└─vgfs-xfsvol  253:6  0  128M  0 lvm  /xfsfs2
```

The outputs reflect the new sizes (128MB) for both file systems. They also indicate their mount status.

This concludes the exercise.

Exercise 14-4: Create and Mount XFS File System in LVM VDO Volume

This exercise should be done on *server2* as *user1* with *sudo* where required.

In this exercise, you will create an LVM VDO volume called *lvvdo1* of virtual size 20GB on the 5GB *sdf* disk in a volume group called *vgvdo1*. You will initialize the volume with the XFS file system type, define it for persistence using its device files, create a mount point called */xfsvdo1*, attach it to the directory structure, and verify its availability and usage.

1. Initialize the *sdf* disk using the *pvcreate* command:

```
[user1@server2 ~]$ sudo pvcreate /dev/sdf
   Physical volume "/dev/sdf" successfully created.
```

2. Create *vgvdo1* volume group using the *vgcreate* command:

```
[user1@server2 ~]$ sudo vgcreate vgvdo1 /dev/sdf
   Volume group "vgvdo1" successfully created
```

3. Display basic information about the volume group:

```
[user1@server2 ~]$ sudo vgdisplay vgvdo1
  --- Volume group ---
  VG Name               vgvdo1
  System ID
  Format                lvm2
  Metadata Areas        1
  Metadata Sequence No  1
  VG Access             read/write
  VG Status             resizable
  MAX LV                0
  Cur LV                0
  Open LV               0
  Max PV                0
  Cur PV                1
  Act PV                1
  VG Size               <5.00 GiB
  PE Size               4.00 MiB
  Total PE              1279
  Alloc PE / Size       0 / 0
  Free  PE / Size       1279 / <5.00 GiB
  VG UUID               VpnIhp-rPb6-iJOJ-Bmwi
```

The volume group contains a total of 1279 PEs.

4. Create a VDO volume called *lvvdo1* using the lvcreate command. Use the -l option to specify the number of logical extents (1279) to be allocated and the -V option for the amount of virtual space (20GB).

```
[user1@server2 ~]$ sudo lvcreate -n lvvdo1 -l 1279 -V 20G --type vdo vgvdo1
WARNING: vdo signature detected on /dev/vgvdo1/vpool0 at offset 0. Wipe it? [y/
n]: y
  Wiping vdo signature on /dev/vgvdo1/vpool0.
    The VDO volume can address 2 GB in 1 data slab.
    It can grow to address at most 16 TB of physical storage in 8192 slabs.
    If a larger maximum size might be needed, use bigger slabs.
  Logical volume "lvvdo1" created.
```

Confirm with a y when prompted to wipe old signatures.

5. Display detailed information about the volume group including the logical volume and the physical volume:

```
[user1@server2 ~]$ sudo vgdisplay -v vgvdo1
........
```

```
--- Logical volume ---
LV Path                    /dev/vgvdo1/vpool0
LV Name                    vpool0
VG Name                    vgvdo1
LV UUID                    yGS8b4-4sdN-LRRr-zpFW-UvPn-vHQn
LV Write Access            read/write
LV Creation host, time     server2.example.com, 2023-02-03
LV VDO Pool data           vpool0_vdata
LV VDO Pool usage          60.00%
LV VDO Pool saving         100.00%
LV VDO Operating mode      normal
LV VDO Index state         online
LV VDO Compression st      online
LV VDO Used size           <3.00 GiB
LV Status                  NOT available
LV Size                    <5.00 GiB
Current LE                 1279
Segments                   1
Allocation                 inherit
Read ahead sectors         auto

--- Logical volume ---
LV Path                    /dev/vgvdo1/lvvdo1
LV Name                    lvvdo1
VG Name                    vgvdo1
LV UUID                    8e4MS4-IAcy-s0zU-QxCm-Xwvy-vHaC
LV Write Access            read/write
LV Creation host, time     server2.example.com, 2023-02-03
LV VDO Pool name           vpool0
LV Status                  available
# open                     0
LV Size                    20.00 GiB
Current LE                 5120
Segments                   1
Allocation                 inherit
Read ahead sectors         auto
- currently set to         256
Block device               253:4
```

The output reflects the creation of two logical volumes: a pool called */dev/vgvdo1/vpool0* and a volume called */dev/vgvdo1/lvvdo1*.

6. Display the new VDO volume creation using the *lsblk* command:

```
[user1@server2 ~]$ sudo lsblk /dev/sdf
NAME                       MAJ:MIN RM SIZE RO TYPE MOUNTPOINTS
sdf                          8:80   0   5G  0 disk
└─vgvdo1-vpool0_vdata       253:2   0   5G  0 lvm
  └─vgvdo1-vpool0-vpool     253:3   0  20G  0 lvm
    └─vgvdo1-lvvdo1         253:4   0  20G  0 lvm
```

The output shows the virtual volume size (20GB) and the underlying disk size (5GB).

7. Initialize the VDO volume with the XFS file system type using the *mkfs.xfs* command. The VDO volume device file is */dev/mapper/vgvdo1-lvvdo1* as indicated in the above output. Add the -f flag to force the removal of any old partitioning or labeling information from the disk.

```
[user1@server2 ~]$ sudo mkfs.xfs /dev/mapper/vgvdo1-lvvdo1
meta-data=/dev/mapper/vgvdo1-lvvdo1 isize=512    agcount=4,
         =                       sectsz=4096  attr=2, projic
         =                       crc=1        finobt=1, spa
         =                       reflink=1    bigtime=1 inol
data     =                       bsize=4096   blocks=524288(
         =                       sunit=0      swidth=0 blks
naming   =version 2              bsize=4096   ascii-ci=0, ft
log      =internal log           bsize=4096   blocks=2560, 
         =                       sectsz=4096  sunit=1 blks,
realtime =none                   extsz=4096   blocks=0, rte
Discarding blocks...
Done.
```

8. Open the */etc/fstab* file, go to the end of the file, and append the following entry for the file system for persistent mounts using its device file:

```
/dev/mapper/vgvdo1-lvvdo1 /xfsvdo1 xfs defaults 0 0
```

9. Create the mount point */xfsvdo1* using the *mkdir* command:

```
[user1@server2 ~]$ sudo mkdir /xfsvdo1
```

10. Mount the new file system using the *mount* command. This command will fail if there are any invalid or missing information in the file.

```
[user1@server2 ~]$ sudo mount -a
```

The *mount* command with the -a flag is a validation test for the *fstab* file. It should always be executed after updating this file and before rebooting the server to avoid landing the system in an unbootable state.

11. View the mount and availability status as well as the type of the VDO file system using the *lsblk* and *df* commands:

```
[user1@server2 ~]$ lsblk /dev/sdf
NAME                      MAJ:MIN RM SIZE RO TYPE MOUNTPOINTS
sdf                          8:80  0   5G  0 disk
└─vgvdo1-vpool0_vdata      253:2  0   5G  0 lvm
  └─vgvdo1-vpool0-vpool 253:3  0  20G  0 lvm
    └─vgvdo1-lvvdo1        253:6  0  20G  0 lvm  /xfsvdo1
[user1@server2 ~]$
[user1@server2 ~]$ df -hT /xfsvdo1
Filesystem                Type  Size  Used Avail Use% Mounted on
/dev/mapper/vgvdo1-lvvdo1 xfs    20G  176M   20G   1% /xfsvdo1
```

The *lsblk* command output illustrates the VDO volume name (*lvvdo1*), the disk it is located on (*sdf*), the actual size (5GB) and the virtual size (20GB), and the mount point (*/xfsvdo1*) where the file system is connected to the directory structure.

The *df* command shows the logical size of the file system that users will see, but it does not reveal the underlying disk information. This file system is added to the *fstab* file for persistence, meaning a future system reboot will remount it automatically. This file system may now be used to store files.

Refer to Chapter 13 "Storage Management" for details on VDO.

Swap and its Management

Physical memory (or main memory) in the system is a finite temporary storage resource employed for loading kernel and running user programs and applications. *Swap space* is an independent region on the physical disk used for holding idle data until it is needed. The system splits the physical memory into small logical chunks called *pages* and maps their physical locations to virtual locations on the swap to facilitate access by system processors. This physical-to-virtual mapping of pages is stored in a data structure called *page table*, and it is maintained by the kernel.

When a program or process is spawned, it requires space in the physical memory to run and be processed. Although many programs can run concurrently, the physical memory cannot hold all of them at once. The kernel monitors the memory usage. As long as the free memory remains above a high threshold, nothing happens. However, when the free memory falls below that threshold, the system starts moving selected idle pages of data from physical memory to the swap space to make room to accommodate other programs. This piece in the process is referred to as *page out*. Since the system CPU performs the process execution in a round-robin fashion, when the system needs this paged-out data for execution, the CPU looks for that data in the physical memory and a *page fault* occurs, resulting in moving the pages back to the physical memory from the swap. This return of data to the physical memory is referred to as *page in*. The entire process of paging data out and in is known as *demand paging*.

RHEL systems with less physical memory but high memory requirements can become over busy with paging out and in. When this happens, they do not have enough cycles to carry out other useful tasks, resulting in degraded system performance. The excessive amount of paging that affects the system performance is called *thrashing*.

When thrashing begins, or when the free physical memory falls below a low threshold, the system deactivates idle processes and prevents new processes from being launched. The idle processes are only reactivated, and new processes are only allowed to be started when the system discovers that the available physical memory has climbed above the threshold level and thrashing has ceased.

Determining Current Swap Usage

The size of a swap area should not be less than the amount of physical memory; however, depending on workload requirements, it may be twice the size or larger. It is also not uncommon to see systems with less swap than the actual amount of physical memory. This is especially witnessed on systems with a huge physical memory size.

RHEL offers the *free* command to view memory and swap space utilization. Use this command to view how much physical memory is installed (total), used (used), available (free), used by shared library routines (shared), holding data before it is written to disk (buffers), and used to store frequently accessed data (cached) on the system. The -h flag may be specified with the command to list the values in human-readable format, otherwise -k for KB, -m for MB, -g for GB, and so on are also supported. Add -t with the command to display a line with the "total" at the bottom of the output. Here is a sample output from *server2*:

```
[user1@server2 ~]$ free -ht
              total      used      free    shared  buff/cache  available
Mem:          1.7Gi     1.0Gi     443Mi      11Mi       430Mi       702Mi
Swap:         2.0Gi        0B     2.0Gi
Total:        3.7Gi     1.0Gi     2.4Gi
```

The output indicates that the system has 1.7GiB of total memory of which 1.0GiB is in use and 443MiB is free. It also shows on the same line the current memory usages by temporary (tmpfs) file systems (11MiB) and kernel buffers and page cache (430MiB). It also illustrates an estimate of free memory available to start new processes (702MiB).

On the subsequent row, it reports the total swap space (2.0GiB) configured on the system with a look at used (0 Bytes) and free (2.0GiB) space. The last line prints the combined utilization of both main memory and swap.

Try **free -hts 3** and **free -htc 2** to refresh the output every three seconds (-s) and to display the output twice (-c).

The *free* command reads memory and swap information from the */proc/meminfo* file to produce the report. The values are shown in KBs by default, and they are slightly off from what is shown in the above screenshot with *free*. Here are the relevant fields from this file:

```
[user1@server2 ~]$ cat /proc/meminfo | grep -E 'Mem|Swap'
MemTotal:        1813400 kB
MemFree:          454280 kB
MemAvailable:     719512 kB
SwapCached:            0 kB
SwapTotal:       2097148 kB
SwapFree:        2097148 kB
```

This data depicts the usage of the system's runtime memory and swap.

Prioritizing Swap Spaces

On many production RHEL servers, you may find multiple swap areas configured and activated to meet the workload demand. The default behavior of RHEL is to use the first activated swap area and move on to the next when the first one is exhausted. The system allows us to prioritize one area over the other by adding the option "pri" to the swap entries in the *fstab* file. This flag supports a value between -2 and 32767 with -2 being the default. A higher value of "pri" sets a higher priority for the corresponding swap region. For swap areas with an identical priority, the system alternates between them.

Swap Administration Commands

In order to create and manage swap spaces on the system, the *mkswap*, *swapon*, and *swapoff* commands are available. Use *mkswap* to initialize a partition for use as a swap space. Once the swap area is ready, you can activate or deactivate it from the command line with the help of the other two commands, or set it up for automatic activation by placing an entry in the *fstab* file. The *fstab* file accepts the swap area's device file, UUID, or label.

Exercise 14-5: Create and Activate Swap in Partition and Logical Volume

This exercise should be done on *server2* as *user1* with *sudo* where required.

In this exercise, you will create one swap area in a new 40MB partition called *sdb3* using the *mkswap* command. You will create another swap area in a 140MB logical volume called *swapvol* in *vgfs*. You will add their entries to the */etc/fstab* file for persistence. You will use the UUID and priority 1 for the partition swap and the device file and priority 2 for the logical volume swap. You will activate them and use appropriate tools to validate the activation.

> **EXAM TIP:** Use the lsblk command to determine available disk space.

1. Use *parted print* on the *sdb* disk and the *vgs* command on the *vgfs* volume group to determine available space for a new 40MB partition and a 144MB logical volume:

```
[user1@server2 ~]$ sudo parted /dev/sdb print
Model: ATA VBOX HARDDISK (scsi)
Disk /dev/sdb: 262MB
Sector size (logical/physical): 512B/512B
Partition Table: msdos
Disk Flags:

Number  Start    End    Size    Type     File system  Flags
 1      1049kB   101MB  99.6MB  primary  ext4
 2      102MB    201MB  99.6MB  primary  fat16
[user1@server2 ~]$
[user1@server2 ~]$ sudo vgs vgfs
  VG    #PV #LV #SN Attr   VSize    VFree
  vgfs  2   2   0 wz--n- 400.00m 144.00m
```

The outputs show 49MB (250MB minus 201MB) free space on the *sdb* disk and 144MB free space in the volume group.

2. Create a partition called *sdb3* of size 40MB using the *parted* command:

```
[user1@server2 ~]$ sudo parted /dev/sdb mkpart primary 202 242
```

3. Create logical volume *swapvol* of size 144MB in *vgs* using the *lvcreate* command:

```
[user1@server2 ~]$ sudo lvcreate -L 144 -n swapvol vgfs
  Logical volume "swapvol" created.
```

4. Construct swap structures in *sdb3* and *swapvol* using the *mkswap* command:

```
[user1@server2 ~]$ sudo mkswap /dev/sdb3
Setting up swapspace version 1, size = 38 MiB (39841792 bytes)
no label, UUID=dcb489c9-5479-473c-96d1-aa2089d76677
[user1@server2 ~]$
[user1@server2 ~]$ sudo mkswap /dev/vgfs/swapvol
Setting up swapspace version 1, size = 144 MiB (150990848 bytes)
no label, UUID=410aff13-15af-47a3-ad9c-bd3bf69b43fb
```

5. Edit the *fstab* file and add entries for both swap areas for auto-activation on reboots. Obtain the UUID for partition swap with **lsblk -f /dev/sdb3** and use the device file for logical volume. Specify their priorities.

```
UUID=dcb489c9-5479-473c-96d1-aa2089d76677  swap  swap pri=1 0 0
/dev/vgfs/swapvol                          swap  swap pri=2 0 0
```

EXAM TIP: You will not be given any credit for this work if you forget to add entries to the fstab file.

6. Determine the current amount of swap space on the system using the *swapon* command:

```
[user1@server2 ~]$ sudo swapon
NAME        TYPE      SIZE USED PRIO
/dev/dm-1 partition   2G   0B   -2
```

There is one 2GB swap area on the system and it is configured at the default priority of -2.

7. Activate the new swap regions using the *swapon* command:

```
[user1@server2 ~]$ sudo swapon -a
```

The command would display errors if there are any issues with swap entries in the *fstab* file.

8. Confirm the activation using the *swapon* command or by viewing the */proc/swaps* file:

```
[user1@server2 ~]$ sudo swapon
NAME        TYPE       SIZE USED PRIO
/dev/dm-1 partition    2G   0B   -2
/dev/sdb3 partition   38M   0B   1
/dev/dm-7 partition  144M   0B   2
[user1@server2 ~]$
[user1@server2 ~]$ cat /proc/swaps
Filename      Type        Size      Used   Priority
/dev/dm-1     partition   2097148   0      -2
/dev/sdb3     partition   38908     0      1
/dev/dm-7     partition   147452    0      2
```

The activation of the two new swap regions is confirmed from the above outputs. Their sizes and priorities are also visible. The device mapper device files for the logical volumes and the device file for the partition swap are also exhibited.

9. Issue the *free* command to view the reflection of swap numbers on the Swap and Total lines:

```
[user1@server2 ~]$ free -ht
            total    used    free    shared  buff/cache  available
Mem:        1.7Gi    1.1Gi   305Mi   11Mi    543Mi       676Mi
Swap:       2.2Gi    0B      2.2Gi
Total:      3.9Gi    1.1Gi   2.5Gi
```

The total swap is now 2.2GiB. This concludes the exercise.

Chapter Summary

This chapter covered two major storage topics: file systems and swap. These structures are created in partitions or VDO/logical volumes irrespective of the underlying storage management solution used to build them.

The chapter began with a detailed look at the concepts, categories, benefits, and types of file systems. We reviewed file system administration and monitoring utilities. We discussed the concepts around mounting and unmounting file systems. We examined the UUID associated with file systems and applied labels to file systems. We analyzed the file system table and added entries for auto-activating file systems at reboots. We explored tools for reporting file system usage and calculating disk usage. We performed a number of exercises on file system creation and administration in partitions and VDO and LVM volumes to reinforce the concepts and theory learned in this and the previous chapters.

We touched upon the concepts of swapping and paging, and studied how they work. We performed exercises on creating, activating, viewing, deactivating, and removing swap spaces, as well as configuring them for auto-activation at system reboots.

Review Questions

1. What type of information does the *blkid* command display?
2. What would the command *xfs_admin -L bootfs /dev/sda1* do?
3. The *lsblk* command cannot be used to view file system UUIDs. True or False?
4. Which two file systems are created in a default RHEL 9 installation?
5. What would the command *lvresize -r -L +30 /dev/vg02/lvol2* do?
6. XFS is the default file system type in RHEL 9. True or False?
7. What is the process of paging out and paging in known as?
8. What would the command *mkswap /dev/sdc2* do?
9. What would happen if you tried to mount a file system on a directory that already contains files in it?
10. A UUID is always assigned to a file system at its creation time. True or False?
11. Arrange the activities to create and activate a swap space while ensuring persistence: (a) swapon, (b) update fstab, (c) mkswap, and (d) reboot?
12. The difference between the primary and backup superblocks is that the primary superblock includes pointers to the data blocks where the actual file contents are stored whereas the backup superblocks don't. True or False?
13. What would the command *mkfs.ext4 /dev/vgtest/lvoltest* do?
14. Arrange the tasks in correct sequence: umount file system, mount file system, create file system, remove file system.
15. Which of these statements is wrong with respect to file systems: (a) optimize each file system independently, (b) keep dissimilar data in separate file systems, (c) grow and shrink a file system independent of other file systems, and (d) file systems cannot be expanded independent of other file systems.
16. Which command can be used to create a label for an XFS file system?
17. Which virtual file contains information about the current swap?
18. The */etc/fstab* file can be used to activate swap spaces automatically at system reboots. True or False?
19. What is the default file system type used for optical media?
20. The *xfs_repair* command must be run on a mounted file system. True or False?

21. Provide two commands that can be used to activate and deactivate swap spaces manually.
22. Provide the *fstab* file entry for an Ext4 file system located in device */dev/mapper/vg20-lv1* and mounted with default options on the */ora1* directory.
23. What is the name of the virtual file that holds currently mounted file system information?
24. Both Ext3 and Ext4 file system types support journaling. True or False?
25. What would the *mount* command do with the -a switch?
26. What would the command *df -t xfs* do?
27. Which command can be used to determine the total and used physical memory and swap in the system?
28. Name three commands that can be employed to view the UUID of an XFS file system?

Answers to Review Questions

1. The *blkid* command displays attributes for block devices.
2. The command provided will apply the specified label to the XFS file system in */dev/sda1*.
3. False.
4. */* and */boot*.
5. The command provided will expand the logical volume *lvol2* in volume group *vg02* along with the file system it contains by 30MB.
6. True.
7. The process of paging out and in is known as demand paging.
8. The command provided will create swap structures in the */dev/vdc2* partition.
9. The files in the directory will hide.
10. True.
11. c/a/b or c/b/a.
12. False.
13. The command provided will format */dev/vgtest/lvoltest* logical volume with Ext4 file system type.
14. Create, mount, unmount, and remove.
15. d is incorrect.
16. The *xfs_admin* command can be used to create a label for an XFS file system.
17. The */proc/swaps* file contains information about the current swap.
18. True.
19. The default file system type for optical devices is ISO9660.
20. False.
21. The *swapon* and *swapoff* commands.
22. /dev/mapper/vg20-lv1 /ora1 ext4 defaults 0 0
23. The *mounts* file under */proc/self* directory.
24. True.
25. The command provided will mount all file systems listed in the */etc/fstab* file but are not currently mounted.
26. The command provided will display all mounted file systems of type XFS.
27. The *free* command.
28. You can use the *xfs_admin*, *lsblk*, and *blkid* commands to view the UUID of an XFS file system.

Do-It-Yourself Challenge Labs

The following labs are useful to strengthen most of the concepts and topics learned in this chapter. It is expected that you perform the labs without external help. A step-by-step guide is not supplied, as the knowledge and skill required to implement the labs have already been disseminated in the chapter; however, hints to the relevant major topic(s) are included.

Use the lab environment built specifically for end-of-chapter labs. See sub-section "Lab Environment for End-of-Chapter Labs" in Chapter 01 "Local Installation" for details.

Lab 14-1: Create VFAT, Ext4, and XFS File Systems in Partitions and Mount Persistently

As *user1* with *sudo* on *server4*, create three 70MB primary partitions on one of the available 250MB disks (*lsblk*) by invoking the *parted* utility directly at the command prompt. Apply label "msdos" if the disk is new. Initialize partition 1 with VFAT, partition 2 with Ext4, and partition 3 with XFS file system types. Create mount points */vfatfs5*, */ext4fs5*, and */xfsfs5*, and mount all three manually. Determine the UUIDs for the three file systems, and add them to the *fstab* file. Unmount all three file systems manually, and execute *mount -a* to mount them all. Run *df -h* for verification. (Hint: File System Management).

Lab 14-2: Create XFS File System in LVM VDO Volume and Mount Persistently

As *user1* with *sudo* on *server4*, ensure that VDO software is installed. Create a volume *vdo5* with a logical size 20GB on a 5GB disk (*lsblk*) using the *lvcreate* command. Initialize the volume with XFS file system type. Create mount point */vdofs5*, and mount it manually. Unmount the file system manually and execute *mount -a* to mount it back. Run *df -h* to confirm. (Hint: File System Management).

Lab 14-3: Create Ext4 and XFS File Systems in LVM Volumes and Mount Persistently

As *user1* with *sudo* on *server4*, initialize an available 250MB disk for use in LVM (*lsblk*). Create volume group *vg200* with PE size 8MB and add the physical volume. Create two logical volumes *lv200* and *lv300* of sizes 120MB and 100MB. Use the *vgs*, *pvs*, *lvs*, and *vgdisplay* commands for verification. Initialize the volumes with Ext4 and XFS file system types. Create mount points */lvmfs5* and */lvmfs6*, and mount them manually. Add the file system information to the *fstab* file using their device files. Unmount the file systems manually, and execute *mount -a* to mount them back. Run *df -h* to confirm. (Hint: File System Management).

Lab 14-4: Extend Ext4 and XFS File Systems in LVM Volumes

As *user1* with *sudo* on *server4*, initialize an available 250MB disk for use in LVM (*lsblk*). Add the new physical volume to volume group *vg200*. Expand logical volumes *lv200* and *lv300* along with the underlying file systems to 200MB and 250MB. Use the *vgs*, *pvs*, *lvs*, *vgdisplay*, and *df* commands for verification. (Hint: File System Management).

Lab 14-5: Create Swap in Partition and LVM Volume and Activate Persistently

As *user1* with *sudo* on *server4*, create two 100MB partitions on an available 250MB disk (*lsblk*) by invoking the *parted* utility directly at the command prompt. Apply label "msdos" if the disk is new. Initialize one of the partitions with swap structures. Apply label *swappart* to the swap partition, and add it to the *fstab* file. Execute *swapon -a* to activate it. Run *swapon -s* to confirm activation.

Initialize the other partition for use in LVM. Expand volume group *vg200* (Lab 14-3) by adding this physical volume to it. Create logical volume *swapvol* of size 180MB. Use the *vgs*, *pvs*, *lvs*, and *vgdisplay* commands for verification. Initialize the logical volume for swap. Add an entry to the *fstab* file for the new swap area using its device file. Execute *swapon -a* to activate it. Run *swapon -s* to confirm activation. (Hint: Swap and its Management).

## Chapter 15

Networking, Network Devices, and Network Connections

This chapter describes the following major topics:

➢ Overview of basic networking concepts: hostname, IPv4, network classes, subnetting, subnet mask, CIDR, protocol, TCP/UDP, well-known ports, ICMP, Ethernet address, IPv6, IPv4/IPv6 differences, consistent device naming, etc.

➢ Change hostname of the system

➢ Understand the concepts of network device and connection

➢ Anatomy of a network connection profile

➢ Know network device and connection management tools and techniques

➢ Configure network connections by hand and using commands

➢ Describe the hosts table

➢ Test network connectivity using hostname and IP address

RHCSA Objectives:

44. Configure IPv4 and IPv6 addresses

A computer network is formed when two or more physical or virtual computers are connected together for sharing resources and data. The computers may be linked via wired or wireless means, and a device such as a switch is used to interconnect several computers to allow them to communicate with one another on the network. There are numerous concepts and terms that need to be grasped in order to work effectively and efficiently with network device and network connection configuration and troubleshooting, and several other network services. This chapter provides a wealth of that information.

For a system to be able to talk to other systems, one of its network devices must have a connection profile attached containing a unique IP address, hostname, and other essential network parameters. The network assignments may be configured statically or obtained automatically from a DHCP server. Few files are involved in the configuration, which may be modified by hand or using commands. Testing follows the configuration to confirm the system's ability to communicate.

Networking Fundamentals

The primary purpose of computer networks is to allow users to share data and resources. A simple network is formed when two computers are interconnected. Using a networking device such as a *switch*, this network can be expanded to include additional computers, as well as printers, scanners, storage, and other devices (collectively referred to as *nodes* or *entities*). A computer on the network can be configured to act as a file server, storage server, or as a gateway to the Internet for the rest of the networked computers. Nodes may be interconnected using wired or wireless means. A corporate network may have thousands of nodes linked via a variety of data transmission media. The Internet is the largest network of networks with millions of nodes interconnected.

There are many elementary concepts and terms that you need to grasp before being able to configure network interfaces, connection profiles, and client/server setups that are elaborated in this and other chapters. As well, there are many configuration files and commands related to various network services that you need to understand thoroughly in order to manage a RHEL-based environment effectively. Some of the concepts, terms, configuration files, and commands are explained in this chapter.

Hostname

A *hostname* is a unique alphanumeric label (the hyphen (-), underscore (_), and period (.) characters are also allowed) that is assigned to a node to identify it on the network. It can consist of up to 253 characters. It is normally allotted based on the purpose and principal use of the system. In RHEL, the hostname is stored in the */etc/hostname* file.

The hostname can be viewed with several different commands, such as *hostname*, *hostnamectl*, *uname*, and *nmcli*, as well as by displaying the content of the */etc/hostname* file. Let's run these commands on *server1*:

```
[user1@server1 ~]$ hostname
server1.example.com
[user1@server1 ~]$ hostnamectl --static
server1.example.com
[user1@server1 ~]$ uname -n
server1.example.com
[user1@server1 ~]$ nmcli general hostname
server1.example.com
[user1@server1 ~]$ cat /etc/hostname
server1.example.com
```

All the above commands displayed the same output.

Exercise 15-1: Change System Hostname

This exercise should be done on both *server1* and *server2* as *user1* with *sudo* where required.

In this exercise, you will change the hostnames of both lab servers persistently. You will rename *server1.example.com* to *server10.example.com* by editing a file and restarting the corresponding service daemon. You will rename *server2.example.com* to *server20.example.com* using a command. You will validate the change on both systems.

On *server1*:

1. Open the */etc/hostname* file in a text editor and change the current entry to the following:

    ```
    server10.example.com
    ```

2. Execute the *systemctl* command to restart the *systemd-hostnamed* service and verify the new hostname with the *hostname* command:

    ```
    [user1@server1 ~]$ sudo systemctl restart systemd-hostnamed
    [user1@server1 ~]$ hostname
    server10.example.com
    ```

3. To view the reflection of the new hostname in the command prompt, log off and log back in as *user1*. The new prompt will look like:

    ```
    [user1@server10 ~]$
    ```

On *server2*:

1. Execute the *hostnamectl* command to change the hostname to *server20.example.com*:

```
[user1@server2 ~]$ sudo hostnamectl set-hostname server20.example.com
```

2. To view the reflection of the new hostname in the command prompt, log off and log back in as *user1*. You can also use the *hostname* command to view the new name.

```
[user1@server20 ~]$
[user1@server20 ~]$ hostname
server20.example.com
```

You can also change the system hostname using the *nmcli* command. For instance, you could have used **nmcli general hostname server20.example.com** to rename *server2.example.com*. The *nmcli* command is explained in detail later in this chapter.

EXAM TIP: You need to know only one of the available methods to change the system hostname.

Going forward, you will be using the new hostnames *server10* and *server20*.

IPv4 Address

IPv4 stands for *Internet Protocol version 4* and represents a unique 32-bit software address that every single entity on the network must have in order to communicate with other entities. It was the first version of IP that was released for public use. IPv4 addresses are also referred to as *dotted-quad* addresses, and they can be assigned on a temporary or permanent basis. Temporary addresses are referred to as *dynamic* addresses and are typically leased from a DHCP server for a specific period of time. Permanent addresses, on the other hand, are called *static* addresses and they are manually set.

You can use the *ip* command with the addr argument to view the current IP assignments on the system. Let's run this command on *server10* and see what it returns:

```
[user1@server10 ~]$ ip addr
1: lo: <LOOPBACK,UP,LOWER_UP> mtu 65536 qdisc noqueue state UNKNOWN ç
len 1000
    link/loopback 00:00:00:00:00:00 brd 00:00:00:00:00:00
    inet 127.0.0.1/8 scope host lo
       valid_lft forever preferred_lft forever
    inet6 ::1/128 scope host
       valid_lft forever preferred_lft forever
2: enp0s3: <BROADCAST,MULTICAST,UP,LOWER_UP> mtu 1500 qdisc fq_codel
 default qlen 1000
    link/ether 08:00:27:5f:fd:43 brd ff:ff:ff:ff:ff:ff
    inet 192.168.0.110/24 brd 192.168.0.255 scope global noprefixrout
       valid_lft forever preferred_lft forever
    inet6 2001:1970:5383:4b00:a00:27ff:fe5f:fd43/64 scope global dyna
ute
       valid_lft 604768sec preferred_lft 86368sec
    inet6 fdaa:bbcc:ddee:0:a00:27ff:fe5f:fd43/64 scope global dynamic

       valid_lft 2006054623sec preferred_lft 2006054623sec
    inet6 fe80::a00:27ff:fe5f:fd43/64 scope link noprefixroute
       valid_lft forever preferred_lft forever
```

The output indicates one configured network connection (number 2 above) called *enp0s3* with IPv4 address 192.168.0.110 assigned to it. The other connection (number 1 above), represented as *lo*, is a special purpose software device reserved for use on every Linux system. Its IPv4 address is always 127.0.0.1, and it is referred to as the system's *loopback* (or *localhost*) address. Network programs and applications that communicate with the local system employ this hostname.

Classful Network Addressing

An IPv4 address is comprised of four period-separated octets (4 x 8 = 32-bit address) that are divided into a *network* portion (or network ID/bits) comprising of the *Most Significant Bits* (MSBs) and a *node* portion (or node/host ID/bits) containing the *Least Significant Bits* (LSBs). The network portion identifies the correct destination network, and the node portion represents the correct destination node on that network. Public network addresses are classified into three categories: class A, class B, and class C. Private network addresses are classified into two categories: class D and class E. Class D addresses are multicast and they are employed in special use cases only. Class E addresses are experimental and are reserved for future use.

Class A

Class A addresses are used for large networks with up to 16 million nodes. This class uses the first octet as the network portion and the rest of the octets as the node portion. The total number of usable network and node addresses can be up to 126 and 16,777,214, respectively. The network address range for class A networks is between 0 and 126. See an example below of a random class A IP address, which also shows two reserved addresses:

10.121.51.209	(class A IP address)
10.121.51.**0**	(network address)
10.121.51.**255**	(broadcast address)

The 0 and 255 (highlighted) are network and broadcast addresses, and they are always reserved.

Class B

Class B addresses are used for mid-sized networks with up to 65 thousand nodes. This class employs the first two octets as the network portion and the other two as the node portion. The total number of usable network and node addresses can be up to 16,384 and 65,534, respectively. The network address range for class B networks is between 128 and 191. See an example below of a random class B IP address, which also shows two reserved addresses:

161.121.51.209	(class B IP address)
161.121.51.**0**	(network address)
161.121.51.**255**	(broadcast address)

The 0 and 255 (highlighted) are network and broadcast addresses, and they are always reserved.

Class C

Class C addresses are employed for small networks with up to 254 nodes. This class uses the first three octets as the network portion and the last octet as the node portion. The total number of usable network and node addresses can be up to 2,097,152 and 254, respectively. The network address range for class C networks is between 192 and 223. See an example below of an arbitrary class C IP address, which also shows two reserved addresses:

215.121.51.209   (class C IP address)
215.121.51.**0**   (network address)
215.121.51.**255**   (broadcast address)

The 0 and 255 (highlighted) are network and broadcast addresses, and they are always reserved.

Class D
Class D addresses range from 224 to 239.

Class E
Class E addresses range from 240 to 255.

Subnetting

Subnetting is a technique by which a large network address space is divided into several smaller and more manageable logical subnetworks, referred to as *subnets*. Subnetting results in reduced network traffic, improved network performance, and de-centralized and easier administration, among other benefits. Subnetting does not touch the network bits; it uses the node bits only.

The following should be kept in mind when dealing with subnetting:

- ✓ Subnetting results in the reduction of usable addresses.
- ✓ All nodes in a given subnet have the same subnet mask.
- ✓ Each subnet acts as an isolated network and requires a router to talk to other subnets.
- ✓ The first and the last IP address in a subnet are reserved. The first address points to the subnet itself, and the last address is the broadcast address.

Subnet Mask

A *subnet mask* or *netmask* is the network portion plus the subnet bits. It segregates the network bits from the node bits. It is used by routers to pinpoint the start and end of the network/subnet portion and the start and end of the node portion for a given IP address.

The subnet mask, like an IP address, can be represented in either decimal or binary notation. The 1s in the subnet mask isolate the subnet bits from the node bits that contain 0s. The default subnet masks for class A, B, and C networks are 255.0.0.0, 255.255.0.0, and 255.255.255.0, respectively.

To determine the subnet address for an arbitrary IP address, such as 192.168.12.72 with netmask 255.255.255.224, write the IP address in binary format. Then write the subnet mask in binary format with all network and subnet bits set to 1 and all node bits set to 0. Then perform a logical AND operation. For each matching 1 you get a 1, otherwise you get a 0. The following highlights the ANDed bits:

```
11000000.10101000.00001100.01001000    (IP address 192.168.12.72)
11111111.11111111.11111111.11100000    (subnet mask 255.255.255.224)
================================
11000000.10101000.00001100.01000000    (subnet IP 192.168.12.64 in binary format)
   192  .   168  .   12  .   64         (subnet IP in decimal format)
```

This calculation enables you to ascertain the subnet address from a given IP and subnet mask.

Classless Network Addressing

Classless Inter-Domain Routing (CIDR) is a technique designed to control the quick depletion of IPv4 addresses and the rapid surge in the number of routing tables required to route IPv4 traffic on the network and the Internet. This technique was introduced as a substitute for the *classful* scheme, which was not scalable and had other limitations. Using CIDR, IPv4 addresses can be allocated in custom blocks suitable for networks of all sizes. This technique has resulted in smaller and less cluttered routing tables. CIDR was originally designed to address IPv4 needs; however, it has been extended to support IPv6 as well.

An IPv4 address written in CIDR notation has a leading forward slash (/) character followed by the number of routing bits. A sample IP address of 192.168.0.20 with the default class C subnet mask of 255.255.255.0 will be written as 192.168.0.20/24. This notation presents a compact method of denoting an IP address along with its subnet mask.

Protocol

A *protocol* is a set of rules governing the exchange of data between two network entities. These rules include how data is formatted, coded, and controlled. The rules also provide error handling, speed matching, and data packet sequencing. In other words, a protocol is a common language that all nodes on the network speak and understand. Protocols are defined in the */etc/protocols* file. An excerpt from this file is provided below:

```
[user1@server10 ~]$ cat /etc/protocols
ip       0      IP        # internet protocol, pseudo protocol number
hopopt   0      HOPOPT    # hop-by-hop options for ipv6
icmp     1      ICMP      # internet control message protocol
igmp     2      IGMP      # internet group management protocol
ggp      3      GGP       # gateway-gateway protocol
ipv4     4      IPv4      # IPv4 encapsulation

........
```

Column 1 in the output lists the name of a protocol, followed by the associated port number, alias, and a short description in columns 2, 3, and 4.

Some common protocols are TCP, UDP, IP, and ICMP.

TCP and UDP Protocols

TCP (*Transmission Control Protocol*) and UDP (*User Datagram Protocol*) protocols are responsible for transporting data packets between network entities. TCP is reliable, connection-oriented, and point-to-point. It inspects for errors and sequencing upon a packet's arrival on the destination node, and returns an acknowledgement to the source node, establishing a point-to-point connection with the peer TCP layer on the source node. If the packet is received with an error or if it is lost in transit, the destination node requests a resend of the packet. This ensures guaranteed data delivery and makes TCP reliable. Due to its reliability and connection-oriented nature, TCP is widely implemented in network applications.

UDP, in contrast, is unreliable, connectionless, and multi-point. If a packet is lost or contains errors upon arrival at the destination, the source node is unaware of it. The destination node does not send an acknowledgment back to the source node. A common use of this protocol is in broadcast-only applications where reliability is not sought.

Well-Known Ports

Both TCP and UDP use ports for data transmission between a client and its server program. Ports are either well-known or private. A well-known port is reserved for an application's exclusive use, and it is standardized across all network operating systems. Well-known ports are defined in the */etc/services* file, an excerpt of which is presented below:

```
[user1@server10 ~]$ cat /etc/services

. . . . . . . .
ftp            21/tcp
ftp            21/udp          fsp fspd
ssh            22/tcp                          # The Secure Shell (SSH) Protocol
ssh            22/udp                          # The Secure Shell (SSH) Protocol
telnet         23/tcp
telnet         23/udp
# 24 - private mail system
lmtp           24/tcp                          # LMTP Mail Delivery
lmtp           24/udp                          # LMTP Mail Delivery
smtp           25/tcp          mail

. . . . . . . .
```

Column 1 lists the official name of a network service, followed by the port number and transport layer protocol the service uses, optional aliases, and comments in successive columns.

Some common services and the ports they listen on are FTP (*File Transfer Protocol*) 21, SSH (*Secure Shell*) 22, SMTP (*Simple Mail Transfer Protocol*) 25, DNS (*Domain Name System*) 53, HTTP (*HyperText Transfer Protocol*) 80, NTP (*Network Time Protocol*) 123, secure HTTP (*HyperText Transfer Protocol Secure*) 443, and rsyslog 514.

A private port, on the other hand, is an arbitrary number generated when a client application attempts to establish a communication session with its server process. This port number no longer exists after the session has ended.

ICMP Protocol

The *Internet Control Message Protocol* (ICMP) is a key protocol. It is primarily used for testing and diagnosing network connections. Commands such as *ping* uses this protocol to send a stream of messages to remote network devices to examine their health and report statistical and diagnostic information. The report includes the number of packets transmitted, received, and lost; a round-trip time for individual packets with an overall average; a percentage of packets lost during the communication; and so on. See a sample below that shows two packets (-c2) sent from *server10* to the IP address of *server20*:

```
[user1@server10 ~]$ ping -c2 192.168.0.120
PING 192.168.0.120 (192.168.0.120) 56(84) bytes of data.
64 bytes from 192.168.0.120: icmp_seq=1 ttl=64 time=0.325 ms
64 bytes from 192.168.0.120: icmp_seq=2 ttl=64 time=0.402 ms

--- 192.168.0.120 ping statistics ---
2 packets transmitted, 2 received, 0% packet loss, time 45ms
rtt min/avg/max/mdev = 0.325/0.363/0.402/0.042 ms
```

Other commands, such as *traceroute*, also employ this protocol for route determination and debugging between network entities. The IPv6 version of ICMP is referred to as *ICMPv6* and it is used by tools such as *ping6* and *tracepath6*.

Ethernet Address

An *Ethernet* address represents an exclusive 48-bit address that is used to identify the correct destination node for data packets transmitted from the source node. The data packets include hardware addresses for the source and the destination node. The Ethernet address is also referred to as the *hardware, physical, link layer,* or *MAC* address.

You can use the *ip* command to list all network interfaces available on the system along with their Ethernet addresses:

```
[user1@server10 ~]$ ip addr | grep ether
    link/ether 08:00:27:5f:fd:43 brd ff:ff:ff:ff:ff:ff
```

IP and hardware addresses work hand in hand, and a combination of both is critical to identifying the correct destination node on the network. A network protocol called *Address Resolution Protocol* (ARP) is used to enable IP and hardware addresses to work in tandem. ARP determines the hardware address of the destination node when its IP address is known.

IPv6 Address

With the explosive growth of the Internet, the presence of an extremely large number of network nodes requiring an IP, and an ever-increasing demand for additional addresses—the conventional IPv4 address space, which provides approximately 4.3 billion addresses—has been exhausted. To meet the future demand, a new version of IP is now available and its use is expanding. This new version is referred to as IPv6 (*IP version 6*) or IPng (*IP next generation*). By default, IPv6 is enabled in RHEL 9 on all configured network connections.

IPv6 is a 128-bit software address, providing access to approximately 340 undecillion (340 followed by 36 zeros) addresses. This is an extremely large space, and it is expected to fulfill the IP requirements for several decades to come.

IPv6 uses a messaging protocol called *Neighbor Discovery Protocol* (NDP) to probe the network to discover neighboring IPv6 devices, determine their reachability, and map their associations. This protocol also includes enhanced functionalities (provided by ICMP and ARP on IPv4 networks) for troubleshooting issues pertaining to connectivity, address duplication, and routing.

Unlike IPv4 addresses, which are represented as four dot-separated octets, IPv6 addresses contain eight colon-separated groups of four hexadecimal numbers. A sample IPv6 would be 2001:1970:5383:4b00:a00:27ff:fe5f:fd43/64. It looks a bit daunting at first sight, but there are methods that will simplify their representation.

The *ip addr* command also shows IPv6 addresses for the interfaces:

```
[user1@server10 ~]$ ip addr | grep inet6
    inet6 ::1/128 scope host
    inet6 2001:1970:5383:4b00:a00:27ff:fe5f:fd43/64
```

It returns two IPv6 addresses. The first one belongs to the loopback interface, and the second one is assigned to the *enp0s3* connection.

Major Differences between IPv4 and IPv6

There are a number of differences between IPv4 and IPv6 protocols. Some of the major ones are highlighted in Table 15-1.

IPv4	IPv6
Uses 4x8-bit, period-separated decimal number format for address representation. Example: 192.168.0.100	Uses 8x16-bit, colon-separated hexadecimal number format for address representation. Example: fe80::a00:27ff:feae:f35b
Number of address bits: 32	Number of address bits: 128
Maximum number of addresses: ~4.3 billion.	Maximum number of addresses: virtually unlimited
Common testing and troubleshooting tools: ping, traceroute, tracepath, etc.	Common testing and troubleshooting tools: ping6, traceroute6, tracepath6, etc.
Support for IP autoconfiguration: no	Support for IP autoconfiguration: yes
Packet size: 576 bytes	Packet size: 1280 bytes

Table 15-1 IPv4 vs IPv6

These and other differences not listed here are due to enhancements and new features added to IPv6.

Network Devices and Connections

Network Interface Cards (NICs) are hardware adapters that provide one or more Ethernet ports for network connectivity. NICs may also be referred to as *network adapters* and individual ports as *network interfaces* or *network devices*. NICs may be built-in to the system board or are add-on adapters. They are available in one, two, and four port designs on a single adapter.

Individual interfaces (devices) can have one or more connection profiles attached to them with different configuration settings. Each connection profile has a unique name and includes settings such as the device name, UUID, hardware address, IP address, and so on. A connection profile can be configured by editing files or using commands. A device can have multiple connection profiles attached, but only one of them can be active at a time.

Consistent Network Device Naming

In RHEL versions 6 and earlier, network interfaces used *eth* (Ethernet), *em* (embedded), and *wlan* (wireless lan) naming and were numbered 0 and onwards as the interfaces were discovered during a system boot. This was the default scheme that had been in place for network device naming for years. Given multiple interfaces located onboard and on add-on NICs, the number assignments could possibly change on the next boot due to failures or errors in their detection, which could possibly result in connectivity and operational issues.

As of RHEL 7, the default naming scheme has been augmented to base on several rules governed by a service called *udevd*. The default ruleset is to assign names using the device's location and topology, and the setting in firmware. The underlying virtualization layer (VMware, VirtualBox, KVM, Hyper-V) also plays a role in the naming. Some sample device names are *enp0s3*, *ens160*, etc.

This advanced ruleset has resulted in consistent and predictable naming, eliminating the odds of re-enumeration during a hardware rescan. Moreover, the designated names are not affected by the addition or removal of interface cards. This naming scheme helps in identifying, configuring, troubleshooting, and replacing the right adapter without hassle.

Exercise 15-2: Add Network Devices to server10 and server20

This exercise will add one network interface to *server10* and one to *server20* using VirtualBox.

In this exercise, you will shut down *server10* and *server20*. You will launch VirtualBox Manager and add one network interface to *server10* and one to *server20*. You will power on both servers and confirm new interfaces.

1. Execute **sudo shutdown now** on *server10*.

2. Start VirtualBox on your Windows/Mac computer and highlight the *RHEL9-VM1* virtual machine.

3. Click Settings at the top and then Network on the window that pops up. Click on "Adapter 2" and check the "Enable Network Adapter" box. Select "Internal Network" from the drop down list next to "Attached to". See Figure 15-1.

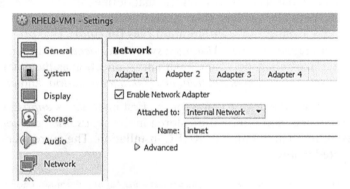

Figure 15-1 VirtualBox Manager | Add Network Interface

4. Click OK to return to the main VirtualBox interface.
5. Power on *RHEL9-VM1* to boot RHEL 9 in it.
6. When the server is up, log on as *user1* and run the *ip* command to verify the new interface:

```
[user1@server10 ~]$ ip a
........
2: enp0s3: <BROADCAST,MULTICAST,UP,LOWER_UP> mtu 1500 qdisc fq_codel stat
len 1000
    link/ether 08:00:27:5f:fd:43 brd ff:ff:ff:ff:ff:ff
    inet 192.168.0.110/24 brd 192.168.0.255 scope global noprefixroute en
        valid_lft forever preferred_lft forever
    inet6 2001:1970:5383:4b00:a00:27ff:fe5f:fd43/64 scope global dynamic
        valid_lft 604785sec preferred_lft 86385sec
    inet6 fdaa:bbcc:ddee:0:a00:27ff:fe5f:fd43/64 scope global dynamic nop
        valid_lft 2006054640sec preferred_lft 2006054640sec
    inet6 fe80::a00:27ff:fe5f:fd43/64 scope link noprefixroute
        valid_lft forever preferred_lft forever
3: enp0s8: <BROADCAST,MULTICAST,UP,LOWER_UP> mtu 1500 qdisc fq_codel stat
len 1000
    link/ether 08:00:27:ca:47:01 brd ff:ff:ff:ff:ff:ff
```

The output reveals a new network device called *enp0s8*. This is the interface that you just added to the VM.

7. Repeat steps 1 through 6 to add a network interface to *server20* and verify.

This completes the addition of new network interfaces to *server10* and *server20*. You are now ready to use them in the upcoming exercises.

The NetworkManager Service

NetworkManager is the default interface and connection configuration, administration, and monitoring service used in RHEL 9. This service has a daemon program called *NetworkManager*, which is responsible for keeping available interfaces and connections up and active. It offers a powerful command line tool called *nmcli* to manage interfaces and connections, and to control the service. This utility offers many options for their effective management. The *NetworkManager* service also furnishes a text-based interface called *nmtui* and a graphical equivalent called *nm-connection-editor* that you may use in lieu of *nmcli*.

Understanding Interface Connection Profile

Each network connection has a configuration file that defines IP assignments and other relevant parameters for it. The networking subsystem reads this file and applies the settings at the time the connection is activated. Connection configuration files (or *connection profiles*) are stored in a central location under the */etc/NetworkManager/system-connections* directory. The filenames are identified by the interface connection names with nmconnection as the extension. Some instances of connection profiles are *enp0s3.nmconnection*, *ens160.nmconnection*, and *em1.nmconnection*.

On *server10* and *server20*, the device name for the first interface is *enp0s3* with connection name *enp0s3* and relevant connection information stored in the *enp0s3.nmconnection* file. This connection was established at the time of RHEL installation. The current content of the file from *server10* are presented below:

```
[user1@server10 ~]$ sudo cat /etc/NetworkManager/system-connections/enp0s3.nmconnec
tion
[connection]
id=enp0s3
uuid=f8ae446e-fb1f-3d57-a0b0-7ddf95a9a899
type=ethernet
autoconnect-priority=-999
interface-name=enp0s3
timestamp=1674768379

[ethernet]

[ipv4]
address1=192.168.0.110/24,192.168.0.1
method=manual

[ipv6]
addr-gen-mode=eui64
method=auto

[proxy]
```

The file has multiple sections. Each section defines a set of networking properties for the connection. The output above shows five sections—connection, ethernet, ipv4, ipv6, and proxy.

There are no settings under ethernet and proxy. The other three have a few properties defined and they are outlined in Table 15-2 in the order in which they are listed.

Property	Description
id	Any description given to this connection. The default matches the interface name.
uuid	The UUID associated with this connection
type	Specifies the type of this connection
autoconnect-priority	If the connection is set to autoconnect, connections with higher priority will be preferred. A higher number means higher priority. The range is between -999 and 999 with 0 being the default.
interface_name	Specifies the device name for the network interface
timestamp	The time, in seconds since the Unix Epoch that the connection was last activated successfully. This field is automatically populated each time the connection is activated.
address1/method	Specifies the static IP for the connection if the method property is set to manual. /24 represents the subnet mask.
addr-gen-mode/method	Generates an IPv6 address based on the hardware address of the interface.

Table 15-2 Network Connection Configuration Directives

There are hundreds of other properties that may be defined in connection profiles depending on the type of interface. Run **man nm-settings** for a description of additional properties.

Network Device and Connection Administration Tools

There are a few tools and methods available for configuring and administering network interfaces, connections, and connection profiles. The *NetworkManager* service includes a toolset for this purpose as well. Let's take a quick look at the basic management tools in Table 15-3.

Command	Description
ip	A powerful and versatile tool for displaying, monitoring, and managing interfaces, connections, routing, traffic, etc.
nmcli	Creates, updates, deletes, activates, and deactivates a connection profile.

Table 15-3 Network Interface Management Tools

You can manually create a connection profile and attach it to a network device. Many Linux administrators prefer this approach. RHEL also offers an alternative method for this purpose, which is discussed later in this chapter.

The ifup, ifdown, and ifconfig commands, and storing interface profiles in the /etc/sysconfig/network-scripts directory are deprecated and should not be used anymore. The NetworkManager service and associated tools are the replacements.

In Exercise 15-3, you'll use the manual method to configure a connection profile for a new network device that was added in Exercise 15-2 and employ the tools listed in Table 15-3.

The nmcli Command

nmcli is a NetworkManager command line tool that is employed to create, view, modify, remove, activate, and deactivate network connections, and to control and report network device status. It operates on seven different object categories, with each category supporting several options to form a complete command. The seven categories are general, networking, connection, device, radio, monitor, and agent. This discussion only focuses on the connection and device object categories. They are described in Table 15-4 along with management operations that they can perform.

Object	Description
Connection: activates, deactivates, and administers network connections	
show	Lists connections
up / down	Activates/deactivates a connection
add	Adds a connection
edit	Edits an existing connection or adds a new one
modify	Modifies one or more properties of a connection
delete	Deletes a connection
reload	Instructs NetworkManager to re-read all connection profiles
load	Instructs NetworkManager to re-read a connection profile
Device: displays and administers network interfaces	
status	Exhibits device status
show	Displays detailed information about all or the specified interface

Table 15-4 Network Connection and Device Administration Tools

Object categories and the objects within them may be written in an abridged form to save typing. For instance, the connection category may be abbreviated as a "c" or "con" and the device category as a "d" or "dev". The same rule applies to object names as well. For instance, add may be specified as an "a", delete as a "d", and so on. Check the manual pages for *nmcli-examples*.

The *nmcli* command supports tab completion to make its use easier. Let's run a few examples on *server10* to understand the command's usage.

To show (s) all available connections (c) including both active and inactive:

```
[user1@server10 ~]$ nmcli c s
NAME     UUID                                    TYPE      DEVICE
enp0s3   f8ae446e-fb1f-3d57-a0b0-7ddf95a9a899    ethernet  enp0s3
enp0s8   f4477190-f17a-3d75-b7db-fdd594a5f476    ethernet  enp0s8
```

The output lists two connection profiles (NAME) and the devices (DEVICE) they are attached to. It also shows their UUID and type.

To deactivate (down) the connection (c) *enp0s8*:

```
[user1@server10 ~]$ sudo nmcli c down enp0s8
Connection 'enp0s8' successfully deactivated (D-Bus active path: /org/freedeskt
p/NetworkManager/ActiveConnection/3)
```

The connection profile is detached from the device, disabling the connection. You can check with **nmcli c s**.

To activate (up) the connection (c) enp0s8:

```
[user1@server10 ~]$ sudo nmcli c up enp0s8
Connection successfully activated (D-Bus active path: /org/freedesktop/NetworkMa
nager/ActiveConnection/4)
```

The connection profile is reattached to the device, enabling the connection. You can check with **nmcli c s**.

To display the status (s) of all available network devices (d):

```
[user1@server10 ~]$ nmcli d s
DEVICE   TYPE      STATE       CONNECTION
enp0s3   ethernet  connected   enp0s3
enp0s8   ethernet  connected   enp0s8
lo       loopback  unmanaged   --
```

The output shows three devices and their types, states, and the connection profiles attached to them. The loopback interface is not managed by the *NetworkManager* service.

Exercise 15-3: Configure New Network Connection Manually

This exercise should be done on *server10* as *user1* with *sudo* where required.

In this exercise, you will create a connection profile for the new network interface *enp0s8* using a text editing tool. You will assign the IP 172.10.10.110/24 with gateway 172.10.10.1 and set it to autoactivate at system reboots. You will deactivate and reactivate this interface at the command prompt.

1. Create a file called *enp0s8-nmconnection* in the */etc/NetworkManager/system-connections* directory and enter the following information to establish a connection profile:

    ```
    [user1@server10 ~]$ sudo cat /etc/NetworkManager/system-connections/enp0s8.nmco
    nnection
    [connection]
    id=enp0s8
    uuid=f4477190-f17a-3d75-b7db-fdd594a5f476
    type=ethernet
    autoconnect-priority=-999
    interface-name=enp0s8

    [ipv4]
    address1=172.10.10.110/24,172.10.10.1
    method=manual
    ```

2. Deactivate and reactivate this interface using the *nmcli* command:

```
[user1@server10 ~]$ sudo nmcli c d enp0s8
Connection 'enp0s8' successfully deactivated (D-Bus active path: /org/freede
op/NetworkManager/ActiveConnection/4)
[user1@server10 ~]$
[user1@server10 ~]$ sudo nmcli c u enp0s8
Connection successfully activated (D-Bus active path: /org/freedesktop/Netwc
anager/ActiveConnection/5)
```

3. Verify the activation of the connection:

```
[user1@server10 ~]$ ip a show enp0s8
3: enp0s8: <BROADCAST,MULTICAST,UP,LOWER_UP> mtu 1500 qdisc fq_codel
roup default qlen 1000
    link/ether 08:00:27:ca:47:01 brd ff:ff:ff:ff:ff:ff
    inet 172.10.10.110/24 brd 172.10.10.255 scope global noprefixrout
        valid_lft forever preferred_lft forever
    inet6 fe80::5ac:8f46:8a79:9c78/64 scope link noprefixroute
        valid_lft forever preferred_lft forever
```

The new connection profile has been applied to the new network device *enp0s8*. The connection is now ready for use. The connectivity to *server10* over this new connection will be tested later in this chapter.

Exercise 15-4: Configure New Network Connection Using nmcli

This exercise should be done on *server20* as *user1* with *sudo* where required.

In this exercise, you will create a connection profile using the *nmcli* command for the new network interface *enp0s8* that was added to *server20* in Exercise 15-2. You will assign the IP 172.10.10.120/24 with gateway 172.10.10.1, and confirm.

1. Check the presence of the new interface:

```
[user1@server20 ~]$ sudo nmcli d status | grep enp
enp0s3   ethernet   connected       enp0s3
enp0s8   ethernet   disconnected    --
```

The output signifies the existence of a new network device called *enp0s8*. It does not have a connection profile attached at the moment.

2. Add (a) a connection profile (c) and attach it to the new interface. Use the type Ethernet, device name (ifname) *enp0s8* with a matching connection name (con-name), CIDR (ip4) 172.10.10.120/24, and gateway (gw4) 172.10.10.1:

```
[user1@server20 ~]$ sudo nmcli c a type Ethernet ifname enp0s8 con-name enp0s8
ip4 172.10.10.120/24 gw4 172.10.10.1
Connection 'enp0s8' (46630ab7-313c-4dea-a635-62bdfcc21872) successfully added.
```

A new connection has been added, attached to the new interface, and activated. In addition, the command has saved the connection information in a new file called *enp0s8-nmconnection* and stored it in the */etc/NetworkManager/system-connections* directory.

3. Confirm the new connection status:

```
[user1@server20 ~]$ sudo nmcli d status | grep enp
enp0s3   ethernet   connected   enp0s3
enp0s8   ethernet   connected   enp0s8
```

The output indicates the association of the new connection with the network device.

4. Check the content of the *enp0s8-nmconnection* file:

```
[user1@server20 ~]$ sudo cat /etc/NetworkManager/system-connections/enp0s8.nmco
nnection
[connection]
id=enp0s8
uuid=46630ab7-313c-4dea-a635-62bdfcc21872
type=ethernet
interface-name=enp0s8

[ethernet]

[ipv4]
address1=172.10.10.120/24,172.10.10.1
method=manual

[ipv6]
addr-gen-mode=default
method=auto

[proxy]
```

There are a number of default directives added to the connection profile in addition to the configuration items you entered with the *nmcli* command above.

5. Check the IP assignments for the new connection:

```
[user1@server20 ~]$ ip a show enp0s8
3: enp0s8: <BROADCAST,MULTICAST,UP,LOWER_UP> mtu 1500 qdisc fq
roup default qlen 1000
    link/ether 08:00:27:bd:33:ff brd ff:ff:ff:ff:ff:ff
    inet 172.10.10.120/24 brd 172.10.10.255 scope global nopre
       valid_lft forever preferred_lft forever
    inet6 fe80::f66b:9af6:5c44:a315/64 scope link noprefixrout
       valid_lft forever preferred_lft forever
```

The IP is assigned to the interface. The connection will be tested later in this chapter.

This brings the exercise to a conclusion.

EXAM TIP: You need to know only one of the available methods to set IP assignments.

Understanding Hosts Table

Each IP address used on the system should have a hostname assigned to it. In an environment with multiple systems on the network, it is prudent to have some sort of a hostname to IP address resolution method in place to avoid typing the destination system IP repeatedly to access it. DNS is one such method. It is designed for large networks such as corporate networks and the Internet. For small, internal networks, the use of a local hosts table (the */etc/hosts* file) is also common. This table is used to maintain hostname to IP mapping for systems on the local network, allowing us to access a system by simply employing its hostname. In this book, there are two systems in place: *server10.example.com* with IP 192.168.0.110 and alias *server10*, and *server20.example.com* with IP 192.168.0.120 and alias *server20*. You can append this information to the */etc/hosts* file on both *server10* and *server20* as shown below:

```
192.168.0.110        server10.example.com      server10
192.168.0.120        server20.example.com      server20
```

Each row in the file contains an IP address in column 1 followed by the *official* (or *canonical*) hostname in column 2, and one or more optional aliases thereafter. The official hostname and one or more aliases give users the flexibility of accessing the system using any of these names.

> **EXAM TIP:** In the presence of an active DNS with all hostnames resolvable, there is no need to worry about updating the hosts file.

As expressed above, the use of the *hosts* file is common on small networks, and it should be updated on each individual system to reflect any changes for best inter-system connectivity experience.

Testing Network Connectivity

RHEL includes the *ping* command to examine network connectivity between two systems. It uses the IP address of the destination system to send a series of 64-byte *Internet Control Message Protocol* (ICMP) test packets to it. A response from the remote system validates connectivity and health. With the -c option, you can specify the number of packets that you want transmitted.

The following sends two packets from *server10* to 192.168.0.120 (*server20*):

```
[user1@server10 ~]$ ping 192.168.0.120 -c 2
PING 192.168.0.120 (192.168.0.120) 56(84) bytes of data.
64 bytes from 192.168.0.120: icmp_seq=1 ttl=64 time=0.406 ms
64 bytes from 192.168.0.120: icmp_seq=2 ttl=64 time=0.418 ms

--- 192.168.0.120 ping statistics ---
2 packets transmitted, 2 received, 0% packet loss, time 38ms
rtt min/avg/max/mdev = 0.406/0.412/0.418/0.006 ms
```

Under "192.168.0.120 ping statistics," the output depicts the number of packets transmitted, received, and lost. The packet loss should be 0%, and the round-trip time should not be too high for a healthy connection. In general, you can use this command to test connectivity with the system's own IP, the loopback IP (127.0.0.1), a static route, the default gateway, and any other address on the local or remote network.

If a *ping* response fails, you need to check if the NIC is seated properly, its driver is installed, network cable is secured appropriately, IP and netmask values are set correctly, and the default or static route is accurate.

Exercise 15-5: Update Hosts Table and Test Connectivity

This exercise should be done on *server10* and *server20* as *user1* with *sudo* where required.

In this exercise, you will update the */etc/hosts* file on *server10* and *server20*. You will add the IP addresses assigned to both connections and map them to hostnames *server10*, *server10s8*, *server20*, and *server20s8* appropriately. You will test connectivity from *server10* to *server20* and from *server10s8* to *server20s8* using their IP addresses and then their hostnames.

On *server20*:

1. Open the */etc/hosts* file and add the following entries:

        192.168.0.110 server10.example.com server10
        192.168.0.120 server20.example.com server20
        172.10.10.110 server10s8.example.com server10s8
        172.10.10.120 server20s8.example.com server20s8

The IP addresses for both connections are added for both servers.

On *server10*:

2. Open the */etc/hosts* file and add the following entries:

        192.168.0.110 server10.example.com server10
        192.168.0.120 server20.example.com server20
        172.10.10.110 server10s8.example.com server10s8
        172.10.10.120 server20s8.example.com server20s8

The IP addresses for both connections are added for both servers.

3. Send two packets from *server10* to the IP address of *server20*:

        [user1@server10 ~]$ ping -c2 192.168.0.120
        PING 192.168.0.120 (192.168.0.120) 56(84) bytes of data.
        64 bytes from 192.168.0.120: icmp_seq=1 ttl=64 time=0.369 ms
        64 bytes from 192.168.0.120: icmp_seq=2 ttl=64 time=0.446 ms

        --- 192.168.0.120 ping statistics ---
        2 packets transmitted, 2 received, 0% packet loss, time 45ms
        rtt min/avg/max/mdev = 0.369/0.407/0.446/0.043 ms

4. Issue two ping packets on *server10* to the hostname of *server20*:

        [user1@server10 ~]$ ping -c2 server20
        PING server20.example.com (192.168.0.120) 56(84) bytes of data.
        64 bytes from server20.example.com (192.168.0.120): icmp_seq=1 ttl=64 time=0.351 ms
        64 bytes from server20.example.com (192.168.0.120): icmp_seq=2 ttl=64 time=0.422 ms

        --- server20.example.com ping statistics ---
        2 packets transmitted, 2 received, 0% packet loss, time 26ms
        rtt min/avg/max/mdev = 0.351/0.386/0.422/0.040 ms

5. Send one packet from *server10* to the IP address of *server20s8*:

```
[user1@server10 ~]$ ping -c1 172.10.10.120
PING 172.10.10.120 (172.10.10.120) 56(84) bytes of data.
64 bytes from 172.10.10.120: icmp_seq=1 ttl=64 time=4.56 ms

--- 172.10.10.120 ping statistics ---
1 packets transmitted, 1 received, 0% packet loss, time 0ms
rtt min/avg/max/mdev = 4.558/4.558/4.558/0.000 ms
```

6.   Issue one ping packet on *server10* to the hostname of *server20s8*:

```
[user1@server10 ~]$ ping -c1 server20s8
PING server20s8.example.com (172.10.10.120) 56(84) bytes of
64 bytes from server20s8.example.com (172.10.10.120): icmp_s
31 ms

--- server20s8.example.com ping statistics ---
1 packets transmitted, 1 received, 0% packet loss, time 0ms
rtt min/avg/max/mdev = 2.313/2.313/2.313/0.000 ms
```

Steps 3 through 6 verified the connectivity to the remote server over both connections. Each server has two IP addresses, and each IP address has a unique hostname assigned to it.

This concludes the exercise.

Chapter Summary

This chapter discussed the rudiments of networking. It began by providing an understanding of various essential networking terms and concepts to build the foundation for networking topics going forward. Topics such as hostname, IPv4, IPv6, classful and classless network addressing, subnetting, subnet mask, protocol, port, Ethernet address, and consistent device naming were covered in sufficient detail.

We modified hostnames on both lab servers by modifying a configuration file and restarting the hostname service on one server and using a single command on the other. We employed two different methods to demonstrate multiple ways of doing the same thing. A third method was also mentioned to rename a hostname.

Next, we described the terms network devices and network connections, and realized the difference between the two. We examined a connection profile and looked at a number of directives that may be defined for a network connection. We added a new network device to each lab server and configured them by employing two different methods. We activated the new connections and performed a ping test for functional validation. Lastly, we populated the hosts tables with the IP and hostname mapping on both lab servers.

Review Questions

1.   Which service is responsible for maintaining consistent device naming?
2.   List three key differences between TCP and UDP protocols.
3.   What is the significance of the NAME and DEVICE directives in a connection profile?
4.   Which class of IP addresses has the least number of node addresses?
5.   Which command can you use to display the hardware address of a network device?
6.   Define protocol.

7. Which directory stores the network connection profiles?
8. True or False. A network device is a physical or virtual network port and a network connection is a configuration file attached to it.
9. IPv4 is a 32-bit software address. How many bits does an IPv6 address have?
10. Which file defines the port and protocol mapping?
11. What would the command *hostnamectl set-hostname host20* do?
12. Name the file that stores the hostname of the system.
13. What would the command *nmcli c s* do?
14. The */etc/hosts* file maintains hostname to hardware address mappings. True or False?
15. Which file contains service, port, and protocol mappings?
16. What would the *ip addr* command produce?
17. Which file would you consult to identify the port number and protocol associated with a network service?
18. Name four commands that can be used to display the hostname.
19. List any two benefits of subnetting.

Answers to Review Questions

1. The *udevd* service handles consistent naming of network devices.
2. TCP is connection-oriented, reliable, and point-to-point; UDP is connectionless, unreliable, and multi-point.
3. The NAME directive sets the name for the network connection and the DEVICE directive defines the network device the connection is associated with.
4. The C class supports the least number of node addresses.
5. The *ip* command.
6. A set of rules that govern the exchange of information between two network entities.
7. The */etc/NetworkManager/system-connections* directory.
8. True.
9. 128.
10. The */etc/protocols* file.
11. The command provided will update the */etc/hostname* file with the specified hostname and restart the *systemd-hostnamed* daemon for the change to take effect.
12. The */etc/hostname* file.
13. The command provided will display the status information for all network connections.
14. False. This file maintains hostname to IP address mapping.
15. The */etc/services* file.
16. This command provided will display information about network connections including IP assignments and hardware address.
17. The */etc/services* file.
18. The *hostname*, *uname*, *hostnamectl*, and *nmcli* commands can be used to view the system hostname.
19. Better manageability and less traffic.

Do-It-Yourself Challenge Labs

The following labs are useful to strengthen most of the concepts and topics learned in this chapter. It is expected that you perform the labs without external help. A step-by-step guide is not supplied, as the knowledge and skill required to implement the labs have already been disseminated in the chapter; however, hints to the relevant major topic(s) are included.

Use the lab environment built specifically for end-of-chapter labs. See sub-section "Lab Environment for End-of-Chapter Labs" in Chapter 01 "Local Installation" for details.

Lab 15-1: Add New Interface and Configure Connection Profile with nmcli

Add a third network interface to *RHEL9-VM3* in VirtualBox.

As *user1* with *sudo* on *server30*, run *ip a* and verify the addition of the new interface. Use the *nmcli* command and assign IP 192.168.0.230/24 and gateway 192.168.0.1. Deactivate and reactivate this connection manually. Add entry *server30-3* to the *hosts* table. (Hint: Exercise 15-2 and Exercise 15-4).

Lab 15-2: Add New Interface and Configure Connection Profile Manually

Add a third network interface to *RHEL9-VM4* in VirtualBox.

As *user1* with *sudo* on *server40*, run *ip a* and verify the addition of the new interface. Make a copy of the *enp0s3.nmconnection* file for the new connection under */etc/NetworkManager/system-connections*. Remove the UUID directive and set CIDR 192.168.0.240/24. Deactivate and reactivate this connection manually. Add entry *server40-3* to the *hosts* table and run ping tests to *server40-3* and its IP address. (Hint: Exercise 15-2 and Exercise 15-3).

Chapter 16

Network File System

This chapter describes the following major topics:

➤ Overview of Network File System service and key components

➤ Network File System benefits and versions

➤ Export a share on NFS server

➤ Mount the share on NFS client using standard mount method

➤ Understand the AutoFS service, and its benefits and functioning

➤ Analyze AutoFS configuration maps

➤ Mount the exported share on NFS client using AutoFS

➤ Configure NFS and AutoFS to share and mount user home directories

RHCSA Objectives:

33. Mount and unmount network file systems using NFS
34. Configure autofs

N etwork shares may be mounted on RHEL and accessed the same way as local file systems. This can be done manually using the same tools that are employed for mounting and unmounting local file systems. An alternative solution is to implement the AutoFS service to automatically mount and unmount them without the need to execute any commands explicitly. AutoFS monitors activities in mount points based on which it triggers a mount or unmount action.

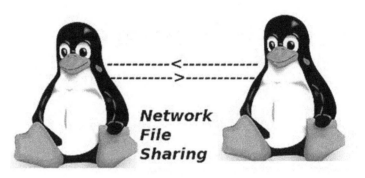

RHEL exports shares using the Network File System service for remote mounting on clients. A combination of this service and AutoFS/standard mount is prevalent in real world scenarios. This chapter elaborates on the benefits of the file sharing solution and expounds upon AutoFS. It demonstrates a series of exercises to detail the server-side and client-side configurations. It also explores the automatic mounting of user home directories on clients.

Network File System

Network File System (NFS) is a networking protocol that allows file sharing over the network. The Network File System service is based upon the client/server architecture whereby users on one system access files, directories, and file systems (collectively called "shares") that reside on a remote system as if they are mounted locally on their system. The remote system that makes its shares available for network access is referred to as an NFS server, and the process of making the shares accessible is referred to as *exporting*. The shares the NFS server exports may be accessed by one or more systems. These systems are called NFS clients, and the process of making the shares accessible on clients is referred to as *mounting*. See Figure 16-1 for a simple NFS client/server arrangement that shows two shares—*/export1* and */export2*—exported on the network to a remote system, which has them mounted there.

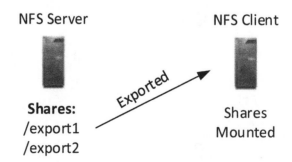

Figure 16-1 NFS Server/Client

A system can provide both server and client functionality concurrently. When a directory or file system share is exported, the entire directory structure beneath it becomes available for mounting on the client. A subdirectory or the parent directory of a share cannot be re-exported if it exists in the same file system. Similarly, a mounted share cannot be exported further. A single exported file share is mounted on a directory mount point.

Benefits of Using NFS

The use of NFS provides several benefits, some of which are highlighted below:

- ✓ Supports a variety of operating system platforms including Linux, UNIX, and Microsoft Windows.
- ✓ Multiple NFS clients can access a single share simultaneously.
- ✓ Enables the sharing of common application binaries and other read-only information, resulting in reduced administration overhead and storage cost.
- ✓ Gives users access to uniform data.
- ✓ Allows the consolidation of scattered user home directories on the NFS server and then exporting them to the clients. This way users will have only one home directory to maintain.

NFS Versions

RHEL 9 provides the support for NFS versions 3, 4.0, 4.1, and 4.2, with version 4.2 being the default. NFSv3 supports both TCP and UDP transport protocols, asynchronous writes, and 64-bit file sizes that gives clients the ability to access files of sizes larger than 2GB.

NFSv4.x are *Internet Engineering Task Force* (IETF) series of protocols that provide all the features of NFSv3, plus the ability to transit firewalls and work on the Internet. They provide enhanced security and support for encrypted transfers, as well as greater scalability, better cross-platform interoperability, and better system crash handling. They use usernames and group names rather than UIDs and GIDs for files located on network shares. NFSv4.0 and NFSv4.1 use the TCP protocol by default, but can work with UDP for backward compatibility. In contrast, NFSv4.2 only supports TCP.

NFS Server and Client Configuration

This section presents two exercises, one demonstrating how to export a share on a server (NFS server) and the other outlines the steps on mounting and accessing a share on a remote system (NFS client). The basic setup of the NFS service is straightforward. It requires adding an entry of the share to a file named */etc/exports* and using a command called *exportfs* to make it available on the network. It also requires the addition of a firewall rule to allow access to the share by NFS clients.

The *mount* command employed on an NFS client is the same command that was used in Chapter 14 "Local File Systems and Swap" to mount local file systems. Moreover, the *fstab* file requires an entry for the NFS share on the client for persistent mounting.

The exercises in this section illustrate the usage of both commands and the syntax of both files.

Exercise 16-1: Export Share on NFS Server

This exercise should be done on *server20* as *user1* with *sudo* where required.

In this exercise, you will create a directory called */common* and export it to *server10* in read/write mode. You will ensure that NFS traffic is allowed through the firewall. You will confirm the export.

---

1. Install the NFS software called *nfs-utils*:

```
[user1@server20 ~]$ sudo dnf -y install nfs-utils

Base OS software                              17 MB/s | 1.7 MB     00:00
Application software                          26 MB/s | 6.1 MB     00:00
Dependencies resolved.
==================================================================================
 Package            Architecture  Version            Repository      Size
==================================================================================
Installing:
 nfs-utils          x86_64        1:2.5.4-15.el9     BaseOS          453 k
Installing dependencies:
 gssproxy           x86_64        0.8.4-4.el9        BaseOS          114 k
 keyutils           x86_64        1.6.1-4.el9        BaseOS           68 k
 libev              x86_64        4.33-5.el9         BaseOS           56 k
 libnfsidmap        x86_64        1:2.5.4-15.el9     BaseOS           67 k
 libverto-libev     x86_64        0.3.2-3.el9        BaseOS           15 k
 rpcbind            x86_64        1.2.6-5.el9        BaseOS           62 k
 sssd-nfs-idmap     x86_64        2.7.3-4.el9        BaseOS           42 k

Transaction Summary
==================================================================================
Install  8 Packages

Total size: 876 k
Installed size: 2.0 M

. . . . . . . .
Installed:
  gssproxy-0.8.4-4.el9.x86_64             keyutils-1.6.1-4.el9.x86_64
  libev-4.33-5.el9.x86_64                 libnfsidmap-1:2.5.4-15.el9.x86_64
  libverto-libev-0.3.2-3.el9.x86_64       nfs-utils-1:2.5.4-15.el9.x86_64
  rpcbind-1.2.6-5.el9.x86_64              sssd-nfs-idmap-2.7.3-4.el9.x86_64

Complete!
```

📝 Follow the instructions outlined in "Exercise 9-1: Mount RHEL 9 ISO Persistently" and "Exercise 10-1: Configure Access to Pre-Built Repositories" to ensure the above software installation works.

2. Create */common* directory to be exported as a share:

```
[user1@server20 ~]$ sudo mkdir /common
```

3. Add full permissions to */common*:

```
[user1@server20 ~]$ sudo chmod 777 /common
```

4. Add the NFS service persistently to the Linux firewall to allow the NFS traffic to pass through it, and load the new rule:

```
[user1@server20 ~]$ sudo firewall-cmd --permanent --add-service nfs
success
[user1@server20 ~]$ sudo firewall-cmd --reload
success
```

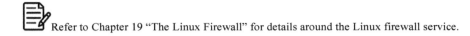 Refer to Chapter 19 "The Linux Firewall" for details around the Linux firewall service.

5. Start the NFS service and enable it to autostart at system reboots:

```
[user1@server20 ~]$ sudo systemctl --now enable nfs-server
Created symlink /etc/systemd/system/multi-user.target.wants/nfs-server.service
→ /usr/lib/systemd/system/nfs-server.service.
```

6. Verify the operational status of the NFS service:

```
[user1@server20 ~]$ sudo systemctl status  nfs-server
● nfs-server.service - NFS server and services
     Loaded: loaded (/usr/lib/systemd/system/nfs-server.service; enabled; vendor>
     Active: active (exited) since Sun 2023-02-05 17:12:47 EST; 37s ago
   Main PID: 32935 (code=exited, status=0/SUCCESS)
        CPU: 79ms

Feb 05 17:12:46 server20.example.com systemd[1]: Starting NFS server and service>
Feb 05 17:12:47 server20.example.com systemd[1]: Finished NFS server and service>
```

7. Open the */etc/exports* file in a text editor and add an entry for */common* to export it to *server10* with read/write option:

```
/common server10(rw)
```

8. Export the entry defined in the */etc/exports* file. The -a option exports all the entries listed in the file and -v displays verbose output.

```
[user1@server20 ~]$ sudo exportfs -av
exporting server10.example.com:/common
```

The NFS service is now set up on *server20* with the */common* share available for mounting on *server10* (NFS client in this case).

For practice, you can unexport the share by issuing the *exportfs* command with the -u flag as follows:

```
[user1@server20 ~]$ sudo exportfs -u server10:/common
```

Before proceeding, re-export the share using **sudo exportfs -av**.

Exercise 16-2: Mount Share on NFS Client

This exercise should be done on *server10* as *user1* with *sudo* where required.

In this exercise, you will mount the */common* share exported in Exercise 16-1. You will create a mount point called */local*, mount the remote share manually, and confirm the mount. You will add the remote share to the file system table for persistence. You will remount the share and confirm the mount. You will create a test file in the mount point and confirm the file creation on the NFS server (*server20*).

---

1. Install the NFS software called *nfs-utils*:

```
[user1@server2 ~]$ sudo dnf -y install nfs-utils
```

2. Create */local* mount point:

```
[user1@server10 ~]$ sudo mkdir /local
```

3. Mount the share manually using the *mount* command:

```
[user1@server10 ~]$ sudo mount server20:/common /local
```

The remote share is successfully mounted on *server10*, and it can be accessed as any other local file system.

4. Confirm the mount using either the *mount* or the *df* command:

```
[user1@server10 ~]$ mount | grep local
server20:/common on /local type nfs4 (rw,relatime,vers=4.2,rsize=262144,wsize=2
62144,namlen=255,hard,proto=tcp,timeo=600,retrans=2,sec=sys,clientaddr=192.168.
0.110,local_lock=none,addr=192.168.0.120)
[user1@server10 ~]$
[user1@server10 ~]$ df -h | grep local
server20:/common        17G   4.0G   14G   24% /local
```

The *mount* command output returns the NFS protocol version (NFS4.2) and all the default options used in mounting the share.

5. Open the */etc/fstab* file and append the following entry for persistence:

```
server20:/common   /local   nfs   _netdev   0   0
```

 The _netdev option will make the system wait for networking to establish before attempting to mount this share.

 A mount point should be empty and must not be in use when an attempt is made to mount a share to it.

6. Unmount the share manually using the *umount* command and remount it via the *fstab* file to validate the accuracy of the entry placed in the file:

```
[user1@server10 ~]$ sudo umount /local
[user1@server10 ~]$ sudo mount -a
```

7. Run **mount** and **df -h** again to verify the remounting.

8. Create a file called *nfsfile* under */local* and verify:

```
[user1@server10 ~]$ touch /local/nfsfile
[user1@server10 ~]$ ls -l /local/
total 0
-rw-r--r--. 1 user1 user1 0 Feb  5 17:31 nfsfile
```

9. Confirm the file creation on the NFS server (*server20*):

```
[user1@server20 ~]$ ls -l /common
total 0
-rw-r--r--. 1 user1 user1 0 Feb  5 17:31 nfsfile
```

EXAM TIP: Do not forget to update the /etc/fstab file on the client.

This completes the setup and testing of mounting, unmounting, and remounting of an NFS share on the client.

Auto File System (AutoFS)

In the previous section, you learned how to attach (mount) an NFS share to the Linux directory tree manually for access by users and applications on an NFS client. Once attached, the share was treated just like any other local file system. You also learned how to detach (unmount) an NFS share manually from the directory tree to make it inaccessible to users and applications. You placed an entry for the share in the *fstab* file to guarantee a remount during system reboots.

RHEL offers an alternative way of mounting and unmounting a share on the clients during runtime as well as system reboots. This feature is delivered by a service called the *Auto File System* (AutoFS). AutoFS is a client-side service, which is employed to mount an NFS share on-demand. With a proper entry placed in AutoFS configuration files, the AutoFS service automatically mounts a share upon detecting an activity in its mount point with a command such as *ls* or *cd*. In the same manner, AutoFS unmounts the share automatically if it has not been accessed for a predefined period of time.

To avoid inconsistencies, mounts managed with AutoFS should not be mounted or unmounted manually or via the /etc/fstab file.

The use of AutoFS saves the kernel from dedicating system resources to maintain unused NFS shares, resulting in slight improvement in system performance.

Benefits of Using AutoFS

There are several benefits associated with using the AutoFS service over placing entries in the */etc/fstab* file. Some of the key benefits are described below:

✓ AutoFS requires that NFS shares be defined in text configuration files called *maps*, which are located in the */etc* or */etc/auto.master.d* directory. AutoFS does not make use of the */etc/fstab* file.

✓ AutoFS does not require *root* privileges to mount an NFS share; manual mounting and mounting via *fstab* do require that privilege.

✓ AutoFS prevents an NFS client from hanging if an NFS server is down or inaccessible. With the other method, the unavailability of the NFS server may cause the NFS client to hang.

✓ With AutoFS, a share is unmounted automatically if it is not accessed for five minutes by default. With the *fstab* method, the share stays mounted until it is either manually unmounted or the client shuts down.

✓ AutoFS supports wildcard characters and environment variables, which the other method does not support.

How AutoFS Works

The AutoFS service consists of a daemon called *automount* in the userland that mounts configured shares automatically upon access. This daemon is invoked at system boot. It reads the AutoFS master map and creates initial mount point entries, but it does not mount any shares yet. When the service detects a user activity under a mount point during runtime, it mounts the requested file system at that time. If a share remains idle for a certain time period, *automount* unmounts it by itself.

AutoFS Configuration File

The configuration file for the AutoFS service is */etc/autofs.conf*, which AutoFS consults at service startup. Some key directives from this file are shown below along with preset values:

```
master_map_name = auto.master
timeout = 300
negative_timeout = 60
mount_nfs_default_protocol = 4
logging = none
```

There are additional directives available in this file and more can be added to modify the default behavior of the AutoFS service. Table 16-1 describes the above directives.

Directive	Description
master_map_name	Defines the name of the master map. The default is auto.master located in the /etc directory.
timeout	Specifies, in seconds, the maximum idle time after which a share is automatically unmounted. The default is five minutes.
negative_timeout	Expresses, in seconds, a timeout value for failed mount attempts. The default is one minute.
mount_nfs_default_protocol	Sets the default NFS version to be used to mount shares.
logging	Configures a logging level. Options are none, verbose, and debug. The default is none (disabled).

Table 16-1 AutoFS Directives

The directives in the *autofs.conf* file are normally left to their default values, but you can alter them if required.

AutoFS Maps

The AutoFS service needs to know the NFS shares to be mounted and their locations. It also needs to know any specific options to use with mounting them. This information is defined in AutoFS files called *maps*. There are three common AutoFS map types: *master*, *direct*, and *indirect*.

The Master Map

The *auto.master* file located in the */etc* directory is the default master map, as defined in the */etc/autofs.conf* configuration file with the master_map_name directive. This map may be used to define entries for direct and indirect maps. However, it is recommended to store user-defined map files in the */etc/auto.master.d* directory, which the AutoFS service automatically parses at startup. The following presents two samples to explain the format of the map entries:

```
/-          /etc/auto.master.d/auto.direct              # Line 1
/misc       /etc/auto.misc                              # Line 2
```

The two entries are explained below.

The Direct Map

The direct map is used to mount shares automatically on any number of unrelated mount points. Some key points to note when working with direct maps are:

- ✓ Direct mounted shares are always visible to users.
- ✓ Local and direct mounted shares can coexist under one parent directory.
- ✓ Accessing a directory containing many direct mount points mounts all shares.

Each direct map entry places a separate share entry to the */etc/mtab* file, which maintains a list of all mounted file systems whether they are local or remote. This file is updated whenever a local file system, removable file system, or a network share is mounted or unmounted.

Line 1 from above defines a direct map and points to the */etc/auto.master.d/auto.direct* file for mount details.

You may append an option to the line entry in the *auto.master* file above; however, that option will apply to all subentries in the specified map file.

The Indirect Map

The indirect map is preferred over the direct map if you want to mount all shares under one common parent directory. Some key points to note when working with indirect maps are:

- ✓ Indirect mounted shares become visible only after they have been accessed.
- ✓ Local and indirect mounted shares cannot coexist under the same parent directory.
- ✓ Each indirect map puts only one entry in the */etc/mtab* mount table.
- ✓ Accessing a directory containing many indirect mount points shows only the shares that are already mounted.

Line 2 from above represents an indirect map, notifying AutoFS to refer to the */etc/auto.misc* file for mount details. The umbrella mount point */misc* will precede all mount point entries listed in the */etc/auto.misc* file. This indirect map entry is normally used to automount removable file systems, such as CD, DVD, external USB disks, and so on. Any custom indirect map file should be located in the */etc/auto.master.d* directory.

You may append an option to the corresponding line entry in the *auto.master* file above; however, that option will apply to all subentries in the specified map file.

Direct Map vs. Indirect Map

Both direct and indirect maps have their own merits and demerits. By comparing their features, it seems more prudent to use the indirect map for automounting NFS shares. However, this statement may not be true for every environment, as there could be specifics that would dictate which option to go with.

Exercise 16-3: Access NFS Share Using Direct Map

This exercise should be done on *server10* as *user1* with *sudo* where required.

In this exercise, you will configure a direct map to automount the NFS share */common* that is available from *server20*. You will install the relevant software, create a local mount point */autodir*, and set up AutoFS maps to support the automatic mounting. Note that */common* is already mounted to */local* on *server10* (NFS client) via the *fstab* file. There should not be any conflict in configuration or functionality between the two.

1. Install the AutoFS software package called *autofs*:

```
[user1@server10 ~]$ sudo dnf install -y autofs
........
Running transaction
  Preparing        :                                                    1/1
  Installing       : libsss_autofs-2.7.3-4.el9.x86_64                   1/2
  Installing       : autofs-1:5.1.7-31.el9.x86_64                       2/2
  Running scriptlet: autofs-1:5.1.7-31.el9.x86_64                       2/2
  Verifying        : autofs-1:5.1.7-31.el9.x86_64                       1/2
  Verifying        : libsss_autofs-2.7.3-4.el9.x86_64                   2/2
Installed products updated.

Installed:
  autofs-1:5.1.7-31.el9.x86_64          libsss_autofs-2.7.3-4.el9.x86_64

Complete!
```

2. Create a mount point */autodir* using the *mkdir* command:

```
[user1@server10 ~]$ sudo mkdir /autodir
```

3. Edit the */etc/auto.master* file and add the following entry at the beginning of the file. This entry will point the AutoFS service to the *auto.dir* file for additional information.

```
/-   /etc/auto.master.d/auto.dir
```

4. Create */etc/auto.master.d/auto.dir* file and add the mount point, NFS server, and share information to it:

```
/autodir   server20:/common
```

5. Start the AutoFS service now and set it to autostart at system reboots:

```
[user1@server10 ~]$ sudo systemctl enable --now autofs
Created symlink /etc/systemd/system/multi-user.target.wants/autofs.service → /u
sr/lib/systemd/system/autofs.service.
```

6. Verify the operational status of the AutoFS service. Use the -l and --no-pager options to show full details without piping the output to a pager program (the *pg* command in this case).

```
[user1@server10 ~]$ sudo systemctl status autofs -l --no-pager
● autofs.service - Automounts filesystems on demand
     Loaded: loaded (/usr/lib/systemd/system/autofs.service; enabled; vendor pr
eset: disabled)
     Active: active (running) since Sun 2023-02-05 18:13:55 EST; 50s ago
   Main PID: 3746 (automount)
      Tasks: 6 (limit: 10944)
     Memory: 3.8M
        CPU: 100ms
     CGroup: /system.slice/autofs.service
             └─3746 /usr/sbin/automount --systemd-service --dont-check-daemon

Feb 05 18:13:55 server10.example.com systemd[1]: Starting Automounts filesystem
s on demand...
Feb 05 18:13:55 server10.example.com systemd[1]: Started Automounts filesystems
 on demand.
```

7. Run the *ls* command on the mount point */autodir* and then issue the *mount* command to verify that the share is automounted and accessible:

```
[user1@server10 ~]$ ls /autodir
nfsfile
[user1@server10 ~]$ mount | grep autodir
/etc/auto.master.d/auto.dir on /autodir type autofs (rw,relatime,fd=5,pgrp=3746
,timeout=300,minproto=5,maxproto=5,direct,pipe_ino=33821)
server20:/common on /autodir type nfs4 (rw,relatime,vers=4.2,rsize=262144,wsize
=262144,namlen=255,hard,proto=tcp,timeo=600,retrans=2,sec=sys,clientaddr=192.16
8.0.110,local_lock=none,addr=192.168.0.120)
```

Observe the above outcomes. An activity in the mount point (the *ls* command) caused AutoFS to mount the share */common* on */autodir*. The *mount* command output depicts the path of the AutoFS map (*/etc/auto.master.d/auto.dir*), the file system type (autofs), and the options used during the mount process. Wait for five minutes and run the *mount* command again. You'll see that the auto file system has disappeared. A *cd*, *ls*, or another activity in the mount point will bring it back.

This completes the AutoFS setup for an NFS share on the client using a direct map.

Exercise 16-4: Access NFS Share Using Indirect Map

This exercise should be done on *server10* as *user1* with *sudo* where required.

In this exercise, you will configure an indirect map to automount the NFS share */common* that is available from *server20*. You will install the relevant software and set up AutoFS maps to support the automatic mounting. You will observe that the specified mount point "autoindir" is created automatically under */misc*.

Note that */common* is already mounted on the */local* mount point via the *fstab* file and it is also configured via a direct map for automounting on */autodir*. There should occur no conflict in configuration or functionality among the three.

1. Install the *autofs* software package if it is not already there:

```
[user1@server10 ~]$ sudo dnf -y install autofs
Last metadata expiration check: 1:53:35 ago on Sun 05 Feb 2023 04:38:58 PM.
Package autofs-1:5.1.7-31.el9.x86_64 is already installed.
Dependencies resolved.
Nothing to do.
Complete!
```

2. Confirm the entry for the indirect map */misc* in the */etc/auto.master* file exists:

```
[user1@server10 ~]$ grep ^/misc /etc/auto.master
/misc    /etc/auto.misc
```

3. Edit the */etc/auto.misc* file and add the mount point, NFS server, and share information to it:

```
autoindir   server20:/common
```

4. Start the AutoFS service now and set it to autostart at system reboots:

```
[user1@server10 ~]$ sudo systemctl enable --now autofs
Created symlink /etc/systemd/system/multi-user.target.wants/autofs.service → /u
sr/lib/systemd/system/autofs.service.
```

5. Verify the operational status of the AutoFS service. Use the -l and --no-pager options to show full details without piping the output to a pager program (the *pg* command in this case):

```
[user1@server10 ~]$ sudo systemctl status autofs -l --no-pager
● autofs.service - Automounts filesystems on demand
     Loaded: loaded (/usr/lib/systemd/system/autofs.service; enabled; vendor pr
eset: disabled)
     Active: active (running) since Sun 2023-02-05 18:35:13 EST; 10s ago
   Main PID: 3872 (automount)
      Tasks: 6 (limit: 10944)
     Memory: 1.8M
        CPU: 76ms
     CGroup: /system.slice/autofs.service
             └─3872 /usr/sbin/automount --systemd-service --dont-check-daemon

Feb 05 18:35:13 server10.example.com systemd[1]: Starting Automounts filesystem
s on demand...
Feb 05 18:35:13 server10.example.com systemd[1]: Started Automounts filesystems
 on demand.
```

6. Run the *ls* command on the mount point */misc/autoindir* and then *grep* for both *auto.misc* and *autoindir* on the *mount* command output to verify that the share is automounted and accessible:

```
[user1@server10 ~]$ ls /misc/autoindir
nfsfile
[user1@server10 ~]$
[user1@server10 ~]$ mount | egrep 'auto.misc|autoindir'
/etc/auto.misc on /misc type autofs (rw,relatime,fd=10,pgrp=3872,timeout=300,mi
nproto=5,maxproto=5,indirect,pipe_ino=34144)
server20:/common on /misc/autoindir type nfs4 (rw,relatime,vers=4.2,rsize=26214
4,wsize=262144,namlen=255,hard,proto=tcp,timeo=600,retrans=2,sec=sys,clientaddr
=192.168.0.110,local_lock=none,addr=192.168.0.120)
```

Observe the above outcomes. An activity in the mount point (*ls* command in this case) caused AutoFS to mount the share */common* on */misc/autoindir*. The *mount* command output illustrates the path of the AutoFS map (*/etc/auto.misc*), the auto-generated mount point (*/misc/autoindir*), file system type (autofs), and the options used during the mount process. You can use the same umbrella mount point */misc* to mount additional auto-generated mount points.

This mount point will automatically disappear after five minutes of idling. You can verify that by issuing the *mount* command again. A *cd*, *ls*, or another activity in the mount point will bring it back.

This completes the AutoFS setup for an NFS share on the client using an indirect map.

Automounting User Home Directories

AutoFS allows us to automount user home directories by exploiting two special characters in indirect maps. The asterisk (*) replaces the references to specific mount points and the ampersand (&) substitutes the references to NFS servers and shared subdirectories. With user home directories located under */home*, on one or more NFS servers, the AutoFS service will connect with all of them simultaneously when a user attempts to log on to a client. The service will mount only that specific user's home directory rather than the entire */home*. The indirect map entry for this type of substitution is defined in an indirect map, such as */etc/auto.master.d/auto.home*, and will look like:

```
*    -rw   &:/home/&
```

With this entry in place, there is no need to update any AutoFS configuration files if additional NFS servers with */home* shared are added or removed. Similarly, if user home directories are added or deleted, there will be no impact on the functionality of AutoFS. If there is only one NFS server sharing the home directories, you can simply specify its name in lieu of the first & symbol in the above entry.

Exercise 16-5: Automount User Home Directories Using Indirect Map

There are two portions for this exercise. The first portion should be done on *server20* (NFS server) and the second portion on *server10* (NFS client) as *user1* with *sudo* where required.

In the first portion, you will create a user account called *user30* with UID 3000. You will add the */home* directory to the list of NFS shares so that it becomes available for remote mount.

In the second portion, you will create a user account called *user30* with UID 3000, base directory */nfshome*, and no home directory. You will create an umbrella mount point called */nfshome* for mounting the user home directory from the NFS server. You will install the relevant software and establish an indirect map to automount the remote home directory of *user30* under */nfshome*. You will observe that the home directory is automounted under */nfshome* when you sign in as *user30*.

On NFS server *server20*:

1. Create a user account called *user30* with UID 3000 (-u) and assign password "password1":

    ```
    [user1@server20 ~]$ sudo useradd -u 3000 user30
    [user1@server20 ~]$ echo password1 | sudo passwd --stdin user30
    Changing password for user user30.
    passwd: all authentication tokens updated successfully.
    ```

2. Edit the */etc/exports* file and add an entry for */home* (do not modify or remove the previous entry):

```
/home server10(rw)
```

3. Export all the shares listed in the */etc/exports* file:

```
[user1@server20 ~]$ sudo exportfs -avr
exporting server10.example.com:/home
exporting server10.example.com:/common
```

On NFS client *server10*:

1. Install the *autofs* software package if it is not already there:

```
[user1@server10 ~]$ sudo dnf install -y autofs
```

2. Create a user account called *user30* with UID 3000 (-u), base home directory location */nfshome* (-b), no home directory (-M), and password "password1":

```
[user1@server10 ~]$ sudo useradd -u 3000 -b /nfshome -M user30
[user1@server10 ~]$ echo password1 | sudo passwd --stdin user30
Changing password for user user30.
passwd: all authentication tokens updated successfully.
```

This is to ensure that the UID for the user is consistent on the server and the client to avoid access issues.

3. Create the umbrella mount point */nfshome* to automount the user's home directory:

```
[user1@server10 ~]$ sudo mkdir /nfshome
```

4. Edit the */etc/auto.master* file and add the mount point and indirect map location to it:

```
/nfshome   /etc/auto.master.d/auto.home
```

5. Create the */etc/auto.master.d/auto.home* file and add the following information to it:

```
*   -rw   server20:/home/&
```

For multiple user setup, you can replace "user30" with the & character, but ensure that those users exist on both the server and the client with consistent UIDs.

6. Start the AutoFS service now and set it to autostart at system reboots. This step is not required if AutoFS is already running and enabled.

```
[user1@server10 ~]$ sudo systemctl enable --now autofs
Created symlink /etc/systemd/system/multi-user.target.wants/autofs.service → /u
sr/lib/systemd/system/autofs.service.
```

7. Verify the operational status of the AutoFS service. Use the -l and --no-pager options to show full details without piping the output to a pager program (the *pg* command):

```
[user1@server10 ~]$ sudo systemctl status autofs -l --no-pager
● autofs.service - Automounts filesystems on demand
     Loaded: loaded (/usr/lib/systemd/system/autofs.service; enabled; vendor pr
eset: disabled)
     Active: active (running) since Sun 2023-02-05 18:51:51 EST; 17s ago
   Main PID: 3977 (automount)
      Tasks: 7 (limit: 10944)
     Memory: 3.9M
        CPU: 47ms
     CGroup: /system.slice/autofs.service
             └─3977 /usr/sbin/automount --systemd-service --dont-check-daemon

Feb 05 18:51:51 server10.example.com systemd[1]: Stopped Automounts filesystems
 on demand.
Feb 05 18:51:51 server10.example.com systemd[1]: Starting Automounts filesystem
s on demand...
Feb 05 18:51:51 server10.example.com systemd[1]: Started Automounts filesystems
 on demand.
```

8. Log in as *user30* and run the *pwd*, *ls*, and *df* commands for verification:

```
[user1@server10 ~]$ su - user30
Password:
[user1@server10 ~]$ pwd
/nfshome/user30
[user1@server10 ~]$ ls -l
total 0
[user1@server10 ~]$ df -h .
Filesystem              Size  Used Avail Use% Mounted on
server20:/home/user30    17G  4.0G   14G  24% /nfshome/user30
```

The user is successfully logged in with their home directory automounted from the NFS server. The *pwd* command confirms the path. The *df* command verifies the NFS server name and the source home directory path for *user30*, as well as the mount location. You can also use the *mount* command and pipe the output to *grep* for *user30* to view mount details (**mount | grep user30**).

> **EXAM TIP:** You may need to configure AutoFS for mounting a remote user home directory.

This completes the setup for an automounted home directory share for a user.

Chapter Summary

This chapter discussed the sharing and mounting of remote file systems using the Network File System protocol. It elucidated the concepts, benefits, and versions of the NFS service, and described the commands and configuration files involved in NFS management on the server and the client.

Next, we performed an exercise to demonstrate the configuration and sharing of a directory on one of the lab servers (NFS server) and another exercise on the second lab system (NFS client) to mount that share manually and persistently using the standard NFS mount method.

We explored the client-side service called AutoFS for automounting NFS shares. We discussed the concepts, benefits, and components associated with AutoFS, and analyzed its maps. We performed exercises to mount, confirm, and unmount the remote NFS share using both direct and indirect methods.

Finally, we described the AutoFS setting to automount user home directories from the NFS server.

Review Questions

1. The name of the AutoFS service daemon is *autofs*. True or False?
2. What would the line entry */dir1 *(rw)* in the */etc/exports* file mean?
3. What type of AutoFS map would have the */- /etc/auto.media* entry in the *auto.master* file?
4. AutoFS requires *root* privileges to automatically mount a network file system. True or False?
5. What is the default timeout value for a file system before AutoFS unmounts it automatically?
6. Name the three common types of maps that AutoFS support.
7. Arrange the tasks in three different correct sequences to export a share using NFS: (a) update */etc/exports*, (b) add service to firewall, (c) run *exportfs*, (d) install *nfs-utils*, and (e) start nfs service.
8. What would the entry * *server10:/home/&* in an AutoFS indirect map imply?
9. Which command is used to export a share?
10. An NFS server exports a share and an NFS server mounts it. True or False?
11. Which command would you use to unexport a share?
12. What is the name of the NFS server configuration file?
13. What is the name of the AutoFS configuration file and where is it located?

Answers to Review Questions

1. False. The name of the AutoFS service daemon is *automount*.
2. The line entry would export */dir1* in read/write mode to all systems.
3. A direct map.
4. False.
5. Five minutes.
6. The three common AutoFS maps are master, direct, and indirect.
7. d/e/b/a/c, d/e/a/c/b, or d/e/a/b/c.
8. This indirect map entry would mount individual user home directories from *server10*.
9. The *exportfs* command.
10. True.
11. The *exportfs* command with the -u switch.
12. The */etc/nfs.conf* file.
13. The name of the AutoFS configuration file is *autofs.conf* and it is located in the */etc* directory.

Do-It-Yourself Challenge Labs

The following labs are useful to strengthen most of the concepts and topics learned in this chapter. It is expected that you perform the labs without external help. A step-by-step guide is not supplied, as the knowledge and skill required to implement the labs have already been disseminated in the chapter; however, hints to the relevant major topic(s) are included.

Use the lab environment built specifically for end-of-chapter labs. See sub-section "Lab Environment for End-of-Chapter Labs" in Chapter 01 "Local Installation" for details.

Lab 16-1: Configure NFS Share and Automount with Direct Map

As *user1* with *sudo* on *server30*, share directory */sharenfs* (create it) in read/write mode using NFS. On *server40* as *user1* with *sudo*, install the AutoFS software and start the service. Configure the master and a direct map to automount the share on */mntauto* (create it). Run *ls* on */mntauto* to trigger the mount. Use *df -h* to confirm. (Hint: NFS Server and Client Configuration, and Auto File System).

Lab 16-2: Automount NFS Share with Indirect Map

As *user1* with *sudo* on *server40*, configure the master and an indirect map to automount the share under */autoindir* (create it). Run *ls* on */autoindir/sharenfs* to trigger the mount. Use *df -h* to confirm. (Hint: Auto File System).

## Chapter 17

Hostname Resolution and Time Synchronization

This chapter describes the following major topics:

➢ Overview of Domain Name System and hostname resolution

➢ Understand various DNS roles

➢ Analyze entries in resolver configuration files

➢ Perform name resolution using a variety of lookup tools

➢ Describe time synchronization and the role of Network Time Protocol

➢ Comprehend the terms: time source, NTP roles, and stratum levels

➢ Anatomy of the Chrony service configuration file

➢ Configure and verify NTP/Chrony client service

➢ View and set system date and time

RHCSA Objectives:

45. Configure hostname resolution
41. Configure time service clients

Domain Name System is an OS- and hardware-independent network service employed for determining the IP address of a system when its hostname is known, and vice versa. This mechanism is implemented to map human-friendly hostnames to their assigned numeric IP addresses by consulting one or more servers offering the hostname resolution service. This service has been used on the Internet and corporate networks as the de facto standard for this purpose. DNS clients use this service to communicate with remote systems. There are several lookup programs that use DNS to obtain information.

The Chrony service, an implementation of the Network Time Protocol, maintains the clock on the system and keeps it synchronized with a more accurate and reliable source of time. Providing accurate and uniform time for systems on the network allows time-sensitive applications such as monitoring software, backup tools, scheduling utilities, billing systems, file sharing protocols, and authentication programs to perform correctly and precisely. It also aids logging and auditing services to capture and record messages and alerts in log files with accurate timestamps.

DNS and Name Resolution

Domain Name System (DNS) is an inverted tree-like structure employed on the Internet and private networks (including home and corporate networks) as the de facto standard for resolving hostnames to their numeric IP addresses. DNS is platform-independent with support integrated in every operating system. DNS is also referred to as BIND, *Berkeley Internet Name Domain*, which is an implementation of DNS, and it has been the most popular DNS application in use. *Name resolution* is the technique that uses DNS/BIND for hostname lookups.

To understand DNS, a brief discussion of its components and roles is imperative. The following subsections provide a look at the client-side configuration files and commands, along with examples on how to use the tools for resolving hostnames.

DNS Name Space and Domains

The DNS *name space* is a hierarchical organization of all the domains on the Internet. The root of the name space is represented by a period (.). The hierarchy below the root (.) denotes the *top-level domains* (TLDs) with names such as .com, .net, .edu, .org, .gov, .ca, and .de. A DNS *domain* is a collection of one or more systems. Subdomains fall under their parent domains and are separated by a period (.). For example, *redhat.com* is a second-level subdomain that falls under .com, and *bugzilla.redhat.com* is a third-level subdomain that falls under *redhat.com*.

Figure 17-1 exhibits a sample hierarchy of the name space, showing the top three domain levels.

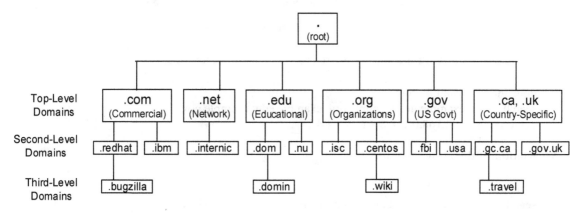

Figure 17-1 Sample DNS Hierarchy

At the deepest level of the hierarchy are the *leaves* (systems, nodes, or any device with an IP address) of the name space. For example, a network switch *net01* in *.travel.gc.ca* subdomain will be known as *net01.travel.gc.ca*. If a period (.) is added to the end of this name to look like *net01.travel.gc.ca.*, it will be referred to as the *Fully Qualified Domain Name* (FQDN) for *net01*.

DNS Roles

From a DNS perspective, a system can be configured to operate as a primary server, secondary server, or client. A DNS server is also referred to as a *nameserver*.

A *primary server* is responsible for its domain (or subdomain). It maintains a master database of all the hostnames and their associated IP addresses that are included in that domain. All changes in the database are done on this server. Each domain must have one primary server with one or more optional *secondary* servers for load balancing and redundancy. A secondary server also stores an updated copy of the master database, and it continues to provide name resolution service in the event the primary server becomes unavailable or inaccessible.

A *DNS client* queries nameservers for name lookups. Every system with access to the Internet or other external networks will have the DNS client functionality configured and operational. Setting up DNS client on Linux involves two text files that are discussed in the next two subsections.

Understanding Resolver Configuration File

The *resolv.conf* file under */etc* is the DNS resolver configuration file where information to support hostname lookups is defined. This file may be edited manually with a text editor. It is referenced by resolver utilities to construct and transmit queries. There are three key directives set in this file—domain, nameserver, and search—and they are described in Table 17-1.

Directive	Description
domain	Identifies the default domain name to be searched for queries
nameserver	Declares up to three DNS server IP addresses to be queried one at a time in the order in which they are listed. Nameserver entries may be defined as separate line items with the directive or on a single line.
search	Specifies up to six domain names, of which the first must be the local domain. No need to define the domain directive if the search directive is used.

Table 17-1 The Resolver Configuration File

A sample entry showing the syntax is provided below for reference:

```
domain      example.com
search      example.net  example.org  example.edu  example.gov
nameserver  192.168.0.1  8.8.8.8  8.8.4.4
```

A variation of the above would be:

```
domain      example.com
search      example.net  example.org  example.edu  example.gov
nameserver  192.168.0.1
nameserver  8.8.8.8
nameserver  8.8.4.4
```

Currently, there are two search and three nameserver entries in the *resolv.conf* file on both *server10* and *server20*. These entries are automatically placed by the NetworkManager service.

```
[user1@server10 ~]$ cat /etc/resolv.conf
# Generated by NetworkManager
search example.com cgocable.net
nameserver 192.168.0.1
nameserver 2001:1970:c06e:c0::93
nameserver 2001:1970:c0c0:6ec0::193
```

On a system with this file absent, the resolver utilities only query the nameserver configured on the localhost, determine the domain name from the hostname of the system, and construct the search path based on the domain name.

Viewing and Adjusting Name Resolution Sources and Order

The *nsswitch.conf* file under */etc* directs the lookup utilities to the correct source to get hostname information. In the presence of multiple sources, this file also identifies the order in which to consult them and an action to be taken next. There are four keywords—success, notfound, unavail, and tryagain—that oversee this behavior, and they are described along with default actions in Table 17-2.

Keyword	Meaning	Default Action
success	Information found in source and provided to the requester	return (do not try the next source)
notfound	Information not found in source	continue (try the next source)
unavail	Source down or not responding; service disabled or not configured	continue (try the next source)
tryagain	Source busy, retry later	continue (try the next source)

Table 17-2 Name Service Source and Order Determination

The following example entry shows the syntax of a relevant entry from the *nsswitch.conf* file. It shows two sources for name resolution: files (*/etc/hosts*) and DNS (*/etc/resolv.conf*).

    hosts: files   dns

Based on the default behavior, the search will terminate if the requested information is found in the *hosts* table. However, you can alter this behavior and instruct the lookup programs to return if the requested information is not found there. The modified entry will look like:

    hosts: files [notfound=return]   dns

This altered entry will ignore the DNS.

See Chapter 15 "Networking, Network Devices, and Network Connections" for details on the /etc/hosts file.

Once the *resolv.conf* and *nsswitch.conf* files are configured appropriately, you can use any of the native client resolver tools for lookups. Common query tools available in RHEL 9 include *dig, host, nslookup,* and *getent.*

Performing Name Resolution with dig

dig (domain information groper) is a DNS lookup utility. It queries the nameserver specified at the command line or consults the *resolv.conf* file to determine the nameservers to be queried. This tool may be used to troubleshoot DNS issues due to its flexibility and verbosity. The following shows a few usage examples.

To get the IP for *redhat.com* using the nameserver listed in the *resolv.conf* file:

    [user1@server10 ~]$ dig redhat.com

    . . . .

```
;; ANSWER SECTION:
redhat.com.                3461    IN       A       52.200.142.250
redhat.com.                3461    IN       A       34.235.198.240

;; Query time: 20 msec
;; SERVER: 2001:1970:c06e:c0::93#53(2001:1970:c06e:c0::93)
;; WHEN: Sun Feb 05 22:28:59 EST 2023
;; MSG SIZE   rcvd: 71
```

The output shows the total time (20 milliseconds) it took to get the result, the IP addresses (52.200.142.250 and 34.235.198.240) of redhat.com, the nameserver IPv6 (2001:1970:xxxxxx) used for the query, query timestamp, the size of the received message (71 bytes), and other information.

To perform a reverse lookup on the redhat.com IP (52.200.142.250), use the -x option with the command:

```
[user1@server10 ~]$ dig -x 209.132.183.105
........
;; ANSWER SECTION:
250.142.200.52.in-addr.arpa. 3600 IN     PTR      ec2-52-200-142-
250.compute-1.amazonaws.com.

;; AUTHORITY SECTION:
142.200.52.in-addr.arpa. 3600    IN       NS       ns1-24-us-east-
1.ec2-rdns.amazonaws.com.
142.200.52.in-addr.arpa. 3600    IN       NS       ns2-24-us-east-
1.ec2-rdns.amazonaws.com.
142.200.52.in-addr.arpa. 3600    IN       NS       ns3-24-us-east-
1.ec2-rdns.amazonaws.com.
142.200.52.in-addr.arpa. 3600    IN       NS       ns4-24-us-east-
1.ec2-rdns.amazonaws.com.

;; Query time: 51 msec
;; SERVER: 2001:1970:c06e:c0::93#53(2001:1970:c06e:c0::93)
;; WHEN: Sun Feb 05 22:33:26 EST 2023
;; MSG SIZE   rcvd: 245
```

Reference the command's manual pages for details and options.

Performing Name Resolution with host

host is an elementary DNS lookup utility that works on the same principles as the *dig* command in terms of nameserver determination. This tool produces lesser data in the output by default; however, you can add the -v option for verbosity.

To perform a lookup on *redhat.com*:

```
[user1@server10 ~]$ host redhat.com
redhat.com has address 52.200.142.250
redhat.com has address 34.235.198.240
redhat.com mail is handled by 10 us-smtp-inbound-2.mimecast.com.
redhat.com mail is handled by 10 us-smtp-inbound-1.mimecast.com.
```

Rerun the above with -v added. The output will be similar to that of the *dig* command.

To perform a reverse lookup on the IP of *redhat.com* using the -v flag to add details:

```
[user1@server10 ~]$ host -v 52.200.142.250
Trying "250.142.200.52.in-addr.arpa"
;; ->>HEADER<<- opcode: QUERY, status: NOERROR, id: 45851
;; flags: qr rd ra; QUERY: 1, ANSWER: 1, AUTHORITY: 0, ADDITIONAL:
 0

;; QUESTION SECTION:
;250.142.200.52.in-addr.arpa.    IN        PTR

;; ANSWER SECTION:
250.142.200.52.in-addr.arpa. 3421 IN      PTR       ec2-52-200-142-250
.compute-1.amazonaws.com.

Received 101 bytes from 2001:1970:c06e:c0::93#53 in 21 ms
```

Refer to the command's manual pages for options and more information.

Performing Name Resolution with nslookup

nslookup queries the nameservers listed in the *resolv.conf* file or specified at the command line. The following shows a few usage examples.

To get the IP for *redhat.com* using nameserver 8.8.8.8 instead of the nameserver defined in *resolv.conf*:

```
[user1@server10 ~]$ nslookup redhat.com 8.8.8.8
Server:         8.8.8.8
Address:        8.8.8.8#53

Non-authoritative answer:
Name:    redhat.com
Address: 52.200.142.250
Name:    redhat.com
Address: 34.235.198.240
```

To perform a reverse lookup on the IP of *redhat.com* using the nameserver from the resolver configuration file:

```
[user1@server10 ~]$ nslookup 52.200.142.250
250.142.200.52.in-addr.arpa     name = ec2-52-200-142-250.compute-
1.amazonaws.com.

Authoritative answers can be found from:
```

Consult the command's manual pages on how to use it in interactive mode.

Performing Name Resolution with getent

The *getent* (*get entries*) command is a rudimentary tool that can fetch matching entries from the databases defined in the *nsswitch.conf* file. This command reads the corresponding database and displays the information if found. For name resolution, use the *hosts* database and *getent* will attempt to resolve the specified hostname or IP address. For instance, run the following for forward and reverse lookups:

```
[user1@server10 ~]$ getent hosts redhat.com
34.235.198.240   redhat.com
52.200.142.250   redhat.com
[user1@server10 ~]$
[user1@server10 ~]$ getent hosts 34.235.198.240
34.235.198.240   ec2-34-235-198-240.compute-1.amazonaws.com
```

Check the command's manual pages for available flags and additional information.

Time Synchronization

Network Time Protocol (NTP) is a networking protocol for synchronizing the system clock with remote time servers for accuracy and reliability. This protocol has been in use with tens of millions of computing devices employing it to synchronize their clocks with tens of thousands of time servers deployed across the globe. Having steady and exact time on networked systems allows time-sensitive applications, such as authentication and email applications, backup and scheduling tools, financial and billing systems, logging and monitoring software, and file and storage sharing protocols, to function with precision.

NTP sends a stream of messages to configured time servers and binds itself to the one with least amount of delay in its responses, the most accurate, and may or may not be the closest distance-wise. The client system maintains a drift in time in a file and references this file for gradual drop in inaccuracy.

RHEL 9 has an implementation of NTP called *Chrony*. Chrony uses the UDP protocol over the well-known port 123. If enabled, it starts at system boot and continuously operates to keep the system clock in sync with a more accurate source of time.

Chrony performs well on computers that are occasionally connected to the network, attached to busy networks, do not run all the time, or have variations in temperature.

Time Sources

A *time source* is any reference device that acts as a provider of time to other devices. The most precise sources of time are the atomic clocks. They use *Universal Time Coordinated* (UTC) for time accuracy. They produce radio signals that radio clocks use for time propagation to computer servers and other devices that require correctness in time. When choosing a time source for a network, preference should be given to the one that takes the least amount of time to respond. This server may or may not be closest physically.

The common sources of time employed on computer networks are the local system clock, an Internet-based public time server, and a radio clock.

The local system clock can be used as a provider of time. This requires the maintenance of correct time on the server either manually or automatically via *cron*. Keep in mind that this server has no way of synchronizing itself with a more reliable and precise external time source. Therefore, using the local system clock as a time server is the least recommended option.

Several public time servers are available over the Internet for general use (visit *www.ntp.org* for a list). These servers are typically operated by government agencies, research and scientific organizations, large software vendors, and universities around the world. One of the systems on the local network is identified and configured to receive time from one or more public time servers. This option is preferred over the use of the local system clock.

RHCSA Red Hat Enterprise Linux 9: Training and Exam Preparation Guide

The official *ntp.org* site also provides a common pool called *pool.ntp.org* for vendors and organizations to register their own NTP servers voluntarily for public use. Examples include *rhel.pool.ntp.org* and *ubuntu.pool.ntp.org* for distribution-specific pools, and *ca.pool.ntp.org* and *oceania.pool.ntp.org* for country and continent/region-specific pools. Under these sub-pools, the owners maintain multiple time servers with enumerated hostnames such as *0.rhel.pool.ntp.org*, *1.rhel.pool.ntp.org*, *2.rhel.pool.ntp.org*, and so on.

A radio clock is regarded as the perfect provider of time, as it receives time updates straight from an atomic clock. *Global Positioning System* (GPS), WWVB, and DCF77 are some popular radio clock methods. A direct use of signals from these sources requires connectivity of some hardware to the computer identified to act as an organizational or site-wide time server.

NTP Roles

From an NTP standpoint, a system can be configured to operate as a primary server, secondary server, peer, or client.

A *primary* server gets time from a time source and provides time to secondary servers or directly to clients.

A *secondary* server receives time from a primary server and can be configured to furnish time to a set of clients to offload the primary or for redundancy. The presence of a secondary server on the network is optional but highly recommended.

A *peer* reciprocates time with an NTP server. All peers work at the same stratum level, and all of them are considered equally reliable.

A *client* receives time from a primary or a secondary server and adjusts its clock accordingly.

Stratum Levels

As mentioned, there are different types of time sources available so you can synchronize the system clock. These time sources are categorized hierarchically into several levels that are referred to as *stratum levels* based on their distance from the reference clocks (atomic, radio, and GPS). The reference clocks operate at stratum level 0 and are the most accurate provider of time with little to no delay. Besides stratum 0, there are fifteen additional levels that range from 1 to 15. Of these, servers operating at stratum 1 are considered perfect, as they get time updates directly from a stratum 0 device. See Figure 17-2 for a sample hierarchy.

A stratum 0 device cannot be used on the network directly. It is attached to a computer, which is then configured to operate at stratum 1. Servers functioning at stratum 1 are called *time servers* and they can be set up to deliver time to stratum 2 servers. Similarly, a stratum 3 server can be configured to synchronize its time with a stratum 2 server and deliver time to the next lower-level servers, and so on. Servers sharing the same stratum can be configured as peers to exchange time updates with one another.

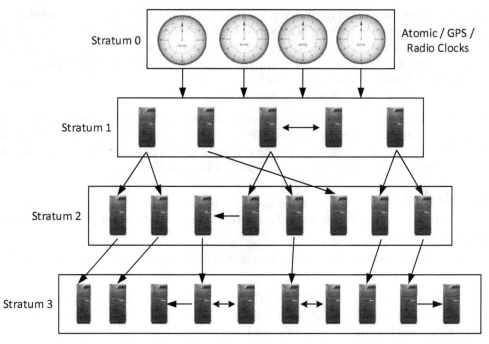

Figure 17-2 NTP Stratum Levels

There are numerous public NTP servers available for free that synchronize time. They normally operate at higher stratum levels such as 2 and 3.

Chrony Configuration File

The key configuration file for the Chrony service is *chrony.conf* located in the */etc* directory. This file is referenced by the Chrony daemon at startup to determine the sources to synchronize the clock, the log file location, and other details. This file can be modified by hand to set or alter directives as required. Some common directives used in this file along with real or mock values are presented below:

```
driftfile     /var/lib/chrony/drift
logdir        /var/log/chrony
pool          0.rhel.pool.ntp.org  iburst
server        server20s8.example.com  iburst
server        127.127.1.0
peer          prodntp1.abc.net
```

Table 17-3 describes these directives.

Directive	Description
driftfile	Indicates the location and name of the drift file to be used to record the rate at which the system clock gains or losses time. This data is used by Chrony to maintain local system clock accuracy.
logdir	Sets the directory location to store the log files in

Directive	Description
pool	Defines the hostname that represents a pool of time servers. Chrony binds itself with one of the servers to get updates. In case of a failure of that server, it automatically switches the binding to another server within the pool. The iburst option dictates the Chrony service to send the first four update requests to the time server every 2 seconds. This allows the daemon to quickly bring the local clock closer to the time server at startup.
server	Defines the hostname or IP address of a single time server. The IP 127.127.1.0 is a special address that epitomizes the local system clock.
peer	Identifies the hostname or IP address of a time server running at the same stratum level. A peer provides time to a server as well as receives time from the same server.

Table 17-3 Chrony Directives

There are plenty of other directives and options available with Chrony that may be defined in this file. Use **man chrony.conf** for details.

Chrony Daemon and Command

The Chrony service runs as a daemon program called *chronyd* that handles time synchronization in the background. It uses the configuration defined in the */etc/chrony.conf* file at startup and sets its behavior accordingly. If the local clock requires a time adjustment, Chrony takes multiple small steps toward minimizing the gap rather than doing it abruptly in a single step. There are a number of additional options available that may be passed to the service daemon if required.

The Chrony service has a command line program called *chronyc* available that can be employed to monitor the performance of the service and control its runtime behavior. There are a few subcommands available with *chronyc*; the *sources* and *tracking* subcommands list current sources of time and view performance statistics, respectively.

Exercise 17-1: Configure NTP Client

This exercise should be done on *server10* as *user1* with *sudo* where required.

In this exercise, you will install the Chrony software package and activate the service without making any changes to the default configuration. You will validate the binding and operation.

1. Install the Chrony package using the *dnf* command:

```
[user1@server10 ~]$ sudo dnf -y install chrony
Package chrony-4.2-1.el9.x86_64 is already installed.
Dependencies resolved.
Nothing to do.
Complete!
```

The software is already installed on the system.

2. Ensure that preconfigured public time server entries are present in the */etc/chrony.conf* file:

```
[user1@server10 ~]$ grep -E 'pool|server' /etc/chrony.conf | grep -v ^#
pool 2.rhel.pool.ntp.org iburst
```

There is a single pool entry set in the file by default. This pool name is backed by multiple NTP servers behind the scenes.

3. Start the Chrony service and set it to autostart at reboots:

```
[user1@server10 ~]$ sudo systemctl --now enable chronyd
Created symlink /etc/systemd/system/multi-user.target.wants/chronyd.service → /usr/li
b/systemd/system/chronyd.service.
```

4. Examine the operational status of Chrony:

```
[user1@server10 ~]$ sudo systemctl status chronyd --no-pager -l
● chronyd.service - NTP client/server
     Loaded: loaded (/usr/lib/systemd/system/chronyd.service; enabled; vend
or preset: enabled)
     Active: active (running) since Mon 2023-02-06 07:28:24 EST; 8s left
       Docs: man:chronyd(8)
             man:chrony.conf(5)
    Process: 2832 ExecStart=/usr/sbin/chronyd $OPTIONS (code=exited, status
=0/SUCCESS)
   Main PID: 2835 (chronyd)
      Tasks: 1 (limit: 10944)
     Memory: 1.2M
        CPU: 116ms
     CGroup: /system.slice/chronyd.service
             └─2835 /usr/sbin/chronyd -F 2

Feb 06 07:28:24 server10.example.com systemd[1]: Starting NTP client/server
...
........
```

The service has started successfully and it is set for autostart.

5. Inspect the binding status using the *sources* subcommand with *chronyc*:

```
[user1@server10 ~]$ chronyc sources
MS Name/IP address         Stratum Poll Reach LastRx Last sample
===============================================================================
^- 2607:5300:201:3100::345c      5   6   377    17  +2414us[+1827us] +/-   24ms
^* ntp3.torix.ca                 1   6   377    21   -571us[-1160us] +/- 7250us
^- 2001:470:b2de::1              2   6   377    89  +2240us[+1781us] +/-   51ms
^- muug.ca                       2   6   377    32  -1309us[-1896us] +/-  103ms
```

The output shows the information in eight columns. Columns 1 to 4—M, S, Name/IP address, and Stratum—illustrate the mode, state, hostname/IP, and stratum level of the source. The ^ means the source is a server and the * implies current association with the source.

Columns 4 to 8—Poll, Reach, LastRx, and Last Sample—display the polling rate (6 means 64 seconds), reachability register (377 indicates a valid response was received), how long ago the last sample was received, and the offset between the local clock and the source at the last measurement. Check out the manual pages of the *chronyc* command and search for the section 'sources' for additional details.

The second time source *ntp3.torix.ca* from the top in the output depicts that *server10* is bound to it. This association is identified with the asterisk character (*) beside the time server.

6. Display the clock performance using the *tracking* subcommand with *chronyc*:

```
[user1@server10 ~]$ chronyc tracking
Reference ID    : CE6C0085 (ntp3.torix.ca)
Stratum         : 2
Ref time (UTC)  : Mon Feb 06 12:47:35 2023
System time     : 0.000830334 seconds fast of NTP time
Last offset     : +0.000982684 seconds
RMS offset      : 0.014357651 seconds
Frequency       : 0.000 ppm fast
Residual freq   : +1.334 ppm
Skew            : 18.330 ppm
Root delay      : 0.022933554 seconds
Root dispersion : 0.002992374 seconds
Update interval : 128.7 seconds
Leap status     : Normal
```

Rows 1 and 2 in the above output identify the current source of time (Reference ID) and the stratum level it is configured at (Stratum). Row 3 shows the reference time at which the last measurement from the time source was processed (Ref time). Row 4 displays the local time offset from the NTP time (System time). Row 5 depicts the last reported offset from the NTP server (Last offset). Row 6 identifies the frequency at which time adjustments are occurring (Frequency). The rest of the rows show additional information. Check out the manual pages of the *chronyc* command and search for the section "tracking" for additional details.

> **EXAM TIP:** You will not have access to the outside network during the exam. You will need to point your system to an NTP server available on the exam network. Simply comment the default server/pool directive(s) and add a single directive "server <hostname>" to the file. Replace <hostname> with the NTP server name or its IP address as provided.

The concludes the exercise.

Displaying and Setting System Date and Time

System date and time can be viewed and manually adjusted with native Linux tools such as the *timedatectl* command. This command can modify the date, time, and time zone. When executed without any option, as shown below, it outputs the local time, Universal time, RTC time (*real-time clock*, a battery-backed hardware clock located on the system board), time zone, and the status of the NTP service:

```
[user1@server10 ~]$ timedatectl
               Local time: Mon 2023-02-06 07:52:31 EST
           Universal time: Mon 2023-02-06 12:52:31 UTC
                 RTC time: Mon 2023-02-06 12:52:31
                Time zone: America/Toronto (EST, -0500)
System clock synchronized: yes
              NTP service: active
          RTC in local TZ: no
```

This command requires that the NTP/Chrony service is deactivated in order to make time adjustments. Run the *timedatectl* command as follows to turn off NTP and verify:

```
[user1@server10 ~]$ sudo timedatectl set-ntp false
[user1@server10 ~]$ timedatectl | grep NTP
            NTP service: inactive
```

To modify the current date to February 28, 2023, and confirm:

```
[user1@server10 ~]$ sudo timedatectl set-time 2023-02-28
[user1@server10 ~]$ timedatectl
                Local time: Tue 2023-02-28 00:00:03 EST
            Universal time: Tue 2023-02-28 05:00:03 UTC
                  RTC time: Tue 2023-02-28 05:00:03
                 Time zone: America/Toronto (EST, -0500)
System clock synchronized: no
               NTP service: inactive
           RTC in local TZ: no
```

To change both date and time in one go (March 18, 2023 11:20 p.m.):

```
[user1@server10 ~]$ sudo timedatectl set-time "2023-03-18 23:20"
[user1@server10 ~]$ timedatectl
                Local time: Sat 2023-03-18 23:20:03 EDT
            Universal time: Sun 2023-03-19 03:20:03 UTC
                  RTC time: Sun 2023-03-19 03:20:04
                 Time zone: America/Toronto (EDT, -0400)
System clock synchronized: no
               NTP service: inactive
           RTC in local TZ: no
```

To reactivate NTP:

```
[user1@server10 ~]$ sudo timedatectl set-ntp true
[user1@server10 ~]$ timedatectl | grep NTP
            NTP service: active
```

Check out the manual pages of the *timedatectl* command for more subcommands and usage examples.

Alternatively, you can use the *date* command to view or modify the system date and time.

To view current date and time:

```
[user1@server10 ~]$ date
Mon 06 Feb 2023 08:01:22 AM EST
```

To change the date and time to February 11, 2023, 8:00 a.m.:

```
[user1@server10 ~]$ sudo date --set "2023-02-11 8:00"
Sat 11 Feb 2023 08:00:00 AM EST
```

There are many options available with the *date* command. Consult its manual pages for details.

To return the system to the current date and time execute **sudo timedatectl set-ntp** with the **false** and then with the **true** argument.

Chapter Summary

The focus of this chapter was on two topics: hostname resolution and network time synchronization.

The chapter began with a discussion of DNS and name resolution. We discussed the concepts and roles, analyzed the resolver configuration file, and examined the source/order determination file. We added required entries to the resolver configuration file and tested the functionality by employing client tools for hostname lookup.

We concluded the chapter with a deliberation of Network Time Protocol, what role it plays in keeping the clocks synchronized, and what is its relationship with the Chrony service. We explored various sources for obtaining time, different roles that systems could play, and the strata paradigm. We analyzed the configuration file to understand some key directives and their possible settings. We performed an exercise to configure the service, display clock association, and analyze the results. We also employed a couple of other RHEL tools to display the system time and set it instantly.

Review Questions

1. Provide the maximum number of nameservers that can be defined in the resolver configuration file.
2. What is the purpose of a drift file in Chrony/NTP?
3. The Chrony client is preconfigured when the *chrony* software package is installed. You just need to start the service to synchronize the clock. True or False?
4. List any three DNS lookup tools.
5. List two utilities that you can use to change system time.
6. What is a relative distinguished name in a DNS hierarchy?
7. What would you add to the Chrony configuration file if you want to use the local system clock as the provider of time?
8. BIND is an implementation of Domain Name System. True or False?
9. Define time source.
10. Name the three DNS roles that a RHEL system can play.
11. Chrony is an implementation of the Network Time Protocol. True or False?
12. What is the name and location of the DNS resolver file?
13. What stratum level do two peer time sources operate on a network?
14. What would you run to check the NTP bind status with time servers?
15. Define DNS name space.
16. Name the four Chrony/NTP roles that a RHEL system can play.
17. Which file defines the name resolution sources and controls the order in which they are consulted?
18. What is the filename and directory location for the Chrony configuration file?

Answers to Review Questions

1. Three.
2. The purpose of a drift file is to keep track of the rate at which the system clock gains or losses time.
3. True.
4. Name resolution tools are *dig*, *host*, *getent*, and *nslookup*.
5. The *timedatectl* and *date* utilities can be used to modify the system time.

6. A relative distinguished name represents individual components of a distinguished name.
7. You will add "server 127.127.1.0" to the Chrony configuration file and restart the service.
8. True.
9. A time source is a reference device that provides time to other devices.
10. From a DNS perspective, a RHEL machine can be a primary server, a secondary server, or a client.
11. True.
12. The DNS resolver file is called *resolv.conf* and it is located in the */etc* directory.
13. Two peers on a network operate at the same stratum level.
14. You will run *chronyc sources* to check the binding status.
15. DNS name space is a hierarchical organization of all the domains on the Internet.
16. From a Chrony/NTP standpoint, a RHEL machine can be a primary server, a secondary server, a peer, or a client.
17. The */etc/nsswitch.conf* file.
18. The name of the Chrony configuration file is *chrony.conf* and it is located in the */etc* directory.

Do-It-Yourself Challenge Labs

The following labs are useful to strengthen most of the concepts and topics learned in this chapter. It is expected that you perform the labs without external help. A step-by-step guide is not supplied, as the knowledge and skill required to implement the labs have already been disseminated in the chapter; however, hints to the relevant major topic(s) are included.

Use the lab environment built specifically for end-of-chapter labs. See sub-section "Lab Environment for End-of-Chapter Labs" in Chapter 01 "Local Installation" for details.

Lab 17-1: Configure Chrony

As *user1* with *sudo* on *server40*, install Chrony and mark the service for autostart on reboots. Edit the Chrony configuration file and comment all line entries that begin with "pool" or "server". Go to the end of the file, and add a new line "server 127.127.1.0". Start the Chrony service and run *chronyc sources* to confirm the binding. (Hint: Time Synchronization).

Lab 17-2: Modify System Date and Time

As *user1* with *sudo* on *server40*, execute the *date* and *timedatectl* commands to check the current system date and time. Identify the distinctions between the two outputs. Use *timedatectl* and change the system date to a future date. Issue the *date* command and change the system time to one hour ahead of the current time. Observe the new date and time with both commands. Reset the date and time to the current actual time by disabling and re-enabling the NTP service using the *timedatectl* command. (Hint: Time Synchronization).

Chapter 18

The Secure Shell Service

This chapter describes the following major topics:

➢ Understand the OpenSSH service, versions, and algorithms

➢ Overview of encryption techniques and authentication methods

➢ Describe OpenSSH administration commands and configuration files

➢ Configure private/public key-based authentication

➢ Access OpenSSH server from other Linux systems

➢ Use OpenSSH client tools to transfer files

➢ Synchronize files remotely over OpenSSH

RHCSA Objectives:

04. Access remote systems using ssh
25. Securely transfer files between systems
54. Configure key-based authentication for SSH

Secure Shell is a network service that delivers a secure mechanism for data transmission between source and destination systems over insecure network paths. It provides a set of utilities that allows users to generate key pairs and use them to set up trusted logins between systems for themselves.

Additional utilities in the set gives remote users the ability to log in, execute commands, and transfer files securely over encrypted network channels. These tools have predominantly supplanted their insecure counterparts in the corporate world.

The OpenSSH Service

Secure Shell (SSH) delivers a secure mechanism for data transmission between source and destination systems over IP networks. It was designed to replace the old remote login programs that transmitted user passwords in clear text and data unencrypted. SSH employs digital signatures for user authentication with encryption to secure a communication channel. As a result, this makes it extremely hard for unauthorized people to gain access to passwords or the data in transit. It also monitors the data being transferred throughout a session to ensure integrity. SSH includes a set of utilities—*ssh* and *sftp*—for remote users to log in, transfer files, and execute commands securely.

Common Encryption Techniques

Encryption is a way of scrambling information with the intent to conceal the real information from unauthorized access. OpenSSH can utilize various encryption techniques during an end-to-end communication session between two entities (client and server). The two common techniques are *symmetric* and *asymmetric*. They are also referred to as *secret key encryption* and *public key encryption* techniques.

Symmetric Technique

This technique uses a single key called a *secret* key that is generated as a result of a negotiation process between two entities at the time of their initial contact. Both sides use the same secret key during subsequent communication for data encryption and decryption.

Asymmetric Technique

This technique uses a combination of *private* and *public* keys, which are randomly generated and mathematically related strings of alphanumeric characters attached to messages being exchanged. The client transmutes the information with a *public* key and the server decrypts it with the paired *private* key. The private key must be kept secure since it is private to a single sender; the public key is disseminated to clients. This technique is used for channel encryption as well as user authentication.

Authentication Methods

Once an encrypted channel is established between the client and server, additional negotiations take place between the two to authenticate the user trying to access the server. OpenSSH offers several methods for this purpose; they are listed below in the order in which they are attempted during the authentication process:

- GSSAPI-based (*Generic Security Service Application Program Interface*) authentication
- Host-based authentication
- Public key-based authentication
- Challenge-response authentication
- Password-based authentication

Let's review each one in detail.

GSSAPI-Based Authentication

GSSAPI provides a standard interface that allows security mechanisms, such as Kerberos, to be plugged in. OpenSSH uses this interface and the underlying Kerberos for authentication. With this method, an exchange of tokens takes place between the client and server to validate user identity.

Host-Based Authentication

This type of authentication allows a single user, a group of users, or all users on the client to be authenticated on the server. A user may be configured to log in with a matching username on the server or as a different user that already exists there. For each user that requires an automatic entry on the server, a *~/.shosts* file is set up containing the client name or IP address, and, optionally, a different username.

The same rule applies to a group of users or all users on the client that require access to the server. In that case, the setup is done in the */etc/ssh/shosts.equiv* file on the server.

Private/Public Key-Based Authentication

This method uses a private/public key combination for user authentication. The user on the client has a private key and the server stores the corresponding public key. At the login attempt, the server prompts the user to enter the passphrase associated with the key and logs the user in if the passphrase and key are validated.

Challenge-Response Authentication

This method is based on the response(s) to one or more arbitrary challenge questions that the user has to answer correctly in order to be allowed to log in to the server.

Password-Based Authentication

This is the last fall back option. The server prompts the user to enter their password. It checks the password against the stored entry in the *shadow* file and allows the user in if the password is confirmed.

Of the five authentication methods, the password-based method is common and requires no further explanation. The GSSAPI-based, host-based, and challenge-response methods are beyond the scope of this book. The public/private authentication and encryption methods will be the focus in the remainder of this chapter.

OpenSSH Protocol Version and Algorithms

OpenSSH has evolved over the years. Its latest and the default version in RHEL 9, version 2, has numerous enhancements, improvements, and sophisticated configuration options. It supports various algorithms for data encryption and user authentication (digital signatures) such as RSA, DSA, and ECDSA. RSA is more prevalent than the rest partly because it supports both encryption and authentication. In contrast, DSA and ECDSA are restricted to authentication only. These algorithms are used to generate public and private key pairs for the asymmetric technique.

RSA stands for *Rivest-Shamir-Adleman*, who first published this algorithm, DSA for *Digital Signature Algorithm*, and ECDSA is an acronym for *Elliptic Curve Digital Signature Algorithm*.

OpenSSH Packages

OpenSSH has three software packages that are of interest. These are *openssh*, *openssh-clients*, and *openssh-server*. The *openssh* package provides the *ssh-keygen* command and some library routines; the *openssh-clients* package includes commands, such as *sftp*, *ssh*, and *ssh-copy-id*, and a client configuration file */etc/ssh/ssh_config*; and the *openssh-server* package contains the *sshd* service daemon, server configuration file */etc/ssh/sshd_config*, and library routines. By default, all three packages are installed during OS installation.

OpenSSH Server Daemon and Client Commands

The OpenSSH server program *sshd* is preconfigured and operational on new RHEL installations, allowing remote users to log in to the system using an ssh client program such as PuTTY or the *ssh* command. This daemon listens on well-known TCP port 22 as documented in the */etc/ssh/sshd_config* file with the Port directive.

A discussion around the *scp* command has been removed from the book, as this tool is not recommended to be used due to some serious security flaws; use *sftp* instead.

The client software includes plenty of utilities such as those listed and described in Table 18-1.

Command	Description
sftp	A secure remote file transfer program
ssh	A secure remote login command
ssh-copy-id	Copies public key to remote systems
ssh-keygen	Generates and manages private and public key pairs

Table 18-1 OpenSSH Client Tools

The use of these commands is demonstrated in the following subsections.

Server Configuration File

The OpenSSH service *sshd* has a configuration file that defines default global settings on how it should operate. This file is located in the */etc/ssh* directory and called *sshd_config*. There are a number of directives preset in this file that affect all inbound ssh communication and are tuned to work as-is for most use cases. In addition, the */var/log/secure* log file is used to capture authentication messages.

A few directives with their default values from the *sshd_config* file are displayed below:

```
[user1@server10 ~]$ sudo cat /etc/ssh/sshd_config
#Port                             22
#Protocol                         2
ListenAddress                     0.0.0.0
SyslogFacility                    AUTHPRIV
#LogLevel                         INFO
PermitRootLogin                   yes
#PubkeyAuthentication             yes
AuthorizedKeysFile                .ssh/authorized_keys
PasswordAuthentication            yes
#PermitEmptyPasswords             no
ChallengeResponseAuthentication   no
UsePAM                            yes
X11Forwarding                     yes
```

The above directives are elaborated in Table 18-2.

Directive	Description
Port	Specifies the port number to listen on. Default is 22.
Protocol	Specifies the default protocol version to use.
ListenAddress	Sets the local addresses the sshd service should listen on. Default is to listen on all local addresses.
SyslogFacility	Defines the facility code to be used when logging messages to the /var/log/secure file. This is based on the configuration in the /etc/rsyslog.conf file. Default is AUTHPRIV.
LogLevel	Identifies the level of criticality for the messages to be logged. Default is INFO.
PermitRootLogin	Allows or disallows the root user to log in directly to the system. Default is yes.
PubKeyAuthentication	Enables or disables public key-based authentication. Default is yes.
AuthorizedKeysFile	Sets the name and location of the file containing a user's authorized keys. Default is ~/.ssh/authorized_keys.
PasswordAuthentication	Enables or disables local password authentication. Default is yes.
PermitEmptyPasswords	Allows or disallows the use of null passwords. Default is no.

Directive	Description
ChallengeResponseAuthentication	Enables or disables challenge-response authentication mechanism. Default is yes.
UsePAM	Enables or disables user authentication via PAM. If enabled, only root will be able to run the sshd daemon. Default is yes.
X11Forwarding	Allows or disallows remote access to graphical applications. Default is yes.

Table 18-2 OpenSSH Server Configuration File

There are many more settings available that may be added to the file for additional control. Check out the manual pages of the *sshd_config* file (**man 5 sshd_config**) for details.

Client Configuration File

Each RHEL client machine that uses ssh to access a remote OpenSSH server has a local configuration file that directs how the client should behave. This file, *ssh_config*, is located in the */etc/ssh* directory. There are a number of directives preset in this file that affect all outbound ssh communication and are tuned to work as-is for most use cases.

A few directives with their default values from the *ssh_config* file are displayed below:

```
[user1@server10 ~]$ sudo more /etc/ssh/ssh_config
# Host   *
# ForwardX11              no
# PasswordAuthentication  yes
# StrictHostKeyChecking   ask
# IdentityFile            ~/.ssh/id_rsa
# IdentityFile            ~/.ssh/id_dsa
# Port                    22
# Protocol                2
```

The above directives are described in Table 18-3.

Directive	Description
Host	Container that declares directives applicable to one host, a group of hosts, or all hosts. It ends when another occurrence of Host or Match is encountered. Default is *, which sets global defaults for all hosts.
ForwardX11	Enables or disables automatic redirection of X11 traffic over SSH connections. Default is no.
PasswordAuthentication	Allows or disallows password authentication. Default is yes.
StrictHostKeyChecking	Controls (1) whether to add host keys (host fingerprints) to ~/.ssh/known_hosts when accessing a host for the first time, and (2) what to do when the keys of a previously accessed host mismatch with what is stored in ~/.ssh/known_hosts. Options are: **no:** adds new host keys and ignores changes to existing keys.

Directive	Description
	yes: adds new host keys and disallows connections to hosts with non-matching keys.
	accept-new: adds new host keys and disallows connections to hosts with non-matching keys.
	ask (default): prompts whether to add new host keys and disallows connections to hosts with non-matching keys.
IdentityFile	Defines the name and location of a file that stores a user's private key for their identity validation. Defaults are id_rsa, id_dsa, and id_ecdsa based on the type of algorithm used. Their corresponding public key files with .pub extension are also stored at the same directory location.
Port	Sets the port number to listen on. Default is 22.
Protocol	Specifies the default protocol version to use

Table 18-3 OpenSSH Client Configuration File

The *~/.ssh* directory does not exist by default; it is created when a user executes the *ssh-keygen* command for the first time to generate a key pair or connects to a remote ssh server and accepts its host key for the first time. In the latter case, the client stores the server's host key locally in a file called *known_hosts* along with its hostname or IP address. On subsequent access attempts, the client will use this information to verify the server's authenticity.

There are a lot more settings available that may be added to the file for additional control. Check out the manual pages of the *ssh_config* file (**man 5 ssh_config**) for details.

System Access and File Transfer

A user must log in to the Linux system in order to use it or transfer files. The login process identifies the user to the system. For accessing a RHEL system remotely, use the *ssh* command, and the *sftp* command for copying files. These tools require either a resolvable hostname of the target system or its IP address in order to establish a connection. Both commands are secure and may be used over secure and unsecure network channels for data exchange.

The following subsections and exercises describe multiple access scenarios including accessing a RHEL system (*server20*) from another RHEL system (*server10*) and a Windows computer, accessing a RHEL system (*server20*) using ssh keys, and transferring files using *sftp*.

Exercise 18-1: Access RHEL System from Another RHEL System

This exercise should be done on *server10* and *server20* as *user1*.

This exercise works under two assumptions: (1) *user1* exists on both *server10* and *server20*, and (2) hostname and IP mapping is in place in the */etc/hosts* file (Chapter 16). Use the IP address in lieu of the hostname if the mapping is unavailable for *server20*.

In this exercise, you will issue the *ssh* command as *user1* on *server10* to log in to *server20*. You will run appropriate commands on *server20* for validation. You will log off and return to the originating system.

1. Issue the *ssh* command as *user1* on *server10*:

```
[user1@server10 ~]$ ssh server20
The authenticity of host 'server20 (192.168.0.120)' can't be established.
ED25519 key fingerprint is SHA256:RATBqZmkp4BOMGNQqAp7Ic5i7I5RX0XfUEp5zlp9c
This key is not known by any other names
Are you sure you want to continue connecting (yes/no/[fingerprint])? yes
Warning: Permanently added 'server20' (ED25519) to the list of known hosts.
user1@server20's password:
Register this system with Red Hat Insights: insights-client --register
Create an account or view all your systems at https://red.ht/insights-dashb
Last login: Sun Feb  5 21:09:12 2023 from 192.168.0.3
```

Answer 'yes' to the question presented and press Enter to continue. This step adds the hostname of *server20* to a file called *known_hosts* under */home/user1/.ssh* directory on the originating computer (*server10*). This message will not reappear on subsequent login attempts to *server20* for this user. Enter the correct password for *user1* to be allowed in. You will be placed in the home directory of *user1* on *server20*. The command prompt will reflect that information.

2. Issue the basic Linux commands *whoami*, *hostname*, and *pwd* to confirm that you are logged in as *user1* on *server20* and placed in the correct home directory:

```
[user1@server20 ~]$ whoami
user1
[user1@server20 ~]$ hostname
server20.example.com
[user1@server20 ~]$ pwd
/home/user1
[user1@server20 ~]$
```

3. Run the *logout* or the *exit* command or simply press the key combination Ctrl+d to log off *server20* and return to *server10*:

```
[user1@server20 ~]$ exit
logout
Connection to server20 closed.
[user1@server10 ~]$
```

This concludes the exercise.

If you wish to log on as a different user such as *user2* (assuming *user2* exists on the target server *server20*), you may run the *ssh* command in either of the following ways:

```
[user1@server10 ~]$ ssh -l user2 server20
[user1@server10 ~]$ ssh user2@server20
```

The above will allow you to log in if the password entered for *user2* is valid.

Exercise 18-2: Generate, Distribute, and Use SSH Keys

This exercise should be done on *server10* and *server20* as *user1* and *sudo* where required.

In this exercise, you will generate a passwordless ssh key pair using RSA algorithm for *user1* on *server10*. You will display the private and public file contents. You will distribute the public key to *server20* and attempt to log on to *server20* from *server10*. You will show the log file message for the login attempt.

1. Log on to *server10* as *user1*.

2. Generate RSA keys without a password (-N) and without detailed output (-q). Press Enter when prompted to provide the filename to store the private key.

   ```
   [user1@server10 ~]$ ssh-keygen -N "" -q
   Enter file in which to save the key (/home/user1/.ssh/id rsa):
   ```

The content of the *id_rsa* (private key) file is shown below:

   ```
   [user1@server10 ~]$ cat .ssh/id rsa
   -----BEGIN OPENSSH PRIVATE KEY-----
   b3BlbnNzaC1rZXktdjEAAAAABG5vbmUAAAEbm9uZQAAAAAAAABAAAB1wAAAdzc2gtcn
   NhAAAAAwEAAQAAAYEAyi9uKKFjA7F1kcApw7F3hKV6rb2hfJ+jY1uMNmWb/VrXrFkvNvlu
   BYY2ZOwAjGJMy41VkLj8cxyzkZcq5NCBCUu45XKFVzT+YCx/2tsHxySgob7lRNmF2TApn2
   o44Htjz/mZB6pJD7DaOP5FX+PCOZiE+ZBPHM8cmYCQzoi6ZaBauO92cg7Gj2pKAQIO4XWD
   ........
   ```

The content of the *id_rsa.pub* (public key) file is displayed below:

   ```
   [user1@server10 ~]$ cat .ssh/id rsa.pub
   ssh-rsa AAAAB3NzaC1yc2EAAAADAQABAAABgQDKL24ooWMDsXWRwCnDsXeEpxQtva
   9WtesWS82+W4FhjZk7ACMYkzLjVWQuPxzHLORlyrk0IEJS7jlcoVXNP5gLH/a2wfHJ
   nfajjge2PP+ZkHqkkPsNo4/kVf48LRmIT5kE8czxyZgJDOiLploFq473ZyDsaPakoB
   4KmqVaaHRLJxF2o7dBQ6b+08O6LCoRfflvc6ZqjmhLJrXjargrATwqLP3n16y8DKr3
   +WrMXFZ3aLG85/xnXQALoEoiOvnvkGzGs14t6I1uufTuUyyNiNBzcHLYT4Teaocupj
   7awS5ZO45WfmWG3eiBQYgLaWpApovf1y2jsd7vvI+0SnlcMgvFXglZcd5IieIkDjX/
   OEC2euOAut3HxANMtXFo1Ow73n97tDUuAANcr6KbpbI9il/GN3vZCcMbFKDv6REigH
   user1@server10.example.com
   ```

3. Copy the public key file to *server20* under */home/user1/.ssh* directory. Accept the fingerprints for *server20* when prompted (only presented on the first login attempt). Enter the password for *user1* set on *server20* to continue with the file copy. The public key will be copied as *authorized_keys*.

   ```
   [user1@server10 ~]$ ssh-copy-id server20
   /usr/bin/ssh-copy-id: INFO: Source of key(s) to be installed: "/home/
   /id rsa.pub"
   /usr/bin/ssh-copy-id: INFO: attempting to log in with the new key(s),
    out any that are already installed
   /usr/bin/ssh-copy-id: INFO: 1 key(s) remain to be installed -- if you
   ted now it is to install the new keys
   user1@server20's password:

   Number of key(s) added: 1

   Now try logging into the machine, with:   "ssh 'server20'"
   and check to make sure that only the key(s) you wanted were added.
   ```

At the same time, this command also creates or updates the *known_hosts* file on *server10* and stores the fingerprints for *server20* in it. Here is what is currently stored in it:

```
[user1@server10 ~]$ cat .ssh/known_hosts
server20 ssh-ed25519 AAAAC3NzaC11ZDI1NTE5AAAAIAqaKM2bW7L2gxRii0gu3
8wf71lzkIo
server20 ssh-rsa AAAAB3NzaC1yc2EAAAADAQABAAABgQC3wWjCi5XCnveMz10dq
LouAzO4IH72NsqcLKJe7RjhVyLVsfkkv4rw6VwGo+uLzCbfCiEyLA+LGGaXlwI7kpT
```

4. On *server10*, run the *ssh* command as *user1* to connect to *server20*. You will not be prompted for a password because there was none assigned to the ssh keys.

```
[user1@server10 ~]$ ssh server20
Register this system with Red Hat Insights: insights-client --register
Create an account or view all your systems at https://red.ht/insights-c
Last login: Mon Feb  6 09:30:08 2023 from 192.168.0.110
[user1@server20 ~]$
```

You can view this login attempt in the */var/log/secure* file on *server20*:

```
[user1@server20 ~]$ sudo tail /var/log/secure
. . . . . . . .
Feb  6 09:40:36 server20 sshd[34097]: Accepted publickey for user1 from 192.168
.0.110 port 48548 ssh2: RSA SHA256:6ppEXfqJIK9CwKRTofSwgxpb0zFxvMwMNEHqTipOvC4
Feb  6 09:40:36 server20 sshd[34097]: pam_unix(sshd:session): session opened fo
r user user1(uid=1000) by (uid=0)
```

The log entry shows the timestamp, hostname, process name and PID, username and source IP, and other relevant information. This file will log all future login attempts for this user.

Executing Commands Remotely Using ssh

The *ssh* command allows you to securely sign in to a remote system or execute a command without actually logging on to it. Exercise 18-2 demonstrated how a user can log in using this command. The following shows a few basic examples on how to use *ssh* to execute a command on a remote system.

Invoke the *ssh* command on *server10* to execute the *hostname* command on *server20*:

```
[user1@server10 ~]$ ssh server20 hostname
server20.example.com
```

Run the *nmcli* command on *server20* to show (s) active network connections (c):

```
[user1@server10 ~]$ ssh server20 nmcli c s
NAME    UUID                                   TYPE      DEVICE
enp0s3  13c6b478-f563-317a-9bb4-8709496d393f   ethernet  enp0s3
enp0s8  46630ab7-313c-4dea-a635-62bdfcc21872   ethernet  enp0s8
```

You can run any command on *server20* this way without having to log in to it.

Transferring Files Remotely Using sftp

The *sftp* command is an interactive file transfer tool. This tool can be launched as follows on *server10* to connect to *server20*:

```
[user1@server10 ~]$ sftp server20
Connected to server20.
sftp> ?
```

Type ? at the prompt to list available commands along with a short description:

```
sftp> ?
Available commands:
bye                                  Quit sftp
cd path                              Change remote directory to 'path'
chgrp grp path                       Change group of file 'path' to 'grp'
chmod mode path                      Change permissions of file 'path' to 'mode'
chown own path                       Change owner of file 'path' to 'own'
df [-hi] [path]                      Display statistics for current directory or
                                     filesystem containing 'path'
exit                                 Quit sftp
get [-afPpRr] remote [local]         Download file
reget [-fPpRr] remote [local]        Resume download file
reput [-fPpRr] [local] remote        Resume upload file
help                                 Display this help text
lcd path                             Change local directory to 'path'
lls [ls-options [path]]              Display local directory listing
lmkdir path                          Create local directory
ln [-s] oldpath newpath              Link remote file (-s for symlink)
lpwd                                 Print local working directory
ls [-1afhlnrSt] [path]               Display remote directory listing
lumask umask                         Set local umask to 'umask'
mkdir path                           Create remote directory
progress                             Toggle display of progress meter
put [-afPpRr] local [remote]         Upload file
pwd                                  Display remote working directory
quit                                 Quit sftp
rename oldpath newpath               Rename remote file
rm path                              Delete remote file
rmdir path                           Remove remote directory
symlink oldpath newpath              Symlink remote file
version                              Show SFTP version
!command                             Execute 'command' in local shell
!                                    Escape to local shell
?                                    Synonym for help
```

As shown in the above screenshot, there are many common commands available at the sftp> prompt. These include *cd* to change directory, *get/put* to download/upload a file, *ls* to list files, *pwd* to print working directory, *mkdir* to create a directory, *rename* to rename a file, *rm* to remove a file, and *bye/quit/exit* to exit the program and return to the command prompt. These commands will run on the remote server (*server20*). The following screenshot shows how these commands are used:

```
sftp> mkdir /tmp/dir10-20
sftp> cd /tmp/dir10-20
sftp> pwd
Remote working directory: /tmp/dir10-20
sftp> put /etc/group
Uploading /etc/group to /tmp/dir10-20/group
group                                        100%   985    310.8KB/s   00:00
sftp> ls -l
-rw-r--r--      1 user1      user1        985 Feb  6 09:45 group
sftp> cd ..
sftp> pwd
Remote working directory: /tmp
sftp> cd /home/user1
sftp> get /usr/bin/gzip
Fetching /usr/bin/gzip to gzip
gzip                                         100%    90KB   4.8MB/s   00:00
sftp>
```

Furthermore, there are four commands beginning with an 'l'—*lcd*, *lls*, *lpwd*, and *lmkdir*—at the sftp> prompt. These commands are intended to be run on the source server (*server10*). Other Linux commands are also available at the sftp> prompt that you may use for basic file management operations on the remote server.

Type *quit* at the sftp> prompt to exit the program when you're done.

Consult the manual pages of the command for options and additional details.

Chapter Summary

This chapter discussed the open-source version of the secure shell service. It started with an overview of the service, and described what it is, how it works, available versions, and algorithms employed. We skimmed through various encryption techniques and authentication methods. We touched upon the service daemon, client and server configuration files, and commands. We demonstrated accessing a lab server from another lab server. We generated and distributed passwordless private/public key pair and employed ssh utilities to remote execute commands and transfer files.

Review Questions

1. Name the SSH client-side configuration file.
2. What would the command *ssh server10 ls* do?
3. What would the command *ssh-keygen -N ""* do?
4. What is the default location to store user SSH keys?
5. What would the command *ssh-copy-id* do?
6. Which two of the five authentication methods mentioned in this chapter are more prevalent?
7. What is the use of the *ssh-keygen* command?
8. Name the default algorithm used with SSH.
9. The primary secure shell server configuration file is *ssh_config*. True or False?
10. Which three common algorithms are used with SSH version 2 for encryption and/or authentication?
11. What kind of information does the *~/.ssh/known_hosts* file store?
12. List the two encryption techniques described in this chapter.
13. What is the default port used by the secure shell service?

---

14. Which log file stores authentication messages?
15. The *ssh* tool provides a non-secure tunnel over a network for accessing a RHEL system. True or False?

Answers to Review Questions

1. The client-side SSH configuration file is *ssh_config* and it is located in the */etc/ssh* directory.
2. The command provided will run the *ls* command on the specified remote ssh server without the need for the user to log in.
3. The command provided will generate a passwordless ssh key pair using the default RSA algorithm.
4. Under the *~/.ssh* directory.
5. The *ssh-copy-id* command is used to distribute the public key to remote systems.
6. The public key-based and password-based authentication methods are more prevalent.
7. The *ssh-keygen* command is used to generate public/private key combination for use with ssh.
8. The default algorithm used with ssh is RSA.
9. False. The primary secure shell configuration file is *sshd_config*.
10. The SSH version 2 uses RSA, DSA, and ECDSA algorithms.
11. The *~/.ssh/known_hosts* file stores fingerprints of remote servers.
12. The two encryption techniques are symmetric (secret key) and asymmetric (public key).
13. The default port used by the secure shell service is 22.
14. The */var/log/secure* file stores authentication messages.
15. False. The *ssh* command provides a secure tunnel over a network.

Do-It-Yourself Challenge Labs

The following labs are useful to strengthen most of the concepts and topics learned in this chapter. It is expected that you perform the labs without external help. A step-by-step guide is not supplied, as the knowledge and skill required to implement the labs have already been disseminated in the chapter; however, hints to the relevant major topic(s) are included.

Use the lab environment built specifically for end-of-chapter labs. See sub-section "Lab Environment for End-of-Chapter Labs" in Chapter 01 "Local Installation" for details.

Lab 18-1: Establish Key-Based Authentication

As *user1* with *sudo* on *server30* and *server40*, create user account *user20* and assign a password. As *user20* on *server40*, generate a private/public key pair without a passphrase using the *ssh-keygen* command. Distribute the public key to *server30* with the *ssh-copy-id* command. Log on to *server30* as *user20* and accept the fingerprints for the server if presented. On subsequent log in attempts from *server40* to *server30*, *user20* should not be prompted for their password. (Hint: System Access and File Transfer).

Lab 18-2: Test the Effect of PermitRootLogin Directive

As *user1* with *sudo* on *server40*, edit the */etc/ssh/sshd_config* file and change the value of the directive PermitRootLogin to "no". Use the *systemctl* command to activate the change. As *root* on *server30*, run *ssh server40* (or use its IP). You'll get permission denied message. Reverse the change on *server40* and retry *ssh server40*. You should be able to log in. (Hint: The OpenSSH Service).

Chapter 19

The Linux Firewall

This chapter describes the following major topics:

➤ Describe Linux firewall for host-based security control

➤ Overview of the firewalld service

➤ Understand the concepts of firewalld zones and services

➤ Analyze zone and service configuration files

➤ Control access to network services and ports through firewalld

➤ Use firewall-cmd command to manage firewall rules

RHCSA Objectives:

47. Restrict network access using firewall-cmd/firewall

52. Configure firewall settings using firewall-cmd/firewalld

Running a system in a networked or an Internet-facing environment requires that some security measures be taken to tighten access to the system in general and individual services in particular. This can be accomplished by implementing a firewall and restricting inbound traffic to allowed ports from valid source IP addresses only. We discuss a host-based firewall solution in this chapter.

Firewall Overview

A *firewall* is a protective layer implemented at the network or server level to secure, monitor, and control inbound and outbound traffic flow. Firewalls employed at the network level use either dedicated hardware or sophisticated software appliances to form a shield around the network. Server level firewalls are referred to as *host-based firewalls* and they run in a computer operating system to monitor and manage traffic in and out. Firewalls defend a network or an individual server from undesired traffic.

RHEL is shipped with a host-based firewall solution that works by filtering data packets. A data packet is formed as a result of a process called *encapsulation* whereby the header information is attached to a message (called *payload*) during packet formation. The header includes information such as source and destination IP addresses, port, and type of data. Based on predefined *rules*, a firewall intercepts each inbound and outbound data packet, inspects its header, and decides whether to allow the packet to pass through.

Ports are defined in the */etc/services* file for common network services that are standardized across all network operating systems, including RHEL. Some common services and the ports they listen on are FTP (*File Transfer Protocol*) on port 21, SSH (*Secure Shell*) 22, Postfix (an email service) 25, HTTP (*HyperText Transfer Protocol*) 80, and NTP (*Network Time Protocol*) on port 123.

The host-based firewall solution employed in RHEL uses a kernel module called *netfilter* together with a filtering and packet classification framework called *nftables* for policing the traffic movement. It also supports other advanced features such as *Network Address Translation* (NAT) and *port forwarding*. This firewall solution inspects, modifies, drops, or routes incoming, outgoing, and forwarded network packets based on defined rulesets.

Overview of the firewalld Service

firewalld is the default host-based firewall management service in RHEL 9. One of the major advantages is its ability to add, modify, or delete firewall rules immediately without disrupting current network connections or restarting the service process. This is especially useful in testing and troubleshooting scenarios. *firewalld* also allows to save rules persistently so that they are activated automatically at system reboots.

The *firewalld* service lets you perform management operations at the command line using the *firewall-cmd* command, graphically using the web console, or manually by editing rules files. *firewalld* stores the default rules in files located in the */usr/lib/firewalld* directory, and those that contain custom rules in the */etc/firewalld* directory. The default rules files may be copied to the custom rules directory and modified.

firewalld Zones

firewalld uses the concept of *zones* for easier and transparent traffic management. Zones define policies based on the trust level of network connections and source IP addresses. A network connection can be part of only one zone at a time; however, a zone can have multiple network connections assigned to it. Zone configuration may include services, ports, and protocols that may be open or closed. It may also include rules for advanced configuration items such as masquerading, port forwarding, NAT'ing, ICMP filters, and rich language. Rules for each zone are defined and manipulated independent of other zones.

firewalld inspects each incoming packet to determine the source IP address and applies the rules of the zone that has a match for the address. In the event no zone configuration matches the address, it associates the packet with the zone that has the network connection defined, and applies the rules of that zone. If neither works, *firewalld* associates the packet with the default zone, and enforces the rules of the default zone on the packet.

The *firewalld* software installs several predefined zone files that may be selected or customized. These files include templates for traffic that must be blocked or dropped, and for traffic that is public-facing, internal, external, home, public, trusted, and work-related. Of these, the *public* zone is the default zone, and it is activated by default when the *firewalld* service is started. Table 19-1 lists and describes the predefined zones sorted based on the trust level from trusted to untrusted.

Zone	Description
trusted	Allow all incoming traffic
internal	Reject all incoming traffic except for what is allowed. Intended for use on internal networks.
home	Reject all incoming traffic except for what is allowed. Intended for use in homes.
work	Reject all incoming traffic except for what is allowed. Intended for use at workplaces.
dmz	Reject all incoming traffic except for what is allowed. Intended for use in publicly accessible demilitarized zones.
external	Reject all incoming traffic except for what is allowed. Outgoing IPv4 traffic forwarded through this zone is masqueraded to look like it originated from the IPv4 address of an outgoing network interface. Intended for use on external networks with masquerading enabled.

Zone	Description
public	Reject all incoming traffic except for what is allowed. It is the default zone for any newly added network interfaces. Intended for us in public places.
block	Reject all incoming traffic with icmp-host-prohibited message returned. Intended for use in secure places.
drop	Drop all incoming traffic without responding with ICMP errors. Intended for use in highly secure places.

Table 19-1 firewalld Default Zones

For all the predefined zones, outgoing traffic is allowed by default.

Zone Configuration Files

firewalld stores zone rules in XML format at two locations: the system-defined rules in the */usr/lib/firewalld/zones* directory, and the user-defined rules in the */etc/firewalld/zones* directory. The files at the former location can be used as templates for adding new rules, or applied instantly to any available network connection. A system zone configuration file is automatically copied to the */etc/firewalld/zones* directory if it is modified with a management tool. Alternatively, you can copy the required zone file to the */etc/firewalld/zones* directory manually, and make the necessary changes. The *firewalld* service reads the files saved in this location, and applies the rules defined in them. A listing of the system zone files is presented below:

```
[user1@server10 ~]$ ll /usr/lib/firewalld/zones/
total 40
-rw-r--r--. 1 root root 312 Aug  5  2022 block.xml
-rw-r--r--. 1 root root 306 Aug  5  2022 dmz.xml
-rw-r--r--. 1 root root 304 Aug  5  2022 drop.xml
-rw-r--r--. 1 root root 317 Aug  5  2022 external.xml
-rw-r--r--. 1 root root 410 Aug  5  2022 home.xml
-rw-r--r--. 1 root root 425 Aug  5  2022 internal.xml
-rw-r--r--. 1 root root 729 Aug 26 09:25 nm-shared.xml
-rw-r--r--. 1 root root 356 Aug  5  2022 public.xml
-rw-r--r--. 1 root root 175 Aug  5  2022 trusted.xml
-rw-r--r--. 1 root root 352 Aug  5  2022 work.xml
```

The default *public* zone file is displayed below:

```
[user1@server10 ~]$ cat /usr/lib/firewalld/zones/public.xml
<?xml version="1.0" encoding="utf-8"?>
<zone>
  <short>Public</short>
  <description>For use in public areas. You do not trust the other computers on
networks to not harm your computer. Only selected incoming connections are accep
ted.</description>
  <service name="ssh"/>
  <service name="dhcpv6-client"/>
  <service name="cockpit"/>
</zone>
```

As depicted in the screenshot, the zone has a name and description, and it contains a list of all the allowed services—*ssh*, *dhcpv6-client*, and *cockpit*. See the manual pages for *firewalld.zone* for details on zone configuration files.

firewalld Services

In addition to the concept of zones, *firewalld* also uses the idea of *services* for easier activation and deactivation of specific rules. *firewalld* services are preconfigured firewall rules delineated for various services and stored in different files. The rules consist of necessary settings, such as the port number, protocol, and possibly helper modules, to support the loading of the service. *firewalld* services can be added to a zone. By default, *firewalld* blocks all traffic unless a service or port is explicitly opened.

Service Configuration Files

firewalld stores service rules in XML format at two locations: the system-defined rules in the */usr/lib/firewalld/services* directory, and the user-defined rules in the */etc/firewalld/services* directory. The files at the former location can be used as templates for adding new service rules, or activated instantly. A system service configuration file is automatically copied to the */etc/firewalld/services* directory if it is modified with a management tool. Alternatively, you can copy the required service file to the */etc/firewalld/services* directory manually, and make the necessary changes. The *firewalld* service reads the files saved in this location, and applies the rules defined in them. A listing of the system service files is presented below:

```
[user1@server10 ~]$ ll /usr/lib/firewalld/services/
total 768
-rw-r--r--. 1 root root 352 Aug  5  2022 afp.xml
-rw-r--r--. 1 root root 399 Aug  5  2022 amanda-client.xml
-rw-r--r--. 1 root root 427 Aug  5  2022 amanda-k5-client.xml
-rw-r--r--. 1 root root 283 Aug  5  2022 amqps.xml
-rw-r--r--. 1 root root 273 Aug  5  2022 amqp.xml
-rw-r--r--. 1 root root 285 Aug  5  2022 apcupsd.xml
-rw-r--r--. 1 root root 301 Aug  5  2022 audit.xml
-rw-r--r--. 1 root root 320 Aug  5  2022 bacula-client.xml
-rw-r--r--. 1 root root 346 Aug  5  2022 bacula.xml
. . . . . . . .
```

The following shows the content of the *ssh* service file:

```
[user1@server10 ~]$ cat /usr/lib/firewalld/services/ssh.xml
<?xml version="1.0" encoding="utf-8"?>
<service>
  <short>SSH</short>
  <description>Secure Shell (SSH) is a protocol for logging into and executing c
ommands on remote machines. It provides secure encrypted communications. If you
plan on accessing your machine remotely via SSH over a firewalled interface, ena
ble this option. You need the openssh-server package installed for this option t
o be useful.</description>
  <port protocol="tcp" port="22"/>
</service>
```

As depicted in the screenshot, the service has a name and description, and it defines the port and protocol for the service. See the manual pages for *firewalld.service* for details on service configuration files.

Firewalld Management

Managing the *firewalld* service involves a number of operations, such as listing, querying, adding, changing, and removing zones, services, ports, IP sources, and network connections. There are three methods available in RHEL 9 to perform the management tasks. They include the *firewall-cmd* utility for those who prefer to work at the command line and the web interface for graphical administration. The third management option is to make use of the zone and service templates, and edit them manually as desired. We use the command line method in this book.

The firewall-cmd Command

The *firewall-cmd* command is a powerful tool to manage the *firewalld* service at the command prompt. This tool can be used to add or remove rules from the runtime configuration, or save any modifications to service configuration for persistence. It supports numerous options for the management of zones, services, ports, connections, and so on; Table 19-2 lists and describes the common options only.

Option	Description
General	
--state	Displays the running status of firewalld
--reload	Reloads firewall rules from zone files. All runtime changes are lost.
--permanent	Stores a change persistently. The change only becomes active after a service reload or restart.
Zones	
--get-default-zone	Shows the name of the default/active zone
--set-default-zone	Changes the default zone for both runtime and permanent configuration
--get-zones	Prints a list of available zones
--get-active-zones	Displays the active zone and the assigned interfaces
--list-all	Lists all settings for a zone
--list-all-zones	Lists the settings for all available zones
--zone	Specifies the name of the zone to work on. Without this option, the default zone is used.
Services	
--get-services	Prints predefined services
--list-services	Lists services for a zone
--add-service	Adds a service to a zone
--remove-service	Removes a service from a zone
--query-service	Queries for the presence of a service
Ports	
--list-ports	Lists network ports
--add-port	Adds a port or a range of ports to a zone
--remove-port	Removes a port from a zone
--query-port	Queries for the presence of a port
Network Connections	
--list-interfaces	Lists network connections assigned to a zone
--add-interface	Binds a network connection to a zone

Option	Description
--change-interface	Changes the binding of a network connection to a different zone
--remove-interface	Unbinds a network connection from a zone
IP Sources	
--list-sources	Lists IP sources assigned to a zone
--add-source	Adds an IP source to a zone
--change-source	Changes an IP source
--remove-source	Removes an IP source from a zone

Table 19-2 Common firewall-cmd Options

With all the --add and --remove options, the --permanent switch may be specified to ensure the rule is stored in the zone configuration file under the */etc/firewalld/zones* directory for persistence. Some of the options from Table 19-2 are used in the upcoming exercises; the rest are beyond the scope of this book. Consult the manual pages of the command for details on the usage of these and other options.

Querying the Operational Status of firewalld

You can check the running status of the *firewalld* service using either the *systemctl* or the *firewall-cmd* command. Both commands will produce different outputs, but the intent here is to ensure the service is in the running state.

```
[user1@server10 ~]$ sudo firewall-cmd --state
running
[user1@server10 ~]$ sudo systemctl status firewalld -l --no-pager
● firewalld.service - firewalld - dynamic firewall daemon
     Loaded: loaded (/usr/lib/systemd/system/firewalld.service; enabled; vendor
preset: enabled)
     Active: active (running) since Sun 2023-02-05 22:02:20 EST; 12h ago
       Docs: man:firewalld(1)
   Main PID: 801 (firewalld)
      Tasks: 2 (limit: 10944)
     Memory: 44.9M
        CPU: 2.069s
     CGroup: /system.slice/firewalld.service
             └─801 /usr/bin/python3 -s /usr/sbin/firewalld --nofork --nopid
```

The output indicates that the *firewalld* service is in the running state on *server10*. The other command outcome also reports that the service is marked for autostart at system reboots. In case *firewalld* is not enabled or is inactive, issue **sudo systemctl --now enable firewalld** to start it immediately, and mark it for autostart on reboots.

You are ready to perform the exercises presented next.

Exercise 19-1: Add Services and Ports, and Manage Zones

This exercise should be done on *server10* as *user1* with *sudo* where required.

In this exercise, you will determine the current active zone. You will add and activate a permanent rule to allow HTTP traffic on port 80, and then add a runtime rule for traffic intended for TCP port 443 (the HTTPS service). You will add a permanent rule to the *internal* zone for TCP port range

5901 to 5910. You will confirm the changes and display the contents of the affected zone files. Lastly, you will switch the default zone to the *internal* zone and activate it.

1. Determine the name of the current default zone:

```
[user1@server10 ~]$ sudo firewall-cmd --get-default-zone
public
```

2. Add a permanent rule to allow HTTP traffic on its default port:

```
[user1@server10 ~]$ sudo firewall-cmd --permanent --add-service http
success
```

The command made a copy of the *public.xml* file from */usr/lib/firewalld/zones* directory into the */etc/firewalld/zones* directory, and added the rule for the HTTP service.

3. Activate the new rule:

```
[user1@server10 ~]$ sudo firewall-cmd --reload
success
```

4. Confirm the activation of the new rule:

```
[user1@server10 ~]$ sudo firewall-cmd --list-services
cockpit dhcpv6-client http ssh
```

5. Display the content of the default zone file to confirm the addition of the permanent rule:

```
[user1@server10 ~]$ sudo cat /etc/firewalld/zones/public.xml
<?xml version="1.0" encoding="utf-8"?>
<zone>
  <short>Public</short>
  <description>For use in public areas. You do not trust the
 networks to not harm your computer. Only selected incoming
epted.</description>
  <service name="ssh"/>
  <service name="dhcpv6-client"/>
  <service name="cockpit"/>
  <service name="http"/>
  <forward/>
</zone>
```

6. Add a runtime rule to allow traffic on TCP port 443 and verify:

```
[user1@server10 ~]$ sudo firewall-cmd --add-port 443/tcp
success
[user1@server10 ~]$ sudo firewall-cmd --list-ports
443/tcp
```

7. Add a permanent rule to the *internal* zone for TCP port range 5901 to 5910:

```
[user1@server10 ~]$ sudo firewall-cmd --add-port 5901-5910/tcp --permanent --zone internal
success
```

8. Display the content of the *internal* zone file to confirm the addition of the permanent rule:

```
[user1@server10 ~]$ sudo cat /etc/firewalld/zones/internal.xml
<?xml version="1.0" encoding="utf-8"?>
<zone>
  <short>Internal</short>
  <description>For use on internal networks. You mostly trust
rs on the networks to not harm your computer. Only selected in
s are accepted.</description>
  <service name="ssh"/>
  <service name="mdns"/>
  <service name="samba-client"/>
  <service name="dhcpv6-client"/>
  <service name="cockpit"/>
  <port port="5901-5910" protocol="tcp"/>
  <forward/>
</zone>
```

The *firewall-cmd* command makes a backup of the affected zone file with a *.old* extension whenever an update is made to a zone.

9. Switch the default zone to internal and confirm:

```
[user1@server10 ~]$ sudo firewall-cmd --set-default-zone internal
success
[user1@server10 ~]$ sudo firewall-cmd --get-default-zone
internal
```

10. Activate the rules defined in the *internal* zone and list the port range added earlier:

```
[user1@server10 ~]$ sudo firewall-cmd --reload
success
[user1@server10 ~]$ sudo firewall-cmd --list-ports
5901-5910/tcp
```

This completes the exercise.

Exercise 19-2: Remove Services and Ports, and Manage Zones

This exercise should be done on *server10* as *user1* with *sudo* where required.

In this exercise, you will remove the two permanent rules that were added in Exercise 19-1. You will switch the *public* zone back as the default zone, and confirm the changes.

1. Remove the permanent rule for HTTP from the *public* zone:

```
[user1@server10 ~]$ sudo firewall-cmd --remove-service=http --zone public --permanent
success
```

Notice the equal sign (=) used with the --remove-service option. The *firewall-cmd* command supports the specification of add, remove, change, and zone options with and without an equal sign (=). The --zone option is used to specify the *public* zone as it is currently not the default.

2. Remove the permanent rule for ports 5901 to 5910 from the *internal* zone:

```
[user1@server10 ~]$ sudo firewall-cmd --remove-port 5901-5910/tcp --permanent
success
```

The --zone option is not used, as 'internal' is currently the default zone.

3. Switch the default zone to *public* and validate:

```
[user1@server10 ~]$ sudo firewall-cmd --set-default-zone=public
success
[user1@server10 ~]$ sudo firewall-cmd --get-default-zone
public
```

4. Activate the *public* zone rules, and list the current services:

```
[user1@server10 ~]$ sudo firewall-cmd --reload
success
[user1@server10 ~]$
[user1@server10 ~]$ sudo firewall-cmd --list-services
cockpit dhcpv6-client ssh
```

The *public* zone reflects the removal of the *http* service. This concludes the exercise.

Exercise 19-3: Test the Effect of Firewall Rule

This exercise should be done on *server10* and *server20* as *user1* with *sudo* where required.

In this exercise, you will remove the *sshd* service rule from the runtime configuration on *server10*, and try to access the server from *server20* using the *ssh* command.

1. Remove the rule for the *sshd* service on *server10*:

```
[user1@server10 ~]$ sudo firewall-cmd --remove-service ssh
success
```

2. Issue the *ssh* command on *server20* to access *server10*:

```
[user1@server20 ~]$ ssh server10
ssh: connect to host server10 port 22: No route to host
```

The error displayed is because the firewall on *server10* blocked the access. Put the rule back on *server10* and try to access it from *server20* again:

3. Add the rule back for *sshd* on *server10*:

```
[user1@server10 ~]$ sudo firewall-cmd --add-service=ssh
success
```

4. Issue the *ssh* command on *server20* to access *server10*. Enter "yes" if prompted and the password for *user1*.

```
[user1@server10 ~]$ ssh server20
Register this system with Red Hat Insights: insights-client --register
Create an account or view all your systems at https://red.ht/insights-das
Last login: Mon Feb  6 09:40:36 2023 from 192.168.0.110
[user1@server20 ~]$
[user1@server20 ~]$
[user1@server20 ~]$ ssh server10
The authenticity of host 'server10 (192.168.0.110)' can't be established.
ED25519 key fingerprint is SHA256:OIaFcWOQCycM7mrWqw4w5DmTHDbXgdzrmJaLyt%
This key is not known by any other names
Are you sure you want to continue connecting (yes/no/[fingerprint])? yes
Warning: Permanently added 'server10' (ED25519) to the list of known host
user1@server10's password:
Register this system with Red Hat Insights: insights-client --register
Create an account or view all your systems at https://red.ht/insights-das
Last login: Sun Feb  5 22:02:32 2023 from 192.168.0.4
[user1@server10 ~]$
```

This brings the exercise to an end.

Chapter Summary

We discussed a native host-based firewall solution for system protection in this chapter. We explored the concepts around firewall and described how it works. We looked at the firewalld service and examined the concepts of zones and services. We reviewed predefined zones and services, and analyzed their configuration files. We studied the lone firewall management command and reviewed options for listing and administering zones, services, ports, network connections, and source IP addresses.

We learned how to change and check the operational state of the firewalld service. We performed exercises to add and remove services and ports persistently and non-persistently, and manage zones. Finally, we tested the effect of deleting a port from the firewall configuration and adding it back.

Review Questions

1. A firewall can be configured between two networks but not between two hosts. True or False?
2. After changing the default firewalld zone to internal, what would you run to verify?
3. What is the process of data packet formation called?
4. What would the command *firewall-cmd --remove-port=5000/tcp* do?
5. What is the primary command line tool for managing firewalld called?
6. What would the command *firewall-cmd --permanent --add-service=nfs --zone=external* do?
7. If you have a set of firewall rules defined for a service stored under both */etc/firewalld* and */usr/lib/firewalld* directories, which of the two sets will take precedence?
8. What is the kernel module in RHEL 9 that implements the host-level protection called?
9. firewalld is the firewall management solution in RHEL 9. True or False?
10. Which directory stores the configuration file for modified firewalld zones?
11. Name the default firewalld zone.
12. What is the purpose of firewalld service configuration files?

Answers to Review Questions

1. False. A firewall can also be configured between two host computers.
2. You run *firewall-cmd --get-default-zone* for validation.
3. The process of data packet formation is called encapsulation.
4. The command provided will remove the runtime firewall rule for TCP port 5000.
5. The primary command line tool for managing *firewalld* is called *firewall-cmd*.
6. The command provided will add the *nfs* service to *external* firewalld zone persistently.
7. The ruleset located in the */etc/firewalld* directory will have precedence.
8. The kernel module that implements the host-level protection is called netfilter.
9. True.
10. The modified *firewalld* zone files are stored under */etc/firewalld/zones* directory.
11. The default firewalld zone is the *public* zone.
12. firewalld service configuration files store service-specific port, protocol, and other details, which makes it easy to activate and deactivate them.

Do-It-Yourself Challenge Labs

The following labs are useful to strengthen most of the concepts and topics learned in this chapter. It is expected that you perform the labs without external help. A step-by-step guide is not supplied, as the knowledge and skill required to implement the labs have already been disseminated in the chapter; however, hints to the relevant major topic(s) are included.

Use the lab environment built specifically for end-of-chapter labs. See sub-section "Lab Environment for End-of-Chapter Labs" in Chapter 01 "Local Installation" for details.

Lab 19-1: Add Service to Firewall

As *user1* with *sudo* on *server30*, add and activate a permanent rule for HTTPs traffic to the default zone. Confirm the change by viewing the zone's XML file and running the *firewall-cmd* command. (Hint: Firewall Management).

Lab 19-2: Add Port Range to Firewall

As *user1* with *sudo* on *server30*, add and activate a permanent rule for the UDP port range 8000 to 8005 to the *trusted* zone. Confirm the change by viewing the zone's XML file and running the *firewall-cmd* command. (Hint: Firewall Management).

## Chapter 20

Security Enhanced Linux

This chapter describes the following major topics:

➢ Describe Security Enhanced Linux and its terminology

➢ Understand SELinux contexts for users, processes, files, and ports

➢ Copy, move, and archive files with and without SELinux context

➢ How domain transitioning works

➢ Overview of SELinux Booleans

➢ Query and manage SELinux via management tools

➢ Modify SELinux contexts for files and ports

➢ Add SELinux rules to policy database

➢ View and analyze SELinux alerts

RHCSA Objectives:

55. Set enforcing and permissive modes for SELinux
56. List and identify SELinux file and process context
57. Restore default file contexts
58. Manage SELinux port labels
59. Use Boolean settings to modify system SELinux settings
60. Diagnose and address routine SELinux policy violations

Security Enhanced Linux is a mechanism that controls who can access and do what on the system. It is part and parcel of the Linux kernel. It handles access beyond what the traditional access control system delivers including file and directory permissions, user and group-level permissions, and shadow password and password aging mechanisms.

The goal of SELinux is to limit the possible damage that could occur to the system due to unauthorized user or program access. This chapter covers SELinux in reasonable detail.

Security Enhanced Linux

Security Enhanced Linux (SELinux) is an implementation of the *Mandatory Access Control* (MAC) architecture developed by the U.S. *National Security Agency* (NSA) in collaboration with other organizations and the Linux community for flexible, enriched, and granular security controls in Linux. MAC is integrated into the Linux kernel as a set of patches using the *Linux Security Modules* (LSM) framework that allows the kernel to support various security implementations, including SELinux.

MAC provides an added layer of protection above and beyond the standard Linux *Discretionary Access Control* (DAC) security architecture. DAC includes the traditional file and directory permissions, extended attribute settings, setuid/setgid bits, su/sudo privileges, and other controls. MAC limits the ability of a *subject* (Linux user or process) to access an *object* (file, directory, file system, device, network interface/connection, port, pipe, socket, etc.) to reduce or eliminate the potential damage the subject may be able to inflict on the system if compromised due to the exploitation of vulnerabilities in services, programs, or applications.

MAC controls are fine-grained; they protect other services in the event one service is negotiated. For instance, if the HTTP service process is compromised, the attacker can only damage the files the hacked process will have access to, and not the other processes running on the system, or the objects the other processes will have access to. To ensure this coarse-grained control, MAC uses a set of defined authorization rules called *policy* to examine security attributes associated with subjects and objects when a subject tries to access an object, and decides whether to permit the access attempt. These attributes are stored in *contexts* (a.k.a. *labels*), and are applied to both subjects and objects.

SELinux decisions are stored in a special cache area called *Access Vector Cache* (AVC). This cache area is checked for each access attempt by a process to determine whether the access attempt was previously allowed. With this mechanism in place, SELinux does not have to check the policy ruleset repeatedly, thus improving performance.

By default, SELinux controls are enabled at the time of RHEL installation with the default configuration, which confines the processes to the bare minimum privileges that they need to function.

Terminology

To comprehend SELinux, an understanding of some key terms is essential. These terms are useful in explaining the concepts and SELinux functionality in the remainder of this chapter.

Subject

A *subject* is any user or process that accesses an object. Examples include system_u for the SELinux system user, and unconfined_u for subjects that are not bound by the SELinux policy. The subject is stored in field 1 of the context.

Object

An *object* is a resource, such as a file, directory, hardware device, network interface/connection, port, pipe, or socket, that a subject accesses. Examples include object_r for general objects, system_r for system-owned objects, and unconfined_r for objects that are not bound by the SELinux policy.

Access

An *access* is an action performed by the subject on an object. Examples include creating, reading, or updating a file, creating or navigating a directory, and accessing a network port or socket.

Policy

A *policy* is a defined ruleset that is enforced system-wide, and is used to analyze security attributes assigned to subjects and objects. This ruleset is referenced to decide whether to permit a subject's access attempt to an object, or a subject's attempt to interact with another subject. The default behavior of SELinux in the absence of a rule is to deny the access. Two standard preconfigured policies are *targeted* and *mls* with targeted being the default.

The targeted policy dictates that any process that is targeted runs in a confined domain, and any process that is not targeted runs in an unconfined domain. For instance, SELinux runs logged-in users in the unconfined domain, and the *httpd* process in a confined domain by default. Any subject running unconfined is more vulnerable than the one running confined.

The mls policy places tight security controls at deeper levels.

A third preconfigured policy called *minimum* is a light version of the targeted policy, and it is designed to protect only selected processes.

Context

A *context* (a.k.a. *label*) is a tag to store security attributes for subjects and objects. In SELinux, every subject and object has a context assigned, which consists of a SELinux user, role, type (or domain), and sensitivity level. SELinux uses this information to make access control decisions.

Labeling

Labeling is the mapping of files with their stored contexts.

SELinux User

SELinux policy has several predefined SELinux user identities that are authorized for a particular set of roles. SELinux policy maintains Linux user to SELinux user identity mapping to place SELinux user restrictions on Linux users. This controls what roles and levels a process (with a particular SELinux user identity) can enter. A Linux user, for instance, cannot run the *su* and *sudo* commands or the programs located in their home directories if they are mapped to the SELinux user user_u.

Role

A *role* is an attribute of the *Role-Based Access Control* (RBAC) security model that is part of SELinux. It classifies who (subject) is allowed to access what (domains or types). SELinux users are authorized for roles, and roles are authorized for domains and types. Each subject has an associated role to ensure that the system and user processes are separated. A subject can transition into a new role to gain access to other domains and types. Examples roles include user_r for ordinary users, sysadm_r for administrators, and system_r for processes that initiate under the system_r role. The role is stored in field 2 of the context.

Type Enforcement

Type enforcement (TE) identifies and limits a subject's ability to access domains for processes, and types for files. It references the contexts of the subjects and objects for this enforcement.

Type and Domain

A *type* is an attribute of type enforcement. It is a group of objects based on uniformity in their security requirements. Objects such as files and directories with common security requirements, are grouped within a specific type. Examples of types include user_home_dir_t for objects located in user home directories, and usr_t for most objects stored in the */usr* directory. The type is stored in field 3 of a file context.

A *domain* determines the type of access that a process has. Processes with common security requirements are grouped within a specific domain type, and they run confined within that domain. Examples of domains include init_t for the *systemd* process, firewalld_t for the *firewalld* process, and unconfined_t for all processes that are not bound by SELinux policy. The domain is stored in field 3 of a process context.

SELinux policy rules outline how types can access each other, domains can access types, and domains can access each other.

Level

A *level* is an attribute of *Multi-Level Security* (MLS) and *Multi-Category Security* (MCS). It is a pair of sensitivity:category values that defines the level of security in the context. A category may be defined as a single value or a range of values, such as c0.c4 to represent c0 through c4. In RHEL 9, the targeted policy is used as the default, which enforces MCS (MCS supports only one sensitivity level (s0) with 0 to 1023 different categories).

SELinux Contexts for Users

SELinux contexts define security attributes placed on subjects and objects. Each context contains a type and a security level with subject and object information. Use the *id* command with the -Z option to view the context set on Linux users. The following example shows the context for *user1*:

```
[user1@server10 ~]$ id -Z
unconfined_u:unconfined_r:unconfined_t:s0-s0:c0.c1023
```

The output indicates that *user1* is mapped to the SELinux unconfined_u user, and that there are no SELinux restrictions placed on this user. You'll get the same result if you run this command for other users. This entails that all Linux users, including *root*, run unconfined by default, which gives them full access to the system.

In addition to the unconfined user with unlimited privileges, SELinux includes seven confined user identities with restricted access to objects. These accounts are mapped to Linux users via SELinux policy. This regulated access helps safeguard the system from potential damage that Linux users might inflict on the system.

You can use the *seinfo* query command to list the SELinux users; however, the *setools-console* software package must be installed before doing so.

```
[user1@server10 ~]$ sudo seinfo -u

Users: 8
   guest_u
   root
   staff_u
   sysadm_u
   system_u
   unconfined_u
   user_u
   xguest_u
```

The output shows the eight predefined SELinux users. You can use the *semanage* command to view the mapping between Linux and SELinux users:

```
[user1@server10 ~]$ sudo semanage login -l

Login Name          SELinux User          MLS/MCS Range          Service

__default__         unconfined_u          s0-s0:c0.c1023         *
root                unconfined_u          s0-s0:c0.c1023         *
```

The output displays Linux users in column 1 (Login Name) and SELinux users they are mapped to in column 2 (SELinux User). Columns 3 and 4 show the associated security level (MLS/MCS Range), and the context for the Linux user (the * represents all services). By default, all non-*root* Linux users are represented as __default__, which is mapped to the unconfined_u user in the policy.

SELinux Contexts for Processes

You can determine the context for processes using the *ps* command with the -Z flag. The following example shows only the first two lines from the command output:

```
[user1@server10 ~]$ ps -eZ
LABEL                             PID TTY          TIME CMD
system_u:system_r:init_t:s0         1 ?        00:00:04 systemd
```

In the output, the subject (system_u) is a SELinux username (mapped to Linux user *root*), object is system_r, domain (init_t) reveals the type of protection applied to the process, and level of security (s0). Any process that is unprotected will run in the unconfined_t domain.

SELinux Contexts for Files

You can spot the context for files and directories. To this end, use the *ls* command with the -Z switch. The following shows the four attributes set on the */etc/passwd* file:

```
[user1@server10 ~]$ ls -lZ /etc/passwd
-rw-r--r--. 1 root root system_u:object_r:passwd_file_t:s0 2496 Feb  5 19:07
/etc/passwd
```

The outcome indicates the subject (system_u), object (object_r), type (passwd_file_t), and security level (s0) for the *passwd* file. Contexts for system-installed and user-created files are stored in the *file_contexts* and *file_contexts.local* files located in the */etc/selinux/targeted/contexts/files* directory. These policy files can be updated using the *semanage* command.

Copying, Moving, and Archiving Files with SELinux Contexts

As mentioned, all files in RHEL are labeled with an SELINUX security context by default. New files inherit the parent directory's context at the time of creation. However, three common file management operations—copy, move, and archive—require special attention. There are certain rules to be kept in mind during their use to ensure correct contexts on affected files. These rules are:

1. If a file is copied to a different directory, the destination file will receive the destination directory's context, unless the --preserve=context switch is specified with the *cp* command to retain the source file's original context.
2. If a copy operation overwrites the destination file in the same or different directory, the file being copied will receive the context of the overwritten file, unless the --preserve=context switch is specified with the *cp* command to preserve the source file's original context.
3. If a file is moved to the same or different directory, the SELinux context will remain intact, which may differ from the destination directory's context.
4. If a file is archived with the *tar* command, use the --selinux option to preserve the context.

Later in the chapter, we will perform an exercise to confirm the behavior of the three operations.

SELinux Contexts for Ports

SELinux contexts define security attributes for network ports, which can be viewed with the *semanage* command . The following illustrates a few entries from the output of this command:

```
[user1@server10 ~]$ sudo semanage port -l
SELinux Port Type              Proto      Port Number
chronyd_port_t                 udp        323
dns_port_t                     tcp        53, 853
ftp_port_t                     tcp        21, 989, 990
http_port_t                    tcp        80, 81, 443, 488, 8008, 8009, 8443, 9000
ntp_port_t                     udp        123
syslogd_port_t                 udp        514, 601, 20514
```

The output is displayed in three columns. Column 1 shows the SELinux type, column 2 depicts the protocol, and column 3 indicates the port number(s). By default, SELinux allows services to listen on a restricted set of network ports only. This is evident from the above output.

Domain Transitioning

SELinux allows a process running in one domain to enter another domain to execute an application that is restricted to run in that domain only, provided a rule exists in the policy to support such transition. SELinux defines a permission setting called *entrypoint* in its policy to control processes that can transition into another domain. To understand how this works, a basic example is provided below that shows what happens when a Linux user attempts to change their password using the */usr/bin/passwd* command.

The *passwd* command is labeled with the passwd_exec_t type, which can be confirmed as follows:

```
[user1@server10 ~]$ ls -lZ /usr/bin/passwd
-rwsr-xr-x. 1 root root system_u:object_r:passwd_exec_t:s0 32648 Aug 10
2021 /usr/bin/passwd
```

The *passwd* command requires access to the */etc/shadow* file in order to modify a user password. The *shadow* file has a different type set on it (shadow_t):

```
[user1@server10 ~]$ ls -lZ /etc/shadow
----------. 1 root root system_u:object_r:shadow_t:s0 1674 Feb   5 18:50
/etc/shadow
```

The SELinux policy has rules that specifically allow processes running in domain passwd_t to read and modify the files with type shadow_t, and allow them entrypoint permission into domain passwd_exec_t. This rule enables the user's shell process executing the *passwd* command to switch into the passwd_t domain and update the *shadow* file.

Open two terminal windows. In window 1, issue the *passwd* command as *user1* and wait at the prompt:

```
[user1@server10 ~]$ passwd
Changing password for user user1.
Current password: _
```

In window 2, run the *ps* command:

```
[user1@server10 ~]$ ps -eZ | grep passwd
unconfined_u:unconfined_r:passwd_t:s0-s0:c0.c1023 3836 pts/1 00:00:00
  passwd
```

As you can see, the *passwd* command (process) transitioned into the passwd_t domain to change the user password. A process running in this domain is allowed to modify the content of the */etc/shadow* file.

SELinux Booleans

Booleans are on/off switches that SELinux uses to determine whether to permit an action. Booleans activate or deactivate certain rule in the SELinux policy immediately and without the need to recompile or reload the policy. For instance, the ftpd_anon_write Boolean can be turned on to enable anonymous users to upload files. This privilege can be revoked by turning this Boolean off. Boolean values are stored in virtual files located in the */sys/fs/selinux/booleans* directory. The filenames match the Boolean names. A sample listing of this directory is provided below:

```
[user1@server10 ~]$ ls -l /sys/fs/selinux/booleans/
total 0
-rw-r--r--. 1 root root 0 Feb  5 22:02 abrt_anon_write
-rw-r--r--. 1 root root 0 Feb  5 22:02 abrt_handle_event
-rw-r--r--. 1 root root 0 Feb  5 22:02 abrt_upload_watch_anon_write
-rw-r--r--. 1 root root 0 Feb  5 22:02 antivirus_can_scan_system
-rw-r--r--. 1 root root 0 Feb  5 22:02 antivirus_use_jit
-rw-r--r--. 1 root root 0 Feb  5 22:02 auditadm_exec_content
........
```

On a typical server, you'll see hundreds of Boolean files in the output.

The manual pages of the Booleans are available through the *selinux-policy-doc* package. Once installed, use the -K option with the *man* command to bring the pages up for a specific Boolean. For instance, issue **man -K abrt_anon_write** to view the manual pages for the abrt_anon_write Boolean.

Boolean values can be viewed, and flipped temporarily or for permanence. The new value takes effect right away. Temporary changes are stored as a "1" or "0" in the corresponding Boolean file in the */sys/fs/selinux/booleans* directory and permanent changes are saved in the policy database.

One of the exercises in the next section demonstrates how to display and change Boolean values.

SELinux Administration

Managing SELinux involves plentiful tasks, including controlling the activation mode, checking operational status, setting security contexts on subjects and objects, and switching Boolean values. RHEL provides a set of commands to perform these operations. These commands are available through multiple packages, such as *libselinux-utils* provides *getenforce*, *getenforce*, and *getsebool* commands, *policycoreutils* contains *sestatus*, *setsebool*, and *restorecon* commands, *policycoreutils-python-utils* provides the *semanage* command, and *setools-console* includes the *seinfo* and *sesearch* commands.

For viewing alerts and debugging SELinux issues, a graphical tool called *SELinux Alert Browser* is available, which is part of the *setroubleshoot-server* package. In order to fully manage SELinux, you need to ensure that all these packages are installed on the system. Besides this toolset, there are additional utilities available to accomplish specific SELinux administration tasks, but their use is not as frequent.

Management Commands

SELinux delivers a variety of commands for effective administration. Table 20-1 lists and describes the commands mentioned above plus a few more under various management categories.

Command	Description
Mode Management	
getenforce	Displays the current mode of operation
grubby	Updates and displays information about the configuration files for the grub2 boot loader
sestatus	Shows SELinux runtime status and Boolean values
setenforce	Switches the operating mode between enforcing and permissive temporarily
Context Management	
chcon	Changes context on files (changes do not survive file system relabeling)
restorecon	Restores default contexts on files by referencing the files in the /etc/selinux/targeted/contexts/files directory
semanage	Changes context on files with the fcontext subcommand (changes survive file system relabeling)
Policy Management	
seinfo	Provides information on policy components
semanage	Manages policy database
sesearch	Searches rules in the policy database
Boolean Management	
getsebool	Displays Booleans and their current settings
setsebool	Modifies Boolean values temporarily, or in the policy database
semanage	Modifies Boolean values in the policy database with the boolean subcommand
Troubleshooting	
sealert	The graphical troubleshooting tool

Table 20-1 SELinux Management Commands

Most of these commands are employed in this chapter.

Viewing and Controlling SELinux Operational State

One of the key configuration files that controls the SELinux operational state, and sets its default type is the *config* file located in the */etc/selinux* directory. The default content of the file is displayed below:

```
[user1@server10 ~]$ cat /etc/selinux/config

# This file controls the state of SELinux on the system.
# SELINUX= can take one of these three values:
#       enforcing - SELinux security policy is enforced.
#       permissive - SELinux prints warnings instead of enforcing.
#       disabled - No SELinux policy is loaded.
```

```
. . . . . . . .
SELINUX=enforcing
# SELINUXTYPE= can take one of these three values:
#       targeted - Targeted processes are protected,
#       minimum - Modification of targeted policy. Only
 are protected.
#       mls - Multi Level Security protection.
SELINUXTYPE=targeted
```

The SELINUX directive sets the activation mode for SELinux. *Enforcing* activates it and allows or denies actions based on the policy rules. *Permissive* activates SELinux, but permits all actions. It records all security violations. This mode is useful for troubleshooting and in developing or tuning the policy. The third option is to completely turn SELinux off. When running in enforcing mode, the SELINUXTYPE directive dictates the type of policy to be enforced. The default is targeted.

Issue the *getenforce* command to determine the current operating mode:

```
[user1@server10 ~]$ getenforce
Enforcing
```

The output returns enforcing as the current active policy. You may flip the state to permissive using the *setenforce* command, and verify the change with *getenforce*:

```
[user1@server10 ~]$ sudo setenforce permissive
[user1@server10 ~]$ getenforce
Permissive
```

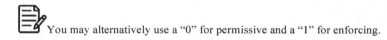 You may alternatively use a "0" for permissive and a "1" for enforcing.

The change takes effect at once; however, it will be lost at the next system reboot. To make it persistent, edit the */etc/selinux/config* file and set the SELINUX directive to the desired mode.

EXAM TIP: You may switch SELinux to permissive for troubleshooting a non-functioning service. Don't forget to change it back to enforcing when the issue is resolved.

To disable SELinux persistently, use the *grubby* command as follows:

```
[user1@server10 ~]$ sudo grubby --update-kernel ALL --args selinux=0
```

The above command appends the selinux=0 setting to the end of the "options" line in the bootloader configuration file located in the */boot/loader/entries* directory:

```
[user1@server10 ~]$ sudo cat /boot/loader/entries/96daf847168342be8233b83a9
2a2a3f0-5.14.0-162.12.1.el9_1.x86_64.conf
title Red Hat Enterprise Linux (5.14.0-162.12.1.el9_1.x86_64) 9.1 (Plow)
version 5.14.0-162.12.1.el9_1.x86_64
linux /vmlinuz-5.14.0-162.12.1.el9_1.x86_64
initrd /initramfs-5.14.0-162.12.1.el9_1.x86_64.img $tuned_initrd
options root=/dev/mapper/rhel-root ro crashkernel=1G-4G:192M,4G-64G:256M,64
G-:512M resume=/dev/mapper/rhel-swap rd.lvm.lv=rhel/root rd.lvm.lv=rhel/swa
p rhgb quiet $tuned_params
```

To revert the above, simply re-run the *grubby* command with the --remove-args option as shown below:

```
[user1@server10 ~]$ sudo grubby --update-kernel ALL --remove-args selinux=0
```

Querying Status

The current runtime status of SELinux can be viewed with the *sestatus* command. This command also displays the location of principal directories, the policy in effect, and the activation mode.

```
[user1@server10 ~]$ sestatus
SELinux status:                 enabled
SELinuxfs mount:                /sys/fs/selinux
SELinux root directory:         /etc/selinux
Loaded policy name:             targeted
Current mode:                   enforcing
Mode from config file:          enforcing
Policy MLS status:              enabled
Policy deny_unknown status:     allowed
Memory protection checking:     actual (secure)
Max kernel policy version:      33
```

The output reveals that SELinux is enabled (SELinux status), and it is running in permissive mode (Current mode) with the targeted policy in effect (Loaded policy name). It also indicates the current mode setting in the *config* file (Mode from config file) along with other information.

The *sestatus* command may be invoked with the -v switch to report on security contexts set on files and processes, as listed in the */etc/sestatus.conf* file. The default content of this file is shown below:

```
[user1@server10 ~]$ cat /etc/sestatus.conf
[files]
/etc/passwd
/etc/shadow
/bin/bash
/bin/login
/bin/sh
/sbin/agetty
/sbin/init
/sbin/mingetty
/usr/sbin/sshd
/lib/libc.so.6
/lib/ld-linux.so.2
/lib/ld.so.1

[process]
/sbin/mingetty
/sbin/agetty
/usr/sbin/sshd
```

Run the *sestatus* command with -v:

```
[user1@server10 ~]$ sestatus -v
SELinux status:               enabled
SELinuxfs mount:              /sys/fs/selinux
SELinux root directory:       /etc/selinux
Loaded policy name:           targeted
Current mode:                 enforcing
Mode from config file:        enforcing
Policy MLS status:            enabled
Policy deny_unknown status:   allowed
Memory protection checking:   actual (secure)
Max kernel policy version:    33

Process contexts:
Current context:              unconfined_u:unconfined_r:unconfin
0-s0:c0.c1023
Init context:                 system_u:system_r:init_t:s0

File contexts:
Controlling terminal:         unconfined_u:object_r:user_devpts_
/etc/passwd                   system_u:object_r:passwd_file_t:s0
/etc/shadow                   system_u:object_r:shadow_t:s0
. . . . . . . .
```

With -v included, the command reports the contexts for the current process (Current context) and the *init* (*systemd*) process (Init context) under Process Contexts. It also reveals the file contexts for the controlling terminal and associated files under File Contexts.

Exercise 20-1: Modify SELinux File Context

This exercise should be done on *server10* as *user1* with *sudo* where required.

In this exercise, you will create a directory *sedir1* under */tmp* and a file *sefile1* under *sedir1*. You will check the context on the directory and file. You will change the SELinux user and type to user_u and public_content_t on both and verify.

1. Create the hierarchy *sedir1/sefile1* under */tmp*:

    ```
    [user1@server10 ~]$ cd /tmp
    [user1@server10 tmp]$ mkdir sedir1
    [user1@server10 tmp]$ touch sedir1/sefile1
    ```

2. Determine the context on the new directory and file:

    ```
    [user1@server10 tmp]$ ls -ldZ sedir1
    drwxr-xr-x. 2 user1 user1 unconfined_u:object_r:user_tmp_t:s0 21 Feb   6
    11:30 sedir1
    [user1@server10 tmp]$ ls -ldZ sedir1/sefile1
    -rw-r--r--. 1 user1 user1 unconfined_u:object_r:user_tmp_t:s0 0 Feb   6
    1:30 sedir1/sefile1
    ```

The directory and the file get unconfined_u and user_tmp_t as the SELinux user and type.

3. Modify the SELinux user (-u) on the directory to user_u and type (-t) to public_content_t recursively (-R) with the *chcon* command:

```
[user1@server10 tmp]$ sudo chcon -vu user_u -t public_content_t sedir1 -R
changing security context of 'sedir1/sefile1'
changing security context of 'sedir1'
```

4. Validate the new context:

```
[user1@server10 tmp]$ ls -ldZ sedir1
drwxr-xr-x. 2 user1 user1 user_u:object_r:public_content_t:s0 21 Feb  6
  11:30 sedir1
[user1@server10 tmp]$ ls -ldZ sedir1/sefile1
-rw-r--r--. 1 user1 user1 user_u:object_r:public_content_t:s0 0 Feb  6
  11:30 sedir1/sefile1
```

This concludes the exercise.

Exercise 20-2: Add and Apply File Context

This exercise should be done on *server10* as *user1* with *sudo* where required.

In this exercise, you will add the current context on *sedir1* to the SELinux policy database to ensure a relabeling will not reset it to its previous value (see Exercise 20-1). Next, you will change the context on the directory to some random values. You will restore the default context from the policy database back to the directory recursively.

1. Determine the current context:

```
[user1@server10 tmp]$ ls -ldZ sedir1
drwxr-xr-x. 2 user1 user1 user_u:object_r:public_content_t:s0 21 Feb  6
  11:30 sedir1
[user1@server10 tmp]$ ls -ldZ sedir1/sefile1
-rw-r--r--. 1 user1 user1 user_u:object_r:public_content_t:s0 0 Feb  6
  11:30 sedir1/sefile1
```

The output indicates the current SELinux user (user_u) and type (public_content_t) set on the directory and the file.

2. Add (-a) the directory recursively to the policy database using the *semanage* command with the *fcontext* subcommand:

```
[user1@server10 tmp]$ sudo semanage fcontext -a -s user_u -t public_con
tent_t '/tmp/sedir1(/.*)?'
```

The regular expression (/.*)? instructs the command to include all files and subdirectories under */tmp/sedir1*. This expression is needed only if recursion is required.

The above command added the context to the */etc/selinux/targeted/contexts/files/file_contexts.local* file. You can use the *cat* command to view the content.

3. Validate the addition by listing (-l) the recent changes (-C) in the policy database:

```
[user1@server10 tmp]$ sudo semanage fcontext -Cl | grep sedir
/tmp/sedir1(/.*)?  all files    user_u:object_r:public_content_t:s0
```

4. Change the current context on *sedir1* to something random (staff_u/etc_t) with the *chcon* command:

```
[user1@server10 tmp]$ sudo chcon -vu staff_u -t etc_t sedir1 -R
changing security context of 'sedir1/sefile1'
changing security context of 'sedir1'
```

5. The security context is changed successfully. Confirm with the *ls* command:

```
[user1@server10 tmp]$ ls -ldZ sedir1 ; ls -lZ sedir1/sefile1
drwxr-xr-x. 2 user1 user1 staff_u:object_r:etc_t:s0 21 Feb  6 11:30
 sedir1
-rw-r--r--. 1 user1 user1 staff_u:object_r:etc_t:s0 0 Feb  6 11:30
sedir1/sefile1
```

6. Reinstate the context on the *sedir1* directory recursively (-R) as stored in the policy database using the *restorecon* command:

```
[user1@server10 tmp]$ sudo restorecon -Rv sedir1
Relabeled /tmp/sedir1 from staff_u:object_r:etc_t:s0 to staff_u:obj
ect_r:public_content_t:s0
Relabeled /tmp/sedir1/sefile1 from staff_u:object_r:etc_t:s0 to sta
ff_u:object_r:public_content_t:s0
```

The output confirms the restoration of the default context on the directory and the file.

EXAM TIP: Use the combination of semanage and restorecon commands to add a file context to the SELinux policy and then apply it. This will prevent the context on file to reset to the original value in the event of SELinux relabeling (disabled to enforcing/permissive).

Exercise 20-3: Add and Delete Network Ports

This exercise should be done on *server10* as *user1* with *sudo* where required.

In this exercise, you will add a non-standard network port 8010 to the SELinux policy database for the *httpd* service and confirm the addition. You will then remove the port from the policy and verify the deletion.

1. List (-l) the ports for the *httpd* service as defined in the SELinux policy database:

```
[user1@server10 ~]$ sudo semanage port -l | grep ^http_port
http_port_t     tcp      80, 81, 443, 488, 8008, 8009, 8443, 9000
```

The output reveals eight network ports the *httpd* process is currently allowed to listen on.

2. Add (-a) port 8010 with type (-t) http_port_t and protocol (-p) tcp to the policy:

```
[user1@server10 ~]$ sudo semanage port -at http_port_t -p tcp 8010
```

3. Confirm the addition:

```
[user1@server10 ~]$ sudo semanage port -l | grep ^http_port
http_port_t  tcp  8010, 80, 81, 443, 488, 8008, 8009, 8443, 9000
```

The new network port is visible in the outcome.

4.   Delete (-d) port 8010 from the policy and confirm:

```
[user1@server10 ~]$ sudo semanage port -dp tcp 8010
[user1@server10 ~]$ sudo semanage port -l | grep ^http_port
http_port_t  tcp  80, 81, 443, 488, 8008, 8009, 8443, 9000
```

The port is removed from the policy database.

> **EXAM TIP:** Any non-standard port you want to use for any service, make certain to add it to the SELinux policy database with the correct type.

Exercise 20-4: Copy Files with and without Context

This exercise should be done on *server10* as *user1* with *sudo* where required.

In this exercise, you will create a file called *sefile2* under */tmp* and display its context. You will copy this file to the */etc/default* directory, and observe the change in the context. You will remove se*file2* from */etc/default*, and copy it again to the same destination, ensuring that the target file receives the source file's context.

1.   Create file *sefile2* under */tmp* and show context:

```
[user1@server10 ~]$ touch /tmp/sefile2
[user1@server10 ~]$ ls -lZ /tmp/sefile2
-rw-r--r--. 1 user1 user1 unconfined_u:object_r:user_tmp_t:s0 0 Feb
   6 11:48 /tmp/sefile2
```

The context on the file is unconfined_u, object_r, and user_tmp_t.

2.   Copy this file to the */etc/default* directory, and check the context again:

```
[user1@server10 ~]$ sudo cp /tmp/sefile2 /etc/default/
[user1@server10 ~]$ ls -lZ /etc/default/sefile2
-rw-r--r--. 1 root root unconfined_u:object_r:etc_t:s0 0 Feb  6 11:
49 /etc/default/sefile2
```

The target file (*/etc/default/sefile2*) received the default context of the destination directory (*/etc/default*).

3.   Erase the */etc/default/sefile2* file, and copy it again with the --preserve=context option:

```
[user1@server10 ~]$ sudo rm /etc/default/sefile2
[user1@server10 ~]$ sudo cp --preserve=context /tmp/sefile2 /etc/de
fault
```

4.   List the file to view the context:

Chapter 20: Security Enhanced Linux   435

```
[user1@server10 ~]$ ls -lZ /etc/default/sefile2
-rw-r--r--. 1 root root unconfined_u:object_r:user_tmp_t:s0 0 Feb
6 11:50 /etc/default/sefile2
```

The original context (user_tmp_t) is preserved on the target file after the copy operation has finished.

Exercise 20-5: View and Toggle SELinux Boolean Values

This exercise should be done on *server10* as *user1* with *sudo* where required.

In this exercise, you will display the current state of the Boolean nfs_export_all_rw. You will toggle its value temporarily, and reboot the system. You will flip its value persistently after the system has been back up.

1. Display the current setting of the Boolean nfs_export_all_rw using three different commands—*getsebool*, *sestatus*, and *semanage*:

```
[user1@server10 ~]$ sudo getsebool -a | grep nfs_export_all_rw
nfs_export_all_rw --> on
[user1@server10 ~]$ sudo sestatus -b | grep nfs_export_all_rw
nfs_export_all_rw                    on
[user1@server10 ~]$ sudo semanage boolean -l | grep nfs_export_
all_rw
nfs_export_all_rw    (on , on)   Allow nfs to export all rw
```

2. Turn off the value of nfs_export_all_rw using the *setsebool* command by simply furnishing "off" or "0" with it and confirm:

```
[user1@server10 ~]$ sudo setsebool nfs_export_all_rw 0
[user1@server10 ~]$ sudo getsebool -a | grep nfs_export_all_rw
nfs_export_all_rw --> off
```

3. Reboot the system and rerun the *getsebool* command to check the Boolean state:

```
[user1@server10 ~]$ sudo getsebool -a | grep nfs_export_all_rw
nfs_export_all_rw --> on
```

The value reverted to its previous state.

4. Set the value of the Boolean persistently (-P or -m as needed) using either of the following:

```
[user1@server10 ~]$ sudo setsebool -P nfs_export_all_rw off
[user1@server10 ~]$ sudo semanage boolean -m -0 nfs_export_all_rw
```

5. Validate the new value using the *getsebool*, *sestatus*, or *semanage* command:

```
[user1@server10 ~]$ sudo getsebool nfs_export_all_rw
nfs_export_all_rw --> off
[user1@server10 ~]$ sudo sestatus -b | grep nfs_export_all_rw
nfs_export_all_rw               off
[user1@server10 ~]$ sudo semanage boolean -l | grep nfs_export_
all_rw
nfs_export_all_rw    (off , off)  Allow nfs to export all rw
```

The command outputs confirm the permanent change.

Monitoring and Analyzing SELinux Violations

SELinux generates alerts for system activities when it runs in enforcing or permissive mode. It writes the alerts to the */var/log/audit/audit.log* file if the *auditd* daemon is running, or to the */var/log/messages* file via the *rsyslog* daemon in the absence of *auditd*. SELinux also logs the alerts that are generated due to denial of an action, and identifies them with a type tag AVC (*Access Vector Cache*) in the *audit.log* file. It also writes the rejection in the *messages* file with a message ID, and how to view the message details.

 If it works with SELinux in permissive mode and not in enforcing, something needs to be adjusted in SELinux.

SELinux denial messages are analyzed, and the audit data is examined to identify the potential cause of the rejection. The results of the analysis are recorded with recommendations on how to fix it. These results can be reviewed to aid in troubleshooting, and recommended actions taken to address the issue. SELinux runs a service daemon called *setroubleshootd* that performs this analysis and examination in the background. This service also has a client interface called *SELinux Troubleshooter* (the *sealert* command) that reads the data and displays it for assessment. The client tool has both text and graphical interfaces. The server and client components are part of the *setroubleshoot-server* software package that must be installed on the system prior to using this service.

Figure 20-1 shows how SELinux handles an incoming access request (from a subject) to a target object.

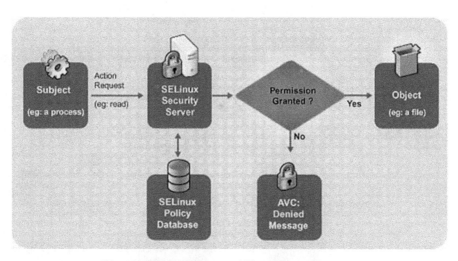

Figure 20-1 SELinux Allow/Deny Process

The following reveals a sample allowed record in raw format from the */var/log/audit/audit.log* file:

```
type=USER_ACCT msg=audit(1575462873.869:744): pid=7496 uid=0 auid=1000 ses=2 subj
=unconfined_u:unconfined_r:unconfined_t:s0-s0:c0.c1023 msg='op=PAM:accounting gra
ntors=pam_succeed_if acct="root" exe="/usr/bin/su" hostname=server10.example.com
addr=? terminal=pts/0 res=success'UID="root" AUID="user1"
```

The record indicates a successful *user1* attempt to *su* into the *root* user account on *server10*.

The following is a sample denial record from the same file in raw format:

```
type=AVC msg=audit(1575464056.692:782): avc:  denied  { create } for  pid=7677 co
mm="passwd" name="nshadow" scontext=unconfined_u:unconfined_r:passwd_t:s0-s0:c0.c
1023 tcontext=system_u:object_r:etc_t:s0 tclass=file permissive=0
```

The message has the AVC type, and it is related to the *passwd* command (comm) with source context (scontext) "unconfined_u:unconfined_r:passwd_t:s0-s0:c0.c1023", and the *nshadow* file (name) with file type (tclass) "file", and target context (tcontext) "system_u:object_r:etc_t:s0". It also indicates the SELinux operating mode, which is enforcing (permissive=0). This message indicates that the */etc/shadow* file does not have the correct context set on it, and that's why SELinux prevented the *passwd* command from updating the user's password.

You can also use the *sealert* command to analyze (-a) all AVC records in the *audit.log* file. This command produces a formatted report with all relevant details:

```
[user1@server10 ~]$ sudo sealert -a /var/log/audit/audit.log
100% done
found 1 alerts in /var/log/audit/audit.log
--------------------------------------------------------------------------

SELinux is preventing /usr/bin/passwd from create access on the file nshadow.

. . . . . . . .
Additional Information:
Source Context                  unconfined_u:unconfined_r:passwd_t:s0-s0:c0.c1023
Target Context                  system_u:object_r:etc_t:s0
Target Objects                  nshadow [ file ]
Source                          passwd
Source Path                     /usr/bin/passwd
Port                            <Unknown>
Host                            <Unknown>
Source RPM Packages             passwd-0.80-12.el9.x86_64
Target RPM Packages
SELinux Policy RPM              selinux-policy-targeted-34.1.43-1.el9.noarch
Local Policy RPM                selinux-policy-targeted-34.1.43-1.el9.noarch
Selinux Enabled                 True
Policy Type                     targeted
Enforcing Mode                  Enforcing
Host Name                       server10.example.com
Platform                        Linux server10.example.com
                                5.14.0-162.12.1.el9_1.x86_64 #1 SMP
                                PREEMPT_DYNAMIC Tue Dec 20 06:06:30 EST 2022
                                x86_64 x86_64
Alert Count                     1
First Seen                      2023-02-16 15:06:21 EST
Last Seen                       2023-02-16 15:06:21 EST
Local ID                        70a2641e-9f46-471d-8587-da639d82c62e

. . . . . . . .
```

The above SELinux denial was due to the fact that I produced the scenario by changing the SELinux type on the *shadow* file to something random (etc_t). I then issued the *passwd* command as *user1* to modify the password. As expected, SELinux disallowed the *passwd* command to write the new password to the *shadow* file, and it logged the password rejection attempt to the audit log. I then restored the type on the *shadow* file with **restorecon /etc/shadow**. I re-tried the password change and it worked.

Chapter Summary

In this chapter, we discussed security enhanced Linux in fair detail. We looked at the concepts, features, and terminology at length. We examined how security contexts are associated with users, processes, files, and ports, and viewed and modified contexts for them. We analyzed the configuration file that controls its state and defines the policy to be enforced. We examined how domain transitioning works. We learned several SELinux administrative commands and performed tasks such as checking and switching activation mode and operational status. We studied the concept of Booleans and learned how to modify certain parts of the SELinux policy temporarily and persistently. Finally, we reviewed the SELinux Troubleshooter program and used it to view and analyze SELinux related messages.

Review Questions

1. What would the command *semanage login -a -s user_u user10* do?
2. Name the two commands that can be used to modify a Boolean value.
3. Which option is used with the *ps* command to view the security contexts for processes?
4. What would the command *restorecon -F /etc/sysconfig* do?
5. What is the name of the default SELinux policy used in RHEL 9?
6. SELinux is an implementation of discretionary access control. True or False?
7. Where are SELinux denial messages logged in the absence of the *auditd* daemon?
8. Name the four parts of a process context.
9. What would the command *sestatus -b | grep nfs_export_all_rw* do?
10. Name the directory that stores SELinux Boolean files.
11. What are the two commands to display and modify the SELinux mode?
12. Name the two SELinux subjects.
13. What one task must be done to change the SELinux mode from enforcing to disabled?
14. Which option with the *cp* command must be specified to preserve SELinux contexts?
15. What is the purpose of the command *sestatus*?
16. What is the name and location of the SELinux configuration file?
17. What would the command *semanage fcontext -Cl* do?
18. Which command can be used to ensure modified contexts will survive file system relabeling?
19. With SELinux running in enforcing mode and one of the services on the system is compromised, all other services will be affected. True or False?
20. Name the command that starts the SELinux Troubleshooter program.

Answers to Review Questions

1. This command provided will map Linux user *user10* with SELinux user user_u.
2. The *semanage* and *setsebool* commands.
3. The -Z option.
4. The command provided will restore the default SELinux contexts on the specified directory.
5. The default SELinux policy used in RHEL 9 is targeted.

6. False. SELinux is an implementation of mandatory access control.
7. The SELinux denial messages are logged to the */var/log/messages* file.
8. The four parts of a process context are user, role, type/domain, and sensitivity level.
9. The command provided will display the current value of the specified Boolean.
10. The */sys/fs/selinux/booleans* directory.
11. The *getenforce* and *setenforce* commands.
12. User and process are two SELinux subjects.
13. The system must be rebooted.
14. The --preserve=context option.
15. The *sestatus* command displays SELinux status information.
16. The SELinux configuration filename is *config* and it is located in the */etc/selinux* directory.
17. The command provided will show recent changes made to the SELinux policy database.
18. The *semanage* command.
19. False.
20. The command name is *sealert*.

Do-It-Yourself Challenge Labs

The following labs are useful to strengthen most of the concepts and topics learned in this chapter. It is expected that you perform the labs without external help. A step-by-step guide is not supplied, as the knowledge and skill required to implement the labs have already been disseminated in the chapter; however, hints to the relevant major topic(s) are included.

Use the lab environment built specifically for end-of-chapter labs. See sub-section "Lab Environment for End-of-Chapter Labs" in Chapter 01 "Local Installation" for details.

Lab 20-1: Disable and Enable the SELinux Operating Mode

As *user1* with *sudo* on *server30*, check and make a note of the current SELinux operating mode. Modify the configuration file and set the mode to disabled. Reboot the system to apply the change. Run *sudo getenforce* to confirm the change when the system is up. Restore the directive's value to enforcing in the configuration file, and reboot to apply the new mode. Run *sudo getenforce* to confirm the mode when the system is up. (Hint: SELinux Administration).

Lab 20-2: Modify Context on Files

As *user1* with *sudo* on *server30*, create directory hierarchy */tmp/d1/d2*. Check the contexts on */tmp/d1* and */tmp/d1/d2*. Change the SELinux type on */tmp/d1* to etc_t recursively with the *chcon* command and confirm. Add */tmp/d1* to the policy database with the *semanage* command to ensure the new context is persistent on the directory hierarchy. (Hint: SELinux Administration).

Lab 20-3: Add Network Port to Policy Database

As *user1* with *sudo* on *server30*, add network port 9005 to the SELinux policy database for the secure HTTP service using the *semanage* command. Verify the addition. (Hint: SELinux Administration).

Lab 20-4: Copy Files with and without Context

As *user1* with *sudo* on *server30*, create file *sef1* under */tmp*. Copy the file to the */usr/local* directory. Check and compare the contexts on both source and destination files. Create another file *sef2* under */tmp* and copy it to the */var/local* directory using the --preserve=context option with the *cp* command. Check and compare the contexts on both source and destination files. (Hint: SELinux Administration).

Lab 20-5: Flip SELinux Booleans

As *user1* with *sudo* on *server30*, check the current value of Boolean *ssh_use_tcpd* using the *getsebool* and *sestatus* commands. Use the *setsebool* command and toggle the value of the directive. Confirm the new value with the *getsebool*, *semanage*, or *sestatus* command. (Hint: SELinux Administration).

Chapter 21

Shell Scripting

This chapter describes the following major topics:

➢ Overview of shell scripts

➢ Write scripts to display basic system information, employ shell and environment variables, use command substitution, and manipulate special and positional parameters

➢ Execute and debug scripts

➢ Know exit codes and test conditions

➢ Understand logical constructs: if-then-fi, if-then-else-fi, and if-then-elif-fi

➢ Write scripts using logical statements

➢ Know arithmetic test conditions

➢ Comprehend looping construct: for-do-done

➢ Write scripts using looping statements

RHCSA Objectives:

12. Conditionally execute code (use of: if, test, [], etc.)
13. Use Looping constructs (for, etc.) to process file, command line input
14. Process script inputs ($1, $2, etc.)
15. Processing output of shell commands within a script

S hell

S hell scripts are essentially a group of Linux commands along with control structures and optional comments stored in a text file. Their primary purpose of creation is the automation of long and repetitive tasks. Scripts may include any simple to complex command and can be executed directly at the Linux command prompt. They do not need to be compiled as they are interpreted by the shell line by line.

I ♥ #/bin/bash

This chapter presents example scripts and analyzes them to solidify the learning. These scripts begin with simple programs and advance to more complicated ones. As with any other programming language, the scripting skill develops over time as more and more scripts are read, written, and examined. This chapter also discusses a debug technique that may be helpful in troubleshooting the code.

Shell Scripts

Shell scripts (a.k.a. *shell programs* or simply *scripts*) are text files that contain Linux commands and control structures to automate lengthy, complex, or repetitive tasks, such as managing packages and users, administering partitions and file systems, monitoring file system utilization, trimming log files, archiving and compressing files, finding and removing unnecessary files, starting and stopping database services and applications, and producing reports. Commands in a script are interpreted and run by the shell one at a time in the order in which they are listed. Each line is executed as if it is typed and run at the command prompt. Control structures are utilized for creating and managing conditional and looping constructs. Comments are also generally included to add information about the script such as the author name, creation date, previous modification dates, purpose, and usage. If the script encounters an error during execution, the error message is printed on the screen.

Scripts presented in this chapter are written in the bash shell and may be used in other Linux shells with slight modifications.

You can use any available text editor to write the scripts; however, it is suggested to use the *vim* editor so that you have an opportunity to practice it as you learn scripting. To quickly identify where things are in your scripts, you can use the *nl* command to enumerate the lines. You can store your scripts in the */usr/local/bin* directory, which is included in the PATH of all users by default.

Script01: Displaying System Information

Let's create the first script called *sys_info.sh* on *server10* in the */usr/local/bin* directory and examine it line by line. Use the *vim* editor with *sudo* to write the script. Type what you see below. Do not enter the line numbers, as they are used for explanation and reference.

```
[user1@server10 ~]$ nl /usr/local/bin/sys_info.sh
     1  #!/bin/bash
     2  # The script name is sys_info.sh
     3  # The script is written by Asghar Ghori on February 6, 2023
     4  # The script should be located in under /usr/local/bin
     5  # The script shows basic system information
     6  echo "Display Basic System Information"
     7  echo "================================="
     8  echo
     9  echo "The hostname, hardware, and OS information is:"
    10  /usr/bin/hostnamectl
    11  echo
    12  echo "The following users are currently logged in:"
    13  /usr/bin/who
```

 Within vim, press the ESC key and then type :set nu to view line numbers associated with each line entry.

In this script, comments and commands are used as follows:

The first line indicates the shell that will run the commands in the script. This line must start with the "#!" character combination (called *shebang*) followed by the full pathname to the shell file.

The next three lines contain comments: the script name, author name, creation time, default directory location for storage, and purpose. The number sign (#) implies that anything to the right of it is informational and will be ignored during script execution. Note that the first line also uses the number character (#), but it is followed by the exclamation mark (!); that combination has a special meaning to the shell.

The fifth line has the first command of the script. The *echo* command prints on the screen whatever follows it ("Display Basic System Information" in this case). This may include general comments, errors, or script usage.

The sixth line will highlight the text "Display Basic System Information" by underlining it.

The seventh line has the *echo* command followed by nothing. This will insert an empty line in the output.

The eighth line will print "The hostname, hardware, and OS information is:".

The ninth line will execute the *hostnamectl* command to display basic information about the system.

The tenth line will insert an empty line.

The eleventh line will print "The following users are currently logged in:" on the screen.

The twelfth line will execute the *who* command to list the logged-in users.

Here is the listing of the *sys_info.sh* file created in the */usr/local/bin* directory:

```
[user1@server10 ~]$ ll /usr/local/bin/sys_info.sh
-rw-r--r--. 1 root root 434 Feb  6 22:31 /usr/local/bin/sys_info.sh
```

Executing a Script

The script created above does not have the execute permission bit since the default umask for the *root* user is set to 0022, which allows read/write access to the owner, and read-only access to the rest. You will need to run the *chmod* command on the file and add an execute bit for everyone:

```
[user1@server10 ~]$ sudo chmod +x /usr/local/bin/sys_info.sh
[user1@server10 ~]$ ll /usr/local/bin/sys_info.sh
-rwxr-xr-x. 1 root root 434 Feb  6 22:31 /usr/local/bin/sys_info.sh
```

Any user on the system can now run this script using either its name or the full path.

Let's run the script and see what the output will look like:

```
[user1@server10 ~]$ sys_info.sh
Display Basic System Information
====================================

The hostname, hardware, and OS information is:
  Static hostname: server10.example.com
        Icon name: computer-vm
          Chassis: vm
       Machine ID: 96daf847168342be8233b83a92a2a3f0
          Boot ID: 2fbfb1f6ed1b485baa71bc0afd894952
   Virtualization: oracle
 Operating System: Red Hat Enterprise Linux 9.1 (Plow)
      CPE OS Name: cpe:/o:redhat:enterprise_linux:9::baseos
           Kernel: Linux 5.14.0-162.12.1.el9_1.x86_64
     Architecture: x86-64
  Hardware Vendor: innotek GmbH
   Hardware Model: VirtualBox

The following users are currently logged in:
user1      pts/0          2023-02-06 22:28 (192.168.0.3)
```

The output reflects the execution of the commands as scripted.

The *hostnamectl* command displays the hostname of the system, type of platform (physical, virtual) it is running on, hypervisor vendor name, operating system name and version, current kernel version, hardware architecture, and other information.

Debugging a Script

Before you have a perfectly working script in place, you may have to run and modify it more than once. You can use a debugging technique that will help identify where the script might have failed or did not function as expected. You can either append the -x option to the "#!/bin/bash" at the beginning of the script to look like "#!/bin/bash -x", or execute the script as follows:

```
[user1@server10 ~]$ bash -x sys_info.sh
+ echo 'Display Basic System Information'
Display Basic System Information
+ echo ================================
================================
+ echo

+ echo 'The hostname, hardware, and OS information is:'
The hostname, hardware, and OS information is:
+ /usr/bin/hostnamectl
  Static hostname: server10.example.com
........
```

The above output now also includes the actual lines from the script prefixed by the + sign and followed by the command execution result. It also shows the line number of the problem line in the output if there is any. This way you can identify any issues pertaining to the path, command name, use of special characters, etc., and address it quickly. Try changing any of the *echo* commands in the script to "iecho" and re-run the script in the debug mode to confirm what has just been said.

Script02: Using Local Variables

You had worked with variables earlier in the book and seen their usage. To recap, there are two types of variables: *local* (also called *private* or *shell*) and *environment*. Both can be defined and used in scripts and at the command line.

The following script called *use_var.sh* will define a local variable and display its value on the screen. You will re-check the value of this variable after the script execution has completed. The comments have been excluded for brevity.

```
[user1@server10 ~]$ cat /usr/local/bin/use_var.sh
#!/bin/bash
echo "Setting a Local Variable"
echo "========================="
SYSNAME=server10.example.com
echo "The hostname of this system is $SYSNAME"
```

Add the execute bit to the script. The following output will be generated when you run it:

```
[user1@server10 ~]$ use_var.sh
Setting a Local Variable
=========================
The hostname of this system is server10.example.com
```

If you run the *echo* command to see what is stored in the SYSNAME variable, you will get nothing:

```
[user1@server10 ~]$ echo $SYSNAME

[user1@server10 ~]$
```

The output is self-explanatory.

Script03: Using Pre-Defined Environment Variables

The following script called *pre_env.sh* will display the values of SHELL and LOGNAME environment variables:

```
[user1@server10 ~]$ cat /usr/local/bin/pre_env.sh
#!/bin/bash
echo "The location of my shell command is:"
echo $SHELL
echo "I am logged in as $LOGNAME"
```

Add the execute bit to the script, and run to view the result:

```
[user1@server10 ~]$ pre_env.sh
The location of my shell command is:
/bin/bash
I am logged in as user1
```

The output is self-explanatory.

Script04: Using Command Substitution

During the execution of a script, you can use the command substitution feature of the bash shell and store the output generated by the command into a variable. For example, the following script called *cmd_out.sh* will run the *hostname* and *uname* commands and save their outputs in variables. This script shows two different ways to use command substitution. Make sure to use the backticks (normally located with the ~ character on the keyboard) to enclose the *uname* command.

```
[user1@server10 ~]$ cat /usr/local/bin/cmd_out.sh
#!/bin/bash
SYSNAME=$(hostname)
KERNVER=`uname -r`
echo "The hostname is $SYSNAME"
echo "The kernel version is $KERNVER"
```

Add the execute bit and run the script:

```
[user1@server10 ~]$ cmd_out.sh
The hostname is server10.example.com
The kernel version is 5.14.0-162.12.1.el9_1.x86_64
```

The output is self-explanatory.

Understanding Shell Parameters

A *shell parameter* (or simply a *parameter*) is an entity that holds a value such as a name, special character, or number. The parameter that holds a name is referred to as a variable; a special character is referred to as a *special parameter*; and one or more digits, except for 0 is referred to as a *positional parameter* (a.k.a. a *command line argument*). A special parameter represents the command or script itself ($0), count of supplied arguments ($* or $@), all arguments ($#), and PID

---

of the process ($$). A positional parameter ($1, $2, $3 . . .) is an argument supplied to a script at the time of its invocation, and its position is determined by the shell based on its location with respect to the calling script. Figure 21-1 gives a pictorial view of the special and positional parameters.

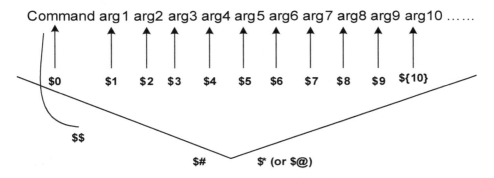

Figure 21-1 Shell Parameters

Figure 21-1 also shows that positional parameters beyond 9 are to be enclosed in curly brackets. Just like the variable and command substitutions, the shell uses the dollar ($) sign for special and positional parameter expansions as well.

Script05: Using Special and Positional Parameters

The script *com_line_arg.sh* below will show the supplied arguments, total count, value of the first argument, and PID of the script:

```
[user1@server10 ~]$ cat /usr/local/bin/com_line_arg.sh
#!/bin/bash
echo "There are $# arguments specified at the command line"
echo "The arguments supplied are: $*"
echo "The first argument is: $1"
echo "The Process ID of the script is: $$"
```

The result will be as follows when the script is executed with four arguments. Do not forget to add the execute bit prior to running it.

```
[user1@server10 ~]$ com_line_arg.sh Toronto Brisbane Doha Milan
There are 4 arguments specified at the command line
The arguments supplied are: Toronto Brisbane Doha Milan
The first argument is: Toronto
The Process ID of the script is: 2719
```

The output is self-explanatory.

Script06: Shifting Command Line Arguments

The *shift* command is used to move arguments one position to the left. During this move, the value of the first argument is lost. The *com_line_arg_shift.sh* script below is an extension to the *com_line_arg.sh* script. It uses the *shift* command to show what happens when arguments are moved.

```
[user1@server10 ~]$ cat /usr/local/bin/com_line_arg_shift.sh
#!/bin/bash
echo "There are $# arguments specified at the command line"
echo "The arguments supplied are: $*"
echo "The first argument is: $1"
echo "The Process ID of the script is: $$"
shift
echo "The new first argument after the first shift is: $1"
shift
echo "The new first argument after the second shift is: $1"
```

Let's execute the script with the same four arguments. Notice that a new value is assigned to $1 after each shift.

```
[user1@server10 ~]$ com_line_arg_shift.sh Toronto Brisbane Doha Milan
There are 4 arguments specified at the command line
The arguments supplied are: Toronto Brisbane Doha Milan
The first argument is: Toronto
The Process ID of the script is: 2727
The new first argument after the first shift is: Brisbane
The new first argument after the second shift is: Doha
```

Multiple shifts in a single attempt may be performed by furnishing a count of desired shifts to the *shift* command as an argument. For example, "*shift* 2" will carry out two shifts, "*shift* 3" will make three shifts, and so on.

Logical Constructs

So far, we have talked about simple scripts that run the code line by line. The shell lets us employ logical constructs to control the flow of scripts. It does this by allowing us to use test conditions, which decides what to do next based on the true or false status of the condition.

The shell offers two logical constructs: the *if-then-fi* construct and the *case* construct. The if-then-fi construct has a few variations and those will be covered as well. A discussion on the case construct is beyond the scope.

Before starting to look at the example scripts and see how logical constructs are used, let's discuss exit codes and various test conditions. You will use them later in the example scripts.

Exit Codes

Exit codes, or *exit values*, refer to the value returned by a command when it finishes execution. This value is based on the outcome of the command. If the command runs successfully, you typically get a zero exit code, otherwise you get a non-zero value. This code is also referred to as a *return code,* and it is stored in a special shell parameter called *?* (question mark). Let's look at the following two examples to understand their usage:

```
[user1@server10 ~]$ pwd
/home/user1
[user1@server10 ~]$ echo $?
0
[user1@server10 ~]$ man
What manual page do you want?
[user1@server10 ~]$ echo $?
1
[user1@server10 ~]$
```

In the first example, the *pwd* command ran successfully and it produced the desired result, hence a zero exit code was returned and stored in the ?. In the second example, the *man* command did not run successfully because of a missing argument, therefore a non-zero exit code was returned and stored in the ?.

You can define exit codes within a script at different locations to help debug the script by knowing where exactly it terminated.

Test Conditions

Test conditions are used in logical constructs to decide what to do next. They can be set on integer values, string values, or files using the *test* command or by enclosing them within the square brackets []. Table 21-1 describes various test condition operators.

Operation on Integer Value	Description
integer1 -eq (-ne) integer2	Integer1 is equal (not equal) to integer2
integer1 -lt (-gt) integer2	Integer1 is less (greater) than integer2
integer1 -le (-ge) integer2	Integer1 is less (greater) than or equal to integer2
Operation on String Value	**Description**
string1=(!=)string2	Tests whether the two strings are identical (not identical)
-l string or -z string	Tests whether the string length is zero
string or -n string	Tests whether the string length is non-zero
Operation on File	**Description**
-b (-c) file	Tests whether the file is a block (character) device file
-d (-f) file	Tests whether the file is a directory (normal file)
-e (-s) file	Tests whether the file exists (non-empty)
-L file	Tests whether the file is a symlink
-r (-w) (-x) file	Tests whether the file is readable (writable) (executable)
-u (-g) (-k) file	Tests whether the file has the setuid (setgid) (sticky) bit
file1 -nt (-ot) file2	Tests whether file1 is newer (older) than file2
Logical Operators	**Description**
!	The logical NOT operator
-a or && (two ampersand characters)	The logical AND operator. Both operands must be true for the condition to be true. Syntax: [-b file1 && -r file1]
-o or || (two pipe characters)	The logical OR operator. Either of the two or both operands must be true for the condition to be true. Syntax: [(x == 1 -o y == 2)]

Table 21-1 Test Conditions

Having described the exit codes and test conditions, let's look at a few example scripts and observe their effects.

The if-then-fi Construct

The if-then-fi statement evaluates the condition for true or false. It executes the specified action if the condition is true; otherwise, it exits the construct. The if-then-fi statement begins with an "if" and ends with a "fi", as depicted in the flow diagram in Figure 21-2:

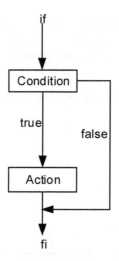

Figure 21-2 The if-then-fi Construct

The general syntax of this statement is as follows:

```
if   condition
then
        action
fi
```

This construct is used in the following script.

Script07: The if-then-fi Construct

You saw earlier how to check the number of arguments supplied at the command line. The following script called *if_then_fi.sh* determines the number of arguments and prints an error message if there are none provided:

```
[user1@server10 ~]$ cat /usr/local/bin/if_then_fi.sh
#!/bin/bash
if [ $# -ne 2 ]   # Ensure there is a space after [ and before ]
then
   echo   "Error: Invalid number of arguments supplied"
   echo   "Usage: $0 source_file destination_file"
exit 2
fi
echo   "Script terminated"
```

This script will display the following messages on the screen if it is executed without exactly two arguments specified at the command line:

```
[user1@server10 ~]$ if_then_fi.sh a
Error: Invalid number of arguments supplied
Usage: /usr/local/bin/if_then_fi.sh source_file destination_file
```

A value of 2 will appear upon examining the return code as follows. This value reflects the exit code that you defined in the script on line 6.

```
[user1@server10 ~]$ echo $?
2
```

Conversely, the return code will be 0 and the message will be as follows if you supply a pair of arguments:

```
[user1@server10 ~]$ if_then_fi.sh a b
Script terminated
[user1@server10 ~]$ echo $?
0
```

The if-then-else-fi Construct

The if-then-fi statement has a limitation and it can execute an action only if the specified condition is true. It quits the statement if the condition is untrue. The if-then-else-fi statement, in contrast, is more advanced in the sense that it can execute an action if the condition is true and another action if the condition is false. The flow diagram for this structure is shown in Figure 21-3:

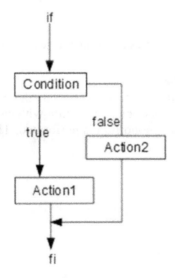

Figure 21-3 The if-then-else-fi Construct

The general syntax of this statement is as follows:

```
if    condition
then
      action1
else
      action2
fi
```

action1 or action2 is performed based on the true or false evaluation of the condition.

Script08: The if-then-else-fi Construct

The following script called *if_then_else_fi.sh* will accept an integer value as an argument and tell if the value is positive or negative:

```
[user1@server10 ~]$ cat /usr/local/bin/if_then_else_fi.sh
#!/bin/bash
if [ $1 -gt 0 ]
then
   echo "$1 is a positive integer value"
else
   echo "$1 is a negative integer value"
fi
```

Run this script one time with a positive integer value and the next time with a negative value:

```
[user1@server10 ~]$ if_then_else_fi.sh 10
10 is a positive integer value
[user1@server10 ~]$ if_then_else_fi.sh -10
-10 is a negative integer value
```

Try the script again but with a non-integer value and see what it does.

The if-then-elif-fi Construct

The if-then-elif-fi is a more sophisticated construct than the other two conditional statements. You can define multiple conditions and associate an action with each one of them. During the evaluation, the action corresponding to the true condition is performed. The flow diagram for this structure is shown in Figure 21-4:

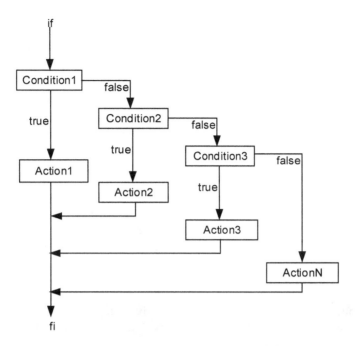

Figure 21-4 The if-then-elif-fi Construct

The general syntax of this statement is as follows:

```
if      condition1
then
        action1
elif    condition2
then
        action2
elif    condition3
then
        action3
………….
else
        action(n)
fi
```

Let's use the if-then-elif-fi construct in the following two example scripts.

Script09: The if-then-elif-fi Construct (Example 1)

The *if_then_elif_fi.sh* script is an enhanced version of the *if_then_else_fi.sh* script. It accepts an integer value as an argument and tells if it is positive, negative, or zero. If a non-integer value or no argument is supplied, the script will complain. Notice that the script employs the *exit* command after each action to help you identify where it exited.

```
[user1@server10 ~]$ cat /usr/local/bin/if_then_elif_fi.sh
#!/bin/bash
if [ $1 -gt 0 ]
then
   echo "$1 is a positive integer value"
exit 1
elif [ $1 -eq 0 ]
then
   echo "$1 is a zero integer value"
exit 2
elif [ $1 -lt 0 ]
then
   echo "$1 is a negative integer value"
exit 3
else
   echo "$1 is not an integer value. Please supply an integer."
exit 4
fi
```

Run this script four times: the first time with a positive integer, the second time with 0, the third time with a negative integer, and the fourth time with a non-integer value. Check the exit code after each execution to know where the script exited.

```
[user1@server10 ~]$ if_then_elif_fi.sh 10
10 is a positive integer value
[user1@server10 ~]$ echo $?
1
[user1@server10 ~]$
[user1@server10 ~]$ if_then_elif_fi.sh 0
0 is a zero integer value
[user1@server10 ~]$ echo $?
2
[user1@server10 ~]$
[user1@server10 ~]$ if_then_elif_fi.sh -10
-10 is a negative integer value
[user1@server10 ~]$ echo $?
3
[user1@server10 ~]$
[user1@server10 ~]$ if_then_elif_fi.sh abd
abd is not an integer value. Please supply an integer.
[user1@server10 ~]$ echo $?
4
```

The outputs and exit values reflect the program code.

Script10: The if-then-elif-fi Construct (Example 2)

The script *ex200_ex294.sh* will display the name of the Red Hat exam RHCSA or RHCE in the output based on the input argument (ex200 or ex294). If a random or no argument is provided, it will print "Usage: Acceptable values are ex200 and ex294". Make sure to add white spaces in the conditions as shown.

```
[user1@server10 ~]$ cat /usr/local/bin/ex200_ex294.sh
#!/bin/bash
if [ "$1" = ex200 ]
then
  echo "RHCSA"
elif [ "$1" = ex294 ]
then
  echo "RHCE"
else
  echo "Usage: Acceptable values are ex200 and ex294"
fi
```

Run this script three times: the first time with argument ex200, the second time with argument ex294, and the third time with something random as an argument:

```
[user1@server10 ~]$ ex200_ex294.sh ex200
RHCSA
[user1@server10 ~]$ ex200_ex294.sh ex294
RHCE
[user1@server10 ~]$ ex200_ex294.sh ex300
Usage: Acceptable values are ex200 and ex294
```

The results are as expected.

EXAM TIP: A good understanding of the usage of logical statements is important.

Looping Constructs

As a Linux user and administrator, you often want to perform certain task on a number of given elements or repeatedly until a specified condition becomes true or false. For instance, if plenty of disks need to be initialized for use in LVM, you can either run the *pvcreate* command on each disk one at a time manually or employ a loop to do it for you. Likewise, based on a condition, you may want a program to continue to run until that condition becomes true or false.

There are three constructs—*for-do-done*, *while-do-done*, and *until-do-done*—that you can use to implement looping.

 The for loop is also referred to as the foreach loop.

The for loop iterates on a list of given values until the list is exhausted. The while loop runs repeatedly until the specified condition becomes false. The until loop does just the opposite of the while loop; it performs an operation repeatedly until the specified condition becomes true. This chapter will discuss the for loop only; the other two are out of scope.

Test Conditions

The *let* command is used in looping constructs to evaluate a condition at each iteration. It compares the value stored in a variable against a pre-defined value. Each time the loop does an iteration, the variable value is altered. You can enclose the condition for arithmetic evaluation within a pair of parentheses (( )) or quotation marks (" ") instead of using the *let* command explicitly.

Table 21-2 lists operators that can be used in test conditions.

Operator	Description
!	Negation
+ / – / * / /	Addition / subtraction / multiplication / division
%	Remainder
< / <=	Less than / less than or equal to
> / >=	Greater than / greater than or equal to
=	Assignment
== / !=	Comparison for equality / non-equality

Table 21-2 Arithmetic Operators

Having described various test condition operators, let's look at the syntax of the for loop and a few example scripts and observe the implications of some of the test conditions.

The for Loop

The for loop is executed on an array of elements until all the elements in the array are consumed. Each element is assigned to a variable one after the other for processing. The flow diagram for this construct is displayed in Figure 21-5:

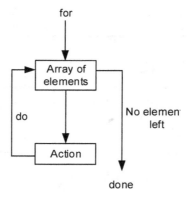

Figure 21-5 The for Loop

The general syntax of this construct is as follows:

```
for  VAR  in  list
do
      action
done
```

Script11: Print Alphabets Using for Loop

The *for_do_done.sh* script initializes the variable COUNT to 0. The for loop will read each letter sequentially from the range placed within curly brackets (no spaces before the letter A and after the letter Z), assign it to another variable LETTER, and display the value on the screen. The *expr* command is an arithmetic processor, and it is used here to increment the COUNT by 1 at each loop iteration.

```
[user1@server10 ~]$ cat /usr/local/bin/for_do_done.sh
#!/bin/bash
COUNT=0
for LETTER in {A..Z}
do
   COUNT=`/usr/bin/expr $COUNT + 1`
   echo "Letter $COUNT is [$LETTER]"
done
```

The output of the script will be:

```
[user1@server10 ~]$ for_do_done.sh
Letter 1 is [A]
Letter 2 is [B]
Letter 3 is [C]
Letter 4 is [D]
Letter 5 is [E]
........
Letter 25 is [Y]
Letter 26 is [Z]
```

Script12: Create Users Using for Loop

The *create_user.sh* script can create several Linux user accounts. As each account is created, the value of the variable ? is checked. If the value is 0, a message saying the account is created successfully will be displayed, otherwise the script will terminate. In case of a successful account creation, the *passwd* command will be invoked to assign the user the same password as their username.

```
[user1@server10 ~]$ cat /usr/local/bin/create_user.sh
#!/bin/bash
for USER in user{10..12}
do
   echo "Creating account for user $USER"
   /usr/sbin/useradd $USER
if [ $? = 0 ]
then
   echo $USER | /usr/bin/passwd --stdin $USER
   echo "$USER is created successfully"
else
   echo "Failed to create account $USER"
exit
fi
done
```

The result of the script execution below confirms the addition of three new user accounts:

```
[user1@server10 ~]$ sudo /usr/local/bin/create_user.sh
Creating account for user user10
Changing password for user user10.
passwd: all authentication tokens updated successfully.
user10 is created successfully
Creating account for user user11
Changing password for user user11.
passwd: all authentication tokens updated successfully.
user11 is created successfully
Creating account for user user12
Changing password for user user12.
passwd: all authentication tokens updated successfully.
user12 is created successfully
```

If this script is re-executed without modifying the list of elements (usernames), the following will appear:

```
[user1@server10 ~]$ sudo /usr/local/bin/create_user.sh
Creating account for user user10
useradd: user 'user10' already exists
Failed to create account user10
```

EXAM TIP: A good understanding of the looping construct will help on the exam.

Chapter Summary

In this chapter, we learned the basics of bash shell scripting. This chapter began with an overview of scripting and then demonstrated how to write and analyze test scripts using various built-in features of the bash shell. We wrote and examined simple code and gradually advanced to more advanced scripts, including those that employed logical and looping constructs. We learned how to identify problem lines in our scripts. After understanding and practicing the scripts presented in this chapter, you should be able to write your own programs, debug them, and examine those authored by others.

Review Questions

1. What are the two types of logical constructs mentioned in this chapter?
2. What would != imply in a looping condition?
3. What is the function of the *shift* command?
4. You can script the startup and shutdown of a database. True or False?
5. What is the difference between a line in a script starting with a "#" and a "#!"?
6. What comments may you want to include in a shell script? Write any six.
7. What is one benefit of writing shell scripts?
8. What are the three major components in a shell script?
9. Which looping construct can be used to perform an action on listed items?
10. What does the *echo* command do without any arguments?
11. What would the command *echo $?* do?
12. When would you want to use an exit code in your script?
13. What would you modify in a shell script to run it in the debug mode?
14. What would the command *bash -x /usr/local/bin/script1.sh* do?

Answers to Review Questions

1. The if and case constructs.
2. != would check the value for non-equality.
3. The *shift* command moves an argument to the left.
4. True.
5. The former is used to include general comments in the script and the latter combination dictates the full path to the shell file that is to be used to execute the script.
6. The author name, creation date, last modification date, location, purpose, and usage.
7. One major benefit of writing shell scripts is to automate lengthy and repetitive tasks.
8. The three major components in a shell script are commands, control structures, and comments.
9. The for loop.
10. The *echo* command inserts an empty line in the output when used without arguments.
11. This command will display the exit code of the last command executed.
12. The purpose of using an exit code is to determine exactly where the script quits.
13. We would specify -x as an argument to the shell path.
14. This command will execute *script1.sh* in debug mode.

Do-It-Yourself Challenge Labs

The following labs are useful to strengthen most of the concepts and topics learned in this chapter. It is expected that you perform the labs without external help. A step-by-step guide is not supplied, as the knowledge and skill required to implement the labs have already been disseminated in the chapter; however, hints to the relevant major topic(s) are included.

Use the lab environment built specifically for end-of-chapter labs. See sub-section "Lab Environment for End-of-Chapter Labs" in Chapter 01 "Local Installation" for details.

Lab 21-1: Write Script to Create Logical Volumes

For this lab, present 2x1GB virtual disks to *server40* in VirtualBox Manager. As *user1* with *sudo* on *server40*, write a single bash script to create 2x800MB partitions on each disk using *parted* and then bring both partitions into LVM control with the *pvcreate* command. Create a volume group called *vgscript* and add both physical volumes to it. Create three logical volumes each of size 500MB and name them *lvscript1*, *lvscript2*, and *lvscript3*.

Lab 21-2: Write Script to Create File Systems

This lab is a continuation of Lab 21-1. Write another bash script to create xfs, ext4, and vfat file system structures in the logical volumes, respectively. Create mount points */mnt/xfs*, */mnt/ext4*, and */mnt/vfat*, and mount the file systems. Include the *df* command with -h in the script to list the mounted file systems.

Lab 21-3: Write Script to Configure New Network Connection Profile

For this lab, present a new network interface to *server40* in VirtualBox Manager. As *user1* with *sudo* on *server40*, write a single bash script to run the *nmcli* command to configure custom IP assignments (choose your own settings) on the new network device. Make a copy of the */etc/hosts* file as part of this script. Choose a hostname of your choice and add a mapping to the *etc/hosts* file without overwriting existing file content.

Chapter 22

Containers

This chapter describes the following major topics:

➢ Understand container technology
➢ Identify key Linux features that establish the foundation to run containers
➢ Analyze container benefits
➢ A better home for containers
➢ Grasp the concepts of container images and registries
➢ Compare pros and cons of root and rootless containers
➢ Examine registry configuration file
➢ Work with container images (find, inspect, pull, list, and delete)
➢ Build container images using custom containerfile
➢ Administer basic containers (start, list, stop, remove, interact with, run commands from outside, attach to, run custom entry point commands, etc.)
➢ Implement advanced container features (port mapping, environment variables, and persistent storage)
➢ Control container operational states via systemd

RHCSA Objectives:

61. Find and retrieve container images from a remote registry
62. Inspect container images
63. Perform container management using commands such as podman and skopeo
64. Build a container from a Containerfile
65. Perform basic container management such as running, starting, stopping, and listing running containers
66. Run a service inside a container
67. Configure a container to start automatically as a systemd service
68. Attach persistent storage to a container

Containers and containerization technologies such as Docker and Kubernetes have received an overwhelming appreciation and massive popularity in recent years. They are part of many new deployments. Containers offer an improved method to package distributed applications, deploy them in a consistent manner, and run them in isolation from one another on the same or different virtual or physical server(s). Containers take advantage of the native virtualization features available in the Linux kernel. Each container typically encapsulates one self-contained application that includes all dependencies such as library files, configuration files, software binaries, and services.

This chapter presents an overview of container images, container registries, and containers. It shows how to interact with images and registries. It demonstrates how to launch, manage, and interact with containers. It discusses advanced topics such as mapping a host port with a container port, passing and setting environment variables, and attaching host storage for data persistence. The chapter ends with a detailed look at controlling the operational states of containers via the systemd service. There are numerous exercises in the chapter to support the concepts learned.

Introduction to Containers

Traditionally, one or more applications are deployed on a single server. These applications may have conflicting requirements in terms of shared library files, package dependencies, and software versioning. Moreover, patching or updating the operating system may result in breaking an application functionality. To address these and other potential challenges, developers perform an analysis on their current deployments before they decide whether to collocate a new application with an existing one or to go with a new server without taking the risk of breaking the current operation.

Fortunately, there is a better choice available now in the form of containers. Developers can now package their application alongside dependencies, shared library files, environment variables, and other specifics in a single image file and use that file to run the application in a unique, isolated "environment" called *container*. A container is essentially a set of processes that runs in complete seclusion on a Linux system. A single Linux system running on bare metal hardware or in a virtual machine may have tens or hundreds of containers running at a time. The underlying hardware may be located either on the ground or in the cloud.

 Containers run on Windows as well.

Each container is treated as a complete whole, which can be tagged, started, stopped, restarted, or even transported to another server without impacting other running containers. This way any conflicts that may exist among applications, within application components, or with the operating system can be evaded. Applications encapsulated to run inside containers are called *containerized applications*. Containerization is a growing trend for architecting and deploying applications, application components, and databases in real world environments.

Containers and the Linux Features

The container technology employs some of the core features available in the Linux kernel. These features include control groups, namespaces, seccomp (*secure computing mode*), and SELinux. A short description of each of these is provided below:

Control Groups

Control groups (abbreviated as *cgroups*) split processes into groups to set limits on their consumption of compute resources—CPU, memory, disk, and network I/O. These restrictions result in controlling individual processes from over utilizing available resources.

Namespaces

Namespaces restrict the ability of process groups from seeing or accessing system resources—PIDs, network interfaces, mount points, hostname, etc.—thus instituting a layer of isolation between process groups and the rest of the system. This feature guarantees a secure, performant, and stable environment for containerized applications as well as the host operating system.

Secure Computing Mode (seccomp) and SELinux

These features impose security constraints thereby protecting processes from one another and the host operating system from running processes.

The container technology employs these characteristics to run processes isolated in a highly secure environment with full control over what they can or cannot do.

Benefits of Using Containers

There are several benefits linked with using containers. These benefits range from security to manageability and from independence to velocity. The following provides a quick look at common containerization benefits:

Isolation

Containers are not affected due to changes in the host operating system or in other hosted or containerized applications, as they run fully isolated from the rest of the environment.

Loose Coupling

Containerized applications are loosely coupled with the underlying operating system due to their self-containment and minimal level of dependency.

Maintenance Independence

Maintenance is performed independently on individual containers.

Less Overhead

Containers require fewer system resources than do bare metal and virtual servers.

Transition Time

Containers require a few seconds to start and stop.

Transition Independence

Transitioning from one state to another (start or stop) is independent of other containers, and it does not affect or require a restart of any underlying host operating system service.

Portability

Containers can be migrated to other servers without modifications to the contained applications. The target servers may be bare metal or virtual and located on-premises or in the cloud.

Reusability

The same container image can be used to run identical containers in development, test, pre-production, and production environments. There is no need to rebuild the image.

Rapidity

The container technology allows for accelerated application development, testing, deployment, patching, and scaling. Also, there is no need for an exhaustive testing.

Version Control

Container images can be version-controlled, which gives users the flexibility in choosing the right version to run a container.

Container Home: Bare Metal or Virtual Machine

A hypervisor software such as VMware ESXi, Oracle VirtualBox VM Manager, Microsoft Hyper-V, or KVM allows multiple virtual machines to run on the same bare metal physical server. Each virtual machine runs an isolated, independent instance of its own guest operating system. All virtual machines run in parallel and share the resources of the underlying hardware of the bare metal server. Each virtual machine may run multiple applications that share the virtualized resources allocated to it. The hypervisor runs a set of services on the bare metal server to enable virtualization and support virtual machines, which introduces management and operational overheads. Besides, any updates to the guest operating system may require a reboot or result in an application failure.

Containers, in contrast, run directly on the underlying operating system whether it be running on a bare metal server or in a virtual machine. They share hardware and operating system resources securely among themselves. This allows containerized applications to stay lightweight and isolated, and run in parallel. Containers share the same Linux kernel and require far fewer hardware resources than do virtual machines, which contributes to their speedy start and stop. Given the presence of an extra layer of hypervisor services, it may be more beneficial and economical to run containers directly on non-virtualized physical servers.

Figure 22-1 depicts how applications are placed on traditional bare metal hardware, in virtual machines, and to run as containers on bare metal servers.

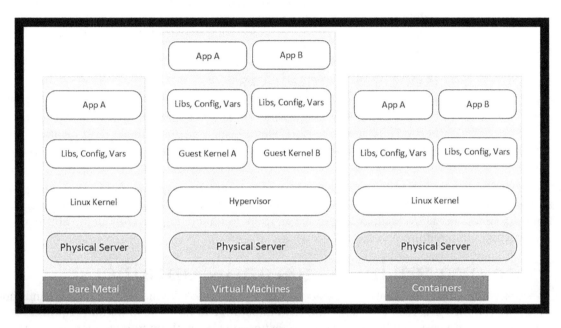

Figure 22-1 Container Home: Bare Metal or Virtual Machine

The added layer of hypervisor is shown in the middle stack. Any of the above implementation can run multiple applications concurrently. A decision as to which option to go with requires a careful use case study; however, the benefits of running containers on bare metal servers are obvious.

Container Images and Container Registries

Launching a container requires a pre-packaged image to be available. A container *image* is essentially a static file that is built with all necessary components—application binaries, library files, configuration settings, environment variables, static data files, etc.—required by an application to run smoothly, securely, and independently. RHEL follows the *open container initiative* (OCI) to allow users to build images based on industry standard specifications that define the image format, host operating system metadata, and supported hardware architectures. An OCI-compliant image can be executed and managed with OCI-compliant tools such as *podman* (*pod manager*) and Docker. Images can be version-controlled giving users the suppleness to use the latest or any of the previous versions to launch their containers. A single image can be used to run several containers at once.

Container images adhere to a standard naming convention for identification. This is referred to as *fully qualified image name* (FQIN). An FQIN is comprised of four components: (1) the storage location (registry_name), (2) the owner or organization name (user_name), (3) a unique repository name (repo_name), and (4) an optional version (tag). The syntax of an FQIN is *registry_hostname/user_name/repo_name:tag*.

Images are stored and maintained in public or private *registries*; however, they need to be downloaded and made locally available for consumption. There are several registries available on the Internet. These include *registry.redhat.io* (images based on official Red Hat products; requires authentication), *registry.access.redhat.com* (requires no authentication), *registry.connect.redhat.com* (images based on third-party products), and *hub.docker.com* (Docker Hub). The three Red Hat registries may be searched using the Red Hat Container Catalog at *catalog.redhat.com/software/containers/search*. Additional registries may be added as required. Private registries may also require authentication for access.

Rootful vs. Rootless Containers

Containers can be launched with the *root* user privileges (*sudo* or directly as the *root* user). This gives containers full access to perform administrative functions including the ability to map privileged network ports (1024 and below). However, launching containers with superuser rights opens a gate to potential unauthorized access to the container host if a container is compromised due to a vulnerability or misconfiguration.

To secure containers and the underlying operating system, containers should be launched and interacted with as normal Linux users. Such containers are referred to as *rootless* containers. Rootless containers allow regular, unprivileged users to run containers without the ability to perform tasks that require privileged access.

Working with Images and Containers

To work with images and containers, a good comprehension of the management commands and the configuration files involved is crucial. It is also imperative to have the minimum required version of the necessary software installed to ensure the features you're looking to implement are available. RHEL offers two commands—*podman* and *skopeo*—to manage and interact with images, registries, and containers. These tools can also be used to troubleshoot issues and to perform advanced management tasks; however, a discussion around debugging and advanced management is beyond the scope of this book.

Exercise 22-1: Install Necessary Container Support

This exercise should be done on *server20* as *user1* with *sudo* where required.

In this exercise, you will install the necessary software to set the foundation for completing the exercises in the remainder of the chapter. The standard RHEL 9.1 image includes a package called *container-tools* that consists of all the required components and commands. You will use the standard *dnf* command to install the package.

1. Install the *container-tools* package:

```
[user1@server20 ~]$ sudo dnf install -y container-tools
Last metadata expiration check: 19:16:45 ago on Mon 06 Feb 2023 04:29:15 PM.
Dependencies resolved.
================================================================================
 Package              Architecture Version            Repository      Size
================================================================================
Installing:
 container-tools      noarch       1-12.el9           AppStream       9.0 k
Installing dependencies:
 podman-docker        noarch       2:4.2.0-3.el9      AppStream        43 k
 podman-remote        x86_64       2:4.2.0-3.el9      AppStream       8.1 M
 python3-podman       noarch       3:4.2.0-1.el9      AppStream       173 k
 python3-pyxdg        noarch       0.27-3.el9         AppStream       108 k
 python3-toml         noarch       0.10.2-6.el9       AppStream        46 k
 skopeo               x86_64       2:1.9.2-1.el9      AppStream       6.6 M
 toolbox              x86_64       0.0.99.3-5.el9     AppStream       2.2 M
 udica                noarch       0.2.6-4.el9        AppStream        54 k

Transaction Summary
================================================================================
Install  9 Packages

Total size: 17 M
Installed size: 59 M
. . . . . . . .
Installed:
  container-tools-1-12.el9.noarch          podman-docker-2:4.2.0-3.el9.noarch
  podman-remote-2:4.2.0-3.el9.x86_64       python3-podman-3:4.2.0-1.el9.noarch
  python3-pyxdg-0.27-3.el9.noarch          python3-toml-0.10.2-6.el9.noarch
  skopeo-2:1.9.2-1.el9.x86_64              toolbox-0.0.99.3-5.el9.x86_64
  udica-0.2.6-4.el9.noarch

Complete!
```

See the *skopeo* and *podman* commands and their versions on the list of installed packages above. They are now available on the system for managing images and containers.

2. Verify the package installation:

```
[user1@server20 ~]$ dnf list container-tools

Installed Packages
container-tools.noarch     1-12.el9        @AppStream
```

The output confirms a successful installation of the *container-tools* package.

This concludes the exercise.

The podman Command

Managing images and containers involves several operations such as finding, inspecting, retrieving, and deleting images and running, stopping, listing, and deleting containers. The *podman* command is used for most of these operations. It supports numerous subcommands and options. Table 22-1 describes the subcommands that are used in this chapter.

Subcommand	Description
Image Management	
build	Builds an image using instructions delineated in a Containerfile
images	Lists downloaded images from local storage
inspect	Examines an image and displays its details
login/logout	Logs in/out to/from a container registry. A login may be required to access private and protected registries.
pull	Downloads an image to local storage from a registry
rmi	Removes an image from local storage
search	Searches for an image. The following options can be included with this subcommand: 1. A partial image name in the search will produce a list of all images containing the partial name. 2. The --no-trunc option makes the command exhibit output without truncating it. 3. The --limit <number> option limits the displayed results to the specified number.
tag	Adds a name to an image. The default is 'latest' to classify the image as the latest version. Older images may have specific version identifiers.
Container Management	
attach	Attaches to a running container
exec	Runs a process in a running container
generate	Generates a systemd unit configuration file that can be used to control the operational state of a container. The --new option is important and is employed in later exercises.
info	Reveals system information, including the defined registries
inspect	Exhibits the configuration of a container
ps	Lists running containers (includes stopped containers with the -a option)
rm	Removes a container
run	Launches a new container from an image. Some options such as -d (detached), -i (interactive), and -t (terminal) are important and are employed in exercises where needed.
start/stop/restart	Starts, stops, or restarts a container

Table 22-1 Common podman Subcommands

Consult the manual pages of the *podman* command for details on the usage of these and other subcommands.

EXAM TIP: A solid understanding of the usage of the podman command is key to completing container tasks.

The skopeo Command

The *skopeo* command is utilized for interacting with local and remote images and registries. It has numerous subcommands available; however, you will be using only the *inspect* subcommand to examine the details of an image stored in a remote registry. View the manual pages of *skopeo* for details on the usage of the *inspect* and other subcommands.

The registries.conf File

The system-wide configuration file for image registries is the *registries.conf* file and it resides in the */etc/containers* directory. Normal Linux users may store a customized copy of this file, if required, under the *~/.config/containers* directory. The settings stored in the per-user file will take precedence over those stored in the system-wide file. This is especially useful for running rootless containers.

The *registries.conf* file defines searchable and blocked registries. The below output shows the uncommented lines from the file:

```
[user1@server20 ~]$ grep -Ev '^#|^$' /etc/containers/registries.conf
unqualified-search-registries = ["registry.access.redhat.com", "regist
ry.redhat.io", "docker.io"]
short-name-mode = "enforcing"
```

The output shows three registries. The *podman* command searches these registries for container images in the given order.

If access to an additional registry is necessary, simply add it to the list and place it according to your preference. For instance, if you want a private registry called *registry.private.myorg.io* to be added with the highest priority, edit this file and make the following change:

> unqualified-search-registries = ["registry.private.myorg.io", "registry.access.redhat.com", "registry.redhat.io", "docker.io"]

If this private registry is the only one to be used, you can take the rest of the registry entries out of the list. In that case, the line entry will look like:

> unqualified-search-registries = ["registry.private.myorg.io"]

EXAM TIP: As there is no Internet access provided during Red Hat exams, you may have to access a network-based registry to download images.

The default content of the file is good for many use cases; however, you may see additional or different entries on busy systems.

Viewing Podman Configuration and Version

The *podman* command references various system runtime and configuration files and runs certain Linux commands in the background to gather and display information. For instance, it looks for registries and storage data in the system-wide and per-user configuration files, pulls memory information from the */proc/meminfo* file, executes **uname -r** to obtain the kernel version, and so on. *podman*'s *info* subcommand shows all this information. Here is a sample when this command is executed as a normal user (*user1*):

```
[user1@server20 ~]$ podman info
host:
  arch: amd64
  buildahVersion: 1.27.0
  cgroupControllers:
  - memory
  - pids
  cgroupManager: systemd
  cgroupVersion: v2
  conmon:
    package: conmon-2.1.4-1.el9.x86_64
    path: /usr/bin/conmon
    version: 'conmon version 2.1.4, co1
39721499e160'
  cpuUtilization:
    idlePercent: 99.7
    systemPercent: 0.23
    userPercent: 0.07
  cpus: 2
  distribution:
    distribution: '"rhel"'
    version: "9.1"
.........
  kernel: 5.14.0-162.6.1.el9_1.x86_64
  linkmode: dynamic
  logDriver: k8s-file
  memFree: 70537216
  memTotal: 1290690560

........
registries:
  search:
  - registry.access.redhat.com
  - registry.redhat.io
  - docker.io
store:
  configFile: /home/user1/.config/containers/storage.conf
  containerStore:
    number: 0
    paused: 0
    running: 0
    stopped: 0
........
  imageStore:
    number: 0
  runRoot: /run/user/1000/containers
  volumePath: /home/user1/.local/share/containers/storage/volumes
........
```

The above output is self-explanatory.

Now, re-run the command as *root* (preceded by *sudo* if running as *user1*) and compare the values for the settings "rootless" under host and "ConfigFile" and "ImageStore" under store. The differences lie between where the root and rootless (normal) users store and obtain configuration data, the number of container images they have locally available, and so on.

Similarly, you can run the *podman* command as follows to check its version:

```
[user1@server20 ~]$ podman version
Client:         Podman Engine
Version:        4.2.0
API Version:    4.2.0
Go Version:     go1.18.4
Built:          Mon Aug 22 08:37:10 2022
OS/Arch:        linux/amd64
```

The output reveals the version (4.2.0) of the *podman* utility, and this is what you will be using to perform the forthcoming exercises.

Image Management

Container images are available from numerous private and public registries. They are pre-built for a variety of use cases. You can search through registries to find the one that suits your needs. You can examine their metadata before downloading them for consumption. Downloaded images can be removed when no longer needed to conserve local storage. The same pair of commands—*podman* and *skopeo*—is employed for these operations.

Exercise 22-2: Search, Examine, Download, and Remove an Image

This exercise should be done on *server20* as *user1* with *sudo* where required.

In this exercise, you will log in to the *registry.access.redhat.com* registry with the Red Hat credentials that you created in Chapter 01 "Local Installation" to download the RHEL 9.1 image. You will look for an image called *mysql-80* in the registry, examine its details, pull it to your system, confirm the retrieval, and finally erase it from the local storage. You will use the *podman* and *skopeo* commands as required for these operations.

1. Log in to the specified Red Hat registry:

    ```
    [user1@server20 ~]$ podman login registry.redhat.io
    Username: ██████
    Password:
    Login Succeeded!
    ```

2. Confirm a successful login:

    ```
    [user1@server20 ~]$ podman login registry.redhat.io --get-login
    ```

You should see your login name in the output.

3. Find the *mysql-80* image in the specified registry. Add the --no-trunc option to view full output.

```
[user1@server20 ~]$ podman search registry.redhat.io/mysql-80 --no-trunc
NAME                                    DESCRIPTION
registry.redhat.io/rhel8/mysql-80       This container image provides a
containerized packaging of the MySQL mysqld daemon and client application
. The mysqld server daemon accepts connections from clients and provides
access to content from MySQL databases on behalf of the clients.
registry.redhat.io/rhel9/mysql-80       rhcc_registry.access.redhat.com_
rhel9/mysql-80
registry.redhat.io/rhscl/mysql-80-rhel7 This container image provides a
containerized packaging of the MySQL mysqld daemon and client application
. The mysqld server daemon accepts connections from clients and provides
access to content from MySQL databases on behalf of the clients.
```

4. Select the second image *rhel9/mysql-80* for this exercise. Inspect the image without downloading it using *skopeo inspect*. A long output will be generated. The command uses the docker:// mechanism to access the image.

```
[user1@server20 ~]$ skopeo inspect docker://registry.redhat.io/rhel9/mysq
l-80
{
    "Name": "registry.redhat.io/rhel9/mysql-80",
    "Digest": "sha256:f20bad15ccf810492c26fd8f8bb44aedd880142d2b1a55a17f7
ce84426929454",
    "RepoTags": [
        "1-228",
        "1-228.1669634586",
        "1-190.1655192188-source",
        "1-206",
. . . . . . . .
        "latest"
    ],
    "Created": "2023-02-07T22:08:28.243932602Z",
    "DockerVersion": "",
    "Labels": {
        "architecture": "x86_64",
        "build-date": "2023-02-07T22:06:13",
        "com.redhat.component": "mysql-80-container",
        "com.redhat.license_terms": "https://www.redhat.com/en/about/red-
hat-end-user-license-agreements#rhel",
        "description": "MySQL is a multi-user, multi-threaded SQL databas
e server. The container image provides a containerized packaging of the M
ySQL mysqld daemon and client application. The mysqld server daemon accep
ts connections from clients and provides access to content from MySQL dat
abases on behalf of the clients.",
. . . . . . . .
```

The output shows older versions under RepoTags, the creation time for the latest version, the build date of the image, a description, and other information. It is a good practice to analyze the metadata of an image prior to downloading and consuming it.

5. Download the image by specifying the fully qualified image name using *podman pull*:

```
[user1@server20 ~]$ podman pull docker://registry.redhat.io/rhel9/mysql-80
Trying to pull registry.redhat.io/rhel9/mysql-80:latest...
Getting image source signatures
Checking if image destination supports signatures
Copying blob a5b9df63f283 done
Copying blob fc07e4fdbabe done
Copying blob 25ead466f550 done
Copying config 3d93d1dfea done
Writing manifest to image destination
Storing signatures
3d93d1dfeacd771a06244b1534b7d7d410d02dc7f33a2f7743ffc2168f44d9aa
```

6. List the image to confirm the retrieval using *podman images*:

```
[user1@server20 ~]$ podman images
REPOSITORY                            TAG      IMAGE ID      CREATED
  SIZE
registry.redhat.io/rhel9/mysql-80   latest   3d93d1dfeacd  39 hours ago
  551 MB
```

The output indicates the FQIN of the image (repository), version (tag), image ID, creation time, and size.

7. Display the image's details using *podman inspect*. The command will generate a long output. You may pipe the output to *less* to view one screenful of information at a time.

```
[user1@server20 ~]$ podman inspect mysql-80
[
    {
        "Id": "3d93d1dfeacd771a06244b1534b7d7d410d02dc7f3
f44d9aa",
        "Digest": "sha256:f20bad15ccf810492c26fd8f8bb44ae
a17f7ce84426929454",
        "RepoTags": [
            "registry.redhat.io/rhel9/mysql-80:latest"
        ],
. . . . . . . .
```

8. Remove the mysql-80 image from local storage using *podman rmi*:

```
[user1@server20 ~]$ podman rmi mysql-80
Untagged: registry.redhat.io/rhel9/mysql-80:latest
Deleted: 3d93d1dfeacd771a06244b1534b7d7d410d02dc7f33a2f7743ff
```

The *podman* command shows the ID of the image after deletion.

9. Confirm the removal using *podman images*:

```
[user1@server20 ~]$ podman images
REPOSITORY   TAG         IMAGE ID    CREATED     SIZE
```

The image is no longer available in the local storage, which confirms the removal.

This concludes the exercise.

Containerfile

For specific use cases where an existing image does not fulfill a requirement, you can build a custom image by outlining the steps you need to be run in a file called *Containerfile*. The *podman* command can then be used to read those instructions and executes them to produce a new image.

 The file name *containerfile* is widespread; however, in reality, you can use any name of your liking.

There are several instructions, Table 22-2, that may be utilized inside a Containerfile to perform specific functions during the build process.

Instruction	Description
CMD	Runs a command
COPY	Copies files to the specified location
ENV	Defines environment variables to be used during the build process
EXPOSE	A port number that will be opened when a container is launched using this image
FROM	Identifies the base container image to use
RUN	Executes the specified commands
USER	Defines a non-*root* user to run the commands as
WORKDIR	Sets the working directory. This directory is automatically created if it does not already exist.

Table 22-2 Common Containerfile Instructions

A sample container file is presented below:

```
[user1@server20 ~]$ cat containerfile
#Use RHEL9 base image
FROM registry.redhat.io/ubi9/ubi

# Install Apache web server software
RUN dnf -y install httpd

# Copy the website
COPY ./index.html /var/www/html/

# Expose Port 80/tcp
EXPOSE 80

# Start Apache web server
CMD ["httpd"]
```

The file contains five instructions with comments to self-explain their purpose. The *index.html* file may contain a basic statement such as "This is a custom-built Apache web server container image based on RHEL 9".

EXAM TIP: A solid understanding of what each command instruction does and how to use it within a containerfile is important.

Exercise 22-3: Use Containerfile to Build Image

This exercise should be done on *server20* as *user1* with *sudo* where required.

In this exercise, you will use a containerfile to build a custom image based on the latest version of the RHEL 9 *universal base image* (ubi) available from a Red Hat container registry. You will confirm the image creation. You will use the *podman* command for these activities.

1. Log in to the specified Red Hat registry:

```
[user1@server20 ~]$ podman login registry.redhat.io
Username: ⬛⬛⬛⬛⬛
Password:
Login Succeeded!
```

2. Confirm a successful login:

```
[user1@server20 ~]$ podman login registry.redhat.io --get-login
```

3. Create a file called *containerfile* with the following code:

```
[user1@server20 ~]$ cat containerfile
#Use RHEL9 base image
FROM registry.redhat.io/ubi9/ubi

# Count the number of characters
CMD echo "RHCSA exam is hands-on." | wc

# Copy a local file to /tmp
COPY ./testfile /tmp
```

4. Create a file called *testfile* with some random text in it and place it in the same directory as the containerfile.

5. Build an image by specifying the containerfile name (-f) and an image tag (-t) such as *ubi9-simple-image*. The period character at the end represents the current directory and this is where both *containerfile* and *testfile* are located.

```
[user1@server20 ~]$ podman image build -f containerfile -t ubi9-simple-image .
STEP 1/3: FROM registry.redhat.io/ubi9/ubi
Trying to pull registry.redhat.io/ubi9/ubi:latest...
Getting image source signatures
Checking if image destination supports signatures
Copying blob fc07e4fdbabe done
Copying config 10acc17441 done
Writing manifest to image destination
Storing signatures
STEP 2/3: CMD echo "RHCSA exam is hands-on." | wc
--> a25953befea
STEP 3/3: COPY ./testfile /tmp
COMMIT ubi9-simple-image
--> 8c2abb5bafb
Successfully tagged localhost/ubi9-simple-image:latest
8c2abb5bafb9daf805b15262c189b57dddd6b3ee9e1e51eb3d8fd260ee257e98
```

The output indicates that *podman* downloaded the latest version of RHEL 9 ubi from the specified registry, ran the *echo* command, uploaded the *testfile* to */tmp*, and applied the tag to the custom image.

6. Confirm image creation:

```
[user1@server20 ~]$ podman image ls
REPOSITORY                      TAG       IMAGE ID      CREATED         SIZE
localhost/ubi9-simple-image     latest    8c2abb5bafb9  14 minutes ago  219 MB
registry.redhat.io/ubi9/ubi     latest    10acc174412e  2 days ago      219 MB
```

The output shows the downloaded image as well as the new custom image along with their image IDs, creation time, and size. Do not remove the custom image yet as you will be using it to launch a container in the next section.

This concludes the exercise.

Basic Container Management

Managing containers involves common tasks such as starting, stopping, listing, viewing information about, and deleting them. Depending on the use case, containers can be launched in different ways. They can have a name assigned or be nameless, have a terminal session opened for interaction, execute an entry point command (the command specified at the launch time) and be auto-terminated right after, and so on. Running containers can be stopped and restarted, or discarded if no longer needed. The *podman* command is utilized to start containers and manage their lifecycle. This command is also employed to list stopped and running containers, and view their details.

Exercise 22-4: Run, Interact with, and Remove a Named Container

This exercise should be done on *server20* as *user1* with *sudo* where required.

In this exercise, you will run a container based on the latest version of the RHEL 8 ubi available in the Red Hat container registry. You will assign this container a name and run a few native Linux commands in a terminal window interactively. You will exit out of the container to mark the completion of the exercise.

1. Launch a container using ubi8 (RHEL 8). Name this container *rhel8-base-os* and open a terminal session (-t) for interaction (-i). Use the *podman run* command.

```
[user1@server20 ~]$ podman run -ti --name rhel8-base-os ubi8
Resolved "ubi8" as an alias (/etc/containers/registries.conf.d.
Trying to pull registry.access.redhat.com/ubi8:latest...
Getting image source signatures
Checking if image destination supports signatures
Copying blob ea0a20a2c448 done
Copying config 55e87c8c55 done
Writing manifest to image destination
Storing signatures
[root@3d284974eddb /]#
```

The above command downloaded the latest version of the specified image automatically even though no FQIN was provided. This is because it searched through the registries listed in the */etc/containers/registries.conf* file and retrieved the image from wherever it found it first (*registry.access.redhat.com*). It also opened a terminal session inside the container as the *root* user to interact with the containerized RHEL 8 OS. The container ID is reflected as the hostname in the container's command prompt (last line in the output). This is an auto-generated ID.

 If you encounter any permission issues, delete the */etc/docker* directory (if it exists) and try again.

2. Run a few basic commands such as *pwd*, *ls*, *cat*, and *date* inside the container for verification:

```
[root@3d284974eddb /]# pwd
/
[root@3d284974eddb /]# ls
bin   dev   home   lib64        media  opt    root  sbin  sys  usr
boot  etc   lib    lost+found   mnt    proc   run   srv   tmp  var
[root@3d284974eddb /]#
[root@3d284974eddb /]# cat /etc/redhat-release
Red Hat Enterprise Linux release 8.7 (Ootpa)
[root@3d284974eddb /]#
[root@3d284974eddb /]# date
Fri Feb 10 13:45:16 UTC 2023
```

3. Close the terminal session when done:

```
[root@3d284974eddb /]# exit
exit
[user1@server20 ~]$
```

4. Delete the container using *podman rm*:

```
[user1@server20 ~]$ podman rm  rhel8-base-os
aab058b49f37696f543766ddf9e6df36ed2fa5c326bde59d6932fbe5c198adc7
```

Confirm the removal with **podman ps**.

This concludes the exercise.

Exercise 22-5: Run a Nameless Container and Auto-Remove it After Entry Point Command Execution

This exercise should be done on *server20* as *user1*.

In this exercise, you will launch a container based on the latest version of RHEL 7 ubi available in a Red Hat container registry. This image provides the base operating system layer to deploy containerized applications. You will enter a Linux command at the command line for execution inside the container as an entry point command and the container should be automatically deleted right after that.

1. Start a container using ubi7 (RHEL 7) and run *ls* as an entry point command. Use *podman run* with the --rm option to remove the container as soon as the entry point command has finished running.

```
[user1@server20 ~]$ podman run --rm ubi7 ls
Resolved "ubi7" as an alias (/etc/containers/registries.conf.d
Trying to pull registry.access.redhat.com/ubi7:latest...
Getting image source signatures
Checking if image destination supports signatures
Copying blob 7597778323f6 done
Copying config f0c1470d8c done
Writing manifest to image destination
Storing signatures
bin
boot
dev
etc
home
lib
lib64
media
. . . . . . . .
```

The *ls* command was executed successfully, and the container was terminated thereafter.

2. Confirm the container removal with *podman ps*:

```
[user1@server20 ~]$ podman ps
CONTAINER ID   IMAGE   COMMAND   CREATED   STATUS   PORTS   NAMES
[user1@server20 ~]$
```

The container no longer exists.

This concludes the exercise.

Advanced Container Management

Containers run a variety of applications and databases that may need to communicate with applications or databases running in other containers on the same or different host system over certain network ports. Preset environment variables may be passed when launching containers or new variables may be set for containerized applications to consume for proper operation. Information stored during an application execution is lost when a container is restarted or erased. This behavior can be overridden by making a directory on the host available inside the container for saving data persistently. Containers may be configured to start and stop with the transitioning of the host system via the systemd service. These advanced tasks are also performed with the *podman* command. Let's take a closer look.

Containers and Port Mapping

Applications running in different containers often need to exchange data for proper operation. For instance, a containerized Apache web server may need to talk to a MySQL database instance running in a different container. It may also need to talk to the outside world over a port such as 80

---

or 8080. To support this traffic flow, appropriate port mappings are established between the host system and each container.

EXAM TIP: As a normal user, you cannot map a host port below 1024 to a container port.

Exercise 22-6: Configure Port Mapping

This exercise should be done on *server20* as *root*.

In this exercise, you will launch a container called *rhel7-port-map* in detached mode (as a daemon) with host port 10000 mapped to port 8000 inside the container. You will use a version of the RHEL 7 image with Apache web server software pre-installed. This image is available from a Red Hat container registry. You will list the running container and confirm the port mapping.

1. Search for an Apache web server image for RHEL 7 using *podman search*:

```
[root@server20 ~]# podman search registry.redhat.io/rhel7/httpd
INDEX        NAME                                        DESCRIPTION
                        STARS    OFFICIAL    AUTOMATED
redhat.io    registry.redhat.io/rhscl/httpd-24-rhel7     Apache HTTP 2.4 Server
                        0
. . . . . . . .
```

The Red Hat Container Registry has an Apache web server image called *httpd-24-rhel7* available as evident from the output.

2. Log in to *registry.redhat.io* using the Red Hat credentials to access the image:

```
[root@server20 ~]# podman login registry.redhat.io
Username:
Password:
Login Succeeded!
[root@server20 ~]#
```

3. Download the latest version of the Apache image using *podman pull*:

```
[root@server20 ~]# podman pull registry.redhat.io/rhscl/httpd-24-rhel7
Trying to pull registry.redhat.io/rhscl/httpd-24-rhel7:latest...
Getting image source signatures
Checking if image destination supports signatures
Copying blob 3a809bec8aaa done
Copying blob 7597778323f6 done
Copying blob aeb95ba4200f done
Copying config 2ffb9643fd done
Writing manifest to image destination
Storing signatures
2ffb9643fd0deec937e860d1b760d72675788cdf29381cbf81b421bdc077fbf2
```

4. Verify the download using *podman images*:

```
[root@server20 ~]# podman images
REPOSITORY                                TAG         IMAGE ID
CREATED         SIZE
registry.redhat.io/rhscl/httpd-24-rhel7   latest      2ffb9643fd0d
3 weeks ago     330 MB
```

5. Launch a container named (--name) *rhel7-port-map* in detached mode (-d) to run the containerized Apache web server with host port 10000 mapped to container port 8000 (-p). Use the *podman run* command with appropriate flags.

```
[root@server20 ~]# podman run -dp 10000:8000 --name rhel7-port-map
httpd-24-rhel7
8a441af1f78befc1f98f7485c9cc3f058bb2884b42de6f3685e45d5b4f97716c
```

6. Verify that the container was launched successfully using *podman ps*:

```
[root@server20 ~]# podman ps
CONTAINER ID  IMAGE                                              COMMAND           CREATED         STATUS
        PORTS                     NAMES
8a441af1f78b  registry.redhat.io/rhscl/httpd-24-rhel7:latest  /usr/bin/run-http...  35 seconds ago  Up 31 secon
ds ago  0.0.0.0:10000->8000/tcp  rhel7-port-map
```

The container is running (up for 31 seconds and created 35 seconds ago). The output also indicates the port mapping.

7. You can also use *podman port* to view the mapping:

```
[root@server20 ~]# podman port rhel7-port-map
8000/tcp -> 0.0.0.0:10000
```

Now any inbound web traffic on host port 10000 will be redirected to the container.

This concludes the exercise.

Exercise 22-7: Stop, Restart, and Remove a Container

This exercise should be done on *server20* as *root*.

This exercise is a continuation of Exercise 22-6 in which a container named *rhel7-port-map* was launched.

In this exercise, you will stop the container, restart it, stop it again, and then erase it. You will use appropriate *podman* subcommands and verify each transition.

1. Verify the current operational state of the container *rhel7-port-map*:

```
[root@server20 ~]# podman ps
CONTAINER ID   IMAGE                                              COMMAND
    CREATED         STATUS          PORTS                     NAMES
8a441af1f78b   registry.redhat.io/rhscl/httpd-24-rhel7:latest  /usr/bin/run-http.
..  16 minutes ago  Up 16 minutes ago  0.0.0.0:10000->8000/tcp  rhel7-port-map
```

The container has been up and running for 16 minutes. It was created 16 minutes ago as well.

2. Stop the container and confirm using the *stop* and *ps* subcommands (the -a option with *ps* also includes the stopped containers in the output):

```
[root@server20 ~]# podman stop rhel7-port-map
rhel7-port-map
[root@server20 ~]#
[root@server20 ~]# podman ps -a
CONTAINER ID  IMAGE                                        COMMAND
    CREATED         STATUS                PORTS           NAMES
8a441af1f78b  registry.redhat.io/rhscl/httpd-24-rhel7:latest  /usr/bin/run-http.
..  16 minutes ago  Exited (0) 11 seconds ago  0.0.0.0:10000->8000/tcp  rhel7-po
rt-map
```

The container has been in stopped (Exited) state for the past 11 seconds.

3. Start the container and confirm with the *start* and *ps* subcommands:

```
[root@server20 ~]# podman start rhel7-port-map
rhel7-port-map
[root@server20 ~]# podman ps -a
CONTAINER ID  IMAGE                                        COMMAND
    CREATED         STATUS                PORTS           NAMES
8a441af1f78b  registry.redhat.io/rhscl/httpd-24-rhel7:latest  /usr/bin/run-http.
..  17 minutes ago  Up 3 seconds ago  0.0.0.0:10000->8000/tcp  rhel7-port-map
```

Observe the creation and running times.

4. Stop the container and remove it using the *stop* and *rm* subcommands:

```
[root@server20 ~]# podman stop rhel7-port-map
rhel7-port-map
[root@server20 ~]# podman rm rhel7-port-map
8a441af1f78befc1f98f7485c9cc3f058bb2884b42de6f3685e45d5b4f97716c
```

5. Confirm the removal using the -a option with *podman ps* to also include any stopped containers:

```
[root@server20 ~]# podman ps -a
CONTAINER ID  IMAGE          COMMAND      CREATED      STATUS      PORTS      NAMES
[root@server20 ~]#
```

The container no longer exists.

This concludes the exercise.

Containers and Environment Variables

Many times it is necessary to pass a host's pre-defined environment variable, such as PATH, to a containerized application for consumption. Moreover, it may also be necessary at times to set new variables to inject debugging flags or sensitive information such as passwords, access keys, or other secrets for use inside containers. Passing host environment variables or setting new environment variables is done at the time of launching a container. The *podman* command allows multiple variables to be passed or set with the -e option.

Refer to Chapter 07 "The Bash Shell" for more information on variables, their types, and how to define and view them.

Exercise 22-8: Pass and Set Environment Variables

This exercise should be done on *server20* as *user1*.

In this exercise, you will launch a container using the latest version of a ubi for RHEL 9 available in a Red Hat container registry. You will inject the HISTSIZE environment variable, and a variable called SECRET with a value "secret123". You will name this container *rhel9-env-vars* and have a shell terminal opened to check the variable settings. Finally, you will remove this container.

1. Launch a container with an interactive terminal session (-it) and inject (-e) variables HISTSIZE and SECRET as directed. Use the specified container image.

```
[user1@server20 ~]$ podman run -it -e HISTSIZE -e SECRET="secret123"
--name rhel9-env-vars ubi9
Resolved "ubi9" as an alias (/etc/containers/registries.conf.d/001-rh
el-shortnames.conf)
Trying to pull registry.access.redhat.com/ubi9:latest...
Getting image source signatures
Checking if image destination supports signatures
Copying blob fc07e4fdbabe skipped: already exists
Copying config 10acc17441 done
Writing manifest to image destination
Storing signatures
[root@57ee5a19622f /]#
```

The container is launched with a terminal opened for interaction.

2. Verify both variables using the *echo* command:

```
[root@b8535edb138d /]# echo $HISTSIZE $SECRET
1000 secret123
```

Both variables are set and show their respective values.

3. Disconnect from the container using the *exit* command, and stop and remove it using the *stop* and *rm* subcommands:

```
[root@57ee5a19622f /]# exit
exit
[user1@server20 ~]$ podman stop rhel9-env-vars
rhel9-env-vars
[user1@server20 ~]$ podman rm rhel9-env-vars
57ee5a19622f60b80e2508be8e80170099c3087f50547879aa7c008b4e155451
```

At this point, you may want to confirm the deletion by running **podman ps -a**.

This concludes the exercise.

Containers and Persistent Storage

Containers are normally launched for a period of time to run an application and then stopped or deleted when their job is finished. Any data that is produced during runtime is lost on their restart, failure, or termination. This data may be saved for persistence on a host directory by attaching the host directory to a container. The containerized application will see the attached directory just like any other local directory and will use it to store data if it is configured to do so. Any data that is saved on the directory will be available even after the container is rebooted or removed. Later, this directory can be re-attached to other containers to give them access to the stored data or to save their own data. The source directory on the host may itself exist on any local or remote file system.

> **EXAM TIP:** Proper ownership, permissions, and SELinux file type must be set to ensure persistent storage is accessed and allows data writes without issues.

There are a few simple steps that should be performed to configure a host directory before it can be attached to a container. These steps include the correct ownership, permissions, and SELinux type (container_file_t). The special SELinux file type is applied to prevent containerized applications (especially those running in root containers) from gaining undesired privileged access to host files and processes, or other running containers on the host if compromised.

Exercise 22-9: Attach Persistent Storage and Access Data Across Containers

This exercise should be done on *server20* as *user1* with *sudo* where required.

In this exercise, you will set up a directory on *server20* and attach it to a new container. You will write some data to the directory while in the container. You will delete the container and launch another container with the same directory attached. You will observe the persistence of saved data in the new container and that it is accessible. Finally, you will remove the container to mark the completion of this exercise.

1. Create a directory called */host_data*, set full permissions on it, and confirm:

```
[user1@server20 ~]$ sudo mkdir /host_data
[user1@server20 ~]$ sudo chmod 777 /host_data/
[user1@server20 ~]$ ll -d /host_data/
drwxrwxrwx. 2 root root 6 Feb 10 12:08 /host_data/
```

2. Launch a root container called *rhel9-persistent-data* (--name) in interactive mode (-it) using the latest ubi9 image. Specify the attachment point (*/container_data*) to be used inside the container for the host directory (*/host_data*) with the -v (volume) option. Add :Z as shown to ensure the SELinux type container_file_t is automatically set on the directory and files within.

```
[user1@server20 ~]$ sudo podman run --name rhel9-persistent-data -v
/host_data:/container_data:Z -it ubi9
Resolved "ubi9" as an alias (/etc/containers/registries.conf.d/001-r
hel-shortnames.conf)
Trying to pull registry.access.redhat.com/ubi9:latest...
Getting image source signatures
Checking if image destination supports signatures
Copying blob fc07e4fdbabe done
Copying config 10acc17441 done
Writing manifest to image destination
Storing signatures
[root@716930e311ab /]#
```

3. Confirm the presence of the directory inside the container with *ls* on */container_data*:

```
[root@716930e311ab /]# ls -ldZ /container_data
drwxrwxrwx. 2 root root system_u:object_r:container_file_t:s0:c399,c
907 6 Feb 10 17:08 /container_data
```

The host directory is available as */container_data* inside the container with the correct SELinux type.

4. Create a file called *testfile* with the *echo* command under */container_data*:

```
[root@716930e311ab /]# echo "This is persistent storage." > /contain
er_data/testfile
```

5. Verify the file creation and the SELinux type on it:

```
[root@716930e311ab /]# ls -lZ /container_data/
total 4
-rw-r--r--. 1 root root system_u:object_r:container_file_t:s0:c399,c
907 28 Feb 10 18:35 testfile
```

The file inherits the SELinux type from the parent directory.

6. Exit out of the container and check the presence of the file in the host directory:

```
[root@716930e311ab /]# exit
exit
[user1@server20 ~]$ ls -lZ /host_data/
total 4
-rw-r--r--. 1 root root system_u:object_r:container_file_t:s0:c399,c
907 28 Feb 10 13:35 testfile
```

The output indicates the exact same attributes on the file.

7. Stop and remove the container using the *stop* and *rm* subcommands:

```
[user1@server20 ~]$ sudo podman stop rhel9-persistent-data
rhel9-persistent-data
[user1@server20 ~]$ sudo podman rm rhel9-persistent-data
716930e311ab815d1b88f353ca294c7d5808e83f3b5706ba42726e2d6ab90a8a
```

8. Launch a new root container called *rhel8-persistent-data* (--name) in interactive mode (-it) using the latest ubi8 image from any of the defined registries. Specify the attachment point (*/container_data2*) to be used inside the container for the host directory (*/host_data*) with the -v (volume) option. Add :Z as shown to ensure the SELinux type container_file_t is automatically set on the directory and files within.

```
[user1@server20 ~]$ sudo podman run -it --name rhel8-persistent-data
 -v /host_data:/container_data2:Z ubi8
Resolved "ubi8" as an alias (/etc/containers/registries.conf.d/001-r
hel-shortnames.conf)
Trying to pull registry.access.redhat.com/ubi8:latest...
Getting image source signatures
Checking if image destination supports signatures
Copying blob ea0a20a2c448 done
Copying config 55e87c8c55 done
Writing manifest to image destination
Storing signatures
[root@8baf28c2c218 /]#
```

9. Confirm the presence of the directory inside the container with *ls* on */container_data2*:

```
[root@8baf28c2c218 /]# ls -ldZ /container_data2/
drwxrwxrwx. 2 root root system_u:object_r:container_file_t:s0:c470,c
613 22 Feb 10 18:35 /container_data2/
[root@8baf28c2c218 /]#
[root@8baf28c2c218 /]# ls -lZ /container_data2/
total 4
-rw-r--r--. 1 root root system_u:object_r:container_file_t:s0:c470,c
613 28 Feb 10 18:35 testfile
[root@8baf28c2c218 /]#
[root@8baf28c2c218 /]# cat /container_data2/testfile
This is persistent storage.
[root@8baf28c2c218 /]#
```

The host directory is available as */container_data2* inside this new container with the correct SELinux type. The output also confirms the persistence of the *testfile* data that was written in the previous container.

10. Create a file called *testfile2* with the *echo* command under */container_data2*:

```
[root@8baf28c2c218 /]# echo "This is persistent storage2." > /contai
ner_data2/testfile2
[root@8baf28c2c218 /]# ls -lZ /container_data2/
total 8
-rw-r--r--. 1 root root system_u:object_r:container_file_t:s0:c470,c
613 28 Feb 10 18:35 testfile
-rw-r--r--. 1 root root system_u:object_r:container_file_t:s0:c470,c
613 29 Feb 10 19:23 testfile2
[root@8baf28c2c218 /]#
```

11. Exit out of the container and confirm the existence of both files in the host directory:

```
[root@8baf28c2c218 /]# exit
exit
[user1@server20 ~]$ ls -lZ /host_data/
total 8
-rw-r--r--. 1 root root system_u:object_r:container_file_t:s0:c470,c
613 28 Feb 10 13:35 testfile
-rw-r--r--. 1 root root system_u:object_r:container_file_t:s0:c470,c
613 29 Feb 10 14:23 testfile2
```

12. Stop and remove the container using the *stop* and *rm* subcommands:

```
[user1@server20 ~]$ sudo podman stop rhel8-persistent-data
rhel8-persistent-data
[user1@server20 ~]$ sudo podman rm rhel8-persistent-data
8baf28c2c218c7b9d356aecb8fd07a36aae936b6221fcbda19d8b9da1f7af322
```

13. Re-check the presence of the files in the host directory:

```
[user1@server20 ~]$ ll /host_data/
total 8
-rw-r--r--. 1 root root 28 Feb 10 13:35 testfile
-rw-r--r--. 1 root root 29 Feb 10 14:23 testfile2
```

Both files still exist and they can be shared with other containers if required.

This concludes the exercise.

Container State Management with systemd

So far you have seen how containers are started, stopped, and deleted by hand using a management command. In real life environments multiple containers run on a single host and it becomes a challenging task to change their operational state or delete them manually. In RHEL 9, these administrative functions can be automated via the *systemd* service (refer to Chapter 12 "System Initialization, Message Logging, and System Tuning" for details on *systemd*).

There are several steps that need to be completed to configure container state management via *systemd*. These steps vary for rootful and rootless container setups and include the creation of service unit files and their storage in appropriate directory locations (*~/.config/systemd/user* for rootless containers and */etc/systemd/system* for rootful containers). Once setup and enabled, the containers will start and stop automatically as a *systemd* service with the host state transition or manually with the *systemctl* command.

The *podman* command to start and stop containers is no longer needed if the *systemd* setup is in place. You may experience issues if you continue to use *podman* for container state transitioning alongside.

The start and stop behavior for rootless containers differs slightly from that of rootful containers. For the rootless setup, the containers are started when the relevant user logs in to the host and stopped when that user logs off from all their open terminal sessions; however, this default behavior can be altered by enabling lingering for that user with the *loginctl* command.

📝 User lingering is a feature that, if enabled for a particular user, spawns a user manager for that user at system startup and keeps it running in the background to support long-running services configured for that user. The user need not log in.

> **EXAM TIP:** Make sure that you use a normal user to launch rootless containers and the root user (or sudo) for rootful containers.

Rootless setup does not require elevated privileges of the *root* user.

Exercise 22-10: Configure a Rootful Container as a systemd Service

This exercise should be done on *server20* as *user1* with *sudo* where required.

In this exercise, you will create a systemd unit configuration file for managing the state of your rootful containers. You will launch a new container and use it as a template to generate a service unit file. You will stop and remove the launched container to avoid conflicts with new containers that will start. You will use the *systemctl* command to verify the automatic container start, stop, and deletion.

1. Launch a new container called *rootful-container* (--name) in detached mode (-d) using the latest ubi9:

   ```
   [user1@server20 ~]$ sudo podman run -dt --name rootful-container ubi9
   16f2b2051af2ca467f4fbe5381c9b2bb7b91bed8ad46cf20138b3e6237892fac
   ```

2. Confirm the new container using *podman ps*. Note the container ID.

   ```
   [user1@server20 ~]$ sudo podman ps
   CONTAINER ID   IMAGE                                         COMMAND     CREATED
                  STATUS                        PORTS      NAMES
   16f2b2051af2   registry.access.redhat.com/ubi9:latest   /bin/bash   About a
   minute ago     Up About a minute ago                    rootful-container
   ```

3. Create (*generate*) a service unit file called *rootful-container.service* under */etc/systemd/system* while ensuring that the next new container that will be launched based on this configuration file will not require the source container (--new) to work. The *tee* command will show the generated file content on the screen as well as store it in the specified file.

```
[user1@server20 ~]$ sudo podman generate systemd --new --name rootful-con
tainer | sudo tee /etc/systemd/system/rootful-container.service
# container-rootful-container.service
# autogenerated by Podman 4.2.0
# Fri Feb 10 14:41:35 EST 2023

[Unit]
Description=Podman container-rootful-container.service
Documentation=man:podman-generate-systemd(1)
Wants=network-online.target
After=network-online.target
RequiresMountsFor=%t/containers

[Service]
Environment=PODMAN_SYSTEMD_UNIT=%n
Restart=on-failure
TimeoutStopSec=70
ExecStartPre=/bin/rm -f %t/%n.ctr-id
ExecStart=/usr/bin/podman run \
        --cidfile=%t/%n.ctr-id \
        --cgroups=no-conmon \
        --rm \
        --sdnotify=conmon \
        --replace \
        -dt \
        --name rootful-container ubi9
ExecStop=/usr/bin/podman stop --ignore --cidfile=%t/%n.ctr-id
ExecStopPost=/usr/bin/podman rm -f --ignore --cidfile=%t/%n.ctr-id
Type=notify
NotifyAccess=all

[Install]
WantedBy=default.target
```

The unit file has the same syntax as any other *systemd* service configuration file. There are three sections—Unit, Service, and Install. (1) The unit section provides a short description of the service, the manual page location, and the dependencies (wants and after). (2) The service section highlights the full commands for starting (ExecStart) and stopping (ExecStop) containers. It also highlights the commands that will be executed before the container start (ExecStartPre) and after the container stop (ExecStopPost). There are a number of options and arguments with the commands to ensure a proper transition. The restart on-failure stipulates that systemd will try to restart the container in the event of a failure. (3) The install section identifies the operational target the host needs to be running in before this container service can start. See Chapter 12 "System Initialization, Message Logging, and System Tuning" for details on systemd units and targets. Also check out the manual pages for *systemd.unit*, *systemd.target*, and *systemd.service* for additional details.

4.   Stop and delete the source container (*rootful-container*) using the *stop* and *rm* subcommands:

```
[user1@server20 ~]$ sudo podman stop rootful-container
WARN[0010] StopSignal SIGTERM failed to stop container rootful-container
in 10 seconds, resorting to SIGKILL
rootful-container
[user1@server20 ~]$ sudo podman rm rootful-container
16f2b2051af2ca467f4fbe5381c9b2bb7b91bed8ad46cf20138b3e6237892fac
```

Verify the removal by running **sudo podman ps -a**.

5. Update *systemd* to bring the new service under its control (reboot the system if required):

```
[user1@server20 ~]$ sudo systemctl daemon-reload
```

6. Enable (enable) and start (--now) the container service using the *systemctl* command:

```
[user1@server20 ~]$ sudo systemctl enable --now rootful-container
Created symlink /etc/systemd/system/default.target.wants/rootful-containe
r.service → /etc/systemd/system/rootful-container.service.
```

7. Check the running status of the new service with the *systemctl* command:

```
[user1@server20 ~]$ sudo systemctl status rootful-container
● rootful-container.service - Podman container-rootful-container.service
     Loaded: loaded (/etc/systemd/system/rootful-container.service; enab>
     Active: active (running) since Fri 2023-02-10 14:46:05 EST; 42s ago
       Docs: man:podman-generate-systemd(1)
    Process: 43922 ExecStartPre=/bin/rm -f /run/rootful-container.servic>
   Main PID: 44000 (conmon)
      Tasks: 1 (limit: 7474)
     Memory: 1.0M
        CPU: 786ms
     CGroup: /system.slice/rootful-container.service
             └─44000 /usr/bin/conmon --api-version 1 -c 255fe5e73a576df6>

Feb 10 14:46:04 server20.example.com systemd[1]: Starting Podman contain>
Feb 10 14:46:04 server20.example.com podman[43923]:
Feb 10 14:46:04 server20.example.com podman[43923]: 2023-02-10 14:46:04.>
Feb 10 14:46:04 server20.example.com podman[43923]: 2023-02-10 14:46:04.>
Feb 10 14:46:05 server20.example.com podman[43923]: 2023-02-10 14:46:05.>
```

8. Verify the launch of a new container (compare the container ID with that of the source root container):

```
[user1@server20 ~]$ sudo podman ps
CONTAINER ID   IMAGE                                        COMMAND      CREATED
               STATUS                   PORTS     NAMES
255fe5e73a57   registry.access.redhat.com/ubi9:latest   /bin/bash    About a
minute ago   Up About a minute ago              rootful-container
```

9. Restart the container service using the *systemctl* command:

```
[user1@server20 ~]$ sudo systemctl restart rootful-container
[user1@server20 ~]$
[user1@server20 ~]$ sudo systemctl status rootful-container
● rootful-container.service - Podman container-rootful-container.service
     Loaded: loaded (/etc/systemd/system/rootful-container.service; enab>
     Active: active (running) since Fri 2023-02-10 14:48:51 EST; 5min ago
       Docs: man:podman-generate-systemd(1)
    Process: 44176 ExecStartPre=/bin/rm -f /run/rootful-container.servic>
   Main PID: 44253 (conmon)
. . . . . . . .
```

10. Check the status of the container again. Observe the removal of the previous container and the launch of a new container (compare container IDs).

```
[user1@server20 ~]$ sudo podman ps
CONTAINER ID  IMAGE                                        COMMAND     CREATED
         STATUS              PORTS          NAMES
00f9c57f3925  registry.access.redhat.com/ubi9:latest  /bin/bash  7 minut
es ago  Up 7 minutes ago                  rootful-container
```

Each time the *rootful-container* service is restarted or *server20* is rebooted, a new container will be launched. You can verify this by comparing their container IDs.

This concludes the exercise.

Exercise 22-11: Configure Rootless Container as a systemd Service

This exercise should be done on *server20* as *user1* with *sudo* where required. Log in as *conuser1* as directed.

In this exercise, you will create a systemd unit configuration file for managing the state of your rootless containers. You will launch a new container as *conuser1* (create this user) and use it as a template to generate a service unit file. You will stop and remove the launched container to avoid conflicts with new containers that will start. You will use the *systemctl* command as *conuser1* to verify the automatic container start, stop, and deletion.

1. Create a user account called *conuser1* and assign a simple password:

```
[user1@server20 ~]$ sudo useradd conuser1
[user1@server20 ~]$ echo conuser1 | sudo passwd --stdin conuser1
Changing password for user conuser1.
passwd: all authentication tokens updated successfully.
```

2. Open a new terminal window on *server20* and log in as *conuser1*. Create directory ~/.config/systemd/user to store a service unit file:

```
[conuser1@server20 ~]$ mkdir ~/.config/systemd/user -p
```

3. Launch a new container called *rootless-container* (--name) in detached mode (-d) using the latest ubi8:

```
[conuser1@server20 ~]$ podman run -dt --name rootless-container ubi8
Resolved "ubi8" as an alias (/etc/containers/registries.conf.d/001-rhel-s
hortnames.conf)
Trying to pull registry.access.redhat.com/ubi8:latest...
Getting image source signatures
Checking if image destination supports signatures
Copying blob ea0a20a2c448 done
Copying config 55e87c8c55 done
Writing manifest to image destination
Storing signatures
47df4c2a19fa4de6ae6cecbb5a896bcfb061cff90c788508551d9fc47866f18b
```

4. Confirm the new container using *podman ps*. Note the container ID.

```
[conuser1@server20 ~]$ podman ps
CONTAINER ID  IMAGE                                 COMMAND     CREATED
              STATUS                    PORTS       NAMES
47df4c2a19fa  registry.access.redhat.com/ubi8:latest  /bin/bash   About a
minute ago  Up About a minute ago                     rootless-container
```

5. Create (*generate*) a service unit file called *rootless-container.service* under
    ~/.config/systemd/user while ensuring that the next new container that will be launched based
    on this configuration will not require the source container (--new) to work:

```
[conuser1@server20 ~]$ podman generate systemd --new --name rootless-cont
ainer > ~/.config/systemd/user/rootless-container.service
```

6. Display the content of the unit file:

```
[conuser1@server20 ~]$ cat ~/.config/systemd/user/rootless-container.serv
ice
# container-rootless-container.service
# autogenerated by Podman 4.2.0
# Fri Feb 10 16:17:05 EST 2023

[Unit]
Description=Podman container-rootless-container.service
Documentation=man:podman-generate-systemd(1)
Wants=network-online.target
After=network-online.target
RequiresMountsFor=%t/containers

[Service]
Environment=PODMAN_SYSTEMD_UNIT=%n
Restart=on-failure
TimeoutStopSec=70
ExecStartPre=/bin/rm -f %t/%n.ctr-id
ExecStart=/usr/bin/podman run \
        --cidfile=%t/%n.ctr-id \
        --cgroups=no-conmon \
        --rm \
        --sdnotify=conmon \
        --replace \
        -dt \
        --name rootless-container ubi8
ExecStop=/usr/bin/podman stop --ignore --cidfile=%t/%n.ctr-id
ExecStopPost=/usr/bin/podman rm -f --ignore --cidfile=%t/%n.ctr-id
Type=notify
NotifyAccess=all

[Install]
WantedBy=default.target
```

See Exercise 22-10 earlier for an analysis of the file content.

7. Stop and delete the source container *rootless-container* using the *stop* and *rm* subcommands:

```
[conuser1@server20 ~]$ podman stop rootless-container
rootless-container
[conuser1@server20 ~]$ podman rm rootless-container
47df4c2a19fa4de6ae6cecbb5a896bcfb061cff90c788508551d9fc47866f18b
```

Verify the removal by running **podman ps -a**.

8. Update *systemd* to bring the new service to its control (reboot the system if required). Use the --user option with the *systemctl* command.

```
[conuser1@server20 ~]$ systemctl --user daemon-reload
```

9. Enable (enable) and start (--now) the container service using the *systemctl* command:

```
[conuser1@server20 ~]$ systemctl --user enable --now rootless-container.service
Created symlink /home/conuser1/.config/systemd/user/multi-user.target.wants/root
less-container.service → /home/conuser1/.config/systemd/user/rootless-container.
service.
Created symlink /home/conuser1/.config/systemd/user/default.target.wants/rootles
s-container.service → /home/conuser1/.config/systemd/user/rootless-container.ser
vice.
```

10. Check the running status of the new service using the *systemctl* command:

```
[conuser1@server20 ~]$ systemctl --user status rootless-container
● rootless-container.service - Podman container-rootless-container.servi>
     Loaded: loaded (/home/conuser1/.config/systemd/user/rootless-contai>
     Active: active (running) since Fri 2023-02-10 16:22:02 EST; 37s ago
       Docs: man:podman-generate-systemd(1)
    Process: 44677 ExecStartPre=/bin/rm -f /run/user/3001/rootless-conta>
   Main PID: 44693 (conmon)
      Tasks: 2 (limit: 7474)
     Memory: 1.7M
        CPU: 688ms
     CGroup: /user.slice/user-3001.slice/user@3001.service/app.slice/roo>
             ├─44690 /usr/bin/slirp4netns --disable-host-loopback --mtu=>
             └─44693 /usr/bin/conmon --api-version 1 -c 3703dc9020a3c4b8>
```

11. Verify the launch of a new container (compare the container ID with that of the source rootless container):

```
[conuser1@server20 ~]$ podman ps
CONTAINER ID   IMAGE                                    COMMAND      CREATED
               STATUS                PORTS       NAMES
3703dc9020a3   registry.access.redhat.com/ubi8:latest  /bin/bash    About a
minute ago  Up About a minute ago                rootless-container
```

12. Enable the container service to start and stop with host transition using the *loginctl* command (systemd login manager) and confirm:

```
[conuser1@server20 ~]$ loginctl enable-linger
[conuser1@server20 ~]$ loginctl show-user conuser1 | grep -i linger
Linger=yes
```

13. Restart the container service using the *systemctl* command:

```
[conuser1@server20 ~]$ systemctl --user restart rootless-container
[conuser1@server20 ~]$ systemctl --user status rootless-container
• rootless-container.service - Podman container-rootless-container.servi>
     Loaded: loaded (/home/conuser1/.config/systemd/user/rootless-contai>
     Active: active (running) since Fri 2023-02-10 16:25:11 EST; 6s ago
       Docs: man:podman-generate-systemd(1)
    Process: 44777 ExecStartPre=/bin/rm -f /run/user/3001/rootless-conta>
   Main PID: 44793 (conmon)
. . . . . . . .
```

14. Check the status of the container again. Observe the removal of the previous container and the launch of a new container (compare container IDs).

```
[conuser1@server20 ~]$ podman ps
CONTAINER ID   IMAGE                                    COMMAND      CREATED
               STATUS                    PORTS     NAMES
5d77bbad6fe1   registry.access.redhat.com/ubi8:latest   /bin/bash    About a
 minute ago   Up About a minute ago               rootless-container
```

Each time the *rootless-container* service is restarted or *server20* is rebooted, a new container will be launched. You can verify this by comparing their container IDs.

This concludes the exercise.

Chapter Summary

In this last chapter, we discussed the container technology that has gained tremendous popularity and been deployed in massive numbers lately. It offers benefits that are unmatched with any previous virtualization technology.

We analyzed the core components of the technology: images, registries, and containers. We interacted with images located in remote registries and local storage. We built a custom container image using a file that consisted of instructions. We looked at a variety of ways to launch containers, with and without a name. We examined the benefits and use cases for mapping network ports, injecting environment variables, and making host storage available inside containers for persistent data storage. The last topic expounded on controlling the operational states of rootful and rootless containers via *systemd* and ensuring that they are auto-started and auto-stopped with the host startup and shutdown. The chapter presented several exercises to reinforce the learning.

Review Questions

1. Rootless containers are less secure than rootful containers. True or False?
2. Which of these—isolation, security, high transition time, less overhead—is not a benefit of the container technology?
3. What is the name and location of the system-wide file that stores a list of insecure registries?
4. What is one thing that you do not get with rootless containers? Select from: security, ability to map privileged ports, ability to pass environment variables, or can be managed via *systemd*.
5. What is the significance of a tag in a container image?
6. Which command would you use to inspect a container image sitting in a remote registry?
7. What would you run to remove all locally stored images in one shot?

8. What is the default tag used with container images?
9. The per-user systemd service configuration file is stored under *etc/systemd/user* directory. True or False?
10. Containers can be run on a bare metal server or in a virtual machine. True or False?
11. Which feature would you use to allow traffic flow for your Apache web server running inside a container?
12. How would you ensure that data stored inside a container will not be deleted automatically when the container is restarted?
13. What is the name of the primary tool that is used for container management?
14. Which option must be included with the *systemctl* command to manage the state of a rootless container?
15. It is mandatory to download an image prior to running a container based off it. True or False?
16. How would you connect to a container running in the background?
17. By default, any data saved inside a container is lost when the container is restarted. True or False?
18. What is the typical name of the file that furnishes instructions to build custom images?
19. Can a single host directory be attached to multiple containers at the same time?
20. How would you ensure that a rootless container for a specific user is automatically started with the host startup without the need for the user to log in?
21. What would you run to remove all stopped containers?

Answers to Review Questions

1. False.
2. High transition time is not a container benefit.
3. The file that stores insecure registry list is called *registries.conf* and it lives in the */etc/containers* directory.
4. The ability to map privileged ports is not directly supported with rootless containers.
5. A tag is typically used to identify a version of the image.
6. The *skopeo* command can be used to inspect an image located in a remote registry.
7. Execute *podman rmi -a* to remove all locally stored images.
8. The default tag is 'latest' that identifies the latest version of an image.
9. False. The per-user systemd unit configuration file is stored under the user's home directory at *~/.config/systemd/user*.
10. True.
11. Map a host port with a container port.
12. Attach a host directory to the container and use it for storing data that requires persistence.
13. The primary container management tool is called *podman*.
14. The --user option is required with the *systemctl* command to control the state of a rootless container.
15. False. The specified image is automatically downloaded when starting a container.
16. Use the *podman attach* command to connect to a running container.
17. True.
18. Containerfile is the typical name; however, you can use any name that you want.
19. Yes, a single host directory can be attached to multiple containers simultaneously.
20. Use the *loginctl* command as that user and enable lingering.
21. Run *podman rm -a* to remove all stopped containers.

DIY Challenge Labs

The following labs are useful to strengthen most of the concepts and topics learned in this chapter. It is expected that you perform the labs without external help. A step-by-step guide is not supplied, as the knowledge and skill required to implement the labs have already been disseminated in the chapter; however, hints to the relevant major topic(s) are included.

Use the lab environment built specifically for end-of-chapter labs. See sub-section "Lab Environment for End-of-Chapter Labs" in Chapter 01 "Local Installation" for details.

Lab 22-1: Launch Named Root Container with Port Mapping

Create a new user account called *conadm* on *server30* and give them full *sudo* rights. As *conadm* with *sudo* (where required) on *server30*, inspect the latest version of ubi9 and then download it to your computer. Launch a container called *rootful-cont-port* in attached terminal mode (-it) with host port 80 mapped to container port 8080. Run a few basic Linux commands such as *ls*, *pwd*, *df*, *cat /etc/redhat-release*, and *os-release* while in the container. Check to confirm the port mapping from *server30*. (Hint: use the *skopeo* and *podman* commands). **Note:** Do not remove the container yet.

Lab 22-2: Launch Nameless Rootless Container with Two Variables

As *conadm* on *server30*, launch a container using the latest version of ubi8 in detached mode (-d) with two environment variables VAR1=lab1 and VAR2=lab2 defined. Use the *exec* subcommand to check the settings for the variables directly from *server30*. Delete the container and the image when done. (Hint: use the *podman* command).

Lab 22-3: Launch Named Rootless Container with Persistent Storage

As *conadm* with *sudo* (where required) on *server30*, create a directory called */host_perm1* with full permissions, and a file called *str1* in it. Launch a container called *rootless-cont-str* in attached terminal mode (-it) with the created directory mapped to */cont_perm1* inside the container. While in the container, check access to the directory and the presence of the file. Create a sub-directory and a file under */cont_perm1* and exit out of the container shell. List */host_perm1* on *server30* to verify the sub-directory and the file. Stop and delete the container. Remove */host_perm1*. (Hint: use the *podman* command).

Lab 22-4: Launch Named Rootless Container with Port Mapping, Environment Variables, and Persistent Storage

As *conadm* with *sudo* (where required) on *server30*, launch a named rootless container called *rootless-cont-adv* in attached mode (-it) with two variables (HISTSIZE=100 and MYNAME=RedHat), host port 9000 mapped to container port 8080, and */host_perm2* mounted at */cont_perm2*. Check and confirm the settings while inside the container. Exit out of the container. **Note:** Do not remove the container yet. (Hint: use the *podman* command).

Lab 22-5: Control Rootless Container States via systemd

As *conadm* on *server30*, use the *rootless-cont-adv* container launched in Lab 22-4 as a template and generate a *systemd* service configuration file and store the file in the appropriate directory. Stop and remove the source container *rootless-cont-adv*. Add the support for the new service to *systemd* and enable the new service to auto-start at system reboots. Perform the required setup to ensure the container is launched without the need for the *conadm* user to log in. Reboot *server30* and confirm a successful start of the container service and the container. (Hint: use the *podman*, *systemctl*, and *loginctl* commands).

Lab 22-6: Control Rootful Container States via systemd

As *conadm* with *sudo* where required on *server10*, use the *rootful-cont-port* container launched in Lab 22-1 as a template and generate a *systemd* service configuration file and store the file in the appropriate directory. Stop and remove the source container *rootful-cont-port*. Add the support for the new service to *systemd* and enable the service to auto-start at system reboots. Reboot *server10* and confirm a successful start of the container service and the container. (Hint: use the *podman* and *systemctl* commands).

Lab 22-7: Build Custom Image Using Containerfile

As *conadm* on *server10*, write a containerfile to use the latest version of ubi8 and create a user account called *user-in-container* in the resultant custom image. Test the image by launching a container in interactive mode and verifying the user. (Hint: use the *podman* command).

Appendix A: Sample RHCSA Exam 1

Time Duration: 3 hours
Passing Score: 70% (210 out of 300)
Instructions: The RHCSA exam, EX200, is offered electronically on a physical computer running RHEL 9 as the base operating system. The computer has two virtual machines with RHEL 9 running in each one of them. The exam presents two sets of tasks that are to be completed within the stipulated time in the identified virtual machine. Firewall and SELinux must be taken into consideration for all network services. All settings performed in the virtual machines must survive system reboots, or you will lose marks. Access to the Internet, printed and electronic material, and electronic devices is prohibited during the exam.

Setup for Sample Exam 1:

Build a virtual machine with RHEL 9 Server with GUI (Exercises 1-1 and 1-2). Use a 20GB disk for the OS with default partitioning. Add 2x300MB disks and a network interface. Do not configure the network interface or create a normal user account during installation.

Instructions:

01: The following tasks are in addition to the exercises and labs presented in the book. No solutions are furnished, but hints to applicable exercises, chapters, or topics are provided in parentheses for reference.

02: Do not browse the Internet or seek help from other sources. However, you can refer to the manual pages, and the documentation under the /usr/share/doc directory. This rule does not apply to the kernel download task if included.

03: All exam tasks must be executed in a terminal window using only the command line interface (no GUI).

04: You can reboot the VM whenever you want during this exam but retest the configuration after each reboot for verification.

05: Use your knowledge and judgement for any missing configuration in task description.

Tasks:

Task 01: Assuming the root user password is lost, and your system is running in multi-user target with no current root session open. Reboot the system into an appropriate target level and reset the root user password to root1234. (Exercise 11-2). After completing this task, log in as the root user and perform the remaining tasks presented below.

Task 02: Using a manual method (create/modify files by hand), configure a network connection on the primary network device with IP address 192.168.0.241/24, gateway 192.168.0.1, and nameserver 192.168.0.1. Use different IP assignments based on your lab setup. (Exercise 15-3).

Task 03: Using a manual method (modify file by hand), set the system hostname to rhcsa1.example.com and alias rhcsa1. Make sure that the new hostname is reflected in the command prompt. (Exercises 15-1 and 15-5).

Task 04: Set the default boot target to multi-user. (Chapter 12, topic: Managing Target Units).

Task 05: Set SELinux to permissive mode. (Chapter 20, topic: Viewing and Controlling SELinux Operational State).

Task 06: Perform a case-insensitive search for all lines in the /usr/share/dict/linux.words file that begin with the pattern "essential". Redirect the output to /var/tmp/pattern.txt file. Make sure that empty lines are omitted. (Chapter 07, topic: Regular Expressions).

Task 07: Change the primary command prompt for the root user to display the hostname, username, and current working directory information in that order. Update the per-user initialization file for permanence. (Exercise 7-1).

Task 08: Create user accounts called user10, user20, and user30. Set their passwords to Temp1234. Make user10 and user30 accounts to expire on December 31, 2023. (Exercise 5-1; Exercise 6-1 or 6-2).

Task 09: Create a group called group10 and add user20 and user30 as secondary members. (Exercise 6-4).

Task 10: Create a user account called user40 with UID 2929. Set the password to user1234. (Exercise 5-2).

Task 11: Attach the RHEL 9 ISO image to the VM and mount it persistently to /mnt/cdrom. Define access to both repositories and confirm. (Exercise 9-1).

Task 12: Create a logical volume called lvol1 of size 280MB in vgtest volume group. Mount the ext4 file system persistently to /mnt/mnt1. (Exercises 13-6, 13-7, and 14-3).

Task 13: Change group membership on /mnt/mnt1 to group10. Set read/write/execute permissions on /mnt/mnt1 for group members and revoke all permissions for public. (Exercises 6-4 and 6-6; Exercise 4-1 or 4-2).

Task 14: Create a logical volume called lvswap of size 280MB in vgtest volume group. Initialize the logical volume for swap use. Use the UUID and place an entry for persistence. (Exercises 13-13-6, 13-7, and 14-5; Chapter 14, topic: Automatically Mounting a File System at Reboots).

Task 15: Use the combination of tar and bzip2 commands to create a compressed archive of the /usr/lib directory. Store the archive under /var/tmp as usr.tar.bz2. (Exercise 3-1).

Task 16: Create a directory hierarchy /dir1/dir2/dir3/dir4 and apply SELinux contexts of /etc on it recursively. (Chapter 03, topic: Creating Files and Directories; and Exercise 20-2).

Task 17: Enable access to the atd service for user20 and deny for user30. (Chapter 08, topic: Controlling User Access).

Task 18: Add a custom message "This is RHCSA sample exam on $(date) by $LOGNAME" to the /var/log/messages file as the root user. Use regular expression to confirm the message entry to the log file. (Chapter 07, topic: Regular Expressions; Chapter 12, topic: Logging Custom Messages).

Task 19: Allow user20 to use sudo without being prompted for their password. (Chapter 06, topic: Doing as Superuser (or Doing as Substitute User)).

Task 20: Write a bash shell script to create three user accounts—user555, user666, and user777—with no login shell and passwords matching their usernames. The script should also extract the three usernames from the /etc/passwd file and redirect them into /var/tmp/newusers. (Chapter 21, topic: Script12; Chapter 07, topic: Regular Expressions, and Input, Output, and Error Redirections).

Task 21: Launch a container as user20 using the latest version of ubi8 image. Configure the container to auto-start at system reboots without the need for user20 to log in. (Exercise 22-11).

Task 22: Launch a container as user20 using the latest version of ubi9 image with two environment variables SHELL and HOSTNAME. Configure the container to auto-start via systemd without the need for user20 to log in. Connect to the container and verify variable settings. (Exercises 22-8 and 22-11).

Reboot the system and validate the configuration.

Appendix B: Sample RHCSA Exam 2

Time Duration: 3 hours
Passing Score: 70% (210 out of 300)
Instructions: The RHCSA exam, EX200, is offered electronically on a physical computer running RHEL 9 as the base operating system. The computer has two virtual machines with RHEL 9 running in each one of them. The exam presents two sets of tasks that are to be completed within the stipulated time in the identified virtual machine. Firewall and SELinux must be taken into consideration for all network services. All settings performed in the virtual machines must survive system reboots, or you will lose marks. Access to the Internet, printed and electronic material, and electronic devices is prohibited during the exam.

Setup for Sample Exam 2:

Build a virtual machine with RHEL 9 Server with GUI (Exercises 1-1 and 1-2). Use a 20GB disk for the OS with default partitioning. Add 1x400MB disk and a network interface. Do not configure the network interface or create a normal user account during installation.

Instructions:

01: The following tasks are in addition to the exercises and labs presented in the book. No solutions are furnished, but hints to applicable exercises, chapters, or topics are provided in parentheses for reference.

02: Do not browse the Internet or seek help from other sources. However, you can refer to the manual pages, and the documentation under the /usr/share/doc directory. This rule does not apply to the kernel download task if included.

03: All exam tasks must be executed in a terminal window using only the command line interface (no GUI).

04: You can reboot the VM whenever you want during this exam but retest the configuration after each reboot for verification.

05: Use your knowledge and judgement for any missing configuration in task description.

06: Read all the storage tasks and set your strategy for disk partitioning prior to attempting them.

Tasks:

Task 01: Using the nmcli command, configure a network connection on the primary network device with IP address 192.168.0.242/24, gateway 192.168.0.1, and nameserver 192.168.0.1. Use different IP assignments based on your lab environment. (Exercise 15-3).

Task 02: Using the hostnamectl command, set the system hostname to rhcsa2.example.com and alias rhcsa2. Make sure that the new hostname is reflected in the command prompt. (Exercises 15-1 and 15-5).

Task 03: Create a user account called user70 with UID 7000 and comments "I am user70". Set the maximum allowable inactivity for this user to 30 days. (Exercises 5-2; Exercise 6-1 or 6-2).

Task 04: Create a user account called user50 with a non-interactive shell. (Exercise 5-4).

Task 05: Attach the RHEL 9 ISO image to the VM and mount it persistently to /mnt/dvdrom. Define access to both repositories and confirm. (Exercise 9-1).

Task 06: Create a logical volume called lv1 of size equal to 10 LEs in vg1 volume group (create vg1 with PE size 8MB in a partition on the 400MB disk). Initialize the logical volume with XFS type and mount it on /mnt/lvfs1. Create a file called lv1file1 in the mount point. Set the file system to automatically mount at each system reboot. (Exercises 13-6, 13-7, and 14-2; Chapter 14, topic: Automatically Mounting a File System at Reboots).

Task 07: Add a group called group20 and change group membership on /mnt/lvfs1 to group20. Set read/write/execute permissions on /mnt/lvfs1 for the owner, group members, and others. (Exercises 6-4 and 6-6; Exercise 4-1 or 4-2).

Task 08: Extend the file system in the logical volume lv1 by 64MB without unmounting it and without losing any data. Confirm the new size for the logical volume and the file system. (Exercise 14-3).

Task 09: Create a swap partition of size 85MB on the 400MB disk. Use its UUID and ensure it is activated after every system reboot. (Exercise 14-5; Chapter 14, topic: Automatically Mounting a File System at Reboots).

Task 10: Create a disk partition of size 100MB on the 400MB disk and format it with Ext4 file system structures. Assign label stdlabel to the file system. Mount the file system on /mnt/stdfs1 persistently using the label. Create file stdfile1 in the mount point. (Exercise 13-2 or 13-4; Chapter 14, topic: Labeling a File System; and Exercise 14-1).

Task 11: Use the tar and gzip command combination to create a compressed archive of the /etc directory. Store the archive under /var/tmp using a filename of your choice. (Exercise 3-1).

Task 12: Create a directory /direct01 and apply SELinux contexts for /root to it. (Exercise 20-2).

Task 13: Set up a cron job for user70 to search for files by the name "core" in the /var directory and copy them to the directory /var/tmp/coredir1. This job should run every Monday at 1:20 a.m. (Chapter 04, topics: Using the find Command and Using find with -exec and -ok Flags; and Exercise 8-4).

Task 14: Search for all files in the entire directory structure that have been modified in the past 30 days and save the file listing in the /var/tmp/modfiles.txt file. (Chapter 04, topics: Using the find Command and Using find with -exec and -ok Flags).

Task 15: Modify the bootloader program and set the default autoboot timer value to 2 seconds. (Exercise 11-1).

Task 16: Determine the recommended tuning profile for the system and apply it. (Exercise 12-2).

Task 17: Configure Chrony to synchronize system time with the hardware clock. Remove all other NTP sources. (Exercise 17-1).

Task 18: Install package group called "Development Tools" and capture its information in /var/tmp/systemtools.out file. (Chapter 03, topic: Regular Expressions; and Exercise 10-3).

Task 19: Lock user account user70. Use regular expressions to capture the line that shows the lock and store the output in file /var/tmp/user70.lock. (Chapter 03, topic: Regular Expressions; and Exercise 6-3).

Task 20: Write a bash shell script so that it prints RHCSA when RHCE is passed as an argument, and vice versa. If no argument is provided, the script should print a usage message and quit with exit value 5. (Chapter 21: Script10).

Task 21: Launch a rootful container and configure it to auto-start via systemd. (Exercise 22-10).

Task 22: Launch a rootless container as user80 with /data01 mapped to /data01 using the latest version of the ubi9 image. Configure a systemd service to auto-start the container on system reboots without the need for user80 to log in. Create files under the shared mount point and validate data persistence. (Exercise 22-7 and 22-10).

Reboot the system and validate the configuration.

Appendix C: Sample RHCSA Exam 3

Time Duration: 3 hours
Passing Score: 70% (210 out of 300)
Instructions: The RHCSA exam, EX200, is offered electronically on a physical computer running RHEL 9 as the base operating system. The computer has two virtual machines with RHEL 9 running in each one of them. The exam presents two sets of tasks that are to be completed within the stipulated time in the identified virtual machine. Firewall and SELinux must be taken into consideration for all network services. All settings performed in the virtual machines must survive system reboots, or you will lose marks. Access to the Internet, printed and electronic material, and electronic devices is prohibited during the exam.

Setup for Sample Exam 3:

Build two virtual machines with RHEL 9 Server with GUI (Exercises 1-1 and 1-2). Use a 20GB disk for the OS with default partitioning. Add 1x5GB disk to VM1 and a network interface to both virtual machines. Do not configure the network interfaces or create a normal user account during installation.

Instructions:

01: The following tasks are in addition to the exercises and labs presented in the book. No solutions are furnished, but hints to applicable exercises, chapters, or topics are provided in parentheses for reference.

02: Do not browse the Internet or seek help from other sources. However, you can refer to the manual pages, and the documentation under the /usr/share/doc directory. This rule does not apply to the kernel download task if included.

03: All exam tasks must be executed in a terminal window using only the command line interface (no GUI).

04: You can reboot the VM whenever you want during this exam but retest the configuration after each reboot for verification.

05: Use your knowledge and judgement for any missing configuration in task description.

Tasks:

Task 01: On VM1, set the system hostname to rhcsa3.example.com and alias rhcsa3 using the hostnamectl command. Make sure that the new hostname is reflected in the command prompt. (Exercises 15-1 and 15-5).

Task 02: On rhcsa3, configure a network connection on the primary network device with IP address 192.168.0.243/24, gateway 192.168.0.1, and nameserver 192.168.0.1 using the nmcli command (use different IP assignments based on your lab environment). (Exercise 15-4).

Task 03: On VM2, set the system hostname to rhcsa4.example.com and alias rhcsa4 using a manual method (modify file by hand). Make sure that the new hostname is reflected in the command prompt. (Exercises 15-1 and 15-5).

Task 04: On rhcsa4, configure a network connection on the primary network device with IP address 192.168.0.244/24, gateway 192.168.0.1, and nameserver 192.168.0.1 using a manual method (create/modify files by hand). Use different IP assignments based on your lab environment. (Exercise 15-3).

Task 05: Run "ping -c2 rhcsa4" on rhcsa3. Run "ping -c2 rhcsa3" on rhcsa4. You should see 0% loss in both outputs. (Exercise 15-5).

Task 06: On rhcsa3 and rhcsa4, attach the RHEL 9 ISO image to the VM and mount it persistently to /mnt/sr0. Define access to both repositories and confirm. (Exercise 9-1).

Task 07: On rhcsa3, add HTTP port 8300/TCP to the SELinux policy database persistently. (Exercise 20-3).

Task 08: On rhcsa3, create LVM VDO volume called vdo1 on the 5GB disk with logical size 20GB and mounted with Ext4 structures on /mnt/vdo1. (Exercises 13-12 and 14-4; Chapter 14, topic: Automatically Mounting a File System at Reboots).

Task 09: Configure NFS service on rhcsa3 and share /rh_share3 with rhcsa4. Configure AutoFS direct map on rhcsa4 to mount /rh_share3 on /mnt/rh_share4. User user80 (create on both systems) should be able to create files under the share on the NFS server as well as under the mount point on the NFS client. (Exercises 5-1, 16-1, and 16-3).

Task 10: Configure NFS service on rhcsa4 and share the home directory for user60 (create user60 on both systems) with rhcsa3. Configure AutoFS indirect map on rhcsa3 to automatically mount the home directory under /nfsdir when user60 logs on to rhcsa3. (Exercises 5-1, 16-1, 16-4, and 16-5).

Task 11: On rhcsa3, create a group called group30 with GID 3000, and add user60 and user80 to this group. Create a directory called /sdata, enable setgid bit on it, and add write permission bit for group members. Set ownership and owning group to root and group30. Create a file called file1 under /sdata as user60 and modify the file as user80 successfully. (Exercises 4-5, 6-4, and 6-6).

Task 12: On rhcsa3, create directory /var/dir1 with full permissions for everyone. Disallow non-owners to remove files. Test by creating file /var/dir1/stkfile1 as user60 and removing it as user80. (Exercise 4-6).

Task 13: On rhcsa3, search for all manual pages for the description containing the keyword "password" and redirect the output to file /var/tmp/man.out. (Chapter 02, topic: Searching by Keyword; Chapter 07, topic: Input, Output, and Error Redirections).

Task 14: On rhcsa3, create file lnfile1 under /var/tmp and create one hard link /var/tmp/lnfile2 and one soft link /boot/file1. Edit lnfile1 using one link at a time and confirm. (Exercises 3-2 and 3-3).

Task 15: On rhcsa3, install software group called "Legacy UNIX Compatibility". (Exercise 10-3).

Task 16: On rhcsa3, add the http service to "external" firewalld zone persistently. (Exercise 19-1).

Task 17: On rhcsa3, set SELinux type shadow_t on a new file testfile1 in /usr and ensure that the context is not affected by a SELinux relabeling. (Chapter 03, topic: File and Directory Operations; Exercises 20-1 and 20-2).

Task 18: Configure passwordless ssh access for user60 from rhcsa3 to rhcsa4. (Exercise 18-2).

Task 19: Write a bash shell script that checks for the existence of files (not directories) under the /usr/bin directory that begin with the letters "ac" and display their statistics (the stat command). (Chapter 21: Table 21-1 and Script07).

Task 20: On rhcsa3, write a containerfile to include the ls and pwd commands in a custom ubi8 image. Launch a named rootless container as user60 using this image. Confirm command execution. (Exercises 22-3 and 22-4).

Task 21: On rhcsa3, launch a named rootless container as user60 with host port 10000 mapped to container port 80. Employ the latest version of the ubi8 image. Configure a systemd service to auto-start the container without the need for user60 to log in. Validate port mapping using an appropriate podman subcommand. (Exercises 22-4 and 22-11).

Task 22: On rhcsa3, launch another named rootless container (use a unique name for the container) as user60 with /host_data01 mapped to /container_data01, one variable ENVIRON=Exam, and host port 1050 mapped to container port 1050. Use the latest version of the ubi9 image. Configure a separate systemd service to auto-start the container without the need for user60 to log in. Create a file under the shared directory and validate data persistence. Verify port mapping and variable settings using appropriate podman subcommands. (Exercises 22-6, 22-8, 22-7, and 22-11).

Reboot the system and validate the configuration.

Appendix D: Sample RHCSA Exam 4

Time Duration: 3 hours
Passing Score: 70% (210 out of 300)
Instructions: The RHCSA exam, EX200, is offered electronically on a physical computer running RHEL 9 as the base operating system. The computer has two virtual machines with RHEL 9 running in each one of them. The exam presents two sets of tasks that are to be completed within the stipulated time in the identified virtual machine. Firewall and SELinux must be taken into consideration for all network services. All settings performed in the virtual machines must survive system reboots, or you will lose marks. Access to the Internet, printed and electronic material, and electronic devices is prohibited during the exam.

Setup for Sample Exam 4:

Build two virtual machines with RHEL 9 Server with GUI (Exercises 1-1 and 1-2). Use a 20GB disk for the OS with default partitioning. Add 1x5GB disk to VM2 and a network interface to both virtual machines. Do not configure the network interfaces or create a normal user account during installation.

Instructions:

01: The following tasks are in addition to the exercises and labs presented in the book. No solutions are furnished, but hints to applicable exercises, chapters, or topics are provided in parentheses for reference.

02: Do not browse the Internet or seek help from other sources. However, you can refer to the manual pages, and the documentation under the /usr/share/doc directory. This rule does not apply to the kernel download task if included.

03: All exam tasks must be executed in a terminal window using only the command line interface (no GUI).

04: You can reboot the VM whenever you want during this exam but retest the configuration after each reboot for verification.

05: Use your knowledge and judgement for any missing configuration in task description.

Tasks:

Task 01: On VM1, set the system hostname to rhcsa5.example.com and alias rhcsa5 using the hostnamectl command. Make sure that the new hostname is reflected in the command prompt. (Exercises 15-1 and 15-5).

Task 02: On rhcsa5, configure a network connection on the primary network device with IP address 192.168.0.245/24, gateway 192.168.0.1, and nameserver 192.168.0.1 using the nmcli command. Use different IP assignments based on your lab environment. (Exercise 15-4).

Task 03: On VM2, set the system hostname to rhcsa6.example.com and alias rhcsa6 using a manual method (modify file by hand). Make sure that the new hostname is reflected in the command prompt. (Exercises 15-1 and 15-5).

Task 04: On rhcsa6, configure a network connection on the primary network device with IP address 192.168.0.246/24, gateway 192.168.0.1, and nameserver 192.168.0.1 using a manual method (create/modify files by hand). Use different IP assignments based on your lab environment. (Exercise 15-3).

Task 05: Run "ping -c2 rhcsa6" on rhcsa5. Run "ping -c2 rhcsa5" on rhcsa6. You should see 0% loss in both outputs. (Exercise 15-5).

Task 06: On rhcsa5 and rhcsa6, attach the RHEL 9 ISO image to the VM and mount it persistently to /mnt/sr0. Define access to both repositories and confirm. (Exercise 9-1).

Task 07: Export /share5 on rhcsa5 and mount it to /share6 persistently on rhcsa6. (Exercises 16-1 and 16-2).

Task 08: Use NFS to export home directories for all users (u1, u2, and u3) on rhcsa6 so that their home directories become available under /home1 when they log on to rhcsa5. Create u1, u2, and u3. (Exercises 5-1, 16-1 and 16-5).

Task 09: On rhcsa5, add HTTP port 8400/UDP to the public firewall zone persistently. (Exercise 19-1).

Task 10: Configure passwordless ssh access for u1 from rhcsa5 to rhcsa6. Copy the directory /etc/sysconfig from rhcsa5 to rhcsa6 under /var/tmp/remote securely. (Exercise 18-2; Chapter 18, topic: Transferring Files Remotely Using sftp).

Task 11: On rhcsa6, create LVM VDO volume vdo2 on the 5GB disk with logical size 20GB and mounted persistently with XFS structures on /mnt/vdo2. (Exercises 13-12 and 14-4).

Task 12: On rhcsa6, flip the value of the Boolean nfs_export_all_rw persistently. (Exercise 20-5).

Task 13: On rhcsa5 and rhcsa6, set the tuning profile to powersave. (Exercise 12-2).

Task 14: On rhcsa5, create file lnfile1 under /var/tmp and create three hard links called hard1, hard2, and hard3 for it. Identify the inode number associated with all four files. Edit any of the files and observe the metadata for all the files for confirmation. (Exercise 3-2).

Task 15: On rhcsa5, members (user100 and user200) of group100 should be able to collaborate on files under /shared but cannot delete each other's files. (Exercises 4-5 and 4-6).

Task 16: On rhcsa6, list all files that are part of the "setup" package, and use regular expressions and I/O redirection to send the output lines containing "hosts" to /var/tmp/setup.pkg. (Exercise 9-2; Chapter 07, topics: Regular Expressions, and Input, Output, and Error Redirections).

Task 17: On rhcsa5, check the current version of the Linux kernel. Download and install the latest version of the kernel from Red Hat website. Ensure that the existing kernel and its configuration remain intact. Reboot the system and confirm the new version is loaded. (Exercise 11-3; Chapter 02, topic: Viewing System Information).

Task 18: On rhcsa5, configure journald to store messages permanently under /var/log/journal and fall back to memory-only option if /var/log/journal directory does not exist or has permission/access issues. (Exercise 12-1).

Task 19: Write a bash shell script that defines an environment variable called ENV1=book1 and creates a user account that matches the value of the variable. (Chapter 21: Script02 and Script03).

Task 20: On rhcsa5, launch a named rootful container with host port 443 mapped to container port 443. Employ the latest version of the ubi9 image. Configure a systemd service to auto-start the container at system reboots. Validate port mapping using an appropriate podman subcommand. (Exercises 22-6 and 22-10).

Task 21: On rhcsa5, launch a named rootless container as user100 with /data01 mapped to /data01 and two variables KERN=$(uname -r) and SHELL defined. Use the latest version of the ubi8 image. Configure a systemd service to auto-start the container at system reboots without the need for user100 to log in. Create a file under the shared mount point and validate data persistence. Verify port mapping using an appropriate podman subcommand. (Exercises 22-6, 22-8, and 22-11).

Task 22: On rhcsa5, write a containerfile to include the PATH environment variable output in a custom ubi9 image. Launch a named rootless container as user100 using this image. Confirm command execution. (Exercises 22-3 and 22-4).

Reboot the system and validate the configuration.

Bibliography

The following websites, forums, and guides were referenced in writing this book:

1. www.virtualbox.org
2. docs.redhat.com/docs/en-US
3. developers.redhat.com
4. registry.redhat.com
5. www.redhat.com
6. www.opensource.org
7. www.systemd.io
8. www.tldp.org
9. wiki.archlinux.org
10. www.ibm.com
11. www.centos.org
12. www.wikipedia.org
13. www.linux.org
14. www.firewalld.org
15. www.apache.org
16. www.gnome.org
17. www.ietf.org
18. www.isc.org
19. www.netfilter.org
20. www.nftables.org
21. www.nsa.gov/research/selinux
22. www.ntp.org
23. www.chrony.tuxfamily.org
24. www.openssh.org
25. www.pathname.com/fhs
26. www.docker.io
27. RHCSA Red Hat Enterprise Linux 8 (UPDATED) book by Asghar Ghori
28. RHCSA Red Hat Enterprise Linux 8 book by Asghar Ghori
29. Red Hat Certified System Administrator & Engineer for RHEL 7 book by Asghar Ghori
30. Red Hat Certified System Administrator & Engineer for RHEL 6 book by Asghar Ghori

Glossary

. (single dot)	Represents current directory.
.. (double dots)	Represents parent directory of the current directory.
Absolute mode	A method of permission allocation to a file or directory.
Absolute path	A pathname that begins with a /.
Access mode	See Permission mode.
Access permission	See File permission.
Access right	See File permission.
Access Vector Cache	A special cache area that SELinux uses to store its decisions.
Address Resolution Protocol	A protocol used to determine a system's Ethernet address when its IP address is known.
Address space	Memory location that a process can refer.
Administrator	See Superuser.
Algorithm	A set of well-defined but complex mathematical instructions used for data encryption and decryption.
Alias	A short name to refer to a lengthy command.
Alias substitution	See Alias.
Anaconda	RHEL's installation program.
Apache	A popular HTTP web server software.
Application stream	A method of making multiple versions of a software application available for installation from the same repository.
AppStream	One of the yum repositories in RHEL 9 that provides a number of add-on software applications along with some core operating system components.
Archive	A file that contains one or more files.
Argument	A value passed to a command or program.
ARP	See Address Resolution Protocol.
ASCII	An acronym for American Standard Code for Information Interchange.
Asymmetric encryption technique	A technique that uses a combination of public/private keys to allow two network entities to communicate privately.
Auditing	System and user activity record and analysis.
Authentication	The process of identifying a user to a system.

AutoFS	The NFS client-side service that automatically mounts and unmounts an NFS share on an as-needed basis.
AutoFS maps	Configuration files to define the directory location to automount a remote share.
Automounter	See AutoFS.
AVC	See Access Vector Cache.
Background process	A process that runs in the background.
Backup	Process of saving data on an alternative media such as a tape or another disk.
BaseOS	One of the yum repositories in RHEL 9 that includes the foundational RHEL components.
Bash shell	A feature-rich default shell available in Red Hat Enterprise Linux.
Berkeley Internet Name Domain	A University of California at Berkeley implementation of DNS for Linux and UNIX platforms. See also Domain Name System.
Binary package	A software package available in a format that dnf/rpm can recognize and install.
BIND	See Berkeley Internet Name Domain.
BIOS	Basic I/O System. Software code that sits in the computer's non-volatile memory and is executed when the system is booted. Also see Firmware.
Block	A collection of bytes of data transmitted as a single unit.
Block device file	A file associated with devices that transfer data randomly in blocks. Common examples are disk, CD, and DVD.
Bluetooth	A wireless technology for communication.
Boolean	The on/off switch to permit or deny an SELinux rule for a service.
Boot	See Boot process.
Bootloader	A small program that loads the operating system in memory.
Boot order	The sequence in which to try devices to boot the system.
Boot process	The process of starting up a system to a usable state.
Bourne Again Shell	See Bash shell.
Bus	Data communication path among devices in a computer system.
Cache	A temporary storage area on the system where frequently accessed information is duplicated for quick future access.
Calling process	See Parent process.
CentOS	Community Enterprise Operating System. A 100% unsponsored rebuild of Red Hat Enterprise Linux OS available for free.
Cgroup	See Control group.
Challenge-response authentication	An authentication method that presents one or more arbitrary challenge questions to the user.
Character special file	A file associated with devices that transfer data serially, one character at a time. Common examples are disk, tape, and mouse.
Child directory	A directory one level below the current directory.

Child process	A sub-process started by a process.
Child shell	A child shell is spawned by the current shell as needed.
Chrony	An implementation of Network Time Protocol for time synchronization on network devices.
CIDR	See Classless Inter-Domain Routing.
Classless Inter-Domain Routing	A technique for better use of IP addresses. It also results in smaller and less cluttered routing tables.
Command	An instruction given to the system to perform a task.
Command aliasing	See Alias.
Command history	See History substitution.
Command interpreter	See Shell.
Command line argument	See Positional parameter.
Command line completion	See Tab completion.
Command line editing	A shell feature that allows editing at the command line.
Command prompt	The OS prompt where you type commands.
Command substitution	A shell feature that allows the assignment of the output of an executed command to a variable.
Compression	The process of compressing data.
Container	A set of processes that runs in complete isolation from rest of the processes on the system.
Containerized application	An application packaged to run inside a container.
Containerfile	A set of instructions to build a custom container image.
Container image	A file that contains all necessary components required by an application to run smoothly and securely.
Container registry	A public or private storage location for container images.
Context (SELinux)	A set of SELinux attributes applied to SELinux subjects and objects.
Contiguous data blocks	A series of data blocks.
Control group	A process management technique.
Core	A core is a processor that shares the chip with other cores. Multi-core processor chips are common.
CPU-intensive	A program or application that heavily uses system processors.
Crash	An abnormal system shutdown caused by electrical outage or kernel malfunction, etc.
Crontable	A table of cron jobs scheduled for a user. Commonly abbreviated as crontab.
Current directory	The present working directory.

Current shell	The shell where a program is launched. Compare with Child shell.
DAC (SELinux)	See Discretionary Access Control.
Daemon	A server process that runs in the background and responds to client requests.
Database	A collection of data.
D-bus	Desktop Bus. Another communication method that allows multiple services running in parallel on a system to talk to one another on the same or remote system. Compare with Socket.
De-duplication	A technique to remove redundant data blocks from storage to conserve space and improve performance.
De-encapsulation	The reverse of encapsulation. See Encapsulation.
Default	Predefined values or settings that are automatically accepted by commands or programs.
Default permissions	Permissions assigned to a file and directory at creation.
Defunct process	See Zombie process.
Desktop bus	See D-bus.
Desktop environment	Software such as GNOME that provides graphical environment for users to interact with the system.
Device	A peripheral such as a printer, disk drive, or a CD/DVD device.
Device driver	The software that controls a device.
Device file	See Special file.
DHCP	See Dynamic Host Configuration Protocol.
Directory structure	Inverted tree-like Linux/UNIX directory structure.
Discretionary Access Control	A rich set of traditional access controls in Linux.
Disk-based file system	A file system created on a non-volatile storage device.
Disk partitioning	Creation of partitions on a given storage device so as to access them as distinct, independent logical containers for data storage.
Display manager	Application that is responsible for the presentation of graphical login screen.
Dnf	An upcoming major enhancement to yum.
DNS	See Domain Name System.
DNS name space	See Name space.
Domain	A group of computers configured to use a service such as DNS or NIS.
Domain Name System	The de facto hostname resolution service used on the Internet and corporate networks.
Domain (SELinux)	It ascertains the type of access that a process has.
Domain transitioning	The ability of a process running in one SELinux domain to enter another domain to execute a task in that domain.
Driver	See Device driver.

Dynamic Host Configuration Protocol	A networking service that provides IP assignments to devices.
Encapsulation	The process of forming a packet through the seven OSI layers.
Encryption	A method of scrambling information for privacy. See asymmetric encryption technique and symmetric encryption technique.
Encryption keys	A single secret key or a pair of private/public keys that is used to encrypt and decrypt data for private communication between two network entities.
Environment variable	A variable whose value is inherited by programs in sub-shells.
EOF	Marks the End OF File.
Error redirection	A shell feature that allows forwarding error messages generated during a command execution to an alternative destination (file, printer, etc.).
Ethernet	A family of networking technologies designed for LANs.
Ethernet address	See MAC address.
Exit code	A value returned by a command when it finishes execution.
Exit value	See Exit code.
Export	See Share.
Exporting	The process of making a directory or file system available over the network for sharing.
Extended file system	A type of file system that has been around in Linux for decades and currently has the fourth generation included and widely used in recent Linux distributions.
Extent	The smallest unit of space allocation in LVM. It is always contiguous. See Logical extent and Physical extent.
External command	A command external to the shell.
Fedora	Red Hat sponsored community project for collaborative enhancement of Red Hat Enterprise Linux OS.
Fibre channel	A family of networking technologies designed for storage networking.
File descriptor	A unique, per-process integer value used to refer to an open file.
File globbing	See Filename expansion.
Filename expansion	A series of characters used in matching filenames. Also see Metacharacters and Wildcard characters.
File permission	Read, write, execute or no permission assigned to a file or directory at the user, group, or public level.
File system	A grouping of files stored in special data structures.
File Transfer Protocol	A widely used protocol for file exchange.
Filter	A command that performs data transformation on the given input.
Firewall	A software or hardware appliance used for blocking inbound unauthorized access.

Firewalld	A dynamic firewall manager.
Firewalld zone	A method of segregating incoming network traffic.
Firmware	The BIOS or the UEFI code in x86-based systems.
FQIN	See Fully Qualified Image Name.
FTP	See File Transfer Protocol.
Full path	See Absolute path.
Fully Qualified Image Name	A container image name that includes all the necessary information to access it.
Gateway	A device that connects two networks.
Gateway address	An IP address that allows a system to communicate with computers on a different network.
GECOS	General Electric Comprehensive Operating System. The comments field in the /etc/passwd file.
GID	See Group ID.
Globally Unique Identifier	See Universally Unique Identifier.
Globbing	See Regular expression.
GNOME	GNU Object Model Environment. An intuitive graphical user environment.
GNU	GNU Not Unix. A project initiated to develop a completely free Unix-like operating system.
GPG	Gnu Privacy Guard. An open-source implementation of PGP. See PGP.
GPL	General Public License that allows the use of software developed under GNU project to be available for free to the general public.
GPT	See GUID Partition Table.
Graphical User Interface	An interface that allows users to interact with the operating system or application graphically.
Group	A collection of users that requires same permissions on files and directories.
Group collaboration	A collection of users from different groups with identical rights on files for the purpose of sharing.
Group ID	A numeric identifier assigned to a group.
GRUB2	Grand Unified Bootloader version 2. The second generation of the GRUB bootloader program that loads the operating system in memory.
GSSAPI-based authentication	An authentication method that provides a standard interface for security mechanisms to be plugged in.
Guest	An operating system instance that runs in a virtual machine.
GUI	See Graphical User Interface.
GUID	See Universally Unique Identifier.
GUID Partition Table	A small disk partition on a UEFI system that stores disk partition information.
Hard link	A mapping between a filename and its inode number.

Hardware address	See MAC address.
Hardware clock	See Real-Time Clock.
Hashing	See Password hashing.
History expansion	See History substitution.
History substitution	A shell feature that enables the storage of previously executed commands.
Home directory	A directory where a user lands when he logs into the system.
Host-based firewall	A firewall service that runs on the Linux system.
Host-based authentication	An authentication method that allows a single user, a group of users, or all users on the client to be authenticated on the server.
Hostname	A unique name assigned to a network node.
Hostname resolution	See Name resolution.
Host table	A file that maintains IP and hostname mappings.
HTTP	See HyperText Transfer Protocol.
HTTPS	See HyperText Transfer Protocol Secure.
HyperText Transfer Protocol	HyperText Transfer Protocol. Allows access to web pages.
HyperText Transfer Protocol Secure	Secure cousin of HTTP. Allows access to secure web pages.
Hypervisor	Software loaded on a computer to virtualize its hardware.
ICMP	See Internet Control Message Protocol.
Index node	An index node number holds a file's properties including permissions, size and creation/modification time as well as contains a pointer to the data blocks that actually store the file data.
Init	An older method of system initialization. It has been replaced by systemd in RHEL versions 7 and up.
Initialization files	See Shell startup files.
Initial permissions	Predefined permission settings that are used to calculate default permissions for new files and directories.
Initial Setup	Program that starts at first system reboot after a system has been installed to customize authentication, firewall, network, time zone and other services.
Inode	See Index node.
Inode table	A table in a file system that keeps a record of inode numbers.
Input redirection	A shell feature that allows supplying input to a command from an alternative source (file, etc.).
Installable package	See Binary package.
Installer program	A program that is launched to install an operating system or application.
Interface card	See Network device.
Internet	A complex network of computers and routers.

Internet Control Message Protocol	A well-known networking protocol that is primarily used for testing and debugging.
Internet Protocol	A protocol that is responsible for relaying traffic between network entities.
Inter-Process Communication	Allows processes to communicate directly with each other by sharing parts of their virtual memory address space, and then reading and writing data stored in that shared virtual memory.
I/O redirection	A shell feature that allows getting input from a non-default location and sending output and error messages to non-default locations.
IP	See Internet Protocol.
IP address	A unique 32- or 128-bit software address assigned to a network node.
IPC	See Inter-Process Communication.
ISO9660	A file system type used to mount optical devices.
Job	A process started in the background.
Job scheduling	Execution of commands, programs, or scripts in future.
Journald	A systemd-based logging service for collecting and storing logging data.
Journaled file system	A file system that uses the journaling mechanism for swift recovery after a system crash.
Journaling	A file system feature that allows it to maintain a journal (log) of its metadata changes to be used to fix any potential anomalies that may arise due to an abnormal system shutdown.
Kerberos	A networking protocol used for user authentication over unsecure networks.
Kernel	Software that controls the entire system including all hardware and software.
Kernel-based Virtual Machine	An open-source hypervisor software used for host virtualization.
Kvdo	A kernel module to support the Virtual Data Optimizer feature.
KVM	See Kernel-based Virtual Machine.
Label (storage)	A unique partition identifier that may be used instead of a UUID or device file.
Label (SELinux)	See Context.
Labeling	The process of mapping files with their stored SELinux contexts.
Latency	The time it takes for a data packet to travel between two network entities.
Link	An object that associates a filename to any type of file.
Link count	Number of links that refers to a file.
Link layer address	See MAC address.
Linux	A UNIX-like, open-source operating system.
Load balancing	A technique whereby more than one server serve client requests to share the load.
Localhost	A reserved, non-networked hostname assigned to every device. It represents the device itself.
Local variable	A variable whose value is private to the shell (current shell) it is defined in.

Logical extent	A unit of space allocation for logical volumes in LVM.
Logical volume	A logical container in LVM that holds a file system or swap.
Login Manager	See Display manager.
Logging	A process of capturing desired alerts and forwarding them to preconfigured locations.
Logical construct	Controls the flow of a script via test conditions.
Logical Volume Manager	A widely used disk partitioning solution.
Login	A process that begins when a user enters a username and password at the login prompt.
Login directory	See Home directory.
Loopback	A reserved IP address assigned to a device for testing and troubleshooting local issues.
Looping construct	Performs an action on a list of elements or repeatedly until a condition becomes true or false.
LVM	See Logical Volume Manager.
MAC address	A unique 48-bit hardware address of a network interface. Also called physical address, Ethernet address, and hardware address.
MAC (SELinux)	See Mandatory Access Control.
Machine	A computer, system, workstation, desktop, or server.
Major number	A number that points to a device driver.
Mandatory Access Control	A rich set of policies for granular access controls.
Map	See AutoFS map.
Masquerading	A variant of NAT.
Master Boot Record	A small region on the disk that stores disk partition information.
MBR	See Master Boot Record.
Memory-based file system	A kernel-managed virtual file system created in memory at system boot and destroyed at system shutdown.
Memory-intensive	A program or application that heavily uses memory.
Metacharacters	A series of characters that have special meaning to the shell and are used in pattern matching and filename globbing. Also see Wildcard characters.
Minor number	A unique number that points to an individual device controlled by a specific device driver.
MLS	See Multi-Level Security.
Module (kernel)	Device drivers used to control hardware devices and software components.
Mounting	Attaching a device (a file system, a CD/DVD) to the directory structure.
Multi-Level Security	One of the two standard SELinux policies that controls access at deeper levels.

Named pipe	Allows two unrelated processes running on the same system or on two different systems to communicate with each other and exchange data.
Name resolution	A technique to determine IP address by providing hostname.
Namespace	A layer of isolation between process groups and the rest of the system.
Name space	A hierarchical organization of DNS domains on the Internet.
NAT	See Network Address Translation.
NDP	See Neighbor Discovery Protocol.
Neighbor Discovery Protocol	A networking protocol that is used to discover Ipv6 devices and troubleshoot networking issues.
Netfilter	A framework that provides a set of hooks within the kernel to enable it to intercept and manipulate data packets.
Netmask	See Subnet mask.
Network	Two or more computers joined together to share resources.
Network Address Translation	Allows systems on an internal network to access external networks using a single IP address.
Network classes	Ranges of IP addresses classified into five distinct categories.
Network connection	A connection profile attached to a network device (interface).
Network device	A physical or virtual network interface assigned to a system for network connectivity.
Network File System	A networking protocol that allows Linux systems to share resources (files, directories, and file systems) on the network.
Network interface	See Network device.
Network interface card	See Network device.
NetworkManager	A Linux service that is used to configure, administer, and monitor network devices and connections.
Network mask	See Subnet mask.
Network Time Protocol	A networking protocol that is used to synchronize the system clock with a reliable time source.
NIC	See Network device.
NFS	See Network File System.
NFS client	A system that mounts an exported Linux resource.
NFS server	A system that exports (shares) a resource for mounting by an NFS client.
Nftables	A packet classification framework to monitor network traffic.
Niceness	It determines the priority of a process.
Nice value	See Niceness.
Node	A network device with a hostname and IP address.
Node name	A unique name assigned to a node.

Nologin (user) account	A user without the ability to log in to the system.
Normal (user) account	A user account with limited privileges on the system.
NTP	See Network Time Protocol.
NTP client	A system that receives time from a primary or secondary NTP server for its clock adjustments.
NTP peer	Two or more time servers that operate at the same stratum level.
NTP pool	A pool of time servers.
NTP server	See Primary NTP server and Secondary NTP server.
Object (SELinux)	A file, directory, file system, device, network connection, network interface, network socket, network port, etc.
Octal mode	A method for setting permissions on a file or directory using octal numbering system.
Octal numbering system	A 3 digit numbering system that represents values from 0 to 7.
On-demand activation	A systemd way of activating a service when needed.
Open source	Any software whose source code is published and is accessible at no cost to the public under GNU GPL for copy, modification and redistribution.
OpenSSH	A free implementation of secure shell services and utilities.
Orphan process	An alive child process of a terminated parent process.
Output redirection	A shell feature that allows forwarding a command output to an alternative destination (file, printer, etc.).
Owner	A user who has ownership rights on a file, directory, or process.
Owning user	The owner of a file or directory.
Owning group	The group of a file or directory.
Package	A set of necessary files and metadata that makes up a software application.
Package credibility	The authenticity or originality of a package.
Package database	A directory location that stores metadata for installed packages.
Package dependency	Additional required packages for a successful installation or functioning of another package.
Package group	A group of similar applications that can be managed as a single entity.
Package integrity	A state of being complete and error-free.
Paging	The process of transferring data between memory and swap space.
PAM	See Pluggable Authentication Module.
Parent directory	A directory one level above the current directory.
Parent process	A process with one or more child processes spawned.
Parent process ID	The ID of a process that starts a child process.

Parallelism	A systemd way of starting multiple services concurrently at system boot.
Partition	A partition created on a storage device.
Password aging	A mechanism that provides enhanced control on user passwords.
Password-based authentication	An authentication method that prompts users to enter their passwords to be signed in.
Password hashing	A one-way process of converting a legible text string into a random but unique string of characters using one of the several available password hashing algorithms.
Pattern matching	See Regular expression.
Peer	See NTP peer.
Per-user startup files	A set of initialization files that defines custom settings for an individual user upon logging in.
Performance-based	Hands-on implementation.
Performance monitoring	The process of acquiring data from system components for analysis and decision-making purposes.
Permission	Right to read, write, or execute.
Permission class	Access rights on files and directories based on an individual user, a group of users, or everyone else on the system.
Permission type	Read, write, or execute permission bits set on files or directories.
Permission mode	Add, revoke, or assign a permission type to a permission class.
Persistent storage	A host directory mounted inside a container to store application-generated data for persistence.
PGP	Pretty Good Privacy. An encryption program to ensure data privacy and secrecy.
Physical address	See MAC address.
Physical extent	A unit of space allocation on physical volumes in LVM.
Physical volume	A disk or a partition logically brought under LVM control.
PID	See Process ID.
Pipe	Sends output of one command as input to the second command.
Pipeline	A command construction with the pipe character used multiple times.
Pluggable Authentication Module	A set of library routines that allows using any authentication service available on a system for user authentication, password modification and user account validation purposes.
Policy (SELinux)	A set of rules enforced system-wide for analysis of security attributes on subjects and objects.
Pool	See Thin pool.
Pool (NTP)	See NTP pool.
Port	A number appended to an IP address. This number could be associated with a well-known service or is randomly generated.
Port forwarding	A method of directing incoming network traffic to an alternative network port.

Port mapping	Allows containerized applications to communicate with one another and with the container host.
Positional parameter	An argument supplied to a script at the time of its invocation, and its position is determined by the shell based on location with reference to the calling script.
POST	Power-On-Self-Test that runs at system boot to test hardware. See BIOS, Firmware, and UEFI.
Postfix	A mail transfer application used for sending and receiving mail.
PPID	See Parent process ID.
Primary DNS	A system that acts as the primary provider of DNS zones.
Primary NTP server	A system that gets time from a more reliable source and provides time to secondary servers or clients.
Primary prompt	The symbol where commands and programs are typed for execution.
Priority	See Process priority.
Private key	A randomly generated portion of the private/public key combination that is used to decode the messages encrypted with the paired public key.
Privilege	An extra right to accomplish something.
Process	Any command, program, or daemon that runs on a system.
Process ID	A numeric identifier assigned by kernel to each process spawned.
Process niceness	See Niceness.
Process priority	The value at which a process is running. This value is determined based on the current niceness setting.
Process state	One of multiple states in which a process is held during its lifecycle.
Processor	A CPU. It may contain more than one cores.
Profile (module)	A list of recommended packages that are organized for purpose-built convenient installations.
Prompt	See Primary prompt and Secondary prompt.
Protocol	A common language that communicating nodes understand.
Proxy	A system that acts on behalf of other systems to access network services.
Public key	A randomly generated portion of the private/public key combination that is used to encode messages destined for a specific user.
Public key-based authentication	An authentication method that uses a public/private key pair for user authentication.
Public key encryption	See Asymmetric encryption technique.
Quoting	Treats the specified special character as a regular character by disabling their special meaning.
Real-Time Clock	A battery-backed hardware clock on the system.
Recovery	A function that recovers a crashed system to its previous normal state. It may require restoring lost data files.
Redhat Package Manager	A file format used for packaging software for RHEL and its clones.

Red Hat Subscription Management	A comprehensive management service provided by Red Hat to its clients.
Redirection	Getting input from and sending output to non-default destinations.
Regex	See Regular expression.
Regexp	See Regular expression.
Registry	See Container registry.
Regular expression	A string of characters commonly used for pattern matching and filename globbing.
Relative path	A path to a file relative to the current user location in the file system hierarchy.
Renicing	Changing the niceness of a running process.
Repository	A URL location that provides access to software packages for installation.
Rescue mode	A special boot mode for fixing and recovering an unbootable system.
Resolver	The client-side of DNS.
Return code	See Exit code.
RHCE	Red Hat Certified Engineer. A designation that may be earned by passing a performance based RHCE exam.
RHCSA	Red Hat Certified System Administrator. A designation that may be earned by passing a performance based RHCSA exam.
RHEL	Red Hat Enterprise Linux.
RHSM	See Red Hat Subscription Management.
Role (SELinux)	It controls who (SELinux subject) is allowed to access what (SELinux domains or types).
Root (user) account	See Superuser.
Router	A device that routes data packets from one network to another.
Routing	The process of choosing a path over which to send a data packet.
Root container	A container launched by the root user or with root privileges.
Rootless container	A container launched by a normal, unprivileged Linux user.
Root servers	The thirteen most accurate root DNS servers.
RPM	See RedHat Package Manager.
Rsyslog	Essential Linux service for capturing system messages and forwarded them to various destinations for storage.
RTC	See Real-Time Clock.
Runtime	The operational state of an operating system.
SAS	Serial Attached SCSI. See Small Computer System Interface.
SATA	Serial Advanced Technology Attachment. This disk technology is a successor to the PATA drives.
Script	A text program written to perform a series of tasks.

SCSI	See Small Computer System Interface.
Search path	A list of directories where the system looks for the specified command.
Seccomp	See Secure Computing Mode.
Secondary DNS	A system that acts as an alternate provider of DNS zones.
Secondary NTP server	A system that gets time from a primary NTP server and provides time to NTP clients.
Secondary prompt	A prompt indicating that the entered command needs more input.
Secret key encryption	See Symmetric encryption technique.
Secure Computing Mode	A Linux feature that impose security constraints to protect processes.
Secure shell	A set of tools that gives secure access to a system.
Security context	SELinux security attributes set on files, processes, users, ports, etc.
Security Enhanced Linux	An implementation of Mandatory Access Control architecture for enhanced and granular control on files, processes, users, ports, etc.
SELinux	See Security Enhanced Linux.
Server (hardware)	Typically, a larger and more powerful system that offers services to network users.
Server (software)	A process or daemon that runs on the system to serve client requests.
Service (user) account	A user account that is used to control an installed application or service.
Set Group ID	Sets effective group ID.
Set User ID	Sets effective user ID.
Setgid	See Set group ID.
Setuid	See Set user ID.
Shadow password	A mechanism to store passwords and password aging data in a secure file.
Share	A directory or file system shared over the network.
Shared memory	A portion in physical memory created by a process to share it with other processes that communicate with that process.
Sharing	See Exporting.
Shell	The Linux command interpreter that sits between a user and kernel.
Shell parameter	An entity that holds a value such as a name, special character, or number.
Shell program	See Script.
Shell script	See Script.
Shell scripting	Programming in a Linux shell to automate one or a series of tasks.
Shell startup files	A set of files that are used to define the environment for a user upon logging in.
Shell variable	See Local variable.
Signal	A software interrupt sent to a process.

Simple Mail Transfer Protocol	A networking protocol used for email transfer over the Internet.
Single user mode	An operating system state in which the system cannot be accessed over the network.
Skeleton directory	A directory location where user default configuration templates are stored.
Small Computer System Interface	A parallel interface used to connect peripheral devices to the system.
SMTP	See Simple Mail Transfer Protocol.
Snapshot	The state of a system at a certain point in time.
Socket	A communication method that allows a process to talk to another process on the same or remote system.
Soft link	See Symbolic link.
Source package	A software package that can be modified and repackaged for a specific purpose.
Special characters	See Metacharacters.
Special file	A file that points to a specific device.
Special file permissions	Additional access permission bits that may be set on files and directories, where applicable, to give extra rights to (or limit rights for) normal users on executable files and shared directories. Also see Set user ID, Set group ID, and Sticky bit.
SSH	See Secure Shell.
Standard error	A standard location to forward error messages to. Also see Error redirection.
Standard input	A standard location to receive input from. Also see Input redirection.
Standard output	A standard location to forward output to. Also see Output redirection.
Startup files	See Shell startup files.
Stderr	See Standard error.
Stdin	See Standard input.
Stdout	See Standard output.
Sticky bit	Disallows non-owners to delete files located in a directory.
Stratum level	The categorization of NTP time sources based on reliability and accuracy.
Stream (module)	Represents a collection of packages that are organized by version.
String	A series of characters.
Subject (SELinux)	A process or user.
Subnet	One of the smaller networks formed using the process of subnetting. See Subnetting.
Subnet mask	Segregates the network bits from the node bits in an IP address.
Subnetting	The process of dividing an IP address into several smaller subnetworks.
Sub-shell	See Child shell. Compare with Current shell.
Substituting users	See Switching users.

Sudo	A method of delegating a portion of superuser privileges to normal users.
Superblock	A small portion in a file system that holds the file system's critical information.
Superuser	A user with full powers on the system.
Swap	Alternative disk or file system location for paging.
Switch	A network device that looks at the MAC address and switches the packet to the correct destination port based on the MAC address.
Switching users	The ability to switch into a different user account provided the target user's password is known.
Symbolic link	A shortcut that points to a file or directory located somewhere in the directory hierarchy. Compare with hard link.
Symbolic mode	A method of setting permissions on a file using non-decimal values.
Symlink	See Symbolic link.
Symmetric encryption technique	A technique that employs a secret key for private communication between two network entities.
Syslog	See rsyslog.
System	A computer or a logical partition in a computer that runs an operating system.
System Administrator	Person responsible for installing, configuring and managing a RHEL system.
System call	A mechanism that applications use to request service from the kernel.
System console	A display terminal that acts as the system console.
Systemd	System daemon. The default method of system initialization and service management starting at RHEL 7.
System recovery	The process of recovering an unbootable system.
System tuning	A service in RHEL 9 to monitor connected devices and dynamically adjust their parameters for performance improvement.
System-wide startup files	A set of initialization files that defines common settings for all users upon logging in.
Tab completion	A shell feature that allows completing a file or command name by typing a partial name at the command line and then hitting the Tab key twice for additional matching possibilities.
Target	A logical collection of systemd units. All units within a target are treated as a single entity.
Targeted policy	An SELinux policy.
TCP	See Transmission Control Protocol.
TCP/IP	Transmission Control Protocol / Internet Protocol. A stacked, standard suite of protocols for computer communication.
Terminal	A window where commands are executed.
Test condition	Used in logical constructs to decide what to do next.
Thin pool	A pool of storage that uses the thin provisioning technology to allow the creation of volumes much larger than their actual physical size.

Thin provisioning	An economical technique of storage allocation and utilization.
Thrashing	Excessive amount of paging.
Throughput	The amount of data transferred between two network entities within a specified period of time.
Tilde expansion	See Tilde substitution.
Tilde substitution	A shell feature that uses the tilde character as a shortcut to navigate within the directory tree.
Time source	A reference device that provides time to other devices.
Transmission Control Protocol	A stateful and reliable transport protocol. Compare with UDP.
Tty	Refers to a terminal.
Tuning profile	A set of attributes that can be applied to a system for improving performance of certain components.
Type enforcement	It controls the ability of an SELinux subject to access domains and types.
Udevd	Dynamic device management service.
UDP	See User Datagram Protocol.
UDS	See Universal De-duplication Service.
UEFI	See Unified Extensible Firmware Interface.
UID	See User ID.
Umask	See User mask.
Unified Extensible Firmware Interface	Software code used in computers for pre-boot system management. Also see Firmware.
Universal De-duplication Service	A kernel module to support data de-duplication.
Universally Unique IDentifier	A unique alphanumeric software identifier used to identify an object, such as a disk or disk partition.
Unmounting	Detaching a mounted file system or a CD/DVD from the directory structure.
Unit	A systemd object used to organize service startups, socket creation, etc.
Universal Time Coordinated	The reference time used around the world to determine the local time and time zone.
USB	Universal Serial Bus. A bus standard to connect peripheral devices.
User Datagram Protocol	A stateless and unreliable transport protocol. Compare with TCP.
User ID	A numeric identifier assigned to a user.
User mask	A value used in calculating default access rights on new files and directories.
User Private Group	Referred to the GID that matches with the user's UID for safeguarding the user's private data from other users.
UTC	See Universal Time Coordinated.
UUID	See Universally Unique IDentifier.

Variable	A temporary storage of data in memory.
Variable substitution	A shell feature that allows the value of a variable to be used in a command.
VDO	See Virtual Data Optimizer.
VFAT	See Virtual File Allocation Table.
VirtualBox	A type II hypervisor to virtualize an operating system.
VirtualBox Manager	The management interface for VirtualBox.
Virtual console	One of several console screens available for system access.
Virtual Data Optimizer	A feature to conserve disk space, improve data throughput, and save cost.
Virtual File Allocation Table	An MSDOS-compatible file system type.
Virtual file system	See memory-based file system.
Virtual host	An approach to host more than one website on a single system using unique or shared IP addresses.
Virtualization	A technology that allows a single physical computer to run several independent logical computers (called virtual machines) with complete isolation from one another.
Virtual machine	A logical computer running within a virtualized environment.
Volume group	A logical container in LVM that holds physical volumes, logical volumes, file systems, and swap.
Wayland	An innovative, superior, faster networking protocol that has replaced the X Window System protocol in RHEL 9. See X Window System protocol.
Web	A system of interlinked hypertext documents accessed over a network or the Internet via a web browser.
Web server	A system or service that provides web clients access to website pages.
Wildcard characters	A subset of metacharacters used for character matching in strings. See also Metacharacters.
Workload	Any application, database, program, or a combination that runs on the system.
XFS	eXtended File System. A high-performance journaling file system type.
X Window System protocol	A networking protocol that lays the foundation to run graphical applications. See Wayland.
Yum repository	See Repository.
Zero-block elimination	A technique to remove empty (zero-byte) data blocks from storage.
Zombie process	A child process that terminated abnormally and whose parent process still waits for it.
Zone (DNS)	A delegated portion of a DNS name space.
Zone (Firewalld)	A firewalld zone for traffic management.

Index

IPv6 address (See Networking)

O